Jackson's Chameleon

MACMILLAN McGRAW-HILL
Science

Lucy H. Daniel
Jay Hackett
Richard H. Moyer
JoAnne Vasquez

About the Cover

Chameleons are known as the masters of camouflage. They have the ability to change their skin color and patterns. Chameleons are slow-moving animals so they rely on protective coloration for defense. For protection, a chameleon might show bright colors, which often means "bad-tasting" or "poison" to predators. If this doesn't work, they may shift to a dull color and play dead.

INQUIRY **What else would you like to know about chameleons? Write your own question or questions to answer.**

Mc Graw Hill **Macmillan McGraw-Hill**

Program Authors

Dr. Lucy H. Daniel
Teacher, Consultant
Rutherford County Schools, North Carolina

Dr. Jay Hackett
Professor Emeritus of Earth Sciences
University of Northern Colorado

Dr. Richard H. Moyer
Professor of Science Education
University of Michigan-Dearborn

Dr. JoAnne Vasquez
Elementary Science Education Consultant
Mesa Public Schools, Arizona
NSTA Past President

Contributing Authors

Lucille Villegas Barrera, M.Ed.
Elementary Science Supervisor
Houston Independent School District
Houston, Texas

Mulugheta Teferi, M.A.
St. Louis Public Schools
St. Louis, Missouri

Dinah Zike, M.Ed.
Dinah Might Adventures LP
San Antonio, Texas

The features in this textbook entitled "Amazing Stories," as well as the unit openers, were developed in collaboration with the National Geographic Society's School Publishing Division.

RFB&D
learning through listening

Students with print disabilities may be eligible to obtain an accessible, audio version of the pupil edition of this textbook. Please call Recording for the Blind & Dyslexic at 1-800-221-4792 for complete information.

The McGraw·Hill Companies

Macmillan McGraw-Hill

Published by Macmillan/McGraw-Hill, of McGraw-Hill Education, a division of The McGraw-Hill Companies, Inc., Two Penn Plaza, New York, New York 10121.

Printed in the United States of America

ISBN 0-02-281862-6 /5

3 4 5 6 7 8 9 058/043 09 08 07 06 05

Teacher Reviewers

Michelle Dunning
Birmingham, Alabama

Donna Bullock
Chandler, Arizona

Debra Allen
Davie, Florida

Lora Meade
Plantation, Florida

Roxanne Laird
Miami, Florida

Karen Gaudy
Satellite Beach, Florida

Stephanie Sirianni
Margate, Florida

Heidi Stephens
South Daytona, Florida

Rosanne Phillips
Miami, Florida

Brenda Crow
Miami, Florida

Kari Pingel
Pella, Iowa

Christie Jones
Springfield, Illinois

Diane Songer
Wabash, Indiana

Lee Arwood
Wabash, Indiana

Margarite Hart
Indianapolis, Indiana

Charlotte Bennett
Newburgh, Indiana

Donna Halverson
Evansville, Indiana

Stephanie Tanke
Crown Point, Indiana

Mindey LeMoine
Marquette, Michigan

Billie Bell
Grand View, Missouri

Charlotte Sharp
Greenville, North Carolina

Pat Shane
Chapel Hill, North Carolina

Karen Daniel
Chapel Hill, North Carolina

Linda Dow
Concord, North Carolina

Consultants

Dr. Carol Baskin
University of Kentucky
Lexington, KY

Dr. Joe W. Crim
University of Georgia
Athens, GA

Dr. Pradeep M. Dass
Appalachian State University
Boone, NC

Dr. Marie DiBerardino
Allegheny University of
Health Sciences
Philadelphia, PA

Dr. R. E. Duhrkopf
Baylor University
Waco, TX

Dr. Dennis L. Nelson
Montana State University
Bozeman, MT

Dr. Fred Sack
Ohio State University
Columbus, OH

Dr. Martin VanDyke
Denver, CO

Dr. E. Peter Volpe
Mercer University
Macon, GA

Consultants

Dr. Clarke Alexander
Skidaway Institute of
Oceanography
Savannah, GA

Dr. Suellen Cabe
Pembroke State University
Pembroke, NC

Dr. Thomas A. Davies
Texas A & M University
College Station, TX

Dr. Ed Geary
Geological Society of America
Boulder, CO

Dr. David C. Kopaska-Merkel
Geological Survey of Alabama
Tuscaloosa, AL

Consultants

Dr. Bonnie Buratti
Jet Propulsion Lab
Pasadena, CA

Dr. Shawn Carlson
Society of Amateur Scientists
San Diego, CA

Dr. Karen Kwitter
Williams College
Williamstown, MA

Dr. Steven Souza
Williamstown, MA

Dr. Joseph P. Straley
University of Kentucky
Lexington, KY

Dr. Thomas Troland
University of Kentucky
Lexington, KY

Dr. Josephine Davis Wallace
University of North Carolina
Charlotte, NC

Consultant for Primary Grades

Donna Harrell Lubcker
East Texas Baptist University
Marshall, TX

Teacher Reviewers (continued)

Beth Lewis
Wilmington, North Carolina

Cindy Hatchell
Wilmington, North Carolina

Cindy Kahler
Carrboro, North Carolina

Diane Leusky
Chapel Hill, North Carolina

Heather Sutton
Wilmington, North Carolina

Crystal Stephens
Valdese, North Carolina

Meg Millard
Chapel Hill, North Carolina

Patricia Underwood
Randleman, North Carolina

E. Joy Mermin
Chapel Hill, North Carolina

Yolanda Evans
Wilmington, North Carolina

Tim Gilbride
Pennsauken, New Jersey

Helene Reifowitz
Nesconset, New York

Tina Craig
Tulsa, Oklahoma

Deborah Harwell
Lawton, Oklahoma

Kathleen Conn
West Chester, Pennsylvania

Heath Renninger Zerbe
Tremont, Pennsylvania

Patricia Armillei
Holland, Pennsylvania

Sue Workman
Cedar City, Utah

Peg Jensen
Hartford, Wisconsin

When I put on my helmet and climbed into the space shuttle I knew I was in for the adventure of a lifetime. That trip into space was a dream come true. The dream began when I was in elementary school. And studying science made it possible! I've always been interested in science. In the fifth grade, I made a mobile of the planets for a class project. Even then I wondered what it would be like to explore Mars.

Neither of my parents were scientists, but that didn't matter. They encouraged me to read books and to explore the things that interested me. And they encouraged me to be curious, to ask questions, and to think about things for myself. All of these things helped me become a scientist and an astronaut.

Maybe some of you have dreams like mine. Maybe you dream of exploring Mars one day. Whatever you dream of doing, it will help you to have the skills of a scientist—ask questions and explore things for yourself! And always

Reach for the stars!

Sally K Ride

Be a Scientist! PAGE S1

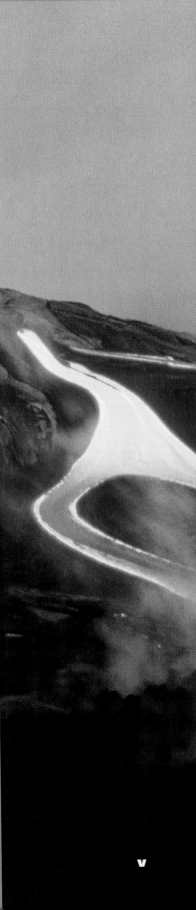

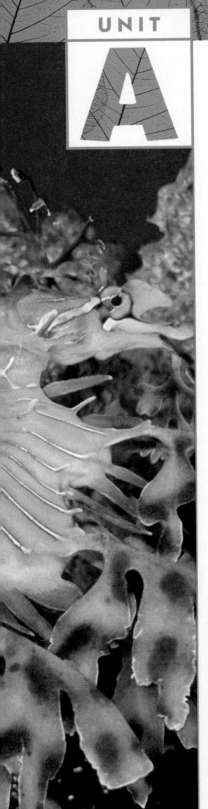

Characteristics of Living Things PAGE A1

Living Things and Their Environments PAGE B1

UNIT C

Earth Science

Earth and Its Resources PAGE C1

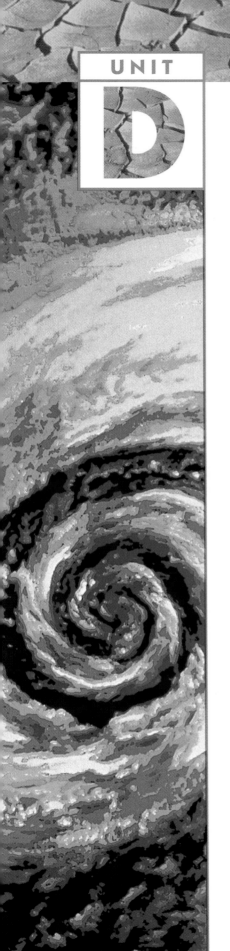

Astronomy, Weather, and Climate PAGE D1

Properties of Matter and Energy PAGE E1

Physical Science

Motion and Energy PAGE F1

Activities

UNIT D

UNIT E

UNIT F

For Your Reference

FOLDABLES™

by Dinah Zike

Using Foldables for Data Collection

A Foldables organizer is a 3-D, interactive graphic organizer. It can be a valuable learning tool to help you organize, review, and remember information. You will find suggestions for using Foldables organizers to help you collect and record data in Quick Lab activities throughout this book.

Basic Shapes

The figures on this page illustrate the basic folds that are the building blocks for all Foldables organizers used in the Quick Labs. The basic folds have friendly names, such as "hot dog fold," so that you can easily visualize and remember what they look like. Step-by-step folding instructions for each type of Foldables organizer used in the Quick Labs are given on pages R41–R44.

Hot Dog Fold

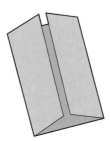

Shutter Fold

Hamburger Fold

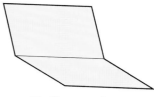

Valley Fold

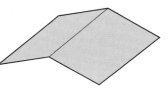

Mountain Fold

Science Safety Tips

In the Classroom

- Read all directions. Make sure you understand them. When you see **BE CAREFUL!**, be sure to follow the safety rule.
- Listen to your teacher for special safety directions. If you don't understand something, ask for help.
- Wash your hands with soap and water before an activity.
- Be careful around a hot plate. Know when it is on and when it is off. Remember that the plate stays hot for a few minutes after it's turned off.
- Wear a safety apron if you work with anything messy or anything that might spill.
- Wipe up a spill right away or ask your teacher for help.
- Tell your teacher if something breaks. If glass breaks, do not clean it up yourself.
- Keep your hair and clothes away from open flames. Tie back long hair, and roll up long sleeves.
- Keep your hands dry around electrical equipment.
- Don't eat or drink anything during an experiment.
- Put equipment back the way your teacher tells you.
- Dispose of things the way your teacher tells you.

- Wear safety goggles when your teacher tells you to wear them. Wear them when working with anything that can fly into your eyes or when working with liquids.
- Clean up your work area after an activity and wash your hands with soap and water.

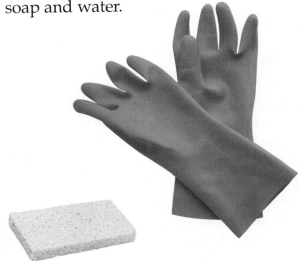

In the Field

- Go with a trusted adult—such as your teacher or a parent or guardian.
- Do not touch animals or plants without an adult's approval. The animal might bite. The plant might be poison ivy or another dangerous plant.

Responsibility

- Treat living things, the environment, and one another with respect.

Be a Scientist!

What on Earth is this?

Volcano!

Science is a way of understanding the world around us. The work of scientists often begins when scientists ask questions about something they observe. Asking and answering questions is the basis of inquiry.

In this section, you will see how scientists use inquiry skills, visual literacy, reading skills, technology and information literacy, math skills, and writing skills as they study volcanoes.

Inquiry Skills

These are the inquiry skills scientists use. You can use these skills, too.

Observe

Infer

Classify

Measure

Use numbers

Communicate

Predict

Interpret data

Form a hypothesis

Use variables

Experiment

Make a model

Define based on observations

The diagram on this page shows what is usually called the "scientific method." Scientists don't always follow all these steps in the same order, but they often start with an observation about the world around us.

You, too, are constantly making observations every moment you are awake. You might look out the window to see if it is raining. You might listen for the sound of thunder to find out if a storm is coming.

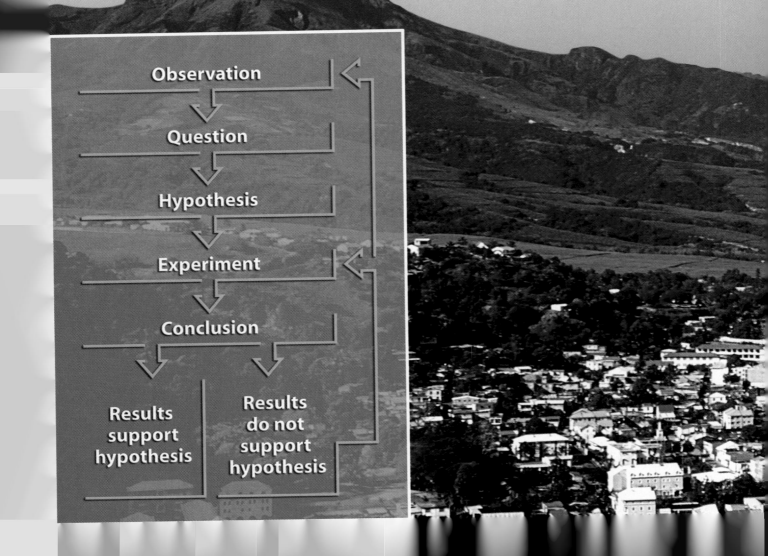

Observation

↓

Question

↓

Hypothesis

↓

Experiment

↓

Conclusion

Results support hypothesis

Results do not support hypothesis

Inquiry Skills

When you make observations, you use these skills.

Observe Use your senses to learn about an object or event.

Classify Place things that share properties together in groups.

Measure Find the size, distance, time, volume, area, mass, weight, or temperature of an object or an event.

Visual Literacy

More than half the information you get comes from pictures, or visuals. Pictures, maps, graphs, charts, and diagrams are tools. When you use them to improve your observation skills and to understand what you read, you are increasing your visual literacy.

This photograph shows the town of St. Pierre on the island of Martinique. It sits at the base of Mt. Pelée, an active volcano. Why do you think scientists might want to closely observe this volcano?

The work of scientists often starts with an unanswered question. If scientists cannot find an answer to a question, they go one step further. They propose a possible answer that can be tested experimentally. This is known as *forming a hypothesis*. A good hypothesis must

▸ be based on what you observe.
▸ be testable by performing an experiment.
▸ be useful in predicting new findings.

   Scientists who study volcanoes are called volcanologists. This volcanologist is examining lava as it flows into the ocean. What do you think happens to the lava when it flows into the ocean water? Form a hypothesis to answer this question.

Reading in Science

Before doing an experiment to answer a question, scientists often read to try to find the answer or to find what others have learned from their experiments. You can use these reading strategies and skills to help you understand science. While you read, ask yourself these questions:

▶ **Compare and Contrast** How are two things alike? How are they different?

▶ **Main Idea and Supporting Details** What is the paragraph about? Which details add more information?

▶ **Predict** What do you think will happen next?

▶ **Cause and Effect** Why did something happen? (This is the cause.) What happened as a result? (This is the effect.)

▶ **Draw Conclusions** What do I know from the evidence?

▶ **Sequence of Events** What happened first, next, and last?

▶ **Summarize** What is this lesson or paragraph about?

Inquiry Skills

When you ask questions and form hypotheses, you use these skills.

Infer Form an idea from facts or observations.

Form a hypothesis Make a statement that can be tested to answer a question.

Define terms based on observations Put together a description that is based on observations and experiences.

A scientific test, or experiment, is used to test a hypothesis. Although scientists don't always wear lab coats and work in a laboratory, every good experiment must

▶ be able to be repeated.
▶ change only one variable at a time.

Why are these two rules important? First, scientists must be able to check each other's work for accuracy. Second, if more than one variable changes in an experiment, it may be difficult to find the variable that was responsible for the results. For example, scientists might measure the temperature of lava at different locations on a volcano. What would happen if they changed both the depth and the location at which they measured the temperature?

Inquiry Skills

When you experiment, you use these skills.

Experiment Perform a test to support or disprove a hypothesis.

Use variables Identify things in an experiment that can be changed or controlled.

Predict State possible results of an event or experiment.

Make a model Make something to represent an object or event.

Technology Literacy

In an experiment, scientists use tools to collect and analyze data. They may use simple tools, such as clocks and rulers. They also use more powerful tools, such as microscopes and computers.

Information Literacy

Information literacy begins with knowing how to search for and use books, magazines, newspapers, and other media. Today, information literacy also includes searching for information on CD-ROMs, DVDs, and the Internet.

In an experiment a scientist tries to observe
carefully and collect good data. Once all the
information has been gathered, it is time to
interpret the data. Collecting and interpreting data
often requires working with numbers.

These volcanologists are taking samples of gases
escaping from vents on the side of a volcano. They
are careful to wear protective clothing and gas
masks. Why is it important to know what gases are
produced by a volcano?

Math Literacy

Scientists often use math skills when they collect and interpret data as part of their experiments. A **Math Link** in each lesson of this book asks you to use several types of math skills, including:

▶ **Number Sense and Operations** This includes estimation, addition, subtraction, multiplication, and division.

▶ **Measurement** This includes using and converting standard and metric units of size, distance, time, volume, area, mass, weight, or temperature.

▶ **Data Analysis and Probability** This includes calculating the likelihood that an event will happen, and making and interpreting bar graphs and line graphs.

▶ **Problem Solving** This means using skills and strategies to solve problems.

Inquiry Skills

When you collect and interpret data, you use these skills.

Use numbers Order, count, add, subtract, multiply, and divide to explain data.

Measure Find the size, distance, time, volume, area, mass, weight, or temperature of an object or an event.

Interpret data Use the information that has been gathered to answer questions or solve a problem.

After interpreting the data, it is time to draw a conclusion. A conclusion is a statement about whether or not the hypothesis is valid based on the data collected. Sometimes the data do not support the hypothesis. Perhaps different experiments and observations are needed. A new question may result.

Scientists also tell other scientists, as well as members of the public, about what they have discovered. The United States Geological Survey (USGS) operates five volcano observatories. They observe activity leading to eruption, provide emergency information about future and ongoing eruptions, identify hazardous areas around active and potentially active volcanoes, and improve public understanding of how volcanoes erupt and

Inquiry Skills

When you draw conclusions and communicate results, you use this skill.

Communicate Share information.

Writing in Science

Writing is a tool you can use to communicate, or share information, about science. A **Writing Link** in each lesson of this book asks you to use one of these types of writing:

▸ A **Personal Narrative** tells about an event in your life.

▸ **Writing a Story** uses characters, setting, and a sequence of events.

▸ **Persuasive Writing** tries to get your readers to agree with your opinion.

▸ **Explanatory Writing** tells how to make or do something.

▸ **Writing That Compares** tells how two things are alike and different.

▸ **Expository Writing** presents facts and explains ideas.

Using Your Book

The **Explore Activity** is a hands-on way to learn about the lesson. The title is in the form of a question that you will answer in the activity.

The **inquiry skills** in the Explore Activity are the same skills that scientists use.

The last step of the activity provides an opportunity for **further inquiry**.

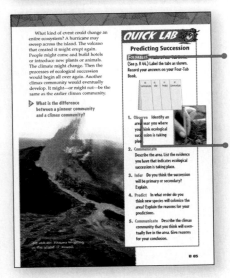

You can use different kinds of **Foldables™ organizers** to collect and record data in the Quick Lab.

Inquiry skills are also used in the Quick Lab.

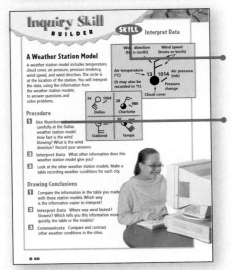

Each Inquiry Skill Builder focuses on a specific **inquiry skill**.

Other **inquiry skills** are also reinforced in the Inquiry Skill Builder.

Learn Through Visuals

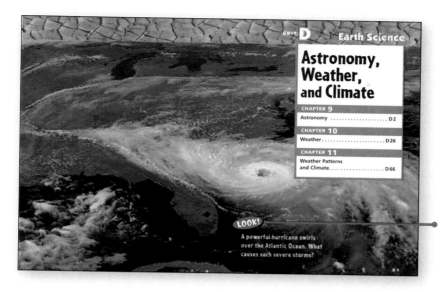

Visuals include both **photographs** and **graphics**. This question will help you get information from the photograph at the beginning of each unit of this book.

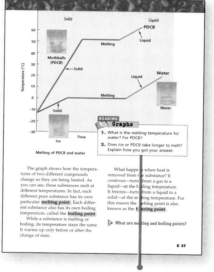

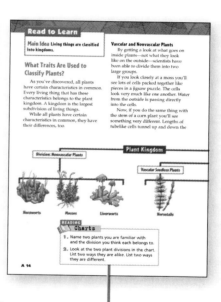

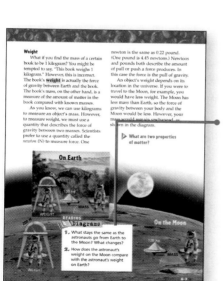

Throughout all chapters of this book you will get information by **reading graphics**. Graphics are pictures such as:
• diagrams
• charts
• maps
• graphs

This box contains the **Main Idea** of the lesson. Keep the main idea of the lesson in mind as you read.

Before Reading Read the large red question before you read the page. Try to answer this question from what you already know.

During Reading Look for new **Vocabulary** words highlighted in yellow. Look at the pictures. They will help you understand what you are reading.

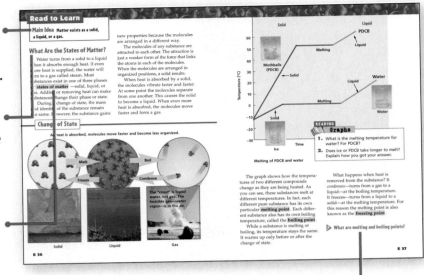

After Reading This arrow points to a question. It will help you check that you understand what you have read. Try to answer the question before you go to the next large red question.

On one page in each lesson, you will find a question that practices the **Chapter Reading Skill.** In any chapter, you will find one of these skills:

- compare and contrast
- main idea and supporting details
- predict
- cause and effect
- draw conclusions
- sequence of events
- summarize

At the end of every lesson, you can log on to **e-Journal** for tips and suggestions about how to write a research report.

Think and Write questions at the end of every lesson give you an opportunity to write about what you learned in the lesson.

A **Writing Link** at the end of every lesson allows you to express yourself through several different types of writing:
- Personal Narrative
- Writing a Story
- Persuasive Writing
- Explanatory Writing
- Writing That Compares
- Expository Writing

A **Technology Link** at the end of every lesson gives you an opportunity to log on to our Web site www.science.mmhschool.com for additional links.

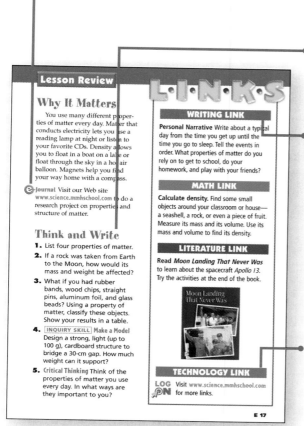

Lesson Review

Why It Matters

You use many different properties of matter every day. Matter that conducts electricity lets you use a reading lamp at night or listen to your favorite CDs. Density allows you to float in a boat on a lake or float through the sky in a hot air balloon. Magnets help you find your way home with a compass.

e-Journal Visit our Web site www.science.mmhschool.com to do a research project on properties and structure of matter.

Think and Write

1. List four properties of matter.
2. If a rock was taken from Earth to the Moon, how would its mass and weight be affected?
3. What if you had rubber bands, wood chips, straight pins, aluminum foil, and glass beads? Using a property of matter, classify these objects. Show your results in a table.
4. INQUIRY SKILL Make a Model Design a strong, light (up to 100 g), cardboard structure to bridge a 30-cm gap. How much weight can it support?
5. Critical Thinking Think of the properties of matter you use every day. In what ways are they important to you?

L·I·N·K·S

WRITING LINK

Personal Narrative Write about a typical day from the time you get up until the time you go to sleep. Tell the events in order. What properties of matter do you rely on to get to school, do your homework, and play with your friends?

MATH LINK

Calculate density. Find some small objects around your classroom or house—a seashell, a rock, or even a piece of fruit. Measure its mass and its volume. Use its mass and volume to find its density.

LITERATURE LINK

Read *Moon Landing That Never Was* to learn about the spacecraft *Apollo 13.* Try the activities at the end of the book.

TECHNOLOGY LINK

LOG ON Visit www.science.mmhschool.com for more links.

E 17

Amazing Stories

PLANETARY WEATHER

What's the weather like on other planets? Knowing about the atmosphere on other planets tells us more about our entire solar system.

D 22

D 23

Write About It questions on selected Sally Ride Science, Time for Kids, and magazine-style features give you an opportunity to write about what you learned.

A **LogOn reference** on every Sally Ride Science, Time for Kids, and magazine-style feature allows you to learn more about each topic.

There are **What Did I Learn? questions** on selected Sally Ride Science, Time for Kids, and magazine-style features. Answering the questions gives you an opportunity to practice using a standardized test, multiple choice format.

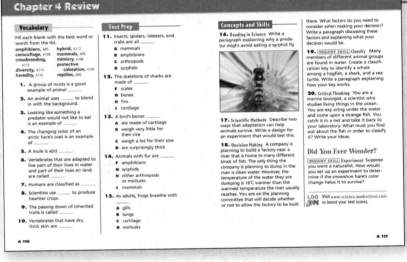

A two-page **review** at the end of each chapter allows you to show what you know using a variety of assessment formats:
• fill-in
• multiple choice
• short answer

Performance Assessment at the end of every unit provides an opportunity to demonstrate what you've learned through hands-on activities and projects.

UNIT A

Characteristics of Living Things

LOOK!

Is it a plant? Is it an animal?
The leafy sea dragon is
actually a fish that looks like
seaweed! How do you think
this helps it to survive?

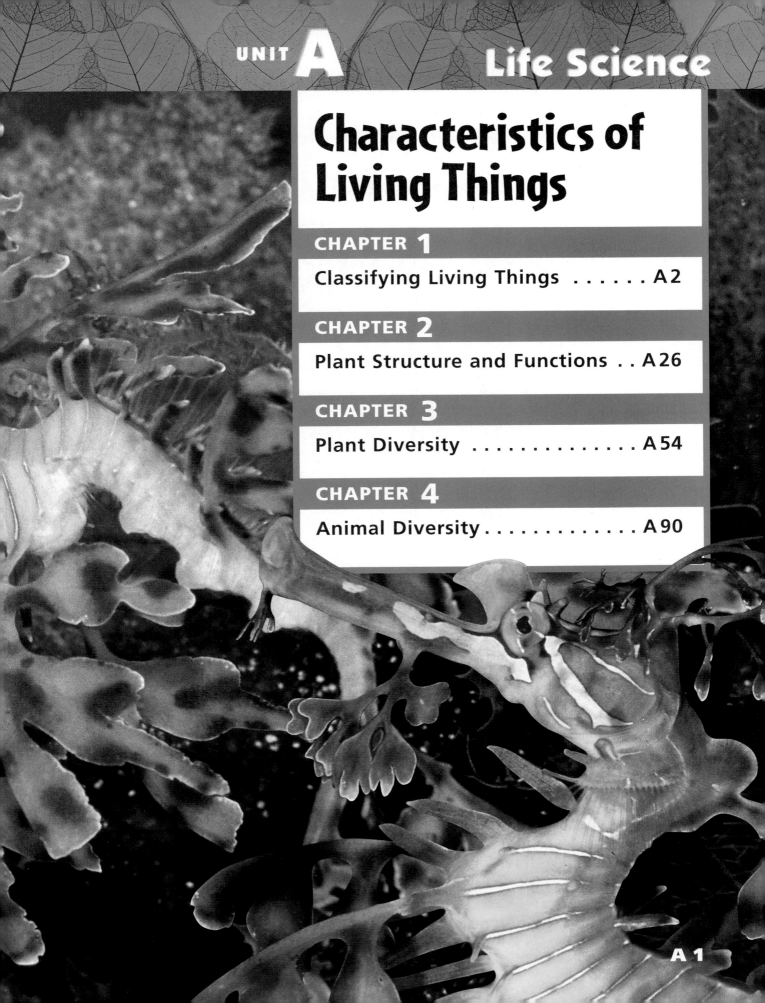

Characteristics of Living Things

Classifying Living Things

Did You Ever Wonder?

How many living things do you see in this picture? There are some living things, smaller than the smallest flea, you won't be able to see. But we know they are there. People have estimated that today there are more than 10 million different kinds of living things on Earth. We have only identified 1.5 million of them.

INQUIRY SKILL **Define based on observations** What makes something a living thing? Think about how you recognized the living things in this picture.

The Basic Unit of Life

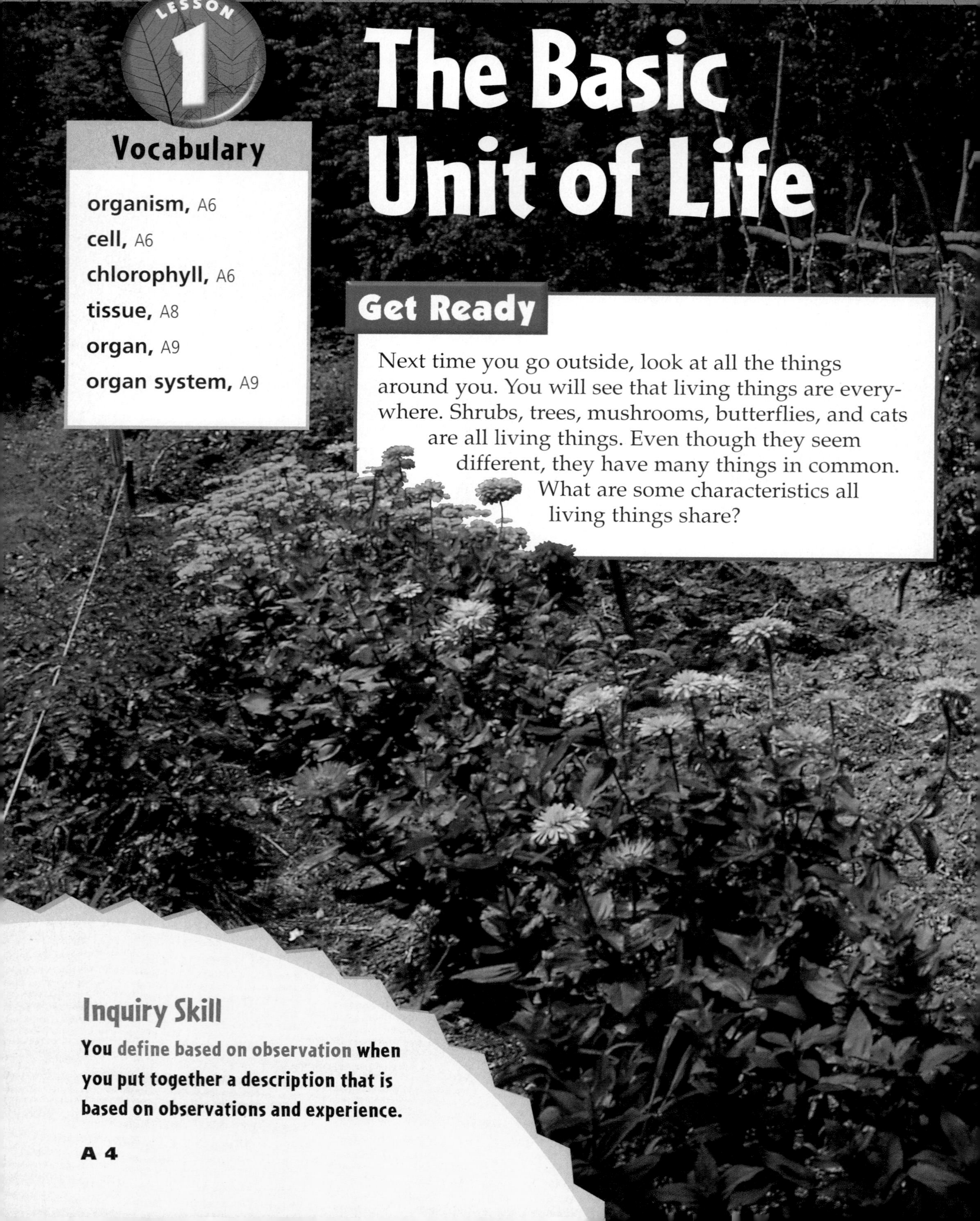

Vocabulary

organism, A6

cell, A6

chlorophyll, A6

tissue, A8

organ, A9

organ system, A9

Get Ready

Next time you go outside, look at all the things around you. You will see that living things are everywhere. Shrubs, trees, mushrooms, butterflies, and cats are all living things. Even though they seem different, they have many things in common. What are some characteristics all living things share?

Inquiry Skill

You define based on observation **when you put together a description that is based on observations and experience.**

Explore Activity

What Is the Basic Unit of Life?

Materials

Elodea, moss, fern, or any flowering plant

prepared slide of human blood

microscope

microscope slide

coverslip

dropper

water

Procedure

1 Your group will need to get a plant and a prepared slide of human blood from your teacher.

2 Make a wet-mount slide of your plant by placing a leaf in a drop of water in the center of the slide and carefully putting a coverslip on top.

3 **Observe** View the slide under low power. Then observe the prepared slide of human blood.

4 **Communicate** Draw what you see.

Drawing Conclusions

1 **Communicate** What common traits did you observe using the microscope?

2 **Communicate** What do the organisms the cells come from have in common?

3 **Define** From what you observed, come up with your own definition of a living thing.

4 **FURTHER INQUIRY** **Hypothesize** Examine the drawings you made and think about the organisms that they come from. Do you see any differences? Why do you think cells vary from one organism to another?

Main Idea All living things are made of cells, the basic unit of life.

What Is the Basic Unit of Life?

Do you know what all living things have in common? From the smallest **organism**, or living thing, to the largest, we are all made of cells. A **cell** is the smallest unit of an organism that is capable of life.

Since the cell is the smallest unit of living matter, the processes of life must be carried out by the cells. To do this, cells have structures that work

together to maintain the life of the cell. Some of these structures make food, some release energy for the cell to use, and some transport materials.

The cells of different organisms are different. For example, plant cells are different from animal cells. Plants have needs that animals don't have and cell parts that meet these needs.

You don't need a microscope to discover that plants are green. That's because their cells contain a green chemical called **chlorophyll** (KLAWR·uh·fil). It allows plants to use the Sun's energy to make their

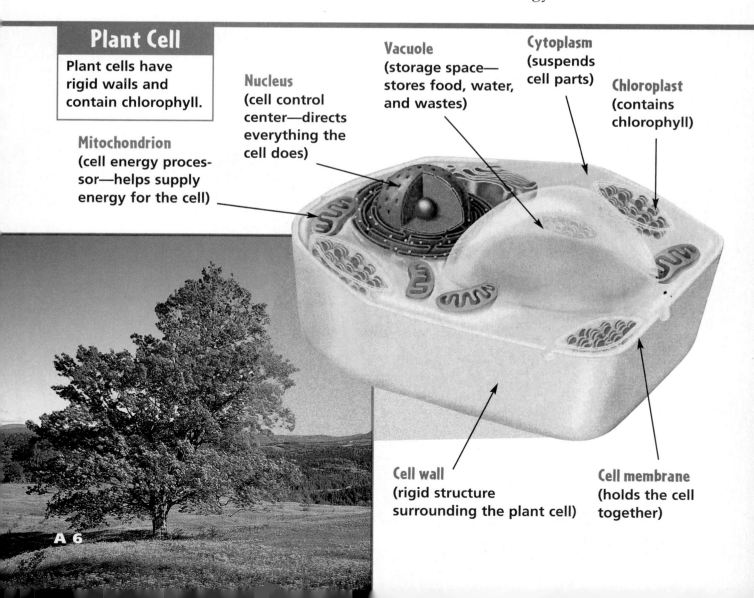

Plant Cell

Plant cells have rigid walls and contain chlorophyll.

Mitochondrion (cell energy processor—helps supply energy for the cell)

Nucleus (cell control center—directs everything the cell does)

Vacuole (storage space—stores food, water, and wastes)

Cytoplasm (suspends cell parts)

Chloroplast (contains chlorophyll)

Cell wall (rigid structure surrounding the plant cell)

Cell membrane (holds the cell together)

own food. This chemical is found in chloroplasts (KLAWR·uh·plasts).

Plant cells also have a cell wall. Let's look at a tree to find out why plants need cell walls. A tree rises up from the ground. Its rigid trunk supports all its weight. The tree must be made of rigid building blocks—rigid cells that support it. The cell walls of the plant cells keep the tree from collapsing.

Animal cells don't have chloroplasts or a cell wall. However, plant and animal cells share many characteristics because they have many of the same needs. For example, plant and animal cells have a nucleus,

cytoplasm, mitochondria, and a cell membrane.

The nucleus of plant and animal cells directs everything the cells do. The cytoplasm is a fluid where all parts of the cell float. The mitochondria release energy the cell needs. Plant vacuoles are used for storing food, water and wastes. The cell membrane holds the cell together.

READING **Draw Conclusions**
What is one of the things plant and animal cells have in common?

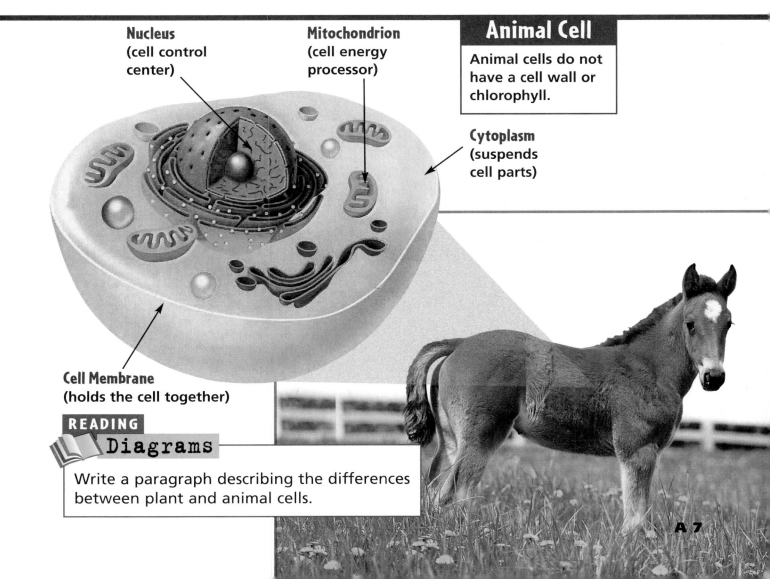

Nucleus
(cell control center)

Mitochondrion
(cell energy processor)

Animal Cell

Animal cells do not have a cell wall or chlorophyll.

Cytoplasm
(suspends cell parts)

Cell Membrane
(holds the cell together)

READING
Diagrams

Write a paragraph describing the differences between plant and animal cells.

What Are Living Things Made Of?

Some organisms, such as bacteria and some fungi, are made of just one cell. Other organisms, such as some algae, are made of many similar cells that benefit from cooperating. They do this by forming colonies of hundreds of cells that move and find food together.

Many-celled living things, such as complex plants and animals, are made of different kinds of cells. The cells of a many-celled organism work together to keep the organism alive. Different kinds of cells do different kinds of jobs. Each cell contributes to the health and survival of the organism in a different way.

For example, in a tree, cells in leaves make the plant's food. Cells in roots, trunk, stems, and branches form tubes through which the food or water is moved, or transported

(trans·PAWRT·uhd). Other cells form flowers, fruits, and seeds that allow the tree to reproduce.

Similarly, the cells of animals, including humans, have different functions. Skin cells are flat and wide to protect the cells beneath them, muscle cells are long threadlike cells that allow body movement, nerve cells are long because they transport messages from one part of the body to another.

Similar cells that have the same job or function come together to make a **tissue** (TISH·ew). The "strings" in celery stalks are examples of plant tissues. These tissues carry water and

READING Charts

Give an example of each level organization in many-celled organisms.

Levels of Organization

Cell

Tissue

Organ

Organ system

Organism

minerals from the roots to the leaves of the plant. Another example of a plant tissue is the flesh of fruits. This tissue's function is to protect the plant's seeds.

Examples of animal tissue are the muscles that allow you to move your arms or to walk. The muscles in your body are tissue made of muscle cells. Different kinds of tissue in an animal's body include muscle, bone, skin, nerve, and blood.

Tissues of different kinds come together to make an **organ**. Stems and fruits are examples of plant organs. The heart, the lungs, and the brain are examples of animal organs.

Finally, a group of organs that work together to do a certain job makes up an **organ system**. For example, a fox's digestive system includes its mouth, stomach, and intestines. The roots of a plant are the main organ in the root system of a plant. The stems and leaves are organs of the shoot system.

Organs systems work together so that life processes like breathing and digestion can be carried out. These are the processes that keep many-celled organisms, like you, healthy and alive.

▷ **What are the levels of organization of many-celled organisms?**

QUICK LAB

Plant Parts

FOLDABLES™ Make a Shutter Fold. (See p. R 42.) Label the tabs as shown.

(See p. R 42.)

1. **Observe** Use a hand lens to observe the parts of a celery plant.

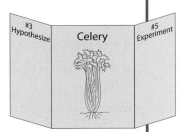

2. **Draw** what you see in your Shutter Fold.

3. **Hypothesize** Make a guess about the function of the stem of the celery plant. Write your hypothesis in the left shutter of your Shutter Fold.

4. Label the plant organs you see on your drawing. What levels of organization does your drawing show? Record your answer below your diagram in your Shutter Fold.

5. **Experiment** Add water to a bottle so the water is about 1 inch deep. Add a few drops of food coloring to the water. Cut a piece of stalk and place it in the colored water. Observe it after a few minutes. Record what you see on the right shutter of your Shutter Fold.

6. **Communicate** Explain to the class why your observation supports or doesn't support your guess.

What Traits Are Used to Classify Organisms?

People have always tried to make sense of their surroundings. One way to do this is to look for patterns. For example, if we find patterns among plants we can answer some very important questions, such as: What plants are good to eat? What plants are poisonous?

The science of finding patterns among living things is called *classification* (klas·uh·fi·KAY·shuhn). Cells are used in classification because cells from different organisms are different. Whether an animal grows hair or feathers depends on the kinds of cells it has.

Ancient scientists came up with very simple classification systems. These were based on characteristics that anyone could see. In 350 B.C. the Greek scientist Aristotle classified plants into three large groups—herbs (little plants), shrubs (bigger plants), and trees (the biggest plants).

This made sense at the time. However, as scientists learned more about plants, they realized that size was not the best way to classify them. For example, today we know that a tiny blade of grass is more like a stalk of corn than a dandelion that grows close to the ground.

When it comes to classifying organisms, cells, tissues, organs, and systems all have to be compared carefully. For example, bats and birds have wings and fly. However, if you were to take a close look at the wing of a bat, you would

Eagle

Bat

Cat

The bones in the diagram above have been color-coded to show similar bones in each animal.

READING

Diagrams

How are the bat's wing and the cat's front leg alike?

find that it is more like the front leg of a cat than like the wing of an eagle.

So bats and cats are in fact more alike than bats and eagles.

▷ **What parts should be analyzed when classifying an organism?**

Lesson Review

Why It Matters

All living things are made of cells. The cell is the basic unit of life because it can carry out all life processes. Some organisms are made of one cell and some are many-celled. Many-celled organisms are organized internally from cells to tissues to organs to organ systems.

Similarities among organisms are found in cells, tissues, organs, and organ systems. All these levels of organization are used to classify organisms.

e-Journal Visit our Web site **www.science.mmhschool.com** to do a research project on the levels of organization of a many-celled organism of your choice.

Think and Write

1. What do all living things have in common?

2. What does the cell wall in plant cells do for plants?

3. What are some examples of animal tissue?

4. What are the two main organ systems in plants?

5. **Critical Thinking** How can cell classification be useful in identifying organisms?

L·I·N·K·S

WRITING LINK

Writing That Compares How are plant and animal cells similar? How are they different? Use a Venn diagram to organize your ideas. Write an essay to present your findings.

MATH LINK

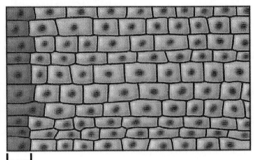

10 cells

Solve this problem. Use a benchmark number to estimate the number of cells in the slide.

ART LINK

Make a poster. Choose a plant and an animal. Make a poster using drawings and/or photographs to show the levels of organization in the plant and the animal you selected. Research the structure of these organisms so you can complete your poster accurately.

TECHNOLOGY LINK

LOG ON Visit www.science.mmhschool.com for more links.

The Kingdoms of Life

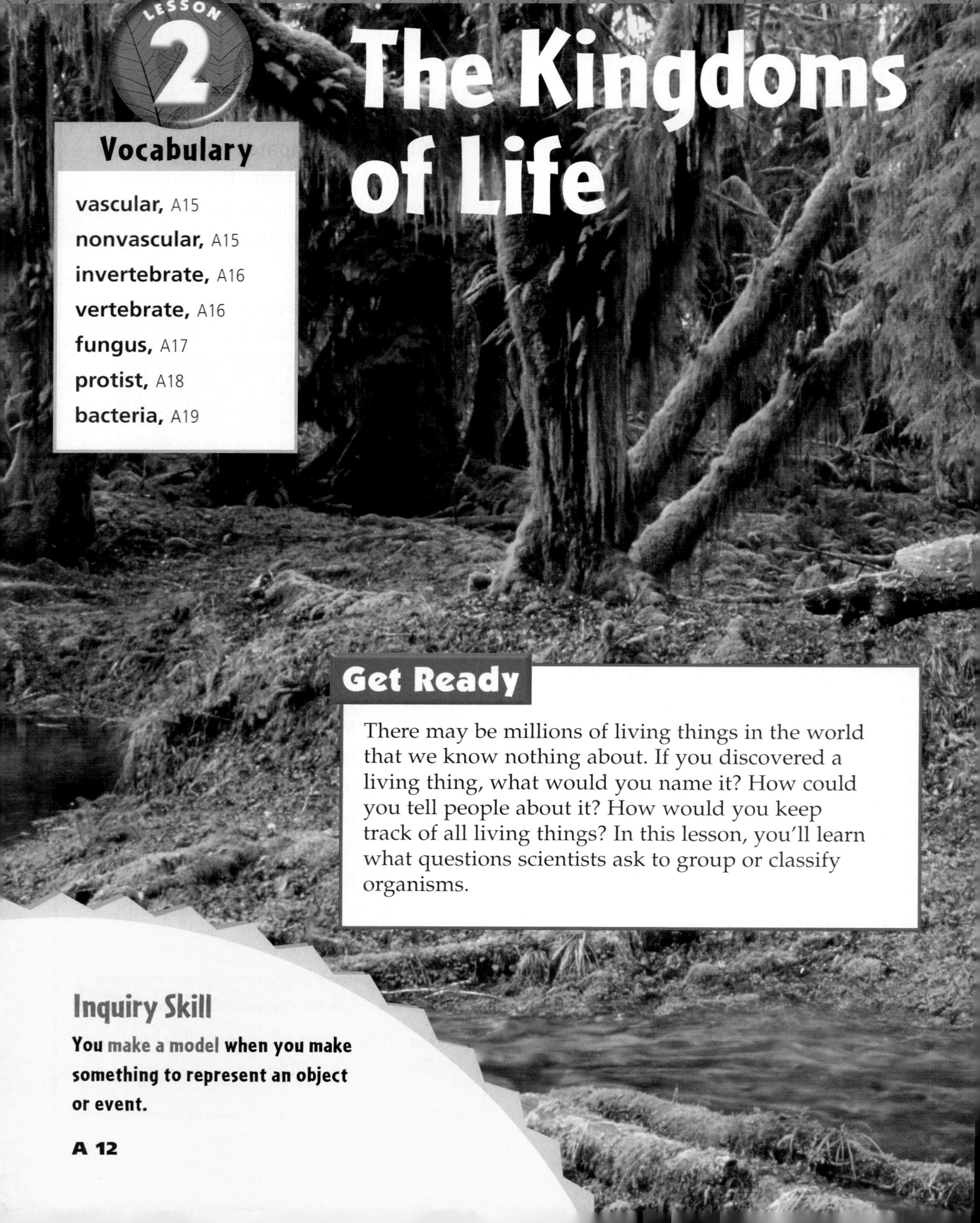

Vocabulary

vascular, A15

nonvascular, A15

invertebrate, A16

vertebrate, A16

fungus, A17

protist, A18

bacteria, A19

Get Ready

There may be millions of living things in the world that we know nothing about. If you discovered a living thing, what would you name it? How could you tell people about it? How would you keep track of all living things? In this lesson, you'll learn what questions scientists ask to group or classify organisms.

Inquiry Skill

You make a model when you make something to represent an object or event.

Explore Activity

What Traits Are Used to Classify Plants?

Materials
lettuce leaf
liverwort plant
stalk of celery
hand lens

Procedure

1 **Observe** Use the hand lens to observe the lettuce leaf and the liverwort.

2 **Communicate** As you observe each plant, draw and describe the plant.

3 **Observe** Break the piece of celery. Pull apart the two pieces. Remove a 1-cm piece of the string from the celery. Observe the string with the hand lens.

4 **Communicate** Draw and describe the string from the celery.

Drawing Conclusions

1 **Communicate** How are the lettuce, liverwort, and celery similar?

2 **Communicate** How are the plants different?

3 **Infer** What is the purpose of the tubelike parts in the lettuce and the celery?

4 **Infer** How can liverworts live and grow without tubelike parts?

5 FURTHER INQUIRY **Make a Model** Design a model to show how both kinds of plants get water and minerals from the soil.

Read to Learn

Main Idea Living things are classified into kingdoms.

What Traits Are Used to Classify Plants?

As you've discovered, all plants have certain characteristics in common. Every living thing that has these characteristics belongs to the plant kingdom. A kingdom is the largest subdivision of living things.

While all plants have certain characteristics in common, they have their differences, too.

Vascular and Nonvascular Plants

By getting a look at what goes on inside plants—not what they look like on the outside—scientists have been able to divide them into two large groups.

If you look closely at a moss you'll see lots of cells packed together like pieces in a jigsaw puzzle. The cells look very much like one another. Water from the outside is passing directly into the cells.

Now, if you do the same thing with the stem of a corn plant you'll see something very different. Lengths of tubelike cells tunnel up and down the

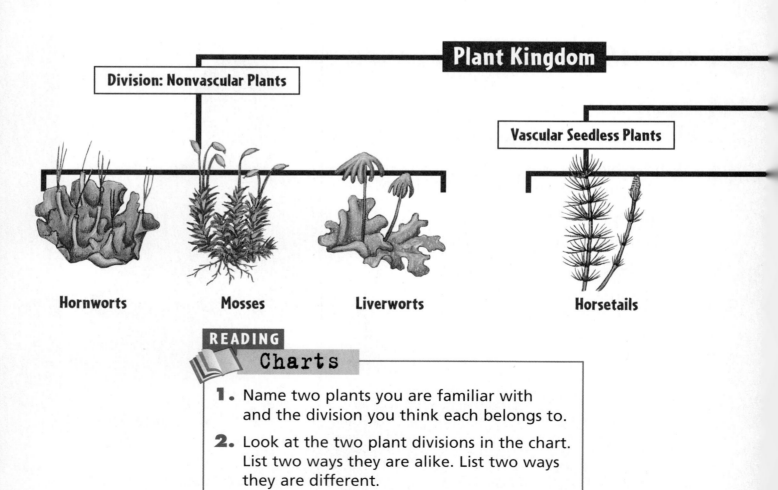

Plant Kingdom

Division: Nonvascular Plants

Vascular Seedless Plants

Hornworts   Mosses   Liverworts   Horsetails

READING Charts

1. Name two plants you are familiar with and the division you think each belongs to.

2. Look at the two plant divisions in the chart. List two ways they are alike. List two ways they are different.

stem. Water taken in by the plant's roots is moving up one set of tubes toward the plant's leaves, flowers, and other parts. At the same time, foods made in the leaves are moving down the other set of tubes, which lead to all the plant's parts. These tubes are called *vascular tissue*.

Scientists call plants that have this kind of tissue—such as trees and flowering plants—**vascular** (VAS·kyuh·luhr) plants. Vascular means "composed of or containing vessels." Scientists call plants that don't have this kind of tissue—such as mosses and other simple plants— **nonvascular** plants. All plants fall into one of these two groups. Each of these groups is called a *division*.

Plants within each of these two divisions are far from identical. This observation prompted scientists to divide these groups even further. They divided vascular plants into seedless plants and plants with seeds. Then they divided seed plants into flowering and nonflowering plants.

The smallest groups have plants most like one another. The larger groups have plants least like one another. This means that the smaller the group, the more closely related its members are.

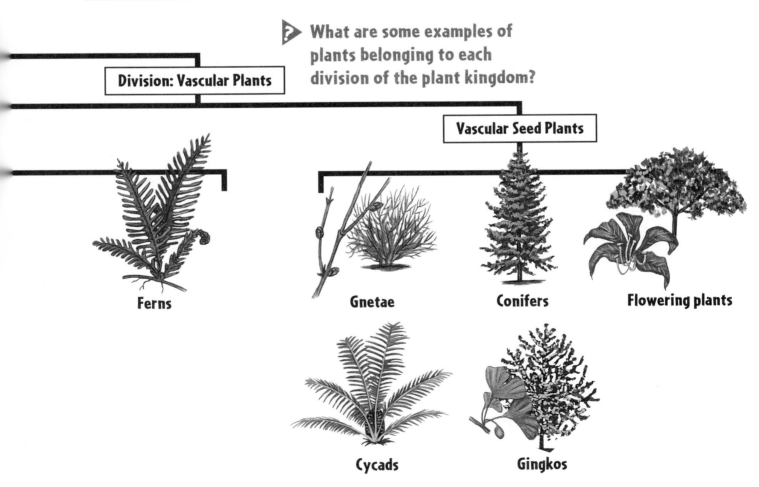

? **What are some examples of plants belonging to each division of the plant kingdom?**

Division: Vascular Plants

Vascular Seed Plants

Ferns

Gnetae

Conifers

Flowering plants

Cycads

Gingkos

What Makes Animals Different from Plants?

Unlike plants, animals cannot make their own food. Animals also differ from plants because most animals can move from one place to another during some parts of their lives.

All animals are grouped into one kingdom, known as the animal kingdom. The animal kingdom is divided into two large groups. One group is made up of animals that have backbones. The members of this group are called **vertebrates**. The members of the other group do not have backbones. They are called **invertebrates**.

Invertebrates are divided into *phyla* (FIGH·luh) (singular, *phylum*). Some examples are shown on the left. The vertebrates are in the Phylum *Chordata*. Phyla are divided in smaller divisions called *classes*. Some classes of vertebrates are shown on the right.

▷ **How are animals different from plants?**

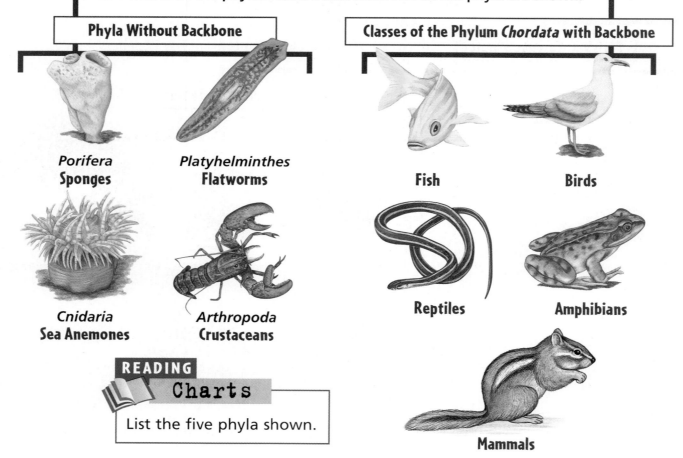

Animal Kingdom

Phyla in the animal kingdom are like divisions in the plant kingdom. On the left are members of four phyla without backbones. On the right are five classes of the phylum with backbones. Not all the phyla are shown.

Phyla Without Backbone

Porifera
Sponges

Platyhelminthes
Flatworms

Cnidaria
Sea Anemones

Arthropoda
Crustaceans

Classes of the Phylum *Chordata* with Backbone

Fish

Birds

Reptiles

Amphibians

Mammals

READING
Charts

List the five phyla shown.

What Is a Fungus?

It may be one celled or many celled. It doesn't make its own food as plants do or eat food as animals do. Instead it simply absorbs (takes in) food from decaying dead organisms and wastes in its environment. What is it? It's a **fungus** (FUNG·guhs).

Fungi (FUN·jigh) is the plural of *fungus*. Fungi can be very useful living things. Some of them have great flavors. Others contain chemicals that fight diseases. Still others help bread to rise or turn cheeses sharp and tangy. Fungi in soil break down decaying plants and animals so that their chemicals can be used by living things. You might say that such fungi clean up our environment.

Unfortunately, the fungus kingdom also contains organisms that cause problems for people. Some fungi are poisonous. Some fungi give people itchy diseases, like athlete's foot. Some fungi can spoil food and make you sick. Some fungi coat bathroom tiles and basement walls with smelly black or white fuzz. In the autumn of 1997, one kind of fungus was even responsible for the closing of a library in Staten Island, a part of New York City. The fungus, which grows in damp places like the library's basement, caused people to cough and sneeze as if they had the flu.

The chart on this page shows the groups of the fungus kingdom.

▷ **How are members of the fungus kingdom different from plants?**

Fungus Kingdom

Yeasts, morels, mildews

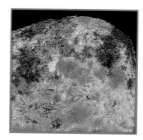

Molds

Mushrooms, smuts, rusts

READING Charts

1. Give examples of the three main groups of fungi.
2. Make a chart listing things useful fungi can do.

What Is a Protist?

What do you see when you look into a lake, pond, river, or ocean? Sometimes it looks like clear water. However, that "clear" water is home to millions of microscopic living things that belong to the **protist** (PROH·tist) kingdom. This kingdom isn't made up of just microscopic living things. It also includes living things you can see without a microscope, such as seaweed and green pond scum, called algae. Protists are very important because they provide food for many marine and freshwater animals. Although most protists live in water, some inhabit the land.

Some protists are single cells that swim in the water in search of smaller living things to eat. Others, like seaweeds, are made up of groups of the same cells that are linked together. Protists such as algae don't have to hunt for food. They contain chlorophyll. All they have to do is float on water in the sunlight, soak up the Sun's rays, and make their own food. Still other kinds of protists are one celled, swim around, and contain chlorophyll.

Members of the protist kingdom certainly seem very different. However, if scientists put them in the same kingdom, they must have something in common. You would discover that "something" if you peered at the cells of protists under a microscope. You'd notice a dense, dark structure, called a *nucleus* (NEW·klee·uhs) inside each cell. If you looked very carefully, you'd see that the nucleus was surrounded by a thin envelope. Scientists call this envelope a *membrane* (MEM·brayn). The chart shows some of the groups of the protist kingdom.

 How are some protists like plants?

Protist Kingdom

Slime molds

Diatoms

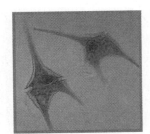
Dinoflagellates

Green algae

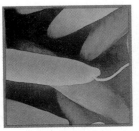
Euglenas

What Are Bacteria?

Bacteria (bak·TEER·ee·uh) are the tiniest living things. They are also very simple. Some can cause a great deal of trouble, like infections. Others are necessary for animals and plants to survive.

Some kinds of bacteria group together in clusters or chains. Other kinds don't. You can only see bacteria under a microscope. Each *bacterium* (bak·TEER·ee·uhm) is a single cell without a nucleus.

Bacteria were once classified in a single kingdom called Monera. However, many scientists today recognize two separate kingdoms; the "ancient" bacteria kingdom and the "true" bacteria kingdom. The "ancient" bacteria kingdom includes some fascinating organisms. One type lives in the digestive system of cows. It helps the cow by digesting cellulose, the main substance in grass, which the cow eats but can't digest. Still another kind of "ancient" bacterium lives deep in the ocean, where lava seeps through cracks in the ocean floor. The red-hot lava heats the water up to 105°C. That's hotter than the temperature of boiling water!

The "true" bacteria kingdom also contains some unusual members. Have you ever seen a blue-green lake? This color is due to the presence of *cyanobacteria* (sigh·uh·noh·bak·TEER·ee·uh). These bacteria release oxygen to the air.

Some true bacteria cause diseases in plants and animals. A "strep" throat is caused by a true bacterium. If your stomach aches after eating spoiled food, the culprit is likely to be another true bacterium. More serious diseases like tuberculosis and certain kinds of pneumonia are also caused by true bacteria.

▷ **How are bacteria different from plants and other organisms?**

Bacteria Kingdoms

"Ancient" Bacteria

These bacteria are methanogens. They use carbon dioxide and produce methane (natural gas).

"True" Bacteria

These bacteria are streptococci—the ones that can give you a strep throat.

Inquiry Skill
BUILDER

SKILL Classify

Using a Key

How should a living thing be classified? Into what group should it be placed?

One way to classify organisms is by using a *classification key*. A classification key lists choices describing characteristics of organisms. It is a series of pairs of statements with directions to follow. These directions will eventually lead you to the identity of the organism you have chosen.

Key to Birds

1. Webbed feet........Go to 3.
   No webbed feet...Go to 2.

2. Hooked bill......Red-tailed hawk
   No hooked bill...Cardinal

3. Flat bill.....Mallard duck
   No flat bill....Go to 4.

4. Pouch...
   Brown pelican
   No pouch...
   Red-faced cormorant

Procedure

1 **Observe** Use the classification key, above right, to identify the birds shown. Starting with the first pair of statements, choose the one that applies to the bird you picked.

2 **Interpret Data** Follow the statement's direction. It will lead you to another pair of statements.

3 Keep following the directions until you come to the identity of the bird you chose.

Drawing Conclusions

Do you think this key would be helpful in identifying birds in your neighborhood? Explain.

A 20

Why It Matters

Nature holds many secrets and presents many mysteries. It is the job of scientists to discover the secrets and solve the mysteries. Classifying helps do this. Among other things, it shows which organisms are most closely related to one another. It can also show the order in which they appeared on Earth. Classification can be thought of as a kind of calendar of life on Earth.

e-Journal Visit our Web site www.science.mmhschool.com to do a research project on the history of classification.

Think and Write

1. What is the main difference between an invertebrate and a vertebrate?

2. How are plants similar to animals, protists, fungi, and bacteria? How are plants different?

3. How are vascular plants different from nonvascular plants?

4. **INQUIRY SKILL** **Classify** Name a trait you would use to classify a fish as belonging to either the Phylum *Chordata* or the Phylum *Arthropoda*.

5. **Critical Thinking** How does classification simplify the study of living things?

L·I·N·K·S

WRITING LINK

Expository Writing Write a paragraph to explain why the smallest classification groups have organisms with more similarities than the larger ones. Give facts and examples to support the main idea.

MATH LINK

Solve this problem. Under ideal conditions a bacterium can divide into two bacteria every 20 minutes. Then each of those bacteria can divide into two new ones after another 20 minutes. If you start with one bacterium, how many will you have after one hour? After two hours? After three hours? Five hours? Eight hours?

LITERATURE LINK

Read *The Power of Green,* the story of some of the plants and protists that live in different areas of the world. Think about the plants and protists that live in your area. Try the activities at the end of the book.

by Lisa Feder-Feitel • Illustrated by Rita Lascaro

TECHNOLOGY LINK

 LOG ON Visit www.science.mmhschool.com for more links.

Biodiversity

Plant Kingdom   Did you know that the bark of the white willow tree has been used to relieve pain for thousands of years? Aspirin is based on ingredients found in this tree.

We share Earth with an amazing variety of other living things, from the tallest redwood tree with trillions of cells to the smallest bacterium with just one. We know of more than 1.5 million different species. Millions more in rain forests and oceans are waiting to be discovered.

Why are there so many species? Because each is adapted to a different environment and to a different way of life. Dolphins swim in the oceans, and eagles soar in the skies. Mushrooms digest dead trees, and algae float in sunlit ponds.

This great variety of life is called biodiversity. Each member of each of the kingdoms contributes to our world in its own way. So when a species disappears or becomes extinct, its unique contribution is lost forever.

We depend on other species and the ecosystems they live in. They keep our planet healthy. They provide us with natural resources such as foods, fibers, and medicines. We enjoy them, and we want future generations to be able to enjoy them, too. We have many reasons to protect the many incredible forms of life on our planet.

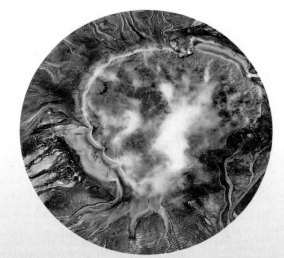

Bacteria Kingdom   The *Thermus aquaticus* bacteria live in the hot springs of Yellowstone National Park. These microscopic organisms thrive at a scalding 160 degrees Fahrenheit! Now they are commercially made in laboratories and used in biomedical tests that help diagnose diseases.

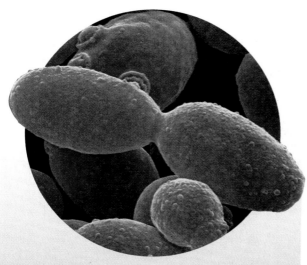

Fungus Kingdom   There's more to fungi than mushrooms. *Saccharomyces cerevisiae,* the fungus known as baker's yeast, feeds on sugars in flour dough. This causes carbon dioxide to be released and bread to rise. Bread would be flat without this fungus.

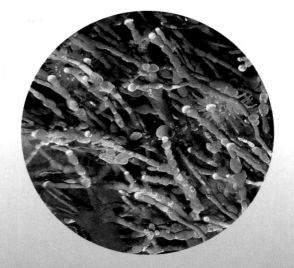

Protist Kingdom   From slime molds to mildew, protists may not seem appealing, but you've probably eaten them. Red algae is a seaweed that contains an ingredient used in ice cream, pudding, and chocolate milk!

Animal Kingdom   They may be as small as sticks of butter at birth, but each new panda that's born is a big boost to an endangered species.

Write About It

1. Why is it worth protecting endangered animals?

2. Plants can be used as medicines. They also have many other uses. Write about a few.

LOG ON Visit www.science.mmhschool.com to learn more about biodiversity.

Chapter 1 Review

Vocabulary

Fill each blank with the best word or words from the list.

chlorophyll, A6
fungus, A17
invertebrate, A16
nonvascular, A15
organ, A9
organ system, A9
protist, A18
tissue, A9
vascular, A15
vertebrate, A16

1. Muscle is an example of a(n) _____.

2. Trees and flowering plants are _____ plants.

3. A group of organs that work together form a(n)_____.

4. A(n) _____ is an organism whose nucleus is surrounded by a membrane.

5. A green chemical called _____ allows plants to use the Sun's energy to make their own foods.

6. A mushroom is a(n) _____.

7. An animal that doesn't have a backbone is a(n) _____.

8. A moss is a(n) _____ plant.

9. Tissues of different kinds come together to make a(n) _____.

10. A bird is a(n) _____.

Test Prep

11. Which of the following is a fungus?

A mold

B moss

C fern

D conifer

12. Similar cells that have the same function come together to make a(n) _____.

F organ system

G organ

H tissue

J organism

13. The green "food factories" of plants are _____.

A chloroplasts

B mitochondria

C vacuoles

D cytoplasm

14. The science of finding patterns among living things is called _____.

F mitochondrion

G classification

H organization

J respiration

15. Where do plant cells store food, water and wastes?

   A nucleus

   B chloroplast

   C vacuole

   D cell membrane

Concepts and Skills

16. Reading in Science Write a paragraph explaining why ferns can grow taller than mosses.

17. Scientific Methods How would you determine if a cell is an animal cell or a plant cell? Write up a design for an experiment to find out.

18. Decision Making Is there a single correct way to classify an organism? Write a paragraph explaining your answer.

19. INQUIRY SKILL **Experiment** Design an experiment to determine how much mosses, ferns, and grasses depend on water for survival. Write how you would set up the experiment. Write down your hypothesis. Tell what variables you would test.

20. Critical Thinking You dig in the ground and find a fossil of a fern. You then dig deeper and find a fossil of a club moss. What reasoning might let you conclude that club mosses existed earlier than ferns? Write a paragraph explaining your reasoning.

Did You Ever Wonder?

INQUIRY SKILL **Communicate** Why are external traits not used to classify living organisms? Explain your answer to your class.

LOG ON Visit **www.science.mmhschool.com** to boost your test scores.

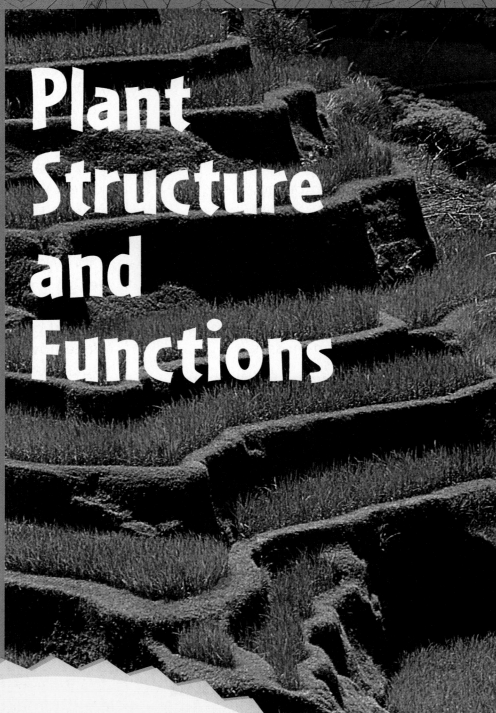

Plant Structure and Functions

Did You Ever Wonder?

Where does rice come from? Most of the world's rice is grown in Asia, often in flooded fields called paddies. It takes 5,000 liters (1,320 gallons) of water to grow 1 kilogram (2.2 pounds) of rice. These rice paddies are growing on terraces—step-like fields cut into a hillside. Why is rice an important food crop?

INQUIRY SKILL Infer Why is rice grown on terraces?

Roots, Stems, and Leaves

Get Ready

What do you have in common with a plant? Would you believe that you and a plant have similar needs? Still, there is a big difference. You can move around to get things. You can change things around you—like your room temperature. Plants stay in one place, yet different kinds of plants can survive in very different places. How? What helps plants survive in their surroundings?

Inquiry Skill

You predict when you state possible results of an event or experiment.

Explore Activity

How Do a Plant's Parts Help It Survive?

Materials

cactus

water plant, such as an *Elodea* or a duckweed

flowering plant, such as a geranium

Procedure

1 **Observe** Look at the physical properties of the leaves of each plant. Note the color, size, and shape of the leaves.

2 **Communicate** List any other plant parts that you see.

3 **Communicate** Observe the physical properties of these parts. Record your observations.

Drawing Conclusions

1 **Interpret Data** How do the parts of a cactus help it survive in a hot, dry desert?

2 **Infer** Would the geranium be able to survive in the desert? Why or why not?

3 **Infer** Could the water plant survive out of water? Why or why not?

4 FURTHER INQUIRY **Predict** Could these plants survive outside where you live? Why or why not? For each plant, what conditions would you have to change so that the plant could survive outside where you live?

Main Idea All plants have certain parts with the same functions.

How Do a Plant's Parts Help It Survive?

Some plant roots help you survive. That's because they are foods. Beets, carrots, sweet potatoes, radishes, and turnips are the roots of different plants. How do roots help a plant survive?

Most plants have roots that hold them in the ground. Some plants, like mosses, don't have true roots. Still, mosses have rootlike structures that anchor them. Roots help keep plants from getting swept away by wind and running water. Roots draw up water and minerals from the soil. Plants must have water and minerals to make their own food. Roots also store food for the plant. That's especially true of sweet potato, sugar beet, and carrot plants.

A root gets its start early in the life of a plant. If you were to look at a lima bean as it sprouted, you would see a tiny piece of the young plant growing straight downward. This is the plant's first root.

This root bores deeper and deeper into the soil. Why don't the rough particles of soil rub away and harm the young root? The tip of the root is protected by a layer of tough cells called the root cap.

Parts of a Root

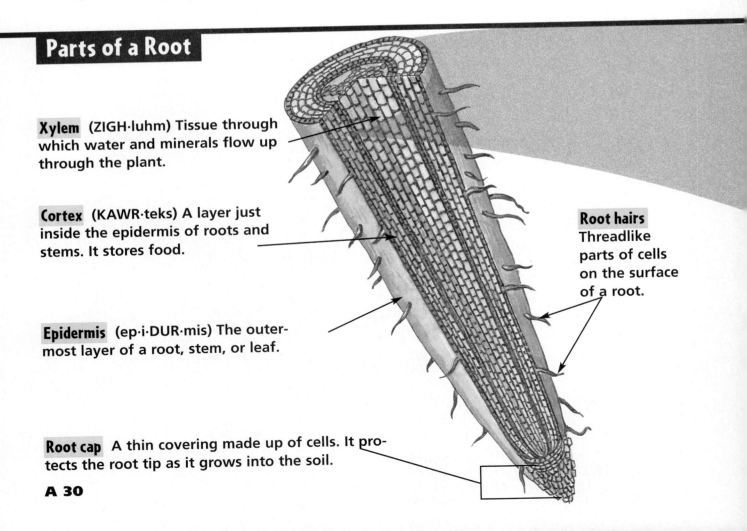

Xylem (ZIGH·luhm) Tissue through which water and minerals flow up through the plant.

Cortex (KAWR·teks) A layer just inside the epidermis of roots and stems. It stores food.

Epidermis (ep·i·DUR·mis) The outermost layer of a root, stem, or leaf.

Root cap A thin covering made up of cells. It protects the root tip as it grows into the soil.

Root hairs Threadlike parts of cells on the surface of a root.

Soon more roots branch out from the sides of the original root. *Taproots* have one large root with a few hairy branching roots. They look like a carrot or a beet. Other roots, like those of grass or rye plants, are made up of only thin hairy branching roots called *fibrous roots*.

Taproots tend to grow deep into the ground and reach water deep down. Fibrous roots spread out near the soil's surface. They collect water where there is little rain that only soaks into the very top layer of soil.

Fibrous roots can make huge networks. The total surface area of the root system of a single rye plant was 639 square meters (6,879 square feet)!

Some plants, like orchids, that grow high in the branches of rain forest trees, have *aerial roots*. These roots never touch the ground. They take in moisture from the air. *Prop roots*, like those of a corn plant, grow like fingers out of the bottom of the stem. These roots help prop up the plant.

The structure of a root helps it absorb water and minerals and send them to other parts of the plant. The diagram shows how this happens.

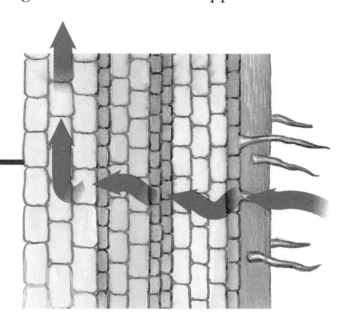

Water and minerals enter the root hairs. They pass through the root's cortex to the xylem. They then move up the xylem, into the plant's stem, and to all parts of the plant.

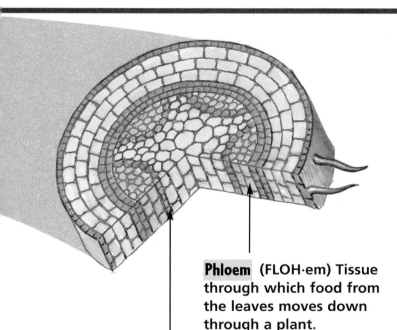

Phloem (FLOH·em) Tissue through which food from the leaves moves down through a plant.

Cambium (KAM·bee·uhm) A layer that separates the xylem from the phloem. The cambium is where new xylem and phloem are produced.

READING Main Idea
How do roots help a plant survive?

How Are Stems Similar?

Some stems are soft and delicate, like those of a young corn plant. Others are hard and tough, like those of a giant redwood tree. No matter what they look like, all stems have certain things in common.

All stems support leaves. Some also support flowers. Stems help leaves reach open places, where the leaves can be bathed in sunlight.

Stems also hold the transportation system for plants. This system lets water and minerals move from the roots to all parts of the plant, especially its leaves. It moves foods made in leaves to all other parts of the plant.

The *xylem* makes up the part of the transportation system that moves water and minerals up from the roots. The *phloem* moves food from the plant's leaves to its other parts. Many stems also have a *cambium*—a layer of cells— that separates the two. In addition, woody stems are protected by a tough outer layer of tissue, called bark.

Soft and woody stems have the same basic parts for transporting water, minerals, and food to all parts of a plant.

Woody stem

Phloem

Cambium

Xylem

Soft stem

READING
Diagrams

How are the xylem, phloem, and cambium arranged differently in a woody stem and in a soft stem?

Strawberry stems, called runners, grow along the ground.

A potato is an underground stem.

Some stems do more than support a plant and give it a transportation system. For example, the stems of plants like potatoes and sugarcane store food for the plants to use later. The potatoes and sugarcane you eat actually are stems. The stems of cactus plants store water, which the plants use during long dry periods in the desert. Still other stems, like those of asparagus, help make the plant's food.

Not all stems grow up into the air. Those of strawberries grow along the ground. That's how a strawberry patch spreads and grows.

The stem of the cactus stores water.

▷ **What are two ways in which all stems are similar?**

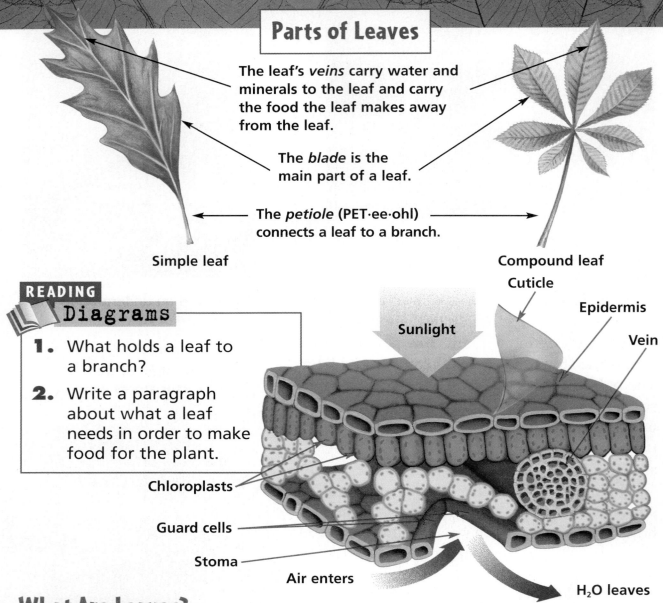

Parts of Leaves

The leaf's *veins* carry water and minerals to the leaf and carry the food the leaf makes away from the leaf.

The *blade* is the main part of a leaf.

The *petiole* (PET·ee·ohl) connects a leaf to a branch.

Simple leaf

Compound leaf

Cuticle

Epidermis

Vein

Sunlight

Chloroplasts

Guard cells

Stoma

Air enters

H_2O leaves

READING Diagrams

1. What holds a leaf to a branch?

2. Write a paragraph about what a leaf needs in order to make food for the plant.

What Are Leaves?

Leaves come in all shapes and sizes. Most of the leaves you see hang from their plants as single leaves or in groups. Maple and oak trees have single leaves. They're called *simple* leaves.

Horse chestnut and locust leaves come in clusters. These are called *compound* leaves.

The parts of a leaf work together to help keep the plant alive.

The outermost layer of a leaf is its *epidermis*. Cells of the epidermis secrete a waxy coating, called a *cuticle*

(KYEW·ti·kuhl). The cuticle helps keep water from leaving the leaf.

The leaf makes food in cells between the layers of the epidermis. These cells contain chloroplasts, the green food factories of plants. In addition to sunlight, these factories need water, minerals, and the carbon dioxide in air to make food.

The air comes through tiny pores in the bottom of the leaves called *stomata* (STOH·muh·tuh) (singular, *stoma*). When the stomata are open to let in air, water can also evaporate from the leaf. The job of opening and closing each stoma is performed by two *guard cells* that surround it.

When the plant has plenty of water, the guard cells swell and pull open the stoma. When the plant has too little water, the guard cells shrink and close the stoma.

Importance of Leaves

Many leaves have green, broad, flat surfaces that help "capture" the sunlight the plant needs to make its food. Other leaves have different shapes for different purposes. The spines on a cactus reduce the leaf's surface area, cutting down water loss. The needles of a pine tree are covered with a wax that keeps the tree from losing too much water. The layers of an onion store food. The leaves of the garden pea plant wind around objects to give the plant added support.

The leaves of the Venus's-flytrap are colorful insect traps. They snap shut when an insect flies inside.

Leaves are often far from roots, yet they help roots take in water from soil. When water evaporates from the leaves, more water moves up through the plant to replace the lost water. This process is called **transpiration** (tran·spuh·RAY·shuhn).

People eat all parts of plants, including leaves such as lettuce, cabbage, parsley, and spinach. Why are leaves important to you?

▷ **What do leaves do for a plant?**

QUICK LAB

Leaves

FOLDABLES™ Make a Pocket Book. (See p. R 42.) Label the pockets as shown.

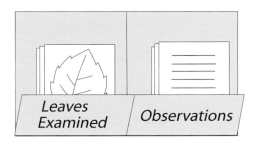

Leaves Examined   Observations

1. Collect a variety of different leaves that you eat as food.

2. **Observe** Examine them with a hand lens.

3. Make a sketch of at least 12 leaves, including their veins, on quarter sheets of photocopy paper.

4. **Classify** Into how many kinds of vein patterns can you group your sketches? Use quarter sheets of notebook paper to explain the similarities and differences you used to classify the leaves. Store your sketches and explanations in your Pocket Book.

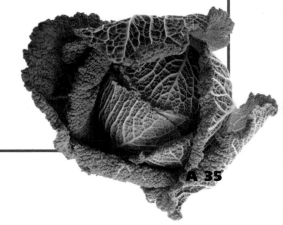

What Is Photosynthesis?

When you walk to a grocery store to buy food, you are really doing two things. You are using energy to get to the store, and you are buying energy at the store. Walking uses energy. Food provides you with energy.

All living things need energy to survive. Where do they get energy? Animals eat food to get energy. Plants make their own food. Where does the plant get energy to make food? It comes from light, especially sunlight.

Light is a form of energy that plants use to make their food. Plants capture the energy of light and trap it in the foods they make. Later, when they need this energy, they get it back from the food. The food-making process is called **photosynthesis** (foh·tuh·SIN·thuh·sis). This term comes from Greek words that mean "putting together by light." The process is very complex, but basically here's how it happens.

First, sunlight strikes a green part of a plant, such as a leaf. The leaf is green because it has a green chemical called chlorophyll. The chlorophyll is found in plant parts called chloroplasts. The chloroplasts act like tiny chemical factories. Inside them water and carbon dioxide from the air combine to make sugar and oxygen. However, this reaction could not happen without the help of light energy. Sugar molecules are only made in the presence of sunlight.

The sugars that the leaf makes go into the leaf's veins and then to all parts of the plant. The oxygen the

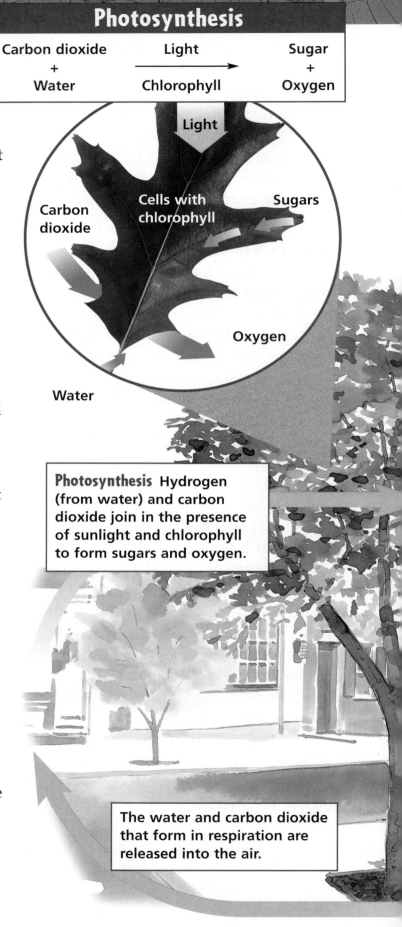

Photosynthesis

Carbon dioxide + Water	Light → Chlorophyll	Sugar + Oxygen

Light

Carbon dioxide

Cells with chlorophyll

Sugars

Oxygen

Water

Photosynthesis Hydrogen (from water) and carbon dioxide join in the presence of sunlight and chlorophyll to form sugars and oxygen.

The water and carbon dioxide that form in respiration are released into the air.

plant makes goes into the air. All animals must breathe in oxygen to stay alive. At the same time, they breathe out carbon dioxide, which the plants need.

Now that the Sun's energy is trapped in the sugars that the plant made, how does the plant get the energy back out? Its cells use oxygen to break apart the sugar. When the sugar breaks apart, it releases energy that the plant uses. This process is called **respiration** (res·puh·RAY·shuhn). This is the same process that releases energy in animals.

About 21 percent of the air you breathe is oxygen. You use this oxygen to release energy from the foods that you eat. The results of the process of respiration are carbon dioxide, water, and energy.

▷ **How is photosynthesis different from respiration?**

The oxygen is released into the air.

The sugars that form are stored in green plants.

READING
Diagrams

In what process is carbon dioxide released?

Respiration In respiration, which occurs in plants and animals, sugars and oxygen join to produce water, carbon dioxide, and energy.

How Does Water Get from Roots to Leaves?

If you were to dry 1,000 g (2.2 lb) of leaves, you would end up with between 50 and 300 g (1.8–11 oz) of crumbly matter. That's because plants are made up of 70–95 percent water.

Cells in all parts of a plant need water to live and grow. They need water to carry out many vital chemical reactions, including photosynthesis. They also need water to stay firm and not wilt.

Plants constantly lose water through transpiration. Over its lifetime an average plant in a mild climate area will lose more than 100 times its weight in water!

It is very important for a plant to efficiently move water from its roots to all its other parts. The diagram on page A39 shows how this is done.

Tropical rain forests pump great amounts of water into the air.

▷ **Why is it important for a plant to move water from its roots?**

If a normal plant (left) gets too little water, it will lose firmness and wilt (right).

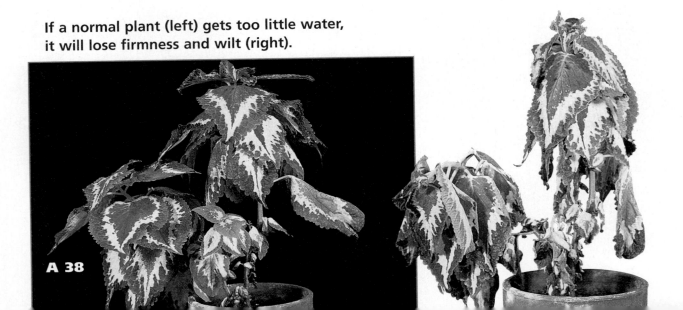

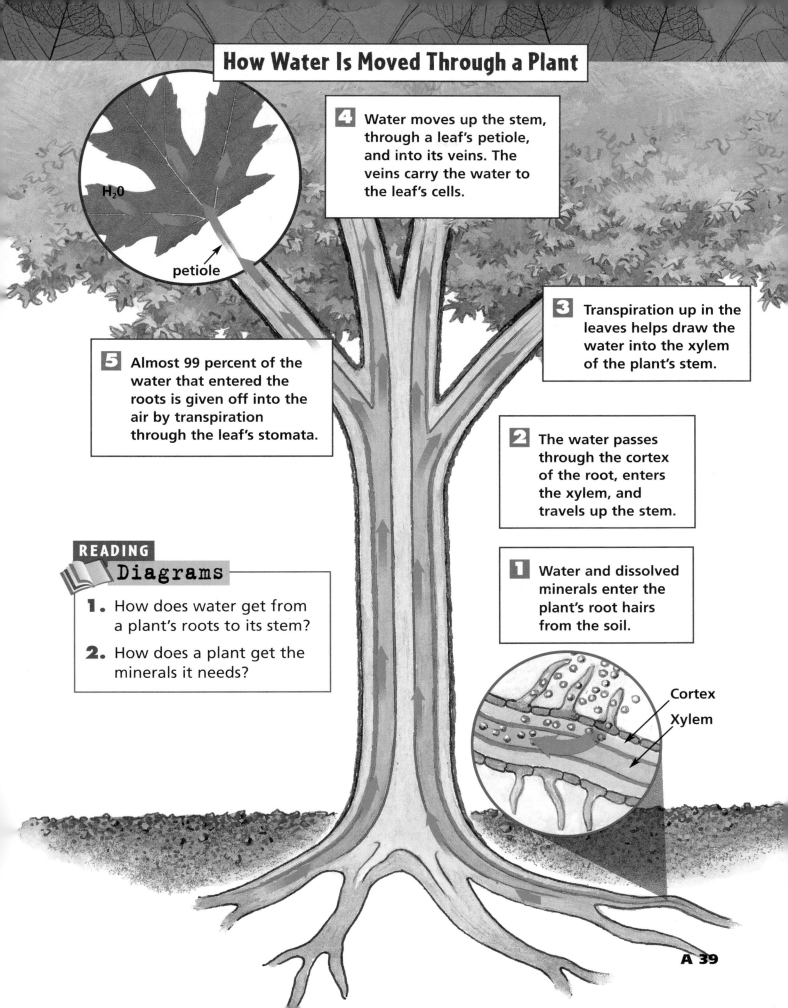

How Water Is Moved Through a Plant

4 Water moves up the stem, through a leaf's petiole, and into its veins. The veins carry the water to the leaf's cells.

H₂0

petiole

3 Transpiration up in the leaves helps draw the water into the xylem of the plant's stem.

5 Almost 99 percent of the water that entered the roots is given off into the air by transpiration through the leaf's stomata.

2 The water passes through the cortex of the root, enters the xylem, and travels up the stem.

READING
Diagrams

1. How does water get from a plant's roots to its stem?

2. How does a plant get the minerals it needs?

1 Water and dissolved minerals enter the plant's root hairs from the soil.

Cortex

Xylem

What Parts of Plants Do You Eat?

There probably isn't a part of a plant that you haven't eaten at one time or another. Whether you know it or not, you've eaten roots, stems, leaves, seeds, fruits, flowers, and even the bark and sap of plants. If you don't believe this is true, look at the chart on this page. Which of these plant parts have you eaten?

▷ **What are five examples of plant parts that people use for food?**

READING
Charts

What part of a plant is a tomato? A peanut?

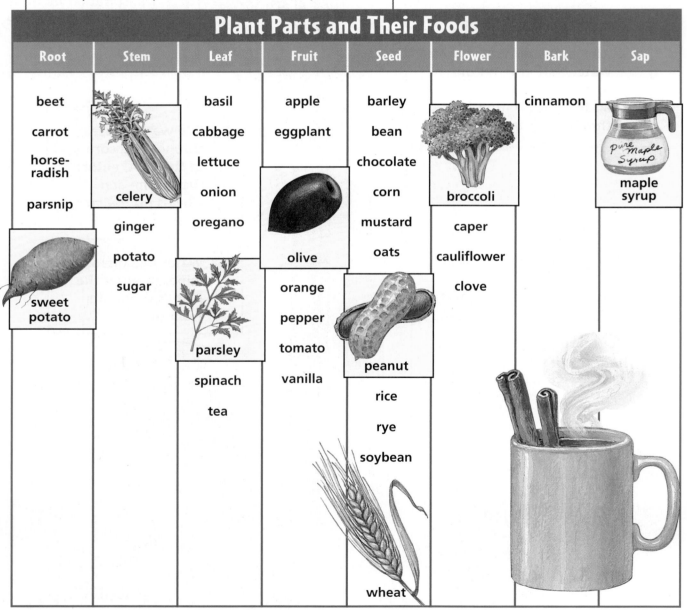

Plant Parts and Their Foods

Root	Stem	Leaf	Fruit	Seed	Flower	Bark	Sap
beet		basil	apple	barley		cinnamon	
carrot		cabbage	eggplant	bean			
horse-radish		lettuce		chocolate			maple syrup
parsnip	celery	onion		corn	broccoli		
	ginger	oregano		mustard	caper		
	potato		olive	oats	cauliflower		
	sugar		orange		clove		
sweet potato		parsley	pepper	peanut			
		spinach	tomato	rice			
		tea	vanilla	rye			
				soybean			
				wheat			

A 40

L·I·N·K·S

Why It Matters

We depend on plants for many things. Among them are food, clothing, and shelter. Since plants are needed by all living things, it is important to know what they need to survive. Part of a plant's ability to survive depends on how well its parts work together to move water and minerals in one direction and food in the other direction. The parts that do this are roots, stems, and leaves.

 e-Journal Visit our Web site **www.science.mmhschool.com** to do a research project on the importance of plants.

Think and Write

1. List three things plants need in order to live and grow.
2. How do roots, stems, and leaves help a plant survive?
3. Describe the process of photosynthesis.
4. Describe the process of respiration in plants.
5. **Critical Thinking** If there were no plants, would animals be able to survive? Explain.

ART LINK

Make a poster. Trace the path of water from the soil, through a plant, and into the air. Make a poster using drawings to show this path.

WRITING LINK

Expository Writing The giant leaves of the royal lily pad are strong enough to hold up the weight of a small child. Search for information about this Amazon plant. Write a research report to present your findings.

MATH LINK

Solve this problem. Find the total surface area of the leaves of a single tree. Use graph paper to estimate the surface area of a single leaf. Then estimate the number of leaves on a single branch. (Find the average of several branches.) Estimate the number of branches on the tree. Find the total number of leaves, then find their total surface area.

TECHNOLOGY LINK

LOG ON Visit **www.science.mmhschool.com** for more links.

Plant Responses and Adaptations

Get Ready

What happens when you jump up? Why don't you just fly up and away from Earth's surface? There is a pull between Earth and everything on it. This pull is called gravity.

Mangrove roots have developed many adaptations to survive in a harsh environment. They filter salt from sea water. They have developed prop roots that arch out from the tree to the soil to help the plant withstand coastal waves. How do these roots respond to gravity?

Inquiry Skill

You predict when you state possible results of an event or experiment.

Explore Activity

How Do Roots Grow?

Materials

petri dish (plastic)

2 paper towels

marking pen

tape

4 bean seeds that have been soaked in water overnight

Procedure

1 Soak two paper towels. Wrinkle the paper towels, and place them in the bottom half of the petri dish.

2 Place the four seeds on top of the wet paper towels as shown in diagram 1. Place the seeds so that the curved part is turned toward the center of the dish.

3 Place the top on the petri dish. The top will hold the seeds in the wet paper towels. Seal the top with transparent tape. Draw an arrow on the petri dish with the marking pen as shown in diagram 2. This will show which direction is down. Write the number or name of your group on the petri dish.

4 In a place your teacher provides, stand the petri dish on its edge so the arrow is pointing downward. Tape the petri dish so that it will remain standing. Do not lay the dish down flat.

5 **Predict** Make and record a prediction about the direction you think the roots will grow.

6 **Communicate** Examine the seeds for the next four days. Record the direction of root growth.

Drawing Conclusions

1 **Observe** In what direction were the roots growing on day 1 of germination? On day 4?

2 **Interpret Data** Is your prediction supported by your data?

3 FURTHER INQUIRY **Predict** What would happen if a seedling were not able to grow its roots down into the soil? Design an experiment to test your prediction. Try it and report your results.

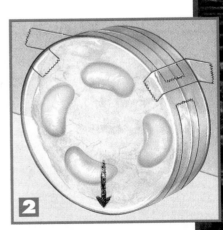

Main Idea Tropisms and other responses and adaptations help plants survive.

What Are Tropisms?

If the flash of a camera goes off near your eyes, you are likely to respond to the bright light by blinking. The flash of light stimulated your blinking. Anything in the environment—light, heat, gravity, and more—that produces such a **response** is called a **stimulus** (STIM·yuh·luhs).

Plants also respond to a stimulus, but they tend to respond more slowly than animals do. Plants slowly bend or curve toward or away from a stimulus. Scientists call this kind of response a **tropism** (TROH·piz·uhm). Tropisms help a plant survive in its environment. For example, as seeds sprout, their roots grow downward. Why do you think the seeds' roots grow downward?

There are several major kinds of tropisms. One of these is *gravitropism*. A plant's roots respond to the stimulus of gravity and grow downward.

The roots of a plant show positive gravitropism. No matter how the plant is tilted, its roots will always grow downward into the soil. The roots grow in the direction Earth's gravity is pulling them. Stems show negative gravitropism. They grow away from the force of gravity. They grow into the air, where their leaves can get the most sunlight.

Light, of course, is very important to plants' survival. Plants respond to changes in light. These responses are called *phototropisms*. (*Photo* comes from a Greek word meaning "light.") If a plant is exposed to light coming from only one direction, its stem will bend in that direction. That is positive phototropism.

If a plant bends toward a stimulus, its change is called a positive tropism. If it bends away, the change is called a negative tropism.

If you examine the roots of a willow tree growing near a stream, you will discover *hydrotropism*. *Hydro* means "water." The willow's roots show positive hydrotropism. They grow toward a source of water.

Some plants, like squash and grape plants, show a response to touch. Grape vines grow around posts farmers stick in the ground. The vines send out threadlike tendrils that coil toward whatever they touch.

People long knew about plant tropisms. However, they didn't always know the process inside a plant that made a plant's parts move. The first clue was discovered by Charles Darwin and his son Francis in the 1870s. Charles Darwin cut off the tips of some very young plant shoots. He left other plants alone. The plants with tips bent toward light. The plants without tips did not. Darwin

The tendrils of this plant respond to touch as they coil around other objects.

concluded that something in the tips was causing the bending, but what?

The second clue was found in the 1920s by Dutch scientist Frits Went. Went guessed that a chemical made only in the shoot's tip was responsible for the bending. He separated many chemicals from shoot tips. One by one he placed them on the cutoff tops of plant shoots. Finally, he found the chemical that let the cut shoots bend toward light.

The chemical is called an *auxin*. Auxins are chemicals that stimulate plant growth. Auxins work on all parts of the plant and cause tropisms of all kinds. How do auxins cause plant parts to bend? When one side of a stem is exposed to light, for example, auxins move to the other side and down. Auxins cause more cells to grow—and some to grow more in length—on the dark side, but not on the side facing the light. This unequal growth causes the stem to bend toward the light.

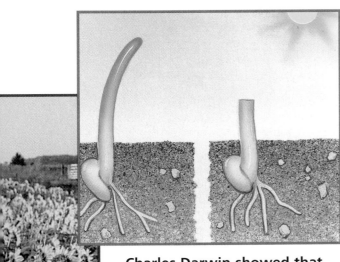

Charles Darwin showed that when the tip of a plant shoot is cut off, the plant will not bend toward light.

▷ **What are examples of a positive tropism and a negative tropism?**

How Do Plants Survive?

Plants survive in deserts, rain forests, and the Arctic. They survive in all these places because they have adapted to their environment. An **adaptation** (ad·uhp·TAY·shuhn) helps an organism survive in its environment.

Desert plants have adaptations for collecting, storing, and saving water. Cactus plants have roots that absorb water very quickly. The water is stored in the center of the plant. A thick, waterproof, waxy coating helps stop water loss. Finally, the plant's stomata open only at night, when temperatures are cooler. Less water is lost through transpiration.

Carnivorous (meat-eating) plants can't get enough nutrients from the soil. These plants trap and digest insects to get some of the nutrients they need.

Plants like spinach, lettuce, and wheat bloom in late spring and early summer. They are called *long-day* plants. That's because when they bloom, there is much more daylight than darkness. By contrast, *short-day* plants, like strawberries, soybeans, and ragweed, bloom in early spring or in the fall. Short-day plants bloom when there is more darkness and less daylight. This flowering response is called *photoperiodism*.

▷ **What adaptations help plants survive water shortages?**

Short-Day, Long-Day Plants

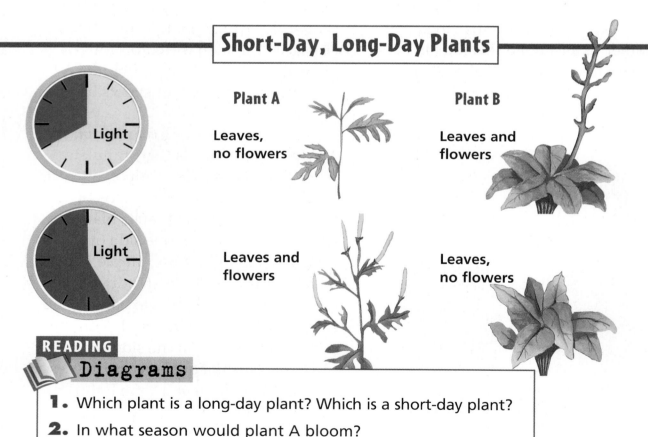

Light

Light

Plant A

Leaves, no flowers

Leaves and flowers

Plant B

Leaves and flowers

Leaves, no flowers

READING
Diagrams

1. Which plant is a long-day plant? Which is a short-day plant?

2. In what season would plant A bloom?

Why Do Plants Compete?

Like all organisms, plants compete with one another for what they need to survive and grow—sunlight, water, and nutrients.

Each plant has its own strategy for winning its battle with other plants. Vines, like ivy and honeysuckle, climb the trunks of trees to get a greater share of sunlight. The trees themselves rise to great heights. They spread their branches to form leafy canopies above the forest. That's why in a forest, trees like oaks and maples have more leaves at their tops.

Have you ever been in a forest full of giant redwoods or other conifers? These trees preserve the nutrients and water in the soil for themselves. They do this by blocking sunlight from reaching the ground. Without sunlight few plants can grow in the soil and soak up nutrients and water near great trees.

Some plants use another strategy for keeping other plants at a distance. They produce chemicals that are poisons to other plants. Creosote bushes, which live in dry areas, release such a poison from their roots. The

Unlike the plant below, which is being eaten by an insect, plants such as the poison ivy, above, produce chemicals that keep insects away or make them sick.

poison keeps the seeds of other plants from germinating. It may even kill other plants that are already growing.

Plants also make chemicals that discourage insects and other animals from feeding on or infecting them. The most powerful insect-fighting plant chemical is made by the neem tree of Africa and Asia. This chemical is so strong that if you dissolved a teaspoon of it in a medium-sized swimming pool and sprayed the water on a plant, insects would not feed on it. Some plants, like the water hemlock, even make poisons that can kill a person.

> **How do plants compete with each other?**

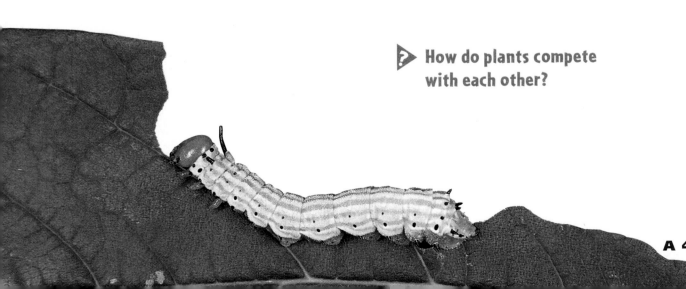

Why Leaves Change Color

To find out why leaves change color in autumn, the first thing you might do is figure out what changes occur in the fall that might cause leaves to change color. Scientists call such changes *variables*. You might identify two of these variables as the amount of daylight and the temperature, both of which go down in the fall.

Next you would make a guess that seems to make sense about which variable causes leaves to change color. This guess is called a *hypothesis*. It is often made in the form of an "*if . . . then . . .*" statement. For example, "*If* the plant doesn't get water, *then* it won't grow." To see if your hypothesis is a good idea, you would perform an experiment. That experiment has to be set up so that it gives a clear answer.

A

Procedure

1. Look at the drawings. They show three experiments—A, B, C. Study the setups.

2. **Observe** What variable or variables are being tested in the first experiment? Record your answer. What variable or variables are being tested in the other two experiments?

B

Drawing Conclusions

1. **Infer** Which experiment is testing to see whether light causes leaves to change color? Explain.

2. **Infer** Which experiment is testing to see whether temperature causes leaves to change color? Explain why.

3. **Infer** Which experiment will not give a clear answer? Explain why not.

C

Why It Matters

Plants respond to changes in their environment. They have to be able to adapt to changes in light, water, and temperature. These adaptations help them survive. Other equally important adaptations help plants reproduce successfully and fight off enemies such as insect pests.

e-Journal Visit our Web site www.science.mmhschool.com to do a research project on how plants adapt to changing seasons.

Think and Write

1. What are tropisms? Give an example of one.

2. How do auxins help plants grow toward the light?

3. Compare the way vines and trees compete for sunlight.

4. INQUIRY SKILL Experiment How would you design an experiment to see if the changing temperature or the changing amount of daylight plays a bigger part in why leaves change color in autumn?

5. Critical Thinking What do you think might happen if all plants bloomed at the same time?

L·I·N·K·S

MATH LINK

Solve this problem. How big does a giant *sequoia* (si·KWOY·uh) grow? Research giant sequoias to find how tall they grow, how big around they get, and how much they weigh. Which weighs more—a giant sequoia or a blue whale?

WRITING LINK

Explanatory Writing Research how a scientist uses a tree's rings to tell about weather conditions. Write an essay that explains the steps in the process. Use time-order words to tell what the scientist does first, next, and last.

ART LINK

Make a poster. Find pictures illustrating several plant tropisms, and use them to help you design a poster. Include a description of each tropism you illustrate.

TECHNOLOGY LINK

Science Newsroom CD-ROM Choose *Color My World* to learn more about how leaves change color.

LOG ON Visit www.science.mmhschool.com for more links.

Cleaning Pollution With Plants

Plants help us in many different ways. They produce oxygen for us to breathe. They provide food for us to eat. We build homes with wood from trees. Lifesaving medicines are made from some plants. Now research shows plants have another amazing use—they help us clean up pollution!

Every year millions of gallons of oil leak into the soil from pipelines, storage tanks, and industrial sites. The usual method of cleanup is to dig up the polluted soil and dispose of it elsewhere. This method is very expensive and disturbs the soil structure.

Researchers Katherine Banks and Paul Schwab have discovered that certain plants—along with tiny soil microbes—will clean up the soil pollutants. The microbes in the soil break down the oil and use it for food. The plants speed up the microbes' activity by getting more oxygen into the soil.

Banks and Schwab have found that certain grasses clean pollution well.

Clover and alfalfa plants also are effective because they increase microbe growth. Finding the right plant, however, can be tricky. Since oil spills occur in different parts of the world, scientists need to use plants that will survive in different climates.

Plants can be used to clean up other kinds of soil pollution, too. Some plants can absorb heavy metals and radioactive material from soil. The plants store the substances in their tissues. Then the plants become toxic and must be destroyed. Mustard plants, for example, can soak up metals, such as lead. In Ukraine, mustard plants were used to remove radiation pollution from the soil around a nuclear plant that exploded.

There are many reasons why using plants may one day be the best way to clean up soil pollution. The method is cheaper, prettier, and powered by an unlimited source of energy—the Sun!

Researchers Katherine Banks and Paul Schwab of Purdue University discovered that grasses with large root surfaces work well at cleaning up polluted soil.

Mustard plants can soak up heavy metals, such as lead. The plants are then burned or dried to recycle the metals.

Sunflowers can be used to clean up radioactive wastes from water.

What Did I Learn?

1. In Ukraine, mustard plants were used to

   A remove pesticides from the soil.
   B clean up oil spills in lakes.
   C remove radiation pollution from soil.
   D clean up oil in parking lots.

2. Plants help clean up oil spills by

   F speeding up the "oil-eating" microbes' activity.
   G using the oil as plant food.
   H absorbing the oil like a paper towel.
   J getting more carbon dioxide into the soil.

LOG ON Visit www.science.mmhschool.com for more information on plants.

Chapter 2 Review

Vocabulary

Fill each blank with the best word or words from the list.

adaptation, A46
cambium, A31
cortex, A30
epidermis, A30
phloem, A31
root cap, A30
stimulus, A44
transpiration, A35
tropism, A44
xylem, A30

1. The outer layer of a root is the _____.

2. Water and minerals flow up through the _____.

3. Foods flow down from the leaves through the _____.

4. Water and minerals pass through the root's _____ to the xylem.

5. A characteristic that helps an organism survive in its environment is a(n)_____.

6. Bending toward or away from a stimulus is a(n)_____.

7. Something in the environment that produces a response in an organism is a(n) _____.

8. The layer of tough cells that protects the root is called the _____.

9. The process by which water goes out of leaves is _____.

10. The _____ separates xylem from phloem.

Test Prep

11. Tropism is the process of _____.

   A movement of a plant toward or away from a stimulus

   B making sugar from sunlight

   C transporting water along a stem

   D adaptation to a hot climate

12. In the process of making food, plants give off _____.

   F sugar

   G carbon dioxide

   H oxygen

   J chloroplasts

13. What causes sunflowers to bend toward the sunlight?

   A positive tropism

   B transporation

   C pollination

   D negative tropism

14. Leaves help roots take in water through a process called _____.

   F photosynthesis

   G transpiration

   H respiration

   J perspiration

15. When plants use stored sugar for energy, they go through a process called _____.

A photosynthesis

B transpiration

C respiration

D perspiration

Concepts and Skills

16. Reading in Science Write a paragraph explaining why light is a stimulus.

17. Scientific Methods How would you determine the length of time a geranium plant needs to be exposed to light daily in order to survive? Write up a design for an experiment that would test this.

18. Decision Making What advice would you give to a friend who is opening a plant store in your neighborhood? What kinds of decisions would your friend need to make regarding the features and the location of the store?

19. INQUIRY SKILL **Experiment** Design an experiment to determine two ways that adaptations can help plants survive. Write how you would set up the experiment. Write down your hypothesis.

20. Critical Thinking If you were lost in the woods in the United States, had no compass, and could not see the sky, how might plants help you infer direction? Write a paragraph explaining your answer.

Did You Ever Wonder?

INQUIRY SKILL **Use Variables** Find two window plants about the same size. Keep all the variables the same except one—give one plant fertilizer. Record your observations every three days for a month.

 LOG ON Visit **www.science.mmhschool.com** to boost your test scores.

3

Plant Diversity

Did You Ever Wonder?

Where do orchids grow? Of the thousands of different kinds
of orchids, many grow in tropical rain forests. However, about
100 kinds of orchids grow in Europe, Asia, and North America.
What do orchids have in common with other flowering plants?

INQUIRY SKILL Form a hypothesis Why are most orchids found in
tropical rain forests?

Plants Without Seeds

Get Ready

Have you ever seen plants like these? If so, there were probably none as tall as these. You are looking at ferns in Costa Rica's Monteverde rain forest, one of Earth's dampest places. These ferns grow taller than a six-story building. Their leaves are more than three times longer than you are tall.

Ferns do best in warm, wet places. So do mosses, but mosses grow low to the ground. Why do ferns grow tall while mosses don't? How do the parts of mosses help them live where they do?

Inquiry Skill

You predict when you state possible results of an event or experiment.

Explore Activity

What Are the Parts of Mosses?

Materials

hand lens

forceps

dropper

3 microscope slides

coverslip

microscope

moss plant

Procedure

1 **Observe** Place a moss on a paper towel. Use a hand lens to find its rootlike, stemlike, and leaflike parts. Record your observations.

2 **Measure** Use the forceps to remove a leaflike part. Make a wet-mount slide of the part. Observe its cells using the microscope on low power. Determine how thick the leaflike part is by moving the focus up and down.

3 **Observe** Find a capsule-shaped object at the end of the brownish stalk. Observe it with the hand lens. Place the capsule on a slide. Add a drop of water. Place a second slide on top of the capsule. Press down on the top slide with your thumb, and crush the capsule. Carefully remove the top slide and place a coverslip over the crushed capsule. Examine the released structures under low power. Draw what you see.

Drawing Conclusions

1 **Observe** Which parts of the moss are green? Explain why they are green.

2 **Observe** How many cell layers did you see in the leaflike structure?

3 **Interpret Data** What structures anchor the moss plant? What was the capsule?

4 [FURTHER INQUIRY] **Predict** What do you think the objects inside the capsule do? How would you test your prediction?

Main Idea Seedless nonvascular plants and seedless vascular plants have different structures but similar life cycles.

What Are Mosses?

Mosses and their close relatives the liverworts are nonvascular plants. They don't have the long tubelike structures vascular plants have. They cling to damp soil, sheltered rocks, and the shady side of trees. Mosses and liverworts are tiny plants, only 2 to 5 centimeters (about 1 to 2 inches) tall. Mosses' leaves are only one or two cells thick.

Mosses and liverworts don't have roots. However, they stay anchored in one place. That's because they have hairlike fibers that do a job much like roots. The fibers are called **rhizoids** (RIGH·zoydz). Rhizoids, like other parts of mosses and liverworts, can take in water from their surroundings. The water then travels directly from one cell to the next.

Most of the plants you see every day grow from seeds. However, mosses and liverworts are seedless plants. They grow from **spores**. Spores are cells that can develop into new organisms.

Nonvascular

Mosses

Liverworts

Mosses and liverworts grow in damp places. Most are tiny plants, growing only 2 to 5 centimeters (about 1 to 2 inches) tall.

Club mosses

Club mosses produce spores at the ends of stems in structures that look like tiny pine cones.

Spores are tiny structures found inside a capsule called a *spore capsule*.

Many mosses look like green, fuzzy pillows. Many liverworts look more like flat leaves. Ancient people thought that the shape of these plants resembled a liver. That's how they got their name.

Seedless Vascular Plants

True mosses and liverworts are seedless plants. So are their more distant relatives club mosses, spike mosses, horsetails, and ferns. All of them use spores to reproduce. However, mosses and liverworts are different from the other four in a very important way.

Mosses and liverworts don't have a vascular system. Club mosses, spike mosses, horsetails, and ferns do.

The vascular tissue in these plants is made up of long tubelike cells. These cells let water and food move easily over long distances. That is why vascular plants can grow very tall and thick. That is also why nonvascular plants like true mosses and liverworts are so short and delicate. The trunks of the largest ferns can be as thick as your body.

▷ **What are mosses like?**

Vascular

Horsetails

The stems of horsetails are hollow, have a ring of vascular tissue and joints, and contain a gritty, sandy substance called silica.

Ferns

Ferns come in all sizes and shapes and live in different kinds of climates.

Spike mosses

Spike mosses, such as this "resurrection plant," live in the desert. Resurrection plants can dry out when there is no rain, but they do not die. They revive when water becomes available again.

QUICK LAB

Ferns

FOLDABLES Make a Folded Table. (See p. R 42.) Label it as shown.

Fern	Form	Function
stem		
leaves		
spores		

1. Use the Folded Table to record your observations.

2. **Observe** Carefully examine a fern plant. Look at the stem. Observe how the leaves grow from the stem. Find the veins in the leaves.

3. **Observe** Find a leaf whose bottom is covered with brownish spots. These are spore cases.

4. **Experiment** Place a drop of water on a clean slide. Use a toothpick to scrape one of the spore cases into the drop of water.

5. **Observe** Examine the spore case under the low power of a microscope. What does the spore case contain?

6. **Infer** Describe what ferns and mosses have in common on the back of your Folded Table.

What Are Ferns?

Ferns once formed huge forests on Earth. You can still find them today in many wooded areas. Many people also grow ferns at home. What are ferns like?

Finding spore cases on the bottom of a fern leaf

Preparing a slide for viewing one spore case

Ferns have leaves that are called **fronds** (FRAHNDZ). They grow above the ground from an underground stem called a **rhizome** (RIGH·zohm). Roots, which anchor the plant to the soil or to a tree, branch out from the rhizome.

The bottom sides of some fronds are covered with rows of brownish or rust-colored spore cases that contain spores. Under the right conditions, the spore cases pop open and spray spores as far away as a few meters. If the spores land in a place where conditions are right for fern growth, the spores will develop into the first stage in a new fern's life cycle.

Spore cases arranged on the bottom of a fern frond will pop open, spraying spores all around. If conditions are right where the spores fall, the spores will produce new fern plants.

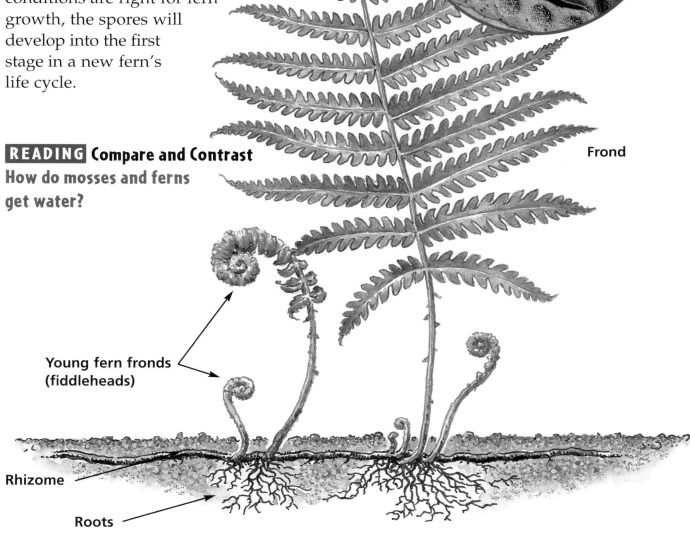

READING **Compare and Contrast**
How do mosses and ferns get water?

Frond

Young fern fronds (fiddleheads)

Rhizome

Roots

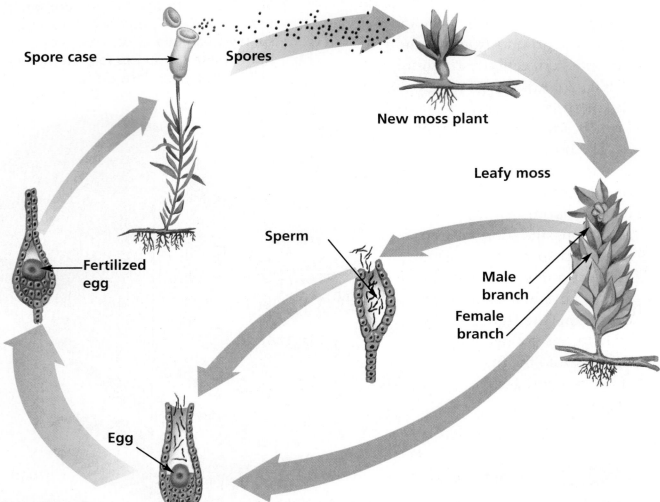

Spore case → Spores

New moss plant

Leafy moss

Fertilized egg

Sperm

Male branch

Female branch

Egg

How Do the Life Cycles of Mosses and Ferns Differ?

Since mosses and ferns use spores to *reproduce* (ree·pruh·DEWS)—make new plants—you might guess that their life cycles are similar. That guess would be correct, but there are differences, too.

The diagrams on these two pages will help you compare and contrast the life cycles of mosses and ferns.

Both mosses and ferns have two separate stages to their life cycles. One stage is when they produce spores. This stage in the life cycle is called

asexual reproduction (ay·SEK·shew·uhl ree·pruh·DUK·shuhn). That's because the plant needs only one type of cell—the spore—in order to reproduce.

Moss spores grow into leafy moss plants that have male branches and female branches. The male branches produce *sperm*—male sex cells. The female branches produce eggs—female sex cells. When a male sex cell meets a female sex cell, the two may join together. This is called **fertilization** (fur·tuh·luh·ZAY·shuhn).

This stage in the cycle is called **sexual reproduction** (SEK·shew·uhl ree·pruh·DUK·shuhn). That's because

Life Cycle of a Fern

READING
Diagrams

Where are a fern's spores produced?

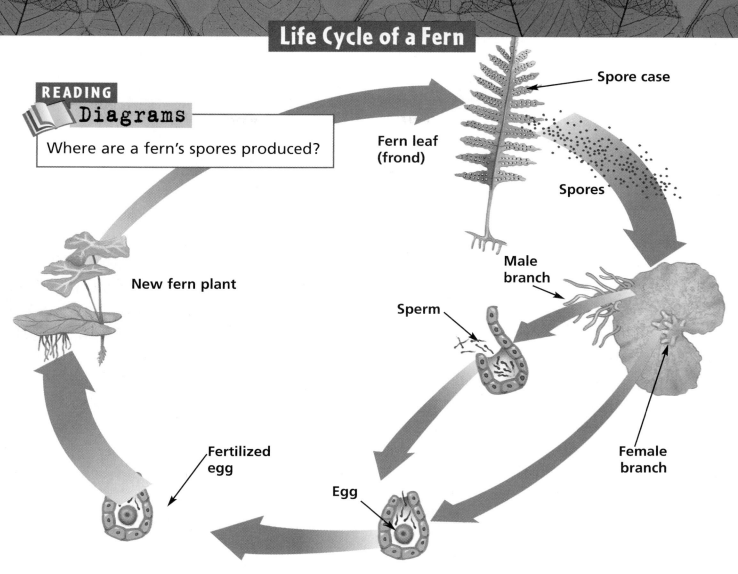

Spore case

Fern leaf (frond)

Spores

New fern plant

Male branch

Sperm

Female branch

Fertilized egg

Egg

the plant needs both male sex cells and female sex cells in order to reproduce.

The fertilized egg eventually becomes a thin stalk with a spore case on top. When the spore case opens, the spores are released. Spores that land on damp ground may grow into new moss plants, and the cycle begins again.

This process of going from sexual reproduction to asexual reproduction to sexual reproduction again is called *alternation of generations*.

Ferns also reproduce by alternation of generations. Leafy fern plants produce spores on the undersides of their fronds.

Spores landing in shady, moist soil are most likely to grow. The spores grow into small, heart-shaped plants. These plants produce male and female sex cells.

If a male sex cell fertilizes a female sex cell, the fertilized egg starts to form a new plant. The new plant develops into a leafy fern plant. Spore cases on the fern's fronds produce spores, and the cycle begins again.

▷ **In what ways are the life cycles of mosses and ferns alike?**

A 63

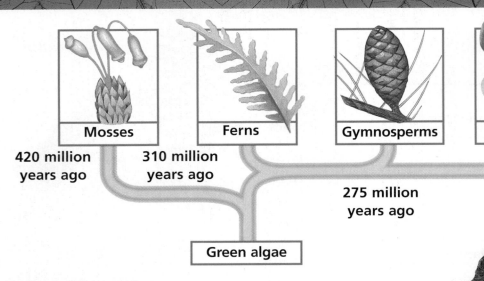

| Mosses | Ferns | Gymnosperms | Angiosperms |

420 million years ago

310 million years ago

275 million years ago

130 million years ago

Green algae

What Were the Ancestors of Plants?

The first land plants developed from living things that lived in the water. Which living things were the ancestors of land plants?

Scientists searched for clues linking organisms that lived in water to those that first grew on land. A good place to start was with photosynthetic organisms. These were living things that made their own food.

To narrow the search, the scientific detectives compared the chlorophyll of various simple organisms living today with that of plants. They found the closest match was with green algae.

Scientists found other clues. The cell walls of both green algae and plants contain cellulose. Cellulose can help plants survive on land, since a strong cell wall helps plants stay upright.

There was another clue. Both green algae and plants store food as starch.

Next, scientists hunted for fossils—the preserved remains of living things.

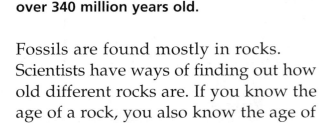

This fernlike plant was found in rock that is over 340 million years old.

Fossils are found mostly in rocks. Scientists have ways of finding out how old different rocks are. If you know the age of a rock, you also know the age of the fossil in it.

Putting all the pieces of this puzzle together, scientists concluded that the first land plants to evolve, or develop, from algae were probably nonvascular plants similar to mosses. These early land plants first appeared about 420 million years ago. Vascular plants appeared more recently. The earliest vascular plants, the ferns, were seedless. The first plants with seeds were gymnosperms, followed by angiosperms, or flowering plants.

▷ **How did scientists find the ancestors of plants?**

Why It Matters

Mosses and ferns were among the first plants to live on land. Today mosses are often the first plants to return to an area where plant life has been destroyed. Mosses help break down rocks into soil. Mosses also help hold on to the soil, making it easier for other plants to survive in the area. Without mosses, perhaps your favorite plants would never have had a chance to grow where they do.

e-Journal Visit our Web site www.science.mmhschool.com to do a research project on mosses and ferns.

Think and Write

1. Why do mosses grow close to the ground?

2. Why do people sometimes add moss to a garden?

3. How do mosses change rocky areas so other plants can grow?

4. List two differences between mosses and ferns.

5. **Critical Thinking** How do cell walls help plants survive on land?

ART LINK

Make a poster. Find pictures of different kinds of ferns, and make a chart. Label each fern, and write a brief description of where each one can be found. Try to include at least one of the following: interrupted fern, leather fern, strap fern, vine fern, shoestring fern, ostrich fern. How do you think these ferns got their names?

WRITING LINK

Expository Writing Write a guidebook about the kinds of ferns found in your area. Use facts and descriptive details. On each page, place a photograph or drawing of one of the ferns. Include a caption that describes the fern as well as information about where it can be found.

MATH LINK

Solve this problem. Study the time line on page A64. About how long after early land plants first appeared did gymnosperms appear? About how long after gymnosperms did angiosperms appear?

TECHNOLOGY LINK

 Visit www.science.mmhschool.com for more links.

Plants with Seeds

Get Ready

What do flowering plants and evergreens have in common? One way they are alike is they produce seeds. They are seed plants.

How are these plants different? One way they are different is that they have different kinds of leaves. How do these differences help the plants survive?

Inquiry Skill

You experiment when you perform a test to support or disprove a hypothesis.

Explore Activity

How Do Seed Plants Differ?

Materials

small pine seedling or other conifer

grass plant

garden plant or houseplant, such as a geranium

hand lens

microscope slide

coverslip

microscope

Procedure

1 **Observe** Examine each plant. Use the hand lens to examine a leaf from each one. Draw each leaf, and label it with the name of the plant it came from.

2 **Observe** Remove a part of the lower epidermis from the grass leaf. Make a wet-mount slide. Examine the slide under low power.

3 **Communicate** Draw what you observe.

4 **Observe** Repeat step 2 with a pine needle and a houseplant leaf (such as a geranium). Draw what you observe.

Drawing Conclusions

1 **Interpret Data** How are the leaves of the three plants alike? How are the leaves of the three plants different from one another?

2 **Infer** Which one of the plants do you think is least like the other two? Explain your reasoning.

3 **FURTHER INQUIRY** **Experiment** Of the plants you examined, predict which could survive best in a dry environment. How do you think the plant's leaves would help it do this? Design an experiment that would test your prediction.

Main Idea One group of seed plants produces seeds on cones, the other group produces seeds inside fruits.

How Do Seed Plants Differ?

How are the leaves of a grass plant, a pine tree, and a geranium different? Two of these plants come from one major group of seed plants, while the other comes from a different group.

Both groups are vascular plants. Both groups reproduce from **seeds**. A seed contains an undeveloped plant and stored food for the young plant.

Most of the plants that you see every day are seed plants. They include grasses, trees, shrubs, and bushes. They all have roots, stems, and leaves. Some, called **angiosperms** (AN·jee·uh·spurmz), produce flowers. The others, called **gymnosperms** (JIM·nuh·spurmz), do not produce flowers. These are the two major groups of seed plants.

The gymnosperms are the oldest seed plants. They include such evergreen trees as pine, fir, cedar, juniper, yew, larch, and spruce.

Gymnosperms first appeared on Earth about 250 million years ago. One hundred million years would pass before the first angiosperms appeared.

The fruits, vegetables, grains, and almost all of the nuts you eat are produced by angiosperms. However, one tasty nut—the pine nut, or pignoli—is a gymnosperm seed. It is the seed of certain pine trees.

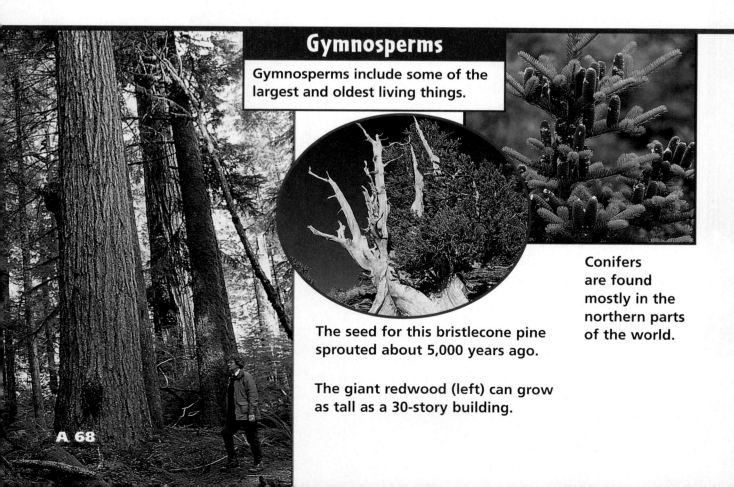

Gymnosperms

Gymnosperms include some of the largest and oldest living things.

The seed for this bristlecone pine sprouted about 5,000 years ago.

Conifers are found mostly in the northern parts of the world.

The giant redwood (left) can grow as tall as a 30-story building.

The gymnosperms are divided into four divisions. They are the *conifers* (KAHN·uh·furz), *cycads* (SIGH·kadz), *ginkgoes* (GING·kohz), and *gnetophytes* (NE·toh·fights). Look at the photographs on these pages. You'll notice that these plants look different. However, they all have certain things in common.

Their seeds are produced on the scales of female cones. The seeds are not surrounded by a fruit. The leaves of most gymnosperms look like needles or scales. Most gymnosperms are *evergreens*. Evergreens lose only a few leaves at a time and constantly replace the leaves they have lost.

Some conifers, such as the larch, dawn redwood, and bald cypress, lose their leaves each fall. Plants that do this are called *deciduous* (di·SIJ·ew·uhs).

When gymnosperms evolved, most of Earth was cold and dry. These plants are well adapted to cold, dry climates. For example, the needles of conifers have a very small surface area and are covered with a thick cuticle. They lose less water than the wider leaves of flowering plants.

READING **Compare and Contrast**
How are angiosperms and gymnosperms different?

Cycads (left) live in warm climates. The red strawberry-shaped structures are not fruits but female cones.

The maidenhair tree (right) is the only member of the ginkgo division. It has fan-shaped leaves and round green fruit.

Gnetophytes (right) are more closely related to flowering plants than any other gymnosperm.

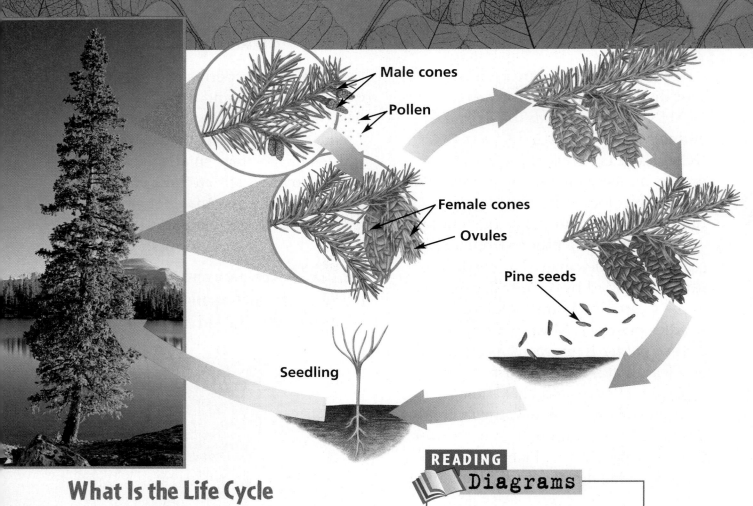

Male cones

Pollen

Female cones

Ovules

Pine seeds

Seedling

What Is the Life Cycle of a Conifer?

Since gymnosperms don't produce flowers or fruits, their life cycle is not the same as the life cycle of angiosperms. However, there are similarities. As you look at the diagram on this page, and later at the life cycle of angiosperms, think of their similarities and differences.

Let's examine the life cycle of a pine tree. A pine tree belongs to a group of gymnosperms called conifers. Pines produce male and female cones on a mature tree. The scales that form the cones carry spore cases that produce the plant's sperm and egg cells. Male cones produce pollen grains, which contain sperm cells.

When pollen grains fall away from a male cone, the wind carries them

READING
Diagrams

What are the steps in the life cycle of a conifer?

through the air. If a pollen grain happens to land on a female cone, a sperm cell from the pollen may fertilize an egg cell in the female cone.

The fertilized cell eventually becomes a seed. As autumn and winter come, the female pine cones fall from the trees. Their seeds scatter on the ground. Sometimes wind or water will carry the seeds far from the tree. If they end up in a place where conditions are right for germination, the seeds will sprout, and a new pine tree will start growing.

▶ **Where are conifer seeds found?**

What Are Angiosperms?

Angiosperms are the most recently evolved and best-adapted division of seed plants. There are about 235,000 different kinds of angiosperms, which makes them the largest division in the plant kingdom.

Some, like duckweed, float on water and are about the size of a large bee's eye. Duckweed is the smallest flowering plant. The largest flowering plant is the giant eucalyptus tree, which can be 100 m (330 ft) tall and 20 m (66 ft) in circumference.

Angiosperms live in all climates and in all parts of the world. The saguaro cactus lives in the hot, dry desert. Duckweed and water lilies grow only

The world's largest flower belongs to this parasitic plant, Rafflesia, which lives in Southeast Asia.

in the water. Some orchids live high in the air attached to trees in hot, damp rain forests. Other angiosperms flower near the Arctic Circle. Oddly, a few angiosperms cannot live on their own. They have little or no chlorophyll and are *parasites*. That is, they live off other plants. The plant with the largest flower is this kind of parasitic angiosperm. The flower can be a meter across, as thick as your thumb, and weigh as much as a small dog.

How can you tell an angiosperm from a gymnosperm? Angiosperms produce flowers; gymnosperms do not. The seeds of angiosperms are inside a fruit. Gymnosperms do not produce fruits.

Flowering trees produce the fruits you eat.

▷ **What are two locations where angiosperms live?**

A 71

What Are Cotyledons?

Scientists divide the angiosperms into two classes. As you might guess, scientists are able to do this because of some particular characteristic that sets the two classes apart. That characteristic turns out to be the number of an angiosperm's **cotyledons** (kaht·uh·LEE·duhnz). A cotyledon, also called a seed leaf, is a tiny leaflike structure inside a seed.

Some angiosperm seeds contain only one cotyledon. Plants whose seeds contain only one cotyledon are called *monocotyledons*, or **monocots** (MAHN·uh·kahts) for short. (The prefix *mono-* comes from a Greek word meaning "one.") There are over 60,000 different kinds of monocots. Corn, rice, wheat, grasses, orchids, and coconut palms are examples of monocots.

Angiosperms whose seeds contain two cotyledons are called *dicotyledons*, or **dicots** (DIGH·kahts) for short. (The prefix *di-* comes from a Greek word meaning "two.") There are over 170,000 kinds of dicots. Bean plants, maple trees, rose plants, and cactuses are some of the dicots.

▷ **What are three differences between monocots and dicots?**

Characteristics of Monocots and Dicots

Characteristics	Monocots	Dicots
Cotyledons	One	Two
Leaf veins	Parallel	Branched
Flower parts	Multiples of three	Multiples of four or five
Vascular system	Scattered in bundles	In rings

Inquiry Skill
BUILDER

Flowering Plants

In this activity you will observe flowering plants in order to try to classify them. That is, you will examine several plants and try to determine whether each is a monocot or a dicot. As you examine each plant sample, refer to the chart on page A72 to help you classify the sample.

Materials
sample leaves and flowers from various angiosperms

Procedure

1 **Observe** Get together with a few of your classmates and go on a leaf- and flower-collecting field trip. (Make sure to avoid poison ivy, poison oak, and poison sumac leaves. Your teacher can tell you how to spot them.)

2 **Observe** Find a number of different angiosperms. Try to get a sample of a leaf and flower from each plant. If you can't get a flower, a leaf will do.

3 **Interpret Data** Look at the chart of Characteristics of Monocots and Dicots. It will give you clues on how to tell if the sample leaves and flowers you chose are monocots or dicots.

Drawing Conclusions

1 **Observe** Examine the plant parts you have chosen. For each sample leaf, describe how the leaf veins look. For each sample flower, tell how many parts the flower has. Record your answers.

2 **Classify** Mount the leaves and flowers on a heavy sheet of cardboard, and indicate whether each came from a monocot or a dicot.

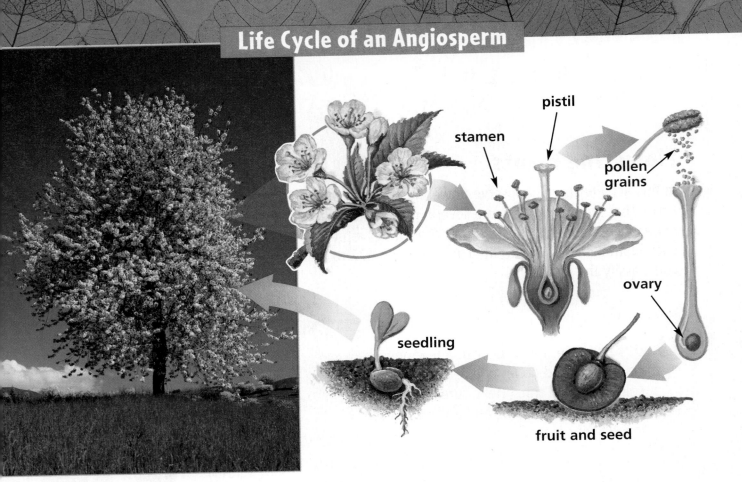

pistil

stamen

pollen grains

ovary

seedling

fruit and seed

What Is the Life Cycle of An Angiosperm?

The life cycle of an angiosperm is similar to the life cycle of a gymnosperm in many ways. The main difference between the two cycles is that angiosperms produce flowers and fruits.

Let's examine the life cycle of a cherry tree. The cherry is an angiosperm. The flowers of angiosperms usually have both male and female parts. The male parts are the stamens. The stamens produce pollen grains, which contain sperm cells. The female part is the pistil. The pistil contains the ovules, which produce the egg cells.

Pollen grains are transferred from a flower's stamen to its pistil, or to another flower's pistil. Pollen grains contain a nucleus. This transfer is called **pollination** (pahl-uh-NAY-shuhn). Once in the stigma, the male nucleus and the egg cell become a seed. As the seeds develop, the surrounding ovary enlarges and becomes the **fruit**. The fruit protects the seeds inside it. If the fruit reaches a place where conditions are right for germination, the seeds will sprout, and a new cherry tree will start growing.

READING **Compare and Contrast**
How are the life cycles of angiosperms and gymnosperms similar?

Why It Matters

Plants with seeds provide us with many useful products such as cotton, paper, foods, and construction materials.

Understanding the life cycles of seed plants is important because it enables people to control the growth and reproduction of the plants. People can change the life cycle of plants to fit their needs.

e-Journal Visit our Web site **www.science.mmhschool.com** to do a research project on the different things plants with seeds provide us.

Think and Write

1. How are the life cycles of gymnosperms and angiosperms different?

2. How are flowers important to a plant?

3. What are the differences between monocots and dicots?

4. INQUIRY SKILL **Observe** List five plants that are angiosperms and five plants that are gymnosperms. Explain what characteristics helped you determine which was which.

5. Critical Thinking How have seed plants become adapted to the environment?

L·I·N·K·S

WRITING LINK

Writing a Story Use your imagination to write a story about a special plant. Classify the plant as an angiosperm or a gymnosperm and as a monocot or dicot. Describe the setting, characters, and problem at the beginning of your story. Solve the problem at the end.

ART LINK

Make your own flip books. Illustrate a "year in the life of an angiosperm" by making a flip book. Do the same for a gymnosperm.

MATH LINK

Make a pie chart. Make a list of the 10 vegetables and fruits you eat the most. Research whether each of these foods are monocots or dicots. Make a pie chart to show the percentage of monocots you eat compared with the percentage of dicots.

TECHNOLOGY LINK

LOG ON Visit **www.science.mmhschool.com** for more links.

Flowers and Seeds

Vocabulary

ovary, A78

self-pollina-tion, A80

cross-pollina-tion, A80

embryo, A82

seed coat, A82

Get Ready

Have you ever seen bees buzzing around flowers? Don't disturb them. From a distance you might watch as a bee goes from flower to flower. What do you think it is doing? Insects and other animals, such as butterflies and hummingbirds, also hover around flowers. What do you think they do for the plants? What do plants use their flowers for?

Inquiry Skill

You infer when you form an idea from facts or observations.

A 76

Explore Activity

How Do Flowers Differ?

Materials

several large flowers from different plants

hand lens

forceps

dropper

toothpick

Procedure: Design Your Own

1 Decide how you will compare the flowers you look at. You may choose to look for parts that they seem to have in common. Describe what the parts are and how they differ from plant to plant.

2 Begin by removing the outer leaflike parts. Examine them. Draw what they look like.

3 Remove the petals. Examine them. Draw what they look like.

4 **Observe** Examine the rest of the flower. Draw what you see.

5 **Communicate** Draw the parts you decided to compare in different flowers.

Drawing Conclusions

1 **Communicate** What color is each flower? What do you think the job of the petals is? How would you design an experiment to find out?

2 **Infer** What do you think the flower parts you chose are for? Do you think the same parts of different flowers do the same kinds of jobs for their plants?

3 FURTHER INQUIRY **Infer** Why do you think a plant has flowers? Design an experiment to test your hypothesis. Try it and report your results.

Read to Learn

Main Idea Fertilized flowers produce seeds that become new plants.

How Do Flowers Differ?

Not all flowers are alike. Some flowers are *complete flowers.* Complete flowers have sepals, petals, stamens, and pistils. *Incomplete flowers* are missing one of these parts. Some flowers are called perfect. *Perfect flowers* have both female and male parts, that is, both pistils (female parts) and stamens (male parts).

Imperfect flowers have either pistils or stamens, but not both. You might think of these flowers as "female" or "male." Some plants, like corn and oak trees, have separate male and female flowers on the same plant. Other plants,

Parts of a Flower

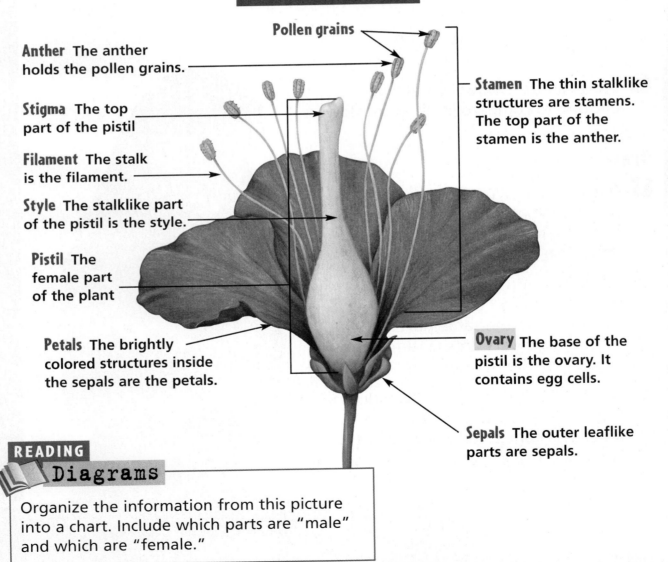

Anther The anther holds the pollen grains.

Stigma The top part of the pistil

Filament The stalk is the filament.

Style The stalklike part of the pistil is the style.

Pistil The female part of the plant

Petals The brightly colored structures inside the sepals are the petals.

Pollen grains

Stamen The thin stalklike structures are stamens. The top part of the stamen is the anther.

Ovary The base of the pistil is the ovary. It contains egg cells.

Sepals The outer leaflike parts are sepals.

READING
Diagrams

Organize the information from this picture into a chart. Include which parts are "male" and which are "female."

Does this holly tree have male flowers or female flowers? How can you tell?

like willow trees and holly trees, have only male flowers or female flowers.

The red holly berries that you see on holly trees in the late fall appear only on holly trees with female flowers. In order to produce the berries (the holly's fruit), the tree with female flowers needs to be fertilized by pollen from a holly tree with male flowers. An oak tree has both male and female flowers on the same tree.

READING **Compare and Contrast**
How do complete and incomplete flowers differ?

An oak tree has tiny green flowers.

What Are Pollination and Fertilization?

Some seeds are very tiny, whereas others are really large. The largest is produced by the double-coconut tree, whose seeds can be about half your weight. Some of the smallest seeds belong to orchid plants. You could put thousands of them in a teaspoon.

No matter how large or small, all seeds develop the same way. Look at the diagram on this page. It will help you understand the difference between pollination and fertilization.

As you learned in Lesson 6, pollination occurs when a pollen grain is transferred from the anther to the stigma. If the pollen is transferred from an anther to a stigma in the same flower, the process is called **self-pollination**. If the transfer is from one flower to the flower of another plant, the process is called **cross-pollination**.

Pollination

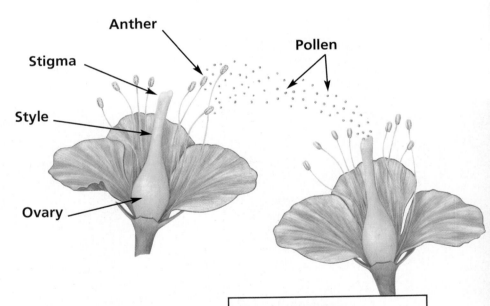

Anther

Pollen

Stigma

Style

Ovary

Self-Pollination
Pollination occurs when a pollen grain from an anther reaches the stigma. This flower is pollinating itself because its own pollen is reaching its own stigma.

Cross-Pollination
Pollination can occur between two or more flowers on separate plants. Here the pollen of one flower reaches the stigma of another.

READING
Diagrams

How are self-pollination and cross-pollination alike? How are they different?

On the stigma a tube forms from the pollen grain. The tube grows down the style and into the flower's ovary. The pollen's nucleus travels down the tube, through the style, and into the ovary. There, it combines with, or fertilizes, an egg cell. This combining is called *fertilization*.

A seed develops from a fertilized egg cell. Under the right conditions, a new plant will develop from the seed. As you have learned, the process of making a new plant from the joining of a sperm and an egg cell is called *sexual reproduction*.

▶ **What are the steps involved in cross-pollination and fertilization?**

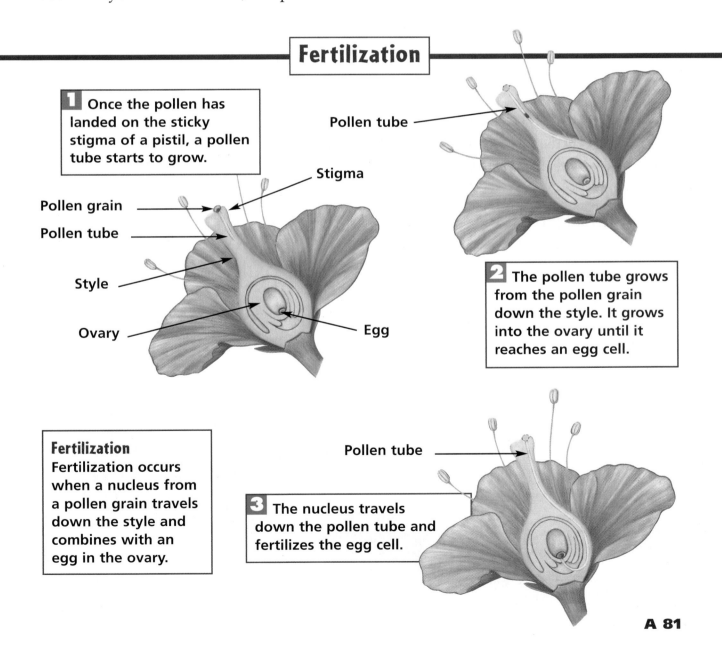

Fertilization

1 Once the pollen has landed on the sticky stigma of a pistil, a pollen tube starts to grow.

Stigma

Pollen grain

Pollen tube

Style

Ovary

Egg

Pollen tube

2 The pollen tube grows from the pollen grain down the style. It grows into the ovary until it reaches an egg cell.

Fertilization
Fertilization occurs when a nucleus from a pollen grain travels down the style and combines with an egg in the ovary.

Pollen tube

3 The nucleus travels down the pollen tube and fertilizes the egg cell.

Inside a Seed

FOLDABLES Make a Two-Tab Book. (See p. R 41.) Label the tabs as shown.

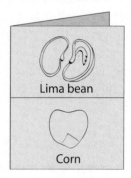

Lima bean

Corn

1. Soak a lima bean in water overnight.

2. **Observe** Carefully pull apart the two halves of the lima bean. Examine the halves with a hand lens. Draw what you see.

3. **Infer** Which part is the embryo?

4. On your drawing, label the seed coat and the cotyledon, where food is stored.

5. **Communicate** Compare a corn kernel with a lima bean. Describe how its parts are similar to or different from the lima bean in your Two-Tab Book.

6. **Classify** Which seed is a dicot? Which is a monocot? Explain how you know which is which in your Two-Tab Book.

What Is in a Seed?

A seed contains an **embryo** (EM·bree·oh). An embryo is an immature plant. Often the embryo includes large cotyledons, where food is stored in the form of starch. A seed also has a **seed coat**. The seed coat encases the whole seed in a tough, protective covering.

Parts of a Seed

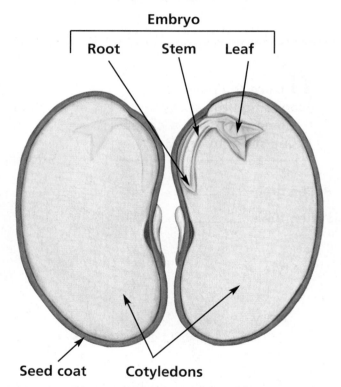

Embryo

Root   Stem   Leaf

Seed coat   Cotyledons

From Seed to Plant

Two things must happen for a seed to produce a new plant. First, the seed must move from the flower to a place where it can sprout. This is called *seed dispersal* (SEED di·SPUR·suhl). Second, the place must provide everything that is needed for sprouting, which is called *germination* (jur·muh·NAY·shuhn). The right temperature and water are the two most important needs for germination. Food is not needed because the seed has its own supply of stored food.

Usually the seed must move a relatively long distance from its parent plant. Why? Competition from its parent, and plants like it, may make the development of a new plant difficult. For example, nearby plants may block sunlight from reaching the young plant. They may soak up the water or minerals from the soil that the new plant needs.

Seeds have evolved all sorts of adaptations for dispersal. For example, dandelion fruits and cottonwood seeds have feathery "parachutes." These parachutes can be blown great distances by the wind. Animals also help move plant seeds.

Animals eat fruits. A fruit is a mature ripened ovary of a plant. The animals digest the soft parts of the fruits, but not the hard seeds inside. As the animals move from place to place, they deposit the seeds in their wastes.

Coconut seeds rely on ocean currents and sea breezes to move them.

The seeds of a cocklebur have tiny hooks that cling to the fur of animals or the clothing of people.

Animals eat fruits and the seeds inside.

How Gymnosperms Spread Seeds

Gymnosperms don't produce fruits. They disperse their seeds in other ways. For example, the cones of the balsam fir tree shatter. When they do this, they release winglike seeds that ride on the wind. Animals move cones from place to place. Heavy rains, floods, and streams can disperse them also.

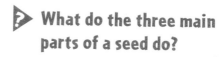

▷ **What do the three main parts of a seed do?**

The awful-smelling jack-in-the-pulpit flower attracts insects that help the plant reproduce.

Why Do Flowers Have Aromas?

The characteristics of living things help them survive in their environment. It would make sense to expect that the aromas of flowers do the same for their plants.

To your nose, some of these aromas are very pleasing. That's why flowers, such as roses and jasmines are used in perfumes. However, some flowers, like those of the jack-in-the-pulpit plant, smell awful. Surprisingly, both beautiful and awful aromas attract insects! What is the advantage of this?

When an insect enters the flower, it brushes against a part of the flower that holds tiny grains of dust, called pollen. These grains contain the plant's male sex cells.

The pollen sticks to the insect. As the insect moves around the flower—

or moves to another flower on the plant—some of the pollen rubs off on parts of the flower that hold female sex cells. The two sex cells join, and the reproduction of a new plant begins.

Many plants attract one particular kind of insect. The jack-in-the-pulpit attracts dung beetles and flies. These insects generally feed on dead or decaying animals or animal wastes, which smell bad. The insects mistake the aroma of the plant for that of a good meal.

Once inside the flower, the insects discover that its sides are so smooth, they can't climb out. As they rush around inside the flower, they keep transferring pollen to the part of the flower that holds female sex cells.

After about 24 hours, something strange happens. The inside of the flower changes from smooth to wrinkled. Their job done, the insects can now get a foothold, escape, and move on to another flower.

▷ How does a flower's aroma help it survive?

L·I·N·K·S

Why It Matters

Almost all of the plants that you eat are flowering plants. Flowering plants also produce food that wild and domesticated animals eat.

Like all plants, flowering plants help keep the balance of gases in the air by using up carbon dioxide and producing oxygen.

Flowering plants also decorate the landscape and homes with beautiful colors. Some produce chemicals that are used in perfumes and other cosmetics.

e-Journal Visit our Web site www.science.mmhschool.com to do a research project on flowers and seeds.

Think and Write

1. Identify the different parts of a flower, and tell what each part does.

2. Explain how seeds are produced.

3. Give at least three examples of how seeds are dispersed.

4. Describe the difference between fertilization and germination.

5. Critical Thinking How do you think trees having flowers that look like bees can help a plant survive?

LITERATURE LINK

Read *Jonathan Chapman: The Appleseed Man,* the story of the man who brought apple trees to the Old West. Think about the pros and cons of moving plants. Try the activities at the end of the book.

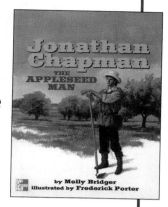

Jonathan Chapman THE APPLESEED MAN

by Molly Bridger
Illustrated by Frederick Porter

WRITING LINK

Persuasive Writing If farmers grow only one kind of plant, other plants become extinct. Research the advantages of plant diversification. Write a persuasive letter to the editor of a farmer's newsletter. Use facts.

MATH LINK

Solve this problem. About 1.8 billion metric tons of rice, wheat, and corn are produced every year. A metric ton equals 2,205 pounds. How many pounds of these grains are produced?

TECHNOLOGY LINK

Science Newsroom CD-ROM Choose *Flower Power* to learn more about how flowers attract pollinators.

 LOG ON Visit www.science.mmhschool.com for more links.

It Takes One to Grow One

What if you could make an exact copy of yourself by removing a part of your body, say a foot, and watching it grow into a new "you"?

It may sound bizarre, but that's actually how some plants make new plants. Reproducing this way is a type of asexual reproduction called vegetative propagation. It's what happens when a part of a plant separates from the main plant, then grows into an exact copy of the plant.

Potatoes are a good example of vegetative propagation. It all starts with the dimples, or "eyes," on a potato. A new plant grows from the potato's eyes, which are actually clusters of tiny buds.

To start their potato crops, farmers cut potatoes into small pieces and plant them. As long as each piece has an eye, a new potato plant can grow. The tiny buds grow roots into the ground and shoots that sprout up through the soil. A new potato plant is born!

Other plants reproduce this way, too. In some species, new plants can grow from the stems, roots, or leaves of a parent plant.

- Strawberry plants send horizontal stems, called runners, that grow along the ground. Shoots and roots grow in places along the runner and develop into new plants.
- When the leaves of African violets are planted, they sprout new African violet plants.

From potatoes to strawberries, this is an amazing way for a part to become a new whole.

Strawberry plants send runners out to form new plants. Young plants that develop this way receive nourishment from the parent plant, so they have a better chance of survival.

A farmer gathers potatoes. With vegetative propagation, plants don't need seeds or partners to reproduce. They can also make many identical plants, helping to ensure the survival of their species.

This potato's "eyes" will grow shoots that can become a new potato. The new plant is genetically identical to its parent.

Write About It

1. What advantages might a farmer identify in vegetative propagation over sexual reproduction?

2. Vegetative propagation produces an exact copy of the parent plant. When could this be a disadvantage to the plant?

LOG ON Visit www.science.mmhschool.com to learn more about vegetative propagation.

Vocabulary

Fill each blank with the best word from the list.

> **angiosperm,** A68
> **conifer,** A69
> **cotyledon,** A72
> **cross-pollination,** A80
> **fertilization,** A62
> **frond,** A61
> **gymnosperm,** A68
> **rhizoid,** A58
> **self-pollination,** A80
> **spore,** A58

1. A plant that has flowers is called a(n) _____.

2. The transfer of a pollen grain from one flower to the stigma of another flower is called _____.

3. Transferring a pollen grain from an anther to a stigma in the same plant is known as _____.

4. A _____ is a gymnosperm.

5. Hairlike fibers that do the same job as roots are _____.

6. A seed plant that does not produce fruits is a(n) _____.

7. A new moss plant is produced by a(n) _____.

8. The leaflike structure of a fern is a(n) _____.

9. A tiny leaflike structure inside a seed is a(n) _____.

10. Male and female cells join together in _____.

Test Prep

11. Unlike other plants angiosperms produce _____.
   A seeds
   B flowers
   C cones
   D spores

12. Which of the following are gymnosperms?
   F apple trees
   G ferns
   H fir trees
   J grains

13. Bees help flowers reproduce through a process called _____.
   A fertilization
   B phototropism
   C transpiration
   D pollination

14. Mosses and liverworts are examples of _____.
   F seedless non-vascular plants
   G seedless vascular plants
   H vascular plants
   J gymnosperms

15. The process of making a new plant from the joining of a sperm and an egg cell is known as _____.

  A asexual reproduction

  B cross-pollination

  C sexual reproduction

  D self-pollination

Concepts and Skills

16. Reading in Science Write a paragraph explaining the difference between a monocot and a dicot.

Rose

Lily

17. Product Ads Look at the ingredients listed on boxes of breakfast foods. What kinds of plants are most commonly used to make breakfast foods? Write a paragraph explaining why.

18. Scientific Methods What would you do to ensure that a plant does not self-pollinate? Make an illustration to explain your answer.

19. INQUIRY SKILL **Observe** Tell which of these plants are angiosperms and which are gymnosperms—bristlecone pine, rose, wheat, oat, fir, cedar, lily, juniper, yew, larch, violet, tomato, spruce, giant redwood tree. Write a paragraph explaining your answer.

20. Critical Thinking How do you think trees that produce seedless oranges are grown? Write down your prediction. Then do library research to see if your prediction was correct.

Did You Ever Wonder?

INQUIRY SKILL **Communicate** The tiger orchid has some fascinating properties. Research this orchid and communicate your findings to the class.

 LOG ON Visit www.science.mmhschool.com to boost your test scores.

Animal Diversity

Did You Ever Wonder?

Where do starfish live? Although starfish live in every ocean on Earth, there are more kinds of starfish in the northern Pacific than anywhere else. Are starfish really fish? What other kinds of animals can you see in this photo?

INQUIRY SKILL Predict What happens when a starfish loses an arm?

Animal Traits

Vocabulary

fish, A95

amphibian, A95

reptile, A95

bird, A95

mammal, A95

Get Ready

What do a tick and a zebra have in common? Animals can be very different from each other. However, all animals have certain traits in common. These traits have been developed as a response to similar needs. Many different kinds of animals visit a watering hole in Africa. What do these animals have in common?

Inquiry Skill

You classify when you place things that share properties together in groups.

Explore Activity

What Are the Traits of Animals?

Materials

25 pictures of animals

5 sheets of paper

tape

scissors

Procedure

BE CAREFUL! Be careful using scissors.

1. Cut out 25 animal pictures from old magazines.

2. **Classify** Think about the kinds of things all of the animals you found need to survive. Then, think about the traits that enable these animals to fulfill those needs.

3. **Communicate** Write why you think these animals are classified as animals.

4. **Classify** Now that you have seen the animals' similarities, look at their differences. What traits would you use to classify the 25 animals you have into different groups? How many groups would you make?

Drawing Conclusions

1. What trait was used most often for grouping the pictures?

2. **Infer** What is the best method for grouping the animals?

3. **FURTHER INQUIRY** **Infer** Why do you think scientists all over the world use a single system for grouping organisms?

Main Idea Animals with similar traits are classified in the same group.

An octopus uses its tentacles to trap a fish.

What Are the Traits of Animals?

You know that a tarantula is an animal. You also know that a donkey is an animal. But do you know what makes an animal an animal?

Animals are many-celled organisms that are made of different kinds of cells. Most animal cells have a nucleus and specialized structures surrounded by a membrane. As you learned in Lesson 1 animal cells are organized to form tissues, organs, and organ systems. Organ systems enable animals to perform different functions such as sensing the environment, getting rid of wastes, and reproducing.

Animals can't make their own food. Some eat plants to supply their energy needs. Some animals eat other animals and some eat both plants and animals.

Most animals can move from place to place. They move to find food, shelter, mates, and to protect

themselves from predators. Animals live in different kinds of environments—from the North Pole to the Amazon forest. They have developed organ systems and behaviors that allow them to survive in these different environments.

For example, since different animals eat different foods, they have developed different methods of getting food. Octopuses have tentacles that they use to capture prey, such as oysters, shrimp, or fish. Frogs have a long and sticky tongue so they can snare prey such as flies.

A frog uses its sticky tongue to trap a fly.

There are as many animal adaptations as there are animal species and there are about 10 million species of animals on Earth! So, how do scientists classify all these animals? Animals are divided into two large groups. Vertebrates are a group made up of animals that have backbones. The members of the invertebrate group do not have backbones. Vertebrates and invertebrates are divided into smaller groups. For example, vertebrates are divided into the following classes:

- **Fish** are the most diverse vertebrate group. Fish are vertebrates that live their whole life in water. Most fish have gills to take oxygen directly from the water. Fish are usually covered by scales.

- **Amphibians** are adapted to live part of their life in water and part of their life on land. Most adult amphibians can live on land, but they need water to reproduce. Amphibians have a thin moist skin and most have four legs.

- Snakes, turtles, alligators, and lizards are **reptiles**. Reptiles can reproduce on land. Unlike the thin moist

A bat is a mammal.

skin of amphibians, reptiles have dry, thick skin covered with scales. Reptiles breathe with lungs.

- **Birds** are different from all other vertebrates in that they have both feathers and wings. Birds also have hollow bones and air sacs that help them to fly.

- **Mammals** are vertebrates whose young drink milk from their mothers' bodies. Humans are mammals, so when you study the traits of mammals, you will learn about yourself too.

On the following pages are some of the groups of invertebrates and vertebrates. They are listed from the simplest to the most complex. Look at each example closely and think about how these different animals carry out different functions.

A cat is a mammal.

READING Summarize
What trait do scientists use to divide all animals into two main groups?

Invertebrates

One of the simplest kinds of animals is a sponge. Sponges belong to a group called *Porifera* (pawr·IF·er·ah). A sponge's body is like a hollow tube with lots of holes in it, called pores. Sponges have different kinds of cells that do different jobs. They have some tissues but no organs. Sponges live in water.

Sponge

Sea anemone

Hydra

Hydras, sea anemones, and jellyfish are the *Cnidaria* (nigh·DAYR·ee·uh). They do not have heads or tails. They live in water. They have soft bodies and tentacles—long threadlike structures. At the end of each tentacle, they have cells that make poisons. They inject the poisons into small animals they kill to eat.

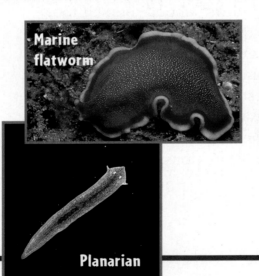

Marine flatworm

Flatworms are *Platyhelminthes* (pla·tee·hel·MIN·theez). Their bodies are flat. They have heads and tails. They also have organs cnidarians do not have. Most flatworms do not have true organ systems. Some flatworms live in water. Some live inside other animals.

Planarian

Roundworms, or *Nematoda* (nee·mah·TOHD·ah), have round bodies, a digestive system, and a simple nervous system. Roundworms live all over Earth, including inside plants and animals.

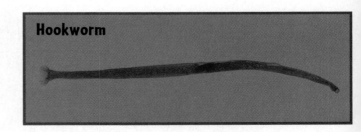

Hookworm

Earthworms belong to a group called segmented worms, or *Annelida* (AN·el·id·ah). Many segmented worms have eyes and other specialized organs, such as jaws or gills. Each of these animals also has a circulatory, digestive, and nervous system.

Earthworm

Snails, clams, and octopuses belong to the *Mollusca* (MAHL·us·kah), the mollusks. Almost all mollusks have a shell. The shell may be either inside or outside the mollusk's body. Mollusks have three main body parts, a kind of foot, a tissue covering called a mantle, and a compartment holding internal organs. They have gills for breathing. They have jaws or other organs for capturing food. They each have a circulatory system for moving blood. More complex mollusks, like octopuses, have a well-developed brain.

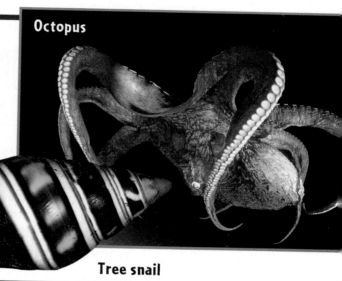

Octopus

Tree snail

Grasshopper

Lobster

What has a tough outer skeleton, jointed legs, and a body made up of two, three, or more sections? It is an arthropod—a member of the group *Arthropoda* (AHR·thruh·pohd·ah). There are more arthropods on Earth than any other kind of animal. They include insects, spiders, centipedes, millipedes, lobsters, and crabs.

Spider

Unlike arthropods, the *Echinodermata* (i·KIGH·noh·durm·ah·tah), or echinoderms, have a skeleton inside their bodies. Most also have a spiny skin and tubelike feet with suction cups.

Starfish

Lamprey

The simplest fish, the *Agnatha* (AG·nah·thuh), do not have jaws or bones. Their skeletons are made of tissue called cartilage. These fish do not have backbones, but each does have a tough nerve cord that runs down its back. They look more like big worms than like fish.

Like those of lampreys and hagfish, the skeletons of sharks and rays are made of cartilage, not bone. However, the cartilage running down their backs is made of a chain of smaller parts called vertebrae. Unlike lampreys and hagfish, sharks and rays have jaws. They also have paired fins. These fish are *Chondrichthyes* (kahn·DRIK·theez).

Shark

Reef sting ray

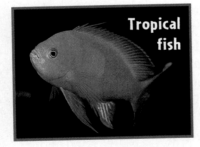

Tropical fish

Bony fish, or *Osteichthys* (AHS·tee·ik·theez), have bones instead of cartilage. Many have fins that look like fans with spokes in them. These fish have a movable flap over their gills. The movement of this flap lets bony fish breathe while staying still. Unlike sharks, most bony fish have an organ called a swim bladder, or air sac, that allows them to hover at any depth.

Frog

Salamander

Frogs, toads, and salamanders are *Amphibia* (am·FIB·ee·uh), the amphibians. Most adult amphibians have four legs and skin that is not covered with scales. Adult amphibians breathe with lungs instead of gills. In their early stages of life, amphibians live in water. As adults, most live on land.

Crocodile

Snake

Turtle

The first vertebrates to grow and develop out of water were the *Reptilia* (rep·TEE·lee·uh), the reptiles. Reptiles breathe through lungs. Most have waterproof scales on their skin that keep them from drying out on land. Their eggs have a leathery or hard covering that protects the eggs from drying out.

Frigate bird

Ostrich

Not all birds can fly, but all birds belong to the group *Aves* (AY·veez). Birds have feathers, walk on two hind limbs, and have front limbs that are wings. Their bones are strong but very lightweight.

Whale

Shrew

You belong to the group called *Mammalia* (mam·AYL·ee·uh), the mammals. All mammals feed their young milk. At one time or another, all mammals have at least some hair or fur. No other animals have these traits. For their size, most mammals have larger brains than other vertebrates.

Inquiry Skill
BUILDER

Model a Backbone

Vertebrates have an internal skeleton with a backbone. Skeletons are made of bones or cartilage that give the body its overall shape. In this activity, you will learn more about the structure of a backbone as you make a model.

Materials

pasta wheels

soft-candy circles

craft sticks

hard-candy circles

BE CAREFUL! Do not eat anything in the lab.

Procedure

1 Use pasta wheels, soft-candy circles, and a craft stick to make a model of a backbone.

2 Alternately string the pasta wheels and the soft-candy circles on the craft stick until the row of candy and pasta is about 10 cm long.

3 Fold each end of the craft stick so the pasta wheels and candy do not come off.

4 Slowly bend the model. Does it move easily?

5 How far can you bend the model?

6 Compare your backbone to the model.

Drawing Conclusions

Build a model using hard-candy circles with the pasta wheels. Compare the two models. Which model allows for more flexibility?

L·I·N·K·S

Why It Matters

Many animal species disappear every year. This is due in part to competition between humans and animals for resources, such as land. Understanding animals and their needs helps us plan our use of resources so that we can coexist with other species.

e-Journal Visit our Web site www.science.mmhschool.com to do a research project on endangered animal species.

Think and Write

1. Name three traits you might use to classify an animal.

2. What is the main difference between an invertebrate and a vertebrate?

3. Name a trait you would use to classify a fish as belonging to either the lamprey and hagfish group or the shark and ray group.

4. INQUIRY SKILL **Make a Model** How would you design a model of the exoskeleton of an invertebrate?

5. **Critical Thinking** Which do you think are more closely related —whales and goldfish or whales and mice? Explain.

LITERATURE LINK

Read *Operation Migration*, the exciting true story about how scientists taught a group of young whooping cranes in Indiana how to migrate. After you finish reading, think about why it is important to save endangered animals. Then try the activities at the end of the book.

Operation Migration

by Emily Laber-Warren

McGraw Hill

WRITING LINK

Expository Writing Look at the picture of the animal shown here. It swims underwater. It has a ducklike bill and webbed feet. It lays eggs like a bird, yet its eggshells are like those of a reptile. It is a *platypus*. Write an essay to explain how you would classify it.

MATH LINK

Solve this problem. The smallest bat is 4 centimeters long. The blue whale is 3,300 centimeters long. How much longer is the blue whale than the smallest bat?

TECHNOLOGY LINK

LOG ON Visit www.science.mmhschool.com for more links.

Animal Life Cycles

What if you saw a tadpole but had never seen a frog? Would people have a hard time convincing you a frog was a grown-up tadpole?

When you see seedlings, you can predict that the fully grown plants will be on stems and have leaves. However, some baby animals look nothing like the adults. They change shape by going through metamorphosis.

Frogs lay eggs in ponds and lakes. The eggs hatch into tadpoles. They must live in water because they have gills, like fish, not lungs.

The tadpoles begin to change. They grow legs. Their tails disappear. They develop lungs and lose their gills. Now they can live on land and in the water!

Insects have two kinds of metamorphosis—complete and incomplete. During complete metamorphosis an egg hatches into a wormlike larva. It eats a lot and grows to become a pupa. This is a resting phase. Many body changes take place. Some larvae spin protective cocoons. Finally, the adult winged insect emerges.

During incomplete metamorphosis the insect changes shape gradually. An egg hatches into a nymph that looks like a small adult without wings. The nymph grows and slowly changes. Finally, it grows wings and becomes an adult.

Eggs

Tadpole with gills

Tadpole with limbs

Young frog

Egg   Larva   Pupa   Adult
butterfly

What Did I Learn?

1. To go from egg to adult, a frog goes through a process called

    A childhood.
    B adolescence.
    C the pupa stage.
    D metamorphosis.

2. The stages of complete metamorphosis are:

    F egg, larva, pupa, adult
    G egg, larva, nymph, pupa, adult
    H egg, nymph, pupa, adult
    J egg, nymph, adult

Egg   Nymph   Adult
grasshopper

LOG ON Visit www.science.mmhschool.com for more links.

Animal Adaptations

Vocabulary

mimicry, A106

camouflage, A108

protective coloration, A109

heredity, A110

hybrid, A112

crossbreeding, A112

diversity, A114

Get Ready

Alaska is home to many animals, including the snowshoe hare. You might think this hare is a little strange. Its fur changes color from white in the winter to brown in the summer. How does this help the snowshoe hare survive in its environment?

Inquiry Skill

You **experiment** when you perform a test to support or disprove a hypothesis.

Explore Activity

How Do Sow Bugs Adapt to Their Environment?

Materials
10 sow bugs
tray
paper towels
water

Procedure

BE CAREFUL! Handle live animals with care. Wash your hands well when you finish this activity.

1. **Observe** Place a sow bug in the center of the tray, and observe it. What traits does it have that enable it to live in the soil and under decaying wood or leaves? Record your observations.

2. **Observe** Touch the sow bug. How does it react?

3. **Experiment** Place all the sow bugs in the center of the tray. Do the animals tend to stay together?

4. **Experiment** Move the sow bugs to one end of the tray. Dampen three or four paper towels, and place them in the opposite end of the tray. Observe for several minutes. Record your observations. When the animals move, do they tend to move faster in the dry section or wet section of the box?

Drawing Conclusions

1. **Infer** How do sow bugs protect themselves?

2. **Infer** Can the behavior of sow bugs when exposed to moisture be related to their survival? If so, how?

3. **FURTHER INQUIRY** **Experiment** Design an experiment to test the reactions of sow bugs to light. Try it and report your results.

Main Idea Animals have certain characteristics, behaviors, and adaptations that help them survive.

How Do Animals Adapt?

Certain traits animals have help them to survive in their environment. Such traits are called adaptations.

An animal has many adaptations. One important group of adaptations helps the animal keep from getting eaten by a *predator* (an animal that might eat it). How can an animal avoid being eaten?

Through experience, you have learned to avoid certain things. For example, if you see a buzzing black-and-yellow striped insect, you are not likely to try to touch it. Why? You have learned that insects that look like this can give you a painful sting. They are called yellow jackets. Animals that feed on insects have also learned to avoid yellow jackets.

They also avoid a harmless insect called a syrphid (SUHR·fuhd) fly. Why? It looks very much like a yellow jacket. In nature, looking like something else—especially something unpleasant—is called **mimicry**.

Mimicry

One of these insects stings. One does not. To be safe, insect-eating animals avoid both. This helps both the wasp (left) and the harmless syrphid fly (right) to survive. Animals avoid the harmless fly because it mimics a stinging wasp.

When food spoils, it tastes bad. If you don't want to get sick, you quickly dispose of spoiled food. Some birds might like to make a meal out of the good-tasting viceroy butterfly. However, birds often avoid gulping down a viceroy. Why? The viceroy looks like a monarch butterfly, which, birds have learned, tastes awful.

Viceroy

Monarch

Birds avoid eating the good-tasting viceroy butterfly (top) because it looks like the awful-tasting monarch butterfly (bottom).

You are probably very careful when you meet a cat you don't know. You have learned that its sharp claws can give you a nasty scratch. Certain predators have learned the same thing about thorny plants. The predators stay away from such plants.

This gives thornbugs protection from being eaten. That's because thornbugs look like thorns. When the bugs cluster on the stem of a plant, a predator mistakes them for the thorns on a plant. The predator stays away, and the thornbugs live to see another day.

▷ **Why is mimicry a good adaptation for an animal to have?**

Monarch larvae (caterpillars) feed on milkweed. Milkweed contains a substance that can make animals ill. Birds that have eaten one monarch butterfly learn to avoid eating both monarchs and look-alike viceroys.

The dark "thorn" on the branch is a thornbug. Because thornbugs look like thorns that can scratch, predators stay away.

What Is Camouflage?

At one time or another, most people have dreamed about being invisible. For one thing, if people can't see you, they can't hurt you. You can't make yourself invisible. Neither can animals. Even so, you can make yourself look so much like your surroundings that you are almost invisible.

An animal that does not move, or moves very, very slowly, and looks like its surroundings is camouflaged. **Camouflage** is another important adaptation that helps animals avoid their predators.

There are two basic kinds of camouflage, or blending in with the environment. One has to do with an animal's shape. The other has to do with its color. Let's start off by exploring how shape can camouflage an animal.

What if you were a bird hunting for a butterfly? You would not be tempted to eat a leaf. That is what protects the leaf butterfly from being eaten. The wings of the leaf butterfly are shaped like the leaves of a plant. When this butterfly is perched on the stem of a plant, or resting on a forest floor littered with leaves, it is very hard to see. A bird passes it by as if it were not there.

Leaf butterflies look so much like leaves that a bird looking for a meal will fly right by.

Birds can more easily spot a light-colored peppered moth (right) against a dark background than a dark-colored peppered moth (left) against a dark background.

About 150 years ago, England was home to two kinds of peppered moths. One kind was light colored. The other kind was dark colored. Birds fed on both kinds of moths, many of which clung to the trunks of trees.

However, gradually the light-colored moths seemed to be disappearing. The birds were eating more of these moths than the dark-colored ones. What was causing this?

Nearby factories were pouring dark, sticky smoke into the air. The smoke stuck to the trunks of trees. The light-colored moths stood out against this background. The dark-colored moths blended in with the background.

Since the birds could more easily see the light-colored moths, the birds were eating more light-colored moths than dark-colored moths. This is an example of a kind of camouflage called **protective coloration**. The color of the dark peppered moths protected them from predators.

▷ **How does camouflage help an animal survive?**

Nest building is an inherited trait. Robins (left) build their nests of twigs. Penguins (above) build their nests of pebbles.

What Is Inherited?

Animals behave in many different ways. They learn some kinds of behavior, like avoiding bad-tasting insects. You may have noticed learned behaviors in your pet. For example, if your cat cries for food every time it hears the electric can opener, your cat has learned that the sound of the can opener can mean mealtime. No wonder your cat acts disappointed when the canned food turns out to be something it doesn't like. However, not all behaviors are learned. Certain other kinds of behavior seem to be automatic.

Young birds will build the same kinds of nests their parents build. They do this even if the young birds have never seen their parents build a nest. In other words, birds do not learn how to build nests. They do it automatically.

Scientists would say that nest building is *inherited*, or passed down from one generation to the next. An inherited behavior is one that is not learned. It is done automatically. This inherited behavior is called *instinct*. The passing of inherited traits from parents to offspring is called **heredity**.

Many physical traits of an animal are also inherited. For example, the shape of a bird's feet and beak is inherited. The color of its feathers is inherited, too. This is easy to see, since young birds have the same-shaped feet and beaks as their parents.

Hawk

Duck

Woodpecker

The feet and beaks of birds are inherited physical traits. All woodpeckers have feet adapted for grasping the sides of tree trunks. All hawks have feet armed with claws adapted for grabbing smaller animals. All ducks have webbed feet adapted for swimming.

What physical traits are not inherited? Those that the environment can change. If there is not much food around, an animal's weight and size may be smaller than normal. Weight and size are physical traits, but they may not be inherited. Of course, certain animals—such as elephants— tend to be bigger and heavier than others—such as mice. Such tendencies are inherited.

The average weight and size of an elephant is greater than the average weight and size of a mouse. Even so, some elephants will be larger and heavier than others. Some mice will be larger and heavier than other mice. In other words, some traits are affected by both heredity and the environment.

▷ **How are animal behaviors that are inherited different from those that are learned?**

Although gerbils are smaller than elephants, the environment can make some gerbils bigger than other gerbils and some elephants bigger than other elephants.

Donkey

Mule

Horse

A mule is the hybrid offspring of the mating of a female horse and a male donkey. Many hybrids are sterile and cannot produce offspring of their own. This is true of mules.

What Is a Hybrid?

What looks a little like a horse and a little like a donkey, but isn't either? The answer to this riddle is . . . a mule! It looks the way it does because its male parent was a donkey and its female parent was a horse.

Living things that have parents that are quite different from each other, such as donkeys and horses, are called **hybrids**. People sometimes breed hybrids on purpose, since a hybrid may have more desirable traits than either of its parents.

A mule can do work that a donkey or a horse cannot do. Mules are often used to carry heavy loads through rugged country. That's because mules do not slip as easily as horses. Mules also have more endurance than

donkeys. Horses and donkeys do not normally mate. Even so, for thousands of years people have been breeding mules.

Crossbreeds

People often mate closely related living things on purpose. They may mate certain crop plants, flowers, dogs, or cats. They do this to produce hearty crops or plants and animals with desirable traits. This process is sometimes called **crossbreeding**. A crossbreed is a product of the mating of individuals from two distinct breeds or varieties of the same *species* (kind of organism). Crossbreeding has produced new breeds of dogs and cats. Cross-breeding has also given us new kinds of corn that resist disease, produce more food on the same area of land, and are more nutritious.

Crossbreeds also occur naturally. If you have found a shady spot under the branches of a London plane tree, you have run across a hybrid. About 2,000 years ago, the oriental plane tree grew in the southern parts of Europe. It was so pretty that people living in northern Europe wanted to grow it there. Unfortunately, the oriental plane tree could not survive the cold northern winters. Then in about 1670, the oriental plane tree crossbred naturally with another kind of plane tree. The offspring, which came to be called the London plane tree, was a new kind of plant that could survive cold winters. Today these lovely trees are found on many streets in northern Europe and in the northern United States.

Cat Breeds

Cat breeds can be divided into two major groups—cats with short hair and cats with long hair. Different breeds of cats also vary in color, in length and texture of hair, and in temperament. Some are quiet and affectionate. Others tend to be vocal and demanding.

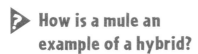 **How is a mule an example of a hybrid?**

QUICK LAB

Find the New Breed

FOLDABLES™ Make a Three-Tab Book. (See p. R 42.) Label it as shown.

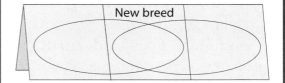

New breed

1. **Observe** Make the Three-Tab Book pictured and use it to record your observations. Look at the picture of the Siamese cat. What traits do you think it has been bred for?

2. **Observe** Look at the picture of the Persian cat. What traits do you think it has been bred for?

3. **Observe** Look at the picture of the Himalayan cat. What traits do you think it has been bred for?

4. **Infer** Which cat do you think is the new breed? Explain your answer.

Himalayan cat

Persian cat

Siamese cat

Why Is Diversity Important?

Would you rather have a mutt or a purebred dog? Purebred dogs—or other animals—look very much like their parents. They are bred to have certain traits. Mutts, on the other hand, may not look much like either parent. However, they do have a great mix of traits.

A group of dogs made up of mutts is a good example of animal **diversity**. *Diversity* means "different." Animal diversity refers to a group of the same kind of animal—like dogs—in which there are lots of animals with different traits. A group of mutts is made up of individual dogs with very different traits. Is there an advantage to being a mutt? The answer can be yes! Mutts may be healthier than certain purebred dogs. Some purebred dogs are known to have breathing problems. Some have hip problems. However, other purebred dogs come from very healthy breeds.

Animal diversity is important. When an environment changes, only those animals that can adapt to the change will survive. If the population is made up of animals with the same traits—and those traits do not help the animals survive in a changing environment—the whole population may die out. This fate threatens the cheetahs of Africa. However, if the population holds animals with different traits, it is more likely that some will survive to keep the population going.

Africa's cheetahs are in trouble. The traits of all cheetahs are so much alike, they have little diversity. This could threaten their survival against a new disease or other changes in their environment.

READING Summarize
Why is diversity important in an animal population?

Why It Matters

Animals need to adapt to changes in their environment to survive. If an animal population is diverse it is likely that at least some of its individuals will be able to adapt to changes in the environment. This ensures species survival.

Sometimes animals carry traits that could be unhealthy for their offspring. Diversity reduces the chances of inheriting such traits. Hybridization, whether natural or artificial, produces animal diversity.

e-Journal Visit our Web site **www.science.mmhschool.com** to do a research project on animal diversity.

Think and Write

1. What is one adaptation that helps an animal escape a predator?

2. What is an example of an inherited behavior?

3. What is an example of an inherited physical trait?

4. Why is diversity important?

5. **Critical Thinking** Dark peppered moths cling to trees covered by black soot from factories. If the factories were not allowed to produce sooty smoke, what might happen to the dark peppered moths? Explain.

L·I·N·K·S

ART LINK

Make a display. Research three hybrid animals other than the ones discussed in this lesson. Make an illustration of these animals and their parents to display.

Tiglon

WRITING LINK

Writing That Compares Think about your favorite animal. Which of its behaviors are automatic? Which are learned? Write an essay that compares the behaviors of your favorite animal with your own behaviors. Which of your responses are automatic? Which are learned? Make a chart of points to compare and contrast before writing.

MATH LINK

Make a bar graph. It is estimated that there were about 100,000 cheetahs in the wild in 1900; about 30,000 in 1950; and there are about 10,000 today. Make a bar graph to show how the population of the cheetah has declined.

TECHNOLOGY LINK

LOG ON Visit **www.science.mmhschool.com** for more links.

Chapter 4 Review

Vocabulary

Fill each blank with the best word or words from the list.

amphibians, A95
camouflage, A108
crossbreeding, A112
diversity, A114
heredity, A110
hybrid, A112
mammals, A95
mimicry, A106
protective coloration, A109
reptiles, A95

1. A group of mutts is a good example of animal _____.

2. An animal uses _____ to blend in with the background.

3. Looking like something a predator would not like to eat is an example of _____.

4. The changing color of an arctic hare's coat is an example of _____.

5. A mule is a(n) _____.

6. Vertebrates that are adapted to live part of their lives in water and part of their lives on land are called _____.

7. Humans are classified as _____.

8. Scientists use _____ to produce heartier crops.

9. The passing down of inherited traits is called _____.

10. Vertebrates that have dry, thick skin are _____.

Test Prep

11. Insects, spiders, lobsters, and crabs are all _____.
    A mammals
    B amphibians
    C arthropods
    D syrphids

12. The skeletons of sharks are made of _____.
    F scales
    G bones
    H fins
    J cartilage

13. A bird's bones _____.
    A are made of cartilage
    B weigh very little for their size
    C weigh a lot for their size
    D are surprisingly thick

14. Animals with fur are _____.
    F amphibians
    G syrphids
    H either arthropods or mollusks
    J mammals

15. As adults, frogs breathe with _____.
    A gills
    B lungs
    C cartilage
    D mollusks

Concepts and Skills

16. Reading in Science Write a paragraph explaining why a predator might avoid eating a syrphid fly.

17. Scientific Methods Describe two ways that adaptation can help animals survive. Write a design for an experiment that would test this.

18. Decision Making A company is planning to build a factory near a river that is home to many different kinds of fish. The only thing the company is planning to dump in the river is clean water. However, the temperature of the water they are dumping is 18°C warmer than the warmest temperature the river usually reaches. You are on the planning committee that will decide whether or not to allow the factory to be built there. What factors do you need to consider when making your decision? Write a paragraph discussing these factors and explaining what your decision would be.

19. INQUIRY SKILL **Classify** Many members of different animal groups are found in water. Create a classification key to identify a whale among a hagfish, a shark, and a sea turtle. Write a paragraph explaining how your key works.

20. Critical Thinking You are a marine biologist, a scientist who studies living things in the ocean. You are exploring under the water and come upon a strange fish. You catch it in a net and take it back to your laboratory. What must you find out about the fish in order to classify it? Write your ideas.

Did You Ever Wonder?

INQUIRY SKILL **Experiment** Suppose you were a naturalist. How would you set up an experiment to determine if the snowshoe hare's color change helps it to survive?

 LOG ON Visit www.science.mmhschool.com to boost your test scores.

Paul Sereno
Paleontologist

Students of Professor Paul Sereno follow him around the world for one of his classes. Sereno is a paleontologist — a scientist who studies the remains of plants and animals that lived millions of years ago. He and his students travel the world in search of dinosaur fossils.

Fossils are the remains of ancient life forms. They can be bones, shells, impressions of feathers—even footprints! They are usually found in rocks. Fossils give scientists information about Earth's past. They can unlock mysteries about what life was like in the past.

Sereno and a team of students working in the field.

Sereno's hand showing jaws of "super croc."

One of Sereno's most interesting finds was the bones of a 40-foot-long crocodile. He found the bones in Niger, a nation in Africa. The "super croc" lived about 110 million years ago. It weighed as much as a small whale. Its jaws were about five feet long!

Sereno knows it's important to back up his discoveries with science that's available today. By measuring live crocodiles in the wild, Sereno and his team were able to figure out how long the super croc may have been and how much it probably weighed. Members of his team literally got on the backs of living crocodiles to measure them!

TOP 5 Most Extreme Dinosaurs

Here are five dinosaurs that paleontologists think were tops in their fields:

1. **Largest dinosaur:** *Seismosaurus* Grew to about 120 feet long
2. **Smallest dinosaur:** *Compsognathus* Weighed about $6\frac{1}{3}$ pounds
3. **Longest neck:** *Mamenchisaurus* Possessed a neck 46 feet long
4. **Fastest:** *Ornithomimu* Could run about 40 to 50 miles per hour
5. **Smartest:** *Troodon* Had the largest brain-to-body ratio of all dinosaurs

Write About It

1. What are fossils?
2. What can paleontologists learn by studying fossils?

LOG ON Visit www.science.mmhschool.com to learn more about the work of paleontologists.

Classifying Your World

Your goal is to design a key to classify living things.

What to Do

Make a list of all the living things you encounter on a daily basis. How would you classify them? Design a key that you can use to classify them.

Analyze **Your Results**

1. Use your key to classify all the living things you listed.

2. Make a diagram to show how you grouped your list of living things.

Plant Parts Do Their Part

Your goal is to identify plant parts and diagram water movement in a plant.

Root	Stem	Leaf	Fruit
Seed	Flower	Bark	Sap

What to Do

1. Using a hand lens, identify veins and petioles in a leaf; root hairs, cortex, and xylem in a root; and xylem and phloem in a stem. Draw and label diagrams of each part.

2. Draw and label a tree. Show water movement from soil to leaf.

Analyze **Your Results**

Using the words *light*, *chlorophyll*, and *energy* describe how leaf cells use water.

Cactus Creature

Your goal is to make a model animal adapted to life in the desert.

What to Do

BE CAREFUL! Handle sharp objects carefully! Examine a cactus with a hand lens. Think of how an animal that lives among cactus would look. Make a model of it.

Analyze **Your Results**

Describe the adaptations you gave your model animal. How would each of these adaptations help the animal survive in the desert? Compare it to a cactus.

UNIT B

Living Things and Their Environments

LOOK!

A tiny leaf-cutter ant carries off a leaf that is much larger than itself. How do leaf-cutter ants interact with other living things in the rain forest?

Living Things and Their Environments

CHAPTER

5

Interactions of Living Things

Did You Ever Wonder?

What happened to the buffalo? The huge herds of buffalo that once roamed the grasslands of the United States were hunted almost to extinction. Today, however, buffalo can once again be seen in places like Yellowstone National Park.

INQUIRY SKILL **Infer** What living and nonliving things affect the life of the buffalo?

Interactions in an Ecosystem

Vocabulary

ecosystem, B6

abiotic factor, B6

biotic factor, B7

population, B11

community, B11

ecology, B11

habitat, B12

niche, B12

Get Ready

What do you need in order to survive? Food? Water? Comfortable temperatures? Shelter?

What kinds of things does the animal shown here need to survive? What kinds of things do the plants need? Where do you think they get these things?

Inquiry Skill

You experiment when you perform a test to support or disprove a hypothesis.

Explore Activity

What Do Living Things Need to Survive?

Procedure: Design Your Own

BE CAREFUL! Handle animals and plants gently.

1 For a water environment, add thoroughly washed sand or gravel to the jar. Fill the jar with water. Add a few floating plants, rooted plants with floating leaves, and submerged plants. Add water snails.

2 For a land environment, place a layer of gravel on the bottom of the jar. Cover the gravel layer with a layer of moistened soil. Add plants, and plant grass seeds. Add earthworms, sow bugs, and snails.

3 Place each jar in a lighted area but not in direct sunlight.

4 Cover each jar with its own lid or with a piece of plastic wrap. Record the number and types of living things you used.

5 **Observe** Examine your jars every other day, and record your observations.

Drawing Conclusions

1 **Infer** What are the nonliving parts of your system? What are the living parts of your system?

2 **Infer** What do the living things need to survive? How do you know?

3 **FURTHER INQUIRY** **Experiment** How could you design an environment that contains land and water areas?

Materials

wide-mouthed, clear container with lid

washed gravel

pond water or aged tap water

water plants

water snails

soil

small rocks

grass seed and small plants

earthworms, land snails, sow bugs, or other small land animals that eat plants

What Is an Ecosystem?

What or whom do you interact with every day? Living things and nonliving things interact in an **ecosystem**. An ecosystem is all the living and nonliving things in an area.

An ecosystem may be very small, such as a backyard or pond. Some ecosystems, like the prairie ecosystem of North America, the deserts of Africa, and the rain forests of Brazil, cover large areas of a country or continent. Freshwater ecosystems cover less space than saltwater ecosystems. Saltwater ecosystems can cover entire oceans. It doesn't matter where they are or what they look like, all ecosystems have the same parts.

Abiotic Factors

The nonliving parts of an ecosystem are the **abiotic** (ay·bigh·AHT·ik) **factors**. All living things need certain nonliving things in order to survive. Abiotic factors include water, minerals, sunlight, air, climate, and soil.

All organisms, or living things, need water. Their bodies are 50 to 95 percent water. The processes that keep living things alive—like photosynthesis and respiration—can only take place in the presence of water. Living things also need minerals, such as calcium, iron, phosphorus, and nitrogen. Some living things, like plants and algae, need

sunlight to make food. Animals need oxygen to produce energy for their bodies. Plants and algae need carbon dioxide. The environment must also have the right temperature for organisms to survive.

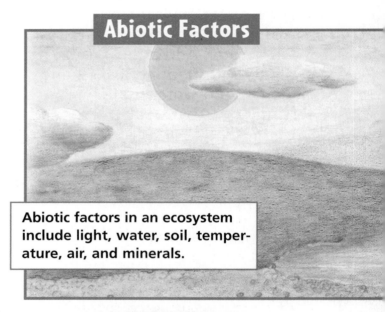

Abiotic Factors

Abiotic factors in an ecosystem include light, water, soil, temperature, air, and minerals.

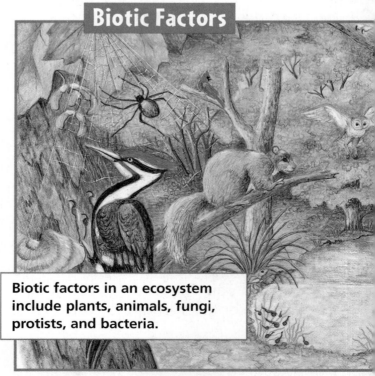

Biotic Factors

Biotic factors in an ecosystem include plants, animals, fungi, protists, and bacteria.

1. How do these two diagrams differ? What does each diagram show?

2. Which of these two diagrams best shows the abiotic factors in the ecosystem? Explain your answer.

Biotic Factors

The living parts of an ecosystem are animals, plants, fungi, protists, and bacteria. These organisms make up the **biotic** (bigh·AHT·ik) **factors** of an ecosystem.

Plants and algae are *producers*. They produce oxygen and food that animals need. Animals are *consumers*. Animals consume, or eat, algae, plants, or animals. Animals also give off carbon dioxide that plants and algae need to make food.

What do the fungi and bacteria contribute? They are a very important part of any ecosystem. Fungi and bacteria are *decomposers*. They *decompose*, or break down, dead plants and animals into useful things like minerals that enrich soil. Plants need these in order to grow. Each kind of organism has a role that helps the others survive.

There are many ecosystems in the world and each has a unique set of biotic and abiotic factors. These factors determine the kinds of organisms that the ecosystem can support. This is why there are different organisms in different ecosystems. For example, you wouldn't find a buffalo in a desert or a forest ecosystem because it needs grass to survive.

▶ **What are five abiotic and five biotic factors in an ecosystem?**

What Is a Prairie Ecosystem Like?

Long ago a "sea of wild grasses" covered North America from central Texas in the south to North Dakota in the north. These were America's prairie lands, the range of the famous song "Home on the Range."

The Blackland Prairie is the largest remaining prairie in America. It stretches 483 km (300 mi) across Texas, from Austin to Clarksville. The Blacklands got their name from the rich black soil the early settlers found there. The settlers found that the summers were hot and long, and that there was enough rain to grow profitable crops, like cotton.

Before the land became farms and ranches, huge herds of buffalo grazed on the prairie grasses. Native Americans once hunted the buffalo on this land for food and clothing as a means of survival.

Buffalo were not the prairie's only inhabitants. Plants and animals of all kinds lived there. At least 50 different kinds of tall and short grasses provided food for plant-eating animals. Many kinds of wildflowers painted the landscape with beautiful colors. These flowers included purple coneflowers, bluebells, yellow sunflowers, and golden daleas. Travelers might have come across oak, hickory, elm, or cedar trees along nearby streams.

The cattle and crops that provide much of our food live on the prairie today. Ranchers and farmers now graze cattle and plant crops such as corn and wheat on the Blacklands.

READING

Sequence of Events
How has the Blackland Prairie ecosystem changed over time?

What Is the Treasure of the Blackland Prairie?

Have you ever read about a buried treasure? Unlike those stories, the treasure of the Blackland Prairie is not buried underground. The treasure of the Blackland Prairie *is* the ground.

Prairie soils can often be identified by their dark brown to black *topsoil*. Topsoil is the top layer of soil. The dark color shows the presence of *humus*. Humus is partly decayed plant matter. The decay is produced by the bacteria and fungi.

The rich topsoil is full of minerals that prairie grasses and crops need. Two of the most important minerals are magnesium and calcium. Plants need magnesium in order to make chlorophyll. Calcium is an important element of cell walls in plants.

The Blackland Prairie covers almost 13 million acres. Many kinds of animals and plants live on a prairie. A prairie is a region of grasses. It may be flat or hilly grassland.

The nutrients in certain prairie soils tend to stay near the surface. That's true because of the low yearly rainfall on prairies. There isn't enough water to carry the nutrients deep into the ground. Farmers take advantage of this by growing crops that have shallow roots, such as corn, wheat, cotton, and sorghum. Sorghum is a grain that is used to feed livestock. What do these crops have in common with the plants that grow naturally on the prairie? They are all classified as grasses.

▷ **How can you describe the soil of the Blackland Prairie?**

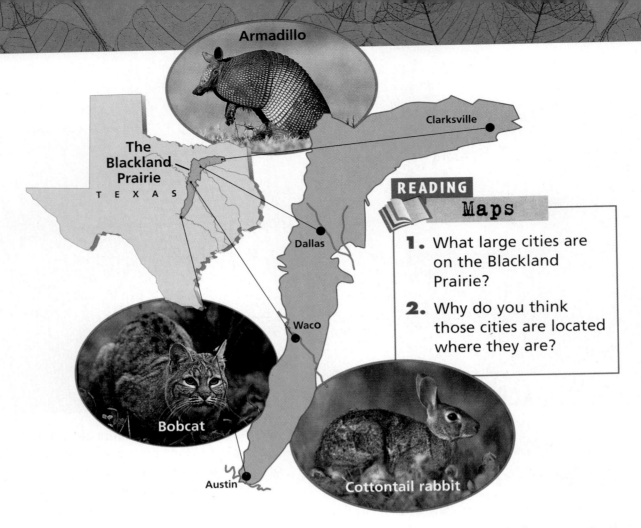

Armadillo

The Blackland Prairie
T E X A S

Clarksville

Dallas

Waco

Bobcat

Austin

Cottontail rabbit

READING
Maps

1. What large cities are on the Blackland Prairie?

2. Why do you think those cities are located where they are?

What Animals Live on the Blackland Prairie?

About 500 species, or different kinds, of animals still live on this prairie. The spotted chorus frog sings in the night near the streams and rivers. Rattlesnakes and lizards seek shelter under rocks.

Birds like pipits, longspurs, and horned larks, as well as 300 other kinds of birds, still live on the Blackland Prairie.

Raccoons, opossums, coyotes, white-tailed deer, and striped skunks live on the Blacklands. Cotton rats, white-footed mice, eastern cottontails, red bats, and bobcats live there, too.

Mountain lions, gray wolves, black bears, and jaguars used to come in search of prey. When people came and built towns, cities, and farms, the buffalo left. The animals that fed on the buffalo left, too. Some animals, however, came to the Blacklands from other places, and stayed. Armadillos arrived from Mexico as the Blacklands' climate warmed up over the past 150 years. Badgers invaded from north-western Texas when their natural homes were cleared for development.

▷ **What are five animals that live on the prairie?**

What Are Populations and Communities?

The Blackland Prairie, like all ecosystems, is home to many different organisms. Each kind of organism, whether an animal, plant, fungus, protist, or bacterium, is a member of a different species. All the organisms of a species living in the same area make up a **population**.

The Blackland Prairie has populations of armadillos and badgers. It has populations of little bluestem grass and Indian grass. It has elm trees. It also has populations of pond algae and soil bacteria. All the populations living in an area make up a **community**.

The populations in a community interact with each other in different ways. Scientists who are interested in these interactions are ecologists.

Ecology is the study of how all things in an ecosystem interact.

Ecologists investigate the activities of animals, plants, fungi, protists, and bacteria in the ecosystem. They want to know which animals prey on others. Which animals eat plants? Which insects eat crops? They are interested in how bacteria and fungi make the soil fertile. All these questions need to be answered to understand how an ecosystem stays healthy.

▷ **What are populations and communities?**

Scientists study the interactions of different populations in an ecosystem's community. This helps them to understand what makes an ecosystem grow.

What Are Niches and Habitats?

The place where an organism lives is called its **habitat**. The chorus frog's habitat is in the scattered ponds of the Blacklands.

Each species in an ecosystem also has a role or place in the activities of its community. The role of an organism in the community is its **niche**.

A species' niche includes many factors. It includes what a species eats and what eats that species. It includes the kind of environment the species needs to live in. It even includes whether the species is active by day or night.

No two populations can have the same niche. Why is this true? To have the same niche, two populations would have to eat the same foods and be eaten by the same predators. They would have to live in the same space and reproduce in the same ways. They would have to grow under the same temperature, moisture, and light conditions, get the same diseases, and look and behave exactly alike. They would have to be identical! No two populations are identical though, so no two populations have the same niche.

Scientists study the habitats and niches of organisms in a community. They do this to see if the community is healthy or in trouble.

The red bat's habitat is above the ground. During the day it hangs from tree branches like a red leaf. At night it streaks through the air looking for food.

▷ **What is the difference between a niche and a habitat?**

The horned lark has its niche on the prairie.

How Do Organisms Change Their Environment?

You have learned how plants and animals adapt to their environment. However, living organisms also change the environment where they live. These changes can be good, neutral, or bad for the ecosystem.

Have you ever seen a beaver pond? Beavers cut down trees by gnawing their way through tree trunks. Then, they use the tree trunks to build dams that back up water into ponds. Beaver ponds filter sediment and organic matter that otherwise would be carried downstream. The filtered organic matter provides nutrients for invertebrates and aquatic plants.

These invertebrates and aquatic plants attract breeding waterfowl and many fish species. Soon fish-eating animals such as otters follow.

Beaver ponds eventually become marshy areas which allow certain trees to grow. Over time, the marshy area becomes a meadow, and later shrubs begin to grow. The shrubs provide shade that allows tree seedlings to get started. The trees eventually grow into a mature forest.

▷ **How do beavers change their environment?**

QUICK LAB

Changing the Environment

FOLDABLES™ Make a Shutter Fold. (See p. R 42.) Label the shutters as shown.

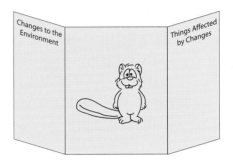

1. Select a wild animal that you find interesting. It can be as small as an insect or as large as whale.

2. Do research to find where this animal lives and what it does to survive in its environment.

3. Draw or find a picture of the animal you selected and paste it in the center of the Shutter Fold.

4. **Communicate** How does the animal you selected change the environment where it lives? What living things are affected by these changes? Write your answers on the Shutter Fold.

5. **Infer** How do the living things you listed above adapt to the changes in their environment? Write your answer on the back of your Shutter Fold.

How Do Organisms Survive in Variable Environments?

The world is a place of changes. As you read on the previous page, some of these changes are caused by living organisms. Some other changes are weather related.

One day the weather may be dry and cold. The next day it may be wet and warm. Heavy rains may drench the land one spring and summer. The next year's spring and summer may have cloudless skies day after day. This makes habitats change.

A good habitat for a certain organism at one time may be a threatening one at another time. How do organisms survive difficult times?

Organisms find new habitats or adapt to the changes in their habitat.

The Eastern Spadefoot Toad

The eastern spadefoot toad lives on the Blackland Prairie. This animal reproduces in water and needs water for its daily life. What happens if a drought strikes the Blacklands?

A close look at the toad's hind feet provided scientists with a clue to the answer. Its hind feet are shaped like little spades. They are adapted for digging. That's just what the spadefoot toad does when water is scarce. It digs into the ground and covers itself with soil. This toad can absorb water through its skin. There's a lot of clay in Blacklands soil, and clay holds water well. Usually there is some water in the soil, even though there may not be any water above it. The toad may be able to survive in the soil even during a drought.

> **What happens to animals when habitats change?**

The eastern spadefoot toad can survive in a dry, hot habitat by burrowing into the soil and absorbing water through its skin.

Why It Matters

Ecosystems in nature tend to stay in balance. This balance, however, can be upset by the actions of people. Cities are built on the land. Crops are cultivated. The land changes. Its natural inhabitants disappear. People gain certain things but lose others. It is important to make wise decisions when you think of changing an ecosystem. Otherwise you may lose more than you gain.

e-Journal Visit our Web site **www.science.mmhschool.com** to do a research project on an ecosystem of your choice.

Think and Write

1. Describe the structure of an ecosystem.

2. What is the difference between a population and a community?

3. How does an animal's habitat relate to its niche?

4. How do light, temperature, and soil composition affect an ecosystem's capacity to support life?

5. **Critical Thinking** Identify changes caused by human activity in your ecosystem. Explain what was lost and what was gained. Evaluate the results.

L·I·N·K·S

ART LINK

Make a poster. Visit a local ecosystem like a park, pond, or even your backyard. Draw all the living and nonliving things you see. Discuss the similarities and differences between the communities and interactions of the ecosystem you visited, and an ecosystem you studied in class.

WRITING LINK

Writing That Compares Research the biotic and abiotic factors of the Blackland Prairie and the Everglades in Florida. Compare these two ecosystems. Tell how the ecosystems are similar. Then write about their differences.

MATH LINK

Problem solving. A group of ecologists has counted 7,522 American Robins, 12,788 Northern Cardinals, and 3,657 Ruby-throated Hummingbirds in the Piedmont area. Order birds from the least number to the greatest.

TECHNOLOGY LINK

 LOG ON Visit **www.science.mmhschool.com** for more links.

Interactions Among Living Things

Get Ready

Populations provide energy-rich food for one another. Grasses and other green plants provide food for gazelles. Lions feed on gazelles. What do you think might happen if a drought reduced the number of grasses? How can changes in a population lead to changes in the ecosystem where it lives?

Inquiry Skill

You predict when you state possible results of an event or experiment.

Explore Activity

How Do Populations Interact?

Materials

tape

string

population cards

Procedure

1. Cut out the cards representing the plants and animals in the ecosystem.

2. Label the top of your paper *Sunlight*.

3. Place the plant cards on the paper, and link each to the sunlight with tape and string.

4. Link each plant-eating animal to a plant card. Link each meat-eating animal to its food source. Only two animals can be attached to a food source. Record the links you have made.

5. Fire destroys half the plants. Remove four plant cards. Rearrange the animal cards. Remove animal cards if more than two animals link to any one food source. Record the changes you have made.

Drawing Conclusions

1. **Observe** What has happened to the plant eaters as a result of the fire? To the animal eaters?

2. **Infer** Half of the plants that were lost in the fire grow back again. What happens to the animal populations?

3. **Experiment** Try adding or removing plant or animal cards. What happens to the rest of the populations?

4. FURTHER INQUIRY **Predict** If plants or prey become scarce, their predators may move to a new area. What will happen to the ecosystem the predators move into?

Grasshopper
Food: prairie plants

Meadowlark
Food: crickets, grasshoppers

Ground Squirrel
Food: prairie plants

Bullsnake
Food: mice, rabbits, ground squirrels, birds and eggs.

Red-Tailed Hawk
Food: ground squirrels, mice, rabbits, snakes, lizards, small birds

Prairie Plants
Food: made from water, carbon dioxide, and sunlight

Coyote
Food: rabbits, ground squirrels, meadow mice, other rodents

Read to Learn

Main Idea Food chains and food webs describe the feeding relationship in an ecosystem.

What Is a Food Chain?

How important is a small change in a population? Changes in one population can affect several other populations in the same ecosystem. Every population needs energy in order to survive. Where does that energy come from? The energy in an ecosystem comes from the Sun.

You can feel the Sun's energy as it warms your skin. A meadow mouse scurrying through a Blacklands cornfield and a red-tailed hawk diving to snare the mouse can feel it, too. Neither of these animals can directly use the Sun's energy. However, they must have it to move, to breathe, to keep their hearts beating, and to stay alive.

The energy of the Sun is stored in food. The energy in food is passed from one organism to another in a **food chain**. A food chain is the path energy takes from producers to consumers to decomposers.

On the prairie the first organisms in a food chain are plants. Plants capture the Sun's energy during photosynthesis. This energy is stored in foods, or sugars, the plant makes for itself.

What happens when a plant eater such as a grasshopper eats the plant? Animals use the oxygen they breathe to release energy from the energy-rich sugars they eat. Some of the energy is released for the grasshopper to use. Some of the energy is also stored in its tissues. Some is lost as heat. A Texas horned lizard may snap up the grasshopper, and a red-tailed hawk may eat the lizard. In the prairie

A Food Chain

A food chain moves the Sun's energy through a community from producers to consumers.

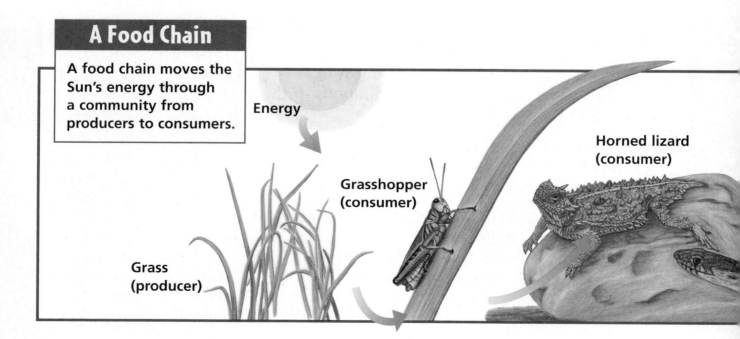

Energy

Grasshopper
(consumer)

Horned lizard
(consumer)

Grass
(producer)

community, the hawk is one of the organisms at the top of the food chain. It eats snakes, mice, lizards, rabbits, and other birds.

The red-tailed hawk doesn't eat plants. However, because of the food chain, it gets some of the Sun's energy that was originally stored in plants.

Plants and animals become food for small organisms like crickets and ants when they die. They are also a food source for microscopic organisms like bacteria.

▷ **What does a food chain show?**

READING
Diagrams

1. What are the members of this food chain?

2. Where does the food chain begin? End?

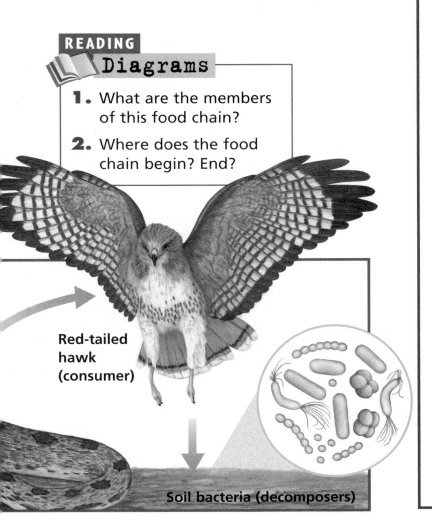

Red-tailed hawk (consumer)

Soil bacteria (decomposers)

QUICK LAB

Getting Food

FOLDABLES Make a Shutter Fold. (See p. R 42.) Label the shutters as shown.

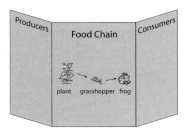

Producers   Food Chain   Consumers

plant   grasshopper   frog

1. Take a walk outdoors around your home or school. Choose a community to study. Make a list of the living things you see. Don't include people or domestic animals like dogs, cats, and farm animals. You may want to take photos to complete your observations.

2. **Classify** Divide the organisms into two groups in your Shutter Fold—those that can make their own food (producers) on the left and those that cannot (consumers) on the right.

3. **Classify** Which organisms did you list as producers?

4. **Classify** Which organisms did you list as consumers?

5. **Communicate** Draw one or more food chains in your Shutter Fold to show how energy moves through this community.

What Is a Food Web?

Do all organisms eat only one food? Are all organisms eaten by only one type of animal? No. Animals often eat or are eaten by many different things. How can we study all of the things that an animal eats or is eaten by? A food chain only shows the path of energy as it moves from one organism to another. A **food web** shows the relationship between all of the species in a community. It shows how populations must compete for food. A food web is a map of overlapping food chains.

Producers

All food webs begin with *producers*. The producers on land include grasses, trees, and all other organisms that use the Sun's energy to make their own food. In oceans the main producers are algae.

Plant Eaters

Organisms that cannot make their own food are *consumers*. Consumers get energy from the food made by other organisms. Consumers can be grouped according to the type of food they eat. **Herbivores** (HUR·buh·vawrz) eat producers. Both Earth's land and waters are filled with herbivores—animals that eat plants, algae, and other producers.

Meat Eaters

Herbivores, in turn, are eaten by **carnivores** (KAHR·nuh·vawrz)—animals that eat other animals. All cats, big and small, are carnivores. So are dogs, wolves, foxes, coyotes, and other sharp-toothed animals. The sea also has carnivores. One of the largest of these is the great white shark.

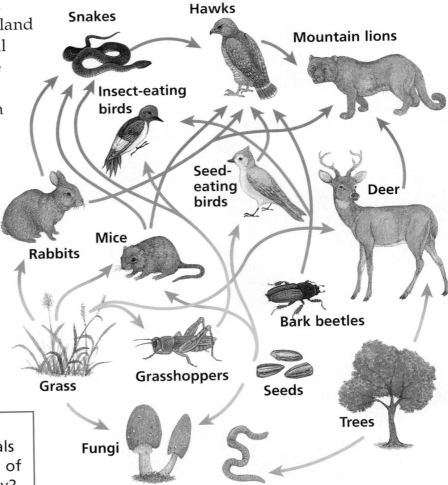

Land Food Web

Snakes
Hawks
Mountain lions
Insect-eating birds
Seed-eating birds
Deer
Rabbits
Mice
Bark beetles
Grass
Grasshoppers
Seeds
Trees
Fungi
Earthworms

READING Diagrams

Which of these animals are predators? Which of these animals are prey?

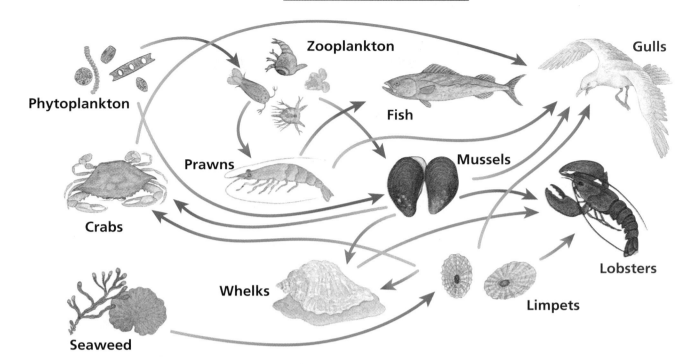

Phytoplankton

Zooplankton

Gulls

Fish

Prawns

Mussels

Crabs

Lobsters

Whelks

Limpets

Seaweed

Other sea dwellers also eat meat. Seals, dolphins, and whales dine on fish, squid, and even penguins.

Living things that hunt other living things for food are **predators**. The hunted are called **prey**. The relationships between predators and prey are a key part of both food chains and food webs.

However, not all meat eaters are predators. Some animals eat meat but don't hunt it. Such meat eaters are called **scavengers**. They feed on the remains of dead animals. Have you ever seen vultures circling a spot of land? Then you have seen scavengers. Crows are also scavengers. You might see them on a road, pecking at the body of an animal.

The sea is home to many scavengers. One of these is the hagfish. It wanders the ocean floor in search of dead or dying fish. Some tiny sea creatures also feed on the remains of dead sea animals.

When an animal eats both animals and plants, it is an **omnivore**. You are an omnivore. Bears are omnivores, too, eating things from berries to salmon.

Decomposers

Every food chain and food web ends with *decomposers* such as worms, insects, bacteria, and fungi. These organisms break down dead matter into substances that can be used by producers. Decomposers break down dead organisms and wastes into simpler substances. Some of these substances are absorbed by the decomposers. Some are returned to the soil.

▷ **What are the parts of a food web?**

How Are Populations Connected?

What would happen if farmers used powerful insecticides to kill pests? What might happen if these pesticides also killed some harmless ants? Ants live in the same habitat as Texas horned lizards. Because the lizards eat ants, changes in the ant population may tell a lot about the future of the lizards.

In the food chain, the relationship doesn't stop there. Birds of prey, such as hawks, feed on the lizards. What happens to the ants will also affect the lives of these birds. A change in one population affects all the other organisms in that food chain.

Animals may adapt to changes in their habitats. A varied diet can be useful. Texas horned lizards eat mainly ants. They also eat other insects such as grasshoppers. If

the ant population decreases, the lizards can feed on grasshoppers instead. This changes the number of grasshoppers in a community, however. The other organisms that eat grasshoppers will be affected, too. A change in the ant population affects more than just a food chain. It affects all of the organisms in a food web.

Food chains and food webs help scientists predict how communities will be affected by change.

Lubber grasshoppers

Ant

Horned lizard

READING **Sequence of Events**
How does a change in a food web affect other populations?

How Do Populations Adapt to Competition for Food?

Food webs show that animals compete for food. Fish and gulls must compete for a dinner of prawns, for example. In order to survive, an organism must adapt to competition. Sometimes this competition causes a population to change its habitat. This is what happened to Florida's green anole.

At one time green anoles could be spotted all over Florida, perched on the trunks of trees and the branches of bushes. Then a new and bigger species of anole arrived in Florida from the island of Cuba. Scientists don't know how it made the 144 km (90 mi) trip. Its size and, perhaps, other characteristics gave it a hunting edge over the small green anole, however.

Soon the smaller green anole seemed to disappear. Was it really gone? No. Scientists found the little green anole high in the trees. It had found a new habitat where it did not have to compete with the Cuban anole for food.

▶ How did the green anole adapt to competition?

The green anole (left), a native of the U.S. southeast, acquired a new habitat when Cuban anoles (above) were introduced.

What Is Symbiosis?

Organisms interact with each other in a number of different ways. You have already seen that some organisms hunt others. Some organisms are predators. Some organisms are prey. You have also seen that organisms may compete with each other for food or territory. Two different kinds of predators may hunt the same prey. However, there are also other kinds of relationships between different kinds of organisms. Some of these relationships are long lasting.

In nature a relationship between two kinds of organisms that lasts over a period of time is called **symbiosis**. There are different kinds of symbiosis. Sometimes both organisms benefit from the relationship. Sometimes one organism benefits while harming the other. Sometimes only one benefits, and the other is not affected. Let's take a closer look at each kind of symbiosis.

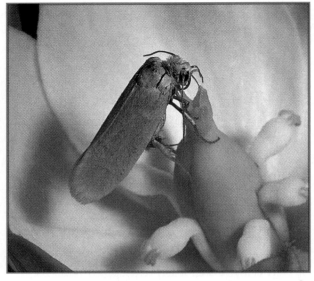

Yucca moth

▷ **What is symbiosis?**

Mojave Desert

READING

Maps

Describe where in the United States the Mojave Desert is.

What Is Mutualism?

When a relationship between two kinds of organisms benefits both of them, it is called **mutualism**.

A strange-looking plant grows in the Mojave Desert of southern California. It's called a Joshua tree, or yucca plant.

When this tree's creamy flowers are in bloom, small gray shadows seem to dart from flower to flower. A more careful look reveals that the "shadows" are actually moths. These are yucca moths.

Yucca trees and yucca moths depend on each other for survival. Each helps the other reproduce.

The Yucca Moth and the Yucca Tree

Yucca moths cannot survive without yucca trees. The yucca trees would also quickly become extinct if the moths vanished. The yucca moths and the yucca trees benefit from each other and share a relationship of mutualism. How does this work?

At night a female yucca moth visits a yucca flower. Inside the flower the moth picks up pollen and rolls it up into a ball, which it holds gently in its mouth. Then the moth flutters over to another flower. There it makes a hole in the flower's ovary. The moth injects its eggs through the hole. Finally, it packs the sticky ball of pollen onto the flower's stigma. The stigma and ovary are female reproductive parts of a flower. Pollen holds male sex cells.

In protecting its eggs, the moth has also pollinated the yucca flower. The pollinated flower can then make seeds. Eventually some of the seeds will sprout into new yucca plants. This means yucca plants will continue to grow in the desert.

The moth's eggs and the tree's seeds develop at the same time. When the eggs hatch into larvae, the larvae will feed on some of the seeds. All this is happening inside the protective ovary wall. The larvae are not only getting needed food, they are also safe from predators.

▷ **How is mutualism an example of symbiosis?**

What Is Parasitism?

A relationship in which one kind of organism lives on or in another organism and may harm that organism is called **parasitism** (PAR·uh·sigh·tiz·uhm). The organisms that live on or in other organisms are called *parasites* (PAR·uh·sights). The organisms they feed on are called *hosts*. The parasites benefit from the relationship. The hosts are harmed by it.

Fleas are parasites of dogs and cats. The fleas live off the blood of these hosts and give nothing back but itching and irritation. Plants also have parasites, which often are other plants.

The bright orange dodder plant has little chlorophyll. This means that it can't make enough food to live on. Instead it winds around a plant that can make its own food. The dodder then sends tubes into the stem of the plant it is coiled around. Next, the dodder gets food from the plant through the tubes. Although the plant it lives on usually does not die, it is weakened, grows more slowly, and is not able to easily fight off diseases.

▷ **How does parasitism differ from mutualism?**

Flea

The coiling dodder plant, which can't make enough of its own food, draws food from other plants.

Mistletoe is another parasitic plant. It is an evergreen that grows on the trunk or branches of trees such as hawthorn, poplar, fir, or apple.

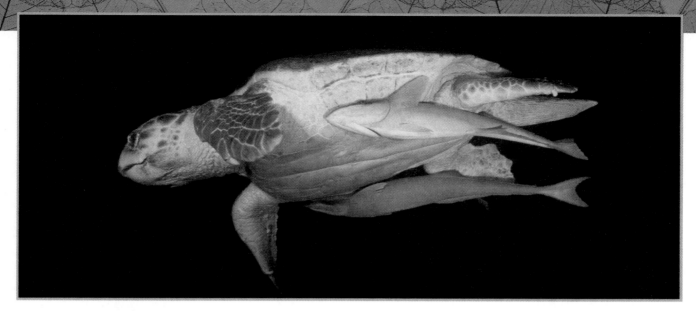

The remora picks up the scraps that the loggerhead sea turtle discards.

Orchids benefit from their position on the trunks of trees.

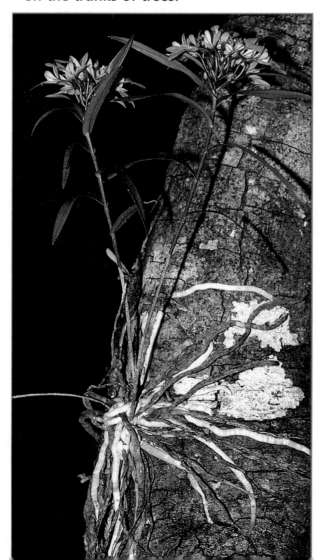

What Is Commensalism?

Few plants can grow on the floor of a rain forest. The thick canopy above keeps light from reaching the ground. Some plants, like orchids, attach themselves to the trunks of trees high above the rain forest floor. The orchids don't take anything from the trees. They simply use the trees to get needed sunlight. This relationship, in which one organism benefits from another without harming or helping it, is called **commensalism** (kuh·MEN·suh·liz·uhm).

Many animals also have this kind of relationship. The remora's dorsal fin is modified into a sucker with which it forms a temporary attachment to the loggerhead sea turtle. When the turtle feeds, the remora picks up scraps. The turtle provides food to the remora. However, the remora neither harms nor helps the loggerhead sea turtle.

▷ **What kind of relationship is commensalism?**

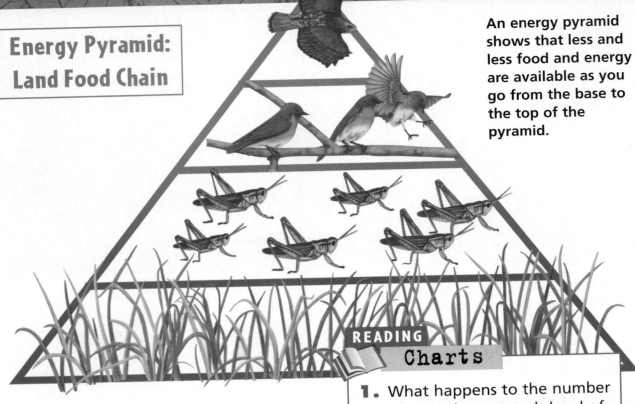

Energy Pyramid: Land Food Chain

An energy pyramid shows that less and less food and energy are available as you go from the base to the top of the pyramid.

READING Charts

1. What happens to the number of organisms at each level of the pyramid starting from the base?

2. How much more energy from the Sun was available to the grass than to the bluebirds?

How Does Energy Move in a Community?

Plants capture energy from sunlight. When you eat a plant, how much of that energy do you get? All organisms need energy to live. Producers get energy from the Sun. Consumers get it from the foods they eat. However, energy is lost as it passes from one organism to another in a food chain.

You can see the effect of this in the drawing of the energy pyramid on this page. An energy pyramid shows a number of things. It shows that there is less food at the top of the pyramid than at the base. It also shows that there are fewer organisms as you move from bottom to top.

Consumers get their energy from food. The less food there is, the less energy is available. Energy decreases from the base to the top of the pyramid.

In an ocean community in the Antarctic, algae form the base. Algae are producers that store energy from the Sun. Small fish that live in the icy waters eat some of these algae. The algae that are not eaten are lost to the community. Their energy is not passed up to the next level of the pyramid. Only some of the energy the fish get is passed up to the next level. The fish use some of the energy in swimming and other activities.

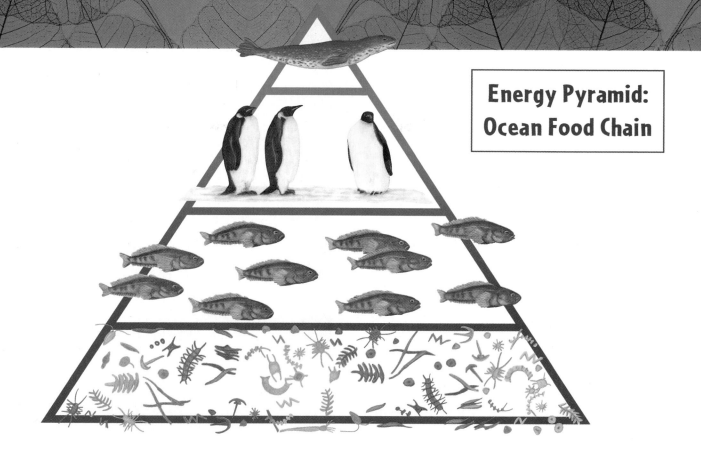

Energy Pyramid: Ocean Food Chain

The penguins dive for the small fish and eat as many as they can catch. Many fish get away. Nevertheless, the penguins have snared some energy-rich fish as food. Some of the energy from the fish is stored in the penguins' tissues. Some of the energy is used to heat their bodies. A dip in the frigid water removes some of this heat from the penguins' bodies. Now they have less energy than they took in from the fish.

Rising from below, a leopard seal clamps its sharp teeth around a helpless penguin and eats it. Does this predator get all the energy that was originally in the algae the fish ate? No. Energy has been lost at each level in the pyramid.

Kilogram for kilogram there are fewer fish than algae. There are fewer penguins than fish. There are fewer leopard seals than penguins. That's because there is less food and energy available at each higher level in the energy pyramid. The less food and energy there are, the fewer living things that can be supported.

How much energy is lost from one level of an energy pyramid to the next? Scientists have actually measured it. The startling figure is 90 percent! Of all the Sun's energy captured by the algae, the leopard seal gets only one-tenth of one percent.

▷ **What does an energy pyramid show?**

How Do Food Webs Affect You?

"Red Tide Observed off the Coast of Maine" might not seem like a scary headline. You might even ignore this important warning. However, it could mean trouble for the average person.

On page B28 you learned that single-celled organisms called algae are at the base of the marine food web. When the algae population increases very rapidly, or blooms, it can turn hundreds of square miles of ocean red. Scientists call this a red tide. Most red tides are not harmful. However, some algae produce poisons. Fire algae are an example. A bloom of these algae is very dangerous to all the species in a food web.

Small fish and mussels feed on the algae. The algae's poison may kill or infect the fish. The decline in the fish population reduces the energy available to the consumers that feed on fish.

How does this affect you? People who eat contaminated fish may become very sick. You are part of a food web, too. Humans are at the top of most food webs. Changes in any population may also affect you.

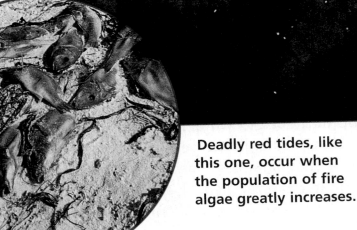

Deadly red tides, like this one, occur when the population of fire algae greatly increases.

▷ How can changes in a food web affect you?

Why It Matters

The lives of all organisms, including humans, are affected by other living things. If the population of one organism in a food chain disappears, the whole food chain is disturbed. If a food chain, food web, or energy pyramid changes, the result will affect humans. By understanding how living things interact with one another people can help preserve the treasures of nature.

e-Journal Visit our Web site **www.science.mmhschool.com** to do a research project on interactions among living things.

Think and Write

1. What is the original source of energy in an ecosystem?

2. Is it possible to have a food chain that has only a producer and a decomposer?

3. What is the relationship between a food chain and a food web?

4. How is mutualism like commensalism? How is it different?

5. **Critical Thinking** Think about human relationships that are symbiotic. Explain what makes the relationship symbiotic. Who is helped? Who is the helper?

L·I·N·K·S

MATH LINK

Use percents. An energy pyramid shows that 90 percent of the energy is lost from one level to the next. If you start with 100,000 units of energy, how much energy does the next level get? The fourth level?

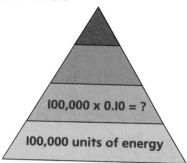

$100,000 \times 0.10 = ?$

100,000 units of energy

WRITING LINK

Writing a Story Stories have a setting, characters, and a sequence of events. They also have a theme, or central idea. Write a story whose theme is a changing ecosystem. Make sure the events in your story involve the lives or activities of your characters.

HEALTH LINK

Investigate parasites. How do parasites affect humans? What do these organisms gain from their host? How do they harm it? Write a paragraph on this topic.

TECHNOLOGY LINK

 LOG ON Visit **www.science.mmhschool.com** for more links.

How Populations Survive

Get Ready

What affects the size of a population? Some forests are so thick with trees and shrubs that you would have a tough time hiking through them. However, hiking through other forests would be as easy as walking down a country road or the street in front of your house. What makes some areas crowded and others empty? What do organisms need in an environment in order to survive?

Inquiry Skill

You communicate when you share information.

Explore Activity

What Controls the Growth of Populations?

Materials

4 small, clean milk cartons with the tops removed

40 pinto bean seeds that have been soaked overnight

soil

water

Procedure

1 Label the cartons 1 to 4. Fill cartons 1 and 2 with dry potting soil. Fill cartons 3 and 4 with moistened potting soil. Fill the cartons to within 2 cm of the top.

2 Plant ten seeds in each carton, and cover the seeds with 0.5 cm of soil.

3 **Use Variables** Place cartons 1 and 3 in a well-lighted area. Place cartons 2 and 4 in a dark place. Label the cartons to show if they are wet or dry and in the light or in the dark.

4 **Observe** Examine the cartons each day for four days. Keep the soil moist in cartons 3 and 4. Record your observations.

5 Observe the plants for two weeks after they sprout. Continue to keep the soil moist in cartons 3 and 4, and record your observations.

Drawing Conclusions

1 **Communicate** How many seeds sprouted in each carton?

2 **Observe** After two weeks how many plants in each carton were still living?

3 Why did some seeds sprout and then die?

4 **FURTHER INQUIRY** **Infer** Use your observations to explain what is needed for seeds to sprout and what is needed for bean plants to grow. Use evidence to support your explanation.

Main Idea Living and nonliving things interact in ecosystems.

What Controls the Growth of Populations?

How much do living things depend on conditions in their environment in order to survive? Certain factors control the growth and survival of living things. What do these factors include?

A dry wind howls across the prairie. The hot Sun bakes the ground below. No rain has fallen in days. Grasses have withered. Plant-eating insects have gone hungry.

High in the bright, cloudless sky, a hawk flies one way and then another. Its sharp eyes sweep over the barren land below. An unsuspecting deer mouse scurries along the ground in search of an insect.

The mouse's tan fur blends in with the dusty soil, but its movement gives it away. The hawk tucks in its wings and dives like a falling rock. In a flash its talons grab the mouse.

Hidden in this story are clues to how the size of a population is limited. Anything that controls the growth or survival of a population is called a **limiting factor**.

Some limiting factors are nonliving. In the story the sunlight, wind, water, and temperature were nonliving limiting factors. They controlled the population of grasses on the prairie.

The grasses, insects, deer mice, and hawks were living limiting factors. The grasses had withered. There was less food for plant-eating insects, so the number of insects living on the prairie decreased. That meant there was less food for the insect-eating deer mice. The deer mouse population was also limited by the hawks, which are predators.

The number of predators in an ecosystem affects the number of prey. The number of prey in an ecosystem can also determine how many predators the ecosystem can support. If there were few hawks, the deer mouse population

Organisms like coyotes (above) and raccoons (left) compete with each other for resources such as food, water, and territory.

might stay steady or even rise. More hawks, however, mean fewer deer mice.

Hawks compete with other predators, like coyotes and raccoons. Coyotes and raccoons hunt many animals, including small rodents like deer mice. Coyotes and raccoons also compete with each other for food, water, and places to live. The population that wins such competitions is likely to grow.

However, even a growing population faces problems. Its size will soon limit its own growth. The organisms in the population will become crowded. They will have to compete with one another for food, water, and shelter. Some will die. Eventually there will be enough resources for the number of organisms that remain. The maximum population size that the resources in an area can support is called the **carrying capacity**.

READING **Sequence of Events** Explain how a change in the coyote population could affect the number of mice in an area.

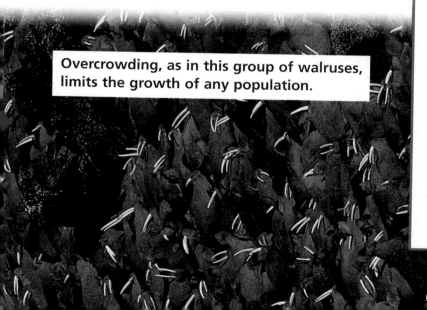

Overcrowding, as in this group of walruses, limits the growth of any population.

QUICK LAB

Playground Space

FOLDABLES Make a Folded Table. (See p. R 44.) Label it as shown. Record your results in the Folded Table.

	How Much Space?
#3 Use Numbers	
#4 Infer	
#5 Infer	

1. **Measure** Use a meterstick to measure the sides of your playground.

2. Multiply the length by the width to find the area in square meters. If your playground is irregular, use triangles and squares to find the area.

3. **Use Numbers** To find out how much space each student has, divide the area of the playground by the number of students.

4. **Infer** What would happen to the space each student had if the number of students doubled?

5. **Infer** Suppose two other classes with the same number of students as yours used the playground at the same time as your class. What effect might this have on your class?

6. Compare your area and space per student with the results that other groups obtained. Are there any discrepancies? Explain.

What Happens When Habitats Are Changed?

Did you know that American bald eagles were once found in almost every part of the United States? When the first European settlers sailed to American shores, bald eagles roamed the skies of the Atlantic and the Pacific coasts. They inhabited every large river and lake in North America.

Bald eagles need wilderness areas with tall trees to nest and perch in, and clean waters to fish in, to survive. However, as the human population settled all over North America, the bald eagle's natural habitat disappeared, and their food supplies decreased. When this happened, eagles started feeding on chickens and other domestic livestock and large numbers were shot by people. By the late 1800s, the population of bald eagles had sharply declined.

In 1940 the Bald Eagle Act was passed. As a result, eagle populations began to recover. At the same time, however, DDT and other pesticides began to be widely used. Pesticides sprayed on plants were eaten by small animals, which were later eaten by birds of prey. The DDT poison harmed both the adult birds and the eggs that they laid. The egg shells became too thin and were often crushed. Eggs that were not crushed during incubation often did not hatch. Large quantities of DDT were discovered in the bodies of adult bald eagles too.

Bald eagles were once common on the Blackland Prairie.

When the effects of DDT were understood, people all over the country worked to help save the bald eagle. DDT was banned and laws continued to protect our national symbol. In 1976, the U. S. Fish and Wildlife Service officially listed the bald eagle as an **endangered species**. This means that a species is in danger of becoming **extinct**. A species is extinct when it has died out completely.

The bald eagle population responded well to these conservation measures. The number of bald eagles went from less than 850 in 1963 to almost 13,000 in 2000 in the lower 48 states. In 1995, the bald eagle's status was upgraded to **threatened species**. This means that the species may become endangered. Today, about half of the world's 70,000 bald eagles live in Alaska.

▷ **Why did bald eagles start feeding on domestic livestock?**

Inquiry Skill BUILDER

Vanishing Bald Eagles

The table below shows the average number of bald eagle eggs that hatched in the wild during a 16-year period. It also shows the level of an insecticide in bald eagle eggs during the same period. What is the relationship between these two variables?

Variables are things that can change. In order to determine what caused the results of an experiment, you need to change one variable at a time. The variable that is changed is called the *independent variable*. A *dependent variable* is one that changes because of the independent variable.

Materials

ruler

Bald Eagle Egg-Hatching Data																
Year	1966	1967	1968	1969	1970	1971	1972*	1973	1974	1975	1976	1977	1978	1979	1980	1981
Average number of young hatched (per nest)	1.28	0.75	0.87	0.82	0.50	0.55	0.60	0.70	0.60	0.81	0.90	0.93	0.91	0.98	1.02	1.27
Insecticide in eggs (parts per million)	42	68	125	119	122	108	82	74	68	59	32	12	13	14	13	13

*pesticide banned

Procedure

1. **Infer** What is the independent variable in the study? What is the dependent variable in the study?

2. **Communicate** Make a line graph showing the average number of young that hatched. Make another line graph showing the amount of insecticide in eggs.

Drawing Conclusions

1. **Use Variables** Based on the graphs, what appears to be the relationship between the amount of insecticide in eggs and the number of young hatched?

2. **Hypothesize** Suggest a reason for the relationship.

How Do People Change the Environment?

The two competitors face off. There is an enormous silence in the tenseness of the moment. Slowly, silently, heads and shoulders are lowered. Then they charge and their massive weights are crashed together. Finally, one retreats in defeat. No, this is not a football game. It is the grandest rivalry in nature: Two rams fighting for the right to breed and pass along his genes to the next generation.

From the high alpine of the Rocky Mountains to the rocky peaks of the southwestern desert, bighorn sheep have adapted and survived in harsh conditions. However, their once huge numbers are declining due to their fiercest predator. It is not the mountain lion or the bobcat, but the human species.

Humans have the most profound effect on the environment. As our population continues to grow, so do the factors that bring about environmental degradation, including pollution, and urban growth. Environmental degradation is the process by which the environment is reduced in quantity and quality.

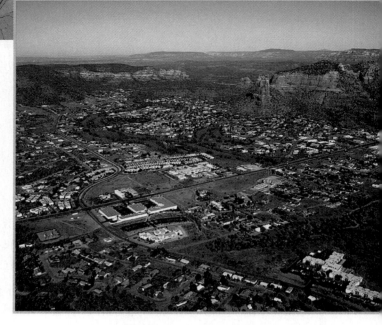

Aerial view of Sedona, Arizona

Urban Growth

During the westward expansion, around 1860, the human population in the U.S. was 31,443,321 and the population per square mile was 7.9. In 2000 the population was 281,421,906 and the population per square mile was 79.6. Since the size of the land is the same, this means that humans are encroaching on more and more land. Humans have the ability to change the course of a river for a new highway or destroy an ecosystem and clear huge tracts of land for apartment complexes and housing developments. However, we also have the ability to make wise land use decisions so we can meet our needs while preserving our natural heritage. This is possible because we understand how ecosystems work and what they need to remain viable.

Pollution

There are different kinds of pollution. Air pollution is produced by fuels that are burned to power industries, transport systems, and homes. To reduce this kind of pollution we should always remember to conserve energy.

Water pollution is caused by different factors. A common problem is excess fertilizers used in agriculture. Rain carries these excess fertilizers to streams and lakes. The algae in these streams and lakes grows excessively because of the fertilizers. When they die, they sink to the bottom where they decay. The decaying process uses the oxygen that other animals and plants need to survive.

Another kind of pollution is garbage. With more people comes more garbage and new places to put it. Landfills are filling quickly and new sites must be developed to accept the tons of garbage produced every day. When the land cannot sufficiently handle it, garbage is shipped out to sea to be dumped and become part of the food chain. To reduce this problem,

Factories produce smoke that pollutes the air.

Garbage disposal landfill

people can apply the three Rs of conservation: reduce, reuse and recycle. For example, we can reduce the amount of paper we use by using both sides of it, we can reuse things like bags and boxes, and we can take paper, plastic, and glass to the local recycling center.

Our use of the land has a constant effect on our natural resources, plants, animals, air, and water. Humans have done a lot to damage the environment. However, human intervention now helps to rehabilitate, recover, and preserve many areas of land that are vital to the survival of many different populations.

▷ **What are some things we can do to conserve the environment?**

How Does Mining Change the Environment?

The soil under your feet looks brown. The rocks are mostly gray. However, both hold a treasure chest of glittering colorful metals—gold, silver, aluminum, iron, copper, and many more.

People use these metals in many ways. Gold is made into jewelry and coins. Silver is, too. Silver is also used in photographic film and tableware.

Fly in an airplane. Ride in an automobile. Open a soft drink can. Squeeze a toothpaste tube. Marvel at fireworks. For all these things, you can thank aluminum. It's in each of these products.

Every large building, bridge, ship, train, and piece of machinery has iron in it—usually as part of steel.

Turn on your TV, your home's lights, a CD player. Electricity flowing through copper wires gets them going.

Clearly metals play an important part in our modern society. However, we pay a price for them—and not only

The easiest way to mine metals that are near the surface is to scrape the surface away. However, this leaves the land barren and often covered with dangerous chemicals.

in money. Since metal-containing rocks are buried in the ground, we must change the ground to get at them. If the rocks are near the surface, we simply carve away huge areas of land. This is called surface mining, open-pit mining, or strip mining.

In the United States alone, about 2,331 km^2 (900 mi^2) of land has been cleared for mining. That's about three-fourths of the area of the entire state of Rhode Island.

Surface-mined land is loaded with substances that are harmful to living things. Rainwater flows easily over this kind of land and carries pollutants into nearby streams, rivers, and lakes. The wind picks up dust, which pollutes the air. In both cases, living things are harmed.

▷ **What is strip mining?**

L·I·N·K·S

Why It Matters

In nature, the size of a population is determined by the resources available and competition for those resources. However, populations today are also dependent on human actions.

People can do good and bad things to the environment. They can interfere with an ecosystem by damming up rivers, using pesticides, and cutting down trees. They can also preserve an ecosystem by passing laws that protect its animals and plants.

e-Journal Visit our Web site **www.science.mmhschool.com** to do a research project on the limiting factors of a species of your choice.

Think and Write

1. Identify two biotic and two abiotic limiting factors.

2. Explain what carrying capacity is using an example.

3. How does the decline in the bald eagle population affect other populations?

4. Make a list of ways you and your community affect your environment.

5. **Critical Thinking** Explain and evaluate some ways that humans affect ecosystems.

LITERATURE LINK

Read *The Eagles Are Back!* to learn about two eaglets named Ross and Betsey who were raised in a safe environment and then were returned to the wild. Try the activities at the end of the book.

MATH LINK

Find the range. Using the data on page B37, determine the range of young hatched and the range of insecticide in eggs from 1966 to 1981.

WRITING LINK

Expository Writing What resources have been exploited in your state? What are the results? Research the topic. Use the facts you find to write an essay. Then use scientific reasoning to end your essay with a recommendation, at the local and global levels, regarding this resource.

TECHNOLOGY LINK

Science Newsroom CD-ROM Choose *Keep Them Alive* to learn how sea turtles and other species get what they need to survive from their environment.

 LOG ON Visit **www.science.mmhschool.com** for more links.

Coral Reefs

Rain Forests of the Sea

They're sometimes called "rain forests of the sea." That's because they're home for an amazing variety and number of creatures—up to a quarter of all the oceans' animals. They can take thousands of years to form. They grow in shallow, warm waters. Creatures smaller than your thumbnail build them, and they can be over a thousand miles long. What are they? Coral reefs!

A coral reef is built by millions of tiny animals called coral polyps. They live together in colonies, or groups. Coral polyps secrete a substance that hardens into skeletons. The hard skeletons build up reefs over time. Special algae live inside coral polyps. The algae produce food for the polyps. Coral reefs form only in shallow waters because the algae need sunlight to produce food.

A coral reef often looks like a sea garden because of its beautiful shades of orange, yellow, purple, and green. The colors come from the different algae and sea animals that live among the corals. Coral reefs provide food and shelter for thousands of ocean plants and animals, including hundreds of kinds of fish.

Some of the more unusual inhabitants of coral reefs include small fish and shrimp known as cleaners. Cleaners eat parasites from larger fish, such as barracudas and eels.

Coral reefs are endangered. As humans develop shorelines near the reefs, soil runs into coastal waters and smothers the fragile reefs. Pollution and destructive fishing practices also threaten reefs. Today many countries are trying to protect and save coral reefs.

What Did I Learn?

1. A coral reef is formed by

- **A** small pieces of rock.
- **B** sea shells.
- **C** tiny animals.
- **D** sand particles.

2. Coral reefs are endangered because of

- **F** severe storms.
- **G** human development. along shorelines.
- **H** lack of sunlight.
- **J** too many animals.

Red and yellow soft coral

Cleaner shrimp at work

LOG ON Visit www.science.mmhschool.com for more amazing stories and facts about ecosystems.

Chapter 5 Review

Vocabulary

Fill each blank with the best word or words from the list.

> **abiotic factor,** B6
> **community,** B11
> **ecology,** B11
> **food chain,** B18
> **mutualism,** B25
> **niche,** B12
> **omnivore,** B21
> **population,** B11
> **predator,** B21
> **symbiosis,** B24

1. A consumer that eats both plants and animals is called a(n) _____.

2. Water is an example of a(n) _____.

3. A(n) _____ includes all the members of a single species in a certain place.

4. Corn, elms, and armadillos are part of the _____ of the prairie ecosystem.

5. The study of how living and nonliving things interact in the same place is called _____.

6. All populations have a unique _____ in their habitat.

7. The relationship of _____ means that both populations benefit.

8. A(n) _____ is a consumer that hunts for its food.

9. A relationship between two organisms that lasts over a period of time is called _____.

10. You can trace how energy moves in a community with a(n) _____.

Test Prep

11. All of the following are abiotic factors in an ecosystem EXCEPT
    A water.
    B minerals.
    C bacteria.
    D soil.

12. A vulture is an example of a
    F predator.
    G scavenger.
    H carnivore.
    J all of the above

13. One example of a parasitic plant is
    A mistletoe.
    B an orchid.
    C a fir tree.
    D seaweed.

14. Surface mining can harm the environment when

    F trees are cut down to clear the land.

    G dust from surface-mined land causes air pollution.

    H rainwater washes pollutants into nearby streams.

    J all of the above

15. A relationship in which one organism benefits from another without helping or harming it is called

    A parasitism.

    B mutualism.

    C commensalism.

    D symbiosis.

Concepts and Skills

16. INQUIRY SKILL **Use Variables** Study the table below. Suggest a reason for the change in the eagle population.

Population Size			
Year	Grasslands (mi^2)	Rabbits	Eagles
1960	10,200	101,000	1,050
1970	9,100	89,000	864
1980	8,200	78,000	782
1990	5,300	42,000	386
2000	5,140	41,900	378

17. Reading in Science Describe the sequence by which the Sun's energy is moved through a community.

18. Scientific Methods You discover that two of your ten ferns have a bacterium living on their stalks. If all the ferns are the same size and age, and you care for them all the same way, how do you determine if the fern and the bacterium have a symbiotic relationship? How would you determine if this relationship is an example of parasitism or mutualism?

19. Critical Thinking What is the relationship between herbivores and carnivores? Explain your answer in a paragraph.

20. Product Ads Advertisements for some products claim that the products are environmentally friendly. What does that mean? What are examples of products that are environmentally friendly and products that are not?

Did You Ever Wonder?

INQUIRY SKILL **Hypothesize** When wildlife are in a limited area and not free to roam, larger animals can be severely affected. What hypothesis explains this?

 LOG ON Visit **www.science.mmhschool.com** to boost your test scores.

Ecosystems

Did You Ever Wonder?

In winter, these caribou leave their home on the tundra and migrate south, where they can find food and give birth to their young. In the summer they will return and usually find the same landscape they left in the winter.

INQUIRY SKILL Hypothesis Why can ecosystems remain unchanged year after year?

Cycles of Life

Get Ready

Have you ever walked in a grassy field early in the morning after a clear night? What did you observe about the grass? It was probably wet with dew. Where did all this water come from? It hadn't rained in the night. Dew comes from water in the air. How is water stored in the air? How does it change to dew?

Inquiry Skill

You infer when you form an idea from facts or observations.

Explore Activity

What Is the Water Cycle?

Materials

plastic food container with clear cover

small bowl or cup filled with water

small tray filled with dry soil

paper towel

100-W lamp (if available)

Procedure

1. Place the dry paper towel, the dry soil, and the bowl of water in the plastic container. Close the container with the lid.

2. **Observe** Place the container under a lamp or in direct sunlight. Observe every ten minutes for a class period. Record your observations.

3. Observe the container on the second day. Record your observations.

Drawing Conclusions

1. What did you observe the first day? What did you observe the second day?

2. **Infer** What was the source of the water? What was the source of the energy that caused changes in the container?

3. What happened to the water?

4. **FURTHER INQUIRY**
   Infer How did the water move? Use your observations to explain how water is recycled.

Read to Learn

Main Idea Earth's systems recycle materials, such as water, carbon, and nitrogen.

What Is the Water Cycle?

What happens to rainwater after it falls? Does it simply vanish? Water moves from one part of the environment to another. It is not lost from an environment. In other words, water is recycled. How is this possible?

Here's how it happens. Heat from the Sun is absorbed by oceans, seas, lakes, streams, ponds, and even puddles. This heat makes the water evaporate and go into the air. **Evaporation** is the process in which a liquid changes into a gas.

As the *water vapor*, or water in its gas state, rises higher and higher into the atmosphere, it cools. When cooled enough, water vapor condenses into tiny water droplets. **Condensation** is

The Water Cycle

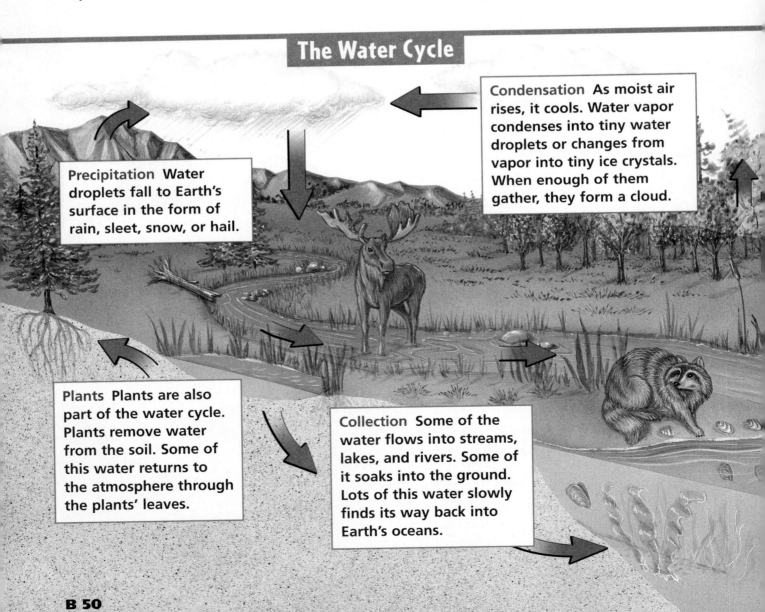

Condensation As moist air rises, it cools. Water vapor condenses into tiny water droplets or changes from vapor into tiny ice crystals. When enough of them gather, they form a cloud.

Precipitation Water droplets fall to Earth's surface in the form of rain, sleet, snow, or hail.

Plants Plants are also part of the water cycle. Plants remove water from the soil. Some of this water returns to the atmosphere through the plants' leaves.

Collection Some of the water flows into streams, lakes, and rivers. Some of it soaks into the ground. Lots of this water slowly finds its way back into Earth's oceans.

the process in which a gas changes into a liquid.

When enough water droplets gather, a cloud is formed. As more and more droplets gather, they become too heavy to stay in the air. They fall to Earth's surface as **precipitation**. Precipitation is any form of water particles—rain, sleet, snow, or hail—that falls to Earth.

On land some of the precipitation seeps into the ground and is stored as *groundwater*. Some of the water, however, lands on the *watershed*.

A watershed is an area on which water flows downhill to a common stream, lake, or river. This water is called *runoff*. It slowly finds its way back to the ocean. Here it absorbs heat and evaporates into the atmosphere again. The **water cycle** is the continuous movement of water between Earth's surface and the air, changing from liquid to gas to liquid.

READING Summarize
What are the stages of the water cycle?

Evaporation Heat from the Sun makes water evaporate and change into the gas state.

Animals Animals take in water. Some of this water returns to the environment through the skin or breathing. Some returns as waste products.

What Is the Carbon Cycle?

Have you ever roasted marshmallows over a fire until the outsides turned black? Have you ever left bread in the toaster for so long that it burned? The "black" that you observe on burnt food is carbon.

Carbon is a very important element. It is one of the elements that make up all living things. It is found in the air as carbon dioxide and is used by plants in photosynthesis. It is found in many of the things we use every day, from fuel to chairs to nonstick pans.

The Carbon Cycle

Carbon enters the air when plants and animals decay. It enters the air when animals breathe out. It enters the air when fossil fuels such as coal, oil, gasoline, and natural gas are burned.

Plants During photosynthesis plants use the carbon from carbon dioxide to make sugars, starches, and proteins. They also give off oxygen, which is used by animals.

Car exhaust

Oil

Like water, carbon is recycled by nature. The process is called the **carbon cycle**. The carbon cycle shows the continuous transfer of carbon between the atmosphere and living things. Read the diagram to learn how nature does this.

▷ **What does the carbon cycle do?**

READING Diagrams

1. When does carbon dioxide enter the air?

2. What happens to carbon when living things die?

Oxygen

Carbon

Death, Decay, Storage When living things die, the carbon in them goes into the air and ground. Some of it is turned into carbon dioxide by decomposers. Some is stored as fossil fuels. This is what happened to the carbon in certain organisms that died millions of years ago.

Animals Animals eat plant sugars, starches, proteins, and other substances. The animals use the carbon in these foods to make their own body chemicals.

Decaying matter

How Is Nitrogen Recycled?

What do you need nitrogen for? When you eat meat, fish, cereal, or vegetables, you are taking in the nutrients that your body needs to make *proteins*. Proteins are a part of your muscles and many cell structures.

Among other things, proteins are rich in the element nitrogen. You need nitrogen to make parts of your body, such as muscles, nerves, skin, bones, blood, and digestive juices.

Since air is 78 percent nitrogen, you might think that you do not need to eat protein to get nitrogen. However, animals and plants cannot use the nitrogen that is in the air. Animals get nitrogen by eating proteins. Plants get nitrogen by absorbing it from the soil. Some plants even get nitrogen with the help of a special group of bacteria.

The way nitrogen moves between the air, soil, plants, and animals is called the **nitrogen cycle**.

▷ **What organisms are involved in the nitrogen cycle?**

The Nitrogen Cycle

Air Air is made up of about 78 percent nitrogen gas.

Nitrogen-Fixing Bacteria Some bacteria that grow on pea and bean roots give those plants the nitrogen they need. The bacteria turn nitrogen gas in the air to nitrogen-containing substances the plants can use to make their proteins.

Decomposers When plants die, decomposers in the soil break down the plant proteins. One product is the nitrogen-containing substance ammonia. Soil bacteria change ammonia into nitrites.

Ammonia

1. Compare the different ways various kinds of bacteria help in the nitrogen cycle.

2. How do pea and bean plants get the nitrogen they need?

Denitrifying Bacteria Some soil bacteria turn nitrates back into nitrogen gas.

Animals Animals eat plant proteins, or they eat other animals that eat plant proteins. Animal wastes contain nitrogen compounds.

Plants Plants absorb nitrates dissolved in water through their roots. The nitrogen is then used by the plant to make proteins.

Nitrites   Nitrates

Nitrogen compounds

Bacteria Certain bacteria can use nitrogen from the air to make nitrogen-containing substances called *nitrites*. Other bacteria can turn nitrites into *nitrates*—another group of nitrogen-containing substances.

Nitrites and ammonia

B 55

This dead tree is being decomposed by fungi, shown here, and microscopic bacteria.

How Are Trees Recycled?

How can a dead tree help living things? Even though the tree is dead, it is being turned into substances other organisms need to survive. Some of these organisms are other trees. The dead tree is providing elements for living trees. When these trees die, they will provide elements that other trees need. The cycling of matter is continuous. How does this happen?

An old, fallen tree is made of wood, bark, and other dead tree tissue. That tissue holds all sorts of complex chemical substances. Most of the chemicals are too complex to be used by other living things. They need to be broken down into simpler chemicals.

This is the job of the decomposers. They are organisms that recycle matter from dead organisms. Worms, crickets, cockroaches, bacteria, and fungi are decomposers. These organisms can break down dead wood and other dead plant parts into carbon dioxide and ammonia. All living plants need carbon dioxide in order to make sugars. Ammonia is a simple substance that contains the element nitrogen. Nitrogen is extremely important for plants. No plant can live or grow without nitrogen. All organisms need nitrogen in order to make proteins.

Nitrogen is a chemical found in plant *fertilizers*. Fertilizers are substances used to add minerals to the soil. Some fertilizers are natural. These are decaying plants and animals, and animal wastes. Other fertilizers are made in factories. Both natural and artificial fertilizers contain nitrogen. The next time you go to a store that sells fertilizers, read the labels. You're sure to find nitrogen as one of the ingredients.

Composting

You can help nature recycle plant material by composting. Gardeners use compost to make soil more fertile. A good mixture for compost is three parts dry leaves and plant material, one part fresh grass clippings, and one part food scraps. Earthworms, insects, fungi, and bacteria break down the leaves, grass, and food scraps into compost. The compost contains nitrogen, phosphorous, and potassium, which enrich the soil.

As you'll soon discover, like water, nitrogen and carbon have their own cycles in nature. Earth is a closed system. With the exception of energy, almost nothing gets out or gets in. It is recycled.

▷ **How do decomposers recycle nutrients?**

Fertilizers sold in stores contain nitrogen. Nitrogen is an element plants need to grow and stay healthy.

Guaranteed Analysis

Total Nitrogen (N) 10%
Available Phosphate (P_2O_5) 10%
Soluble Potash (K_2O) 10%
The Plant Foods used in   Garden Food are Ammonium
Sulfate, Triple Superphosphate and Potash. Also contained
in Garden Food is the natural mineral limestone.

~~~~d 10-10-10 is an agricult~~~~

QUICK LAB

Soil Sample

FOLDABLES™ Make a Half-Book.
(See p. R 41.)

Core sample

BE CAREFUL! Do not touch the sharp edges of the can.

1. Go to a wooded area in a park or other location near your school. Find a patch of soft, moist soil.

2. Press a can, open side down, into the soil to get a core sample. You might have to gently rotate the can so it cuts into the soil.

3. **Observe** Carefully remove the core so it stays in one piece. Use your Half-Book to describe and draw the core.

4. **Infer** From top to bottom, what kind of matter does the core hold? In what order did the layers form?

5. **Infer** Which layer holds the most available nutrients? Explain.

Why Recycle?

Have you ever seen a paper bag with a symbol that says "Printed on recycled paper"? Why is this important?

The environment provides the materials people use to make products. Sunlight is an *inexhaustible resource*. The Sun will last for millions, if not billions, of years. Other resources, however, are not inexhaustible. The paper to make books, magazines, newspapers, and containers comes from the wood in trees. Metals mined from the ground are used to make cars, ships, pots and pans, appliances, and many other things. Glass is made from sand. Plastics are made from chemicals in oil found deep underground.

Wood, metals, sand, and oil are called *raw materials*. Raw materials are the building blocks of products.

Many raw materials, such as oil and metals, are *nonrenewable resources*. Earth's oil was formed millions of years ago. There's a limited amount of it. When it's gone, it's gone forever.

Certain other resources, such as plants and animals, are *renewable resources*. If trees are cut down for lumber and paper, more can be planted to replace them. Even so, trees take years to grow. This is why it is important to remember and practice the three Rs of conservation: reduce, reuse, and recycle.

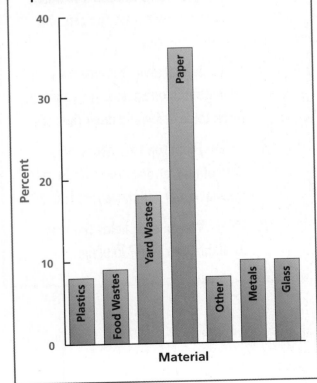

Garbage Thrown Away Daily in the United States

This graph shows the percent of different materials in garbage thrown away each day by each person in the United States.

Percent (y-axis): 0, 10, 20, 30, 40

Material (x-axis): Plastics, Food Wastes, Yard Wastes, Paper, Other, Metals, Glass

> ▷ **Why is it important to recycle both renewable and nonrenewable resources?**

READING
Graphs

Let's say there are 280,000,000 people in the United States. Each person throws away 1.8 kg (4 lb) of garbage each day. How much garbage is thrown away by all the people each day?

L·I·N·K·S

Why It Matters

The environment will continue to provide all the things we need as long as we let it recycle the substances that make life possible. People can either help or hinder the process.

To help we can conserve raw materials by recycling them—just as nature recycles water, carbon, and nitrogen. Many communities have recycling programs to do this.

e-Journal Visit our Web site **www.science.mmhschool.com** to do a research project on the recycling and waste reduction laws in your state.

Think and Write

1. By what process does water move from oceans, lakes, rivers, and streams into the air?

2. What organisms turn a dead tree into substances that can be used by living trees?

3. Describe three ways that carbon dioxide gets into the air.

4. Name two substances that contain nitrogen.

5. **Critical Thinking** Many people use disposable products because they are safe and less expensive. What are the environmental costs of disposable products?

MATH LINK

Make a circle graph. Use the data from page B58. Calculate (in kilograms) how much of each type of garbage Americans produce every day.

ART LINK

Make a collage. Weigh the amount of garbage you throw away each day. Estimate how much of it is paper, glass, plastic, and food scraps. Represent this in a collage.

WRITING LINK

Writing That Compares How can people help save the environment by reducing waste, reusing, and recycling? Choose one product you use regularly and compare the three conservation strategies to see which one you think is the best for this product. Plan your writing in a three-column chart. Label each column with one of these labels: Reducing, Reusing, or Recycling. List the benefits of each for this product. Then use your chart to write an essay that compares.

TECHNOLOGY LINK

LOG ON Visit **www.science.mmhschool.com** for more links.

Recycling

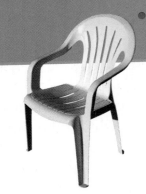

Soccer practice just ended, and you're in a hurry. You gulp down your last drop of water. Now what do you do with the plastic bottle?

Your friends are waiting, so you toss the bottle in the nearest trash can. The plastic bottle will make its way to a landfill. There it could decorate the landscape for hundreds of years!

If you recycle the bottle instead, it could take on another life. Like many recycled materials, plastic can be made into other things. In recycling facilities, plastic bottles and jugs are sorted, chopped, and melted. Then the melted plastic is cooled and formed into beads. The beads can be used to make everything from picnic tables to carpets.

A lot of other things that we use can be recycled too. When a tree is turned into paper, it can start a loop that just keeps going. If you recycle things like paper, you're part of the loop. The paper that's recycled is shredded, boiled in water, and then made into paper again. So, when you use recycled paper, you're closing the loop.

And, don't let that banana peel slip into a landfill either. Even that can be recycled. If you have plants in your house or a yard, your family can make a compost pile of food scraps. In a few weeks, the scraps will decompose— break down into small pieces. The compost will make the soil rich in nutrients.

Recycle those water bottles!

We can all do our part. Let's all recycle!

Plastic bottles and jugs arrive at a recycling facility.

How long does it take trash to decompose?	
Paper and newspaper	4 weeks
Banana and orange peels	5 weeks
Plastic bags	20 years
Styrofoam cup	50 years
Aluminum can	100 years
Plastic bottle	700 years
Glass bottle	1,000,000 years

But there's something even better than recycling. It's throwing away less trash in the first place! At the grocery store, next time they ask, "Paper or plastic?" say, "Neither. I brought my own canvas bag."

LOG ON Visit **www.science.mmhschool.com** to learn more about recycling.

What Did I Learn?

1. How are plastic bottles recycled?

 A They are washed and refilled.
 B They can't be recycled.
 C They are chopped, melted, and made into beads.
 D They are shredded.

2. As responsible citizens, you should do all of the following things. Which one is the most important recycling strategy?

 F Cut down on waste in the first place.
 G Recycle bottles and cans.
 H Buy recycled products.
 J Compost food scraps.

They are sorted and chopped into small pieces.

Recycled plastic beads come in different colors.

Biomes

Vocabulary

biome, B64

grasslands, B66

taiga, B67

tundra, B68

desert, B69

deciduous forest, B70

tropical rain forest, B71

Get Ready

What kinds of plants and animals live in the tropical rain forest? Are they the same as the ones that live in your community? Why do certain plants live in some areas and not others?

Soil varies greatly and is a distinctive factor in each area. Soil content can determine what plants and animals can live there.

Inquiry Skill

You observe when you use your senses to learn about an object or event.

Explore Activity

Why Is Soil Important?

Materials

washed sand

soil

hydrogen peroxide

2 plastic cups

2 plastic teaspoons

dropper

goggles

apron

Procedure

BE CAREFUL! Wear goggles and an apron.

1. Place 1 tsp. of washed sand in a plastic cup.

2. **Observe** Using the dropper, add hydrogen peroxide to the sand, drop by drop. Count each drop. Bubbles will form as the hydrogen peroxide breaks down any decayed matter.

3. **Communicate** Record the number of drops you add until the bubbles stop forming.

4. **Experiment** Repeat steps 1–3 using the soil.

Drawing Conclusions

1. Which sample—soil or sand—gave off more bubbles?

2. **Infer** Why was the sand used?

3. **Infer** Decayed materials in soil release their nutrients to form humus. The amount of humus in soil depends on the rate of decay and the rate at which plants absorb the nutrients. Which sample had more humus?

4. **FURTHER INQUIRY** **Infer** Use your observations to identify in which sample you could grow larger, healthier plants. Give evidence to support your answer.

Main Idea The world has six major biomes.

Taiga

What Is a Biome?

The land on Earth is divided into six major kinds of large eco-systems, called **biomes** (BIGH·ohmz). Each biome has its own kind of climate, soil, plants, and animals. Each biome can be found in different parts of the world. A desert biome is found in North America. Another is found in Africa. Still others are found in South America, Asia, and Australia. The map shows where Earth's six biomes are located around our planet.

Deciduous forest

Tropical rain forest

▷ **What are the six major biomes?**

Taiga

Location: Mid- to high latitudes
Climate: Very cold winters, cool summers; about 50 cm (20 in.) of precipitation a year
Soil: Acidic, mineral-poor, decayed pine and spruce needles on surface
Plants: Mostly spruce, fir, and other evergreens
Animals: Rodents, snowshoe hares, lynx, sables, ermine, caribou, bears, wolves, birds in summer

Deciduous Forest

Location: Midlatitudes
Climate: Relatively mild summers and cold winters, 76–127 cm (30–50 in.) of precip-itation a year
Soil: Rich topsoil over clay
Plants: Hardwoods such as oaks, beeches, hickories, maples
Animals: Wolves, deer, bears, and a wide variety of small mammals, birds, amphibians, reptiles, and insects

Tropical Rain Forest

Location: Near the equator
Climate: Hot all year round, 200–460 cm (80–180 in.) of rain a year
Soil: Nutrient-poor
Plants: Greatest diversity of any biome; vines, orchids, ferns, and a wide variety of trees
Animals: More species of insects, reptiles, and amphibians than any place else; monkeys, other small and large mammals, including in some places elephants, all sorts of colorful birds

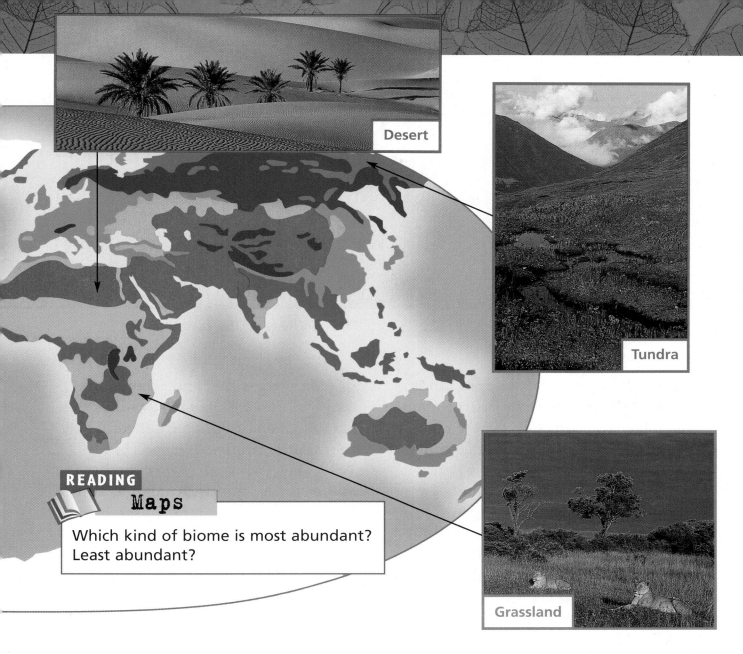

Desert

Tundra

Grassland

READING

Maps

Which kind of biome is most abundant? Least abundant?

Desert

Location: Midlatitudes
Climate: Generally very hot days, cool nights; precipitation less than 4 cm (10 in.) a year
Soil: Poor in animal and plant decay products but often rich in minerals
Plants: None to cacti, yuccas, bunch grasses, shrubs, and a few trees
Animals: Rodents, snakes, lizards, tortoises, insects, and some birds. The Sahara in Africa is home to camels, gazelles, antelopes, small foxes, snakes, lizards, and gerbils.

Tundra

Location: High northern latitudes
Climate: Very cold, harsh, and long winters; short and cool summers; 10–25 cm (4–10 in.) of precipitation a year
Soil: Nutrient-poor, permafrost layer a few inches down
Plants: Grasses, wildflowers, mosses, small shrubs
Animals: Musk oxen, migrating caribou, arctic foxes, weasels, snowshoe hares, owls, hawks, various rodents, occasional polar bears

Grassland

Location: Midlatitudes, interiors of continents
Climate: Cool in winter, hot in summer; 25–75 cm (10–30 in.) of precipitation a year
Soil: Rich topsoil
Plants: Mostly grasses and small shrubs, some trees near sources of water
Animals: American grasslands include prairie dogs, foxes, small mammals, snakes, insects, various birds. African grasslands include elephants, lions, zebras, giraffes.

The lion lives on the savanna.

What Are Grasslands?

As the name tells you, **grasslands** are biomes where grasses are the main plant life. They are areas where rainfall is irregular and not usually plentiful.

Prairies, like the Blackland Prairie, are one kind of grassland. Called the "bread baskets" of the world, few temperate grasslands look as they did years ago. *Temperate* means "mild." It refers to grasslands such as those in the United States and Ukraine. Today many of these grasslands are covered with crops such as wheat, corn, and oats.

However, large parts of the world's tropical grasslands still look much as they have for hundreds of years. *Savannas* are grasslands that stay warm all year round. Their soil is not as fertile as that of temperate grasslands. However, they get more rain—about 86–152 cm (34–60 in.) a year.

The most famous savanna covers the middle third of Africa. Here the dust rises as countless hoofed animals thunder across the land. There are more hoofed animals in savannas than anywhere else on Earth. Graceful zebras and giraffes live here. Wildebeests travel in awesome herds of tens of thousands. Antelopes run from sprinting cheetahs. In the heat of the afternoon, lions rest in the shade of a thorny acacia tree. Nearby, hyenas prowl through the low grasses in search of dead or weak animals.

If you want to get a glimpse of a savanna while it still looks like this, you'd better do so soon. The land on savannas is being used more and more to graze domestic cattle. It won't be long until they replace the native animals, at least in unprotected parts of the savanna.

▷ **What are two types of grasslands? How are they different?**

What Is the Taiga Like?

Evidence indicates that about 15,000 years ago, huge fingers of ice, called glaciers, inched down from Earth's arctic regions. The ice was hundreds of feet thick. As it moved southward, it gouged great chunks of land out of northern Europe, Asia, and North America.

Some of the sediment carried by the glaciers dammed up streams, forming ponds and lakes. More lakes formed when the ice began to pull back. Holes dug by the glaciers filled with fresh water. These are the lakes and ponds of a cool, forested biome called the **taiga** (TIGH·guh).

Taigas are mostly conifer forests. They spread out over 11 percent of Earth's land. They are located in the upper latitudes of the Northern Hemisphere—in Alaska, Canada, Norway, Sweden, Finland, and Russia.

If you visit the taiga in the summer, you may hear the pleasant songs of birds. Many different kinds migrate to the taiga in summer. However, they head for warmer regions in the fall. You might also hear the whining sound of chain saws. That's because the taiga is a major source of lumber and pulpwood. Much of the lumber is used for making houses for the world's growing population. The pulpwood is turned into paper products of all kinds, such as the pages of this book.

READING Summarize
What are the main characteristics of the taiga?

Thousands of years ago, moving sheets of ice dug away the land of the taiga. The dug-out land would become some of its lakes and ponds. Today these bodies of water are guarded by great stands of evergreen trees.

The caribou, a member of the deer family, is among the large animals of the tundra.

What Is the Tundra?

Where is the ground frozen even in summer? Only 10–25 cm (4–10 in.) of precipitation fall here each year. Winters are long and icy cold. Summers are short and cool. Just a few inches below the surface, the ground is frozen all the time.

You can't find many plants taller than about 30 cm (12 in.). However, you have no trouble spotting weasels, arctic foxes, snowshoe hares, hawks, musk oxen, and caribou. Near the coast you see a polar bear. When warmer weather comes, mosquitoes by the millions buzz through the air. Where are you?

You are in the far north. You're between the taiga and the polar ice sheets. It could be northern Alaska or northern Canada. It could be Greenland or frigid parts of Europe or Asia. No matter which of these places you are in, you are in the same biome. This cold biome of the far north is the **tundra**.

Why is it so cold? Even in summer the Sun's rays only strike the tundra at a low, glancing angle. The Sun melts ice in the top layer of the soil. However, this water is kept from flowing downward by a layer of *permafrost*, or permanently frozen soil, underneath. The top layer of soil acts like a vast sponge for the melted ice.

Many tundra plants are wildflowers and grasses. The permafrost keeps large plants from developing the deep root systems they need. The growing season is very short—as little as 50 days in some places. The tundra soil is poor in nutrients, so the tundra cannot support large plants.

▷ **What are conditions in the tundra like?**

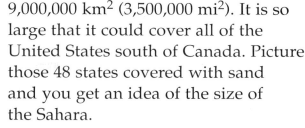

What Is the Desert Biome Like?

Sahara, Gobi, and Atacama stir up thoughts of adventures in strange, dangerous places. These are among the world's greatest **deserts**. A desert is a sandy or rocky biome, with little precipitation and little plant life.

Every continent has at least one desert. Africa has an enormous desert called the Sahara. Its sands dip down to the Atlantic Ocean in the west, the Mediterranean Sea to the north, and the Red Sea to the east. It is the largest desert on Earth, with an area of about 9,000,000 km^2 (3,500,000 mi^2). It is so large that it could cover all of the United States south of Canada. Picture those 48 states covered with sand and you get an idea of the size of the Sahara.

The Gobi Desert in China and Mongolia is the world's second largest desert. It is about 1,300,000 km^2 (500,000 mi^2). That's about twice the size of Texas.

You'll find the Atacama Desert in South America. It runs 968 km (600 mi) from the southern tip of Peru down through Chile. It lies between the Andes Mountains to the east and the Pacific Ocean in the west. The driest place on Earth is found in Arica, Chile. It averages only about 0.08 cm (0.03 in.) of rain a year. That's about the depth of six sheets of paper.

Few animals and plants live in deserts. Those that do are very hardy. They are well adapted to living in the desert.

> **How is the desert similar to and different from the tundra?**

To reach water, the roots of the mesquite plant (above) have been known to grow more than 79 m (260 ft) deep. That's the height of a 26-story building. Elf owls (left) build nests in cacti.

What Is a Deciduous Forest?

Have you ever seen leaves on trees change color in the fall? If you have, you have seen the **deciduous** (di·SIJ·ew·uhs) **forest** biome. This is a forest biome with many trees that lose their leaves each year.

This is where broad-leaved trees grow. Each autumn the leaves turn shades of yellow, orange, and red, giving the land beautiful colors. Then the leaves fall to the ground—which is what *deciduous* means—and decay. The dead leaves help make the soil rich and fertile.

Deciduous forests once covered most of the United States east of the Mississippi River and almost all of western Europe. Much has been cut down to make room for towns, cities, farms, and factories.

Many animals that once lived in deciduous forests still live on the land that was cleared for suburbs, farms, and towns. Chipmunks dart around bushes. Squirrels leap from branch to branch. Raccoons turn over trash cans. Skunks meander through the underbrush.

Birds like cardinals, robins, crows, and hawks, and insects such as bees still live in deciduous forests. Turn over a rock and you might discover a salamander or garter snake.

Many deciduous forests in the United States and Europe are now part of national parks or are in places where few people live. As long as they stay that way, people will be able to see the changing seasons.

▷ **What are the main characteristics of the deciduous forest?**

The trees of a deciduous forest shed their leaves each autumn, painting the land yellow, orange, and red.

Although you'd probably not enjoy an encounter with this family, it's an important part of the deciduous forest biome.

What Are Tropical Rain Forests?

In areas along and near Earth's equator are **tropical rain forests**. These biomes are hot and humid, with much rainfall. They support a wide variety of life.

The canopy of a tropical rain forest spreads like a huge umbrella. It is so thick that little sunlight ever reaches the ground. With little light few plants can grow on the ground. Most of the life is up high in the branches, where howler monkeys and purple orchids cling.

There are no tropical rain forests in North America or Europe. They are too far from the tropics. However, Central America, South America, India, Africa, Southeast Asia, Australia, and many Pacific Islands have rain forests. Each has its own kinds of plants and animals.

Millions of species of animals live in the world's tropical rain forests. Many species have yet to be discovered.

In Africa you might see a silverback gorilla or a troop of playful chimpanzees.

On the island of Borneo, you might see a red-haired, long-armed orangutan (uh·RANG·oo·tan) swinging through the trees.

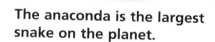

The anaconda is the largest snake on the planet.

The world's most colorful birds—such as toucans (TEW·kanz) and quetzals (ket·SAHLZ)—live in tropical rain forests. Giant snakes like the 9 m (30 ft), 136 kg (300 lb) South American anaconda also live in tropical rain forests.

The world's tropical rain forests have been victims of people's needs for lumber, farmland, and minerals. Fortunately, people are now replanting and restoring tropical rain forests. Still, some of their millions of undiscovered plant and animal species may become extinct before they are discovered.

> **What are some characteristics of the tropical rain forest?**

Some of the most colorful birds on Earth, like this toucan, live in tropical rain forests like those of South America.

QUICK LAB

Freshwater Communities

FOLDABLES Make a Three-Tab Book. (See p. R 43.) Label the tabs as shown.

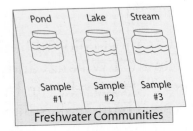

Pond	Lake	Stream
Sample #1	Sample #2	Sample #3

Freshwater Communities

1. **Obtain** from your teacher samples of pond, lake, or stream water taken at different locations. Use a different container for each sample. Record on the container the location each sample came from.

2. **Observe** Place a drop of water on a slide, and carefully place a coverslip over it. Use low power and high power to examine the slide under a microscope.

3. **Communicate** Sketch what you see under the appropriate tab of your Three-Tab Book.

4. **Interpret Data** What does this tell you about aquatic ecosystems?

What Are Water Ecosystems Like?

Temperature and precipitation differ among ecosystems on land. For Earth's watery ecosystems, the main difference is saltiness.

Lakes, streams, rivers, ponds, and certain marshes, swamps, and bogs tend to have little salt in them. They're all freshwater ecosystems. Oceans and seas are saltwater ecosystems.

In fresh water or salt water, organisms can be divided into three main categories. *Plankton* (PLANGK·tuhn) are organisms that float on the water. *Nekton* (NEK·tahn) are organisms that swim through the water. *Benthos* (BEN·thahs) are bottom-dwelling organisms.

Freshwater Organisms

Many plants live in the shallow waters of lakes, ponds, and other bodies of fresh water. If you were to wade here, you might get your feet tangled in cattails, bur reeds, wild rice, and arrowheads. You might also spot a frog, a turtle, or maybe a crayfish.

Farther out, where the water gets deeper, are microscopic plankton like algae and protozoa.

Look beneath the surface, and nekton come into view. There might be large trout or other game fish. All the way to the bottom, an aquatic worm might be burrowing into the mud.

Saltwater Organisms

Like the freshwater ecosystem, the marine, or ocean, ecosystem is divided into several sections.

The shallowest is the *intertidal zone*. There the ocean floor is covered and uncovered as the tide goes in and out. Crabs burrow into the sand so they won't be washed away. Mussels and barnacles attach themselves to rocks.

The open ocean is divided into two regions. The first region is up to 200 m (656 ft) deep. In this upper region are many kinds of fish and whales. The world's largest animals—the 150-ton blue whales—live here.

The lower region goes from 200 m (656 ft) to the ocean bottom—perhaps 10.5 km (6.5 mi) down. At depths greater than about 1,000 m (3,281 ft), there is no sunlight. It is completely black!

Photosynthetic organisms, like algae, can only live where there is sunlight. They are found in the intertidal zone and in waters up to about 100 m (328 ft) deep. Many fantastic creatures live on the dark ocean bottom. Some of these fish "light up" like underwater fireflies. Other bottom-dwelling fish are blind. There are even bacteria that live in boiling water where fiery lava seeps out of the sea floor.

▷ **What are two-water ecosystems? How do they differ?**

The types of animals you see in the ocean change as you go deeper.

Will the remaining whale populations survive? Will the eerie song of the humpback no longer be heard?

Can Humans Change Water Ecosystems?

People started hunting whales for their meat and oil at least 4,000 years ago. However, back then oceans held so many whales that hunting didn't have much effect on their populations.

As the centuries passed, however, whale hunting increased. So did the technology of finding and killing these gentle mammals. By 1850 American whalers alone accounted for the killing of 10,000 a year.

Over the next 100 years, new technologies made whale hunting easier and more efficient. In 1962 alone 66,000 whales were killed. The whales could not reproduce fast enough to replace those that were being killed. Many species, like blue whales, humpbacks, bowheads, and right whales, became threatened with extinction.

The whales were being used for human and animal food, oil for lamps, and fertilizer. However, there were other sources of such products. Recognizing this and the danger to whale populations, the major whaling countries formed the International Whaling Commission (IWC) in 1946.

In 1971 the United States banned its citizens from whaling for profit or even buying products made from whales. By the 1990s the IWC had succeeded in getting whaling countries to reduce or stop hunting threatened whales.

> **How have humans affected the whale population?**

Why It Matters

The world's biomes remain constant as long as their climates and populations do not change greatly. However, climates and populations change naturally. Also, human activity has affected both populations and climates. Changes in a biome can affect the kinds of plants and animals that can live there. It can also affect people's lifestyles. It is important to know if, how, and why these factors are changing before we make irreversible changes.

e-Journal Visit our Web site www.science.mmhschool.com to do a research project on climate changes caused by human activity.

Think and Write

1. Describe the taiga biome in terms of its climate, soil, and inhabitants.

2. How do organisms found in desert and tundra biomes adapt to their environments?

3. Explain why few plants live on the floor of tropical rain forests.

4. Briefly describe the two types of aquatic ecosystems.

5. **Critical Thinking** Choose one biome, and explain how a change in its climate might affect its populations.

L·I·N·K·S

MATH LINK

Find the range. The monthly precipitation in a tropical rain forest in a year is 9 in., 6 in., 4 in., 21 in., 17 in., 8 in., 0 in., 3 in., 7 in., 25 in., 15 in., and 15 in. What is the range of the annual precipitation?

LITERATURE LINK

Read *Antarctica,* the story of the coldest continent on Earth. Try the activities at the end of the book.

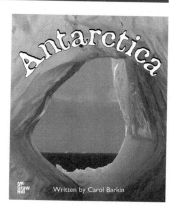

Written by Carol Barkin

WRITING LINK

Personal Narrative What would you do if the biome where you lived suddenly got warmer or colder? How would you adapt if the precipitation suddenly increased or decreased? Write a personal narrative about an adventure you might have if the biome where you lived suddenly changed. Use the "I" point of view to tell your story.

TECHNOLOGY LINK

LOG ON Visit www.science.mmhschool.com for more links.

Agriculture

Humans have adapted to living in every biome on Earth, from the tropical rain forests to the deserts. But we have adapted our environment to fit our own needs, too.

Until about ten thousand years ago, our ancestors were continually on the move. They relied on the food they could gather and the animals they could hunt. Then they learned how to take the seeds of plants and grow their own food. Agriculture was born.

After that, humans began to settle down in one place and to domesticate animals. Attaching plows to horses and oxen let us farm larger areas and grow more crops.

Growing the same plant in the same area year after year exhausts the soil, draining its nutrients. Cutting down forests to make room for crops causes soil to erode. Planting the same plant in large areas encourages certain species of insects and weeds. These opportunists quickly become pests, harming other species, sometimes to the point of extinction.

It takes centuries for soil to become fertile. When too many trees are cut down in a forest, the soil washes off the land into rivers like this one.

New computerized irrigation systems use less water and chemicals. This saves money. It also reduces the amount of chemicals seeping into the ground.

To make farming easier, we invented steel plows and then tractors to help plant and harvest crops. We cleared forests, filled wetlands, and let cattle graze on grasslands.

We redirected rivers to bring water to dry deserts, destroying natural habitats. We also began to use chemicals to fertilize crops and kill the bugs and weeds. These chemicals seep into the soil and groundwater, and many pests become immune to the toxins.

Today, agricultural practices are changing. Some farmers are using organic, or chemical-free, methods to grow crops. These methods are safer, even though an acre will only produce half as many organic crops as regular ones. Some farmers are using natural pest control that uses insect predators such as spiders and ladybugs to kill pests.

Computerized irrigation systems are cutting down on the amount of water and chemicals used. These techniques and new ones are letting us grow food in smarter ways—ways that are protecting our planet.

Write About It

1. What are two technological advancements in agriculture, and how have they changed farming?

2. How can farming damage the land?

LOG ON Visit **www.science.mmhschool.com** to learn more about agriculture.

LESSON

6

Vocabulary

ecological
    succession, B82

pioneer species, B83

pioneer
    community, B83

climax
    community, B84

How Ecosystems Change

Get Ready

Before May 18, 1980, the area around Mount Saint Helens in the state of Washington was decorated with wildflowers and beautiful groves of Douglas fir and western hemlock trees. Animals of many kinds made their home here. Then the mountain exploded. What happened to the community? How did this ecosystem change?

Inquiry Skill

You predict when you state possible results of an event or experiment.

Explore Activity

How Do Ecosystems Change?

Procedure

1 Observe Examine the photograph.

2 Communicate Describe what you see.

Drawing Conclusions

1 Infer What happened to this farm after the owner left and moved to the city?

2 Infer Think about how this farm might have looked ten years ago. What kinds of plants lived there then?

3 Interpret Data How can one ecosystem be changed into another?

4 Compare what you think will happen to the abandoned farm with what happened at Mount Saint Helens. In what ways would the changes in ecosystems be similar? In what ways would they be different?

5 **FURTHER INQUIRY** **Predict** Think of another ecosystem that might be changed by nature. Think of an ecosystem that might be changed by humans. Describe how such ecosystems might continue to change over time.

Main Idea Ecosystems go through both slow and sudden changes.

Abandoned cities of Angkor in Cambodia became covered by jungle.

How Do Ecosystems Change?

Changes happen everywhere on Earth. They can occur in your backyard. They can happen in an empty city lot or on one of its abandoned streets. If given a chance, nature will change an existing ecosystem or produce a new one. How does nature change an abandoned farm's field into a flourishing forest?

In the first year, a community of crabgrass, insects, and mice invades the field where corn or another crop once grew.

Tall weeds, such as asters, ragweed, and goldenrod, and tall grasses grow among the crabgrass. The crabgrass can't easily survive in the shade cast by the taller weeds. It begins to die out in the second and third year. Rabbits and seed-eating birds move in.

The hot, dry field of tall weeds provides a perfect environment for

From Farmland to Forest

Abandoned Farm—First Year

Second and Third Years

pine seeds to sprout. By the fourth year, pine trees begin to grow and shade the weeds, which begin to die out. More birds join the community, as do small mammals like opossums and skunks.

A pine forest has replaced the old farm field within twenty-five years. The number of new pine seedlings drops, however, because they can't grow in the shade. Seeds of deciduous trees, such as maple, hickory, and oak, sprout and take root. Larger animals like raccoons and foxes begin to visit.

The forest is now mostly deciduous trees. These trees are the habitats of many different kinds of birds and small animals, such as squirrels. Deer, raccoons, and foxes also live in the forest.

▶ **How can an abandoned farm become a deciduous forest ecosystem?**

Four to Six Years Later

Twenty-Five Years Later

One Hundred Years Later

How Do Communities Change?

The abandoned farm field you just read about gave way to short crabgrass, then tall grasses and shrubs. Later, pine trees and, finally, deciduous trees grew there. Scientists call the gradual replacement of one community by another ecological succession .

Ecological succession can begin in two different kinds of places. It can begin where a community already exists—such as in an abandoned farm field. Ecological succession in a place where a community already exists is called *secondary succession*.

Ecological succession can also happen where there are few, if any, living things. This is called *primary succession*. Primary succession can begin where communities were wiped out. Such places would include land swept clean by a volcanic eruption or forest fire. It can also begin where communities never existed before, such as on a new island that rises out of the sea.

Mount Saint Helens

Explore what happened to Mount Saint Helens in the state of Washington shortly after May 18, 1980.

Mount Saint Helens had just erupted. The blast from the volcano knocked down thousands of trees. The whole area was covered knee-deep with hot volcanic ash and finely smashed-up rock.

The landscape was different shades of gray as far as you could see. No spot of green greeted your eyes, not even a blade of grass. If you didn't

Ecological Succession on Mount Saint Helens

1 year The rose-purple flowers of fireweed announced that life was returning to the destroyed land.

4 years Seedlings of Douglas fir trees began to take root in the rubble of the volcano.

know better, you might have thought you were on the Moon.

A year passes. You return to the slopes of Mount Saint Helens expecting to see unbroken stretches of rock and stumps of dead trees. However, something has happened in the year you were gone. Wind and rain have cleared some of the ash and dust, especially from steep slopes. The wind has also blown in some seeds and fruits from nearby forests. You see a scattering of rose-purple objects among the charred and fallen tree trunks. They are the flowers of a plant called fireweed. It gets its name from the fact that it is often the first plant to grow after a forest fire.

Scientists would call the fireweed a **pioneer species**. That's because it is the first species to be living in an otherwise lifeless area. You notice that the blooming of fireweed has attracted animals, such as insects and an occasional insect-eating bird. A new community, called a **pioneer community**, is beginning to thrive around Mount Saint Helens.

You return in 1984 and almost step on a little green shoot. You bend down and take a closer look. The shoot has little needlelike leaves. It is the sprout of a Douglas fir tree. Its seed was probably blown here from a forest miles away.

Now picture the land around Mount Saint Helens 100 or 200 years in the future. It is covered with a dense forest of evergreens. The forest is much like the one that spread around it before that explosive day in 1980.

▷ **How does ecological succession change communities?**

11 years Young fir trees grow tall 11 years after the blast.

13 years Fir tree revegetation was further along 13 years after the eruption.

What Happens to Pioneer Communities?

Are the first organisms in a pioneer community always plants? In some places the answer is no. This is usually the case in newly formed, fiery volcanic islands that rise from the sea. Here the pioneer community is often made up of bacteria, fungi, and algae. Over many years these organisms slowly break down the volcanic rock into soil.

What happens when there is enough soil, and other conditions are right for plants to grow? A seed blown to the island by the wind or dropped by a passing bird will take root. The new plant, and others like it, will gradually spread over the land.

During their life cycles, plants will die and further enrich the soil.

Perhaps a coconut will drift ashore. When it germinates, its roots will find a good supply of nutrients. A coconut palm will spring up, and a new island paradise will be created.

Climax Communities

More years will pass—perhaps hundreds of them. The climate of the island will remain almost unchanged. Its community will grow. Its populations will become balanced and stable. Few new animals and plants will arrive. Few will leave. Ecological succession will slow down or stop altogether. This is a **climax community**, a final stage of succession. This community will stay largely unchanged unless some major event occurs.

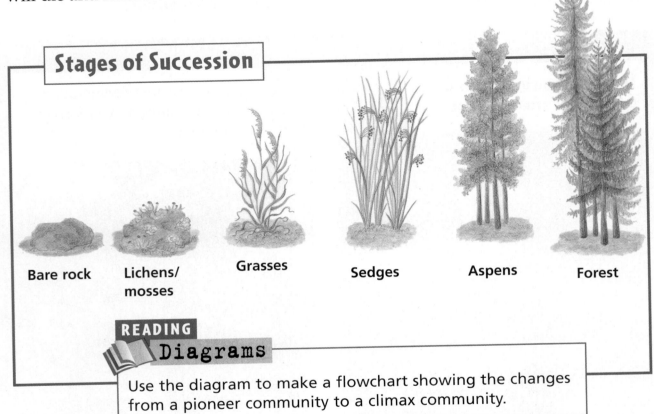

Stages of Succession

Bare rock   Lichens/mosses   Grasses   Sedges   Aspens   Forest

READING Diagrams

Use the diagram to make a flowchart showing the changes from a pioneer community to a climax community.

What kind of event could change an entire ecosystem? A hurricane may sweep across the island. The volcano that created it might erupt again. People might come and build hotels or introduce new plants or animals. The climate might change. Then the processes of ecological succession would begin all over again. Another climax community would eventually develop. It might—or might not—be the same as the earlier climax community.

▷ **What is the difference between a pioneer community and a climax community?**

The volcano Kilauea erupting on the island of Hawaii.

QUICK LAB

Predicting Succession

FOLDABLES Make a Four-Tab Book. (See p. R 44.) Label the tabs as shown. Record your answers on your Four-Tab Book.

| #2 Communicate | #3 Infer | #4 Predict | #5 Communicate |

1. **Observe** Identify an area near you where you think ecological succession is taking place.

2. **Communicate** Describe the area. List the evidence you have that indicates ecological succession is taking place.

3. **Infer** Do you think the succession will be primary or secondary? Explain.

4. **Predict** In what order do you think new species will colonize the area? Explain the reasons for your predictions.

5. **Communicate** Describe the climax community that you think will eventually live in the area. Give reasons for your conclusion.

What's Living on Surtsey?

In 1963 the island of Surtsey, near Iceland, was formed from a volcano. Between 1963 and 1996, at least 45 types of plants were seen growing there. Several kinds of birds, such as snow buntings, were also found raising their young on the island. Flying insects have also been found there. Scientists expect that more types of plants and birds will live on Surtsey in the future.

▷ **How is Surtsey an example of ecological succession?**

Surtsey, a volcanic island, rose from the sea near Iceland in 1963.

By 1996 many plants and birds lived on Surtsey.

Comparing Ecosystems in Volcanic Areas

In this activity you will collect data and infer about the ecosystems of two volcanic areas.

Data are different kinds of facts. They might include observations, measurements, calculations, and other kinds of information. Scientists collect data about an event to better understand what caused it, what it will cause, and how it will affect other events.

What do these data tell the scientist? The scientist first organizes the data in some way—perhaps a table, chart, or graph. The scientist then studies the organized data and makes inferences. To infer means to form an idea from facts or observations. In this case you will infer about which plants will return to a volcanic area.

Materials

research books

Internet

Procedure

1 Collect data on two volcanic areas, such as Mount Saint Helens and the Soufriere Hills volcano on the island of Montserrat or the active volcanoes of Hawaii. Organize the data.

2 **Communicate** Describe the sequence of events that has taken place.

3 **Interpret Data** Draw a conclusion about why certain plants return when they do.

Drawing Conclusions

1 In what ways is succession in the two areas alike? In what ways is it different?

2 **Infer** Why is the succession in these two areas similar or different?

3 **Infer** What abiotic factors must you consider when drawing conclusions? What biotic factors must you consider?

How Do Populations Survive Earth's Changes?

Earth is constantly changing. About 18,000 years ago, great sheets of ice moved deep into the heartland of what is now the United States. Vast ice sheets also covered much of Europe and parts of South America. Sea levels dropped as more and more water froze. New land was exposed. Earth was a cold place.

Slowly Earth began to warm up. The ice melted. Sea levels rose. Coastal land became flooded.

These kinds of changes have occurred no fewer than seven times during the past 700,000 years. Scientists call these cold periods *ice ages*.

Earth has also changed in other ways. Over millions of years, continents have moved north and south, east and west. Huge mountain-sized rocks have crashed into Earth. Volcanoes have poured gases and dust into the air.

Each of these events has had an effect on living things. Some organisms have survived these changes, while others have died out, or become extinct. Why have some of these organisms vanished while others survived?

To answer this, let's look at the age of the dinosaurs. Fossils from about 65 million years ago suggest that dinosaurs shared the land with many other animals. These animals included frogs, snails, insects, turtles, snakes, and some small furry mammals. Plants of all kinds grew everywhere. The seas were full of organisms like fish, sea urchins, clams, and algae.

Dinosaur footprints

Scientific evidence suggests that a meteorite up to 10 km (6 mi) in diameter struck Earth from outer space. One theory states that the impact created a huge explosion. It gouged out a crater 64 km (40 mi) across and threw huge amounts of dust into the sky. The dust may have hung in the sky for months, even years. Sunlight was probably blocked from reaching the ground.

Plants needing lots of sunlight may have died out. That means that the large plant-eating dinosaurs could not get enough food. They would have died out. The large dinosaurs preying on plant eaters would have also died out. It may have been that every animal weighing more than about 55 kg (121 lb) became extinct.

However, many of the smaller animals could have survived. They needed less food to live. They could have moved more easily from habitat to habitat. They would no longer have been in competition with the dinosaurs. They would have been free to grow in size and variety. Possibly this is how a world once ruled by dinosaurs became ruled by mammals.

▶ **How do changes on Earth affect organisms?**

Dinosaurs became extinct about 65 million years ago. Scientists can study them today, however, by searching for fossils, such as footprints and skeletons.

What Do Fossils Tell Us About Changes in the Environment?

Scientists have developed hypotheses to solve the following mystery.

- Scientists gathering fossils in Italy make a discovery. About six million years ago, fish and other sea creatures disappeared from the Mediterranean Sea.

- Other fossils from a slightly later period reveal that horselike animals from Africa arrived in Europe.

- The fossil of an ancient African hippopotamus is found on an island in the middle of the Mediterranean.

- Fossil palm trees of the same age are dug up in Switzerland.

- Then there is another surprising discovery. Five-million-year-old fossils of fish turn up in the Mediterranean area.

What could have gone on back then to have these clues make sense? One theory is called *plate tectonics*.

Earth's crust is made up of moving plates—pieces of crust. About six million years ago, two plates—the African and the Eurasian—collided. The continents of Africa and Europe bumped into each other. This happened at what is now the Strait of Gibraltar. This collision created a natural dam between the Atlantic Ocean and the Mediterranean Sea.

Without a source of water from the ocean, the sea dried up in perhaps as little as 1,000 years. The Mediterranean Sea became a desert. The sea's fish and other marine life died out. Animals from Africa migrated across the desert to Europe. Palm trees sprouted in Switzerland.

Then about five million years ago, the dam began to crumble. A gigantic waterfall poured water into the desert. It carried many kinds of marine life from the Atlantic Ocean. The Mediterranean became a sea again.

READING Summarize

How did changes in the Mediterranean affect populations?

6 million years ago

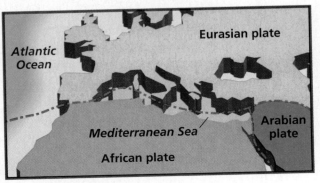

Present day

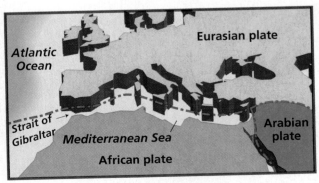

Why It Matters

Once an ecosystem is disturbed it begins to change until a stable climax community is reached. A climax community is an area where biotic and abiotic factors interact to maintain a stable environment.

Ecosystems change and recover from natural disasters and human activities in predictable ways. Understanding of succession and climax communities can prevent human-made ecological disasters and can help us set the right conditions to help environments recover faster.

 e-Journal Visit our Web site www.science.mmhschool.com to do a research project on what fossils can tell us about environmental changes. Find a specific example.

Think and Write

1. Describe how an abandoned farm field becomes a deciduous forest.

2. Give an example of a pioneer and a climax community.

3. List the evidence that supports the conclusion that the Mediterranean Sea once dried up.

4. **Infer** How might a volcanic eruption affect an ecosystem?

5. **Critical Thinking** How would succession be affected if animals did not return to an area after a fire?

L·I·N·K·S

LITERATURE LINK

Read *Wildfire* to learn about the true story of a wildfire that destroyed 5,000 acres of land in New York. Try the activities in the back of the book.

WRITING LINK

Expository Writing How do ecosystems change over time? Research what happened to Angkor. What was the culture like? Why did the people leave their city? Write a research report on your findings.

MATH LINK

Divide by one-digit numbers. Iceland has an area of 39,756 mi. Surtsey has an area of 2 mi. How many times larger is Iceland than Surtsey?

TECHNOLOGY LINK

 Science Newsroom CD-ROM Choose *From the Ground Up* to learn how ecosystems change.

LOG ON Visit www.science.mmhschool.com for more links.

Fill each blank with the best word or words from the list.

biome, B64
carbon cycle, B53
climax community, B84
desert, B69
ecological succession, B82
evaporation, B50
pioneer community, B83
precipitation, B51
taiga, B67
tundra, B68

1. Part of the soil of the _____ is frozen all year round.

2. The gradual change from one community to another is called _____.

3. The _____ shows the continuous transfer of carbon between living and nonliving things.

4. The _____ has many evergreen trees.

5. A(n) _____ is made up of the first organisms to colonize an area.

6. Sleet and snow are examples of _____.

7. When ecological succession slows down, a(n) _____ has formed.

8. A deciduous forest is an example of a(n) _____.

9. The process in which a liquid becomes a gas is called _____.

10. The Gobi and Mojave are examples of _____.

11. All of the following are abiotic factors in an ecosystem EXCEPT
  A water.
  B minerals.
  C bacteria.
  D soil.

12. A vulture is an example of a
  F predator.
  G scavenger.
  H carnivore.
  J all of the above

13. Plants absorb nitrogen
  A from the soil.
  B from the atmosphere.
  C from the Sun.
  D from insects.

14. A _____ is an example of a biome.
  F pond
  G bacteria
  H grassland
  J mammal

15. Scientists call _____ a pioneer species.

   A grasses

   B fir trees

   C fireweed

   D fallen tree trunks

Concepts and Skills

16. Reading in Science Summarize the steps in the nitrogen cycle.

17. Scientific Methods You discover that there are no fossils of dinosaurs above a certain layer of rock, but there are below it. The rock in this layer has more in common with rocks from space than with Earth rocks. Hypothesize how these two discoveries may be linked.

18. INQUIRY SKILL **Infer** What can you infer from the data below?

Pond Populations and Acid Content

Acid	Yellow Perch	Brown Trout	Salamanders	Mayflies
High	23	6	2	0
Medium	28	11	7	2
Low	36	18	10	14

19. Critical Thinking How might a change in the biome you live in affect your way of life?

20. Decision Making Is it important to recycle the waste you produce? Why or why not?

Did You Ever Wonder?

INQUIRY SKILL **Observe** Choose an area near your school or in your neighborhood. Determine how materials in this area are recycled by nature. Would you add or remove any elements to help the natural recycling process?

LOG ON Visit www.science.mmhschool.com to boost your test scores.

Dr. Catherine Toft

POPULATION ECOLOGIST

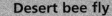

Desert bee fly

Dr. Catherine Toft is a population ecologist. Population ecology is the study of populations in nature. "It focuses on how numbers of individuals in a population change through time or vary from place to place," Dr. Toft says. Toft explains that a population is a group of individuals of the same type that mate within the group and produce offspring.

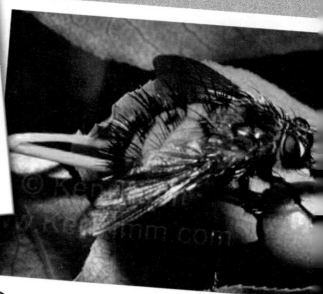

Desert Bee Fly

Dr. Toft loves discovering new things about nature. She spends most of her time in the field. She studies her subjects in their natural environments. "I study desert plants and desert insects," Dr. Toft says.

One of Dr. Toft's favorite subjects is the desert bee fly. The males gather in groups, called leks, to fight over the females. "These leks are in the same place every year even though the male flies live only one season. It is a mystery how the flies know to come to the same place every year, which looks like any other place in the sand dunes where they live."

Dr. Toft's work can help change the way we think about nature. "I hope that I can help people live lives that are more environmentally healthy."

TOP 5 Longest-Living Animals

Do you want to work with living things? A population ecologist such as Dr. Toft studies how long organisms live. Here are the animals that live the longest and the oldest known age for each.

1. Giant tortoise: 200 years
2. Human: 122 years
3. Sturgeon (a type of fish): 100 years
4. Blue whale and golden eagle: 80 years
5. African elephant: 77 years

Write About It

1. What is a lek?
2. Why do leks fascinate Dr. Toft?

 LOG ON Visit www.science.mmhschool.com to learn more about the work of population ecologists.

Ecosystem Discovery

Your goal is to invent and describe a new ecosystem.

What to Do

1. Imagine you are an explorer. You have found the world's last unexplored ecosystem. Give your ecosystem a name.

2. Describe this new ecosystem. Write about the plants and animals there. Tell what each one needs to survive.

3. Draw a picture of your ecosystem.

Analyze Your Results

1. Tell how each plant and animal gets what it needs to survive in your ecosystem.

2. What nonliving things help plants and animals survive in your ecosystem?

3. Draw an energy pyramid to show how energy moves in your ecosystem. What belongs at the bottom of the pyramid? At the top?

Will Succession Succeed?

Your goal is to identify a place where ecological succession is taking place.

What to Do

1. Write a short paragraph describing what ecological succession is.

2. Think of an area you have visited where succession is taking place. If you can't think of an area near you, describe a place you have read about. Write down the name of the place or tell its location. Draw a picture.

Analyze Your Results

1. List evidence that succession is taking place in your area.

2. In what order will new species come to live in your area? Explain.

3. What could happen to prevent succession in your area?

UNIT C
Earth and Its Resources

LOOK!

A spectacular cavern is lit up
with beautiful colored lights.
What causes a cavern to form?

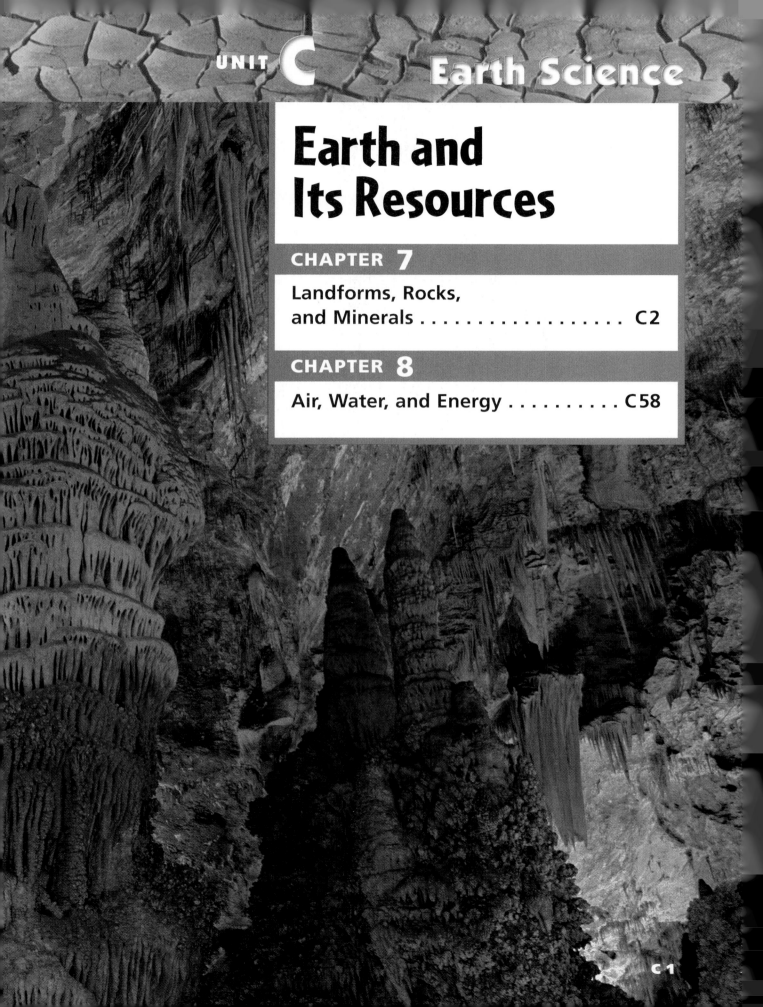

Earth and Its Resources

CHAPTER

7

Landforms, Rocks, and Minerals

Did You Ever Wonder?

What is this strange-looking rock formation? Did someone build it here in Zion National Park? No. This fantastic shape is a natural rock formation called a hoodoo. What natural processes could have produced a hoodoo and other unusual rock formations?

INQUIRY SKILL **Communicate** Select and research a rock or mineral. Become an "expert" on your choice. Prepare a report and make an oral presentation to the class.

Earth's Changing Crust

Vocabulary

fault, C6

geologist, C6

magma, C9

lava, C9

weathering, C10

erosion, C10

deposition, C13

meteorite, C14

Get Ready

What causes an earthquake? An earthquake seems to happen without warning. The ground shakes suddenly, often with enough power to damage objects on the surface.

Where do earthquakes happen? Earthquakes are common in places where the crust (Earth's surface layer) is "cracked." One such crack extends through much of the state of California. Why do you think earthquakes happen along this crack?

Inquiry Skill

You experiment when you perform a test to support or disprove a hypothesis.

Explore Activity

What Makes the Crust Move?

Materials

4–6 matching books (optional)

layers of clay or modeling compound (optional)

plastic knife

cubes

wax paper

Procedure: Design Your Own

1 **Make a Model** Work with a partner to model layers of rock. You may use books, clay, or other materials to represent rock layers. Build your model on wax paper. Include a "crack" down through the layers. Stack cubes on the top of the model to represent buildings and other surface features.

2 **Experiment** Find as many ways of moving the model as you can to show how the crust may move during an earthquake. What happens to the surface features as you move the model each way? Draw and describe each.

3 **Experiment** How can you show movement without causing any visible effect on the surface features?

Drawing Conclusions

1 How many different ways could you move your model? How were they different?

2 **Communicate** How did each way you moved the model affect the surface features? How did each way change the positions of the layers? Explain.

3 **Communicate** How did you move the model without moving the surface features? Did the model change in any way? Explain.

4 FURTHER INQUIRY **Experiment** How can you use your model to show how a mountain might rise up high above sea level? Explain and demonstrate.

Main Idea Forces on and under Earth shape its surface.

What Makes the Crust Move?

Earth's crust is constantly moving, if not in one place then in another. Sometimes it moves quickly enough to be seen and felt. People who have been through an earthquake tell of seeing the ground heave up and down like an ocean wave.

Earthquakes are related to cracks in the crust called **faults**. These faults may have formed from earlier earthquakes. Sometimes they form while the earthquake happens. During an earthquake the crust on either side, or on both sides, of a fault is in motion.

During an earthquake vibrations travel through the crust. The farther away people are from the earthquake, the harder it is for them to feel the vibrations. However, delicate devices called *seismographs* (SIGHZ·muh·grafs) can record this motion at locations all around the crust.

Most of the time, however, the crust moves very slowly. Rocks can move slowly on either side of a fault over centuries. People realize there is movement only when something visibly changes position. Not all motion happens along faults, either. Often, layers of the crust bend, as shown in the picture below. Bending, like motion along a fault, may happen gradually over time.

To measure crust movement, *surveyors* (suhr·VAY·uhrz) measure *elevation*—how high a place is above sea level. They leave plaques called *bench marks* that tell the exact location and elevation of a place. When some bench marks are remeasured, they are found to have risen or sunk.

Geologists (jee·AHL·uh·jists), scientists who study Earth, place sensitive devices all along faults, such as the San Andreas Fault in California. They hope that records of tiny movements can be used to predict an earthquake.

Fossils in mountain areas

Remains of ancient sea life are sometimes found in rock layers high up in mountains.

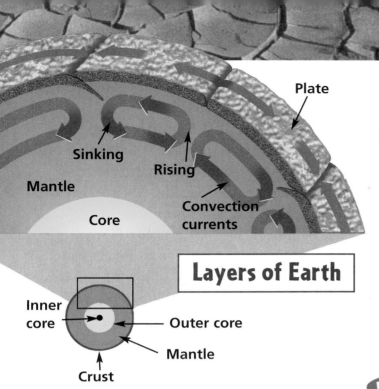

Plate

Sinking

Rising

Mantle

Core

Convection currents

Layers of Earth

Inner core

Outer core

Mantle

Crust

Plate Tectonics

The crust is Earth's hard surface. Compared with the distance to Earth's center, it is very thin. It is only about one-thousandth of Earth's thickness.

Under the crust is the mantle, Earth's thickest layer. The rock material here is solid. However, it can flow like a liquid—as putty can "flow" when you squeeze it between your hands. Below the mantle is Earth's core. It is in two parts, a liquid outer core and a solid inner core.

The rock material in the mantle is in motion, something like heated water in a pot. It rises and pushes against the bottom of the crust. This movement causes the thin, brittle crust at the surface to break into pieces, or *plates*. The plates themselves can move along Earth's surface. Earthquakes and the slow motions of the crust all result from moving plates.

▷ **How are earthquakes related to faults and plates in the crust?**

QUICK LAB

Model of Earth

FOLDABLES Make a Four-Tab Book. (See p. R 44.) Label the tabs as shown.

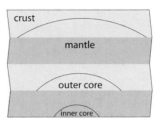

crust

mantle

outer core

inner core

BE CAREFUL! Students who are allergic to peanuts should not do this activity.

1. **Infer** You will use four materials to make a model of Earth on wax paper. Each material is one of Earth's layers. Read step 2. Decide which material represents which layer. Decide how thick each layer needs to be.

2. **Make a Model** Wash your hands. Cover a hazelnut with a layer of peanut butter. Put the covered nut in a plastic bag of mashed banana so that banana covers it completely. Roll the result into graham cracker crumbs on wax paper.

3. **Draw Conclusions** How does each material represent a different layer? Make your book and use it to record your response.

4. How thick did you decide to make each layer? Explain your reasoning.

What Forces Act on the Crust?

As the plates of the crust move, they can collide. They can pull away from each other. They can also slide past each other. These movements cause three kinds of forces to act on the crust.

- *Tension* stretches or pulls apart the crust.

- *Compression* squeezes or pushes together the crust.

- *Shear* twists, tears, or pushes one part of the crust past another.

Each of these forces can cause a fault to form in the crust. Each can cause movement along a fault. These forces can also result in other kinds of motion in the crust.

As forces inside Earth cause the crust to move upward, the land is built up. Compression can crumple rock layers into wavy folds. Mountains can be formed when two pieces of crust crash together.

The impact squeezes the crust, causing it to crumple into huge folds. Mountains made of crumpled and folded layers of rock are called *fold mountains.* The Appalachians, the Alps, and the Himalayas are all ranges of fold mountains.

Tension and shear can also build up the crust. Mountains can be formed as the crust is pulled apart. How?

Forces in the Crust

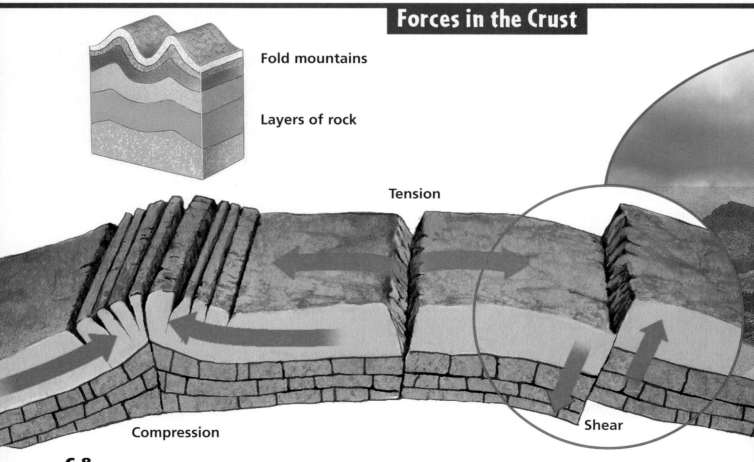

Fold mountains

Layers of rock

Tension

Compression

Shear

Hot molten rock deep below Earth's surface, called **magma**, rises upward. If magma reaches the surface, it may flow out as **lava**.

Lava flows out or is hurled out when a volcano erupts. A volcano is building a new island off the coast of Iceland. Its lava is gushing up through a crack between two pieces of crust that are being pulled apart.

Tension and shear also cause great blocks of crust to break apart cleanly and move along faults. Blocks of crust moving along a fault can form *fault-block mountains*. A vast region of fault-block mountains known as the Basin and Range Province blankets several western states (see map).

Surtsey, an island near Iceland, is forming from an undersea volcano.

▷ **What are three forces that act on Earth's crust?**

Fault-block mountains

Basin and Range Province

What Other Forces Shape Earth's Surface?

While movements of the crust are building up Earth's surface, other forces are at work breaking it down. These processes are known as **weathering** (WETH·uhr·ing) and **erosion** (i·ROH·zhuhn). Weathering is the breaking down of the materials of Earth's crust into smaller pieces. Erosion is the picking up and carrying away of the pieces. Weathering and erosion have been going on for billions of years. They both happen in many ways.

Physical Weathering

Weathering happens when the crust is exposed to water, air, and changes in temperature. How do these break down rocks?

Water can break down the crust in many ways. Water can dissolve some minerals right out of the crust. Moving water can make pieces of rock bang into each other. Small chips can break

Rounded pebbles worn down by moving water.

off the surface of the rock. This causes the rock to get smaller and rounder. The churning waters of a stream can wear down big pieces of rock into small rounded pebbles.

Wind is moving air. The wind blows sand and other broken bits of rock over Earth's surface. These particles also wear away rock.

If the temperature drops low enough, water can freeze. When water freezes it expands, or takes up more space. Water freezing in cracks in rocks expands against the rock. The force of the expanding water is so great that it can split the rock apart.

Limestone cavern

Rock formation carved by water and wind-blown sand

The action of plant roots also causes rocks to weather and erode.

Changes in temperature also cause rock to expand and contract. A rock may be made of a number of different materials. Sometimes one part of a rock expands or contracts more than another part. This difference can cause one part of the rock to push or pull against another part of the rock. Some geologists think that this eventually can cause the rock to break.

Chemical Weathering

Air contains gases that react chemically to form new substances. Oxygen in air reacts with iron to form rust. Carbon dioxide and sulfur dioxide in air react with rain to form acids. These acids eat away at limestone rocks. A limestone cavern was once solid rock. Acid rainwater seeping through the rock dissolved part of it. It "ate away" a huge hole—the cavern.

Houses near the shore may be affected by erosion.

Erosion

Erosion is the carrying away of pieces of weathered rock by gravity, water, wind, and ice. Piece by piece erosion can carry away a boulder, a hill, or even a whole mountain range!

The greatest agent of erosion is water. From the moment a drop of water falling from the sky first hits the ground, it erodes the land.

It may not seem like much, but think of how many raindrops fall in a rainstorm. Altogether they can move a lot of soil.

Once water reaches the ground, it begins to flow downhill. Moving water can push and carry things along with it. Water running downhill picks up pieces of rock and carries them downhill. The faster the water is moving, the bigger the pieces of rock it can move.

▷ **How do weathering and erosion work together to shape Earth's surface?**

How Can Wind and Ice Erode Rock?

Wind is moving air. Wind can push things along with it, just like moving water. Wind does not exert as hard a push as water moving at the same speed, however. Therefore, wind mostly erodes pieces of rock that are the size of sand particles or smaller.

Ice also causes a lot of erosion. The Margerie Glacier in Alaska is a moving river of ice. It may not move as quickly as water, but don't underestimate its power. When the ice of a glacier freezes onto rock and then the glacier moves downhill, the rock is torn right out of the ground. This glacier can carry chunks of rock bigger than your house with ease.

Glaciers also wear away the land as they flow over it. Place an ice cube in some sand for a minute or two. Then look at the bottom of the ice cube. What has become frozen into the bottom of the ice cube? Now rub the bottom of the ice cube on a bar of soap. What happens to the surface of the bar of soap?

Rocks of all sizes become frozen into the bottom of a glacier. As the glacier moves, the rock beneath it is scratched and worn down.

▷ **How do wind and ice cause erosion?**

The Margerie Glacier in Alaska

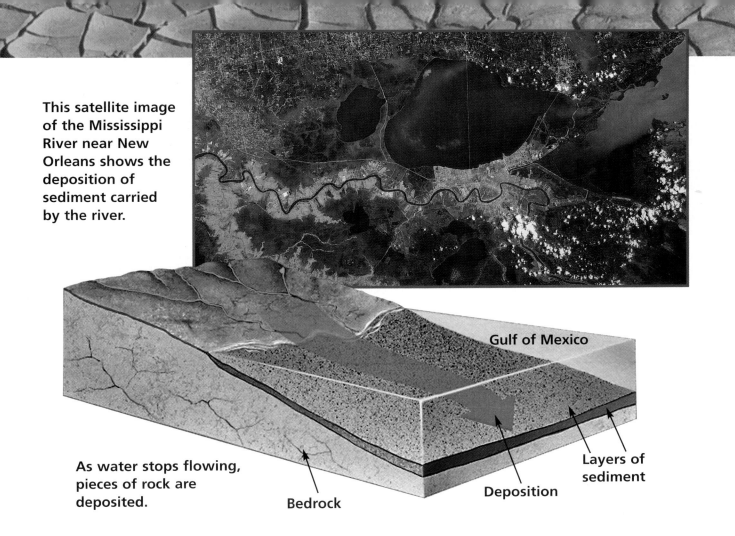

This satellite image of the Mississippi River near New Orleans shows the deposition of sediment carried by the river.

Gulf of Mexico

Layers of sediment

Deposition

Bedrock

As water stops flowing, pieces of rock are deposited.

Where Do Eroded Rocks Go?

What happens to pieces of rock that are carried along by wind, moving ice, or moving water? A fast wind eventually slows down. A glacier stops moving and eventually melts at its front end and sides. All streams eventually slow down and end when they flow into a large body of water, such as a lake or ocean.

When water stops moving, it also stops carrying along bits and pieces of rock. The pieces of rock are dropped to the bottom of the stream, lake, or ocean. The dropping off of bits of eroded rock is called **deposition** (dep·uh·ZISH·uhn).

Deposition also takes place when glaciers melt and winds stop blowing. Layer by layer, pile after pile, bits and pieces of rock deposited by water, wind, and ice build up Earth's surface.

Very slowly deposition may fill up depressions, or basins, in Earth's surface. It can build up land along shorelines and at the end of rivers. Deposition does not seem as dramatic as colliding continents. However, the slow, steady work of deposition is one of the greatest constructive actions on Earth.

READING Sequence of Events
What happens to rocks after they break down?

What Forces Shape the Moon's Surface?

Earth's Moon, our nearest neighbor in space, is a far different place from Earth. There is no evidence of earthquake faults as on Earth's crust. There are no erupting volcanoes. In fact, there is no evidence of any of the kinds of motion that Earth's crust has.

Without air and water, there can be very little weathering or erosion. The Moon has almost no air or water. There are no streams, no glaciers, and no wind. The only weathering and erosion is due to the impact of rocks from space hitting the Moon's surface.

These rocks from space that strike a surface are called **meteorites**. Some craters formed by the impact of meteorites are big enough to be seen from Earth. Others are so tiny the entire crater is on a single mineral crystal.

Can meteorites also strike Earth's surface and produce craters? Yes. However, Earth's atmosphere protects its surface from many such impacts.

Meteorite impacts have been recorded on the Moon's surface.

Rocks from space "burn up" as they pass through Earth's atmosphere. The Moon has little atmosphere. How does that fact affect the Moon's surface?

Meteorite impacts shatter rocks on the Moon and also create a lot of heat. The heat melts the rock. Pieces of rock may melt together, and droplets and globs of molten rock can splatter outward. Over time continual meteorite impacts break down the rock. The end result is a mixture of shattered pieces of rock, rock droplets, and melted-together bits of rock.

▷ **How do meteorites shape the Moon's surface?**

Why It Matters

Natural forces change Earth and the other planets in our solar system. Evidence of surface changes and erosion has been found on other worlds. There are perhaps thousands of volcanoes on Venus. The largest volcano in the solar system is Mars's Olympus Mons. It is 24 km (15 mi) high and 550 km (344 mi) across.

Some of Jupiter's moons also show evidence of constructive and destructive forces. Io has erupting volcanoes. The moons Ganymede, Callisto, and Europa have water and ice. The presence of water, organic compounds, and internal heat mean life may be possible on Europa.

e-Journal Visit our Web site **www.science.mmhschool.com** to do a research project on plate tectonics.

Think and Write

1. What are some types of evidence that show Earth's crust has moved?

2. What are three types of forces acting on Earth's crust?

3. How are earthquakes measured?

4. What is the difference between weathering and erosion?

5. Critical Thinking How do fault-block mountains compare with fold mountains?

L·I·N·K·S

WRITING LINK

Explanatory Writing How can people prepare for an earthquake or another force that can suddenly change Earth's crust? Make a poster that shows people how to prepare for an earthquake or a similar disaster. Give step-by-step instructions. Include illustrations that show the steps.

LITERATURE LINK

Read *Quinto's Volcano* to learn about a boy who overcomes his fear of the sea and saves his village. Try the activities at the end of the book.

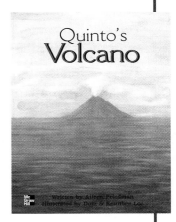

Quinto's Volcano

Written by Aileen Friedman
Illustrated by Dom & Keunhee Lee

MATH LINK

Calculate percentages. Scientists estimate they can detect about 500,000 earthquakes worldwide each year. Of these, 100,000 can be felt, and 100 cause damage. What percent can be felt? What percent cause damage?

TECHNOLOGY LINK

 LOG ON Visit **www.science.mmhschool.com** for more links.

The Sounds of Earthquakes

The ground begins vibrating wildly. Rising from Earth are seismic (SIGHZ·mik) waves—they're like huge sound waves. It's an earthquake!

This simple seismograph has a pen held delicately against a rolling drum with graph paper on it. The pen records the seismic waves.

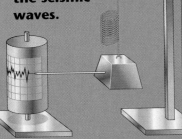

As soon as an earthquake begins, seismic waves travel out in all directions from the focus—where the quake began. They also travel inside Earth. Scientists used seismic waves to piece together a model of the inside of Earth.

Surface waves

Fault

FOCUS

Secondary waves

Primary waves

Seismic waves get weaker the farther they get from the focus. Even so they can still be detected by very sensitive devices called seismographs (SIGHZ·muh·grafs).

The fastest, or primary, waves are recorded soon after an earthquake occurs. Slower, secondary waves come later. Surface waves, the slowest, come even later.

Scientists found that seismic waves change speeds at certain depths below Earth's surface. They speed up when they reach about 30–60 kilometers (19–37 miles) below the surface. Why? This depth, called the Moho (after its discoverer), is a boundary between two of Earth's layers—the outer layer, or thin crust, and the next layer, or thick mantle.

The primary waves slow down when they reach Earth's outer core, a layer of thick liquid. Secondary waves completely stop there. The primary waves speed up again as they reach Earth's solid, inner core.

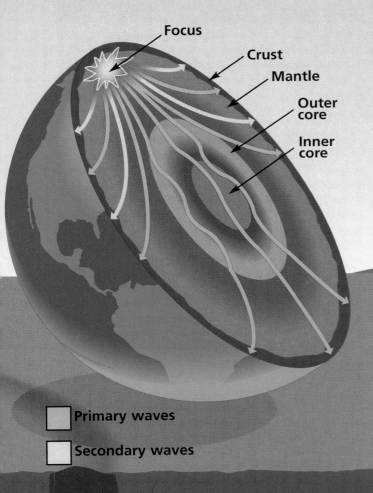

Focus

Crust

Mantle

Outer core

Inner core

Primary waves

Secondary waves

What Did I Learn?

1. An instrument that detects earthquakes is a

A mantle.
B seismic wave.
C seismograph.
D Moho.

2. The boundary between Earth's crust and mantle is called the

F outer core.
G inner core.
H secondary core.
J Moho.

LOG ON Visit www.science.mmhschool.com to learn more about earthquakes.

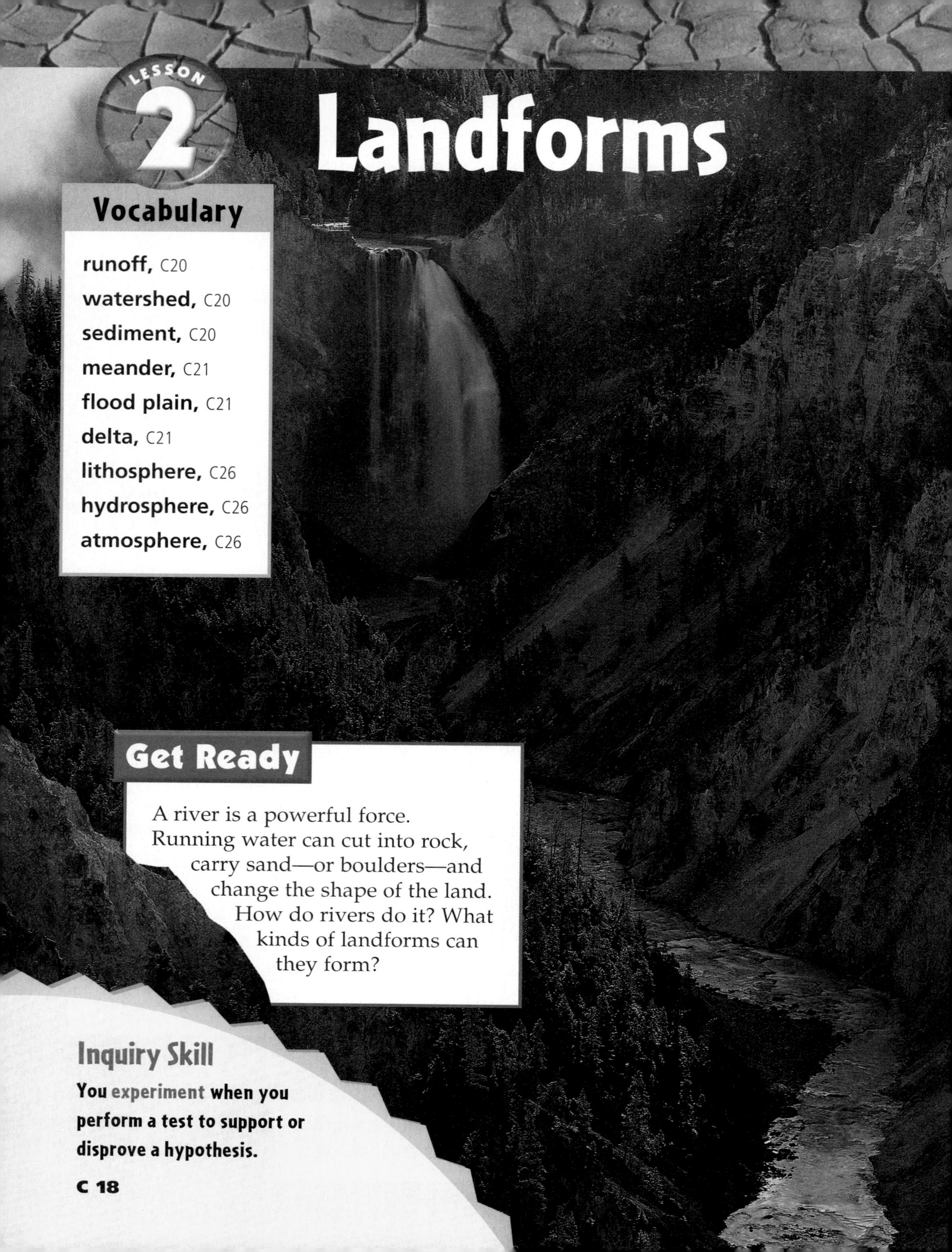

Landforms

Vocabulary

runoff, C20

watershed, C20

sediment, C20

meander, C21

flood plain, C21

delta, C21

lithosphere, C26

hydrosphere, C26

atmosphere, C26

Get Ready

A river is a powerful force. Running water can cut into rock, carry sand—or boulders—and change the shape of the land. How do rivers do it? What kinds of landforms can they form?

Inquiry Skill

You experiment when you perform a test to support or disprove a hypothesis.

Explore Activity

How Does Steepness of Slope Affect Stream Erosion?

Materials

long cake pan

mixture of sand, coarse gravel, pebbles

sprinkle bottle

water

books or wood blocks

Procedure: Design Your Own

1 **Hypothesize** Water flowing in rivers and streams can pick up and carry sediments like silt, sand, and gravel. How does steepness of slope affect how fast a stream flows? How does this affect the size and amount of material rivers can carry? Write a possible explanation, or hypothesis, to answer this question.

2 **Make a Model** Make a model to test your hypothesis. What materials will you need? What will you do? Which factors will you control? What factor will you manipulate?

3 **Experiment** Set up your model and carry out your experiment. Make a chart to organize your data.

Drawing Conclusions

1 **Interpret Data** Do the data you collected support your hypothesis? Explain. Compare your data with others.

2 **Communicate** Write a short newspaper article explaining how steepness of slope affects stream erosion.

3 FURTHER INQUIRY **Experiment** How does the volume of water affect stream erosion? Propose a hypothesis and experiment to test it.

Read to Learn

Main Idea Running water is a major factor in changing the surface of Earth.

How Do Rivers Change the Land?

Earth's surface has been constantly changing. Some changes occur in minutes. Other changes are very slow. Some changes happen over millions of years. One of the most important causes of change on Earth is running water.

Rivers begin high in the mountains or hills as small *tributaries*, or "feeder streams." Tributaries are fed by **runoff** —water that runs off Earth's solid surface. The areas from which the water is drained are called **watersheds**. Tributaries keep merging until they form larger streams or rivers.

The force of gravity keeps water flowing downhill. Where slopes are steep, the water in streams and rivers flows very fast. Rivers flowing along gentle slopes move more slowly. The moving water carries **sediment**

Water flows down a straight path on a steep slope much faster than it flows down a winding, gentle slope. You may want to keep this in mind the next time you visit a water park!

(pieces of material) with it. The amount of sediment a stream or river can carry depends on how much water there is and how fast it is flowing. Larger, faster-flowing streams can carry much larger loads of sediment.

Sediments can range in size from small boulders to gravel, sand, silt, and

Slow-flowing rivers may form bends, or meanders.

Deltas often change shape as channels become clogged with sediments and water is diverted to new outlets.

dissolved materials. The force of running water with its load of sediment can erode the stream bed.

As a stream moves down the slope and into gentler, flatter land, it begins to slow down. When the stream or river slows down, sediments are dropped or deposited on the river floor. Where river valleys are nearly flat and sediments are thick, rivers form bends. These bends or S-shapes are called **meanders**. Here the river erodes material on the outer side of the meanders and deposits material on the inner side. This process makes the river valley wider. As the landscape continues to flatten, **flood plains** may form along the banks of a river. Some of the world's most important agricultural areas are found in flood plains. A river might overflow its banks following

a heavy rain. As the water covers the surrounding land, it releases sediments. Over time, these sediments build up, creating fertile farmlands.

All rivers eventually end as they empty into a lake or ocean. The place where a river empties into the ocean is called the *mouth* of the river. The water slows down so much at its mouth, that it unloads most of its sediment there. This sediment forms a fan-shaped deposit called a **delta**. Deltas are very important agricultural areas. That is because they are a source of fertile soil.

▷ **Why are river deltas important?**

How Do Water Gaps, Canyons, and Valleys Form?

River valleys form from small channels that are deepened and widened by erosion. Small gullies become deeper and wider as their walls are eroded and the sediments are carried away. Where downward cutting is greater than valley widening, narrow V-shaped valleys form. Deep V-shaped valleys are often called canyons. Usually more than one process is involved in the formation of canyons and other landforms. For example, the Grand Canyon would not exist if the surrounding plateaus had not been pushed upward as the Colorado River cut deeper and deeper.

Water gaps are rare. The Delaware Water Gap began forming millions of years ago. It was formed by the river flowing over a sediment-covered plain. As geologic forces pushed the land upward, the river began cutting deeper into the plain. In time, the river encountered a more resistant rock formation below. Instead of changing course, the river slowly cut its way across and down into the resistant rock. Over time, this formed a narrow steep-walled canyon called a water gap. Eventually, much of the surrounding area eroded away. What is left today is a long ridge with the river still flowing through the gap.

▷ **How are valleys and canyons related?**

The Grand Canyon formed over millions of years.

The Delaware Water Gap is known for its depth, width, and spectacular beauty.

Dune plants should not be disturbed. They help anchor the sand and prevent beach erosion.

How Do Beaches, Dunes, and Landslides Form?

Gravity, wind, waves, and glaciers can also reshape the land.

Waves can erode land along coast lines or deposit sand and sediment, forming beaches. Sediment can also be picked up at one point on the shoreline and deposited at another. Sometimes beaches can change shape overnight.

Along the shoreline, windblown sand creates dunes. Wind picks up the sand particles and carries them until some obstacle, such as a rock or bush, slows the wind speed. When it slows down it begins to deposit sediment. As more sand is deposited, the sand dunes grow. Sand dunes help protect shorelines from further erosion. Dunes are formed in a similar manner in some desert areas.

Gravity can pull rocks and soil down slopes. A landslide is an example of a rapid movement of materials down a slope. Rapid landslides can be set off by earthquakes or volcanic activity. They can also occur when heavy rains *saturate* (soak) and loosen the soil.

QUICK LAB

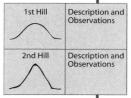

Erosion Challenge

FOLDABLES Make a Two-Column Chart. (See p. R 44.) Label as shown.

| 1st Hill | Description and Observations |
| 2nd Hill | Description and Observations |

1. Cover your workspace with newspaper. Gather materials from your teacher (soil, sand, gravel, plastic plants) and a foil pan to build in.

2. Design a "hill" that is resistant to erosion. Choose which materials to use and how to place them. Think about the effects of slope on the rate of water flow. Sketch and describe your hill on your chart.

3. Use a sprinkling can to create a rain shower over your hill. Compare your results with your classmates'.

4. **Use Variables** Repeat step 2 to see how you could improve your hill's rate of erosion.

5. **Observe** How did the slope of the hill affect the rate of runoff?

6. **Observe** What other factors affected the rate of runoff?

7. **Infer** How could a farmer use this information to help prevent erosion?

▷ **What are three forces of erosion?**

How Do You Read Topographic Maps?

Topographic maps use contour lines to show the shape of Earth's surface. A contour line is an imaginary line drawn on a map. It connects points of equal height above or below sea level. Sea level is the mean level of the surface of the sea between high and low tides and is considered as 0 elevation.

The satellite photo above shows part of the eastern coastline of the United States. The contour map below shows the elevations in the same area.

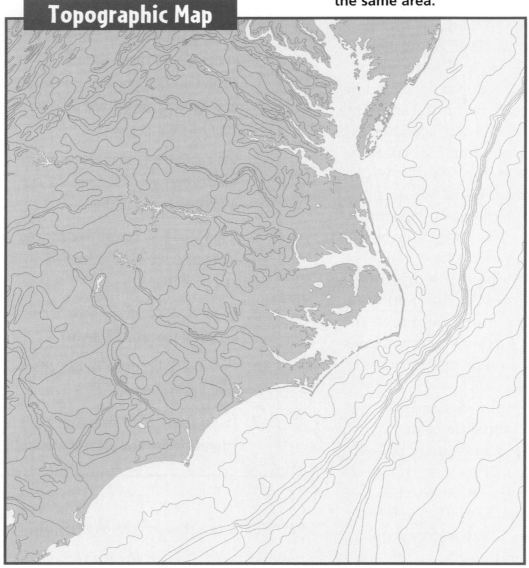

Topographic Map

The spacing of contour lines indicates how steep a slope is. Contour lines that are farther apart indicate a gentler slope. Contour lines that are closer together indicate a steeper slope.

Bodies of water, such as oceans, rivers, and lakes, are also indicated on topographic maps. Symbols are used to locate forests, roads, railroad tracks, and buildings.

Shaded relief maps indicate height by using shading instead of contour lines. The shading makes it easier to recognize sloping hills, steep mountains, and deep valleys. Some topographic maps combine shaded relief maps with contour lines to give an even clearer idea of the geology of an area.

▷ **How do topographic maps and relief maps compare?**

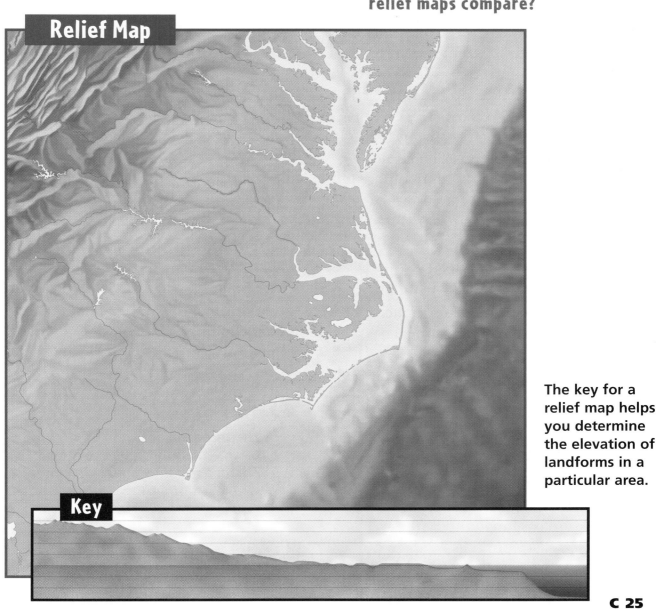

Relief Map

Key

The key for a relief map helps you determine the elevation of landforms in a particular area.

Sea level

Atmosphere

Lithosphere

Hydrosphere

What Are Earth's Major Layers?

Earth has a solid surface layer, mostly covered by a layer of water, and surrounded by layers of gases.

- The **lithosphere** (LITH-uh-sfeer) is the hard, outer layer of Earth, about 100 km (62.14 mi) thick. The rocky surface that makes up the top of the lithosphere is the crust. The crust is thinnest under the oceans and thickest at continents. The crust includes the soil and many other *resources*. Earth's resources are materials that help support life on Earth.

- The **hydrosphere** (HIGH-druh-sfeer) is Earth's water—trillions of liters of water. There is so much water that it covers most of the lithosphere. Most of this water is in the oceans. Ocean water is salty because of minerals that have been deposited in it over the ages. The hydrosphere also includes all of Earth's fresh water found in lakes, rivers, streams, groundwater, and ice. This is the water we use for drinking, cooking, and bathing. Water is also found as a gas in our atmosphere.

The hydrosphere acts as a big heat absorber. Water changes temperature slowly compared to land. The oceans keep temperatures on Earth from changing too drastically.

- Pictures of Earth taken from space show lots of white clouds swirling in the **atmosphere**—layers of gases that surround Earth. There are four major layers of the atmosphere. The one nearest to the surface of Earth is the troposphere. It contains the oxygen needed for living things. It is also where almost all of Earth's weather occurs. Other layers of the atmosphere help protect Earth against harmful energy from the Sun.

The three major layers of Earth – the lithosphere, hydrosphere, and atmosphere – all interact with each other.

READING Sequence of Events
What is the order of Earth's layers?

Why It Matters

Since Earth first formed it has changed, renewed, and recycled itself through natural processes. Perhaps the most powerful force of erosion is running water. Running water and the sediments it carries are vital to the environment and to the quality of our lives. The constant cycling of water and sediments provides fresh water and fertile soils. Before we remove vegetation, build dams, or re-channel streams and rivers, we must consider the short-term benefits against the long-term effects on Earth.

e-Journal Visit our Web site **www.science.mmhschool.com** to do a research project on the effects of altering river systems.

Think and Write

1. Why do gentle, sloping, wide rivers have more meanders than steep, fast-flowing rivers?

2. How does the slope of a hill affect the runoff of surface water?

3. What processes are involved in the formation of a delta?

4. How do topographic maps differ from relief maps?

5. **Critical Thinking** Why are farms often found near rivers?

L·I·N·K·S

WRITING LINK

Persuasive Writing State officials want to build a dam in the river near your town. Research the advantages and disadvantages of building a dam. Take a position on the issue. Write a persuasive speech to present your point of view. Save your strongest argument for last.

MATH LINK

Make a bar graph. Find the elevations of three mountains from around the world. Make a bar graph showing the differences in elevation.

SOCIAL STUDIES LINK

Research ancient and modern civilizations. Learn more about how floodplains affected the establishment and growth of ancient civilizations. How did the annual flooding of the Nile affect the growth of civilization? How does the growth of this ancient civilization compare with the development of towns and cities along other major rivers?

TECHNOLOGY LINK

LOG ON Visit **www.science.mmhschool.com** for more links.

Science, Technology,

Waves of Erosion

Have you ever stood by the ocean and felt a wave pull the sand from under your feet? Waves constantly carry sand away from a beach, bit by bit.

People who live by beaches can watch their "front yards" slowly disappear. Many beach homes are built on stilts. That puts the buildings above water during high tides and storms. However, if the sand supporting the stilts washes away, the houses fall!

If there are cliffs on a shoreline, the pounding waves can wear away the lowest parts. Eventually the cliffs collapse and fall into the water. Then waves slowly break the rocks into smaller pieces. In time the cliffs will become sand.

Stormy winter weather increases erosion. Fierce winds push the waves, giving them the strength to pick up and carry small stones. The stones pound cliffs along with the waves and help to break the rocks. The stronger wind also pushes waves farther inland.

Some towns truck in sand to replace what's lost. Other towns build breakwaters close to shore. The stone and concrete breakwaters reduce the force of the waves before they reach shore. An island or a sandbar close to shore serves as a natural breakwater.

Nearly all sand and rock removed by wave erosion is deposited elsewhere. Only a small percentage is carried out to sea.

Waves can wear away the sand that supports a beachfront home.

and Society

People sometimes build sea walls to try to protect the beaches from pounding waves.

What Did I Learn?

1. Beach homes may be protected from high tides by

   A sea walls.
   B stilts.
   C breakwaters.
   D all of the above

2. The main idea of this story is that

   F people should not live near the beach.
   G beaches are affected by erosion.
   H towns should build sea walls to protect beaches.
   J all of the above

 LOG ON Visit **www.science.mmhschool.com** to learn more about erosion.

Minerals of Earth's Crust

Vocabulary

mineral, C32
luster, C33
streak, C34
hardness, C34
cleavage, C34
ore, C38
gem, C38

Get Ready

How many substances do you think make up Earth's solid surface, the crust? Would you believe about 2,000? The substances that make up Earth's crust are minerals. The formations you see here at Mono Lake in California are made entirely of a mineral called calcium carbonate. How can you tell one mineral from another?

Inquiry Skill

You observe when you use one or more of the senses to identify or learn about an object or event.

Explore Activity

How Can You Identify a Mineral?

Materials

mineral samples

clear tape

red marker

copper penny or wire

porcelain tile

hand lens

nail

Procedure

1 **Communicate** Use tape and a marker to label each sample with a number. Make a table with the column headings shown. Fill in numbers under "Mineral" to match your samples.

2 **Observe** Use the table shown as a guide to collect data on each sample. Fill in the data in your table. Turn to the table on page C35 for more ideas to fill in "Other."

Drawing Conclusions

1 Use your data and the table below to identify your samples. Were you sure of all your samples? Explain.

2 Which observations were most helpful? Explain.

3 FURTHER INQUIRY **Experiment** How could you make a better Scratch (Hardness) test?

Color = color of surface

Porcelain Plate Test = the color you see when you rub the sample gently on porcelain

Shiny Like a Metal = reflects light like a metal, such as aluminum foil or metal coins

Scratch (Hardness): Does it scratch copper? A piece of glass?

Other: Is it very dense? (Is a small piece heavy?) Has it got flat surfaces?

Mineral	Color	Shiny Like a Metal (Yes/No)	Porcelain Plate Test	Scratch (Hardness)	Other

Main Idea Earth's crust contains many types of minerals with important uses.

How Can You Identify a Mineral?

What do diamond rings, talcum powder, and aluminum foil have in common? They are made from **minerals**. So are copper wire, teeth fillings, china dishes, and table salt.

With so many differences in minerals, what can they have in common? Minerals are solid materials of Earth's crust. Like all matter they are made of elements. Some minerals, like gold, silver, copper, and carbon, are made of one element. Most minerals are chemical compounds, that is, two or more elements joined together.

Whether it is an element or a compound, each mineral has a definite chemical composition. Scientists can classify minerals by identifying the elements or compounds they are made of.

As minerals form, their atoms and molecules fall into fixed patterns. These patterns cause minerals to form geometric shapes, called *crystals*. Different patterns form different crystal shapes. You can see the six main crystal shapes on these pages.

No two minerals are exactly alike. Each mineral has a different composition. Each has its own set of properties

Crystal Shapes

Hexagonal

The "lead" in a lead pencil is not the metal element lead at all. It is the mineral graphite (GRAF·ight), which is a form of the element carbon.

Tetragonal

The mineral chalcopyrite (kal·kuh·PIGH·right) is a compound made of the elements copper, iron, and sulfur. It is where much of our copper comes from. Copper is used for wire, coins, pots, and pans.

Cubic

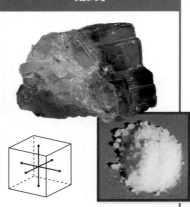

Rock salt, which is used to melt ice, is the mineral halite (HAL·ight). It is a compound made of the elements sodium and chlorine.

that you can use to tell them apart. Crystal shape is one property. However, telling the exact chemical composition of most minerals or their crystal shape isn't easy. This requires special instruments.

Here are some simpler properties to use.

- The color of the outer surface of the mineral is the first thing you see. However, if a mineral is exposed to weather, it can become discolored. Therefore, you should always observe color on a fresh surface. Color alone cannot be used to identify most minerals. Why not? Some minerals come in a variety of colors, and some colors are common to many minerals.

- **Luster** is the way light bounces off a mineral. Minerals with a metallic luster are shiny, like metals. Graphite has a metallic luster.

Minerals with a nonmetallic luster may look shiny or dull. Nonmetallic luster can be described as glassy, waxy, pearly, earthy, oily, or silky. Talc has a nonmetallic luster often described as oily.

▷ **What are the characteristics of a mineral?**

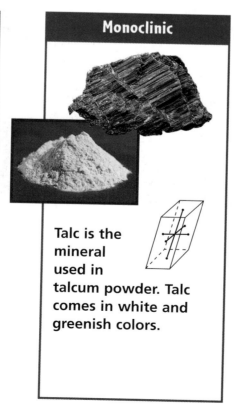

Orthorhombic

Topaz is a mineral used in many kinds of jewelry. It comes in many colors—pink, pale blue, and even yellow or white.

Monoclinic

Talc is the mineral used in talcum powder. Talc comes in white and greenish colors.

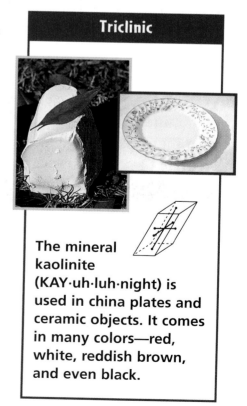

Triclinic

The mineral kaolinite (KAY·uh·luh·night) is used in china plates and ceramic objects. It comes in many colors—red, white, reddish brown, and even black.

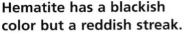

Hematite has a blackish color but a reddish streak.

Galena has three cleavage planes. It breaks into cubes.

Mica has one cleavage plane. It breaks into sheets.

How Else Can You Identify Minerals?

Here are three other ways to identify a mineral.

- **Streak** is the color of the powder left when a mineral is rubbed against a hard, rough surface. Rub it against a porcelain streak plate. The streak is always the same for a given mineral, even if the mineral varies in color.

  The streak may not be the color of the outer surface of the mineral. Fool's gold, pyrite, is brassy yellow, but it has a greenish black streak. Gold has a yellow streak. You would need a streak plate to identify real gold.

- **Hardness** is a measure of how well a mineral resists scratching. Soft minerals are easily scratched. Mohs' scale of hardness is a numbered list of minerals. Talc, number 1, is the softest mineral. It can be scratched with your fingernail. Any item on the list, including the tools, can scratch something above it. You can use the tools to help find the hardness.

- The way a mineral breaks is also helpful. Some minerals have **cleavage**. This property is the tendency of a mineral to break along flat surfaces. Cleavage is described by the number of directions, or planes, along which the mineral breaks.

READING Tables

Which mineral does a fingernail scratch? Which does a glass plate scratch?

Mohs' Scale of Hardness		
Hardness	Sample Mineral	Tool
1 2	Talc Gypsum	
		Fingernail
3	Calcite	
		Copper penny/wire
4	Fluorite	
		Iron nail
5	Apatite	
		Glass plate
6	Feldspar	
		Steel file
7	Quartz	
		Streak plate
8 9 10	Topaz Corundum Diamond	

A form of calcite shows double image because it refracts light twice as you look through it.

READING

Tables

How is hornblende different from quartz? From feldspar? From mica?

Properties of Minerals

Mineral	Color(s)	Luster (Shiny as Metals)	Porcelain Plate Test (Streak)	Cleavage (Number)	Hardness (Tools Scratched By)	Density (Compared with Water)
Gypsum	colorless, gray, white, brown	no	white	varies	2 (all six tools)	2.3
Quartz	colorless, various colors	no	none	no	7 (streak plate)	2.6
Pyrite	brassy, yellow	yes	greenish black	no	6 (steel file, streak plate)	5.0
Calcite	colorless, white, pale blue	no	colorless, white	yes—3	3 (all but fingernail)	2.7
Galena	steel gray	yes	gray to black	yes—3 (cubes)	2.5 (all but fingernail)	7.5
Feldspar	gray, green, yellow, white	no	colorless	yes—2	6 (steel file, streak plate)	2.5
Mica	colorless, silvery, black	no	white	yes—1 (thin sheets)	2–3 (all but fingernail)	3.0
Hornblende	green to black	no	gray to white	yes—2	5–6 (steel file, streak plate)	3.4
Bauxite	gray, red, brown, white	no	gray	no	1–3 (all but fingernail)	2.0–2.5
Hematite	black, gray, red-brown	yes	red or red-brown	no	1–6 (all)	5.3

Many minerals do not break smoothly. They are said to have *fracture*. Quartz, for example, shows jagged edges when it breaks.

Some minerals have special properties that help you identify them. Magnetite, for example, is attracted by a magnet. Some minerals are more *dense* than others. That means they have a lot of mass packed into a given volume. *High density* makes a sample feel quite heavy. Gold, silver, and galena are examples of dense minerals.

▷ **How do tests for streak, hardness, and cleavage help you tell minerals apart?**

How Do Minerals Form?

Where do you find minerals? The answer is simple–in the ground. Minerals make up the rocks of the crust. If you examine rocks with a hand lens, you can often find some of the most common rock-forming minerals in the rock.

How do minerals form? Many form when hot liquid rock, or magma, cools and hardens into a solid. Magma is very hot, and its molecules move very fast. When magma cools, its molecules slow down and get closer together. Then they connect into a pattern, forming crystals. The longer it takes magma to cool, the more time the crystals have to grow, and the larger they get.

Some of the rarest minerals form deep within Earth. The temperatures are high at great depths. The weight of rocks overhead presses down on rocks below, like a huge pressure cooker. The heat and pressure produce minerals such as diamonds. Movements of Earth's crust then bring the minerals near the surface, where they can be mined.

Diamond

Crystals can form from the cooling of hot water. Water heated by magma inside the Earth is rich in dissolved minerals. Hot water can hold more dissolved minerals than cold water. As the water cools, it is able to hold less of the dissolved minerals. The minerals that can no longer stay dissolved form crystals. The huge quartz crystal shown below formed in this way.

The specks you see in this rock include minerals such as quartz, feldspar, hornblende, and mica.

Granite quarry

Quartz crystal

The piles of brightly colored minerals in this hot spring form when the heated water cools as it is exposed to the air.

These crystals then slowly settle to the bottom of the water.

Minerals can also form from evaporation. Ocean water contains many dissolved substances. As the ocean water evaporates, the substances that were dissolved form crystals. Common table salt is mined in areas that were once covered with salt water. The salt is a mineral, halite. It was left behind when an ancient sea evaporated.

READING Sequence of Events
In what ways do minerals form?

QUICK LAB

Growing Crystals

FOLDABLES Make a Six-Row Table. (See p. R 44.) Label the rows as shown.

Date:	Observation:
Date:	Observation:
Date:	Observation:
Date:	Observation:
Date:	Observation:
Date:	Observation:

Your teacher will put a cup of hot water onto a counter for you.

BE CAREFUL! Wear goggles. Use a kitchen mitt if you need to hold or move the cup. Don't touch the hot water.

1. Use a plastic spoon to gradually add small amounts of salt to the water. Stir. Keep adding and stirring until no more will dissolve.

2. Tie one end of a 15-cm piece of string to a crystal of rock salt. Tie the other end to a pencil. Lay the pencil across the cup so that the crystal hangs in the hot salt water without touching the sides or bottom.

3. Observe Observe the setup for several days. Record what you see.

4. Did any crystals grow? If so, did they have many shapes or just one? Explain your answer. If not, how would you change what you did if you tried again?

What Are Minerals Used For?

Can you find minerals being used at home or school? Minerals are used to make many products, from steel to electric light bulbs.

Some of the most useful minerals are called **ores** (AWRZ). An ore is a mineral that contains a useful substance. Ores contain enough useful substances to make them valuable to mine.

For example, iron comes from the mineral hematite (HEE·muh·tight). Iron is used to make nails, buildings, and even ships. Aluminum comes from the mineral bauxite. It is used for food-wrap foil, soft-drink cans, and pie tins, just to name a few uses.

The iron and aluminum that come from these two ores are *metals*. Metals

Gemstones mark special occasions—such as weddings and birthdays. What is your birthstone? Birthstones are gemstones.

Gypsum is used in drywall, or wallboard, for construction of buildings.

have many useful properties. Metals conduct electricity and can be stretched into wires. The metal copper, for example, comes from a mineral ore. It is used to make electrical wires.

Aluminum is lightweight and strong. It shares these properties with another metal that comes from an ore, magnesium. These metals are ideal for use in building jets and spacecraft.

If you look in a jewelry store window, you'll probably see some minerals called **gems**. Gems are minerals that are valued for being rare and beautiful. You may have seen diamond rings. Rubies and sapphires are two other gemstones.

▷ **What are two types of useful minerals?**

L·I·N·K·S

Why It Matters

Minerals are *nonrenewable resources*. They take so long to form that they cannot be replaced in your lifetime.

Because minerals are nonrenewable, they must be *conserved*. To *conserve* means to "use wisely or avoid waste." One way people can conserve minerals is by recycling them—finding ways to treat them or use them again. Researchers also develop substitutes to use in place of natural minerals. Many diamonds used in industry for cutting stone, for example, are not natural diamonds.

e-Journal Visit our Web site www.science.mmhschool.com to do a research project on minerals.

Think and Write

1. Which properties are most useful to identify a mineral? Explain your answer.

2. What if you had two white samples of talc and gypsum? How could you tell them apart in one step?

3. How does time affect crystals?

4. How useful are metallic ores? Give some ways you use them.

5. **Critical Thinking** How could you avoid the mistake that miners made, thinking fool's gold was real? What observations help you tell them apart?

SOCIAL STUDIES LINK

Research minerals. Learn about ways to conserve and recycle minerals. Use the Internet or an encyclopedia.

WRITING LINK

Expository Writing Research the mineral resources in your state. How can these resources be conserved or recycled? Record your findings in a research report.

MATH LINK

Think about shapes. You have learned about the three-dimensional shapes of minerals. How many other regular 3-D shapes do you know? Make a poster illustrating different 3-D shapes.

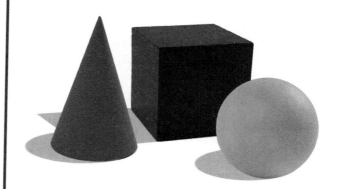

TECHNOLOGY LINK

 LOG ON Visit www.science.mmhschool.com for more links.

LESSON 4

Earth's Rocks and Soil

Vocabulary

rock, C42

igneous rock, C43

sedimentary rock, C44

fossil, C45

metamorphic rock, C46

humus, C49

pollution, C50

rock cycle, C52

Get Ready

What do we walk on, sail over, climb, fly over, live in, and even sit on?

Rocks! Rocks make up Earth's crust. Are all rocks the same? Are the rocks shown here just like any other rocks? How can we tell one rock from another?

Inquiry Skill

You **infer** when you form an idea from facts or observations.

C 40

Explore Activity

How Are Rocks Alike and Different?

Materials

samples of rocks

clear tape

red marker

hand lens

copper wire

streak plate

balance

metric ruler

calculator

Procedure: Design Your Own

1 Use the tape to number each sample in a group of rocks.

2 **Classify** Find a way to sort the group into smaller groups. Determine what properties you will use. Group the rocks that share one or more properties. Your fingernail, the copper wire, and the edge of a streak plate are tools you might use. Scratch gently. Record your results.

3 **Use Numbers** You might estimate the density of each sample. Use a balance to find the mass. Use a metric ruler to estimate the length, width, and height.
Length × width × height = volume
Density = mass ÷ volume

Drawing Conclusions

1 How were you able to make smaller groups? Give supporting details from the notes you recorded.

2 Could you find more than one way to sort the rocks into groups? Give examples of how rocks from two different smaller groups may have a property in common.

3 **Communicate** Share your results with others. Compare your systems for sorting the rocks.

4 **FURTHER INQUIRY** **Infer** How might a sample be useful based on the properties that you observed?

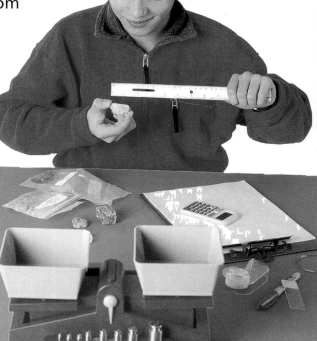

Read to Learn

Main Idea Rocks can be classified according to their composition and properties.

How Are Rocks Alike and Different?

Rocks are mineral treasure chests. A **rock** is any naturally formed solid in the crust made up of one or more kinds of minerals. You can often see mineral crystals in a rock. Sometimes the crystals are too small to see easily.

Look with a hand lens at a piece of granite. You can often find crystals of quartz (whitish), feldspar (pink), mica (black), and even hornblende (black).

Each mineral in a rock has its own streak, hardness, or crystal shape. A rock with several minerals may have a mixture of properties. For example, it may have both hard and soft minerals. It may make both light and dark streaks.

The most exact way to identify a rock is to name the minerals it contains. However, color, density, and the way the rock's surface feels, or its *texture*, are also identifying features. The texture comes from the size, shape, and arrangement of the mineral crystals or grains in a rock. Are the grains large (coarse) or small (fine)? Do they interlock, or can you see each clearly? Are they soft edged or jagged?

A rock's color, density, and texture result from how the rock was formed. Rocks are grouped into three types according to how they were formed.

▷ **What are the characteristics of rocks?**

Igneous Rocks

Extrusive—Cooled Above Ground

Rhyolite (RIGH·uh·light) has a fine texture and is light colored.

Obsidian (uhb·SID·ee·uhn) has no mineral grains and is dark colored.

Basalt (buh·SAWLT) has a fine texture and is dark colored.

What Are Igneous Rocks?

All the rocks on these two pages were at one time deep below Earth's surface. There it is hot enough for some rocks to be melted, or molten. Molten rock material deep below the surface is called magma.

Magma is less dense than the material surrounding it, so it rises toward the surface. Before magma reaches the surface, however, it may cool and harden into solid rock. Rocks that form when melted rock material cools and hardens are called **igneous rocks**.

Often magma makes it to the surface before hardening. Magma reaching the surface is called *lava*. Exposed to the air above ground, lava, too, hardens and cools, forming igneous rocks.

Below ground magma cools slowly. Crystals take a long time to grow. They grow to large (coarse) sizes.

Above ground cooling is much quicker. Crystals are smaller. Lava may cool so quickly that no crystals have a chance to form. What results is obsidian, a solid piece of volcanic glass.

The granite and gabbro shown on this page formed below ground. They both have large mineral crystals. However, granite contains lighter-colored minerals than gabbro.

All the rocks on page C42 formed above ground. They have small crystals or no crystals at all. How do they differ in color?

The texture and color make a difference in how an igneous rock is used. If you were making a monument, which of these rocks might you choose?

▷ **How are igneous rocks formed?**

READING **Charts**

How could you classify the rocks shown on these two pages? Show your results by making a table with two or three columns and rows. Use the properties as headings, and fill in the table with rock names.

Intrusive—Cooled Below Ground

Granite has a coarse texture. The crystals are large enough to be seen. It is a light-colored rock.

Gabbro (GAB·roh) has a coarse texture, but it is dark colored.

What Are Sedimentary Rocks?

How do the rocks here compare with igneous rocks? These rocks are **sedimentary rocks**. Sedimentary rocks are made of small bits of matter joined together. These bits of matter, or sediments, may be bits of weathered rocks. They may be shells or other remains of living things. Long ago water, wind, and ice picked up sediment and carried it. Eventually they dropped the sediment in places where it collected into layers.

Most common sedimentary rocks are formed when sediment is compacted or cemented together. The weight of layer upon layer of sediment on top of each other compacts or squeezes sediment together.

Coarser sediments are cemented by bits of minerals that "glue" the sediments together. Water that contains dissolved minerals seeps between the coarse pieces of sediment. The water evaporates, and mineral crystals form. These crystals hold together the coarse sediment, turning it into a solid rock.

You can see the pieces of sediment that make up these rocks. These rocks are named by the kind of sediment they contain.

Some sedimentary rocks are made of crystals of minerals that were once dissolved in water. The crystals were left behind when the water evaporated. Halite, the rock salt that is used to melt snow and ice, is formed this way.

One type of limestone consists mostly of a mineral called calcite that was once dissolved in ocean water. As the water evaporated in certain areas, the calcite was left behind as solid limestone.

Some sedimentary rocks are made of substances that were once part of, or made by, living things. Cemented-together shells form *coquina* (koh·KEE·nuh). Coral skeletons form coral limestone.

> ▷ **How are sedimentary rocks formed?**

Coquina

Sediment (Small to Large)	Rock
Clay	Shale
Silt	Siltstone
Sand	Sandstone
Gravel	Conglomerate

How Are Sedimentary Rocks Useful?

They may be just clumps of bits and pieces, but sedimentary rocks are very useful. Sandstone, for example, is used for buildings and trim. Limestone is used for buildings, trim, monuments, and even park benches. Limestone is often ground up to make cement and then used to make concrete.

Sedimentary rocks are very useful in helping to piece together Earth's history. They often contain clues, called **fossils**, to life long ago. Fossils are the remains or imprints of living things of the past.

The remains of dead organisms were often covered with mud, sand, or other sediment. Sometimes a living thing left an imprint, such as a footprint, in soft mud. Over centuries of time, the sediment and the remains or imprint hardened into rock. Almost all fossils are found in sedimentary rocks. Why do you think fossils could not be found in an igneous rock?

Bituminous (bigh·TEW·muh·nuhs) coal, or soft coal, is a sedimentary rock. Earth's supplies of coal were formed millions of years ago from dead plants buried in ancient swamps and forests. Coal today is a source of energy, the energy that comes from those ancient forms of life.

▷ **What are some ways sedimentary rocks are used?**

Fossils

Limestone blocks

Bituminous coal lights quickly and provides much energy, but it burns with a lot of soot and yellow smoke.

C 45

What Are Metamorphic Rocks?

Deep below Earth's surface, rocks can undergo great change. They are heated by the high temperatures at great depths. They are under pressure from the rocks lying above.

Great heat and pressure can change one rock into another rock. A rock formed under heat and pressure from another kind of rock is called a **metamorphic** (met·uh·MAWR·fik) **rock**. In the process the original rock does not melt under heat and pressure. If it did, it would become an igneous rock. Instead the original rock remains solid, but

- the mineral grains in the original rock may flatten and line up

- the minerals may change their identity; substances in a mineral may be exchanged with substances in surrounding minerals

- the minerals in the original rock may separate into layers of different densities

In each case the result is a rock different from the original.

Original Rock	Metamorphic Rock
Granite (igneous rock)	gneiss (NIGHS)
Shale (sedimentary rock)	slate
Sandstone (sedimentary rock)	quartzite
Limestone (sedimentary rock)	marble
Slate (metamorphic rock)	schist

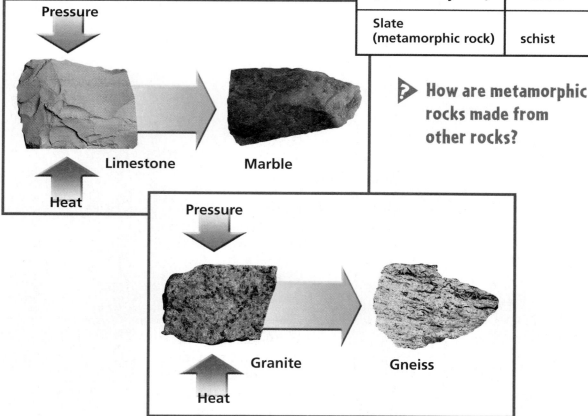

Pressure

Heat

Limestone   Marble

Pressure

Heat

Granite   Gneiss

▶ **How are metamorphic rocks made from other rocks?**

How Are Metamorphic Rocks Used?

Metamorphic rocks are "rock makeovers." In their remade form, these rocks have new properties that are very useful.

Slate, for example, breaks into thin sheets. The minerals in slate are so tightly packed together that water cannot seep through this rock. This makes slate useful as roofing shingles as well as stepping stones and outdoor floors.

Marble is often shiny. It often contains minerals that give it brilliant colors, from greenish to red. It is easy to carve. It is often a first choice for making statues, floors, countertops, and monuments.

One kind of coal is a metamorphic rock. It is called anthracite, or hard coal. Anthracite is formed from soft coal.

> ❓ **Where might you find metamorphic rocks used in your community?**

Anthracite, hard coal, burns cleaner and longer than soft coal, but does not provide as much energy.

The Story of Coal

Millions of Years Ago					
300	280	220	150	10	Present
A forest swamp	Plants die and sink to the bottom.	A thick layer of peat, partly decayed plants, builds up.	The swamp dries up. Buried under layers of sediment, the peat changes to a sedimentary rock called lignite (LIG·night).	Buried by more and more layers of sediment, the lignite becomes more compacted. It forms bituminous coal.	Buried even deeper, bituminous coal is changed by great heat and pressure. It forms anthracite, a metamorphic rock.

Peat

Lignite

Bituminous (soft) coal (sedimentary rock)

Anthracite (hard) coal (metamorphic rock)

READING Diagrams

1. How is the position of the fuel layer changing from picture to picture?
2. How does this position affect what happens to the layer?

Defining Soil

Earth's crust is made up of rocks and minerals. However, to get to the rocks, you usually have to dig through layers of soil.

Soil looks different at different places. It has different properties. Soil can be sandy. It can be moist.

Just what is soil? Make some observations. Write a definition that fits your observations.

Procedure

1 **Observe** Use a hand lens to examine a sample of moist soil. What materials can you find? How do their sizes compare? Write a description.

2 Some soils are more like sand. How does a sample of sand compare with your moist soil sample?

3 **Use Variables** Which sample absorbs water more quickly? Fill a cup halfway with sand and another with moist soil. Pour a spoonful of water in each at the same time.

4 **Experiment** Which absorbs more water? Make a prediction. Find a way to test your prediction.

5 **Experiment** Make any other observations. Look for other differences.

Drawing Conclusions

1 Based on your observations, what is soil made up of?

2 How may soils differ?

3 **Define** Write a definition for *soil*. Take into account all your observations.

> ### Materials
> **moist soil sample in plastic bag**
>
> **sand sample in plastic bag**
>
> **hand lens**
>
> **2 cups**
>
> **2 plastic spoons**

Where Does Soil Come From?

Under a hand lens, you can see that any soil shows that it is a mixture of many things. The main ingredient in soil is weathered rock. Soil may also contain water, air, bacteria, and **humus**. Humus is decayed plant or animal material.

Where does soil come from? A layer of solid rock weathers into chunks. The chunks weather into smaller pieces. Living things die and decay and form humus.

Gradually layers of soil, or soil horizons, develop. If you dig down through soil, you can see many layers and the solid rock, bedrock, beneath it. How do the horizons differ?

Soils differ in different locations. In polar deserts there is no A horizon at the top. However, grassland and forest soils can have very thick A horizons. Why do you think this is so? Some soils are very sandy. Why? How would they differ from soils in many farms?

Sometimes the materials in soil match the bedrock below it. Sometimes they do not match. Can you explain why?

Soil is Earth's greatest treasure. Most plants need soil to grow. Therefore, almost all living things depend on soil for food—and survival. One of the most important uses of soil is farming. All of the food you eat depends on soil.

▶ **What is soil made up of?**

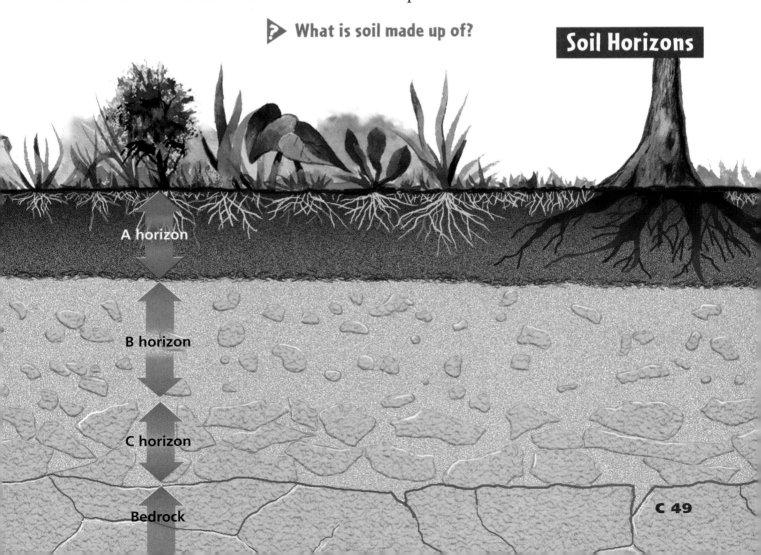

Soil Horizons

A horizon

B horizon

C horizon

Bedrock

How Can People Ruin Soil?

People depend on soil. Would you believe people ruin and waste soil? That might include you! It may be people in general or industries—such as factories or farms.

People often get rid of garbage and hazardous wastes by burying them in soil. Hazardous wastes are wastes that may be poisonous or cause diseases, such as cancer.

Spraying chemicals on soil to kill unwanted animals and plants also affects the soil. These chemicals become a part of the soil.

Tossing materials such as foam cups and plastic wrappers onto the ground, instead of using trash baskets, harms the soil. They do not decay. They remain as wastes in the soil. They may build up and make the soil unusable.

All these materials add up to **pollution**. *Pollution* means any harmful substances added to Earth's land, water, or air. The substances are called *pollutants*. When people cause pollution, we say they *pollute* soil, water, or air.

Not only do people pollute soil, but they often waste it, too. For example, soil needs plants. When plants die and decay, they add valuable substances back into the soil. When a crop is harvested, the plants are removed. They do not decay and return nutrients back into the soil. Growing the same crop year after year uses up the nutrients in soil. Plants don't grow well in nutrient-poor soil.

Plant roots hold soil particles together. They protect soil from being blown away by wind or washed away by water. If plants are removed or if weak, sickly plants are growing in an area, the soil is exposed to erosion by wind and rain.

Letting cattle graze in the same area for a long time also exposes soil. Cutting down forests for lumber exposes soil, too. As a result of any of these practices, soil that took centuries to form may be removed in weeks.

▷ **How do people pollute and waste the soil?**

Each piece of garbage was thrown away by somebody. It takes people to make garbage. What are some ways to prevent this kind of pollution?

By building terraces people in Bali have been able to farm steep hillsides.

Contour means "shape." How does contour plowing prevent water from running downhill?

How Can People Protect the Soil?

People need to take care of soil. We have to protect it from being polluted and wasted. Farmers take care of soil by

- *adding fertilizers and humus.* After growing crops, farmers add these materials to replace minerals removed by crops.

- *using crop rotation.* Each year farmers grow different crops. In this way the soil does not use up the same kinds of minerals year after year. Crops from one year may help replace minerals in the soil that are used up another year.

- *strip farming.* Many crops have stems spaced far apart. Rainwater can run off between the stems and wash soil away. In strip farming strips of tightly growing grasses are grown between more widely spaced crops. The grasses trap runoff and the soil it carries. The next year the position of the strips is switched.

- *contour plowing.* Farmers plow furrows across a slope rather than up and down a slope. Each furrow traps rainwater and keeps it from eroding the soil.

- *terracing.* A hillside is shaped into a series of steps. Runoff water and eroded soil get trapped on the steps. Planting rows of trees to block the wind prevents soil from being blown away.

What can you do to prevent soil from being polluted or wasted? Think about what you toss away as garbage. Is there any way to throw it away to make sure it does not simply end up in the soil? Is there any way to keep from throwing as much garbage away each day as you might?

▷ **What are two ways people can protect the soil?**

What Is the Rock Cycle?

Where do rocks and soil come from? Igneous rocks come from magma or lava. Where did the magma and lava come from?

Sedimentary rock is made of broken-up pieces of rock. However, where did the pieces of rock come from?

All rocks come from other rocks. Rocks are constantly changing from one rock into another. They change in a never-ending series of processes called the **rock cycle**. Part of this cycle is the weathering of rocks into bits and pieces—some of which may eventually become soil.

Rocks are constantly forming—one changing into another. However, any rock takes a really long time to form. When we dig up a deposit of sandstone or use up the coal in an area, it cannot be replaced. Rocks are a nonrenewable resource.

People get into the rock-making process, too. Concrete, porcelain, and brick are all artificial rocks.

READING **Sequence of Events**
What is the path of a rock through the rock cycle?

Rock Cycle

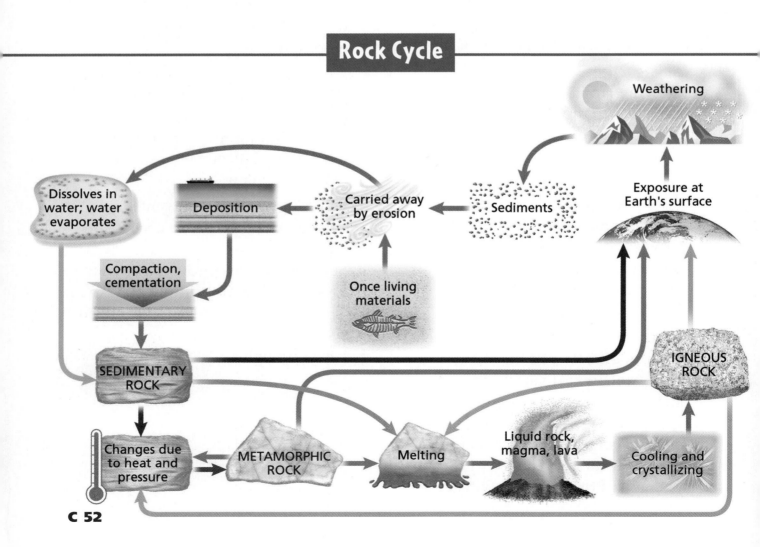

Weathering

Exposure at Earth's surface

Dissolves in water; water evaporates

Deposition

Carried away by erosion

Sediments

Compaction, cementation

Once living materials

SEDIMENTARY ROCK

IGNEOUS ROCK

Changes due to heat and pressure

METAMORPHIC ROCK

Melting

Liquid rock, magma, lava

Cooling and crystallizing

L·I·N·K·S

Why It Matters

It is important to be able to tell one type of rock from another. Just think of all the ways you use rocks. What would life be like without them? There would be no mountains to climb, no beaches to walk on. There would be no soil—so that means no food, or forests, or fields. There would be no metals, because metals come from mineral ores that are found in rocks. There would be no bricks, no concrete, no buildings, no . . .

e-**Journal** Visit our Web site **www.science.mmhschool.com** to do a research project on rocks.

Think and Write

1. How are soils alike? How are they different?

2. How can you tell igneous rocks apart?

3. You pick up a rock. How can you tell if it is a sedimentary rock?

4. **Define** How can you tell rocks apart? Why are they identified in a different way from minerals?

5. **Critical Thinking** How can an igneous rock become a metamorphic rock? Think of three different ways.

WRITING LINK

Writing a Story What would life be like without soil? Write a science-fiction story. Tell how people might live without food or fields, without metals or buildings. Describe the setting of your story in detail. Develop characters and a plot. Include a problem that is solved at the end.

MATH LINK

Do metric conversions. A kilogram is 2.2 pounds. What is the mass in kilograms of a 13.2 pound rock?

ART LINK

Make a diagram. Where do igneous rocks come from? Draw a picture to show how igneous rocks form.

TECHNOLOGY LINK

LOG ON Visit **www.science.mmhschool.com** for more links.

RECORD IN THE ROCKS

How did the age of ancient glass found in Mexico help scientists solve the mystery of what killed off the dinosaurs?

Fossils show that dinosaurs and most reptiles, plants, and fish vanished about 65 million years ago. Scientists suspected that a huge asteroid, a rock from space, was to blame. They needed proof.

They studied rocks around a huge crater called Chicxulub (cheek-SHEW-lewb) in the Yucatan Peninsula of Mexico. Some chemical elements in rocks work like a clock. They decay (give off radiation) at a steady rate, and in the process turn into other elements. The clock starts ticking when the rock forms.

By measuring what is left of these elements in rocks at Chicxulub today, scientists backtracked to the crater's age—65 million years old. Glass beads found nearby could only have been formed by extreme temperatures and pressures like those never seen on Earth. The glass had to be the leftovers of melted rocks from a huge collision. Geologists dated the glass using the same methods they used to date the other rocks.

The ages matched. An asteroid must have hit 65 million years ago. The impact blasted a crater 110 miles wide and launched an enormous cloud of hot vapor and dust into the air. Eventually, the cloud circled the world and wiped out most of Earth's plants and animals.

The "lines" in this quartz grain show that part of the crystal structure was "shifted" by the intense impact of the meteorite. "Shocked quartz" like this is not formed naturally on Earth.

LOG ON Visit www.science.mmhschool.com to learn more about rocks.

An artist's drawing of the huge impact that carved the Chicxulub crater and caused the extinction of the dinosaurs.

Write About It

1. Why is it useful to know how old rocks are?

2. Why might some plants and animals have survived even after an asteroid struck Earth?

How Do You Know the Age of Rocks?

Earth's long history is recorded in the rocks on its surface. These rocks were laid down layer after layer like a stack of books. The top layers are younger than the bottom layers. This can be used to determine a rock's age compared to other rocks.

Another way to date rocks is by using the fossils in rocks. The same kinds of fossils often appear in the same rock layers around the world. In some cases, the living things that formed these fossils lived only during a brief time in history. Their remains are called "index fossils" because their relative ages are known. An index fossil can be used to identify the age of a rock layer containing it.

Chapter 7 Review

Vocabulary

Fill each blank with the best word or words from the list.

erosion, C10
fossil, C45
geologist, C6
hydrosphere, C26
igneous rock, C43
lithosphere, C26
metamorphic rock, C46
mineral, C32
ore, C38
sedimentary rock, C44

1. Rock that changes due to heat and pressure is _____.

2. The oceans are part of Earth's _____.

3. Picking up and carrying away pieces of Earth material is _____.

4. A scientist who studies Earth is called a(n) _____.

5. Rock that forms when melted rock material cools and hardens is _____.

6. A(n) _____ is the imprint of a living thing from the past.

7. _____ is made of small bits of matter joined together.

8. The _____ is the hard outer layer of Earth.

9. A solid material in Earth's crust is called a(n) _____.

10. _____ is a mineral containing a useful substance.

Test Prep

11. The Moon is unlivable compared with Earth because _____.
   A there is no air to breathe
   B there is no water to drink
   C the surface temperature can be hotter than boiling water
   D all of the above

12. Earth's thickest layer is called the _____.
   F mantle
   G crust
   H inner core
   J outer core

13. Fossils are most often found in _____.
   A sedimentary rock
   B lava
   C sand
   D igneous rock

14. Igneous rock is formed from
_____.

    F crystals left behind when
water evaporated

    G meteorites that fell to Earth

    H melted rock material that
cooled and hardened

    J layers of sediment that were
squeezed together

15. The main ingredient in soil is
_____.

    A bacteria

    B weathered rock

    C decayed animal material

    D decayed plant material

Concepts and Skills

16. INQUIRY SKILL **Define** You find
a rock that is made up of different-
colored layers. It seems to be made of
different-sized grains. Some of it
looks as though it is made of tiny
seashells glued together. What type
of rock is it?

17. Critical Thinking Describe two
tests you can use to determine what
minerals a rock is made of.

18. Reading in Science Explain the
sequence of events that turns peat
into anthracite coal.

19. Scientific Methods Explain what
tests you would do to tell real gold
from fool's gold. What would you do
to tell quartz from diamond?

20. Decision Making What would
you need to consider before building
a dam on a river. Explain.

Did You Ever Wonder?

INQUIRY SKILL **Infer** Between
1969-1972, American astronauts
brought back from the Moon 382
kilograms (842 pounds) of rocks and
dust. The samples are kept in special
cabinets filled with nitrogen gas.
Why are the Moon samples
protected this way?

LOG ON Visit **www.science.mmhschool.com**
to boost your test scores.

Air, Water, and Energy

Did You Ever Wonder?

When you look at the spectacular waterfalls of Iguazu in Argentina, you might think that there is an endless supply of fresh water on Earth. Is this true? Might we run out of clean drinking water?

INQUIRY SKILL **Interpret Data** The following shows the gallons per capita (each individual person) use of bottled water. Graph these data: 1998=15.3; 1999=16.8; 2000=17.8; 2001=19.3; and 2002=21.2. What does the data show?

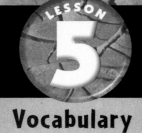

Earth's Atmosphere

Vocabulary

renewable resource, C62

ozone layer, C63

fossil fuel, C64

nonrenewable resource, C64

smog, C64

acid rain, C65

Get Ready

From space Earth's atmosphere appears as a thin blue layer surrounding the planet. From the ground the air may appear different from day to day.

The air may seem clear and clean on some days. If you live in or near a big city, you may have days when the air seems smoky, or "hazy." Why? What kinds of pollutants are in the air that can make it look that way?

Inquiry Skill

You interpret data when you use the information that has been gathered to answer questions or solve a problem.

Explore Activity

What Makes Air Dirty?

Materials

12 cardboard strips

petroleum jelly

plastic knife

transparent tape

string

hand lens

metric ruler

marker

Procedure

1 Make square "frames" by taping together the corners of four cardboard strips. Make three frames, and label them A, B, and C. Tie a 30-cm string to a corner of each frame.

2 Stretch and attach three strips of tape across each frame, with all sticky sides facing the same way. Use a plastic knife to spread a thin coat of petroleum jelly across each sticky side.

3 **Use Variables** Hang the frames in different places to try to collect pollutants. Decide on places indoors or outdoors. Be sure to tell a parent or teacher the places you choose.

4 **Observe** Observe each frame over four days. Record the weather and air condition each day.

5 **Measure** Collect the frames. Observe the sticky sides with a hand lens and a metric ruler to compare particles.

Drawing Conclusions

1 **Interpret Data** How did the frames change over time? How did the hand lens and ruler help you describe any pollution?

2 **Communicate** Present your data in a graph to show differences in amounts.

3 FURTHER INQUIRY **Use Variables** What kinds of pollutants would your frames not collect? How might you design a collector for them? How might you extend this activity over different periods of time?

Why Do Living Things Need the Atmosphere?

Why couldn't humans live on a planet that does not have an atmosphere like that on Earth? Every minute of every day, you need air.

Air is a mixture of nitrogen, oxygen, and a few traces of other gases, including water vapor. This mixture is a vital resource. It supports and protects life on Earth in many ways.

Almost all organisms need air to live. Actually, they need oxygen, one of the gases that is in air. On land living things have structures that enable them to get oxygen directly from the air. Living things in water habitats take in oxygen that is dissolved in the water.

What is oxygen for? Living things take in oxygen for respiration. In this process oxygen is used to break down food so that energy can be gotten from it. As a result of this process, living things give off wastes, including the gas carbon dioxide.

Why doesn't the atmosphere fill up with carbon dioxide? Plants and other producers, living things that have the green substance chlorophyll, take in carbon dioxide. They use it for making food. In the presence of light, these organisms carry on the process called photosynthesis. In this process they make food and give off oxygen.

Producers range in size from green plants to one-celled algae. They replace oxygen in the atmosphere. This makes oxygen a naturally **renewable resource**. A renewable resource is one that can be replaced. It can be replaced in a short enough period of time, such as a human lifetime, to support life on Earth.

Protection

The atmosphere also acts as a protective shield. It shields Earth's surface from harmful energy that comes from

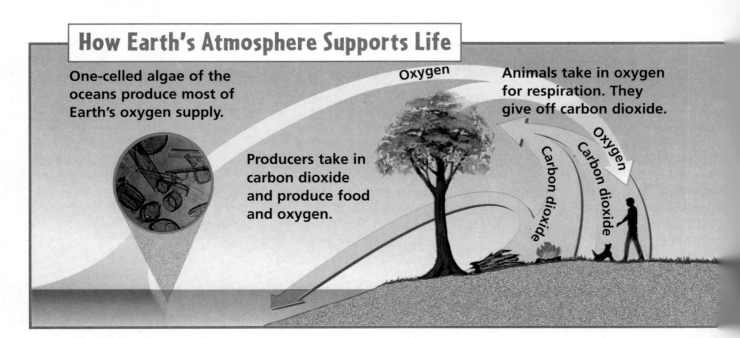

How Earth's Atmosphere Supports Life

One-celled algae of the oceans produce most of Earth's oxygen supply.

Producers take in carbon dioxide and produce food and oxygen.

Oxygen

Animals take in oxygen for respiration. They give off carbon dioxide.

Oxygen

Carbon dioxide

Carbon dioxide

Oxygen

Carbon dioxide

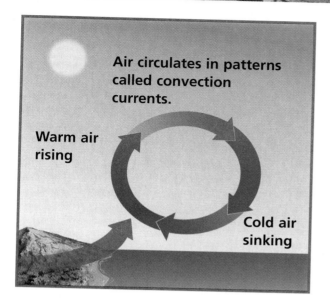

Air circulates in patterns called convection currents.

Warm air rising

Cold air sinking

the Sun. The atmosphere helps screen out harmful ultraviolet rays (UV rays) from the Sun. About 30 km (18.6 mi) above your head is a layer of gas called ozone (OH·zohn). This **ozone layer** screens out from 95 to 99 percent of the Sun's UV rays.

The atmosphere also shields Earth from rocks from space. The "shooting stars" you see on a clear night are not stars. They are rocks from space that burn up due to friction with the air as they speed through the atmosphere.

The atmosphere also protects life from extremes of temperature. Clouds block sunlight during the day. At night they keep much of the heat from escaping into space, so that the planet does not "cool off." Whenever one part of the atmosphere gets hotter than another, the air moves, or circulates, and spreads the heat around.

Most of the air, about 78 percent, is nitrogen. Nitrogen is an important ingredient in food, namely proteins. How does it get into proteins? Nitrogen is taken from the air by

certain kinds of bacteria. These bacteria change the nitrogen into a form that stays in the soil.

Plants use this nitrogen in the soil to make proteins. As living things eat the plants, nitrogen is passed along. It is returned to the soil when living things die.

▷ **What does the atmosphere provide for living things?**

READING Diagrams

1. Do you see any cycles in this diagram? Cycles are continuous processes, where one thing happens after another over and over in the same order.

2. Explain any cycles you see.

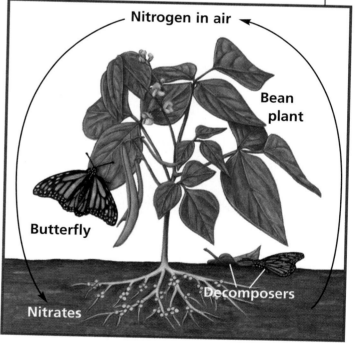

Nitrogen in air

Bean plant

Butterfly

Decomposers

Nitrates

Nitrogen goes from air to plants to all living things. When living things die, nitrogen is returned to the soil.

Natural events can add to air pollution.

Industries produce wastes that add to air pollution.

Wearing a mask helps when smog is very heavy.

What Causes Pollution?

Many of the things humans do add pollution to the air. There are harmful solids, gases, and liquids in the air. Where do they come from?

Many pollutants get into the air from burning **fossil fuels**. These fuels were formed from the decay of ancient forms of life. Fossil fuels are **nonrenewable resources**. They cannot be replaced in your lifetime. Fossil fuels include coal, oil, and natural gas. Cars, buses, trucks, and planes burn these fuels, as do many homes and power plants. The wastes from burning these fuels add pollution to the air.

Burning trash adds smoke to the air. Dust comes from plowed fields. It comes from construction sites and from mines. Factories add chemical wastes to the air.

Other events also add to air pollution. Volcanoes erupt and shoot gases and particles into the air. Forest fires and grass fires can spread smoke over great distances.

All these pollutants can build up into thick clouds called **smog**. Smog is a mixture of smoke and fog. It forms when smoke and fumes collect in moist, calm air. Smog irritates the eyes, nose, and throat. People with breathing problems have died from heavy smog.

Smog hangs like a brown cloud over many cities. Why do you think it is most common in big coastal cities like Los Angeles?

Sometimes ozone can form in smog. High up in the atmosphere, remember, ozone protects Earth from UV radiation. However, at ground level this gas can make people sick.

▷ **What are five sources of air pollution?**

What Is Acid Rain?

What can destroy forests, kill animals and plants in lakes, and even eat away at buildings? Part of the answer comes from power plants that burn coal to produce energy. Another part comes from motor vehicles that burn gasoline.

Wastes that come from burning these fossil fuels travel into the air. In the air the wastes mix with moisture. They can form chemicals called acids in the moisture. The moisture with acids can eventually fall to Earth's surface as **acid rain**. This term includes all forms of precipitation—rain, snow, hail, and sleet.

Acid rain can harm soil and water supplies. Some trees sicken and die if there is too much acid in the soil. Fish die when water in lakes contains too much acid. The acid weathers away statues and buildings. It can cause metal surfaces on cars to crumble.

READING Draw Conclusions

Why is acid rain harmful?

Trees yellow and die due to acid rain.

QUICK LAB

Acids

FOLDABLES™ Make a Four-Column Chart. (See p. R 44.) Label as shown.

Your teacher will give you a stick of chalk and some rock samples.

Sample	Observation
Chalk	
Rocks That Change	
Rocks That Do Not Change	

BE CAREFUL! Wear goggles.

1. **Use Variables** Break a stick of chalk into smaller pieces. Place some small pieces in a plastic cup. Place each rock sample in its own cup. Slowly pour vinegar into each cup to cover each object.

2. Cover each cup using plastic wrap and a rubber band to help keep the vinegar from evaporating.

3. **Observe** Watch for any changes in the chalk and the rocks. Watch for several minutes and then at later times in the day. Record your observations.

4. Vinegar is a mild acid. How did it change the chalk? Make a chart and use it to record your observations.

5. Do all rocks change the same way? Explain based on your results.

How Can We Clean Up the Air?

Cleaning up the air is a job that all nations must work on. That is why the Congress of the United States passed laws to protect the air. It passed the Clean Air Act in 1967 and added more parts in 1970, 1977, and 1990.

As a result of these laws, cars now release lowered amounts of harmful wastes. "Clean coal" methods were introduced to lower the amount of harmful wastes that result in acid rain. Power plants that burn coal can wash coal before burning it, to remove sulfur. Sulfur can result in acid rain when the coal burns.

In 1970 the first Earth Day was celebrated. People were becoming very concerned about the health of planet Earth. That year the Environmental Protection Agency (EPA) was formed. The EPA is part of the United States government. It has the job of checking that laws are being followed. It investigates new dangers and offers solutions and guidelines.

The photograph shows a "hole" in the ozone layer. The ozone layer, remember, is a layer high up in the atmosphere that protects Earth from harmful UV radiation. However, it seems humans have caused holes to form in this layer. The holes are letting UV radiation through.

How did the holes get there? Scientists are not totally sure. Much evidence points to certain substances that have been widely used. These

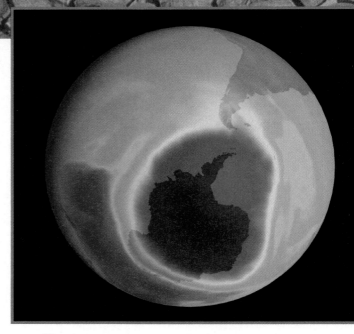

Satellite image shows a "hole" in Earth's ozone layer

substances are called CFCs, which is short for chlorofluorocarbons (klawr·oh·floor·oh·KAHR·buhnz). They are gases used in such things as refrigerators, freezers, and air conditioners. CFCs were also used in many aerosol spray cans. Spray paints, hair sprays, and even shaving foams released CFCs. When the CFCs leak out from these products, they rise into the atmosphere. There they can affect the ozone layer.

In 1990 a group of representatives from around the world met in London. They signed an agreement to ban the use of CFCs worldwide in just ten years.

Aerosol spray cans now use substitutes for CFCs. Just read the label on a spray can, and you can see for yourself.

▷ **What are some ways we can reduce air pollution?**

Why It Matters

Air pollution harms trees, lakes, and buildings. It can also affect you directly. Air pollution can make people sick. It can make your eyes and nose feel like they are burning. It can make your throat feel itchy and irritated.

Laws help to protect the air. However, it takes people to save the air. The Clean Air Act can work only if people work together. For example, using less electricity can save fuel. Finding ways to cut down on using cars saves fuel, too. Cutting down on burning fuel lowers air pollution.

e-Journal Visit our Web site **www.science.mmhschool.com** to do a research project on the EPA.

Think and Write

1. Why is air important to living things?

2. How does the atmosphere protect Earth?

3. How do people pollute the air?

4. What causes acid rain? How does acid rain affect land and water?

5. Critical Thinking How can using less electricity cut down on the use of fossil fuels?

LITERATURE LINK

Read *The Greenhouse Effect and Earth* to learn about how Earth's gases affect its temperatures. Try the activities at the end of the book.

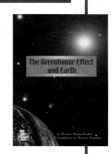

MATH LINK

Plot data. Air samples are graded by how many parts per million (ppm) of various pollutants they contain. Watch the news and note the air quality each night for a week. Show the range of air quality and the average air quality in your community by plotting the data on a number line.

WRITING LINK

Explanatory Writing How can you cut down on using electricity and fuel? Think about all the things that you and your family can do. Make a list. Use your list to write an essay about how you can save energy.

SOCIAL STUDIES LINK

Conduct research. Research the Clean Air Act using the Internet or an encyclopedia.

TECHNOLOGY LINK

LOG ON Visit **www.science.mmhschool.com** for more links.

Clean Watersheds, Clean Water

Keeping our water clean is a big job—from making sure our drinking water is safe, to protecting the fish and other animals that live in lakes and rivers. How do we do this? One way is to monitor our watersheds.

What's a watershed? It's an area of land that drains into a single stream or river. The boundary of each watershed is formed by a ridge or a mountain. When rain or snow falls on a mountain, it trickles down the mountainside into streams. Streams flow downhill and merge into a river.

The United States has 18 major watersheds. The Mississippi River Watershed extends across one-third of the United States. Each watershed includes the land the water runs through and everything on the land— from towns to farms and factories.

Since rain falls everywhere and must drain somewhere, the community each of us lives in is part of a watershed. Everyone who lives in a particular watershed shares the water that drains through it. So our activities play a big role in the quality of water downstream from us. What watershed do you live in? How can you help keep your water supply clean?

Before the Clean Water Act was passed in 1972, waste could be dumped directly into rivers!

The boundaries of watersheds are often determined by geographical features, such as mountain ridges.

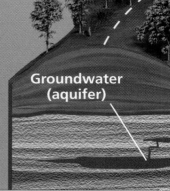

Groundwater (aquifer)

LOG ON Visit www.science.mmhschool.com to learn more about watersheds.

Snowpack

Precipitation

Tributaries

Ridge

Wetland

Watershed divide

Forestry

Town

Write About It

1. What is a watershed?

2. Clean water is important for people's health. What do you think are some other reasons it is important?

Earth's Fresh Water

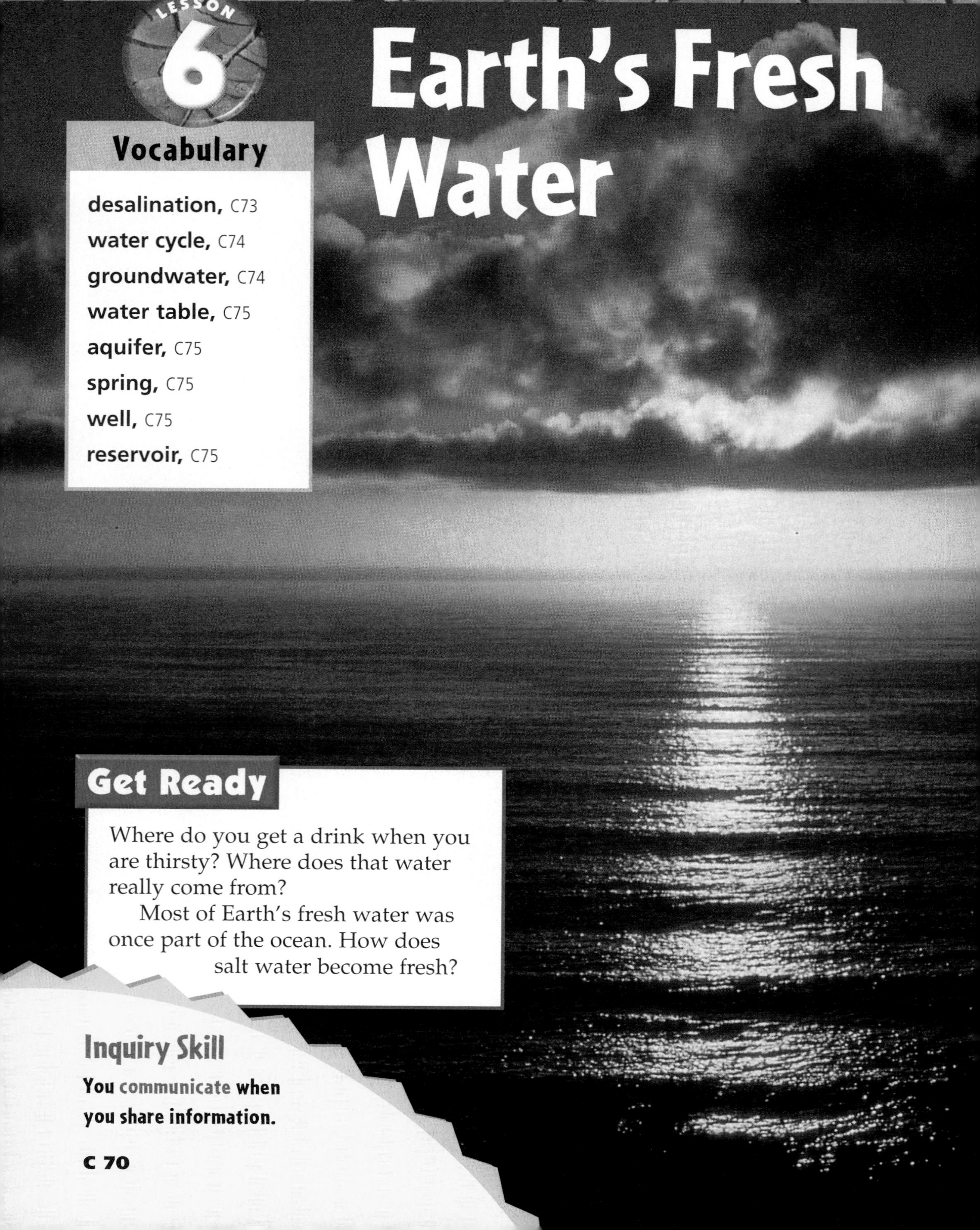

Vocabulary

desalination, C73

water cycle, C74

groundwater, C74

water table, C75

aquifer, C75

spring, C75

well, C75

reservoir, C75

Get Ready

Where do you get a drink when you are thirsty? Where does that water really come from?

Most of Earth's fresh water was once part of the ocean. How does salt water become fresh?

Inquiry Skill

You communicate when you share information.

Explore Activity

Investigate How to Make Salt Water Usable

Materials

tea bag

deep pan

plastic cup

saucer (or petri dish)

large, clear bowl or container

water

Procedure

1. **Make a Model** Keep a tea bag in a cup of water until the water is orange.

2. **Make a Model** Place a pan where there is strong light (sunlight, if possible). Pour some tea water into the saucer. Put the saucer in the pan. Cover the saucer with a large bowl.

3. **Observe** Look at the bowl and pan several times during the day and the next day. Note any water you see on the bowl or in the pan. Record your observations.

Drawing Conclusions

1. How was the water that collected in the bowl or pan different from the tea water?

2. **Infer** What do you think caused the water to collect in the bowl and pan?

3. How does this model represent what might happen to salt water, the water of Earth's oceans?

4. **Use Variables** How long did it take for water to collect in the bowl and pan? How might this process be speeded up?

5. FURTHER INQUIRY **Communicate** Suppose you added salt to the water instead of using a tea bag. How could you tell if the salt had been removed? Try it. Might this model work as a way to get fresh water from ocean water? Explain.

Main Idea Fresh water is constantly renewed by the water cycle.

How Do We Use Earth's Oceans?

If all the water in Earth's hydrosphere was represented by 100 cents, not even 3 cents would represent fresh water. Over 97 cents would be salt water. Salt water is water in the oceans as well as saltwater lakes and inland seas.

Much of the salt in salt water is halite, common rock salt. Salt water has seven times more salt than a person can stand. A person cannot survive drinking it. However, Earth's oceans and inland seas are still useful for the resources they contain.

- **Seafood** What kinds of seafood do you eat? Why are these foods healthful? The oceans support many forms of life. The water has dissolved gases, oxygen, and carbon dioxide, as well as minerals. Plants and other producers of the sea are able to get sunlight so that they can make food. They become food for other forms of sea life, which become food for us.

- **Minerals** Almost everything dissolves in water, at least a little. A pail of seawater contains almost every known element. It contains more minerals than just rock salt.

Hot water bubbling out of underwater volcanoes is especially mineral rich. It leaves rich deposits of minerals on the sea floor. Nodules, or lumps, of minerals can be picked up from the sea floor. They contain manganese and iron. Metals such as tin and gold are also found on the sea floor.

READING Graphs

1. Order the items in the bar graph from greatest to least.
2. Where is most of Earth's fresh water found?

Earth's Water Supply

Fresh water: 2.8%

Salt water: 97.2%

Lakes and streams: 0.01%

Surface water and groundwater: 0.6%

Ice caps and glaciers: 2.2%

Water vapor in atmosphere: 0.001%

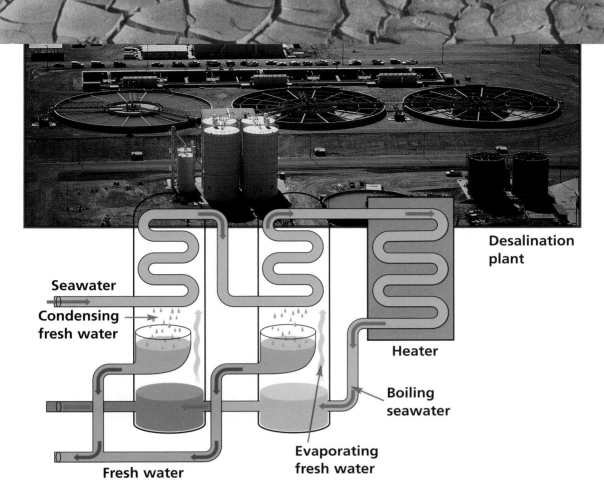

Seawater

Condensing fresh water

Fresh water

Evaporating fresh water

Boiling seawater

Heater

Desalination plant

- **Fossil fuels** Offshore rigs pump oil and natural gas from beneath the ocean floor in many places around the globe. This fuel is worth more than all other resources taken from the oceans.

- **Fresh water** You can't drink seawater or use it to water plants. You need fresh water. Your fresh water comes mostly from freshwater lakes and rivers.

Some areas have very little fresh water available. The islands of Malta, for example, are surrounded by the Mediterranean Sea. However, they have no permanent lakes or rivers. Over two-thirds of the water used by people who live there comes from seawater.

Getting fresh water from seawater takes a process called **desalination** (dee·sal·uh·NAY·shuhn). Desalination helps to remove dissolved salts and materials from seawater to make it usable. A desalination plant aids in this process. Seawater entering the plant is heated. The boiling seawater is then pushed into another chamber. As water evaporates, it leaves the dissolved materials behind. The liquid water that collects at the end of the process is free of dissolved materials.

READING Draw Conclusions

Why are oceans a valuable resource?

Water Cycle

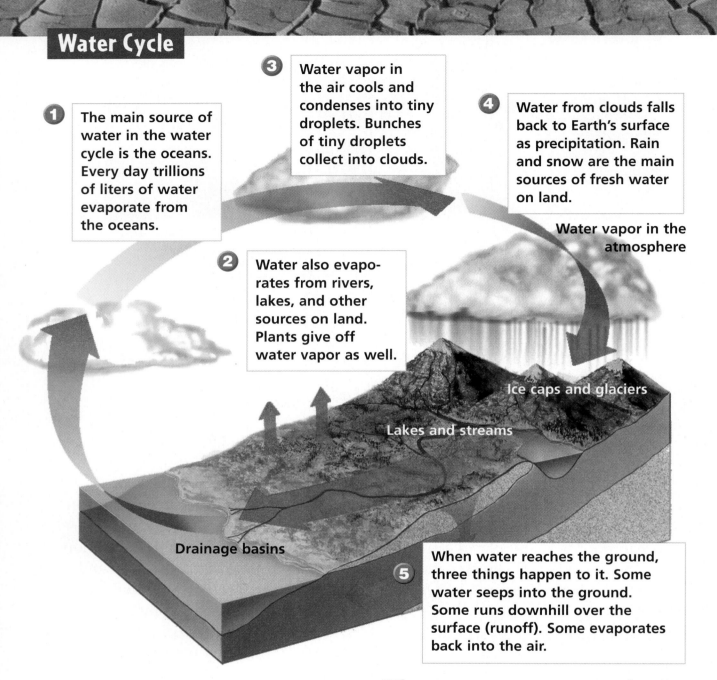

1 The main source of water in the water cycle is the oceans. Every day trillions of liters of water evaporate from the oceans.

3 Water vapor in the air cools and condenses into tiny droplets. Bunches of tiny droplets collect into clouds.

4 Water from clouds falls back to Earth's surface as precipitation. Rain and snow are the main sources of fresh water on land.

Water vapor in the atmosphere

2 Water also evaporates from rivers, lakes, and other sources on land. Plants give off water vapor as well.

Ice caps and glaciers

Lakes and streams

Drainage basins

5 When water reaches the ground, three things happen to it. Some water seeps into the ground. Some runs downhill over the surface (runoff). Some evaporates back into the air.

Where Is Fresh Water From?

Only a tiny fraction of Earth's water is usable fresh water. People use so much fresh water each day, you might wonder why it doesn't run out. Fresh water doesn't run out because it is constantly renewed by the **water cycle**.

In the water cycle, water is on the move—as a liquid that changes to a gas (water vapor) and back to liquid.

When water evaporates, remember, it leaves behind the material it contained. The water vapor is not salt water.

When water falls back to Earth, where does it go? Some water seeps into the ground. It becomes **groundwater**. Groundwater seeps into the spaces between bits of rock and soil. It seeps downward until it is blocked by a kind of rock that is so tightly packed that it has few spaces.

Then the water starts to back up and fill the spaces in the soil and rocks above. The top of the water-filled spaces is called the **water table**. If the water table reaches above the surface, a pond, a lake, or a stream forms.

Ponds and lakes are still bodies of water. They form where water fills up low-lying places. Streams, however, flow downhill. As they flow, they join with other streams, becoming a river. Eventually rivers reach the oceans or other large bodies of water.

An underground layer of rock or soil that is filled with water is called an **aquifer** (AK·wuh·fuhr). Water can move through an aquifer for great distances.

Some groundwater seeps out of the ground in a **spring**. Springs occur where the water table meets the surface. They feed water into streams and lakes long after it stops raining.

Long ago people learned to tap into groundwater by digging **wells**. Wells are holes dug below the water table. The water seeps into the hole. In some wells people get the water out of the hole with pumps. Wells can also be dug deep into aquifers that are sandwiched between tightly packed layers of rock. Water spouts up in these wells because it is being squeezed by the rock layers.

Most supplies of fresh water for large towns and cities come from **reservoirs** (REZ·uhr·vwahrz). Reservoirs are storage areas for freshwater supplies. They may be human-made or natural lakes or ponds. Pipelines transport the water from reservoirs.

▷ **Why is groundwater an important part of the water cycle?**

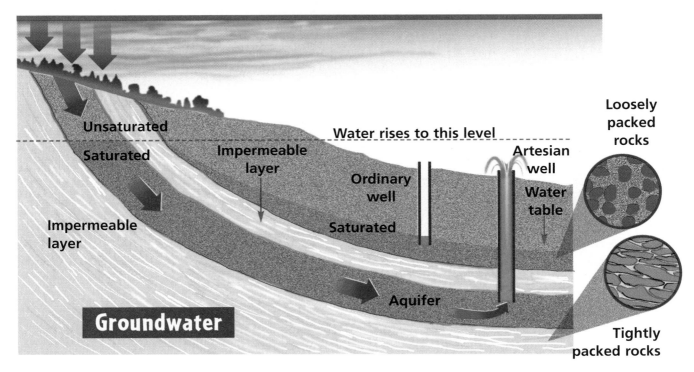

Unsaturated

Saturated

Impermeable layer

Impermeable layer

Water rises to this level

Ordinary well

Saturated

Artesian well

Water table

Aquifer

Loosely packed rocks

Tightly packed rocks

Groundwater

How Can Fresh Water Be Polluted?

Oceans are polluted by people dumping wastes and spilling chemicals. Fresh water can be polluted, too, in many ways.

- **Precipitation** Rain or snow may pick up pollutants from the air. Some chemicals in the air make the rain turn into an acid. Acid rain harms living things and property.

- **Runoff water** Fresh water also gets polluted as it runs off over the land. Water that runs over dumped garbage can end up in streams and lakes. In some cases garbage is dumped into rivers.

- **Groundwater** As water soaks down through the soil, it can pick up chemicals, such as pesticides.

- **Industry** Water used by industry gets polluted as it is used. For example, water that is used to help produce paper is filled with fibers and chemicals.

- **Household waste** You pollute water, too. Every time you flush the toilet, take a bath, brush your teeth, or wash dishes or clothes, water is polluted with wastes. Where do you think this water ends up?

Because of local pollution, many families use water-treatment devices in their faucets. Some families have to use bottled water for cooking and drinking.

▷ **What are four sources of water pollution?**

Inquiry Skill
BUILDER

How Do Wastes from Land Get into Lakes and Rivers?

In seeking an answer to a question, the first thing you might do is find out as much as possible. You make observations. You might look up information.

Next, you would think of an explanation for these observations. That explanation is a hypothesis. It may be stated as an "If . . . then" sentence. "If water runs over land where garbage is dumped, then . . ." Sometimes you can test a hypothesis by making and observing a model.

Materials

soil

food color

foam bits

2 aluminum pans

water

2 textbooks

Procedure

1. **Hypothesize** Write a hypothesis to answer the question above.

2. **Make a Model** Pack moist soil to fill one-half (one side) of one aluminum pan. As you pack the soil, add 10–20 drops of food color to the soil just below the surface. Sprinkle crumbled bits of foam over the top.

3. **Experiment** Use two books to tilt the pan with the soil side up. Place the lower edge of the soil-filled pan in the other pan. Pour water over the uppermost edge of the pan. Describe what happens. Let your model stand for some time, and observe it again.

Drawing Conclusions

1. How does this model represent wastes on land?

2. Based on the model, how do wastes from land get into water? Does the model support your hypothesis? Explain.

3. **Hypothesize** How can some wastes be removed from water? Form a hypothesis, and test your ideas.

How Can We Purify Water?

Can polluted water be cleaned up? Yes, it can be—in many ways. For example, the water cycle helps clean water. Remember that when water evaporates, it leaves behind materials it contained. The water vapor and eventually the rain that forms no longer contain those materials.

When water seeps into the ground, the ground acts as a fine screen, or filter.

Most dirt particles in water are trapped, or filtered out, as water seeps down through the ground. As a result, a well that is dug down deep in the ground collects water that has been filtered.

Freshwater supplies for large areas can be cleaned on a large scale. Follow the steps in the process.

> ## What are three ways that water is purified?

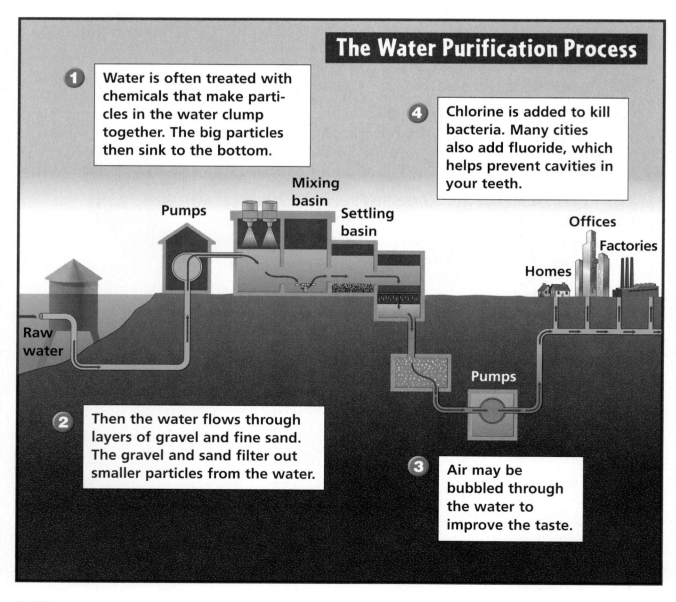

The Water Purification Process

1 Water is often treated with chemicals that make particles in the water clump together. The big particles then sink to the bottom.

4 Chlorine is added to kill bacteria. Many cities also add fluoride, which helps prevent cavities in your teeth.

Pumps

Mixing basin

Settling basin

Offices

Factories

Homes

Raw water

2 Then the water flows through layers of gravel and fine sand. The gravel and sand filter out smaller particles from the water.

Pumps

3 Air may be bubbled through the water to improve the taste.

L·I·N·K·S

Why It Matters

The United States Congress has passed laws such as the Safe Drinking Water Act and the Clean Water Act. These laws set standards for water purity.

Laws are important. However, it takes people—like you—to help save water and keep it clean.

People waste fresh water more than they realize. Often water can become safely reused. At times when the rainfall is low, water supplies may become very low. Saving and recycling water should be part of your daily routine.

e-Journal Visit our Web site www.science.mmhschool.com to do a research project on water resources.

Think and Write

1. How do you depend on the oceans, even if you don't live near one?

2. How can freshwater supplies be cleaned up?

3. How do wastes get into ocean water? Fresh water?

4. Hypothesize How does the Sun help provide you with freshwater supplies?

5. Critical Thinking How can you tell the amount of water wasted in a day by a leaky faucet? Find a way to tell without wasting any.

WRITING LINK

Persuasive Writing Sometimes without even knowing it, people waste fresh water. Write an editorial for your school newspaper. Try to convince your readers that saving and recycling water should be something they do every day.

MATH LINK

Make a graph. Graph how much water is used in different tasks.

Daily Uses of Water	
Activity	**Amount Used**
Flushing a toilet	16–24 liters
Washing dishes	32–80 liters
Taking a shower	80–120 liters
Taking a bath	120–160 liters

LITERATURE LINK

Read *Our Riverkeeper* to learn about cleaning up polluted waters. Try the activities at the end of the book.

TECHNOLOGY LINK

LOG ON Visit www.science.mmhschool.com for more links.

What's the Point?

When you think of pollution, you probably picture big factories pouring solid and liquid waste into rivers and dirty smoke into the air. This nasty stuff is called "point source pollution," because its source can be easily pinpointed. But every day you contribute to what's called "nonpoint source pollution," whose sources are less direct and more difficult to pinpoint. This pollution also finds its way into the air you breathe and the water you drink.

Every day, exhaust from millions of cars enters the air. Rain washes garbage, waste, and chemicals into nearby rivers, lakes, and wetlands. Fertilizer is washed off farms. Motor oil and garbage are washed down city streets. That weed killer you use in your garden runs off the lawn. City sewer systems collect some of this. Even then, leaks and overflows can add raw sewage to the water we use.

Nonpoint source pollution doesn't affect only people; it also affects wildlife. After your garden chemicals kill weeds, they may go on to contaminate water used by other plants and animals. Drastic changes in natural habitats have put over 1,000 plants and animals on the Endangered Species List.

In 1987, Congress amended the Clean Water Act to reduce nonpoint source pollution. These laws control the disposal of pollutants into the water. They also set standards for how clean different bodies of water should be. The standards depend on how the water is used. Do we swim in it? eat fish from it? Or do we drink it?

Most important, the Clean Water Act gives us the power to decide how clean the water should be. You can help make laws to keep local rivers and lakes clean. It's your water—do everything you can to protect it.

Down the drain! Urban runoff, which includes chemicals, oils, and heavy metals like lead, mercury, and zinc, drains into local water supplies.

 LOG ON Visit www.science.mmhschool.com to learn more about pollution.

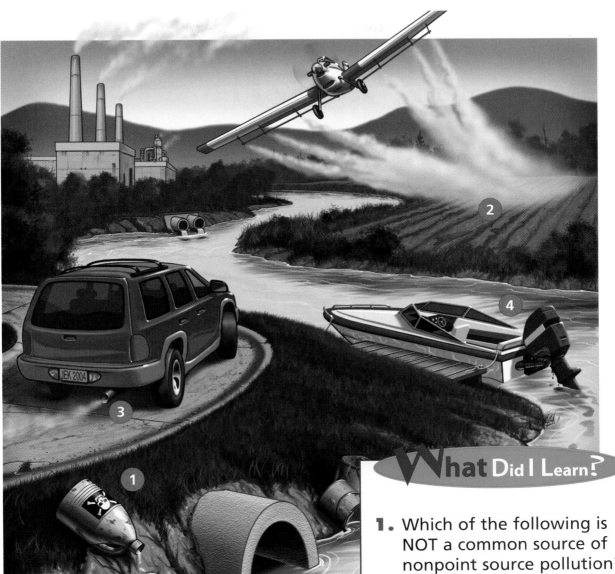

1. If you use chemicals like paints and weed killers, be sure to dispose of them properly.

2. Deforestation and agriculture let soil and natural organisms wash into local waterways and also increase flooding. These changes can hurt the local habitat.

3. Car exhaust contains nitrogen oxides that combine with water in the atmosphere to form acid rain.

4. Boats release pollutants.

What Did I Learn?

1. Which of the following is NOT a common source of nonpoint source pollution?

A mines
B farms
C cars
D books

2. Which of the following is NOT a common pollutant?

F fertilizer
G milk
H chemicals
J manure

Earth's Oceans

Vocabulary

basin, C84

current, C86

continental shelf, C90

continental slope, C90

continental rise, C90

abyssal plain, C90

seamount, C90

trench, C91

mid-ocean ridge, C91

Get Ready

Nearly three-fourths (71 percent) of Earth's surface is covered by water. In fact, you could call Earth a "water planet." Most of Earth's water is contained in the oceans that encircle our planet. How do ocean and fresh water compare?

Inquiry Skill

You **experiment** when you perform a test to support or disprove a hypothesis.

Explore Activity

How Do Ocean and Fresh Water Compare?

Materials

3 small plastic cups

"ocean water"

"fresh water"

clear-plastic straw

waterproof marking pen

wax paper

ruler

Procedure

1. Spread wax paper on your desk before you begin to work.

2. **Predict** What happens when you mix fresh and ocean water?

3. **Experiment** From the bottom of the straw, make a mark every 4 cm. Gently place the bottom of the straw 4 cm under the surface of the "ocean water." Seal the top of the straw with your finger. With your finger still sealing the straw, lift it out of the water. Keeping your finger on top of the straw, place the bottom of the straw 8 cm down in the "fresh water." Lift your finger off the straw, and then put it back again and lift the straw out of the water.

4. **Observe** What happened? Record the results. Now try it again, starting with "fresh water" first. Observe and record what happens.

Drawing Conclusions

1. **Communicate** Which liquid combinations mixed in the straw and which made layers?

2. FURTHER INQUIRY **Experiment** Make a third liquid by mixing equal parts of ocean water and fresh water. How will the mixture compare to fresh and ocean water? Make your prediction, then test it.

Main Idea Ninety-seven percent of Earth's water comes from oceans. Oceans are an important natural resource.

What Are Oceans, Seas, and Basins?

Most of Earth's water is contained in large bodies of salt water called oceans. Examples include the Atlantic and Pacific Oceans.

If all the water evaporated from the oceans, a layer of salt about 60 m (200 ft) thick would be left on the ocean floor. Not all of this salt is table salt. There are many other forms of salt, too. Where does all this salt come from?

One source is the rocks on Earth's surface. Rocks break down through weathering. Their minerals flow into streams. Eventually, the minerals end up in the ocean—more than 2,500 million tons each year.

The other source is from deep inside Earth. When volcanoes erupt, they let out water vapor and other gases. The water vapor is the major source of Earth's water. The other gases include some of the salts that are found in the ocean.

Why doesn't the ocean get saltier and saltier? Because the salts are removed as fast as they are added. Plants and animals use them as they build shells and skeletons. Other minerals fall out of the water to become part of the ocean floor.

Although you may have heard the ocean called the "sea," a sea is actually a body of water much smaller than an ocean. Some seas are part of an ocean. The North Sea, for example, is connected to the Atlantic Ocean and the Arctic Ocean, just north of Europe.

The ocean floor, or **basin**, is as varied as Earth's continents. It contains mountains, valleys, and plains.

Resources from the Ocean

As you saw in Lesson 6, the oceans are rich in natural resources. Seawater is an important source of minerals. To obtain these minerals, people use the heat of the Sun to evaporate water. The minerals left behind are then harvested.

Some resources, such as oil, natural gas, and coal, lie beneath the ocean floor. Drilling rigs, such as the one shown, are used to extract oil and natural gas from beneath the sea.

The ocean's living creatures are also a valuable resource. People use fish, crabs, and squid for food. They eat

From space it is easy to see that 71 percent of Earth's surface is covered by water. Oceans contain valuable resources such as fish and oil.

some kinds of seaweed. A product made from seaweed, *carrageenan,* is used as an ingredient in everything from toothpaste to ice cream.

Other resources are too difficult for us to take from the ocean at this time. For example, certain parts of the ocean floor are covered with lumps called nodules. These nodules contain manganese, iron, and other useful minerals. Gold is an example of a mineral that is dissolved in ocean water. However, we do not yet know how to mine these minerals economically.

 **What are oceans like?**

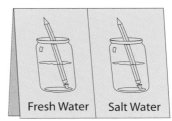

QUICK LAB

Salt Water, Fresh Water

FOLDABLES™ Make a Two-Tab Book. (See p. R 41.) Label the tabs as shown.

Fresh Water   Salt Water

1. Fill a jar with fresh water to about 1 cm from the top. Carefully push a thumbtack into the center of the eraser of a pencil.

2. **Observe** Place the pencil, eraser side down, in the water. Let go. Record what happens.

3. **Measure** Mark the pencil to show where the water line is. Measure and record the length of the pencil above the water mark.

4. Fill the jar with salt water. Repeat steps 2–3. Record your results. Compare with your results for fresh water.

5. **Predict** What do you think will happen if you add a tablespoon of salt to your salt water? Test your prediction.

What Causes Ocean Currents?

Ocean waters are constantly pushed around the planet by currents. A **current** is a stream of water that flows through the ocean like a river. Some currents are on the surface. Others move deep beneath the surface.

Surface currents are driven by the wind. As the winds blow steadily across the ocean, they cause the top layer of water to move in huge circular patterns. A current may move water hundreds of kilometers through the ocean.

Earth's rotation also affects surface currents. As Earth rotates, it pulls great masses of water on the surface along with it. This causes currents to bend to the right in the Northern Hemisphere and to the left in the Southern Hemisphere. The currents start flowing in huge circles.

Surface currents move at a speed of about 220 km (137 mi) a day. Some of these currents are huge. A surface current may move water hundreds of kilometers through the ocean and may carry more water than the Amazon River.

READING Maps

What if you enclosed a message in a bottle and dropped it in the ocean off the California coast? Where might the bottle be found?

The Gulf Stream is a surface current that begins near the equator and flows north past the United States, bringing warm waters to the eastern coast. What causes surface currents like the Gulf Stream?

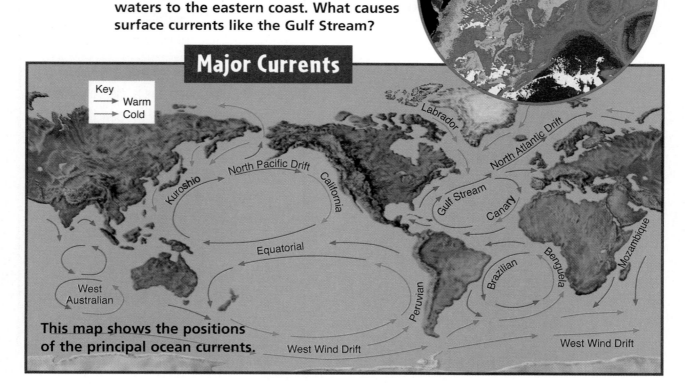

Major Currents

Key
→ Warm
→ Cold

Labrador
North Atlantic Drift
Kuroshio
North Pacific Drift
California
Gulf Stream
Canary
Mozambique
Equatorial
Peruvian
Brazilian
Benguela
West Australian
West Wind Drift
West Wind Drift

This map shows the positions of the principal ocean currents.

As ocean water freezes, the salts do not become part of the ice. The remaining water becomes saltier, causing it to become more dense. It begins to flow to the bottom of the ocean.

As ocean currents flow along the edges of continents, they affect the land's climate. The California current carries cold water along the West Coast of our country, helping it to stay cool there. On the East Coast, the Gulf Stream keeps the climate warm.

Deep-water currents move far beneath the ocean. They are set in motion by differences in the temperature and saltiness of water.

Near Earth's poles, water at the surface of the ocean loses heat to the atmosphere. It may also become saltier as water is removed by evaporation or freezing. This colder, saltier water is *denser* than the water below it. It slowly sinks toward the ocean bottom.

The less dense water below flows in to replace it closer to the surface.

In this way, a deep-water current is set up. The water in a deep-water current moves much slower than the water in a surface current—just a few meters a day.

Dense water forms mainly in Antarctica and in the North Atlantic Ocean. From there the water sinks and spreads slowly outward toward the equator. The water may not resurface for another 500 years.

▷ **What are three ways an ocean current may form?**

How Does the Water in a Wave Move?

Have you ever watched a toy boat bobbing on the surface of a lake or ocean? As the waves go by, the boat moves up, around, down, and then back. It returns to almost the same position where it started. This is exactly what happens to the water particles in waves—they move in circles.

All waves carry energy from place to place. In the ocean the winds blow across the surface, passing energy to the water. The energy of a wave moves forward across the water, but not the water particles themselves. As a wave passes through the ocean, each water particle moves in a circle, returning to almost its original position.

As the winds blow across the ocean, they also drag the water forward slightly, causing the surface currents you read about on page C86. However,

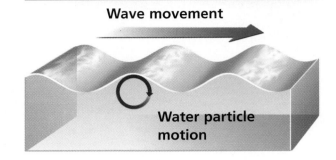

How Water Moves in a Wave

Wave movement

Water particle motion

most of the energy passes through the water as waves, as shown in the illustration above.

When a wave approaches the shore, it begins to slow down. At the same time, it gets higher. The tall wave reaches a point where it collapses, or breaks, against the shore.

The force of breaking waves can be very powerful. Each wave may hurl thousands of tons of water against the shore, breaking rocks apart and smoothing the fragments into pebbles and sand.

▷ **What is the motion of water particles as a wave passes through water?**

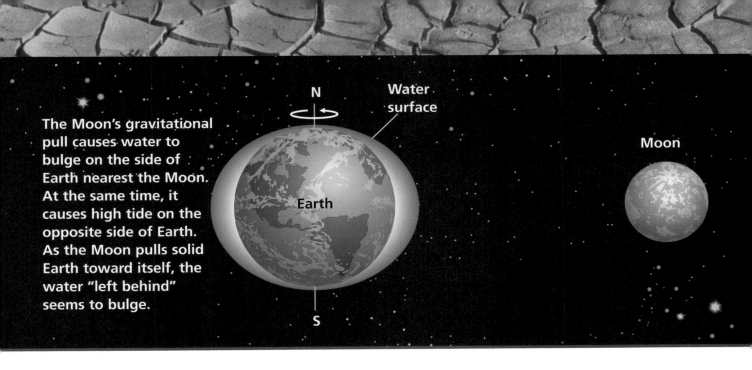

The Moon's gravitational pull causes water to bulge on the side of Earth nearest the Moon. At the same time, it causes high tide on the opposite side of Earth. As the Moon pulls solid Earth toward itself, the water "left behind" seems to bulge.

N

Water surface

Earth

S

Moon

What Causes the Tides?

People living along the coasts are familiar with the rise and fall of the ocean's surface, called the *tide*. Tides result from the pull of the Moon's and the Sun's gravity on Earth. Although the Moon is much smaller than the Sun, it is also much closer to Earth. It is the Moon that has the greatest effect on the tides.

The Sun also influences the tides. However, it is so far away that it has less than half the pull of the Moon. About twice a month, near the times of new and full Moons, the Sun and the Moon line up. Their combined pull causes the highest high tides and lowest low tides, called *spring tides*.

The tides with the smallest range, called *neap tides*, occur between spring tides. During a neap tide, the Moon and the Sun are at right angles to Earth, and their pulls partly cancel each other.

Spring Tides

Full Moon

Earth

New Moon

Sun

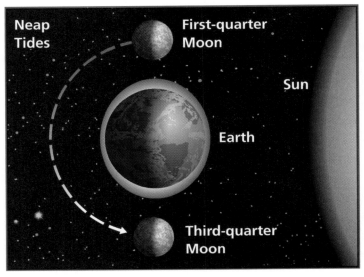

Neap Tides

First-quarter Moon

Earth

Sun

Third-quarter Moon

READING Drawing Conclusions

What are tides the result of?

What Is the Ocean Floor Like?

If you could ride in a submarine from the shore of the Atlantic Ocean out to its deepest part, you would see a varied landscape of mountains, valleys, and plains. As you left the shore, your trip would start above the **continental shelf**, the underwater edge of a continent. It extends from the shore to a depth of about 200 m (600 ft) and has a gentle slope.

About 80 km (50 mi) out from the shore, the land would slope steeply down. You would now be above the **continental slope**. The continental slope leads from the continental shelf toward the sea floor. It is steeper, deeper, and narrower than the shelf.

After traveling another 20 km (12.4 mi) out into the ocean, you would find yourself above the **continental rise**. The continental rise is a buildup of sediment on the sea floor at the bottom of the continental slope. It is a zone of sand and mud that stretches from the slope down to the deep-sea floor.

At the end of the continental rise, you would reach one of the flattest places on Earth—the **abyssal** (uh·BIS·uhl) **plain**. Most of the hills and valleys at the bottom of the ocean were buried under a layer of sand and mud long ago. This created the level abyssal plains. These vast, flat lands cover almost half of the deep ocean floor.

As your trip continued across the abyssal plain, you might come to a huge underwater mountain called a **seamount**. The peak of a seamount rises thousands of meters above the ocean floor. A seamount is a volcano. It is formed in the same way as a volcano on land—hot molten rock from inside Earth rises to the surface and cools to a solid.

A seamount may never cross the surface of the ocean. However, if it

Ocean Floor

Continental shelf

Abyssal plains

Continental slope

Continental rise

grows large enough, it may emerge as an island. The Hawaiian Islands are an example of a chain of seamounts.

As your travels continued, your submarine might come to a long, narrow V-shaped valley known as a **trench**. Deep-sea trenches are the deepest points on Earth. They plunge as far down as 8,000–10,000 m (5–6 mi) below sea level. One is more than 11,000 m (7 mi) deep. If you could put the tallest mountain on Earth—Mount Everest—in the trench, its tip would still be about 2,000 m (1.25 mi) below the ocean surface.

The trenches are too deep beneath the ocean to ever see the sunlight. They are pitch black and freezing cold. Your submarine couldn't dive to the bottom of a trench—the pressure of the water above is so great that it would crush a normal submarine.

As you reached the middle of the Atlantic Ocean, you would see a mountain range rising above the ocean floor. This is known as the mid-Atlantic ridge. It is part of the chain of mountains, called **mid-ocean ridges**, that winds its way through all the world's major oceans. The mid-Atlantic ridge runs the entire length of the Atlantic Ocean. Like seamounts, these mountain ranges were formed by molten rock that cooled and hardened.

▷ **What are some of the features of the ocean floor?**

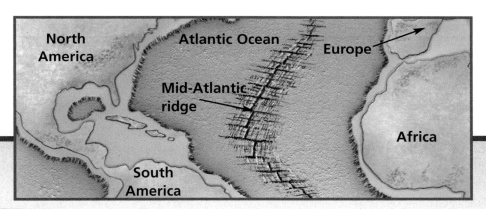

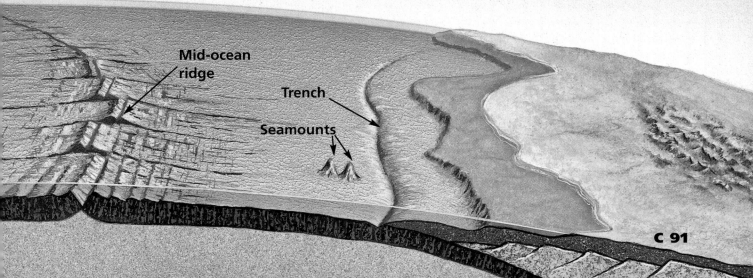

How Do We Explore the Oceans?

Today ocean scientists explore the oceans using a variety of techniques. One of the first breakthroughs in technology came in the 1920s, when sonar equipment was invented. Sonar helps scientists map the ocean floor. Sonar instruments give out sound waves that hit the ocean floor and send back echoes. The echoes are recorded. Their pattern is traced on paper to make a "sound map" of features like underwater mountains and trenches.

The ability of people to move about underwater was aided by the invention in the 1940s of scuba (self-contained underwater breathing apparatus). Scuba was invented by Jacques Cousteau and Emile Gagnan. For the first time, divers had their own air supply.

A diver wearing scuba gear can explore the ocean to about 50 m. After that, the water pressure is too great for the human body to handle safely.

Starting in the 1960s, scientists began using deep-diving research vessels called *submersibles* to explore the ocean. They can go much deeper than a diver can go. Using submersibles like *Alvin*, scientists have found a new world deep beneath the sea. They have studied new

The *Titanic*

animals like tube worms. Submersibles also helped locate and explore the ocean liner *Titanic*. The ship lies on the Atlantic floor almost 4,000 m (2.5 mi) below the surface.

Satellites are yet another way to study the ocean. Satellites can measure surface temperature, wave height and direction, sea level, currents, sea ice, and levels of marine plant life. This information can be used in different ways. For example, patterns in ocean temperatures and currents can be used to predict the weather. Satellites can also monitor ocean pollution.

Deep-sea drilling is also used to study the ocean. Research vessels collect samples from beneath the sea floor. The sediment gathered allows scientists to understand how the oceans have changed over time.

Sea-Floor Vents

In 1977 scientists in a submersible traveled deep below the ocean to one of the mid-ocean ridges. They were there to study hot springs called *sea-floor vents*. These vents are formed when seawater trickles down into the hot, newly formed oceanic crust. The water becomes saturated with minerals. Eventually, it boils out of a vent in the crust.

To the scientists' amazement, large wormlike animals were waving in the water near some of the vents. They named the animals *tube worms*. Tube worms get nourishment from bacteria living inside them. The bacteria, in

Tube worms are found deep beneath the ocean near vents in the ocean floor. How can tube worms get nutrients in these deep, dark waters?

turn, use the hydrogen sulfide and oxygen taken in by the worms to create nutrients through a process called *chemosynthesis* (kee·moh·SIN·thuh·sis).

Recall that photosynthesis is the food-making process in green plants that uses sunlight. Never before had scientists seen a food chain that did not rely on photosynthesis for energy and food. Instead, the bacteria–tube worm food chain gets its food and energy from the mineral-rich waters and the heat energy from the hot vents.

Since that first discovery, more than 400 species new to science have been found living in and around sea-floor vents.

▷ **What are some of the ways that today's scientists explore the oceans?**

People can help clean up polluted waters.

How Do People Affect the Oceans?

The oceans have a tremendous ability to absorb human waste. Unfortunately, at some point the pollution becomes too much for the water to handle. Marine pollution has become a serious problem for the world's oceans.

Each year sewage, waste from factories, and fertilizers and other farm wastes are dumped into rivers that flow into the sea or into the ocean itself. Ships may spill oil or dump sewage overboard. Offshore drilling for oil and natural gas also harms the environment.

Ocean pollution can harm or kill marine animals and plants. It is also dangerous to people who eat seafood from the polluted waters.

Overfishing is another threat to marine animals. People around the world depend on fish and marine animals, such as crabs and lobsters, for food. According to the United Nations Food and Agriculture Organization, 70 percent of the fish species caught to be sold are being overfished. If this continues, entire species may die out.

▶ **What are some of the ways that people affect the ocean environment?**

A factory fishing boat is a huge boat where thousands of fish at a time can be caught, cleaned, and quick frozen. How might such a boat contribute to overfishing?

L·I·N·K·S

Why It Matters

Oceans provide many valuable resources. Most of the world's nations are now aware of the need to protect their coasts and water from pollution. They have begun to enforce laws to keep sewage, chemicals, and other waste out of the water.

Many countries limit the number of fish that can be caught in their waters. Many governments have also set aside protected areas in their waters where marine animals can live undisturbed.

e-Journal Visit our Web site **www.science.mmhschool.com** to do a research project on the oceans.

Think and Write

1. What resources are found in oceans?

2. Where do the oceans' salts come from?

3. How does the water in waves move? In currents?

4. What does the ocean floor look like?

5. **Critical Thinking** In the Indian Ocean, there are seasonal wind shifts known as the summer and winter monsoons. What do you think happens to the surface currents when the winds change direction? Explain.

MATH LINK

Compare ocean depths. The deepest region in the Atlantic Ocean is the Puerto Rico Trench. It is over 8,600 m deep. The deepest region in the Pacific Ocean is the Mariana Trench. It is more than 11,000 m deep. About how much deeper is the Mariana Trench than the Puerto Rico Trench?

WRITING LINK

Writing a Poem Which ocean resources do you use? Write a poem about them. Use words to create images that will appeal to your reader's sense of sight, touch, taste, hearing, or smell.

TECHNOLOGY LINK

Science Newsroom CD-ROM Choose *Sea to Shining Sea* to learn more about Earth's water and how it moves through the water cycle.

 LOG ON Visit **www.science.mmhschool.com** for more links.

DANGER: TSUNAMIS

Imagine a wave speeding across the ocean as fast as a jet plane. Then imagine it slamming into your house as a wall of water five stories high. Say hello to a tsunami.

Tsunamis (soo-nah-mees) are giant ocean waves that can be caused by volcanoes, landslides, even meteorites. More frequently, however, they are caused by earthquakes on the bottom of the ocean.

When huge chunks of the ocean floor buckle up or down during an earthquake, the surrounding water moves up and down, too. This causes ripples that travel through the ocean as waves until they reach land. In deep water, the waves may rise only a few feet. However, they can travel at jet speeds (more than 500 miles per hour) for thousands of miles. As a tsunami approaches the shore, it slows and grows. In the shallower waters near shore, the waves bunch up and can grow into a huge wall of water—sometimes taller than a ten-story building.

Tsunamis can hit land as a single wall of water, as a series of waves, or as a rapidly rising flood. However they arrive, tsunamis can damage everything in their path. They wash away beaches, smash up coastal communities, and endanger lives.

In 1964, an earthquake off the coast of Alaska triggered a tsunami that barreled across the entire Pacific Ocean. In Alaska alone it was responsible for taking the lives of 106 people and causing $84 million in damage.

The seaport town of Seward, Alaska, received heavy damage from a 1964 tsunami. It prompted the formation of the Alaska Tsunami Warning Center. The Center quickly alerts towns of any threats of tsunamis.

Write About It

1. How do tsunamis in the deep ocean differ from those approaching shore?

2. How can damage from tsunamis be reduced?

LOG ON Visit www.science.mmhschool.com to learn more about tsunamis.

Energy Resources

Get Ready

How many hours a day do you use energy? What kinds do you use, and what do you use them for? You use energy all the time. How is that possible? How many different ways is energy being used in this picture?

Inquiry Skill

You hypothesize when you make a statement that can be tested to answer a question.

Explore Activity

How Do People Use Energy?

Procedure

1 **Communicate** Make a list of all the different ways you use energy.

2 Make a table listing all the kinds of energy you use in a day, how you use that energy, and how many hours you use each kind.

Drawing Conclusions

1 How many different ways do you use electricity each day? How many hours a day do you use electricity? What other sources of energy do you use? How many hours a day do you use each?

2 **Infer** Make a log to keep track of your energy use at home and at school. How can you use that information to help you make a plan to save energy?

3 **Use Numbers** If it costs you an average of ten cents an hour for the energy you use, how much would the energy you use cost each week? About how much would it cost each month?

4 FURTHER INQUIRY
Hypothesize How can you use less electricity? How much money do you think you could save on energy use in a month? Design and carry out a test of your hypothesis.

Main Idea Some energy sources will last forever, while others will run out eventually.

How Are Fossil Fuels Turned into Energy?

You use a number of different energy sources each day. Where does the energy you use come from? Try tracing it back to its source. Many homes, schools, and businesses get heat by burning oil or natural gas. Some older buildings still burn coal for heat. Some homes burn wood for heat.

The heat in many other homes and businesses comes from electricity. So does the energy to run many common devices, such as lights, computers, radios, TVs, and washers. Some small devices, such as flashlights and portable CD players, get their electricity from batteries. Most of the other devices use electricity from a wall outlet. That electricity comes from a power plant. Electricity from that plant reaches your home through wires. However, the power plant makes electricity by using energy from burning fuels such as coal, oil, and natural gas.

It takes a lot of energy to move a car, bus, or train. Public and private transportation is one of the greatest uses of energy in today's world. Most vehicles get their energy from burning fuels, such as gasoline or diesel oil. Others run on electricity, propane, or liquefied natural gas.

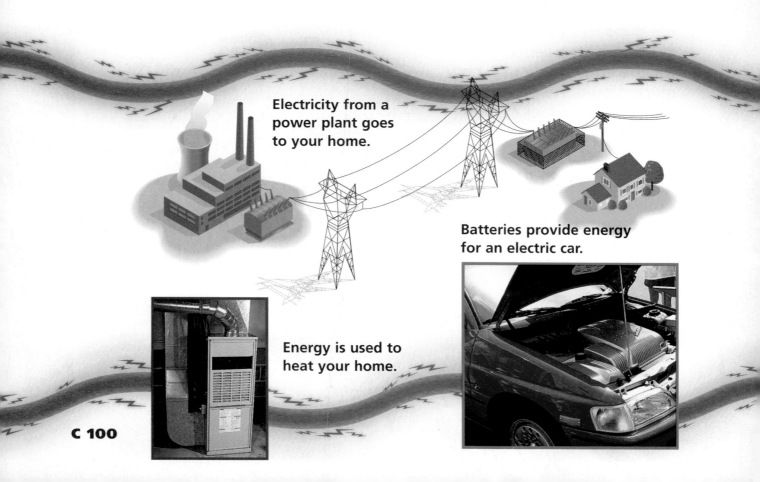

Electricity from a power plant goes to your home.

Batteries provide energy for an electric car.

Energy is used to heat your home.

Smog is air pollution that is a mixture of smoke and fog. Smog also occurs when sunlight reacts with exhaust fumes from cars and factories. Smog can make people ill.

As you can see, most of the energy you use can be traced back to fossil fuels—coal, oil, or natural gas. The energy in fossil fuels, in turn, can be traced back to the Sun.

Heat from burning fossil fuels can be used directly to heat homes, schools, businesses, and factories.

The heat can also be used to generate electricity. The heat is used to boil water and turn it into steam. The steam is trapped, and pressure builds up. Then the steam is released. The steam is directed at a big, pinwheel-like turbine. When the steam hits the turbine, it causes it to spin. The spinning turbine turns a generator to make electricity.

All fuels have advantages and disadvantages. The advantage of using fossil fuels is that they contain a lot of energy. However, fossil fuels take millions of years to form. Once used they cannot be replaced fast enough for future use. Therefore, they are nonrenewable.

Burning a fossil fuel also gives off smoke, gases, and other by-products. These pollute the environment. That is why the search is on for other, cleaner fuels.

▷ **What are some energy sources that come from fossil fuels?**

Where Do Fossil Fuels Come From?

Fossil fuels are the remains of once-living things. Coal formed from the remains of dead plants buried in ancient swamps and forests. Natural gas and oil formed from the remains of tiny ocean plants and animals. These sea creatures died and fell to the bottom of the ocean. There their bodies were buried by layers of sand and mud. As more and more layers covered these remains, pressure on them built up. Eventually, the layers of sediments turned into sedimentary rock. Over millions of years, the plant and animal remains changed into oil and natural gas. Plants and animals get their energy from the Sun. Therefore, the source of energy in fossil fuels can be traced back to the Sun.

Our supplies of fossil fuels are limited, and fossil fuels are not a renewable energy source.

With the growth of industry, the demand for and use of energy also grows. The United States is the world's largest consumer of energy. The energy we use makes our lives easier.

How Fossil Fuels Are Formed

1 Dead plants and animals fall to the ocean floor.

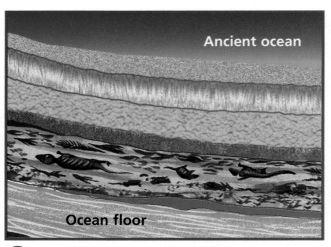

2 Dead plants and animals are covered with layers of sand and mud.

However, energy use pollutes the environment. It also speeds up the rate at which Earth's energy resources are used up.

If we continue to use fossil fuels at our present rate, we will run out of them. There are two possible solutions to this problem. One is to conserve our energy resources so that they will last longer. Another is to search for other sources of energy.

▷ **How do fossil fuels form?**

READING

Diagrams

What were oil and natural gas made from?

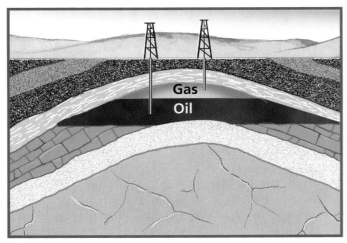

3 Over millions of years, pressure and heat help to turn the dead plant and animal remains into oil and natural gas.

QUICK LAB

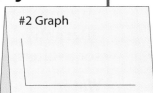

Fuel Supply

FOLDABLES Make a Half-Book. (See p. R 41.) Label the book as shown.

#2 Graph

This table shows how fast we are using up oil and natural gas.

World Supply of Oil and Natural Gas (as of January 1, 1996)	
Oil	1,007 billion barrels (1,007,000,000,000)
Natural gas	4,900 trillion cubic feet
World Use of Oil and Natural Gas for 1995	
Oil	about 70 million barrels a day (70,000,000)
Natural gas	about 78 trillion cubic feet

1. **Observe** Examine the data in the table.

2. **Communicate** Make a Half-Book. On the front draw a graph showing how long the fossil fuels we know about will last, based on the data in the table.

3. **Infer** Inside your book, explain how long it will be until we run out of each type of fossil fuel. Assume that the rate of use remains the same.

What Other Sources of Energy Are There?

Sources of energy other than the burning of fossil fuels are called **alternative energy sources**. Here are some alternative energy sources.

Water

Any whitewater rafter can tell you that running water has a lot of energy. That energy can be harnessed to do work using waterwheels. Running or falling water turns the wheel. The turning wheel spins an axle, which is attached to various machines to do work.

In a mill the axle turns a big stone that grinds up grain. In a sawmill it spins a blade to cut wood. In a *hydroelectric* (high·droh·i·LEK·trik) *plant*, running or falling water spins a generator to make electricity.

Wind

Wind, or moving air, can also spin a wheel. Windmills generate electricity in the same way waterwheels do.

Internal Heat

The Earth's interior is very hot. The most common evidence of that heat is simply hot water or steam coming out of the ground. The water is heated below the surface in places where magma collects. Earth's internal heat is called **geothermal** (jee·oh·THUR·muhl) **energy**. Geothermal energy can be used to heat homes and produce electricity.

- Homes in Boise, Idaho, have been heated by hot springs since the 1890s.
- At The Geysers in California, steam drives turbines that generate electricity. The steam comes from underground water heated by geothermal energy.

Hydroelectric plant

Geothermal energy helps keep the country of Iceland warm.

Solar houses use solar cells for electric energy and solar collectors for heat.

The Sun

Every day the Sun bathes Earth in energy. We usually think of that solar energy simply as sunlight. Plants harness the Sun's energy through photosynthesis to make chemical compounds rich in energy. When you burn wood, you are releasing energy that a tree absorbed from the Sun.

Sunlight also gives water the energy to evaporate and rise into the atmosphere. In this way the energy of running water can also be traced back to sunlight.

Today people are using new ways to harness the power of sunlight. One way is to trap or concentrate sunlight with the use of solar panels, or collectors. The trapped sunlight can be used to heat water or entire homes. Another way to use it is with solar cells. Solar cells are devices that convert sunlight into electric energy.

Tides

Every day the tide causes the water level to rise and drop along the world's coastlines. Now imagine a big tank built just below the high-water level. The tide rises, and water fills the tank. When the tide drops, the water flows out of the tank. Add a waterwheel so the water flowing out of the tank spins the wheel. Now you have a spinning axle that can be used to do work. That's the idea behind tidal power plants.

▷ **What are five alternative energy sources?**

The windmills in this array spin generators to make electricity.

Tidal power plant in Holland

C 105

Cars can be powered by a special mixture that combines alcohol from biomass with gasoline.

How Can We Conserve Energy?

Unfortunately, alternative energy sources are not fully replacing fossil fuels. Therefore, we need to conserve these nonrenewable resources.

What does it mean to conserve our resources? It means we don't waste what we have and we use as little of what we have as possible. Take a typical house as an example. Better insulation of homes has cut United States' consumption of fuel oil almost in half. Newly designed bodies and engines have doubled the gasoline

mileage of most cars. If we could cut our present consumption in half, our oil reserves would last twice as long! How can we do that?

One way is to use alternative energy sources, such as water, wind, and solar energy. Every watt of electricity we get from a solar cell is one less watt we have to get by burning oil or coal.

You have learned that fossil fuels are the stored energy that came from once-living plants and animals. Fossil fuels are nonrenewable. However, plant matter and animal wastes or other remains—called **biomass**—can be used as a renewable energy source. Plant material and animal wastes that might wind up as garbage can be processed to form fuel. This is done in waste-treatment plants. The treated wastes can then be burned. Special devices called scrubbers help prevent pollutants from entering the air when these wastes are burned. Solid wastes can also be digested by bacteria. The bacteria produce methane gas in the process. Methane gas can be used as fuel.

Corn and other grains, and even sugarcane, can also be turned into fuel. This fuel can be used to heat foods. It can also be mixed with gasoline to help run cars while saving gasoline supplies.

READING **Draw Conclusions**
How can biomass help conserve energy?

Why It Matters

You probably look forward to driving a car someday. Think about this: Cars run on gasoline, and gasoline comes from oil. Remember the graph you did comparing known oil reserves with our current rate of use? If we don't conserve, will there be enough gas for your children's cars? Will there be enough gas for their children?

 e-Journal Visit our Web site **www.science.mmhschool.com** to do a research project on energy sources.

Think and Write

1. How do you use energy each day?

2. Why are coal, oil, and natural gas called "fossil" fuels?

3. How does burning fossil fuels pollute the environment?

4. List five ways people can help to conserve fossil fuels. Which of these suggestions do you think would conserve the most fuel? Which of these suggestions do you think more people would try?

5. **Critical Thinking** What alternatives do we have to using fossil fuels for energy? What are some of the advantages and disadvantages to using these energy sources?

L·I·N·K·S

WRITING LINK

Writing That Compares Compare two types of alternative energy sources, such as wind power and solar energy. Write about their similarities and differences. Then draw a conclusion about which of these energy sources might be used someday to replace fossil fuels.

MATH LINK

Calculate percents.
A barrel of crude oil contains 42 gallons. When refined, it produces 21 gallons of gasoline, 9 gallons of fuel oils, 5 gallons of jet fuel, 4 gallons of lubricants, and 3 gallons of asphalt. Convert these numbers to percents and make a circle graph with your results.

TECHNOLOGY LINK

 Science Newsroom CD-ROM Choose *Fuel Rush In* to learn how fossil fuels are formed and used.

LOG ON Visit **www.science.mmhschool.com** for more links.

Chapter 8 Review

Vocabulary

Fill each blank with the best word or words from the list.

acid rain, C65
biomass, C106
continental shelf, C90
continental slope, C90
fossil fuel, C64
geothermal energy, C104
ozone layer, C63
reservoir, C75
smog, C64
water table, C75

1. The _____ screens out much of the Sun's UV rays.

2. The top of the water-filled spaces in the ground is the _____.

3. Dangerous air pollution is called _____.

4. A(n) _____ is a storage area for fresh water.

5. A type of precipitation caused by air pollution is _____.

The **6.** _____ of the ocean floor is steeper and deeper than the **7.** _____.

8. _____ and **9.** _____ are alternative energy sources to **10.** _____.

Test Prep

11. Most of Earth's oxygen supply is produced by _____.
   A bacteria in the soil
   B one-celled algae of the ocean
   C green plants
   D the ozone layer

12. All of the following are examples of nonrenewable resources EXCEPT _____.
   F oil
   G coal
   H oxygen
   J natural gas

13. Geothermal energy comes from _____.
   A the Sun
   B falling water
   C fossil fuels
   D Earth's internal heat

14. Fossil fuels are stored energy that came from _____.
   F sedimentary rocks
   G wind and water
   H once-living plants and animals
   J waste-treatment plants

15. An underground layer of rock or soil that is filled with water is _____.

   A a reservoir

   B an aquifer

   C a lake

   D groundwater

Concepts and Skills

16. `INQUIRY SKILL` **Hypothesize** Does rain remove pollutant particles from the air? Form a hypothesis. What could you do to test your hypothesis?

17. Reading in Science All electricity is made by burning fossil fuels. Is this true or false? Explain your answer.

18. Scientific Methods How can salt water be turned into drinkable water?

19. Critical Thinking Does filtering water remove all impurities? Explain your answer. How would you prove your answer?

20. Making Decisions Solar energy is considered "too expensive" to use in the Northeast. However, sunlight is a renewable resource. Is it better to use solar energy or depend on fossil fuels? What are the benefits and disadvantages of each?

Did You Ever Wonder?

`INQUIRY SKILL` **Form a Hypothesis** Icebergs are fresh water. Can icebergs be a source of water for areas of the Earth lacking fresh water?

LOG ON Visit **www.science.mmhschool.com** to boost your test scores.

Evan B. Forde

Oceanographer

Oceans cover two-thirds of Earth's surface. In this underwater environment, new species wait to be discovered. Amazing rock formations, resources, and unusual-looking creatures are waiting to be studied.

Oceanographers use ideas from geology, chemistry, biology, geography, and physics to study the oceans.

Evan B. Forde is an oceanographer. He works at the National Oceanic and Atmospheric Administration (NOAA) in Florida. About 25 years ago, Forde came up with some original ideas about the formation and structure of the underwater canyons off the Northeast coast of the United States. Some of the canyons are much larger than the Grand Canyon.

To study them, Forde traveled in *Alvin*—a tiny vehicle that carries scientists deep beneath the sea. Oceanographers on *Alvin* have gone to depths of more than two miles! Thanks to *Alvin* and to other deep-diving submarines, Forde was able to explore underwater canyons and landscapes beneath the Atlantic Ocean. It was a sight that few people have ever seen!

These days Forde is using satellite sensors to study ocean conditions that lead to hurricanes. This information will help scientists predict more accurately when a hurricane will form. Evan B. Forde knows his oceans!

Deep Oceans and Seas

The oceans are very deep. The deepest known spot is about 29 times as deep as the Empire State Building is tall!

Ocean or Sea	Greatest Depth (in feet)
1. Pacific Ocean	35,840
2. Indian Ocean	23,376
3. Atlantic Ocean	28,374
4. Caribbean Sea	22,788
5. South China Sea	16,456

Write About It

1. How did *Alvin* help Forde study underwater canyons?
2. Why do some people say the oceans are one of Earth's last frontiers?

LOG ON Visit www.science.mmhschool.com to learn more about the work of oceanographers.

Name That MINERAL

Your goal is to test properties of minerals to determine their identity.

What to Do

1. Make a table with the column headings shown below.

2. Do the following tests to determine properties. Record data in your table for each sample.

   Color(s): What color is its surface?

   Luster: How shiny is the sample?

   Porcelain plate test: What color is the powder when the mineral streaks?

Cleavage: How many directions does it break into?

Hardness: How well does the mineral resist scratching?

Density: How heavy does the sample feel compared with a sample of water with the same volume?

Analyze Your Results

Complete the table. Use the results of your tests and the chart Properties of Minerals (page C35) to name each mineral.

SPOT the SOURCE

Your goal is to make a brochure to educate people about air pollution.

What to Do

1. Look at pictures in a newspaper or magazine. Which of the pictures show things that cause air pollution?

2. Create a brochure about air pollution. Your brochure should do three things:

   a. explain what air pollution is

b. name the sources of air pollution in the pictures

c. describe how those sources pollute

Analyze Your Results

1. Name one way that people use energy that causes air pollution.

2. How are air pollution and water pollution alike?

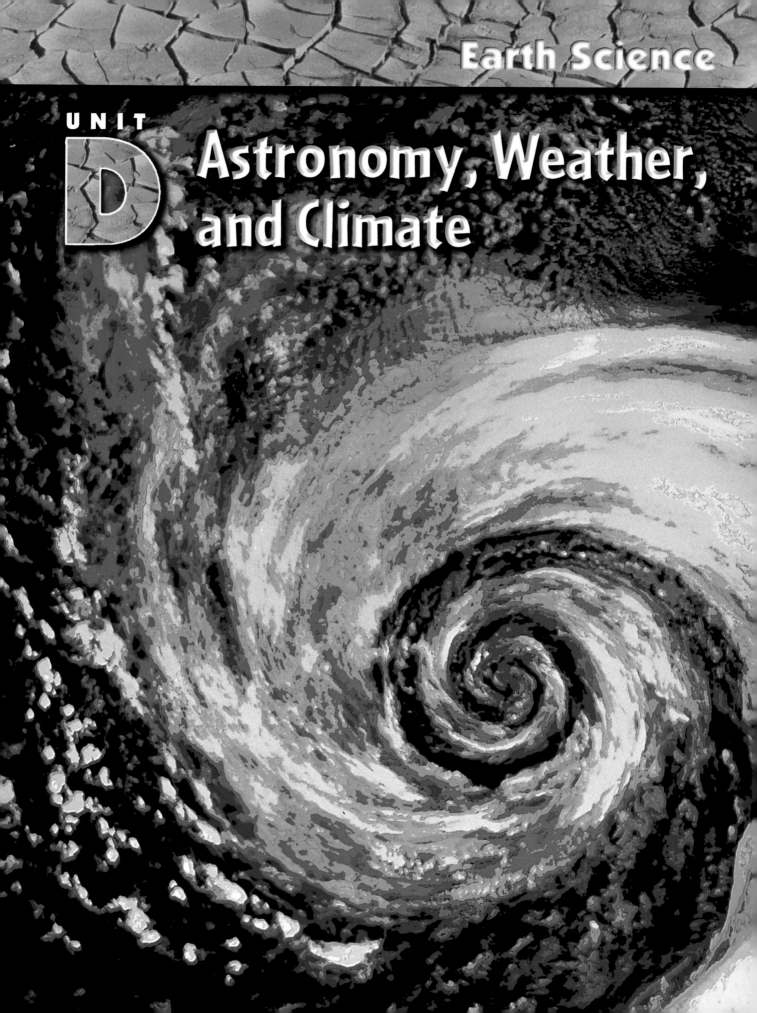

UNIT D
Astronomy, Weather, and Climate

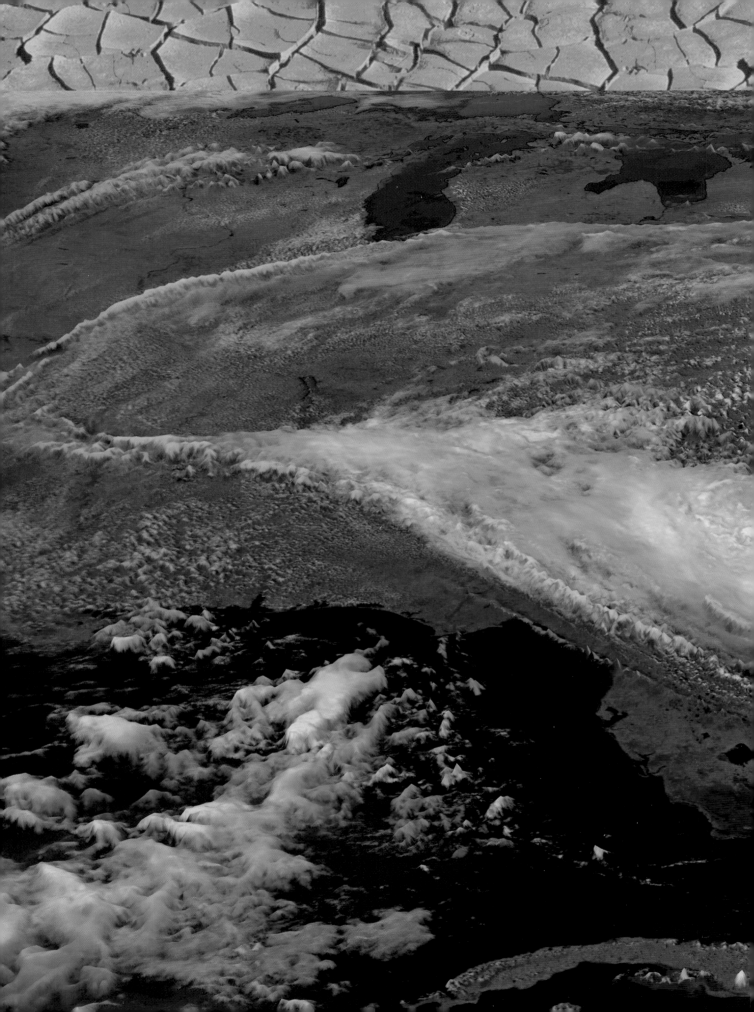

Astronomy, Weather, and Climate

LOOK!

A powerful hurricane swirls over the Atlantic Ocean. What causes such severe storms?

Astronomy

Did You Ever Wonder?

Did you ever see the clear night sky far from city lights? Did it ever seem to you that the stars formed patterns in the sky? Have you watched for one especially bright light that does not twinkle? A light that people call "the evening star"? It is not a star at all. It is the planet Venus. Venus and Earth are only two of many planets in our solar system. What are the other planets like?

INQUIRY SKILL **Make a Model** The Moon orbits Earth each month. Why does the Moon seem to change shape from night to night? Make a hypothesis. Design a model to test your hypothesis.

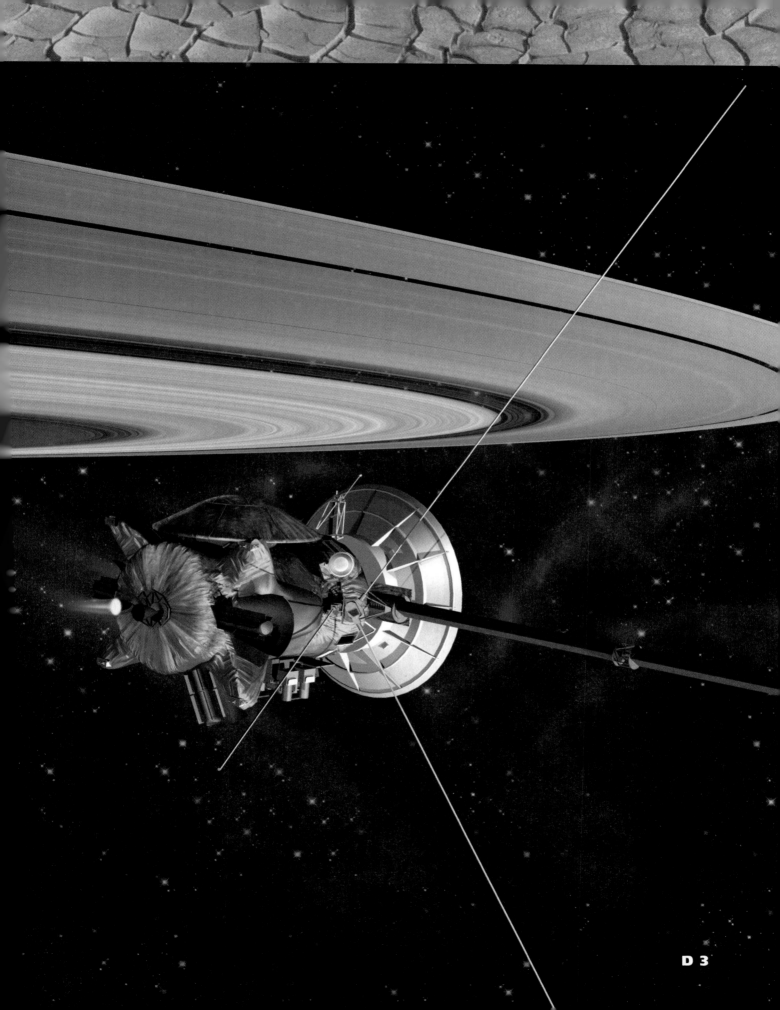

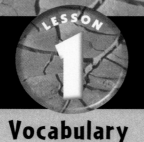
Earth and Its Neighbors

Vocabulary

solar system, D6

planet, D6

gravity, D8

inertia, D8

revolve, D10

constellation, D12

Get Ready

Saturn is not standing still in one spot. It is moving around the Sun in an almost circular path. What holds Saturn, and all the other planets, near the Sun? What keeps each planet on its path?

Inquiry Skill

You use variables when you identify and separate things in an experiment that can be changed or controlled.

Explore Activity

How Are Earth and the Sun Held Together?

Materials

clay
string
scissors
meterstick
goggles

Procedure

BE CAREFUL! Wear goggles. Twirl the model close to the ground.

1. **Make a Model** Cut a 40-cm length of string. Wrap it around a small, round lump of clay in several directions. Tie the ends to make a tight knot. Measure 60 cm of string, and tie it to the string around the ball.

2. **Observe** Spin the ball of clay slowly—just fast enough to keep the string tight and the ball off the ground. Keep the ball close to the ground. Describe the path of the ball.

3. **Experiment** At one point while spinning, let the string go. What happens? Describe the path of the ball of clay. Repeat until you get a clear picture of what happens.

Drawing Conclusions

1. How did your model represent Earth and the Sun? What represented Earth? Where was the Sun located? How did you represent the force between them?

2. **Infer** Explain what happened when you let the string go. Why do you think this happened?

3. **FURTHER INQUIRY** **Use Variables** How would your results change if the mass of the clay were doubled? Tripled? How does the mass affect the pull on the string? Make a prediction. Try it.

Main Idea The solar system consists of nine planets, many moons, and many other bodies orbiting the Sun.

What Is the Solar System?

If you were traveling in a spaceship through space as fast as light, you would be passing stars. Perhaps in time you would approach one star in particular, the star you know as the Sun. If so, you would be approaching your home address, the **solar system**. The solar system is the Sun and the objects that are traveling around it.

Our Sun is an average-size star similar to many other stars in the night sky. It appears so large and bright to us because it is much closer to Earth. The Sun is composed mostly of hydrogen and helium. The formation of helium from hydrogen is what generates light and heat from the Sun.

The objects around the Sun include nine **planets**. Planets are objects that travel around a star in a path. That path is called an *orbit*. The planets are held in orbit around the Sun. The planets do not give off light, as stars do. They reflect light from their star, the Sun.

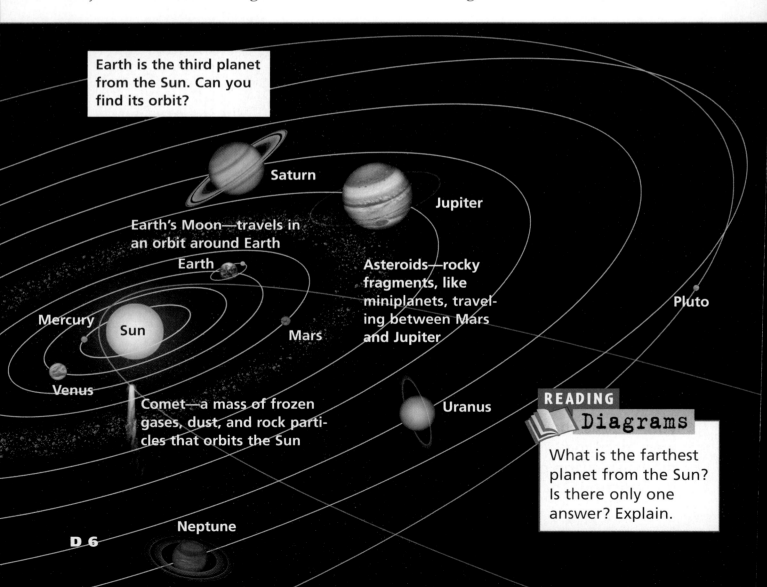

Earth is the third planet from the Sun. Can you find its orbit?

Saturn

Jupiter

Earth's Moon—travels in an orbit around Earth

Earth

Asteroids—rocky fragments, like miniplanets, traveling between Mars and Jupiter

Mercury

Sun

Mars

Pluto

Venus

Comet—a mass of frozen gases, dust, and rock particles that orbits the Sun

Uranus

READING
Diagrams

What is the farthest planet from the Sun? Is there only one answer? Explain.

Neptune

Except for Pluto, the orbit of each planet is almost a circle. Each orbit is slightly oval. What effect does an orbit of this shape have on the distance from a planet to the Sun?

One complete trip of an object in its orbit around the Sun takes one *year*. A year is different from planet to planet. For Earth one year is 365.25 days. The table shows how long a year takes for each planet. The time is given in days as days are timed on Earth.

▷ **What are the parts of the solar system?**

Planet	Average Distance to the Sun (million km)	Year Time for complete orbit around the Sun (in Earth days)
Mercury	57.9	88 days
Venus	108.2	225 days
Earth	149.6	365 days
Mars	227.9	687 days
Jupiter	778.4	4,331 days
Saturn	1,427	10,756 days
Uranus	2,871	30,687 days
Neptune	4,498	60,190 days
Pluto	5,906	90,553 days

QUICK LAB

Orbit Times

FOLDABLES™ Make a Folded Graph using graph paper as shown. (See p. R 41.)

1. **Communicate** Use graph paper to draw a bar graph to compare the revolution times for the planets. Tape the ends of the graph paper together to make an accordian graph. The horizontal axis represents time. Decide how much time each square represents. The vertical axis represents the planets. How many pieces of graph paper will you need?

2. **Interpret Data** What relationship can you find between the length of the year (time) and the planet's location in the solar system?

3. How could you change your graph to show the relationship even better? What might your new graph reveal?

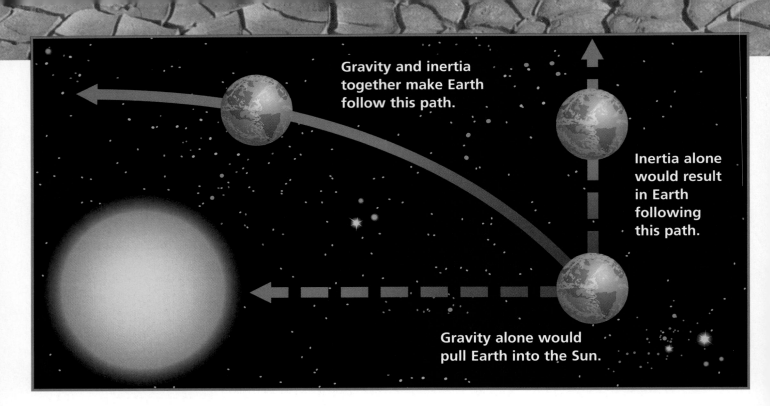

Gravity and inertia together make Earth follow this path.

Inertia alone would result in Earth following this path.

Gravity alone would pull Earth into the Sun.

What Keeps the Planets in Orbit?

The planets orbit the Sun, but what holds them in their paths? What keeps them from flying off into space?

Gravity

Over 300 years ago, Sir Isaac Newton described an invisible force holding the Sun and a planet together. He called the invisible force **gravity**. He described gravity as a property of all matter. It is a force of attraction, or pull, between any object and any other objects around it.

Gravity depends on two measurements—mass and distance. The more matter, or mass, in an object, the greater the pull in the object's direction. The closer two objects are, the stronger the pull of gravity between them.

The Sun has far more mass than any of the planets, so its gravity is much stronger, too. The Sun's gravity holds all of the objects in the solar

system together. Without gravity, everything orbiting the Sun would go flying off into space.

Inertia

Gravity is not the only reason the planets stay in their orbits. Gravity alone would pull the planets into the Sun, because the Sun is so massive. That doesn't happen because the planets are moving. All objects—including the planets—have a property called **inertia** (i·NUR·shuh). Inertia is the tendency of a moving object to keep moving in a straight line.

Without gravity, the planets' inertia would keep them moving in straight lines. Gravity "steers" the planets in their oval paths around the Sun. Together, gravity and inertia keep the planets in their orbits.

READING Sequence of Events
How do gravity and inertia keep a planet in orbit?

What Makes a Day?

The Sun does more than just hold the planets in their orbits in the solar system. It also provides them with light and warmth. The Sun is the reason for day and night. All planets spin, or *rotate*, like huge spinning tops.

READING
Tables

Make a list of planets in order from the shortest day to the longest day.

Length of Day	
Planet	**Day = time for complete spin (in Earth hours or days)**
Mercury	59 days
Venus	243 days
Earth	24 hours
Mars	24 hours 37 minutes
Jupiter	9 hours 56 minutes
Saturn	10 hours 40 minutes
Uranus	17 hours 14 minutes
Neptune	16 hours 7 minutes
Pluto	6.39 days

At any point in time, half of a planet is facing the Sun—it has daylight on that half. At the same time, half is facing away from the Sun—that half is in darkness, night.

As a planet rotates, places that are in darkness eventually turn to face the Sun, and those in daylight eventually turn away. Each planet makes one complete spin in its day. Each planet has its own speed of turning. The length of a day (that is, one complete day-night cycle) is different for each planet.

How much light and warmth a planet receives depends on how far it is from the Sun. Light spreads out as it travels outward from the Sun. An area of one square meter on the planet Mercury receives much more energy than an area of one square meter on a farther planet—such as Pluto. That is why Mercury is much hotter than Pluto.

What is a day?

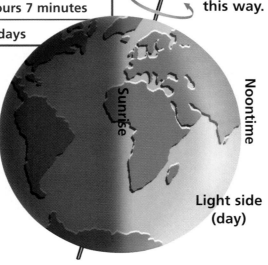

Earth turns this way.

Sunrise

Noontime

Sunlight

Dark side (night)

Light side (day)

What Is the Moon Like?

The Moon is Earth's nearest neighbor—"only" 384,000 km (240,000 mi) away. However, the Moon is not like Earth. There is no water to drink, no air to breathe. There is no weather, either. Without an atmosphere and oceans to trap and circulate heat, temperatures change greatly during a lunar day. With the Sun overhead, temperatures climb to over 123°C (253 °F). During a lunar night, temperatures can drop to -110°C (-170°F) or lower. At the Moon's shaded south pole, temperatures can drop to -233°C (-387°F).

The Moon has a rocky surface. With a telescope you can see its surface features. These include dark-colored regions called *maria* (MAHR·ee·uh). Maria is Latin for "seas." In the past, people thought these areas were oceans. The maria are really dry, flat land surrounded by mountains and ridges. Much of the Moon's surface is covered with huge dents, called craters. Some craters have trails of rock and dust extending out from them. The trails reflect sunlight and look like rays coming out of the crater.

At the same time Earth is **revolving**, or orbiting, around the Sun, the Moon is revolving around Earth. The Moon rotates on its axis once in the time it takes to orbit once around Earth. That means that the same side of the Moon is always facing Earth. However, the Moon seems to change shape, or phase, from day to day.

How Do Moon Phases Happen?

The light of the Moon comes from the Sun's rays striking it. Half of the Moon always faces the Sun, while the other half is in darkness. As the Moon travels around Earth we see different amounts of the lighted half. These are known as the Moon's phases. The phase we see depends on where the Moon is in relation to Earth and the Sun. It takes the Moon 29.5 days to complete all its phases.

▷ How does the Moon differ from Earth?

Earth's nearest neighbor looks nothing much like Earth.

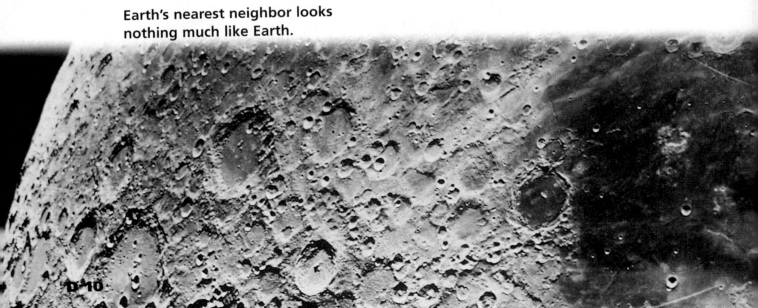

Phases of the Moon

Third Quarter Moon

The Moon is three quarters of the way around Earth. This is sometimes called a half Moon.

Waning Crescent Moon

The left sliver of the Moon is the only part that you can see lighted.

Waning Gibbous Moon

As the Moon continues to move in its orbit, less of the lighted side is visible from Earth.

New Moon

The Moon is between the Sun and Earth.

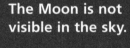

The Moon is not visible in the sky.

Full Moon

Earth is between the Moon and the Sun.

The entire lighted side of the Moon is visible.

Waxing Crescent Moon

As the Moon moves in its orbit, more of the lighted side becomes visible from Earth.

First Quarter Moon

The Moon is a quarter of the way around Earth. This is sometimes called a half Moon.

Waxing Gibbous Moon

The gibbous Moon is almost full.

What Are Constellations?

When you look into the night sky, what else can you see besides the Moon? If the sky is dark enough, you can also see the stars. What are stars? A star is a large, hot ball of gas that is held together by gravity and gives off its own light. Stars look like points of light in the night sky. Unlike the Moon, stars are far outside the solar system.

In the past people looked at the stars and saw them arranged in groups that formed patterns in the sky. These patterns are called **constellations**. To these people the patterns looked like pictures of animals or people.

How can you find a star like Rigel in the night sky? The easiest way is by looking for its constellation. Rigel, for example, is a star in the constellation Orion, the hunter.

The pattern of stars in a constellation always looks the same even though the constellations appear to change position during the night and from season to season. As Earth travels in its orbit

The constellation Orion

around the Sun, its night side faces different directions. You see only the constellations that are in that direction. For example, in the Northern Hemisphere, we see the constellation Orion in the winter months.

▶ **Why do constellations appear to move across the sky?**

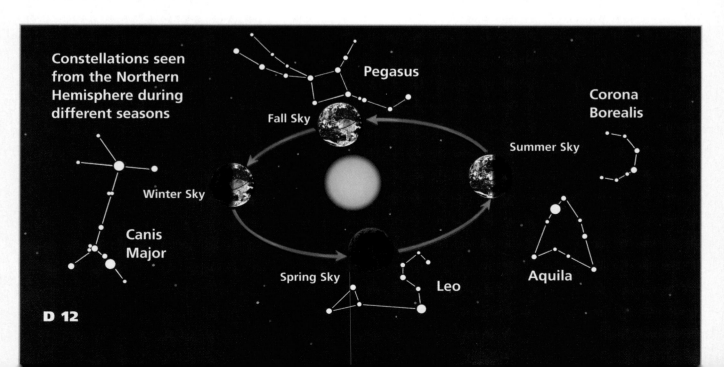

Constellations seen from the Northern Hemisphere during different seasons

Pegasus

Corona Borealis

Fall Sky

Summer Sky

Winter Sky

Canis Major

Spring Sky

Leo

Aquila

L·I·N·K·S

Why It Matters

Earth is teeming with life and movement. The Sun's energy helps produce seasons, day-to-day weather, and climates.

When astronauts first visited the Moon in 1969, they faced a tough problem. How do you survive in such a place? They had to bring all of the things they needed to stay alive all the way from Earth.

Earth is the only member of the solar system that supports life as we know it.

e-Journal Visit our Web site www.science.mmhschool.com to do a research project on the solar system.

Think and Write

1. How would you state your address in space? Explain your answer.

2. How is gravity important for Earth?

3. What keeps the planets in orbit around the Sun? Explain.

4. Why is the Moon unlivable compared with Earth?

5. **Critical Thinking** Would you weigh the same on the Sun as you do on Earth? Explain your answer.

MATH LINK

Estimate sizes. Stars come in different colors and sizes. Rigel is a blue supergiant with a diameter about 100 times larger than the Sun. Red supergiant Betelgeuse has a diameter about 1,000 times larger than the Sun. About how much larger is Betelgeuse than Rigel?

SOCIAL STUDIES LINK

Research the planets. Learn more about Earth's neighbors. Which planets have moons? Rings? Which planets are most likely to support life? Use the Internet or an encyclopedia.

WRITING LINK

Expository Writing How are telescopes used to magnify distant objects in the sky, such as the Moon and the planets? Use the Internet or an encyclopedia for your research. Write an essay about your findings.

TECHNOLOGY LINK

 LOG ON Visit www.science.mmhschool.com for more links.

The Solar System

Get Ready

This is an artist's idea of what a spaceprobe would look like as it passes one of Earth's neighbors. Do you know which planet this is? Even without a telescope you can see several planets during the year. How big is the solar system? How do the distances between planets compare? Construct a model to find out.

Inquiry Skills

You make a model when you make something to represent an object or an event.

Explore Activity

How Do the Distances Between Planets Compare?

Materials

roll of paper towels

markers

tape (optional)

ruler

Procedure

1 **Use Numbers** Study the chart. Distances are in Astronomical Units (A.U.). One A.U. is the distance from Earth to the Sun. How far from the Sun is Mars? Pluto?

2 **Make a Model** Let the width of one paper towel be one A.U. Lay out the length of paper towels you need to show the distance from the Sun to Pluto. Measure and mark the location of each planet.

Planet	Distance (A.U.)
Mercury	0.39
Venus	0.7
Earth	1.0
Mars	1.5
Jupiter	5.2
Saturn	9.5
Uranus	19.2
Neptune	30
Pluto	39.4

Drawing Conclusions

1 **Interpret Data** Describe how the planets are spaced.

2 **Use Numbers** It takes 8 minutes for light to travel from the Sun to Earth. How long does it take for light to travel to Jupiter? To Pluto?

3 **FURTHER INQUIRY** **Make a Model** Your model has all the planets lined up. Actually, the planets are scattered in different places in their orbits. How can you change your model to be more accurate? Make a plan and try it.

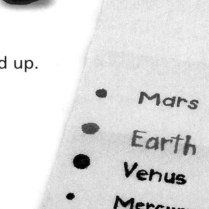

Read to Learn

Main Idea Our solar system consists of four inner planets, five outer planets, moons, and other small bodies.

How Do the Inner Planets Compare?

The planets of our solar system can be divided into two groups. Those closest to the Sun are the **inner planets**. Those beyond the asteroid belt are the **outer planets**.

Small and warm, the inner planets are Mercury, Venus, Earth, and Mars.

The inner planets have solid, rocky crusts. They are much denser than the outer planets. The craters on their surfaces are "scars" left by space debris that constantly bombarded them in their early years. Except for Mercury, they are all geologically active. In this group is the only planet known to support life, Earth. All of these planets are formed from the same materials. As a result, studies of Earth have given us a lot of knowledge about the other inner planets. None of the inner planets have rings. They all have atmospheres. They have few, if any, moons.

Mercury

Mercury is the closest planet to the Sun and orbits the Sun in the shortest time. Mercury rotates three times on its axis for every two revolutions around the Sun. This results in extremely hot temperatures on one side of the planet and extremely cold temperatures on the other side. Mercury has no moons.

Venus

Venus is the hottest planet. Its dense cloud cover holds in the Sun's heat and the heat given off by its volcanoes. Temperatures on Venus reach 482°C (900°F) and surface pressures are high enough to crush spacecraft. Venus also rotates backwards, and a day on Venus is longer than its year. Venus has no moons.

Earth

Earth is the water planet. It is our home. It has the right temperatures and resources for life as we know it to exist. Earth has one Moon.

Mars

The largest volcano in our solar system, Olympus Mons, is found on Mars. Mars has a thin atmosphere, but has strong winds and pink dust storms. There may once have been liquid water on Mars' surface. From the surface of Mars, its two moons, Phobos and Deimos, seem to move in opposite directions. Swift Phobos rises in the west and sets in the east usually twice a Martian day.

▶ **How does Venus compare to Earth?**

Inquiry Skill BUILDER

Making a Model of the Solar System

In this activity you will make a model to compare the sizes of the planets in the solar system. The table "Comparing a Planet's Radius with Earth's" will tell you how the radius of each "model planet" you make would compare to your model of Earth.

Materials

construction paper

white paper

pencil

string 25 cm long

metric ruler

colored markers or colored pencils

tape

Procedure

1 **Use Numbers** Look at the table. How much bigger is Jupiter's radius than Earth's radius? How much smaller is Mars' radius than Earth's?

2 **Measure** Let your model Earth's radius be 1 cm. Using this scale, how big would you need to make the radius of Jupiter? How big would you need to make the radius of Mars?

Comparing a Planet's Radius with Earth's			
Planet	**Radius (in Earth radii)**	**Planet**	**Radius (in Earth radii)**
Mercury	0.38 x Earth	Jupiter	11.2 x Earth
Venus	0.95 x Earth	Saturn	9.5 x Earth
Earth	1 x Earth	Uranus	4.0 x Earth
Mars	0.53 x Earth	Neptune	3.9 x Earth
		Pluto	0.18 x Earth

3 **Make a Model** Draw a model Earth with a 1cm radius. Cut out your model. Repeat this process for each planet.

Drawing Conclusions

1 **Compare** Look at the sizes of your model planets. Which planets are almost the same size?

2 **Compare** The radius for Saturn and its rings is over 28.5 times Earth's radius. How much larger is that than Jupiter's radius?

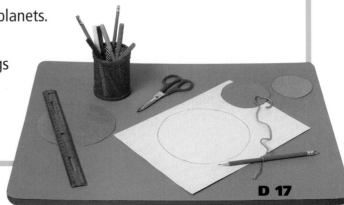

How Do the Outer Planets Compare?

Beyond the asteroid belt lie the outer planets. They are Jupiter, Saturn, Uranus, and Neptune—the gas giants— and tiny, icy Pluto. These planets formed in an area where temperatures were lower. This allowed lighter, less dense materials to clump together and form planets. The cores of the gas giants are dense and rocky. Surrounding the core of each planet are layers of dense liquids. Each gas giant is surrounded by large envelopes of gases. The gas giants also have rings. These range from the breathtaking rings of Saturn to the faint gray rings of Uranus. All of the outer planets have many moons, except for Pluto, which has only one. The period of revolution is much slower among the outer planets. The outer planets take many years to orbit the Sun. However, the gas giants rotate in a period of hours, not days.

Jupiter
The largest planet is the fastest spinner. A "day" on Jupiter is less than 10 hours long. Jupiter has a giant red spot—a storm—that has lasted over 300 years. Lightning bolts and auroras can be seen on Jupiter's night side.

Saturn
Find an ocean big enough and this "Lord of the Rings" would float! Giant Saturn is less dense than water! Saturn has the most visible and beautiful rings of all the planets. Saturn is almost twice as far from the Sun as Jupiter.

Between and Beyond the Planets

Between the orbits of Mars and Jupiter is the **asteroid belt**. Here, many small, rocky objects orbit the Sun. These are the **asteroids**. The largest asteroid, Ceres, is about one-fourth the diameter of Earth's Moon.

Pieces of space rock sometimes fall through Earth's atmosphere. Most of them burn up before they hit the ground. These are the "shooting stars," or **meteors**. Space rocks that reach the ground are called **meteorites**. Meteors can come from asteroids. They can also come from material left behind by **comets** as they orbit the Sun.

Comets are "dirty snowballs"— mixtures of ice, rock, and dust "left over" from the formation of the solar system. Beyond Neptune's orbit, 30 to 100 A.U. from the Sun, is the Kuiper Belt. *Short-period comets*—those that take less than 200 years to orbit the Sun—come from here. Beyond Pluto, about 100,000 A.U. from the Sun, is the Oort cloud. *Long-period comets*—those taking up to 30 million years to orbit the Sun—come from here.

What are comets made of? In January, 2004, the spacecraft *Stardust* flew past Comet Wild 2 and collected material from the comet. It also photographed what may be boulders, high cliffs, and impact craters on the comet's surface

Uranus
Uranus has been called "the planet that was knocked on its side." As a result of its tilt, its poles take turns pointing toward the Sun. Even so, Uranus is hotter at its equator, though scientists don't yet know why. Uranus is about twice as far from the Sun as Saturn. A day on Uranus is $17\frac{1}{4}$ hours long, but it takes 84 Earth-years to orbit the Sun. As springtime comes to Uranus, the planet shows that it has the brightest clouds in the outer solar system.

Neptune
Distant Neptune is almost 4.5 billion km from the Sun. Neptune's year is 165 Earth-years long, but its day is only about 16 hours long. Winds whip around Neptune at almost 1250 miles an hour (2000 km/hr).

Pluto
Tiny Pluto is farthest from the Sun. It is made up of frozen gases with lesser amounts of rocky materials. It is the only planet that has not yet been visited by spacecraft. Little is known about Pluto and its moon, Charon. There has even been some debate among astronomers over whether Pluto should be called a planet.

Are There Other Solar Systems?

Our Sun is only one of billions of stars in our own Milky Way **galaxy**. The Milky Way is only one of billions of star systems in the universe. Are there other Earth-like planets? Might some form of life exist elsewhere in the universe? Scientists are trying to find out.

So far, astronomers have discovered more than 100 giant planets orbiting other stars. These giant planets are more like Jupiter than like Earth. Does that mean there are no Earth-size planets elsewhere? No. It simply means small, Earth-size planets are much harder to detect.

In the next few years, scientists at NASA hope to launch a number of missions to look for planets around other stars. Two missions, in particular, will search for Earth-like planets. The first of those missions is *Kepler*, now scheduled to be launched in 2007. *Kepler* will study 100,000 sun-like stars. It will look for planets orbiting their stars at distances where liquid water could exist.

In 2013, NASA plans to launch the *Terrestrial Planet Finder*—a space telescope that will be able to find small, rocky planets orbiting other stars. The *Terrestrial Planet Finder* would also examine any atmospheres around those planets.

A possible future mission, *Life Finder*, would search such planets for seasonal changes in their atmospheres. It would also search for other changes that might indicate the presence of life.

▷ **Why is it harder to search for Earth-like planets than Jupiter-like planets orbiting other stars?**

Are there other Earth-like planets elsewhere in the galaxy? Astronomers are trying to find out.

Why It Matters

What was the early solar system like? Scientists hope to learn more when *Stardust* returns to Earth with its samples from Comet Wild 2. How likely are there to be Earth-like planets elsewhere in the universe? Scientists may find answers as they study distant solar systems. Might life forms exist on other worlds? Future space missions to Mars and to three of Jupiter's largest moons—which may have oceans below their icy crusts—may give us clues. They may also help us to remember how special our own planet Earth really is.

e-Journal Visit our Web site **www.science.mmhschool.com** to do a research project on space missions.

Think and Write

1. How do the inner planets compare with the outer planets?

2. Name one way Saturn differs from the other gas giants.

3. Name one thing that makes Uranus unusual.

4. INQUIRY SKILL **Make a Model** Model how our solar system might look from another star. (Hint: The Sun's radius is about 100 times Earth's.)

5. **Critical Thinking** Why is it so difficult to design a real-scale model of the solar system?

L·I·N·K·S

MATH LINK

Build a model solar system. The distance from Earth to the Sun (1 A.U.) is about 23,500 times the length of Earth's radius. If you let Earth's radius be one centimeter, about how far away would you have to place your model Pluto from your model Sun?

WRITING LINK

Writing That Compares What do all comets have in common? How do they differ? Compare Comet Hale-Bopp and Halley's Comet. Research both comets. List their similarities and differences in a Venn diagram. Use your Venn diagram to write an essay that compares and contrasts comets.

LITERATURE LINK

Read *2061: Photographing Mars* to learn about a teacher's trip to Mars. Try the activities at the end of the book.

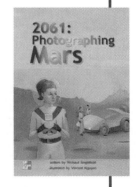

2061: Photographing Mars

TECHNOLOGY LINK

 LOG ON Visit **www.science.mmhschool.com** for more links.

PLANETARY WEATHER

What's the weather like on other planets? Knowing about the atmosphere on other planets tells us more about our entire solar system.

Over the years scientists have learned that Venus's atmosphere is 97 percent carbon dioxide. A greenhouse effect occurs when the layer of carbon dioxide traps the Sun's heat, making Venus's average temperature 460°C (860°F).

Like Earth, Jupiter has storms. The Sun heats our atmosphere which creates conditions that cause storms. But Jupiter receives less of the Sun's heat than Earth. Scientists believe that storms on Jupiter might originate with heat rising from the planet's own hot interior. When it rains on Jupiter it rains liquid helium!

Venus has yellow clouds of sulfuric acid. Precipitation from these clouds is like acid rain on Earth, only worse.

One of Jupiter's storms, the Great Red Spot, is about two times the size of Earth. It began before telescopes were invented.

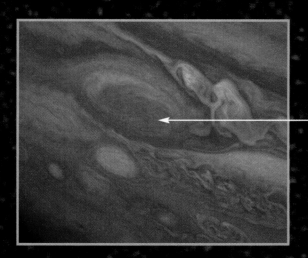

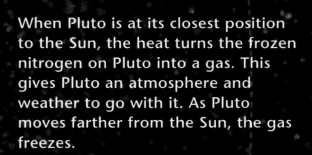

Saturn has three cloud layers—water clouds, ammonia clouds, and ammonium hydrosulfide clouds. Together they form smog!

There is lightning on Venus, Jupiter, and Saturn. Uranus and Neptune are believed to have lightning as well. The lightning is from electrical discharges. Flashes on Jupiter may be 500 kilometers (310 miles) across.

Pluto has the greatest atmospheric changes of all the planets. That's because its orbit is irregular.

When Pluto is at its closest position to the Sun, the heat turns the frozen nitrogen on Pluto into a gas. This gives Pluto an atmosphere and weather to go with it. As Pluto moves farther from the Sun, the gas freezes.

ABOUT IT

1. Why should the atmosphere on Venus be a warning to us on Earth?

2. What forms of weather do we share with other planets?

LOG ON Visit www.science.mmhschool.com to learn more about weather on other planets.

Chapter 9 Review

Vocabulary

Fill each blank with the best word or words from the list

comet, D19
constellation, D12
galaxy, D20
gravity, D8
inner planet, D16
meteor, D19
meteorite, D19
outer planet, D16
planet, D6
solar system, D6

1. The Sun and planets are part of the _____.

2. Earth is a(n) _____ that orbits the Sun.

3. The force of _____ keeps planets from flying off into space away from the Sun.

4. A planet between the Sun and the asteroid belt is called a(n) _____

5. A planet beyond the asteroid belt is known as a(n) _____.

6. Our Milky Way is a star system known as a(n) _____.

7. Stars that seem to form a pattern in the night sky are called a(n) _____.

8. A piece of space rock that burns up in the atmosphere is called a(n) _____.

9. A piece of space rock that survives its fall through the atmosphere and lands on the surface is called a(n) _____.

10. An object that comes from the Oort cloud is a(n) _____.

Test Prep

11. The Moon is unlivable compared with Earth because _____.
   A there is too much water
   B there is too much snow
   C there is too much smog
   D there is no air to breathe

12. The planet Saturn could _____.
   F fit inside Jupiter's Great Red Spot
   G fit in the Atlantic Ocean
   H float if there were an ocean big enough to hold it
   J fit inside the Grand Canyon

13. A year on Mercury is _____.
   A shorter than a year on Venus
   B longer than a year on Jupiter
   C the same as a year on Earth
   D the same as a year on Mars

14. A day on Venus is _____.
   F shorter than a day on Earth
   G shorter than a day on Mars
   H shorter than a day on Jupiter
   J longer than its year

15. Which planets have rings?

A Mars, Jupiter, and Saturn

B Saturn, Pluto, Neptune, and Venus

C Jupiter, Saturn, Neptune, and Venus

D Jupiter, Saturn, Uranus, and Neptune

Concepts and Skills

16. INQUIRY SKILL **Make a Model** Explain how you would model the distances between planets if you were using a football field and put your model Earth on the 2-yard line.

17. Critical Thinking Why is it difficult to find Earth-like planets elsewhere in the galaxy?

18. Reading in Science Explain the sequence of events that would happen if the force that keeps the planets orbiting the Sun did not exist.

19. Scientific Methods Design an experiment to show why Mercury gets much hotter than Pluto.

20. Decision Making What would you need to bring along on a space mission to another planet? Explain your choices.

Did You Ever Wonder?

INQUIRY SKILL **Infer** You want to send a spacecraft to visit each of the giant planets. What do you need to consider in planning your mission?

LOG ON Visit www.science.mmhschool.com to boost your test scores.

Did You Ever Wonder?

What causes frost to form? Frost forms when it is cold enough for water vapor in the air to change from gas to ice crystals on grass and other objects. In warmer weather dew would form instead of frost.

INQUIRY SKILL Experiment Make frost in your classroom! Layer salt and ice in a metal container. Observe the outside of the container.

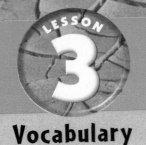

LESSON

3

Atmosphere and Air Temperature

Vocabulary

insolation, D30

atmosphere, D32

troposphere, D32

air pressure, D33

weather, D34

barometer, D34

Get Ready

If it's summer, is it always hot? These animals may find it warmer in summer than in winter. However, it isn't exactly hot here on this beautiful summer day. How can summer be hot in some places and so cold in others?

How does the angle at which the Sun's energy hits Earth affect the warming of Earth?

Inquiry Skill

You experiment when you perform a test to support or disprove a hypothesis.

Explore Activity

Does the Sun's Angle Matter?

Procedure

BE CAREFUL! Do not look into the lamplight.

1. Place a thermometer onto each of the three blocks, as shown. Cover each with black paper. Put the blocks 20 cm from the light bulb, level with its filament (curly wire).

2. **Observe** Measure the starting temperature at each block. Record the temperatures.

3. **Predict** What will happen when the lamp is turned on? Turn the lamp on. Record the temperature at each block every two minutes for ten minutes.

4. **Communicate** Make a line graph showing the change in temperature at each block over time.

5. **Use Variables** Repeat the activity with white paper.

Drawing Conclusions

1. **Communicate** Which block's surface was warmed most by the lamplight? Which block's surface was warmed the least?

2. **Infer** How does the angle at which light hits a surface affect how much the surface is heated? How does the surface color affect how much it is heated?

3. **FURTHER INQUIRY** **Experiment** What other factors might affect how much a surface is warmed by sunlight? How would you test your ideas?

Materials

3 thermometers
triangular blocks
black paper
white paper
centimeter ruler
scissors
tape
150-W clear-bulb lamp
stopwatch
foam bowl
clay

Main Idea The Sun warms Earth's surface, which transmits heat to the air above it.

Does the Sun's Angle Matter?

Where do you think you might find warm temperatures all year long? Where would you find very cold weather? That depends a lot on the angle at which sunlight hits a region. Angles make a difference in how much the Sun warms an area. The areas around the equator are hottest. That's because the Sun's path is high over-head at midday. In those areas the Sun's rays hit Earth at their strongest.

The areas around the North and South Poles are coldest. In those areas the Sun is much lower at midday. The Sun's rays hit Earth's surface at a low angle. The strength of the rays is much weaker at this angle.

The angle at which sunlight strikes Earth's surface is called the angle of **insolation**. *Insolation* is short for *in*coming *solar* radi*ation*. It means the amount of the Sun's energy that reaches Earth at a given place and time.

The diagram shows how sunlight warms Earth in summer and winter. The amount of warming depends on the angle of insolation. The greater the angle, the warmer it gets. The angle of insolation is always smaller near the poles than near the equator. That means while it's freezing cold in one part of the world, it's hot in another.

▷ **How do differing angles of insolation cause differences in warming?**

How Sunlight Warms Earth

The Sun's rays strike the surface at different angles as Earth travels around the Sun.

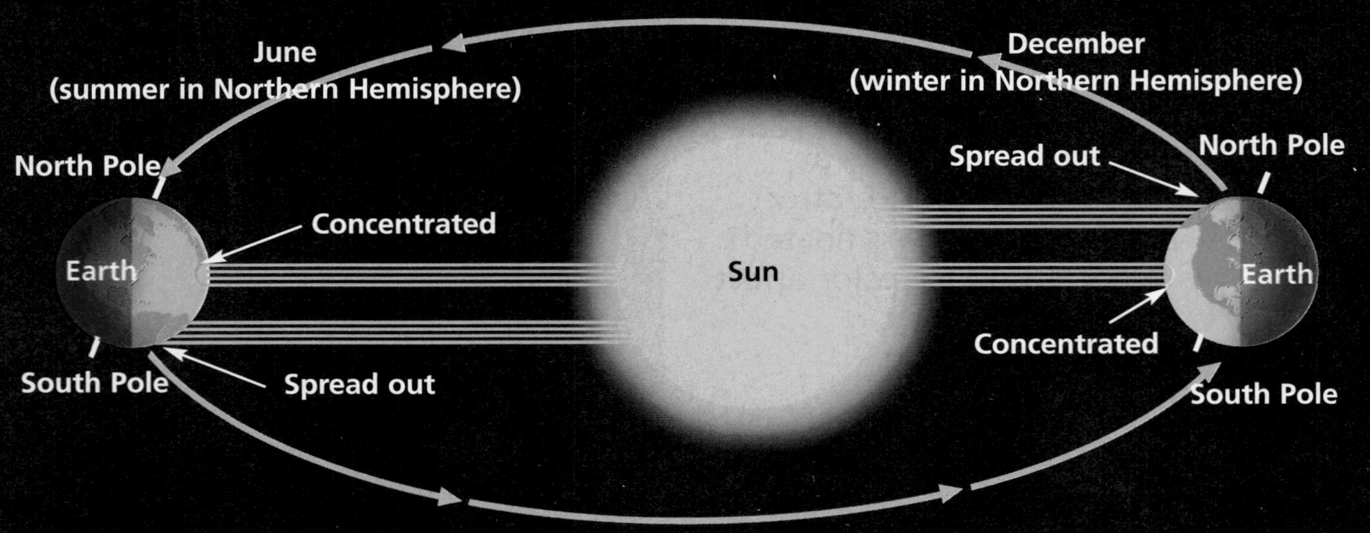

June
(summer in Northern Hemisphere)

North Pole

Concentrated

Earth

South Pole — Spread out

Sun

December
(winter in Northern Hemisphere)

Spread out — North Pole

Earth

Concentrated

South Pole

Angles count! Earth is actually closer to the Sun when it's winter in the Northern Hemisphere.

What Affects Insolation?

In the morning the Sun is close to the horizon. What happens as time goes by? At midday the Sun is high up in the sky, as high as it gets during the day. After midday the Sun is lower and lower in the sky.

How does this affect the angle of insolation? How do we measure it? Look at the shadows cast by objects they strike! The lower the angle of the light rays, the longer the shadows. As you can see in the diagram, the angle of insolation is the same as the angle between the ground and the line from the tip of the shadow to the top of the wall.

▷ **How does the time of day affect the angle of insolation?**

Angle of Insolation

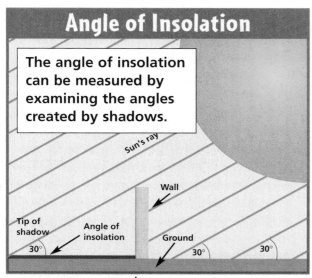

The angle of insolation can be measured by examining the angles created by shadows.

Sun's ray

Wall

Tip of shadow

Angle of insolation

Ground

30°   30°   30°

◄─Shadow of wall─►|

READING
Diagrams

What will happen to the angle as the Sun gets higher in the sky? How will this affect the temperature?

QUICK LAB

Investigating Angles

FOLDABLES Make a Trifold Book. (See p. R 42.)

1. Fold a sheet of graph paper lengthwise in three equal parts. Put a small lump of clay in the middle of each part. Stand a toothpick straight up in each lump of clay.

2. Hold a flashlight directly over the first toothpick. Have a partner trace a line around the circle of light and trace the toothpick's shadow.

3. **Use Variables** Repeat step 2 for the other two toothpicks, changing only the angle of the flashlight.

4. **Measure** Count the number of boxes in each circle. Measure the lengths of the toothpick shadows. Record your results.

5. **Infer** Use the Trifold Book to record how the length of the shadow is related to the angle.

6. **Infer** Record how the number of boxes in the circle is related to the angle.

Why Do You Cool Down As You Go Up?

Did you ever climb a high mountain? As you go higher and higher above sea level, air temperatures drop. The natural drop in air temperature with altitude is about 2°C (3.6°F) for every 305 meters (1,000 ft).

Climbing up a mountain is really a journey up into the **atmosphere**, the air that surrounds Earth. The atmosphere reaches from Earth's surface to the edge of space. What if you could travel to the top part of the atmosphere? The diagram of the atmosphere shows what you would find.

You would find that the temperature does not fall steadily with altitude. It changes abruptly several times. These changes mark the boundaries of four main layers. These layers surround Earth like huge shells.

The layer closest to Earth's surface is the **troposphere** (TROP·uh·sfeer). It's the narrowest layer—between 8 and 18 kilometers (5–11 miles) thick—but it contains most of the air in the atmosphere. All life on Earth exists here. In this layer all moisture is found and all clouds, rain, snow, and thunderstorms form. Above this layer the air gradually thins out to the near-emptiness of space, with no exact upper boundary.

READING
Diagrams

Describe how the temperature changes in each layer of the atmosphere.

▷ **What is the relationship between altitude and temperature?**

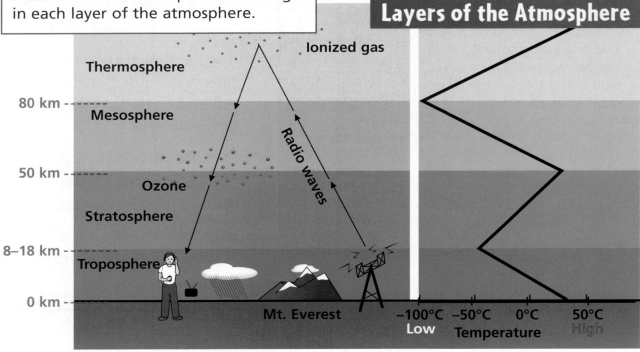

Most weather occurs in the troposphere. The ozone layer in the stratosphere helps shield us from the Sun's ultraviolet light. *Auroras* (the northern and southern lights) may form in the *ionized* (electrically charged) gas in the thermosphere.

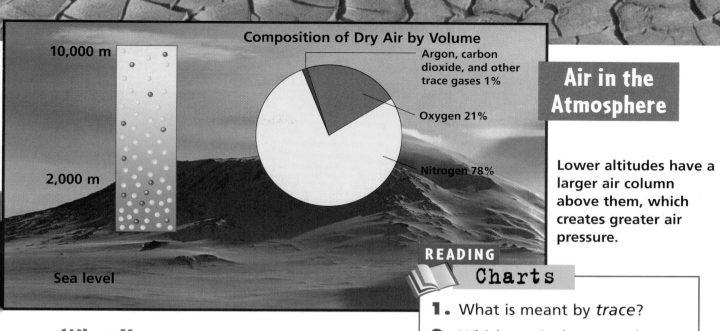

Composition of Dry Air by Volume

10,000 m

2,000 m

Sea level

Argon, carbon dioxide, and other trace gases 1%

Oxygen 21%

Nitrogen 78%

Air in the Atmosphere

Lower altitudes have a larger air column above them, which creates greater air pressure.

READING Charts

1. What is meant by *trace*?

2. Which gas is the most abundant in the atmosphere?

What Happens to the Air Pressure?

As you go higher in altitude, **air pressure** decreases steadily. Air pressure is the force put on a given area by the weight of the air above it. Air is a mixture of gases. It is made up mostly of *molecules* of nitrogen and oxygen. Molecules are the smallest pieces that a substance can be broken into without changing what the substance is.

The molecules have mass. They are attracted to Earth by gravity, so they have weight.

Normal air pressure is greatest at sea level. There the column of air extending above the surface to the top of the atmosphere is tallest. Sea level air pressure is about 1.04 kilograms per square centimeter (14.7 pounds per square inch). As you go higher in altitude, the height of the air column above you becomes shorter. Therefore the weight of that column—or air pressure—becomes less.

In the lower atmosphere, the composition of air varies very little. Up to an altitude of about 100 km (62 mi), air consists of a mixture of gases, water vapor, and dust particles. Nitrogen and oxygen make up 99 percent of the gases in dry air.

Water vapor is a gas. It should not be confused with clouds or fog, which are made of liquid or solid water. The amount of water vapor in air varies from $\frac{1}{10,000}$ of air in dry arctic regions to $\frac{1}{25}$ of air in moist equatorial regions.

The dust in air is made of particles so tiny that 100,000 lined up would only form a row 1 cm (0.4 in.) long. Some of it comes from Earth's surface, from fires and volcanic eruptions, or from tiny crystals of salt.

▷ **How does air pressure change with altitude?**

What Is Weather?

When you say, "It sure is hot today!" the *it* is the air. You really mean that the air around you is hot. The same is true if you say, "It is windy, " or "It is cloudy," or give any other similar description of the **weather**. The weather is simply what the lower atmosphere, or troposphere, is like at any given place and time.

The conditions that make up weather are the characteristics that change. They are air temperature, air pressure, amount of moisture in the air, wind, clouds, and rain or snow.

Measuring Temperature

You can measure temperature with a thermometer. Thermometers can use two different temperature scales. The Celsius scale is marked with the letter *C*. The Fahrenheit scale is shown by the letter *F*.

Measuring Air Pressure

Air pressure is measured with a **barometer** (buh·ROM·i·tuhr). Two common types of barometers are the mercury barometer and the aneroid barometer.

Mercury barometers use a mercury-filled glass tube with one closed end. The open end is submerged in liquid mercury. Air pressure on the mercury pushes it up into the tube. When the weight of the mercury column equals the air pressure, the mercury stops rising.

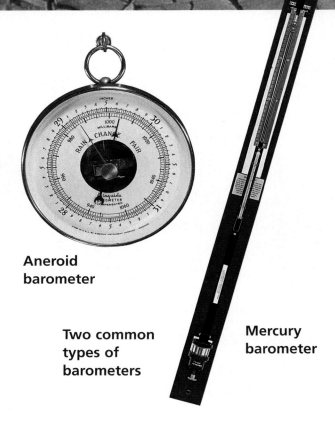

Aneroid barometer

Two common types of barometers

Mercury barometer

An *aneroid* (AN·uh·royd) barometer is an accordion-like metal can with most of the air removed. Inside, a spring balances the outside air pressure. When outside air pressure increases, the can squeezes the spring. When air pressure decreases, the spring pushes outward. A needle inside indicates changes in pressure.

You can monitor and record weather conditions for your own weather station. Measure and record air temperature several times a day. Record daily air pressure by using a barometer or by getting air pressure readings from weather reports.

READING Main Idea

What conditions make up weather?

Why It Matters

Have you ever heard a day called a "scorcher"? That means a really hot day. On really hot days, your body can lose a lot of moisture. Your body gives off sweat gradually most of the time. On a hot day, your body tends to give off more and more. That's why it's important to have plenty of drinking water handy on a hot day.

On really cold days, many people have other problems—such as frostbite. You have to cover your face, ears, and hands to avoid contact with air at extremely low temperatures.

 e-Journal Visit our Web site **www.science.mmhschool.com** to do a research project on the atmosphere.

Think and Write

1. How do temperatures on Earth depend on angles?

2. List factors that affect temperatures of places on Earth.

3. What is air pressure? How does it change in the atmosphere?

4. What is the troposphere? What happens there?

5. **Critical Thinking** Is the weather one or more than just one thing? Defend your answer.

L·I·N·K·S

MATH LINK

Solve this problem. The sunniest place on Earth is in the eastern Sahara Desert, where sunlight shines an average of 4,300 hours per year. Calculate the percentage of possible sunlight hours a year this number represents. (Assume 12 hours of daylight per day.)

WRITING LINK

Writing a Poem Write a poem about how the weather affects your life. Use words, such as *splash*, that imitate the sound of the weather.

SOCIAL STUDIES LINK

Research the history of the thermometer. The maximum-and-minimum thermometer was invented in 1780 by English scientist James Six. A column of mercury moves up and down a U-shaped tube. An index moves with it, recording the highest and lowest temperatures. Research the history of the thermometer, and write a report for the class.

TECHNOLOGY LINK

LOG ON Visit **www.science.mmhschool.com** for more links.

Water Vapor and Humidity

Vocabulary

water vapor, D38

humidity, D38

evaporation, D38

condensation, D39

relative humidity, D39

Get Ready

What if you were walking on this bridge? What would you see and feel all around you? It's fog. What is fog made of? Here's a hint. What if you put a cold glass of lemonade outside on a table on a hot, humid day? What would you see and feel on the outside of the glass?

What is a humid day like? Where is the moisture on a humid day?

Inquiry Skill

You use variables when you identify and separate things in an experiment that can be changed or controlled.

Explore Activity

Where Does the Puddle Come From?

Materials

plastic cups

ice

paper towels

food coloring

thermometer

goggles

Procedure: Design Your Own

BE CAREFUL! Wear goggles.

1 Form a Hypothesis Write down your idea about why a puddle forms around a frosty drink. Where do you think the puddle came from?

2 Experiment Describe what you would do to test your idea. How would your test support or reject your idea?

3 Communicate Draw a diagram showing how you would use the materials. Keep a record of your observations.

Drawing Conclusions

1 Communicate Describe the results of your investigation.

2 Communicate What evidence did you gather? Explain what happened.

3 Infer How does this evidence support or reject your explanation?

4 FURTHER INQUIRY Use Variables Do you get the same results on a cool day as on a warm day? Do you get the same results on a humid day as on a dry day? Investigate to test your hypothesis.

Read to Learn

Main Idea Water on Earth's surface and in the atmosphere changes form and affects the weather.

Where Does Water Vapor Come From?

Put a frosty glass of lemonade on a table on a hot day. What happens? A puddle forms on the table. Where does the puddle come from? The water level in the glass does not drop as the puddle forms. The water in the puddle isn't lemonade.

The water in the puddle comes from the air around the glass. When the warm air touches the cold glass, the air cools. Droplets of water form, run down the side of the glass, and make a puddle on the table.

The water in the air is **water vapor**. Water vapor is water in the form of a

gas. Water vapor is invisible, colorless, odorless, and tasteless. The amount of water vapor in the air is called **humidity**. Do not confuse humidity with droplets of liquid water you see in rain, fog, or clouds.

How does water vapor get into the air in the first place? More than two-thirds of planet Earth is covered with liquid water—oceans, rivers, and lakes. There is also water in the ground and in plants. To get into the air, this liquid water must be changed into water vapor.

The changing of a liquid into a gas is called **evaporation**. This takes lots of energy. The main energy source for Earth is the Sun. Each day the Sun turns trillions of tons of ocean water into water vapor.

Water molecules absorb the Sun's energy and speed up. "Speedy" water molecules near the surface of the liquid "escape" or evaporate into the atmos-

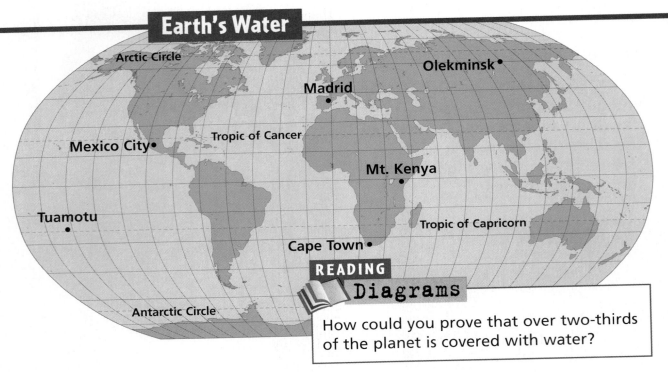

Earth's Water

Arctic Circle

Olekminsk•

Madrid
•

Mexico City•

Tropic of Cancer

Mt. Kenya
•

Tuamotu
•

Tropic of Capricorn

Cape Town •

READING
Diagrams

Antarctic Circle

How could you prove that over two-thirds of the planet is covered with water?

phere as water vapor. Some hit other molecules and return to the liquid. When air is cooled, molecules in the air slow down. The molecules of water vapor in the air also slow down. If they slow enough, water vapor molecules change to molecules of liquid water that collide and stick together to form droplets on cool surfaces. **Condensation** is the changing of a gas into a liquid. You see condensation on shower doors, on cold drink glasses, and as dew on grass in the early morning.

Plants' roots absorb water that has seeped into the ground. Plants transport the liquid water through their roots and stems to their leaves. The leaves then give off water in the process called transpiration. This is the second-largest source of water vapor in the atmosphere.

Two factors determine the amount of humidity in the air. First, there has to be water available to evaporate. Second, the warmer the temperature, the faster the water evaporates. This means that if water is available, warm air will take on more water vapor than cold air.

Relative humidity is a comparison between how much water vapor is in the air and how much the air could hold—at a given temperature.

Relative humidity can affect how a person feels. The higher the relative humidity, the less water can evaporate into the air. The less water, such as sweat, can evaporate from our skin, the warmer and "stickier" we feel.

QUICK LAB

Transpiration

FOLDABLES™ Make a Two-Column Table. (See p. R 41.) Label as shown.

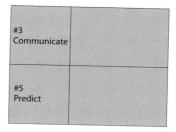

#3 Communicate	
#5 Predict	

1. Place a clear-plastic bag completely over a houseplant. Tie the bag tightly around the base of the stem. Do not put the soil-filled pot in the bag.

2. **Observe** Place the plant in a sunny location. Observe it several times a day. When you are done, remove the plastic bag from the plant.

3. **Communicate** Use the table to describe what you see inside the bag. Explain what happened.

4. **Draw Conclusions** *Transpiration* sounds like *perspiration*–sweating. How might the two processes be alike?

5. **Predict** How would your results vary if you put the plant in the shade?

READING Main Idea

How does water get into the air?

What Happens When Warm, Moist Air Cools?

How can warm, moist air cool off? In the lower atmosphere, the air gets colder with increasing altitude.

- Air can cool by being pushed upward over mountains by winds.

- Heating the air also causes it to rise. When the Sun heats the ground, air above the ground warms and rises. As it rises, it expands and cools.

- Air can also be pushed upward when cooler air and warmer air meet. When the two meet, they don't mix. The lighter, warm air is pushed up over the heavier, cold air. As a result, the warm air, pushed higher into the atmosphere, cools.

In each case the end result is the same. As the air rises and cools, the water vapor in it condenses into tiny water droplets, forming clouds.

If the temperature is below the freezing point of water, its water vapor will form a cloud of tiny ice crystals.

In order for water vapor to condense, it must have a surface on which the liquid droplet or ice crystal will form. This surface is provided by tiny dust particles in the air. You will learn more about clouds in the next lesson.

▷ **How can warm air rise and cool?**

How Clouds Form

① Warm air — Cloud forms

② Cloud forms — Warm air

③ Cloud forms — Warm air — Cool air

READING Diagrams

1. What can cause air to rise?

2. What happens to the air temperature as air rises?

Why It Matters

Have you ever had sweat trickle down your face on a hot day? People sweat every day. Sweating is a way our bodies release wastes. We don't always feel the sweat because we sweat gradually, and it evaporates.

As sweat evaporates, the water droplets absorb heat from the skin's surface, cooling it. In this way your body controls surface temperature.

On very hot days and when you are physically active, you may sweat a lot. The sweat builds up, does not evaporate fast, and collects. On a high-humidity day, you feel even "stickier." On a low-humidity day, the sweat evaporates more quickly.

e-Journal Visit our Web site www.science.mmhschool.com to do a research project on humidity.

Think and Write

1. Where does water vapor in the air come from? What process produces it?

2. How is relative humidity different from humidity?

3. What causes water vapor to change into droplets of liquid water?

4. How does water vapor get cooled in the atmosphere?

5. **Critical Thinking** Would you say that the Sun is a cause of clouds? Defend your answer.

WRITING LINK

Personal Narrative Why are you less comfortable in higher relative humidity? Write about a day in your life when higher relative humidity affected you.

MATH LINK

Find the heat index. Use an almanac to find a heat index prepared by the weather service. This chart tells how warm a person feels at a particular temperature and humidity level. Using the chart, find the heat index for each of the days in the table below. Then use newspaper weather reports for one week last summer. Find the heat index for each of those days.

	Mon	Tues	Wed	Thurs	Fri
High temp.	25°C	35°C	30°C	35°C	25°C
Relative humidity	90%	97%	89%	48%	45%

ART LINK

Make a poster. Very hot, humid weather can be dangerous. Make a poster warning about the dangers of very hot, humid weather. Include a list of safety tips.

TECHNOLOGY LINK

LOG ON Visit www.science.mmhschool.com for more links.

Clouds and Precipitation

Get Ready

How can you predict the weather without using the instruments weather forecasters use? Look at the sky. There are clues up there. They're called clouds. Different kinds of clouds bring different kinds of weather. What is a cloud? What makes a cloud form? What do evaporation and condensation have to do with it?

Inquiry Skill

You infer when you form an idea from facts or observations.

Explore Activity

How Do Clouds Form?

Materials

hot tap water

2 identical clear containers

mug

3 ice cubes

Procedure

BE CAREFUL! Be careful handling the hot water.

1. Chill container 1 by putting it in a refrigerator or on ice for about ten minutes.

2. Fill a mug with hot water.

3. **Make a Model** Fill container 2 with the hot water. Place empty cold container 1 upside down on top of container 2 with the water. Fit the mouths together carefully. Place the ice cubes on top of container 1.

4. **Observe** Record your observations.

Drawing Conclusions

1. **Communicate** What did you observe?

2. **Communicate** Where did this take place?

3. **Infer** Where did the water come from? Explain what made it happen.

4. **FURTHER INQUIRY** **Infer** Do clouds form better in dry or moist air? Conduct an experiment to test your inference. What materials will you need? What will you do?

Main Idea Water vapor and ice form clouds that produce precipitation.

How Do Clouds Form?

What has to happen for a cloud to form? Clouds are made up of tiny water droplets or ice crystals. The air is filled with water vapor. When the air is cooled, the water vapor condenses. That is, the water molecules clump together around dust and other particles in the air. They form droplets of water.

Clouds look different depending on what they are made of. Water-droplet clouds tend to have sharp, well-defined edges. If the cloud is very thick, it may look gray, or even black. That's because sunlight is unable to pass through. Ice-crystal clouds tend to have fuzzy, less distinct edges. They also look whiter.

All clouds form in the troposphere. There are three basic cloud forms. **Stratus clouds** form in blanketlike layers. **Cumulus clouds** are puffy clouds that appear to rise up from a flat bottom. **Cirrus clouds** form at very high altitudes out of ice crystals and have a wispy, featherlike shape. If rain or snow falls from a cloud, the term *nimbo* or *nimbus*—for "rain"—is added to the cloud's name.

Clouds are further grouped into families by height and form. There are low clouds, middle clouds, high clouds, and clouds that develop upward— clouds of vertical development. Cumulonimbus clouds develop upward. These clouds bring thunderstorms.

Stratus clouds

Cumulus clouds

Cirrus clouds

They can start as low clouds and reach up to the highest clouds. If moist air at ground level cools, a cloud can form right there. A cloud at ground level is called **fog**.

▷ **What are three basic cloud forms?**

Types of Clouds

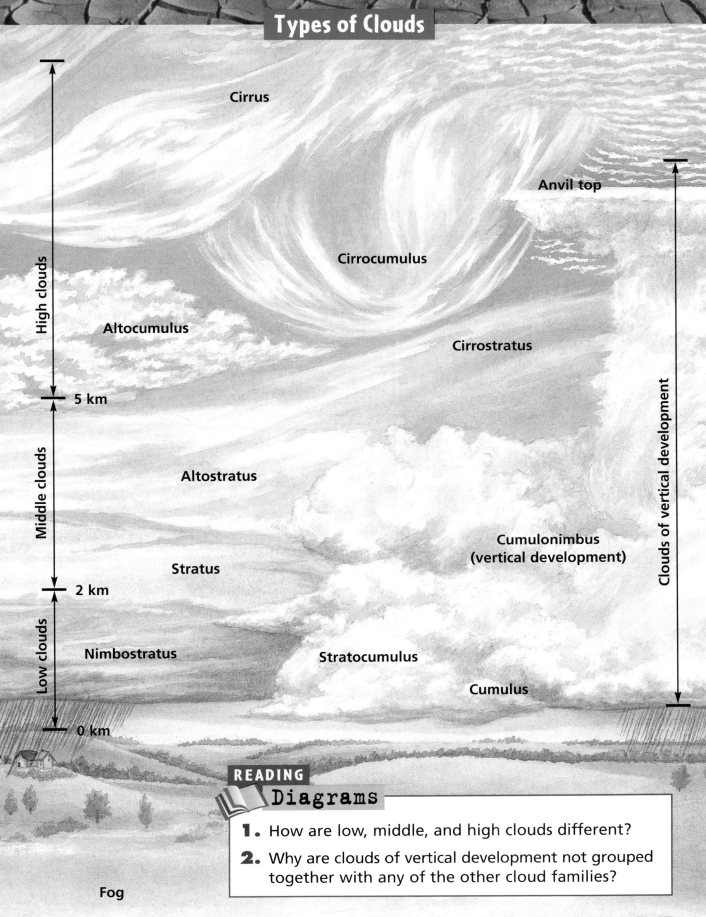

Cirrus

Anvil top

Cirrocumulus

High clouds

Altocumulus

Cirrostratus

5 km

Middle clouds

Altostratus

Clouds of vertical development

Cumulonimbus (vertical development)

Stratus

2 km

Low clouds

Nimbostratus

Stratocumulus

Cumulus

0 km

Fog

READING
Diagrams

1. How are low, middle, and high clouds different?

2. Why are clouds of vertical development not grouped together with any of the other cloud families?

What Is Precipitation?

How do rain and snow form and fall? **Precipitation** is any form of water particles that falls from the atmosphere and reaches the ground. Precipitation can be liquid (rain) or solid (such as snow).

Clouds are made up of tiny water droplets or ice crystals—only about $\frac{1}{50}$ of a millimeter across. These tiny particles are so light that they remain "hanging" in the air. This is why many clouds do not form precipitation.

Precipitation occurs when cloud droplets or ice crystals join together and become heavy enough to fall. They clump around particles of dust in the air. Each particle is like a *nucleus* that the water molecules condense around. The chart shows the different types of precipitation and how they form.

▷ **When does precipitation occur?**

READING Diagrams

1. Classify the types of precipitation into two groups—solids and liquids.

2. Which types of precipitation form in similar ways?

Types of Precipitation

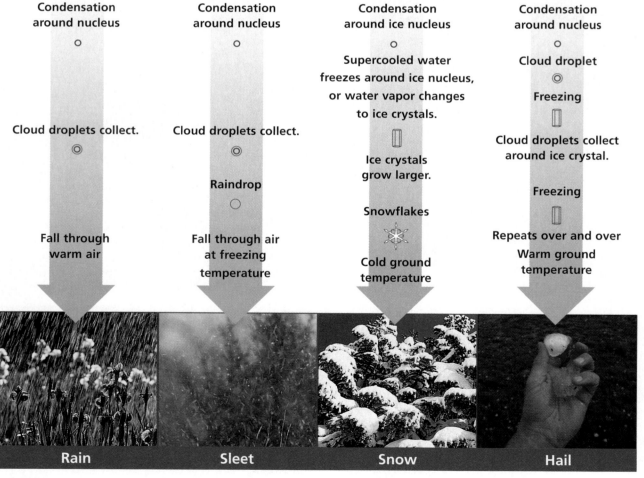

Condensation around nucleus
○
Cloud droplets collect.
◎
Fall through warm air
Rain

Condensation around nucleus
○
Cloud droplets collect.
◎
Raindrop
○
Fall through air at freezing temperature
Sleet

Condensation around ice nucleus
○
Supercooled water freezes around ice nucleus, or water vapor changes to ice crystals.
▯
Ice crystals grow larger.
Snowflakes
✳
Cold ground temperature
Snow

Condensation around nucleus
○
Cloud droplet
◎
Freezing
▯
Cloud droplets collect around ice crystal.
Freezing
▯
Repeats over and over
Warm ground temperature
Hail

Are Cloud Type and Precipitation Related?

Do certain kinds of clouds give certain kinds of precipitation? Yes.

- In tall clouds there is more chance for droplets to run into one another and combine, making larger raindrops.

- Precipitation from large cumulus clouds is often heavy rain or snow showers that don't last too long.

- Precipitation from stratus clouds is usually long lasting, with smaller drops of rain or snowflakes.

- Clouds with great vertical development hold a lot of water. These clouds are very *turbulent*, or violent. Their tops often reach heights where it is below freezing. They often produce great downpours. They also sometimes produce *hail*. Hail is pellets or lumps of ice.

These clouds have updrafts—strong winds that move up inside. Hail forms when updrafts in these huge clouds hurl ice pellets upward again and again. As the pellets fall, they become coated with water. As they rise, the water freezes into an icy outer shell. This process usually happens over and over, adding more and more layers to the hailstones. The more violent the updrafts, the bigger the hailstones can get before they fall to the ground.

READING Main Idea

What kind of cloud can produce hail? Why?

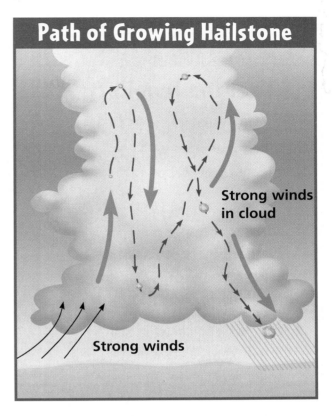

Path of Growing Hailstone

Strong winds in cloud

Strong winds

Hailstones form in layers and can sometimes grow very large. Hailstorms can be very dangerous.

QUICK LAB

Feel the Humidity

FOLDABLES Make an Eight-Row Chart. (See p. R 44.) Label as shown.

Time		Humid Day	Dry Day
1 min.	30 s		
	30 s		
2 min.	30 s		
	30 s		
3 min.	30 s		
	30 s		
#5 Infer			

1. **Observe** Use a thermometer to determine the air temperature. Use the chart to record the air temperature.

2. Put the thermometer in cold water. Slowly add warm water until the water temperature matches the air temperature.

3. Wrap a 5-cm-square piece of old cotton cloth around the bulb of the thermometer. Gently hold it with a rubber band. Dampen the cloth in the water.

4. **Observe** Gently wave the thermometer in the air. Note the temperatures every 30 seconds for 3 minutes. Record them on your chart.

5. **Infer** What happened to the temperature of the wet cloth? How does the cloth feel? Explain on the bottom of your chart.

6. **Infer** If you try this experiment on a day that is humid and on a day that is dry will you get the same results?

How Do You Record How Cloudy It Is?

As you observe the weather each day, you might wish to record the types of clouds you see in the sky. You can use the charts in this lesson to indicate the cloud family and the types of clouds.

Try to estimate the cloud cover— that is, the amount of the sky covered by clouds. Use the terms *clear, scattered clouds, partly cloudy, mostly cloudy,* or *overcast* to describe cloud cover.

One way to record cloud cover is to make a weather station model. Start by drawing a circle for each day. An empty circle means "clear skies." A fully shaded circle means "completely overcast." Portions of a circle are shaded to show different amounts of cloud cover.

Precipitation is measured with a rain gauge. You can make a simple rain gauge from an empty coffee can. Place it outside, open end up, away from buildings or trees. When the precipitation stops, measure its depth in the can. Keep track of the type of precipitation and how much falls.

> **What are the terms used to record cloud cover?**

○	Clear
●	Overcast
◔	Scattered clouds
◑	Partly cloudy
◕	Mostly cloudy

Symbols are used to show cloud cover on a weather station model.

Why It Matters

If you ever had a baseball game rained out, you know how rain can ruin your day.

Rain may ruin your plans for a day, and flooding can sometimes cause disasters. However, rain is vital for life on Earth. Rain helps crops grow. Rain helps build the amount of water in wells and water-collecting areas, such as reservoirs. If you ever had a drought in your area, a time when there is little or no precipitation, you know how scarce water can be.

e-Journal Visit our Web site **www.science.mmhschool.com** to do a research project on clouds.

Think and Write

1. How do clouds form?

2. What are some different types of precipitation? Why are there different types?

3. Explain the difference between the way hail forms and the way sleet forms.

4. How can you measure and describe the amount of precipitation and cloud cover on a given day?

5. **Critical Thinking** "Sun showers" are sudden rainfalls on a sunny day. How can a sun shower happen?

L·I·N·K·S

LITERATURE LINK

Read *The Great Johnstown Flood,* the story of the storm that destroyed a town. When you finish reading, think about how you would prepare for a flood. Try the activities at the end of the book.

The Great Johnstown Flood
by Lisa Norby

MATH LINK

Calculate accuracy. Observe clouds in your area each day for a week. Predict weather based on precipitation those clouds are likely to produce. Record how accurate your predictions are. Then, calculate your accuracy in percent.

WRITING LINK

Writing a Story The Inuit have more than 20 different words for snow. Why do you think this is so? Write a "how" or "why" story about why the Inuit have so many words for snow.

TECHNOLOGY LINK

Science Newsroom CD-ROM Choose *On the Vapor Trail* to learn more about how warm, moist air reacts when it cools.

LOG ON Visit **www.science.mmhschool.com** for more links.

Flood: Good News or Bad?

Can you imagine a flood being good news? It was to many ancient Egyptians living near the Nile River. They looked forward to its annual summer flood. Land that was flooded was better for crops!

No one knew for sure why the flood came. Some people believed that great rains fell near the source of the Nile to start the flood. Much of the water actually comes from rains that fall in the mountains of Ethiopia.

Ethiopia has many mountains over 4,000 meters (13,000 feet) tall. In June the monsoons blow from the South Atlantic over the rain forests of Africa. When the winds reach the mountains of Ethiopia, giant rain clouds let loose their water in great thunderstorms. Rain-filled mountain streams join to form a great river. The river carries the water to the Nile. By July the water reaches Egypt and produces the flood.

Summer winds

MEDITERRANEAN SEA

EGYPT

SAUDI ARABIA

NILE RIVER

RED SEA

SUDAN

ETHIOPIA

and Society

Aswan Dam, Egypt

Today the flood waters are stopped soon after they reach Egypt. A high dam holds back the water to form a great lake. The good news is that buildings on the shore are no longer swept away. Farmers no longer depend on floods to plant one crop each year. Now they have water to plant during summer and winter.

Stopping the flood has changed the environment, and that's bad news. The flood kept the fields fertile; but now farmers must use fertilizer. The Mediterranean Sea was nourished by mud from the Nile. Now fish that were common are gone, and a serious disease is spread by snails thriving in the Nile's slow waters.

What Did I Learn?

1. Where did the Nile flooding start?

A in the Red Sea
B in the Mediterranean Sea
C in the mountains of Ethiopia
D in Saudi Arabia

2. Stopping the Nile flooding

F kept the fields fertile.
G increased the fish population.
H killed off the snails.
J changed the environment.

LOG ON Visit **www.science.mmhschool.com** to learn more about floods.

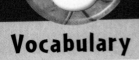

LESSON
6

Air Pressure and Wind

Vocabulary

wind, D55

convection cell, D55

sea breeze, D56

land breeze, D56

Coriolis effect, D57

isobar, D59

Get Ready

What makes the air move? What causes wind? Winds make these kites fly. Some winds move so fast and powerfully, they can knock down trees or even lift trucks into the air. Some winds can be so gentle, they hardly ruffle your hair. Air moves from one place to another because of differences in air pressure. What causes these differences?

Inquiry Skill

You use variables when you identify and separate things in an experiment that can be changed or controlled.

Explore Activity

What Can Change Air Pressure?

Materials

plastic jar with hole in bottom

plastic sandwich bag

rubber band

masking tape

Procedure

1 **Make a Model** Set up a bag-and-jar system as shown. Make sure the masking tape covers the hole in the jar. Have a partner place both hands on the jar and hold it firmly. Reach in and slowly pull up on the bottom of the bag. Describe what happens.

2 **Experiment** Pull the small piece of tape off the hole in the bottom of the jar. Repeat step 1. Push in on the bag. Record your results.

3 **Observe** Place some small bits of paper on the table. Hold the jar close to the table. Point the hole toward the bits of paper. Pull up on the bag, and observe and record what happens.

4 **Experiment** Do just the opposite. Push the bag back into the jar. What happened?

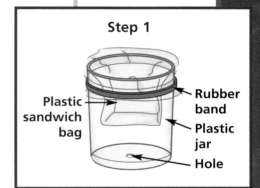

Step 1

Plastic sandwich bag

Rubber band

Plastic jar

Hole

Drawing Conclusions

1 **Observe** What differences did you observe with the hole taped and with the tape removed?

2 **Infer** Explain what happened each time you pushed the bag back into the jar. How does this model show air pressure changes?

3 FURTHER INQUIRY **Use Variables** What happens to the amount of space air takes up if it is warmed? Use the model to test your hypothesis.

Main Idea Differences in air pressure on Earth's surface cause wind.

How Can Air Pressure Change?

Many factors affect the pressure.

Volume

Pulling up on the bag in the diagram below increases the volume inside the bag-jar system. The amount of air inside stays the same. The air inside the jar spreads out into the larger volume. The air pressure inside the bag-jar becomes less. The outside air pushes in harder than the inside air pushes out. That extra force pushing in is what you pull against as you pull up on the bag.

Height Above Earth's Surface

Air pressure depends on the weight of its molecules pressing down on a given area. Molecules are closer together, or more dense, at sea level than high in the atmosphere. Denser air weighs more than an equal volume of less dense air and pushes down harder. That is why air pressure is higher at sea level than high in the atmosphere.

Temperature

Air pressure also depends on temperature. When air is heated, its molecules speed up and spread out into a larger space. The same volume of air weighs less, and the pressure decreases.

Amount of Water Vapor

Air is a mixture of nitrogen, oxygen, and other gases. Adding water vapor to air also affects air pressure. Water vapor molecules weigh less than oxygen or nitrogen molecules. Moist air exerts less pressure than dry air.

READING Diagrams

Explain what happens to the air pressure inside the jar as you push down on the bag.

> How would an increase in temperature affect air pressure?

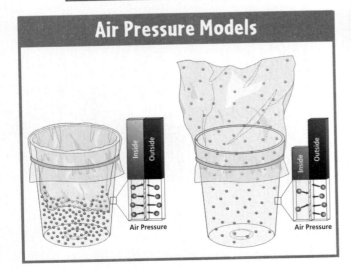

Air Pressure Models

Inside Outside Air Pressure

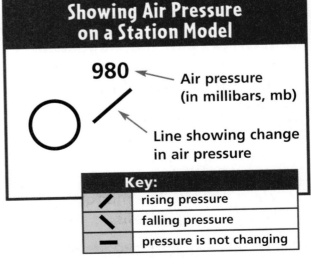

Showing Air Pressure on a Station Model

980 — Air pressure (in millibars, mb)

Line showing change in air pressure

Key:	
⟋	rising pressure
⟍	falling pressure
—	pressure is not changing

Why Do Winds Blow?

Think of what happens if you put a blob of soft clay on a table and push down on it, using a flat hand. The clay squishes out from under your fingers, where the pressure is high. It moves to the spaces between your fingers, where the pressure is lower.

Air acts in a similar way. Denser air exerts a higher pressure than less dense air. Like the clay, denser air flows toward less dense air. This flow of air is wind. Air that moves horizontally is called **wind**. Air that rises is an *updraft*. Air that sinks is a *downdraft*.

Convection Cells

How can air become more or less dense? As the Sun's rays hit an area, they transfer energy to the air. The air heats up. Because it is warmer, the heated air is less dense. Then, just like a cork in water, the warm air rises above the surrounding cooler, denser air. On the other hand, if a region of air is cooled, it becomes denser and sinks.

This unequal heating and cooling of the air often makes a pattern of rising air, sinking air, and winds, called a **convection** (kuhn·VEK·shuhn) **cell**. A convection cell is a part of the atmosphere where air moves in a circular pattern because of unequal heating and cooling.

The drawing shows how a convection cell forms. Cities A and B have the same air pressure. Then direct sunlight heats city A. The air above it warms and expands. It becomes less dense and rises, forming an updraft. The air pressure goes down. The unheated air on either side has a higher pressure. This air moves in toward the low-pressure area, making a surface wind.

▶ **How are winds produced?**

READING
Diagrams

Use the diagram to explain what happens to city B during the formation of the convection cell.

Updraft | Downdraft
Warm air rising | Cool air sinking
Wind
CITY A | CITY B

Warm air

Cold air

Sea breeze

Warm air

Cold air

Valley breeze

What Are Sea and Land Breezes?

An example of convection is a breeze that occurs along a coastline. Land warms faster than water. On sunny days air over land warms faster than air next to it over the sea. The warm air expands and rises. Cooler air from over the ocean replaces the rising warm air. A wind blows onto the land. A wind that blows from the sea toward the land is called a **sea breeze**.

At night the reverse happens. The air over the land cools more rapidly than the air over the water. A **land breeze** blows from land toward the water.

Convection cells also occur along mountains. As the Sun shines on a mountain during the day, the slope heats up faster than the valley below. Air over the slope warms and rises.

READING Diagrams

These pictures show what happens during the day. How would you show what happens at night?

Cooler air over the valley replaces the rising warm air, creating a *valley breeze* that blows up the slope. At night the mountain slope cools rapidly. This causes a *mountain breeze* to blow down the slope.

▷ **How are sea and land breezes produced?**

What Is the Coriolis Effect?

Earth's rotation affects winds blowing across its surface. As Earth rotates, every spot on its surface moves with it. However, in the same 24-hour period, places near the poles travel a shorter distance than places near the equator. This means that places near the poles are moving slower!

Now what if you are in an airplane flying in a straight line from the North Pole to Chicago? While you are in the air, Earth is *rotating*, or spinning, underneath you. Earth rotates counterclockwise as seen from the North Pole. As Earth rotates, Chicago is moving west to east. To someone in Chicago, though, the plane's flight path seems to curve to the southwest.

The same thing happens with winds blowing from the North Pole. Because Earth rotates, the winds seem to curve to the right as they head southward.

No matter which way the wind blows, it will curve to the right in the Northern Hemisphere. This curving is known as the **Coriolis effect**. In the Southern Hemisphere, the Coriolis effect causes winds to curve to the left. This is because, as viewed from the South Pole, Earth rotates clockwise. The effect works on other moving objects as well, such as missiles and rockets.

▷ **What causes the Coriolis effect?**

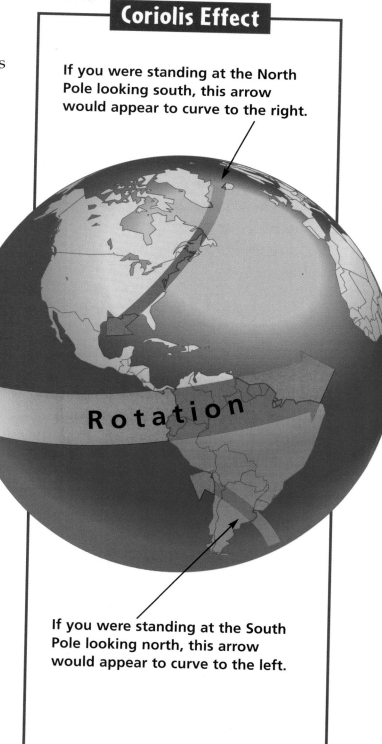

Coriolis Effect

If you were standing at the North Pole looking south, this arrow would appear to curve to the right.

R o t a t i o n

If you were standing at the South Pole looking north, this arrow would appear to curve to the left.

How Are Global Wind Patterns Produced?

Year round the equator is heated strongly by sunlight. The air becomes very warm. Heat also causes evaporation, so the air becomes moist. Warm, moist air over the equator creates a zone of low pressure around the globe.

As the air at the equator warms, it becomes less dense and rises. It rises to the top of the troposphere and spreads out, moving north and south. As the air moves away from the equator, it cools and becomes denser. At about 30° north and south latitudes, the cold air begins to sink toward the surface. This sinking air creates a high-pressure zone on both sides of the equator at these latitudes. A belt of winds is set in motion around Earth by air moving from these high-pressure zones toward the low pressure at the equator. These are the *trade winds*. The Coriolis effect curves these winds, as you see in the diagram.

The poles get very low-angle sunlight, and the air there is very cold. Cold, dense air can hold very little water vapor. Cold, dry air over the poles has high pressure. Air at the poles moves toward 60° latitude, forming winds. Because of the Coriolis effect, the winds curve. These are the polar *easterly winds*. *Easterly* means the wind blows "from the east."

Other winds occur between 60° latitude and the poles as well as between 30° and 60° latitudes. Between 30° and 60° latitudes is the zone of *westerly winds*. The continental United States is in the zone of westerly winds.

▷ **What causes the global trade winds?**

Global Wind Zones

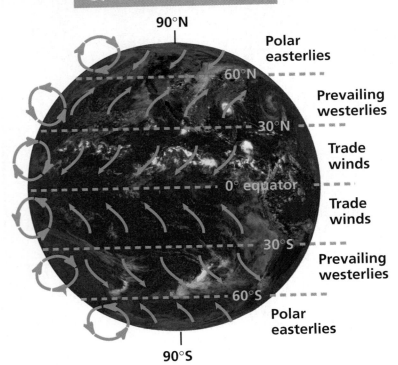

90°N

Polar easterlies

60°N

Prevailing westerlies

30°N

Trade winds

0° equator

Trade winds

30°S

Prevailing westerlies

60°S

Polar easterlies

90°S

READING
Diagrams

Make a table listing different global wind zones and a description of the directions in which winds move in each zone.

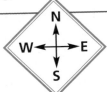

What Are Isobars?

Why is it important to know about air pressure? Knowing where the air pressure is high or low allows you to predict which way air will move. This is why weather scientists make maps showing air pressure. They start by plotting the air pressure at many different locations on a map. Then they connect all places with the same air pressure with a line. A line on a map connecting places with equal air pressure is called an **isobar**. Isobars make pressure patterns easier to see.

Find the series of circular isobars in the west, surrounding a region of high pressure (H). This pattern is called a *high-pressure system*. Since the center has higher pressure than its surroundings, winds blow outward from the center in a clockwise pattern.

A similar set of isobars in the east marks a *low-pressure system* (L). In a low-pressure system, the central region is surrounded by higher pressure. The winds blow in toward the center in a counterclockwise pattern.

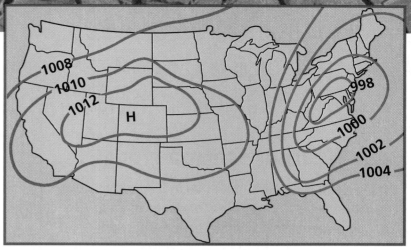

The pressure on each isobar is in millibars (mb).

Isobars also help scientists predict how fast air will move. Big differences in air pressure over short distances cause strong winds. This is shown on a map by drawing closely spaced isobars. Small differences in air pressure cause gentle winds. This is shown by widely spaced isobars.

You show wind on a station model with a straight line touching the circle. The line tells where the wind is blowing from. "Feathers" are used to show speed.

READING **Main Idea**
How do isobars help scientists predict how air will move?

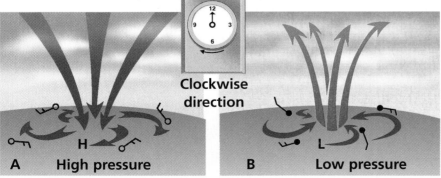

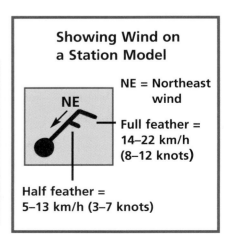

Showing Wind on a Station Model

NE = Northeast wind

Full feather = 14–22 km/h (8–12 knots)

Half feather = 5–13 km/h (3–7 knots)

Inquiry Skill
BUILDER

A Weather Station Model

A weather station model includes temperature, cloud cover, air pressure, pressure tendency, wind speed, and wind direction. The circle is at the location of the station. You will interpret the data, using the information from the weather station models to answer questions and solve problems.

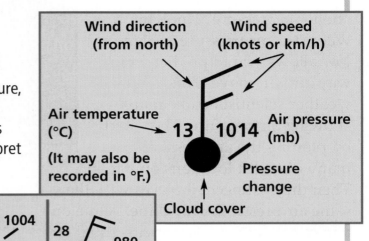

Wind direction (from north)
Wind speed (knots or km/h)
Air temperature (°C)
(It may also be recorded in °F.)
13 | 1014
Air pressure (mb)
Pressure change
Cloud cover

34 🔵 1004 — Dallas

28 ⦿ 980 — Charlotte

14 🔵 1012 — Oakland

30 ◑ 996 — Tampa

Procedure

1 **Use Numbers** Look carefully at the Dallas weather station model. How fast is the wind blowing? What is the wind direction? Record your answers.

2 **Interpret Data** What other information does this weather station model give you?

3 Look at the other weather station models. Make a table recording weather conditions for each city.

Drawing Conclusions

1 Compare the information in the table you made with these station models. Which way is the information easier to interpret?

2 **Interpret Data** Where was wind fastest? Slowest? Which tells you this information more quickly, the table or the models?

3 **Communicate** Compare and contrast other weather conditions in the cities.

Why It Matters

Wind can be very useful. It is often used as a source of power. Wind turns windmills, special machines that produce electricity. They run the machinery that grinds grain. Windmills are also used to pump water.

Wind carries pollen to flowers. Seeds form as a result. Many kinds of seeds, in turn, are carried by wind to new places.

e-Journal Visit our Web site **www.science.mmhschool.com** to do a research project on wind.

Think and Write

1. What makes air pressure change?

2. What causes wind to blow in a particular direction?

3. Why are there zones of winds around the world?

4. **Interpret Data** On a weather map, how can you compare the speed and direction of winds in different locations?

5. **Critical Thinking** How might temperatures near the ocean compare with those inland in winter? In summer? Explain.

L·I·N·K·S

LITERATURE LINK

Read *The Sky-Watchers,* the story of how two students maintained a weather station. When you finish reading, think about how you would build a weather station. Try the activities at the end of the book.

WRITING LINK

Expository Writing Research and write a report on the Beaufort Wind Scale. Include its history. Draw a conclusion about its importance.

MATH LINK

Calculate weather factors. Collect a week's worth of national weather maps from a newspaper. Select a region of the country, such as the Midwest or Southeast. Calculate its average temperature, wind speed, and air pressure.

SOCIAL STUDIES LINK

Write a report. Research the origin of the term "trade winds," and write a report on your findings.

TECHNOLOGY LINK

LOG ON Visit **www.science.mmhschool.com** for more links.

Weather: It's Instrumental!

You turn on the TV to catch the weather forecast. The satellite image looks cool, but all you want to know is how warm it is, whether it's windy, and if you're going to get wet on your way to school. Where does that information come from? Not from space, but from a set of instruments at a nearby weather station.

To find the temperature, you need a thermometer. To find how much rain has fallen, you need a rain gauge. Put a straight-sided bucket outside to collect rain water. Later, stick a ruler in the bucket to measure how much rain fell.

Wonder how much moisture is in the air? Your hair is a good indicator! It gets frizzier when it's raining or very humid outside. That's because hair lengthens (and kinks up) when the air is moist. Forecasters use "hair hygrometers" to measure humidity. Hygrometers have pens that are attached to human or horse hairs. As the hair changes length, the pen graphs the change in humidity.

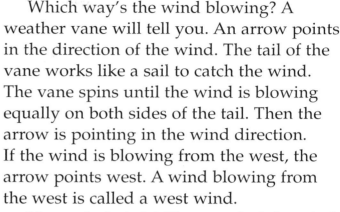

Which way's the wind blowing? A weather vane will tell you. An arrow points in the direction of the wind. The tail of the vane works like a sail to catch the wind. The vane spins until the wind is blowing equally on both sides of the tail. Then the arrow is pointing in the wind direction. If the wind is blowing from the west, the arrow points west. A wind blowing from the west is called a west wind.

How windy is it? The speed of the wind is measured with an anemometer. It uses a set of cups attached to a central pole. As the cups catch the wind, they spin around like a pinwheel. The faster the wind, the faster they spin. Now you can set up a weather station right in your own backyard!

Write **About It**

1. What weather information do you need before you go outside? What instruments help get that information?

2. What would it take to set up a weather station in your neighborhood or outside your window?

LOG ON Visit **www.science.mmhschool.com** to learn more about measuring weather.

Chapter 10 Review

Vocabulary

Fill each blank with the best word or words from the list.

barometer, D34
cirrus cloud, D44
condensation, D39
Coriolis effect, D57
evaporation, D38
humidity, D38
land breeze, D56
precipitation, D46
sea breeze, D56
stratus cloud, D44

1. Rain, snow, and sleet are kinds of _____.

2. The _____ causes winds to follow a curved path over Earth's surface.

3. A(n) _____ forms in blanketlike layers.

4. Liquid changes directly to a gas by the process called _____.

5. The amount of water vapor in the air is called _____.

6. Wind blowing from the ocean toward the land is called a(n) _____.

7. Wind blowing from the land toward the ocean is called a(n) _____.

8. The process that turns water vapor into raindrops is called _____.

9. A high, wispy cloud made of ice crystals is a(n) _____.

10. A(n) _____ measures air pressure.

Test Prep

11. In a low-presure system _____.
   A winds blow out
   B winds blow clockwise
   C winds blow west
   D winds blow inward, counterclockwise

12. Weather takes place in the _____.
   F thermosphere
   G mesosphere
   H troposphere
   J stratosphere

13. Water drops that collect on a cold glass of lemonade come from _____.
   A the lemonade
   B the air
   C a puddle
   D the glass itself

14. Isobars indicate _____.
   F humidity
   G temperature
   H air pressure
   J cloud cover

15. On a hot day, a lake is likely to be _____.

 A cooler than nearby land

 B hotter than nearby land

 C the same temperature as the land

 D the cause of the heat

Concepts and Skills

16. Reading in Science Write a paragraph explaining why north winds blow to the southwest.

17. Safety Why do you need to be careful on hot days when the relative humidity is high? Write a paragraph explaining your answer.

18. Scientific Methods How much does humidity change over a day? Write a design for an experiment that would test this.

19. INQUIRY SKILL Interpret Data You are given this information on a weather map: What kind of weather is city A having? What kind of weather is city B having? Write a paragraph explaining your answer.

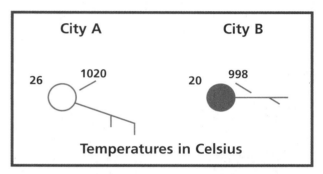

City A   City B

26   1020   20   998

Temperatures in Celsius

20. Critical Thinking What if there were no plants? Do you think Earth would still get as much rain as it does now? Write your ideas. Describe how you might test them.

Did You Ever Wonder?

INQUIRY SKILL Infer You look up in the sky and see clouds. Why don't those clouds fall to the ground?

 LOG ON Visit www.science.mmhschool.com to boost your test scores.

Weather Patterns and Climate

Did You Ever Wonder?

Why is a desert hot and dry? Conditions in the Mojave Desert in California are partly caused by the mountains you see in the background. Rain falls on the other side of the mountains before it can reach the Mojave. Why does one side of a mountain get a lot of rain while the other side gets very little?

INQUIRY SKILL **Infer** Deserts are hot during the day. How can they get so cool at night?

Air Masses and Fronts

Get Ready

Have you ever watched a "wall" of clouds heading toward you? Did the clouds bring gentle, steady rain or heavy downpours? Knowing what kind of weather is on the way can help you make plans.

Part of what weather forecasters need to watch for is approaching air masses and fronts. Why might your weather today depend on what someone else's weather was like yesterday?

Inquiry Skill

You interpret data when you use the information that has been gathered to answer questions or solve a problem.

Explore Activity

How Can You Compare Weather?

Materials

station model key

newspaper weather map (optional)

pencil

crayons

Procedure

Communicate Think of the country in large regions—the Northeast, the Southwest, and the coasts. Write a report for the weather in each region based on the map you see here.

Drawing Conclusions

1 **Infer** Which areas are having warm, rainy weather?

2 **Infer** Where is the weather cool and dry?

3 **Predict** How do you think weather in any part of the country may change, based on the data in this map? Give reasons for your answer. How would you check your predictions?

4 FURTHER INQUIRY **Interpret Data** What will tomorrow's weather be like? Interpret the information on the weather map in the morning paper. Compare your interpretation to the actual weather during the day.

W   E

San Francisco

Lines are drawn to show wind direction, not speed. This is a wind coming from the east, going west—an east wind.

Temperatures here are given in degrees Fahrenheit.

Main Idea Weather changes often occur at fronts, where different air masses meet.

How Do Air Masses Affect Weather?

Weather maps show that cities across a large region can share the same weather. They also show how the weather in different areas can differ.

Why are weather conditions in one part of a country different from those in another part? Look back at the map on page D69. Some of the cities are having clear, cool weather. The air throughout this region is cool and dry. Other cities are having warmer, cloudy weather. The air throughout this region is warm and moist. A large region of the atmosphere where the air has similar properties throughout is called an air mass.

An air mass gets its properties from the region where it forms. Air over the Gulf of Mexico is above very warm water. The water warms the air, and evaporation from the Gulf adds water vapor. The air becomes warm and moist. Air masses are named for the region they come from.

As air masses move, they bring these conditions with them. What happens if a cool, moist air mass moves over an area that has warm, dry weather? The warm, dry weather will change.

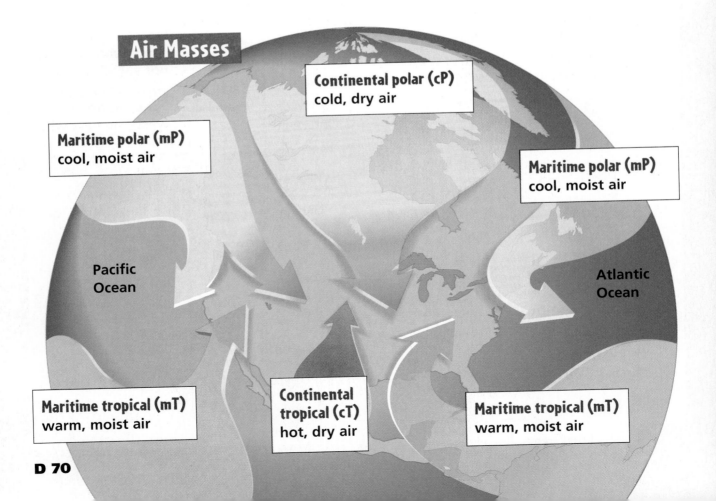

Air Masses

Continental polar (cP)
cold, dry air

Maritime polar (mP)
cool, moist air

Maritime polar (mP)
cool, moist air

Pacific Ocean

Atlantic Ocean

Maritime tropical (mT)
warm, moist air

Continental tropical (cT)
hot, dry air

Maritime tropical (mT)
warm, moist air

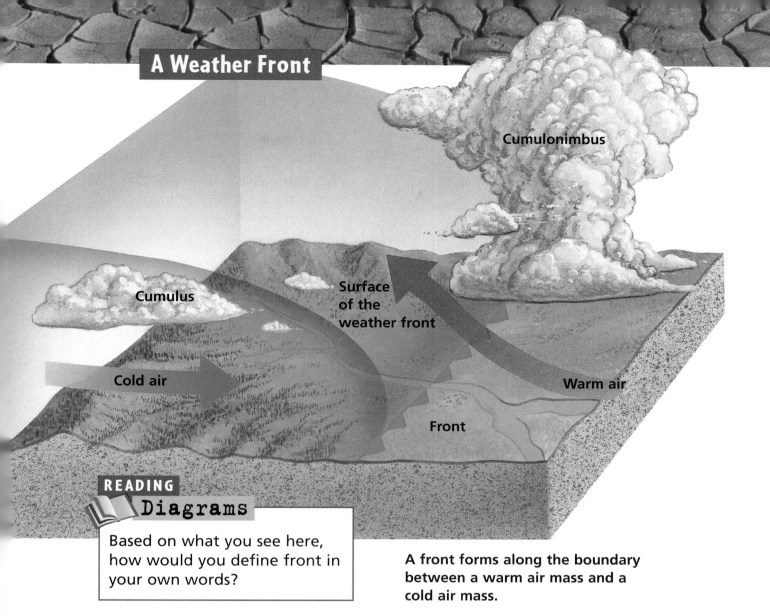

A Weather Front

Cumulonimbus

Cumulus

Surface
of the
weather front

Cold air

Warm air

Front

READING
Diagrams

Based on what you see here, how would you define front in your own words?

A front forms along the boundary between a warm air mass and a cold air mass.

Once an air mass is formed, it is moved by global winds. In the United States, global winds tend to move air masses from west to east.

Air masses with different conditions can "meet." That is, one runs into another. What happens when air masses with different temperatures meet? They don't mix together. Instead, a narrow boundary forms between them. This boundary is called a **front**. It marks the leading edge, or front, of

an air mass that is moving into an area where another air mass is moving out. Weather changes rapidly at fronts. That's because you pass from one kind of air mass into another. Fronts often cause rainy, unsettled weather.

READING Sequence of Events
What happens when a cold air mass meets with a warm air mass?

Weather Prediction

FOLDABLES™ Make a Four-Door Book. (See p. R 44.) Label the tabs as shown.

1. Find a weather map in a newspaper that shows the weather across the United States. Be sure the map shows at least one cold front or warm front in the western part of the country. Look at your map. Use the book to describe the weather in your state.

2. Use your book to describe the weather in each region of the country—northwest, southwest, southeast, northeast.

3. **Infer** Weather patterns move from west to east across the United States. How do you think the weather just east of the front will change in the next day or so? Explain under the tabs of your Four-Door Book.

> **What kind of weather does a cold front usually produce?**

How Do Fronts Affect Weather?

- In a **cold front**, cold air moves in under a warm air mass. Cold fronts often bring brief, heavy storms. There may be thunderstorms and strong winds. After the storm the skies are usually clearer, and the weather is usually cooler and drier.

- In a **warm front**, warm air moves in over a cold air mass. Warm fronts often bring light, steady rain or snow. The precipitation may last for days. Winds are usually light. Warm fronts may also bring fog— stratus clouds that form near the ground. Afterward the weather is usually warmer and more humid.

READING Diagrams

Write a paragraph comparing a warm front with a cold front.

Cold Front

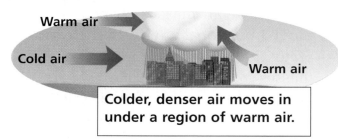

Colder, denser air moves in under a region of warm air.

Warm Front

Warm air moves into a region, rising up and over the colder air mass already there.

Why It Matters

Weather forecasting is hard. Knowing how the atmosphere is moving lets you predict the weather. The problem is that the atmosphere is huge and complex. A weather forecaster might predict clear weather for tomorrow. However, another air mass might move in. Everything can change.

Computers do high-speed calculations to predict the atmosphere's motion. Predictions are compared with forecasts to account for any differences. Two-day forecasts are calculated every 12 hours. A five-day forecast is calculated daily.

 e-Journal Visit our Web site **www.science.mmhschool.com** to do a research project on weather forecasting.

Think and Write

1. What are four different kinds of air masses? How are they different?

2. What kind of weather is produced by a cold front?

3. What kind of weather is produced by a warm front?

4. How can you use weather maps to predict weather?

5. **Critical Thinking** How can you tell the kind of front passing by just observing the weather?

L·I·N·K·S

WRITING LINK

Expository Writing Write an interview for the local TV news. Explain how changes in the weather affected the way three people spent their day.

MATH LINK

Graph weather data. Research local newspapers to learn what kinds of fronts have moved through your area and the kind of weather each front brought. Do this for a month. Graph your data. Report what you found.

TECHNOLOGY LINK

 Science Newsroom CD-ROM Choose *It's Up in the Air* to learn more about how air masses affect weather conditions.

LOG ON Visit **www.science.mmhschool.com** for more links.

Severe Storms

Vocabulary

thunderstorm, D76

tornado, D77

hurricane, D78

storm surge, D79

Get Ready

What's it like to be in the path of a tornado? People have reported a sound like the rumble of an approaching freight train. Tornadoes are the most powerful storms on Earth. Although most tornadoes are not very wide and they don't last too long, when they touch down watch out! Like deadly whirling brooms, they can sweep away anything in their path. Tornadoes strike all parts of the United States, but they are more frequent in some regions than in others. Where in the United States is "tornado country"?

Inquiry Skill

You use numbers when you use ordering, counting, adding, subtracting, multiplying, and dividing to explain data.

Explore Activity

Where Do Tornadoes Occur?

Materials

map of U.S., including Alaska and Hawaii

blue marker

red marker

Procedure

1 Infer The table shown here lists how many tornadoes occurred in each state over a 30-year period. It also shows about how many tornadoes occur in each state each year. Look at the data in the table for two minutes. Now write what part of the country you think gets the most tornadoes.

2 Use the red marker to record on the map the number of tornadoes that occurred in each state over the 30-year period. Use the blue marker to record the average number of tornadoes that occurred in a year in each state.

Drawing Conclusions

1 Use Numbers Which states had fewer than 10 tornadoes a year? Which states had more than 20 tornadoes a year?

2 Interpret Data Which six states had the most tornadoes during the 30-year period?

3 Interpret Data Which part of the country had the most tornadoes?

4 **FURTHER INQUIRY** **Communicate** Many people refer to a certain part of the country as "Tornado Alley." Which part of the country do you think that is? Why do you think people call it that? What else might these states have in common? Describe how you would go about finding the answer to that question.

State	Total	Average per year
AL	668	22
AK	0	0
AZ	106	4
AR	596	20
CA	148	5
CO	781	26
CT	37	1
DE	31	1
FL	1,590	53
GA	615	21
HI	25	1
ID	80	3
IL	798	27
IN	604	20
IA	1,079	36
KS	1,198	40
KY	296	10
LA	831	28
ME	50	2
MD	86	3
MA	89	3
MI	567	19
MN	607	20
MS	775	26
MO	781	26
MT	175	6
NE	1,118	37
NV	41	1
NH	56	2
NJ	78	3
NM	276	9
NY	169	6
NC	435	15
ND	621	21
OH	463	15
OK	1,412	47
OR	34	1
PA	310	10
RI	7	0
SC	307	10
SD	864	29
TN	360	12
TX	4,174	139
UT	58	2
VT	21	1
VA	188	6
WA	45	2
WV	69	2
WI	625	21
WY	356	12

Main Idea Thunderstorms, tornadoes, and hurricanes are severe storms that can cause great damage.

What Are Thunderstorms?

A tornado is a violent kind of storm that forms under special conditions. Often, such storms grow out of a **thunderstorm**, another, more common kind of storm.

Thunderstorms are the most common kind of severe storm. They form in clouds called *thunderheads*, or cumulonimbus clouds. The storms cause huge electric sparks called *lightning*. The lightning heats the air and causes the noise called *thunder*. Thunderstorms usually have heavy rains and strong winds. Some thunderstorms also produce hail. A thunderstorm starts when intense heating causes air to rise very quickly. A cloud forms where there is an upward rush of heated air, an updraft. As more warm, moist air is carried upward, the cloud grows larger. Strong updrafts keep water droplets and ice crystals in the cloud, so they grow in size, too. When the updrafts can't support them anymore, they fall as heavy rain or even hail.

Once the rain falls, it causes downdrafts in the cloud. When the air going up rubs against air going down, static electricity builds up. When enough builds up, there's a huge spark—lightning. Lightning may jump within a cloud, between two clouds, or between a cloud and the ground.

Thunderstorms usually form in warm air just ahead of a cold front. They most often occur in hot humid weather, but can also occur during snow storms, as *thundersnow*.

How a Thunderstorm Forms

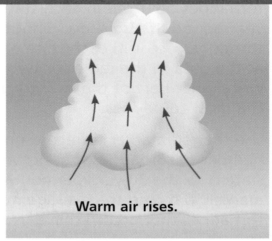

Warm air rises.

1 Strong updrafts form inside the cloud.

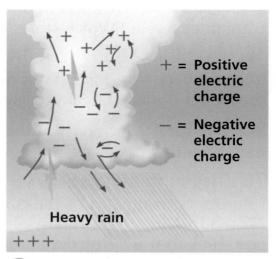

+ = Positive electric charge

− = Negative electric charge

Heavy rain

2 Electric charges build up inside the cloud.

READING Diagrams

Describe how a thunderstorm forms.

The most violent thunderstorms often spin off even more dangerous storms, called **tornadoes**. A tornado is a violent whirling wind that moves across the ground in a narrow path.

How Tornadoes Happen

Late in the day, when Earth's surface is very warm, convection can get very strong. This can lead to a tornado. A tornado is a sort of runaway convection cell.

When the updraft in a convection cell is really strong, the air rushes in from all sides at high speeds. The air curves into a spin. This lowers the pressure even more. Air rushes in even faster, and the pressure gets even lower, and so on. Like a spinning skater who pulls her arms in close to her sides, the spinning tornado gets faster and faster.

As the tornado gets stronger, a funnel forms that eventually touches the ground. In the center of a tornado, winds can reach speeds of 500 km per hour (about 300 mi per hour) or more. At such high speeds, winds can destroy anything in their path.

The speed of the wind in the tornado is not the speed with which the tornado moves across the ground. It moves across the ground very fast but can change its direction continually.

Most tornadoes in the United States occur in the Midwest and the South—especially in the area known as Tornado Alley.

▷ **How are tornadoes related to thunderstorms?**

QUICK LAB

Tornado in a Bottle

FOLDABLES™ Make a Half-Book. (See p. R 41.)

1. **Make a Model** Fill a 2-L plastic bottle one-third full of water. Dry the neck of the bottle, and tape over the top with duct tape. Use a pencil to poke a hole in the tape.

2. Place another 2-L plastic bottle upside down over the mouth of the first bottle. Tape the two bottles together.

3. **Observe** Hold the bottles by the necks so the one with the water is on top. Swirl them around while your partner gently squeezes on the empty bottle. Then place the bottles on a desk with the water bottle on top. Draw what you see on the front of your book and describe your observations under the tab.

4. **Infer** How is this like what happens when a tornado forms? Explain.

How Do Hurricanes Form?

If you live near an ocean or the Gulf Coast, you may have experienced a **hurricane**. Hurricanes are very large, swirling storms with very low pressure at their center. They form over tropical oceans near the equator.

Air masses near the equator tend to be very much alike. They don't form the fronts that you learned about in Lesson 7. Instead, they form lots of thunderstorms.

- Strong heating and lots of evaporation over the ocean can cause a large low-pressure center to form. If this happens, winds begin to blow in toward the low. As this rushing air nears the center, it moves upward and forms a ring of tall thunderstorms.

- The Coriolis effect causes winds to spiral counterclockwise in the Northern Hemisphere. Clusters of thunderstorms are pulled into the spiral. The thunderstorms merge, forming a single large storm.

- As water vapor in the storms condenses, heat is released. The air is

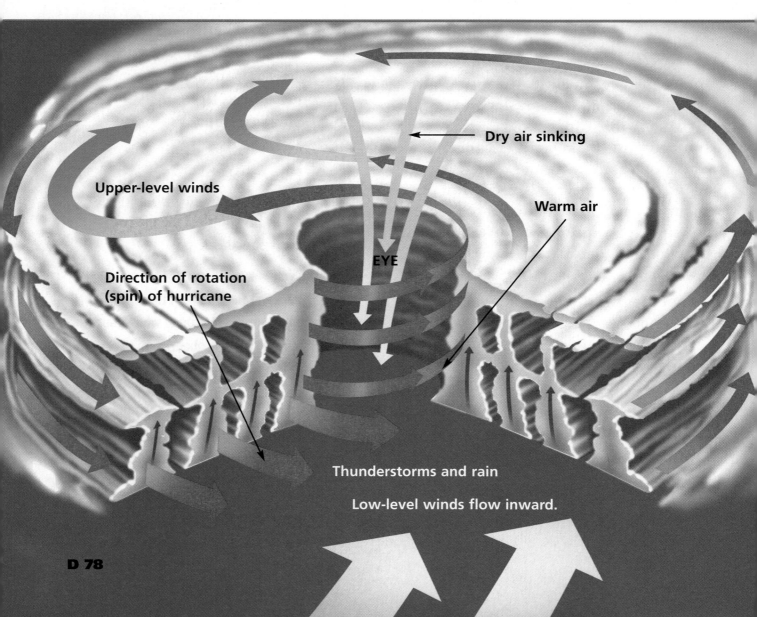

Dry air sinking

Upper-level winds

Warm air

EYE

Direction of rotation (spin) of hurricane

Thunderstorms and rain

Low-level winds flow inward.

warmed. This decreases the air's density and pressure. Moisture evaporating into the air decreases the air's density and pressure even more. Low air pressure favors more evaporation. This lowers the pressure even more.

- The lower the air pressure, the faster are the winds that blow in toward the center of the storm. When the winds reach speeds of 120 km per hour (about 75 mi per hour) or higher, the storm is a hurricane.

- As the moist air in the storm rises and cools, condensation takes place. The clouds thicken. Heavy rains fall through the high winds. When fully formed, a hurricane has an eye at its center. The eye is an area of light winds and skies that are nearly clear.

Hurricane winds whip up large waves in the ocean. These waves move outward from the storm and pound against a shore for days before the storm arrives. However, it is the storm surge that causes the most destruction. Storm surge is a great rise of the sea along a shore. Its main cause is low air pressure.

Air pressure normally presses down on the surface of the sea. When the pressure drops in a hurricane, the surface of the sea rises, forming a bulge beneath a hurricane.

When the hurricane moves over a coast, the bulge can cause water levels to suddenly rise several feet, or surge.

Hurricane winds also push water ahead of the storm, forcing water onshore and adding to the storm surge. If the storm surge comes at high tide, it can raise the water level by 7 meters (about 20 feet) or more.

READING **Sequence of Events**

How does lower and lower air pressure lead to the formation of a hurricane?

This satellite photograph shows a hurricane and its eye. Hurricanes can easily grow to more than 700 km (about 400 mi) in diameter. Hurricanes can pick up about 20 billion tons of water a day from the oceans. Much of this water falls as rain over land areas.

Direction of wind

How Can Radar Track Storms?

Storms are hard to predict because they form so quickly. Scientists use the best methods possible to try to identify conditions long before a storm occurs. They look for clues, like the movement of fronts and the formation of very low pressure areas. Once these conditions are located, scientists keep a "weather eye" on them to see how they develop.

Special methods are used to find storms as they form. One such method is Doppler radar. The word *radar* stands for *ra*dio *d*etection *a*nd *r*anging. Radar works by sending out radio waves and recording their echo. The change in the radio signal from the original to the echo tells us something about where it reflected.

Doppler radar looks at how the echoes have changed in frequency from the original signals. This information gives clues about the movement of the reflective surface. Doppler radar is a very good tool for scientists to track storms. The radio waves reflect off storm clouds and are picked back up again at the radar stations.

With Doppler radar scientists can tell if rain is moving toward or away from them. Doppler radar can also spot spinning motions of clouds. These motions help warn scientists that tornadoes or hurricanes may be forming. Scientists use Doppler radar to find and track thunderstorms, tornadoes, and hurricanes. Doppler radar helps forecasters predict which way the storms will travel.

▷ **How can Doppler radar help in predicting severe storms?**

Radar helps forecasters watch how storms form and move.

L·I·N·K·S

Why It Matters

Scientists have used radar systems to track storms since the 1950s. NEXRAD—"NEXt generation of weather RADar"—is a newer form of Doppler radar that is replacing older radar systems. NEXRAD can spot small particles such as blowing dust, very light snow, and even drizzle. NEXRAD is more accurate than conventional radar at predicting floods and flash floods. It can show the exact locations of different fronts. It also shows changes in wind speed and direction. This helps scientists make more accurate weather predictions.

e-Journal Visit our Web site www.science.mmhschool.com to do a research project on storms.

Think and Write

1. How does a thunderstorm form?

2. How is a tornado related to a thunderstorm?

3. What causes a hurricane to form? What makes its winds move in a certain direction?

4. Why can hurricanes cause so much damage?

5. **Critical Thinking** Why do you think predicting a severe storm is so difficult?

WRITING LINK

Explanatory Writing How can you stay safe during an ice storm or a blizzard? Research the ways. Then use the information you find to write a safety manual on how to stay safe during these storms. Include an illustration for each step you list. Be that your safety manual tells people what to do first, next, and last.

ART LINK

Make a poster. Let others know what to do in a thunderstorm, tornado, or hurricane. Make a poster illustrating important storm safety rules.

MATH LINK

Find the number of tornadoes. Research how many tornadoes hit your state in the past year. Compare that number with the average number listed for your state in the chart on page D75. Were the number of tornadoes in your state last year higher, lower, or the same as the listed average?

TECHNOLOGY LINK

 LOG ON Visit www.science.mmhschool.com for more links.

Climate

Get Ready

What if you lived here, in this desert? What would summers be like? What would winters be like?

Think about what factors are used to describe the average weather pattern of a region. How might you use graphs of year-round weather in different places to test your ideas?

Inquiry Skill

You **communicate** when you share information.

Explore Activity

What Do Weather Patterns Tell You?

Procedure

1 **Use Numbers** Look at the graph for City 1. The bottom is labeled with the months of the year. The left side is labeled with the temperature in degrees Celsius. Use this scale to read the temperature line. What is City 1's average temperature in July?

2 **Use Numbers** The right side of the graph shows millimeters (mm) of precipitation. Use this scale to read precipitation bars. What is City 1's average precipitation in July?

3 Repeat steps 1 and 2 for City 2.

Drawing Conclusions

1 **Use Numbers** How does the annual precipitation of the two cities compare?

2 **Interpret Data** When is the average temperature highest for each city? Lowest? When does each city receive the greatest amount of precipitation?

3 **Interpret Data** Describe the average weather pattern for each city. Be sure to include temperature and precipitation, and their relationship to the seasons.

4 FURTHER INQUIRY **Communicate** What would a yearly graph for your community look like? Gather monthly temperature and precipitation data. Construct your graph. Compare it to City 1 and City 2.

City 1

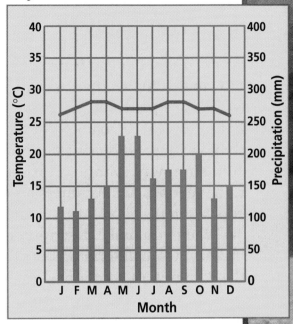

City 2

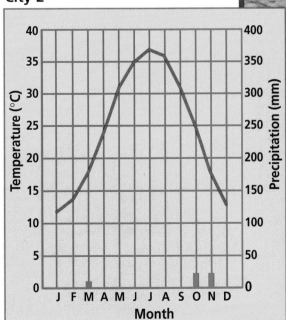

—— Temperature (in Celsius)
■ Precipitation (in millimeters)

Main Idea Long-term weather patterns determine climates, which can change over time.

What Is Climate?

Weather changes from day to day. However, the weather in any area tends to follow a pattern throughout the year. For example, Fairbanks, Alaska, tends to have long, cold winters and short, cool summers. Miami, Florida, tends to have long, hot summers and short, cool winters.

When you make descriptions such as these, you are describing the **climate** (KLIGH·mit) of a region. Climate is the average weather pattern of a region. One way to describe a region's climate is with a temperature-precipitation graph.

The climate of a region can also be described by some other factors, such as winds, distance from a coast, mountain ranges, and ocean currents. The *climate zones* shown here take all these factors into account.

Another way to describe the climate of a region is by the plants that grow there, such as grasslands or coniferous forests. Each kind of plant requires its own conditions for growth, such as amount of sunlight, precipitation, and temperature.

▶ **What factors describe climate?**

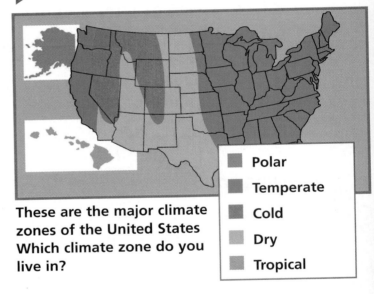

These are the major climate zones of the United States Which climate zone do you live in?

■ Polar
■ Temperate
■ Cold
■ Dry
■ Tropical

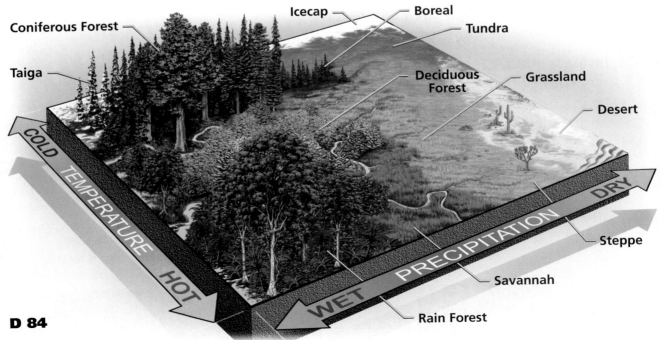

Coniferous Forest — Taiga — Icecap — Boreal — Tundra — Deciduous Forest — Grassland — Desert — Steppe — Savannah — Rain Forest

COLD — TEMPERATURE — HOT — WET — PRECIPITATION — DRY

Modeling Climates

In this activity you will make a model of the soil conditions in two cities. Use the information in the graphs on page D83. The soil conditions you set up will model—or represent—the climates of the two cities. To do this, you will need to measure the amount of water you use and the amount of time you use the lamp.

Materials

stick-on notepaper
marking pencil or pen
2 trays of dry soil
spray bottle of water
lamp
thermometer

Procedure

1 **Measure** Put 3 cm of dry soil into each tray. Label one tray City 1 and the other tray City 2.

2 **Use Numbers** What do the bars on each graph represent?

3 **Measure** Model the yearly precipitation and temperature like this: Let 5 minutes equal 1 month. One squeeze of water sprayed on the tray equals 10 millimeters of precipitation. Every minute the lamp is on equals 20 degrees of temperature. That means that from 0 to 5 minutes is January. During January the City 2 tray gets no water and the lamp shines on it for $\frac{3}{4}$ minute. The City 1 tray gets 12 squeezes of water and the lamp shines on it for $1\frac{1}{4}$ minutes.

4 **Make a Model** Model the two cities for all 12 months. Record your observations.

Drawing Conclusions

1 **Observe** Examine the soil in the trays. Compare them for the same months. How do they differ?

2 **Communicate** How did measuring help you model climates?

What Affects Climate?

Several things affect temperature and precipitation over a long period of time.

Latitude

One way to describe location is to tell the latitude of a place. Latitude is a measure of how far north or south a place is from the equator. The angle of insolation is different at different latitudes. As a result, the temperatures are different at different latitudes.

- **Tropical Zone** Near the equator temperatures are high all year. Rainfall is plentiful. At about 30° latitude in each hemisphere are deserts, areas of high temperatures and low precipitation.

- **Temperate Zones** In the middle latitudes, summers are warm, and winters are cool or cold. Precipitation may be plentiful.

- **Polar Zones** At high latitudes winters are long and cold. Summers are short and warm. Precipitation all year is low.

Bodies of Water

A glance at any globe shows that land and water are not evenly distributed. Most of the globe is covered with water. However, some places on a continent can be more than 1,600 km (1,000 mi) from any large body of water. Land

and water heat and cool at different rates. Land heats up faster in the sunlight than water does. Land also cools off faster than water. As a result, air temperatures over land are warmer in summer and cooler in winter than they are over oceans at the same latitude.

Winds and Ocean Currents

In Lesson 6 you learned that wind patterns circle the globe. These patterns are not the day-to-day winds. Instead they are winds that blow continually above Earth's surface.

- **Wind Patterns** For example, just above and below the equator, the trade winds blow continually. In the middle latitudes are the westerlies. In the polar areas are the easterlies. Westerlies blow across the continental United States from west (the Pacific) to east (the Atlantic). They bring warm, moist air to the west coast. They push air masses and fronts across the country.

North Pole

Polar zone — Sparse precipitation

Temperate zone — Ample precipitation

Tropical zone — Abundant rainfall

Temperate zone — Ample precipitation

Polar zone — Sparse precipitation

South Pole

- **Currents** These winds also move water across the surface of the ocean. As ocean water moves, it moves warm or cool air with it. A warm current, the Gulf Stream, flows up along the east coast. The California Current, a cool current, moves down along the west coast.

Altitude

Altitude is a measure of how high above sea level a place is. The higher a place is above sea level, the cooler its climate is.

- **Mountains** Along the base of a high mountain, you may find tropical plants growing. Halfway up you might find pine forests. At the mountain peaks, you will find permanent ice and snow. Mountain ranges affect climate, too. The Alps protect the Mediterranean coast from cold polar air. The Himalayas protect the lowlands of India from cold Siberian air. Mountain ranges also affect rain patterns. Often one side of the mountain gets lots of rain while the other side gets very little.

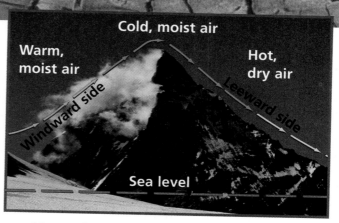

Air passing over a mountain cools. Rain clouds may form and drop their moisture on that side of the mountain. Air reaching the other side is often dry.

- **Rain Shadow** Global wind patterns can force air up along the side of a mountain. For example, warm, moist air from the Pacific Ocean is blown up the side of the Sierra Nevada and the Cascades. As the air moves up, there is precipitation on the windward side. Having lost the moisture, dry air descends down the leeward side of the mountain. This side is said to be in a *rain shadow.*

 **How does latitude affect climate?**

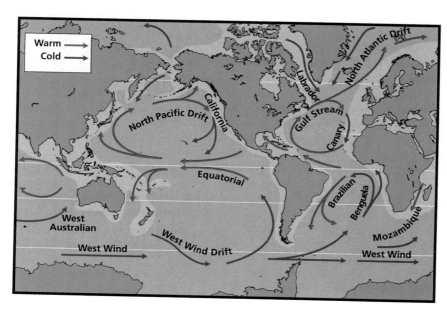

Ocean currents move surface water in huge circular patterns. As ocean currents flow past land areas, they affect the land's climate.

What Causes Climate Change?

There is much evidence that over long periods of time, Earth goes through warming and cooling trends. Warming and cooling are signs that Earth's radiative (energy) balance has shifted. What causes such shifts?

The shifts are caused by changes in sunlight. They are also caused by changes in the movements of air, water, landmasses, and Earth itself.

The Sun's Output

The amount of energy the Sun sends out changes. One clue to how the Sun's output may be changing comes from sunspots. Sunspots are dark areas that appear on the surface of the Sun. They appear dark because they are cooler than the surrounding regions. They appear to be "storms" on the Sun.

Sunspots have been observed for centuries. However, they are not permanent. They appear and disappear over several days or several months.

At times there are many large sunspots. Such a high count is called a *sunspot maximum*. The last sunspot maximum was in 2001.

A sunspot maximum appears to happen about every 11 years. Scientists also record changes in Earth's temperatures about the same times. Around the time of a sunspot maximum, Earth's average temperature has gone up. The pattern is not exact or complete. However, it has led some scientists to suggest that droughts, rainfall, and very cold winters might be related to times when sunspots are very numerous or very few.

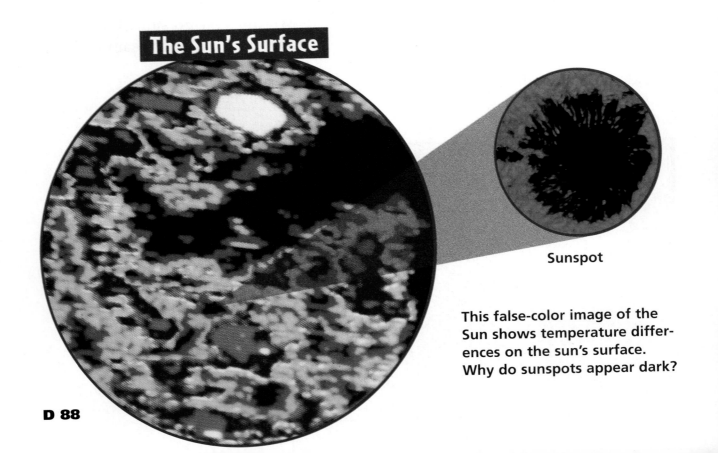

The Sun's Surface

Sunspot

This false-color image of the Sun shows temperature differences on the sun's surface. Why do sunspots appear dark?

Currents and Landmasses

How do the oceans help move Earth's heat around? Ocean currents act like huge conveyor belts, carrying heat from the equator to the poles. Changes in the speed and direction of these currents could explain sudden and long-term climate changes.

The continents have changed their positions over time. In fact, the continents are still moving very gradually. Their climates are likely to change with their locations.

Volcanoes

When volcanoes erupt, they send dust and gases into the atmosphere. Atmospheric dust can block sunlight, causing cooling. In the past eruptions were more frequent. The dust from all of those eruptions may have caused enough cooling to trigger ice ages. Volcanic eruptions are not as common today as they were in the past. While eruptions still cause cooling, they probably don't affect long-term climate as much as in the past.

READING Sequence of Events

How might frequent volcanic eruptions change the climate?

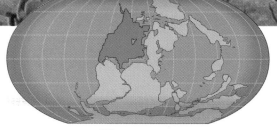

300 Million Years Ago

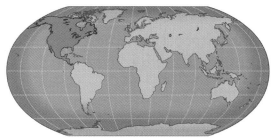

Present

Do you think the ocean currents were the same 300 million years ago as they are today? Changes in ocean currents would profoundly affect climates.

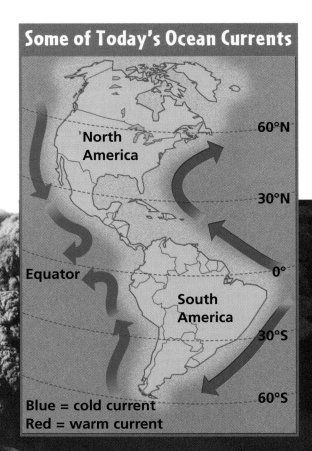

Some of Today's Ocean Currents

North America

Equator

South America

60°N

30°N

0°

30°S

60°S

Blue = cold current
Red = warm current

How Can Climate Affect You?

How do you deal with cold weather? Cold weather cools the surface of the body. The body responds by circulating warm blood faster to counteract the cooling. The heart pumps faster. Blood pressure increases and puts a strain on the heart.

Cold Climates

How can you stay warm in cold weather? Use proper clothing and shelter. Clothing traps body heat to warm the air close to your body. Cold-weather clothes are often made with materials that trap air between loose fibers. Dressing in layers helps. Your body heats trapped air, and soon a thin, warm layer of air surrounds you.

Hot Climates

In hot, dry climates, the main health problem is water loss. Heating the body triggers sweating. When sweat evaporates, it cools the skin. However, if you don't drink enough water, your body eventually stops sweating. No sweat, no cooling. Body temperature rises. This can cause *hyperthermia* (overheating), which can be fatal.

Clothing can help you deal with the heat. Light-colored fabric protects the skin and reflects a lot of the sunlight. Loose clothing lets air circulate so sweat can evaporate and cool the body.

▷ **What is the main health problem in hot, dry climates?**

How to Dress in Hot Weather
Wear light-colored, loose clothing that protects you from the Sun and lets your skin breathe.
Wear a sun hat.
Use sunscreen.

How to Dress in Cold Weather
Protect nose and ears on blustery, cold days.
Keep hands, head, and feet warm.
Dress in layers to trap body heat.

Why It Matters

Since 1900, Earth's average temperature has increased by about 0.5°C (1°F). Most of the warming has come in two periods—from 1920 to 1940 and since the mid-1970s. A drought during the 1920s–1940s led to the Dust Bowl days. Millions of acres of United States farmland dried out. Crops failed. Farmers went broke trying to pay their bills. Many families lost their homes and farms.

Today the warming trend continues.

e-Journal Visit our Web site **www.science.mmhschool.com** to do a research project on global warming.

Think and Write

1. What is climate? What are the main factors that are used to describe the climate of an area?

2. What is a rain shadow?

3. Why are climates different at different places on Earth?

4. **Measure** What variables do you have to measure to describe the average weather pattern, or climate, of a region?

5. **Critical Thinking** Do you think people can live in all climates? Explain your answer.

L·I·N·K·S

WRITING LINK

Persuasive Writing "Greenhouse gases" in the atmosphere let in sunlight, but trap heat. Research what these gases are and how they affect Earth's climate. Write a letter to a politician. Convince this person to pass a law preventing people from placing these gases into the atmosphere.

SOCIAL STUDIES LINK

Report on changing climates. The illustration shows a winter fair on the Thames River in England during the Little Ice Age. Research how Earth's climate changed since farming began. Write a report.

MATH LINK

Make a pie graph. Find out what proportions of greenhouse gases exist in the atmosphere. Make a pie graph.

TECHNOLOGY LINK

 LOG ON Visit **www.science.mmhschool.com** for more links.

Chapter 11 Review

Vocabulary

Fill each blank with the best word or words from the list.

air mass, D70
climate, D84
cold front, D72
front, D71
hurricane, D78
lightning, D76
storm surge, D79
thunderstorm, D76
tornado, D77
warm front, D72

1. A boundary between air masses of different temperatures is called a(n) _____.

2. A storm often created in thunderstorms is a(n) _____.

3. A(n) _____ may bring fog.

4. A storm that produces light-ning is a(n) _____.

5. A great rise of sea level at a shore due to a hurricane is a(n) _____.

6. Thunderstorms cause large electric sparks called _____.

7. A large region of the atmos-phere in which the air has similar properties is a(n) _____.

8. A dangerous storm that forms over warm ocean waters is a(n) _____.

9. A(n) _____ forms when cold air moves in under a warm air mass.

10. The average weather pattern of a region is its _____.

Test Prep

11. Thunderheads are also known as _____.
   A cumulus clouds
   B cumulonimbus clouds
   C stratus clouds
   D cirrus clouds

12. Winds curve to the right in the northern hemisphere because of the _____.
   F Coriolis Effect
   G relative humidity
   H Sun
   J Moon

13. A _____ usually brings cooler, drier air.
   A warm front
   B humid day
   C storm surge
   D cold front

14. The side of a mountain that usually does not get rain is _____.

   F in a rain shadow

   G facing the Pacific coast

   H on the windward side

   J facing the wind

15. A hurricane can cause sea level to rise because the air pressure under the hurricane _____.

   A is higher than normal

   B is lower than normal

   C is the same as usual

   D does not affect why a hurricane makes the sea level rise

Concepts and Skills

16. Reading in Science Write a paragraph explaining how a thunderstorm forms.

17. Scientific Methods Design a research project to determine whether sunspot activity affects Earth's climate.

18. Product Ads What products are advertised to protect you from the weather in the winter? In the summer? What is each product supposed to do? Are the products as good as the ads say? Write a paragraph explaining your answer.

19. INQUIRY SKILL **Measure** What if your area were to get twice as much rain as usual for the next ten years? Write a paragraph explaining how you would make a model of your climate as it is now. How would you adjust it to study the effect of extra rainfall?

20. Critical Thinking Do you think that Earth is getting warmer? Write a paragraph explaining your hypothesis. Describe what you might do to test your ideas.

Did You Ever Wonder?

INQUIRY SKILL **Form a hypothesis** Are cities warmer than their surrounding areas? How can you test this?

LOG ON Visit www.science.mmhschool.com to boost your test scores.

Tim Samaras

TORNADO CHASER

Tornadoes are nature's most powerful storms. They can produce winds that blow at speeds of 300 miles an hour. Tornadoes can destroy homes and kill people. Sometimes people don't have enough warning that a tornado is headed their way. That's where tornado chasers come in. They work to give scientists information to develop warning systems.

Tim Samaras looks for a storm that he thinks will spin off a tornado. Once he spots a tornado, Samaras does the opposite of what most people do. He drives his minivan *toward* the storm to study it.

Inside his minivan are instruments to record weather and wind data. There is also a powerful computer with mapping software to track the storm.

Samaras has also created a tough instrument, or probe. It takes readings from *inside* a tornado. Getting a probe inside a tornado is tricky. Tornadoes don't follow straight paths, so it's hard to guess where they will head next.

In May 2002, near Dodge City, Kansas, Samaras placed a probe in a spot where he hoped a twister would hit. Later, Samaras recovered the probe. It had been inside the twister! The probe had recorded barometric pressure, wind speed, and temperature.

Thanks to the work of storm chasers, scientists are learning why some storms produce tornadoes. They also can be more certain of where a tornado will form. With this information, they are improving storm prediction and saving lives.

Tim Samaras in the field

TOP 5 Worst Years for Tornadoes

The United States has more tornadoes than any other country—about 1,000 a year. Each year, about 38 tornadoes get rated very strong to violent on a scale of wind speed.

1. 1975: 116 strong tornadoes
2. 1965: 75 strong tornadoes
3. 1957: 64 strong tornadoes
4. 1973 and 1976: 59 strong tornadoes
5. 1971: 56 strong tornadoes

Write About It

1. Why is it hard to place a probe in the path of a tornado?
2. Why is the work of storm chasers important?

LOG ON Visit **www.science.mmhschool.com** to learn more about storm chasers and tornadoes.

Football-Field Solar System

Your goal is to make a model of the solar system.

What to Do

Use the data tables from the Explore activity on page D15 and from the Inquiry Skill Builder on page D17.

Explain how you would make a model solar system on a 100-yard football field, if you placed your model Sun at one end and your model Earth two yards away. Include approximate positions for the asteroid belt, the Kuiper Belt, and the Oort Cloud.

Analyze Your Results

1. Where would Jupiter be placed? Where would Pluto be placed?

2. Approximately where would you place the asteroid belt? Where would you place the Kuiper Belt? The Oort cloud?

3. What else would you have to do if you wanted to make a true scale model of the solar system?

CLIMATE on a CHART

Your goal is to make a climate chart of your local area.

What to Do

A climate chart shows average values for temperature (°C) and precipitation (mm). Use local data to make a climate chart for your area.

Analyze Your Results

1. What is the rainiest month where you live? The least rainy month?

2. What is the hottest month where you live? The coldest?

3. Describe your local climate in words based on your climate chart.

UNIT E

Properties of Matter and Energy

LOOK!

With a mighty roar, the space shuttle blasts off. What kind of energy powers the space shuttle's engines?

Properties of Matter and Energy

CHAPTER 12

Properties and Structure of Matter

LESSON 1
Physical Properties, E4

LESSON 2
Elements and Compounds, E20

LESSON 3
Solids, Liquids, and Gases, E34

Did You Ever Wonder?

How can potters use their talent and creativity to turn clay and water into beautiful vases? When wet, clay has certain physical properties that allow potters to shape it into different forms. What happens to the clay when the vases are dried in a hot kiln, or oven?

INQUIRY SKILL Classify One property of clay is that it is heavy. Make a list of movable things you have touched in the last hour. Rearrange the list from the heaviest to the lightest items.

E 2

Physical Properties

Vocabulary

matter, E6
mass, E6
volume, E6
weight, E7
density, E8
conduct, E14
insulate, E14

Get Ready

When you say something is "bigger" than something else, what does "bigger" mean? What is bigger than a hot air balloon? How can the balloon float in the air?

If the balloon is empty and folded up, is it smaller? Will it float now?

Bigger or smaller. More or less. How could you test different ways that things can be "more" or "less" than other things?

Inquiry Skill

You experiment when you perform a test to support or disprove a hypothesis.

Explore Activity

Which Is More?

Procedure: Design Your Own

1 **Observe** Look at the golf ball (or wooden block) and blown-up balloon. Which is "more"? Think of how one object could be "more":
- more when you use a balance
- more when you put it in water and see how much the water level goes up, and so on

Record your observations.

2 Use the equipment to verify one way that one object is more than another. Decide which of the two objects is "more" and which one is "less."

3 Repeat your measurements to verify your answer.

4 Now use different equipment to compare the two objects. Is the same object still "more"? Explain.

5 Repeat your measurements to verify your answer.

Drawing Conclusions

1 **Communicate** Identify the equipment you used. Report your results.

2 For each test, which object was more? In what way was it more than the other object?

3 FURTHER INQUIRY **Experiment** What if you were given a large box of puffed oats and a small box of oatmeal? Which do you think would be more? Design an experiment to test your hypothesis. Tell what equipment you would use.

Materials

golf ball or wooden block

blown-up balloon

equal-pan balance

ruler

string

box, such as a shoe box

pail of water

Main Idea Matter is anything that has mass and occupies space.

What Is Matter?

All of the gases, liquids, and solids in the world around you—the air you breathe, the water you drink, and the chair you sit on—are made of **matter**. Testing to see whether a golf ball or a balloon is "more" measures *properties* of the matter in these objects.

A golf ball has more **mass** because it tips the balance more. However, a balloon has more **volume** because it fills up a greater amount of space.

Mass is a measure of the amount of matter in an object. The photo shows how a balance is used to measure mass. Mass is often measured in kilograms.

Volume describes how much space a sample of matter takes up. Volumes are often measured in milliliters (mL). As the photo shows, the volume of a liquid may be measured using a graduated cylinder, a beaker, or a measuring cup. The volume of a solid may be measured by multiplying its height times its length times its width. Solids don't always have regular shapes, however. We can also measure the volume of a solid by seeing how much water it displaces from a container. A solid with a volume of 1 cm³ will make the water rise 1 mL, for example. A volume of 1 cm³ equals 1 mL.

Matter is defined using the properties of mass and volume. Matter is anything that has mass and takes up space.

Measuring Mass and Volume

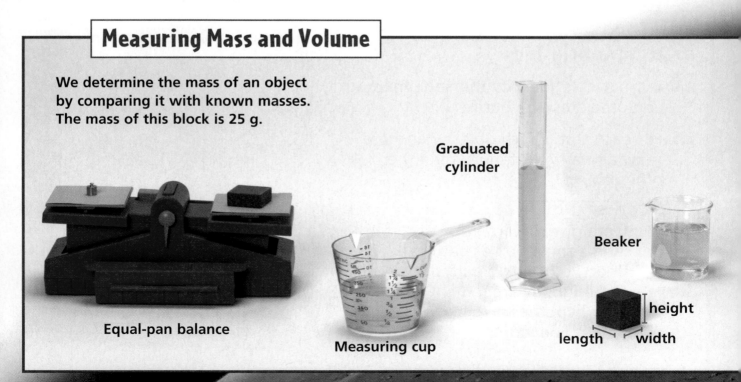

We determine the mass of an object by comparing it with known masses. The mass of this block is 25 g.

Equal-pan balance

Measuring cup

Graduated cylinder

Beaker

height
length   width

Weight

What if you find the mass of a certain book to be 1 kilogram? You might be tempted to say, "This book weighs 1 kilogram." However, this is incorrect. The book's **weight** is actually the force of gravity between Earth and the book. The book's mass, on the other hand, is a measure of the amount of matter in the book compared with known masses.

As you know, we can use kilograms to measure an object's mass. However, to measure weight, we must use a quantity that describes the force of gravity between two masses. Scientists prefer to use a quantity called the *newton* (N) to measure force. One newton is the same as 0.22 pound. (One pound is 4.45 newtons.) Newtons and pounds both describe the amount of pull or push a force produces. In this case the force is the pull of gravity.

An object's weight depends on its location in the universe. If you were to travel to the Moon, for example, you would have less weight. The Moon has less mass than Earth, so the force of gravity between your body and the Moon would be less. However, your mass would remain unchanged, as shown in the diagram.

▷ **What are two properties of matter?**

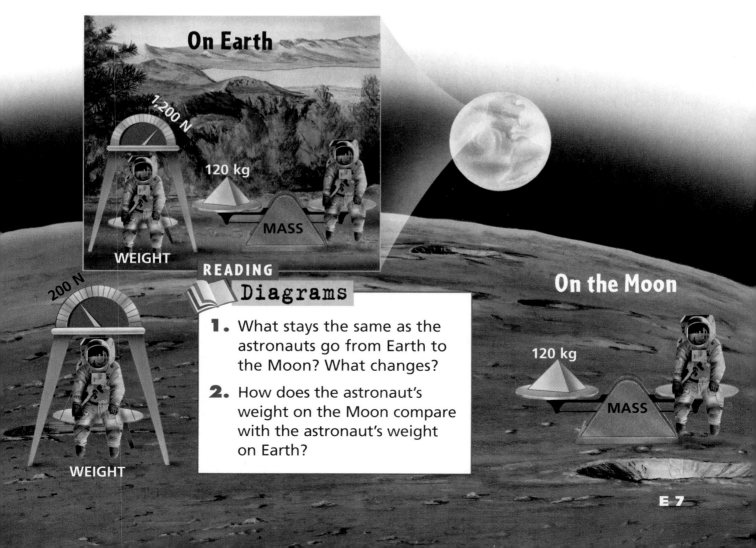

On Earth

1,200 N

120 kg

MASS

WEIGHT

200 N

On the Moon

120 kg

MASS

WEIGHT

READING
Diagrams

1. What stays the same as the astronauts go from Earth to the Moon? What changes?

2. How does the astronaut's weight on the Moon compare with the astronaut's weight on Earth?

What Is Density?

As you learned on page E6, mass and volume are two properties of matter. Can we use these properties to tell us more about matter? How can these two measurements tell us something new?

If we divide the mass of a sample by its volume, we get a new measurement of matter. This property is called **density** . The density of an object tells us how massive something is for its size. It compares an object's mass with its volume.

Let's look at an example. If 2 mL of water has a mass of 2 g, then 2 g divided by 2 mL equals 1 g per mL.

The density is 1 g per mL. If we combined that water sample with another 2 mL sample, we would have 4 mL and 4 g of water. The density would still be 1 g per mL.

As long as conditions, such as temperature, do not change, the density of a substance does not change. The size of the sample does not matter. Density can be used to help identify materials because of this. If you had a piece of metal with a density of 11.3 g per mL, it would probably be lead. A similar-looking piece with a density of 2.7 g per mL, however, would probably be aluminum. Each material has its own density.

▷ **How can density be measured?**

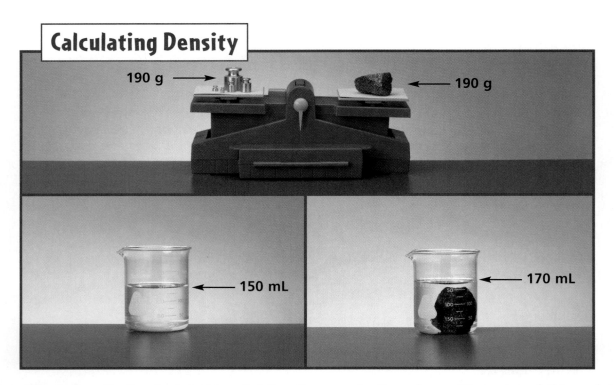

Calculating Density

190 g ⟶ ⟵ 190 g

150 mL

170 mL

An object's density is calculated by dividing its mass by its volume. The mass of this rock is 190 g. Its volume can be determined by calculating how much water it displaces from the beaker. If you subtract the volume of the water from the volume of the water plus the rock, you get the volume of the rock. (170 mL – 150 mL = 20 mL). The volume of this rock is 20 mL. The density of this rock is: 190 g ÷ 20 mL = 9.5 g per mL.

How Metal Boats Float

Think about objects that have more matter packed into the space they take up than water does. Will such objects sink or float in water? You have probably seen how a metal object like a nail or a spoon sinks in water. However, huge ships made of similar metal float even when they carry large cargoes. How is this possible? In this activity you will make different sized models of a metal boat. Scientists use models to help them understand properties of matter. Models also make experimenting easier. Try different designs to see how well the model boats can carry heavy cargo.

Materials

aluminum foil

large paper clips

pan of water

Procedure

1 **Make a Model** Prepare 3 sheets of aluminum foil of different sizes. Record their lengths and widths and use them to make 3 boats. Experiment with different designs and float them on water.

2 **Predict** Write down what you think will happen when you place more and more matter in the empty space of the boat. What steps should you follow to test your prediction? Be sure to use only the materials listed above.

3 **Experiment** Carry out your procedure, keeping a written record of what you observe.

Drawing Conclusions

1 **Communicate** How well did your results agree with your prediction?

2 Compare your model with those of your classmates. Which boat held the most clips? Why?

3 **Make a Model** The aluminum foil boat is a model of a steel ship. Use the way your boat floats to explain how a steel ship floats. Why was using a model of a large ship helpful?

4 **Communicate** What changed as more and more matter was added to the empty space of the boat? What happened as a result of this change?

How Dense Are Solids, Liquids, and Gases?

Think of cutting a piece of aluminum foil into smaller and smaller pieces until the pieces are tinier than specks of dust. All matter—solids, liquids, and gases—is made of similar tiny particles. An object's mass is related to the number and type of particles it has.

Density describes how tightly these particles are packed together. A high density means that many particles are packed tightly into a given space. A low density means that only a few particles fill the same amount of space.

The particles of a solid tend to be packed tightly together. They don't have a lot of room to move around. However, the particles of a gas usually spread out. In general, matter in the solid state is more dense than in the liquid state. Likewise, matter in the liquid state tends to be more dense than in the gaseous state.

READING Main Idea
How do the densities of solids, liquids, and gases compare?

Water is special! Solid water, ice, is less dense than liquid water. The particles in ice are more spread out than the particles in liquid water.

Gas (steam)

Solid (ice)

Liquid (water)

Densities of Common Substances

State	Substance		Density (g/cm³)
Solid	Aluminum	Gold	Aluminum, 2.7 Gold, 18.9
Liquid	Water	Mercury	Water, 1.0 Mercury, 13.5
Gas	Helium	Air	Helium, 0.00018 Air at sea level, 0.0012

READING Charts

1. Which is denser—aluminum or gold? Mercury or gold?
2. Organize the substances in the chart from the least dense to the most dense. Make a bar graph with the densities of these substances.

How Does Density Make Things Sink or Float?

Have you ever observed a beach ball floating in a pool? Have you ever dropped your towel in the water, only to see it sink to the bottom? What makes some things float, and others sink?

Density determines an object's ability to sink or float. An object floats in a liquid when its density is less than the liquid's density. A beach ball is filled with air. Air is less dense than water, so the beach ball floats. We describe an object's ability to float as its *buoyancy* (BOY·uhn·see).

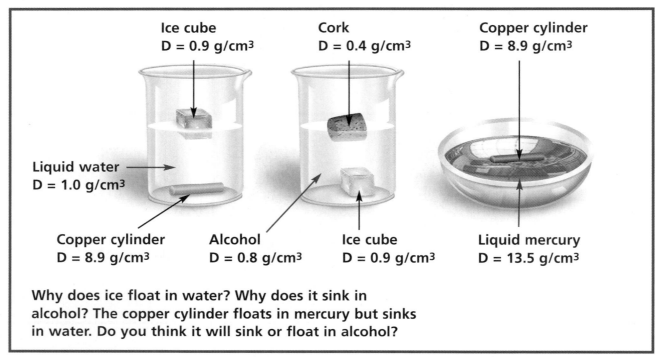

Ice cube
D = 0.9 g/cm³

Cork
D = 0.4 g/cm³

Copper cylinder
D = 8.9 g/cm³

Liquid water
D = 1.0 g/cm³

Copper cylinder
D = 8.9 g/cm³

Alcohol
D = 0.8 g/cm³

Ice cube
D = 0.9 g/cm³

Liquid mercury
D = 13.5 g/cm³

Why does ice float in water? Why does it sink in alcohol? The copper cylinder floats in mercury but sinks in water. Do you think it will sink or float in alcohol?

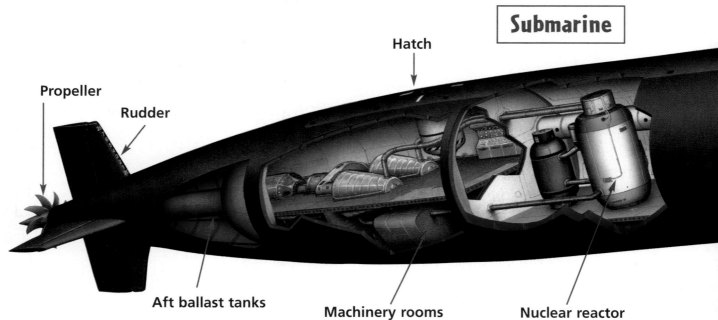

Submarine

Hatch

Propeller

Rudder

Aft ballast tanks

Machinery rooms

Nuclear reactor

Helium balloons can float, too. However, they float in air instead of water. Helium is less dense than air, so helium balloons rise into the sky.

As you know, not all objects float. An object sinks in a liquid when it is more dense than the liquid. The copper cylinder shown in the diagram sinks in water. The ice cube sinks in alcohol.

It's easy to float in the Dead Sea because salt water is denser than fresh water. The Dead Sea has the densest saltiest water on Earth. Swimmers float higher in this sea than in ocean water.

▷ **How does density determine an object's ability to float in water?**

Sailors pump seawater into ballast tanks on a submarine to bring its average density close to the density of the surrounding water. This makes the sub have little tendency to rise or sink.

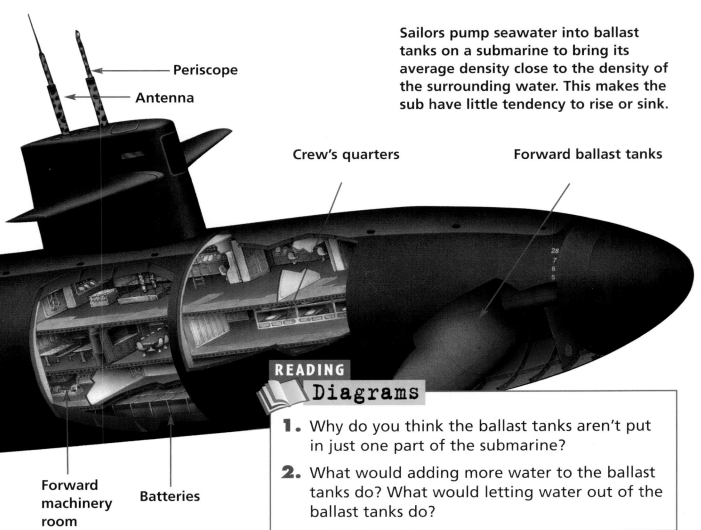

Periscope

Antenna

Crew's quarters

Forward ballast tanks

Forward machinery room

Batteries

READING
Diagrams

1. Why do you think the ballast tanks aren't put in just one part of the submarine?

2. What would adding more water to the ballast tanks do? What would letting water out of the ballast tanks do?

What Are Conductors and Insulators?

Matter has many important properties besides density. For example, some materials **conduct** energy very well. These materials allow energy to flow through them easily. However, other materials **insulate** against the passage of energy. They do not readily permit energy to flow. Look carefully at the photographs to learn about materials that conduct or insulate.

Cooking pots and pans are made of metal because metal conducts heat well. However, they should have wooden or ceramic handles. Such handles insulate against heat so you don't get burned when you touch the handles.

Metals, like the copper in the wire, are also good conductors of electricity.

Which material in this pan is a conductor? Which is an insulator?

The electricity flows from the battery to the light bulb through the wire, producing light and heat. The plastic that coats the wire is an insulator. Anyone who touches the plastic coating will not be shocked, because the electricity cannot pass through it.

Sound booths are made of materials that insulate the room from outside noise. This property is important for musicians who are recording a new CD.

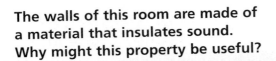

The walls of this room are made of a material that insulates sound. Why might this property be useful?

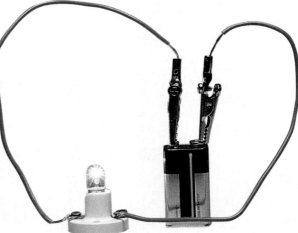

The wire is a good conductor of electricity. The plastic that coats the wire is an insulator. Why must electrical wire be insulated?

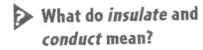

▶ What do *insulate* and *conduct* mean?

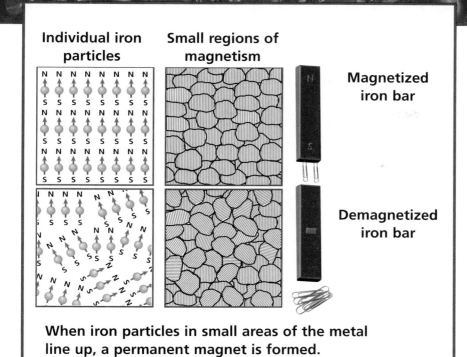

Individual iron particles

Small regions of magnetism

Magnetized iron bar

Demagnetized iron bar

When iron particles in small areas of the metal line up, a permanent magnet is formed.

> **What makes a material magnetic?**

What Is Magnetism?

Certain objects push or pull on each other because they are *magnetic*. Magnetism is another property of some kinds of matter. A magnet has a north pole and a south pole. North poles and south poles of magnets attract, but two poles that are alike repel. Magnets can also attract certain materials that are made of a metal like iron.

Like density, magnetism results from the combined effect of the properties of tiny particles. In iron, for example, each tiny particle of iron is itself a magnet.

Look at the diagram above. Each particle has a north and a south pole. When the particles line up, the material is magnetic. When the particles do not line up pole to pole, however, the material is not magnetic.

Earth acts like a huge magnet. A compass needle is a magnet that points to the Earth's magnetic North pole.

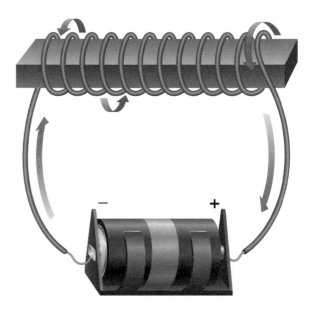

The electric current flowing through the coils lines up the iron core particles pole to pole, making a strong electromagnet. Without the current, the lineup ends and the magnetism disappears.

How Do We Use Properties of Matter?

Engineers and scientists use properties of matter when they design and build new things.

Aerogels are new materials with very low density and relatively great strength. They are made of tiny pockets of air surrounded by thin walls of silica. Silica is the same material found in sand and in window glass.

Aerogels are very good insulators of heat. Insulated windows containing aerogel would be from 10 to 20 times better at holding in heat than ordinary glass windows.

Scientists have discovered that some materials become perfect conductors of electricity when they are very cold. The photo shows a ceramic, glasslike material that conducts perfectly when cooled to −196°C (−320.8°F).

This white aerogel has such a low density that it can float on top of soap bubbles.

▷ **How are properties of matter used?**

A magnetic cube floats above a disk made of a "superconducting" ceramic material. This effect can lift trains above the rails so that they can travel faster.

Why It Matters

You use many different properties of matter every day. Matter that conducts electricity lets you use a reading lamp at night or listen to your favorite CDs. Density allows you to float in a boat on a lake or float through the sky in a hot air balloon. Magnets help you find your way home with a compass.

e-Journal Visit our Web site www.science.mmhschool.com to do a research project on properties and structure of matter.

Think and Write

1. List four properties of matter.

2. If a rock was taken from Earth to the Moon, how would its mass and weight be affected?

3. What if you had rubber bands, wood chips, straight pins, aluminum foil, and glass beads? Using a property of matter, classify these objects. Show your results in a table.

4. **INQUIRY SKILL** **Make a Model** Design a strong, light (up to 100 g), cardboard structure to bridge a 30-cm gap. How much weight can it support?

5. **Critical Thinking** Think of the properties of matter you use every day. In what ways are they important to you?

L·I·N·K·S

WRITING LINK

Personal Narrative Write about a typical day from the time you get up until the time you go to sleep. Tell the events in order. What properties of matter do you rely on to get to school, do your homework, and play with your friends?

MATH LINK

Calculate density. Find some small objects around your classroom or house— a seashell, a rock, or even a piece of fruit. Measure its mass and its volume. Use its mass and volume to find its density.

LITERATURE LINK

Read *Moon Landing That Never Was* to learn about the spacecraft *Apollo 13*. Try the activities at the end of the book.

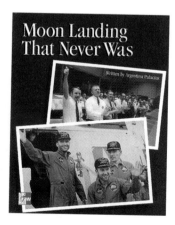

TECHNOLOGY LINK

 LOG ON Visit www.science.mmhschool.com for more links.

ANIMALS: icy SURVIVAL

Imagine a world where water's like most other substances—it becomes denser as it freezes. Ice, now heavier than water, sinks to the bottoms of ponds. The water quickly freezes from the bottom up into solid blocks of ice. Fish in the ponds freeze, too. That's the end of most freshwater fish.

In summer the ice near the tops of the ponds melts, but not the ice at the bottom. That ice never melts. Each summer things get worse. Before long there's no liquid water left on Earth!

Luckily that scenario is science fiction, but real water is stranger than science fiction! Why doesn't it become denser when it turns solid? The answer lies in what happens when water molecules get cold enough to freeze.

As you know, water molecules are made of two hydrogen atoms and one oxygen atom. When water freezes, the molecules are kept farther apart than they are in liquid water.

Ice is only nine-tenths as dense as liquid water, so when water freezes, it expands. A given volume of ice weighs

Water molecules

Ice molecules

less than the same volume of water. That's why ice floats in your lemonade!

Ice forms a protective covering for ponds. Under the ice the water stays liquid, allowing plants and animals to survive the winter. Because ice floats, oceans have icebergs. They can mean trouble for ships, because most of an iceberg is underwater. Look at the ice cube in your next drink. How much of it is under the surface?

What Did I Learn?

1. Water is different from other substances because

  A it is less dense as a solid than as a liquid.

  B it is more dense as a solid than as a liquid.

  C its molecules are packed more tightly as a solid.

  D none of the above

2. Ice helps plants and animals in ponds survive by

  F preserving their habitat.

  G providing more molecules of water.

  H keeping the temperature low.

  J forming a protective covering.

LOG ON Visit www.science.mmhschool.com to learn more about survival in cold.

Elements and Compounds

Get Ready

Look at Jupiter! It's hidden by dense clouds. Are they similar to Earth's clouds? What is Jupiter made of "beneath" its clouds?

Here's a similar question. What is matter made of? Scientists share information as they seek answers to their questions.

If you cannot "look inside" something—a planet or a piece of matter—how can scientists tell what a planet or any piece of matter is made of?

Inquiry Skill

You communicate when you share information.

Explore Activity

How Do We Know What's "Inside" Matter?

Materials

3 identical, sealed, opaque boxes

equal-pan balance with set of masses

magnet

Procedure

1. **Observe** Examine the three boxes, but do not open them. You can lift them, shake them, listen to the noises they make, feel the way their contents shift as you move them, and so on. Use the magnet and balance to obtain more data about the unknown contents. Record your observations.

2. **Infer** Try to determine what is in each box.

Drawing Conclusions

1. **Communicate** Describe what you think is in each box.

2. How did you make your decisions?

3. Do these boxes have anything in common? In what ways are they similar? In what ways are they different?

4. FURTHER INQUIRY **Experiment** What if you have a can of peanuts and a can of stewed tomatoes? The cans look the same except for the labels. Now what if your baby brother takes the labels off? You want the peanuts, but you don't want to open the tomatoes by mistake. What experiments can you do to find out what is inside—before you open the cans?

Main Idea All matter is made of elements.

What Is Matter Made Of?

In studying matter scientists face a challenge. The basic particles that make up matter are too small to be seen directly. In the past the tests scientists performed on matter gave only hints about how matter is put together. That's because particles of matter cannot be observed.

People have experimented with matter for thousands of years. In ancient times the goal was often a practical product like a colorful dye, a metal sword, or a plow. In recent centuries matter has also been studied with carefully planned scientific experiments.

The ancient Greek philosopher Aristotle believed that all matter was composed of four elements—earth, air, fire, and water. However, during the last three centuries, scientists have identified the true chemical **elements**. These substances are the basic building blocks of all matter. One of the most interesting elements is shown in the photograph at the bottom of the page. It expands evenly when warmed and makes a good liquid for thermometers. What is it?

This bronze coin was made about 2,500 years ago. Bronze is made by mixing the metals copper and tin.

The element mercury is also known as liquid silver. It is beautiful but highly poisonous. Mercury is often used in thermometers. Why?

The Elements

Elements are pure substances that cannot be broken down into any simpler substances. You are probably familiar with many of them. Several are shown in the photographs. How many do you recognize?

Many elements have been known since ancient times but were not truly recognized as elements until the last few centuries. Other elements were found for the first time only recently. For example, germanium was not discovered until 1885. Also, some elements are not even found in nature. They have been made by scientists in nuclear reactors and huge machines called particle accelerators. Even though there are many different elements, living organisms and most materials are made up of just a few elements.

Each element is given a special symbol of one or two letters. The first letter is always a capital. The second letter is never a capital. Sometimes the letters match the English name, such as Ni for nickel or Zn for zinc. In other cases the symbol comes from an ancient name. Gold, for instance, is given the symbol Au from its Latin name, *aurum*.

READING **Main Idea**
What are the building blocks of matter?

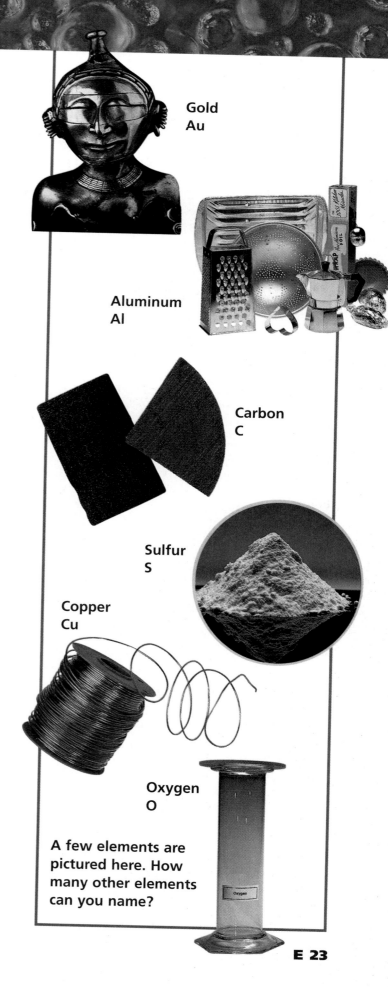

Gold
Au

Aluminum
Al

Carbon
C

Sulfur
S

Copper
Cu

Oxygen
O

A few elements are pictured here. How many other elements can you name?

What Are Compounds?

Imagine looking at pure water through a microscope. It would look the same everywhere. Water has this appearance because it is a single substance. However, the photograph below shows how passing electricity through water breaks it apart into two elements, hydrogen and oxygen. If water is a single substance, how could it contain the elements hydrogen and oxygen?

Actually, the hydrogen and oxygen in water are chemically combined. This makes them act like a single substance. Any substance that is formed by the chemical combination of two or more elements is called a **compound**.

All compounds are single substances that can only be broken into simpler substances by chemical reactions. Compounds have different properties than the elements that make them up, as the lower photographs show.

Water is made of hydrogen and oxygen, as this experiment shows.

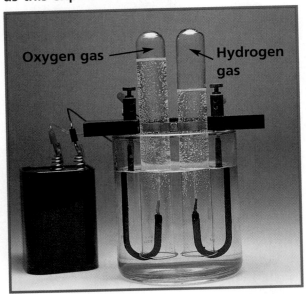

Oxygen gas → ← Hydrogen gas

▷ **How is a compound different from an element?**

The compound sodium chloride is a solid at room temperature. We use it on our foods to give them more flavor. It belongs to a group of compounds called salts. Salts are always made up of a metal and a nonmetal.

Sodium and chlorine combine to make sodium chloride. Sodium is a soft, reactive metal that can explode on contact with water. Chlorine is a very poisonous gas.

Sodium

+

Chlorine

=

Sodium chloride (table salt)

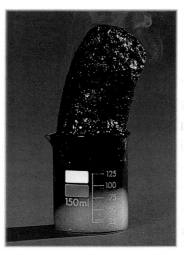

1 When sulfuric acid is added to sugar, it breaks the compound into its elements.

2 The steamy cloud you observe is condensing water vapor, composed of hydrogen and oxygen.

3 The black solid left behind is carbon.

How Do You Write a Compound's Name?

As you know, each element has a one or two letter symbol. Scientists also write symbols for compounds, which are called *chemical formulas*. A compound's chemical formula contains the symbols for the elements that make it up.

The formula also contains numbers below the element symbols called *subscripts*. The table shows chemical formulas for some familiar compounds.

The subscripts in a chemical formula tell us the number of particles that combine in a compound. For example, water is made up of two elements—hydrogen and oxygen. For every oxygen particle, there are two hydrogen particles. The formula for water is written H_2O.

Table sugar is made up of the elements carbon, hydrogen, and oxygen.

Common Compounds	
Compound	**Chemical Formula**
Water	H_2O
Carbon dioxide	CO_2
Baking soda	$NaHCO_3$
Table salt	$NaCl$
Table sugar	$C_{12}H_{22}O_{11}$
Glucose (a sugar)	$C_6H_{12}O_6$

For every 12 carbon particles, there are 22 hydrogen particles and 11 oxygen particles. We write $C_{12}H_{22}O_{11}$ for table sugar's chemical formula.

The photo shows what happens to table sugar when it is treated with strong sulfuric acid. **(Warning: sulfuric acid is a dangerous substance.)** The acid takes out all the hydrogen and oxygen, leaving a black mass, carbon.

▷ **What is a chemical formula?**

What Are Elements Made Of?

In 1803 an English scientist named John Dalton stated an important theory: Matter is made up of tiny particles that cannot be cut into smaller pieces. Today we call Dalton's tiny particles **atoms** .

According to Dalton, the atoms of one element were all alike. Each element was made up of one kind of atom. However, the atoms of one element were different from the atoms of any other element. While many parts of Dalton's theory have been improved since 1803, the basic idea of atoms is correct. An atom is the smallest unit of an element that retains the properties of the element.

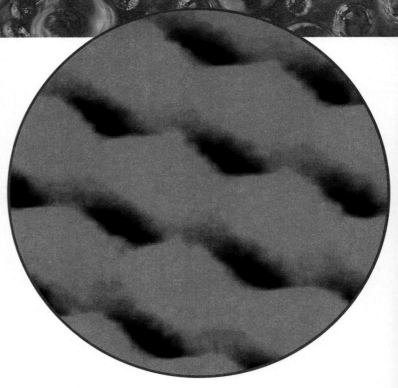

Individual carbon atoms

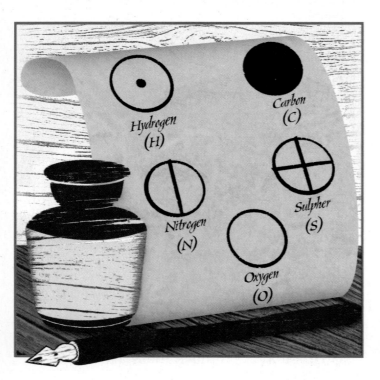

Dalton drew the symbols above for atoms. He believed that each element's atoms weighed a different amount from the atoms of other elements.

Many experiments since Dalton's day have shown us what atoms are like. Atoms are so small that we cannot see them directly, even through a microscope. Scientists have had to observe atoms indirectly. A special microscope called a *scanning tunneling microscope* uses a very sharp needle that can trace the bumps in a surface made by individual atoms. The photograph above shows some of what such special microscopes can "see."

Images made by these microscopes show that atoms are discrete and often occur in well-ordered arrays. For example, the carbon atoms in the photo are arranged in rings of six atoms each.

 **What is an atom?**

What Is Inside Atoms?

John Dalton imagined that atoms were like tiny steel marbles—solid and unbreakable. However, we now know that atoms are made of still smaller particles. Atoms are far from being solid—they are mostly empty space!

Atoms contain three kinds of particles called **protons** (PROH·tahnz), **neutrons** (NEW·trahnz), and **electrons** (i·LEK·trahnz). The protons and neutrons are located in a tiny, very dense body in the atom's center, called the atomic **nucleus** (NEW·klee·uhs). The electrons are in the space outside the nucleus.

Protons and neutrons have nearly the same mass, but electrons are about 2,000 times less massive than protons and neutrons.

Protons carry one unit of positive electric charge, while electrons carry one unit of negative electric charge.

Neutrons have no electric charge. All atoms have equal numbers of electrons and protons, so they have no overall electric charge.

The number of protons in an atom determines what element it is. For example, any atom with six protons is a carbon atom. Any atom with eight protons is an oxygen atom.

Look carefully at the diagrams on this page to see how atoms are put together.

▷ **What are the three particles that make up an atom?**

Atoms are made of protons, neutrons, and electrons. The number of protons an atom has determines what element it is.

Electron

Proton

Neutron

Helium

Hydrogen

Carbon

What Properties Do Elements Have?

We now know of 112 elements. These substances have many different properties. There are patterns in the properties of the elements. Study the photographs on this page to learn about properties that can demonstrate these patterns.

Chemical Reactivity

Some elements take part in chemical reactions much more easily than others. A few elements like helium, a noble gas, are chemically inactive, or inert. Reactive elements, like magnesium, are usually combined with other elements when found in nature.

Metal Versus Nonmetal

About three-fourths of the elements are metallic, like copper, gold, silver, aluminum, iron, and nickel. Metals conduct electricity and heat well. Metals are also shiny when freshly polished, and many can be worked into thin sheets or different shapes. In contrast nonmetals, like iodine, phosphorus, and carbon, are often poor conductors of heat and electricity. They are not reflective like metals.

States at Room Temperature

The elements shown are all at room temperature, about 22°C (71.6°F). Copper, aluminum, and iodine are solids at 22°C. Bromine, though, is a liquid at 22°C. Neon is a gas at 22°C.

▷ **How can elements be classified?**

Property: Chemical Reactivity

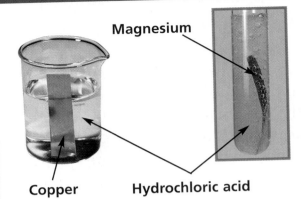

Magnesium

Copper   Hydrochloric acid

Magnesium takes part in chemical reactions much more easily than copper. Here the magnesium reacts rapidly with the acid. The copper hardly reacts at all.

Property: Metal Versus Nonmetal

Metals

Goldleaf

Aluminum

Copper

Nonmetals

Iodine

Neon

Bromine

Metals, like copper, gold, silver, aluminum, iron, and nickel, are good conductors of heat and electricity. Nonmetals are often poor conductors of heat and electricity.

How Can the Elements Be Grouped?

In 1869 a Russian scientist named Dmitry Mendeleyev found that the properties of the elements went through repeating cycles. Mendeleyev created a table of elements based on these cycles. Each group in his table contains elements with similar chemical properties. For example, one group contains lithium (Li), sodium (Na), potassium (K), rubidium (Rb), and cesium (Cs). All of these elements combine with chlorine in the same way. The formulas for their chlorine compounds are LiCl, NaCl, KCl, RbCl, and CsCl.

We call Mendeleyev's table the periodic table after the "periodic" changes he found in the elements' properties.

The metals lie on the left, and the nonmetals lie mainly on the right, with elements called metalloids in between.

Most elements are solids at 20°C, two are liquids, and the rest are gases.

The most reactive metals are at the left, the inert noble gases are on the right, and the most reactive nonmetals are in the second column from the right.

▷ **What is the periodic table? How is it organized?**

The Modern Periodic Table

The number in each box is the number of protons an atom of that element has.

Metallic Properties
- Li — Metal
- B — Metalloid
- C — Nonmetal

Phase at 20°C
- C — Solid
- Br — Liquid
- H — Gas

H 1																	He 2
Li 3	Be 4											B 5	C 6	N 7	O 8	F 9	Ne 10
Na 11	Mg 12											Al 13	Si 14	P 15	S 16	Cl 17	Ar 18
K 19	Ca 20	Sc 21	Ti 22	V 23	Cr 24	Mn 25	Fe 26	Co 27	Ni 28	Cu 29	Zn 30	Ga 31	Ge 32	As 33	Se 34	Br 35	Kr 36
Rb 37	Sr 38	Y 39	Zr 40	Nb 41	Mo 42	Tc 43	Ru 44	Rh 45	Pd 46	Ag 47	Cd 48	In 49	Sn 50	Sb 51	Te 52	I 53	Xe 54
Cs 55	Ba 56	Lu 71	Hf 72	Ta 73	W 74	Re 75	Os 76	Ir 77	Pt 78	Au 79	Hg 80	Tl 81	Pb 82	Bi 83	Po 84	At 85	Rn 86
Fr 87	Ra 88	Lr 103	Rf 104	Db 105	Sg 106	Bh 107	Hs 108	Mt 109	110	111	112		114		116		118

La 57	Ce 58	Pr 59	Nd 60	Pm 61	Sm 62	Eu 63	Gd 64	Tb 65	Dy 66	Ho 67	Er 68	Tm 69	Yb 70
Ac 89	Th 90	Pa 91	U 92	Np 93	Pu 94	Am 95	Cm 96	Bk 97	Cf 98	Es 99	Fm 100	Md 101	No 102

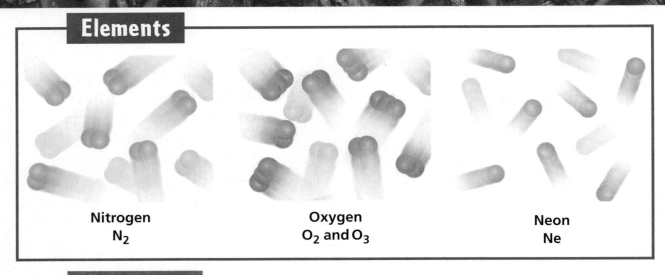

Elements

Nitrogen
N_2

Oxygen
O_2 and O_3

Neon
Ne

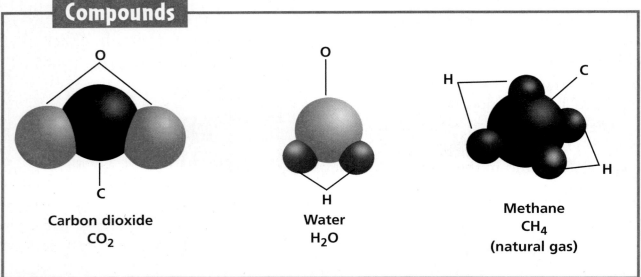

Compounds

O
C
Carbon dioxide
CO_2

O
H
Water
H_2O

H
C
H
Methane
CH_4
(natural gas)

What Are Molecules?

Some elements, such as neon, are made up of single atoms that do not attach to any other atoms. Other elements have atoms that attach to one or more additional atoms. Particles that contain more than one atom joined together are called **molecules**.

Nitrogen is an example of an element that is made up of molecules. Its molecules are made up of two nitrogen atoms. Some elements even exist in more than one form, such as oxygen. Oxygen is usually made up of two-atom

molecules, much like nitrogen, but oxygen can also exist as three-atom molecules. The three-atom form of oxygen is known as ozone. The three-atom ozone has properties different from the two-atom oxygen.

Molecules of elements always contain only one kind of atom. Compounds are made up of molecules that have different kinds of atoms joined together, as the lower diagram shows.

Note how the chemical formulas in both diagrams tell you the number of atoms in the molecules.

When a compound forms from elements, changes occur in the way that atoms are linked together. This causes the compound to have properties different from the elements. For example, water is a liquid, yet it is formed from two gases, hydrogen and oxygen. The diagram shows why water has properties different from hydrogen and oxygen gas—the atoms are linked in a new way when water forms.

▷ **What is the difference between a molecule of oxygen and a molecule of methane?**

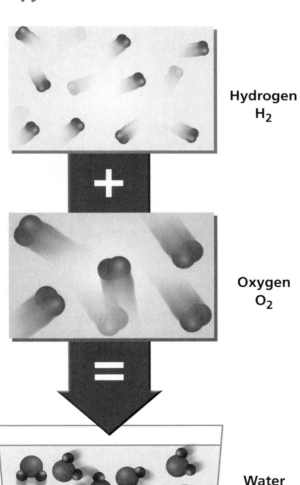

Hydrogen
H_2

+

Oxygen
O_2

=

Water
H_2O

Hydrogen plus oxygen makes water.

QUICK LAB

Modeling Molecules

FOLDABLES™ Make a Three-Tab Book. (See p. R 43.) Label as shown.

Hydrogen Molecules	Oxygen Molecules	Water Molecules
H_2	O_2	H_2O

1. Using small marshmallows for hydrogen atoms and large marshmallows for oxygen atoms, make two H_2 molecules and one O_2 molecule. Join the atoms with toothpicks.

2. **Use Numbers** Count the number of atoms of each type you have in your molecules. Record these numbers under the H_2 and O_2 tabs in your Three-Tab Book. Take these same marshmallows and make as many water molecules as you can, using toothpicks to join the atoms.

3. **Observe** How many water molecules did you make? Record under the H_2O tab.

4. **Infer** Why would real water molecules have properties different from real hydrogen and oxygen molecules?

How Do We Use Compounds?

By studying matter scientists have learned how to prepare compounds that are very useful. Many things are made from the atoms of just a small number of elements. The photographs on this page show several compounds that we depend on a great deal in modern life.

Take petroleum, for example. Petroleum is a complex mixture of *hydrocarbons*—compounds made of hydrogen and carbon atoms. Gasoline comes from petroleum. Its molecules usually have from 5 to 12 carbon atoms in chains. Gasoline gives off a lot of energy when it is burned, so we use it as a fuel in cars.

Many kinds of plastics are also made from hydrocarbons in petroleum or natural gas.

▷ **What are some useful compounds?**

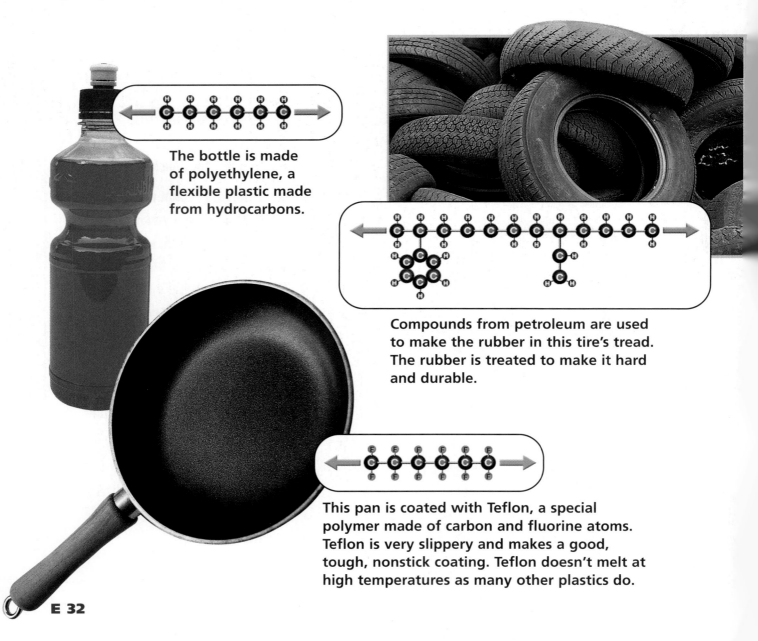

The bottle is made of polyethylene, a flexible plastic made from hydrocarbons.

Compounds from petroleum are used to make the rubber in this tire's tread. The rubber is treated to make it hard and durable.

This pan is coated with Teflon, a special polymer made of carbon and fluorine atoms. Teflon is very slippery and makes a good, tough, nonstick coating. Teflon doesn't melt at high temperatures as many other plastics do.

Why It Matters

Think what the world would be like if there were no compounds. There wouldn't be any plants. There wouldn't be any water or food or animals or things people build. In fact, there wouldn't be any people, either.

New compounds are discovered in nature every day. Scientists also develop new compounds in labs. Many compounds are used to help make life better.

e-Journal Visit our Web site **www.science.mmhschool.com** to do a research project on the uses of new compounds.

Think and Write

1. Why must some element symbols have two letters instead of just one?

2. A beryllium atom is made of four protons, five neutrons, and four electrons. Draw a model of this type of atom.

3. Name a compound whose properties are much different from the elements it is made of. How is it different?

4. Why do scientists use models to study atoms and molecules?

5. **Critical Thinking** Are all molecules compounds? Explain.

L·I·N·K·S

WRITING LINK

Expository Writing John Dalton was the scientist who defined atoms. Research his life and write a biography. Use print and online sources. List your sources at the end of your report.

MATH LINK

Solve this problem. Find the minimum daily requirement of calcium for someone your age. Calculate how much of a calcium-rich food you need to consume to meet this goal.

ART LINK

Make a model. What is your favorite element? Helium? Oxygen? Copper or iron? Draw a picture or make a model of this element. Include its protons, electrons, and neutrons.

TECHNOLOGY LINK

 LOG ON Visit **www.science.mmhschool.com** for more links.

Solids, Liquids, and Gases

Vocabulary

state of matter, E36
melting point, E37
boiling point, E37
freezing point, E37

Get Ready

How many different kinds of matter do you see here? How are they changing?

Glaciers are huge sheets of moving ice and snow. At a shoreline chunks of ice fall off and float away as icebergs.

Ice is solid water. You are looking at solid and liquid water. What does it take for solid ice to become liquid—to melt?

Inquiry Skill

You predict when you state possible results of an event or experiment.

Explore Activity

What Happens When Ice Melts?

Materials

ice cubes

water

graduated cylinder

plastic or
paper cup

thermometer

heat source (lamp or
sunlight)

watch or clock

equal-pan balance
with set of masses

Procedure

1 **Predict** You are going to explore the effect of heat on ice cubes as they melt. How do you think the temperature and mass of a cup of ice will change as it melts? Make a graph showing your prediction of how the temperature will change.

2 **Measure** Put ice cubes in the cup. Add 50 mL of water. Find and record the mass of the mixture. Swirl the mixture for 15 seconds.

3 **Measure** Place the thermometer in the cup. Wait 15 seconds. Then read and record the temperature. Put the cup under a heat source (lamp or sunlight). Take temperature readings every 3 minutes. Record each result.

4 **Measure** After all the ice has melted, find and record the mass of the cup of water again. Take and record 5 more water temperature readings at 3-minute intervals.

Drawing Conclusions

1 **Observe** What happened to the mass and temperature as the ice melted?

2 **Hypothesize** Why do you think you got the results described in question 1?

3 FURTHER INQUIRY **Predict** Design an experiment to test each of your predictions. What do you think will happen as you freeze water? Design an experiment to test your prediction.

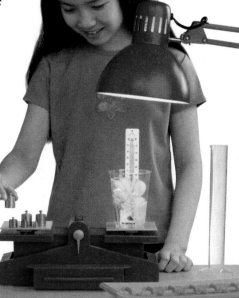

Main Idea Matter exists as a solid, a liquid, or a gas.

What Are the States of Matter?

Water turns from a solid to a liquid when it absorbs enough heat. If even more heat is supplied, the water will turn to a gas called steam. Most substances exist in one of three phases or states of matter —solid, liquid, or gas. Adding or removing heat can make substances change their phase or state.

During a change of state, the mass and identity of the substance remain the same. However, the substance gains new properties because the molecules are arranged in a different way.

The molecules of any substance are attracted to each other. The attraction is just a weaker form of the force that links the atoms in each of the molecules. When the molecules are arranged in organized positions, a solid results.

When heat is absorbed by a solid, the molecules vibrate faster and faster. At some point the molecules separate from one another. This causes the solid to become a liquid. When even more heat is absorbed, the molecules move faster and form a gas.

Change of State

As heat is absorbed, molecules move faster and become less organized.

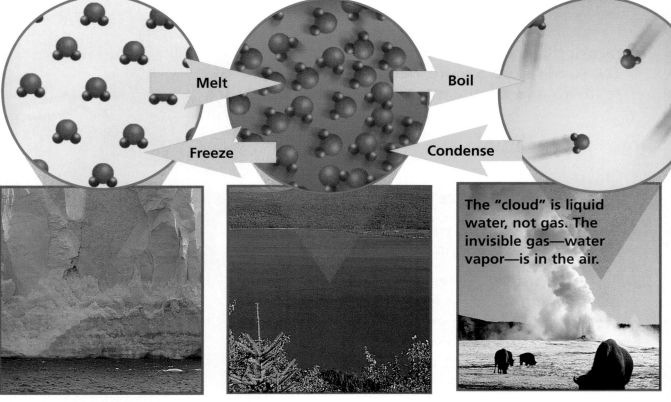

Melt

Boil

Freeze

Condense

The "cloud" is liquid water, not gas. The invisible gas—water vapor—is in the air.

Solid

Liquid

Gas

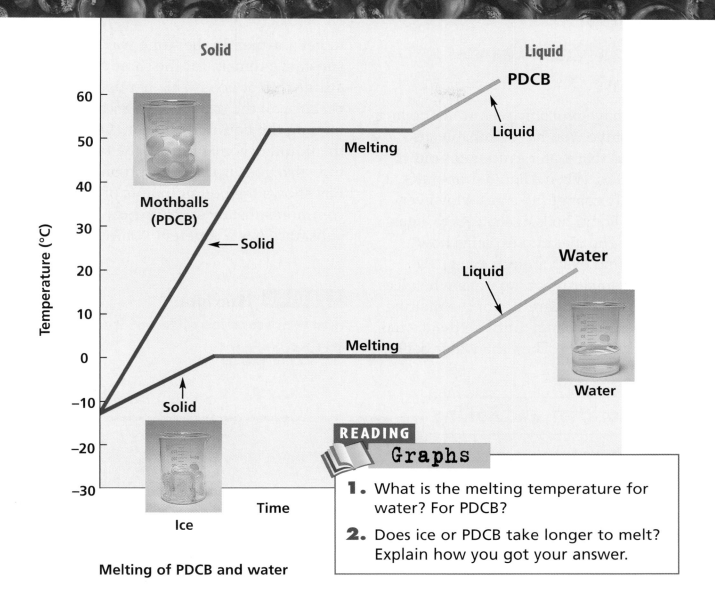

Melting of PDCB and water

READING Graphs

1. What is the melting temperature for water? For PDCB?

2. Does ice or PDCB take longer to melt? Explain how you got your answer.

The graph shows how the temperatures of two different compounds change as they are being heated. As you can see, these substances melt at different temperatures. In fact, each different pure substance has its own particular **melting point**. Each different substance also has its own boiling temperature, called the **boiling point**.

While a substance is melting or boiling, its temperature stays the same. It warms up only before or after the change of state.

What happens when heat is removed from the substance? It *condenses*—turns from a gas to a liquid—at the boiling temperature. It freezes—turns from a liquid to a solid—at the melting temperature. For this reason the melting point is also known as the **freezing point**.

▶ **What are melting and boiling points?**

E 37

How Can Matter Change to a Gas?

You have probably seen water boiling on the stove. You have probably also observed that water evaporates out of wet clothes. When a liquid evaporates, it gradually changes to a gas. However, when a liquid boils, it changes to a gas rapidly. The diagram explains how boiling and evaporation occur.

Remember what happens when ice melts? The temperature of the melting ice does not change until all the ice has turned to water. Then the water begins to get warmer. In the same way, a substance remains at the same temperature while it boils. This happens because all the heat energy goes into turning the liquid into steam. Once all the liquid becomes steam, the temperature also goes up. The graph on page E39 shows the boiling points of common substances. Note how each substance has a different boiling point.

READING **Main Idea**

How is evaporation different from boiling?

Evaporation and Boiling

1 A few molecules escape into the air, causing evaporation at room temperature.

2 When the liquid is heated, more molecules escape. The liquid evaporates faster.

3 As more heat is absorbed over time, the liquid reaches its boiling temperature. Boiling begins at the boiling point.

1. Is butane a liquid or a gas at 10°C?

2. Which boils at a lower temperature, rubbing alcohol or oxygen?

3. Which state of matter is lead at 80°C?

Solid and Liquid Ranges of Common Substances (in degrees Celsius)

Name	Formula	Melting Point	Boiling Point
Oxygen	O_2	−218°	−183°
Nitrogen	N_2	−210°	−196°
Butane	C_4H_{10}	−138°	−0.5°
Rubbing alcohol	C_3H_8O	−90°	82.4°
Water	H_2O	0°	100°
Mercury	Hg	−39°	357°
Lead	Pb	327°	1,740°

The table lists the melting points and boiling points of some common substances.

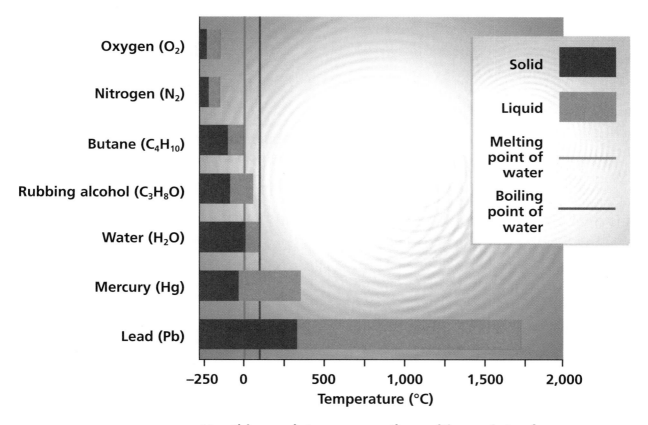

Use this graph to compare the melting points of the substances listed in the table.

What Are the Properties of Solids, Liquids, and Gases?

Solids keep their shape.

The aluminum cube in the first photo is a typical solid. It shows that solids retain their shape. Solids have the same volume no matter what container they are placed in. Also, solids cannot be poured, so they are not fluid.

Many solids form crystals, as in the second photograph. A gemlike crystal of alum is shown. The shape of such crystals results from the way the particles are arranged. The particles link together in an organized pattern.

Many solids form crystals.

Liquids have different properties from solids. Compare the first and third photographs. In the third photograph, the same volume of a colored liquid has been placed in two different containers. This shows that liquids, unlike solids, take on the shape of their containers. However, liquids do have a definite volume—they settle to the bottom of their containers. Also, as you know from pouring water, liquids are fluid.

Liquids take the shape of their containers.

Gases do not have a fixed volume of their own. The volume of a gas is determined by its container. The last photograph shows a yellowish gas in a tube separated from a second tube by a glass plate. When the plate is removed, the gas expands to fill both tubes. Gases always fill the full volume of their containers. Also, gases are fluid—they can be pumped through pipelines just like liquids.

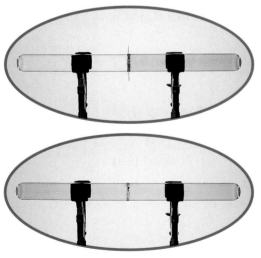

Gases fill the volume of their containers.

Expansion and Contraction

When the temperature of a material increases, its particles move faster. On average these particles tend to spread out more. This causes materials to *expand*—spread out—as they get hotter. The opposite happens when the temperature of a material decreases. Cool materials tend to *contract*—shrink. The material's particles tend to slow down and stay closer together. Gases expand or contract the most with changing temperature, but liquids and solids are also affected by temperature.

You have probably observed expansion and contraction in your everyday life. This property of matter makes bicycle tires and basketballs flat on cold days and your classroom door stick and be difficult to open on hot days. Can you think of other examples?

> ▷ How are solids, liquids, and gases different?

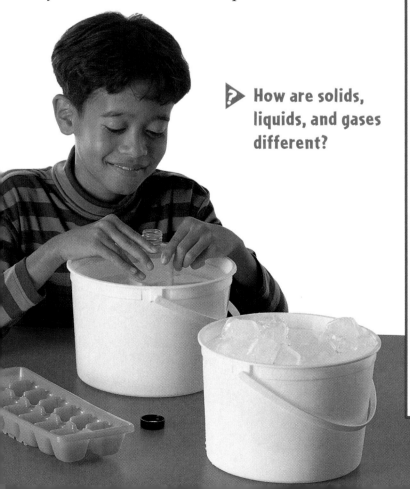

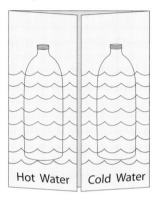

QUICK LAB

Collapsing Bottles

FOLDABLES Make a Shutter Fold. (See p. R 42.) Label it as shown.

Hot Water | Cold Water

1. **Predict** How does heat affect an empty plastic bottle? What do you think will happen to the bottle when it is warmed? What do you think will happen to it when it is cooled? Record your predictions.

2. With the cap off, hold the bottle for a minute or two in a pail of hot tap water. Then screw the cap on tightly while the bottle is still sitting in the hot water.

3. **Experiment** Now hold the bottle in a pail of ice water for a few minutes.

4. **Communicate** Record all your observations in the Shutter Fold.

5. **Infer** Write out an explanation of why the bottle changed as it did. Be sure to use the idea of how molecules move at different temperatures.

How Can Expansion and Contraction Be Used?

You have probably had your temperature taken with a thermometer. Thermometers have liquid mercury or colored alcohol in a bulb connected to a very thin tube. The liquid expands or contracts with changes in temperature and moves up or down in the tube. The position of the liquid in the tube gives the temperature.

In the cylinders of a car's engine, burning fuel produces hot, expanding gases. The expanded gas pushes on the pistons in the cylinders. The pistons in turn provide the power that drives the car forward.

The solid materials that make up a bridge or sidewalk expand when

Expansion joints keep roads and bridges from cracking on hot days when the road expands.

warmed. If the sections are assembled tightly on a normal day, they will expand against each other on very hot days. This expansion can cause cracks to form. To guard against this problem, engineers leave some space between the sections and fill it with a flexible material. Look for these "expansion joints" in the photograph above.

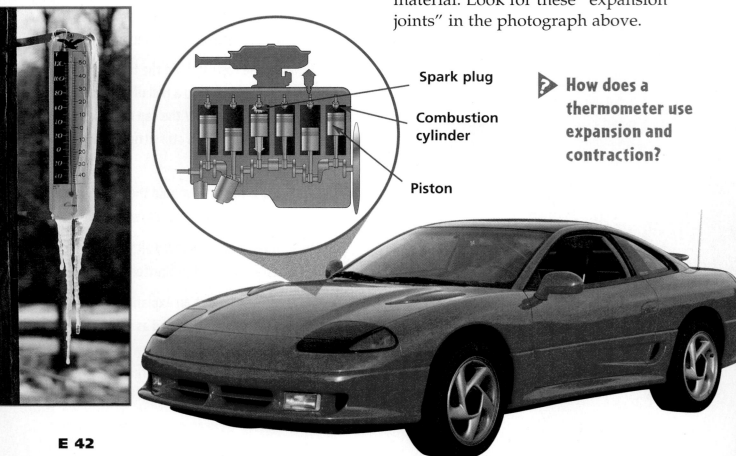

Spark plug

Combustion cylinder

Piston

▷ **How does a thermometer use expansion and contraction?**

Why It Matters

You sit, write, and climb on solids. Liquids allow you to bathe, swim, and drink. You breathe gases every day. They allow you to smell odors at a distance. Gases always fill the full volume of their containers. You notice this property every time you are in your room and smell food cooking in the kitchen.

e-Journal Visit our Web site **www.science.mmhschool.com** to do a research project on states of matter.

Think and Write

1. Explain what happens to the temperature of ice as it melts.

2. Acetone freezes at 95.35°C below 0°C and boils at 56.2°C. At 42°C what state of matter would acetone be in? At 84°C?

3. Gases can be easily squeezed into a smaller volume. Why is this so?

4. Explain why on a humid day, drops of water will form on the outside of a glass containing an ice cold drink.

5. **Critical Thinking** Water boils at 100°C at sea level. High up in the mountains, water boils at a lower temperature. Why does it take longer to cook potatoes high up in the mountains than it does to cook potatoes at sea level?

L·I·N·K·S

LITERATURE LINK

Read *Chilled to the Bone* to learn about icy places. Try the activities in the end of the book.

WRITING LINK

Explanatory Writing Exhale on a mirror and then fan the mirror with your hand. What happens? Write an explanatory essay to describe the task and explain the changes that you observe. Use time-order words, such as first, next, and then to present the steps in the process.

MATH LINK

Predict and try. How long will it take for different volumes of warm tap water to cool 10 degrees? Will the volume affect the cooling time? Plan the experiment. What measurement tools will you need? Try it.

TECHNOLOGY LINK

 LOG ON Visit **www.science.mmhschool.com** for more links.

The Hunt for Helium

It's colorless, odorless, and a gas. It's not very common on Earth. And this chemical element doesn't react with other elements—it doesn't form chemical compounds. No wonder it took so long to discover—even though it's the second most common element in the universe!

What is it?

In the nineteenth century, scientists were on the path to discovering all the elements. By 1868, more than 60 elements were known (today we know of over 110). That year, scientists used a spectroscope to study the Sun. They discovered a new element not yet found on Earth. They didn't know its properties, but they named it helium after *helios*, the Greek word for Sun.

Then scientists wondered if another undiscovered element was hiding in the air. Sure enough, when nitrogen was removed from a sample of air, a tiny amount of another gas was left behind. This was a new, colorless, odorless gas that didn't react with other elements. They named it argon.

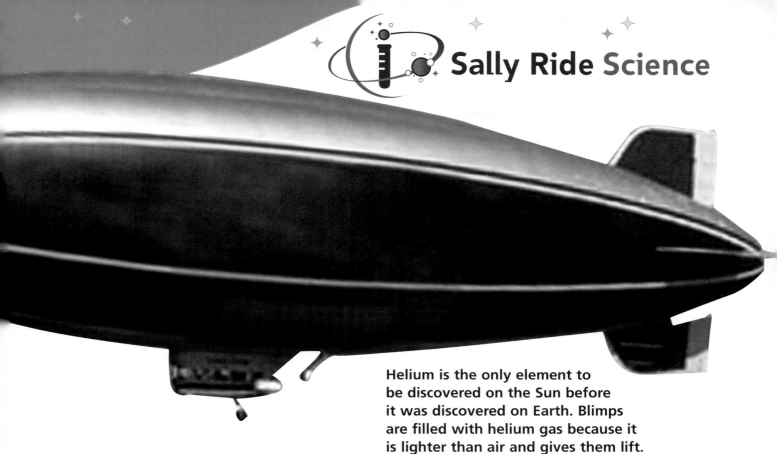

Helium is the only element to be discovered on the Sun before it was discovered on Earth. Blimps are filled with helium gas because it is lighter than air and gives them lift.

Once argon was discovered, scientists knew there must be other elements with similar properties. That's when chemists discovered a strange gas seeping out of a mineral. Much to their surprise, it matched what astronomers had seen years earlier on the Sun. Did you guess it was helium?

After that, it took only four more years to track down the other elements in this unreactive family: neon, krypton, xenon, and radon. Helium and its kin used to be called "noble" gases. The reason was that, just like nobility, they had little to do with the "common" elements.

What Did I Learn?

1. Why were the noble gases hard to discover?

  A They are colorless, odorless, and unreactive.
  B They aren't very plentiful.
  C They're not found on Earth.
  D They react with many other elements.

2. How did helium get its name?

  F It is heavier than air.
  G It is used to fill balloons.
  H It was named after the Sun.
  J It was named after a mineral.

LOG ON Visit www.science.mmhschool.com to learn more about the search for new elements.

Chapter 12 Review

Vocabulary

Fill each blank with the best word or words from the list.

atom, E26
boiling point, E37
density, E8
electron, E27
mass, E6
molecule, E30
nucleus, E27
proton, E27
state of matter, E36
weight, E7

1. An atomic particle that has a positive charge is called a(n) _____.

2. A particle made of different atoms linked together is called a(n) _____.

3. A measure of the force of gravity between Earth and an object is _____.

4. The smallest unit of an element is a(n) _____.

A substance rapidly changes its **5.** _____ to a gas at its **6.** _____ .

A negatively charged particle in the space outside an atom's **7.** _____ is a(n) **8.** _____.

A substance's **9.** _____ divided by its volume is a measure of its **10.** _____.

Test Prep

11. An object's ability to float depends on its _____.
  A size
  B temperature
  C insulation
  D density

12. Water can turn from liquid to gas by evaporating or _____.
  F condensing
  G pouring
  H boiling
  J freezing

13. Mass is the measure of the _____.
  A amount of material in an object
  B weight of an object
  C space an object takes up
  D density of an object

14. The molecules of a _____ tend to be packed tightly in an organized way.
  F gas
  G solid
  H liquid
  J neutron

15. The number of _____ an atom has determines what element it is.

    A electrons

    B neutrons

    C protons

    D charges

Concepts and Skills

16. **INQUIRY SKILL** **Make a Model** Scientists use a variety of models to understand and explain the natural world. A formula, such as H_2O, is a model for water. Tell what the formula means. Give another example of a chemical formula, and tell what it means.

17. **Reading in Science** What is the main difference between mass and weight? Support your answers with any facts or details necessary.

18. **Scientific Methods** Which do you think would evaporate faster—pure water or salt water? Why? Describe an experiment that would test your idea.

19. **Critical Thinking** Are all molecules compounds? Explain your answer.

20. **Product Ads** Teflon® is an artificial compound. It is a "nonstick" plastic. What products might advertise the use of this material?

Did You Ever Wonder?

INQUIRY SKILL **Classify** Use your list from the Inquiry Skill on page E2. Add three column headings: mass, density, and volume. Write the names of the objects with the greatest mass, density, and volume under the headings. An object can be listed under more than one heading.

LOG ON Visit www.science.mmhschool.com to boost your test scores.

CHAPTER
13

Forms of Matter and Energy

Did You Ever Wonder?

Where does the steel used to build bridges and skyscrapers come from? Steel is a mixture of several different elements, including iron, carbon, and nickel. Is the process of making steel a physical change or a chemical change? How are the properties of steel different from the properties of the metals that make it up?

INQUIRY SKILL Experiment Observe objects in your classroom. Infer which objects are made of iron or steel. Use a magnet to test your inferences.

Mixtures and Solutions

Get Ready

Why do people call the Mississippi River the "muddy Mississippi"? What happens when the muddy Mississippi flows into the Gulf of Mexico?

The flowing water of the river joins with standing water in the gulf. The river drops much of what it is carrying.

The Mississippi is made of things mixed together. How many other examples can you give of things that are mixed together?

Inquiry Skill

You observe when you use one or more of the senses to identify or learn about an object or event.

Explore Activity

How Can You Take Apart Things That Are Mixed Together?

Materials

sample of substances mixed together

hand lens

toothpicks

magnet

paper (coffee) filters

2 cups or beakers

water

goggles

Procedure: Design Your Own

BE CAREFUL! Wear goggles. Do not taste your sample.

1 Observe Examine the sample your teacher gives you. It is made of different substances. One of the substances is table salt. What else does it seem to be made of? Record your observations.

2 Experiment Design and carry out an experiment to separate the various ingredients in your sample.

Drawing Conclusions

1 Infer How many parts or substances were mixed into your sample? How did you reach that conclusion?

2 You knew one substance was salt. What properties of salt might help you separate it from the rest? Could you separate salt first? Why or why not?

3 How did you separate out the substances? How did you use the properties of these substances to separate them?

4 FURTHER INQUIRY **Experiment** What if you were given white sand and sugar mixed together? How would you separate the two ingredients?

Main Idea Substances can combine to form mixtures.

What Is a Mixture?

The iron filings and yellow sulfur powder in the first photo have been stirred together. The two materials were *physically* combined. The result is a **mixture**.

The substance shown in the second photograph, iron disulfide, also contains both iron and sulfur. However, now the iron and sulfur are *chemically* combined, and a new substance is formed, a compound.

How do mixtures and compounds differ? Compounds are produced by chemically combining substances. Mixtures are produced by a physical combination of substances. In mixtures the parts simply blend together without forming new substances. Differences in chemical and physical properties of substances are used to separate mixtures and identify compounds.

A compound has different properties from the substances it contains. For example, iron disulfide is not magnetic, while pure iron is. In contrast, the parts of a mixture keep their original properties. Even though the iron has been mixed with sulfur in the first picture, it remains magnetic. You could use a magnet to remove the iron filings from the mixture.

Iron filings   Sulfur powder

When iron filings and yellow sulfur powder are stirred together to make a *mixture*, the substances keep their original properties. The iron remains magnetic. You could use a magnet to remove the iron filings.

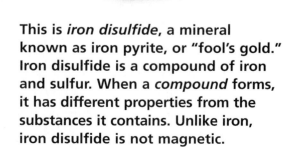

This is *iron disulfide*, a mineral known as iron pyrite, or "fool's gold." Iron disulfide is a compound of iron and sulfur. When a *compound* forms, it has different properties from the substances it contains. Unlike iron, iron disulfide is not magnetic.

Here are a number of household materials. Which are mixtures? Which are either elements or compounds?

What if you stir one spoonful of sugar into a glass of water to make a sugar-water mixture? A friend could stir two spoonfuls of sugar into the same amount of water. You would both have the same kind of mixture. However, your friend's drink would have a much sweeter taste.

Like the sugar water, any type of mixture can contain varying amounts of the parts that make it up. Salt water could be barely salty or very salty. Granola cereal could have many or few raisins. Tea could be strong or weak, and so on.

On the other hand, compounds are always made up in the same way. For example, about two-fifths of the mass of any sample of table salt is sodium, and three-fifths is chlorine.

▷ **What is the difference between compounds and mixtures?**

How Can Mixtures Be Classified?

Mixtures are not pure substances because they contain more than one element or compound. If the substances in a mixture are blended completely, the mixture looks the same everywhere, or is *homogeneous* (hoh·muh·JEE·nee·uhs). We call such mixtures **solutions**. There are many different types of solutions. Look at the table on page E55 for examples of some common solutions.

On the other hand, the parts of a mixture may be only partly blended. The mixture may look "speckled," either to your eye or through a microscope. This type of mixture is said to be *heterogeneous* (het·uhr·uh·JEE·nee·uhs). Most mixtures are heterogeneous. Rivers contain a mixture of water, rock, and soil. Stones are heterogeneous, too.

Some mixtures are neither solutions nor heterogeneous mixtures. These mixtures are called **colloids** . Colloids have properties in between those of solutions and heterogeneous mixtures. Like solutions, there are many types of colloids. The chart on page E55 shows some of these.

▷ **What are three types of mixtures?**

A lunch of a chicken salad sandwich, tea, and gelatin dessert with whipped cream contains each type of mixture. Can you tell which one is which?

Types of Solutions

Substance	Dissolved In	Examples
Liquid	liquid	cranberry juice in water
	gas	water dissolved in air
	solid	mercury in silver (dental fillings)
Gas	liquid	carbon dioxide under pressure dissolved in water to make soda
	gas	oxygen and nitrogen in air
Solid	liquid	salt in water
	solid	copper and zinc mixed in brass

Types of Colloids

Substance	Mixed In	Examples
Liquid	liquid	mayonnaise
	gas	clouds
	solid	jam
Gas	liquid	shaving cream
	solid	marshmallows
Solid	liquid	toothpaste
	gas	smog

What Kinds of Solutions Are There?

You are already familiar with many solutions. In fact, you are surrounded by them all the time. The atmosphere contains a very important solution—air. Seawater is another type of solution.

Solutions are usually transparent or are evenly colored. They never settle into layers. They are the same all the way through.

Solutions come in many different forms. Air is an example of a gaseous solution. Nitrogen, oxygen, and a small amount of other gases mix evenly together. One breath of air is always made up of 78 percent nitrogen and 20 percent oxygen gas.

Seawater is an example of a liquid solution. Tea and your favorite fruit punch are other examples. These solutions are all made from solids that dissolve in a liquid—water. Liquid solutions can also be made by mixing two liquids together, as in nail polish

Not all solutions are liquid. The flask contains a solution of two gaseous compounds, NO_2 and N_2O_4. NO_2 is red-brown, while N_2O_4 is colorless.

remover. Mixing a liquid with a gas, as in a bottle of soda, is another way to form a liquid solution.

Solutions may also be solid. Alloys are solid solutions. They are made by mixing two or more metals together. Bronze, steel, and brass are all alloys.

The properties of an alloy can be varied by changing the amounts of pure metals it contains. The stainless steel used in silverware uses only a slightly different mixture of elements than the

This bridge is made of an alloy, steel.

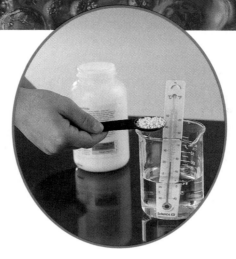

Heat is released when calcium chloride dissolves in water. Hot packs can be used to warm your hands on a cold day for this reason.

high-strength steel you might find in construction.

Solutes and Solvents

Solutions may form in many different ways. However, no matter how they form, all solutions have two parts. The substance that makes up the smaller part of a solution is called the *solute.* The substance that makes up the larger amount is the *solvent.* The solute dissolves in the solvent to form a homogeneous mixture. All solutions consist of at least one solute and one solvent.

Think about the examples on page E56. What is the solvent in fruit punch? What is the solute in seawater? Think about which of the substances is in the greater amount.

Water is an important solvent. Many different kinds of compounds can dissolve in water, such as salts, minerals, proteins, and sugars. Nutrients from food dissolve and are carried through your body because of the water in blood.

Some solute and solvent pairs give off or absorb heat when they are combined. Hot and cold packs use this property of solutions. Calcium chloride is a salt that releases a great deal of heat when it is mixed with water. A hot pack often contains a small pouch of this salt in a sealed package of water. When the package is struck, the pouch of salt breaks open. This allows the salt to dissolve. Heat is then released.

▶ **What are five types of solutions?**

QUICK LAB

Solubility

FOLDABLES Make a Folded Table (See p. R 44.) Label as shown.

Cup	Dissolving Time	
	Prediction	Actual
1		
2		
3		

1. **Measure** Add 100 mL of water to each of three cups. Place a sugar cube in one. Stir until it dissolves. Record the time it took to dissolve.

2. **Predict** Break a second sugar cube into two pieces. How long will they take to dissolve? Place them in a second cup. Stir until they dissolve. Record the dissolving time.

3. **Use Variables** Fold a piece of paper around a sugar cube. Break the cube into many pieces. Pour the pieces in the third cup. Stir until dissolved. Record the dissolving time.

4. **Interpret Data** Construct a graph that illustrates your findings. Which sugar cube dissolved the fastest?

5. What conclusion can you make regarding dissolving time based on the experiment?

What Is Solubility?

Have you ever tried making fruit punch from a mix? How easy is it to get all of the mix to dissolve? Solutes act differently in different solvents. This property describes *solubility.* Solubility explains the ability of a solute to dissolve in a solvent.

Many things affect solubility. Temperature is an example. Most solutes dissolve more quickly when a solvent is hot. Sugar is more soluble in hot tea than in cold, iced tea.

The structure of a solute affects its solubility in various solvents. Oil will not dissolve in water. Their structures are different. Oil dissolves in dish detergent. They have similar structures.

Most solute-solvent combinations have a limit of how much solute will dissolve in a volume of solvent. After that limit is reached, no more solute will dissolve. The concentration of a solution is a measure of the amount of solute dissolved in a solvent. A solution becomes saturated when no more solute can dissolve in it. You may observe this when you add sugar to a glass of lemonade. After a few teaspoons, the sugar settles to the bottom of the glass, and no more sugar will dissolve.

▷ **What are some factors that affect solubility?**

What Are Heterogeneous Mixtures Like?

Rocks are an example of heterogeneous mixtures. Tomato sauce, casseroles, and taco salads are also familiar examples.

Heterogeneous mixtures are even more common than solutions. Heterogeneous mixtures, unlike solutions, settle into layers in a fluid. Oil-and-vinegar salad dressing separates when it is left alone, for example.

Heterogeneous mixtures are either cloudy or opaque. They are not evenly mixed. Think of a pot of chicken soup. One ladle may have a lot of carrots. The next may have few carrots and a lot of rice. One part of a mixture may have more of one substance than another.

Mixtures like clay and water, with particles that are easily seen, are called

Rocks are heterogeneous mixtures. They are composed of pieces or layers of different minerals.

suspensions. Suspensions form when one substance is insoluble, or does not dissolve in a solvent.

▶ **What are the characteristics of heterogeneous mixtures?**

Heterogeneous Mixtures Can Settle into Layers

Clay and water   Oil and water

Freshly shaken mixtures of clay and water, and oil and water

Water
Clay

Oil
Water

The mixtures after they were allowed to stand for a length of time

The fog in this scene is a colloid called an aerosol. Aerosols have either liquid drops or solid particles spread through a gas. Fog is made of tiny drops of water suspended in air.

What Types of Colloids Are There?

Milk is not transparent, so it cannot be a solution. It does not settle out into layers, so it is not a heterogeneous mixture. Milk is a colloid. Like milk, all colloids have properties between those of solutions and heterogeneous mixtures.

The photograph on page E61 shows what milk looks like under a microscope—droplets of fat spread throughout water. Other colloids are similar. They have particles of one material scattered through another. The particles are big enough to block or scatter light but not big enough to settle out.

There are many types of colloids. Milk is an example of an **emulsion**, a liquid (fat) spread through another liquid (water).

Another type of colloid is called an **aerosol**. Aerosols have either liquid drops or solid particles spread through a gas. Fog is made of tiny drops of water suspended in air.

Many food products are colloids. Gelatin dessert is a **gel**. A gel is a solid spread through a liquid. The solid in the gelatin is protein. The liquid in the gelatin is water.

Whipped cream is a **foam**. A foam is a gas spread through a liquid. The gas in the whipped cream is air. The

Fat

Water

(See p. R 41.)

QUICK LAB

Kitchen Colloids

FOLDABLES Make a Two-Tab Book. (See p. R 41.) Label as shown.

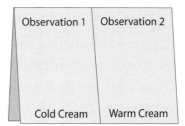

Observation 1	Observation 2
Cold Cream	Warm Cream

1. **Pour** some whipping cream into a bowl. Set it in a bed of ice in another bowl. Let the cream and bowl chill. Whip the cream until it is fluffy.

2. **Observe** Let the cream warm. Whip it more. How does it change? Record your observations under the tabs.

3. **Interpret Data** What kind of colloids did you make in steps 1 and 2?

4. **Infer** What are these colloids commonly known as?

liquid in the whipped cream is water and fat. Marshmallows are a solid foam—a gas spread through a solid. The gas in the marshmallows is air. The solid in the marshmallows is a sweetened gelatin.

▶ **What are four types of colloids?**

How Can Mixtures Be Separated?

We can separate the parts of mixtures using methods called physical separations. A physical separation gets the parts of a mixture away from one another without changing their identities.

We can use the different properties of matter to separate mixtures. Density, magnetism, and boiling and melting temperatures are all helpful tools.

The illustrations on these pages show examples of physical separation methods. Study them to see the steps and equipment needed.

▷ **What properties might you use to separate mixtures?**

The mud particles cannot pass through the pores in the paper, but the water molecules can. The mud collects in the paper, while the water drips through.

Muddy water

Filter

Funnel

Mud particles

Water

1 To separate a mixture of sand and salt, pour in water and stir. The salt dissolves, but the sand doesn't.

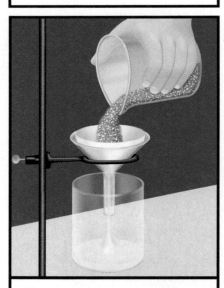

2 Use a filter to separate the sand from the salt water.

3 Then let the water evaporate to get back the salt.

Separating Sand and Wood Chips

To separate sand and wood chips, first pour in water. Stir briefly.

The wood chips float to the top, while the sand settles to the bottom. The wood chips can be skimmed off and dried. The water can be poured off, and the sand dried.

Separating Alcohol and Water

You could separate alcohol and water by heating them in this apparatus.

Alcohol and water are heated. Alcohol boils at a lower temperature than water, so at the beginning, more of the vapor will be alcohol than water.

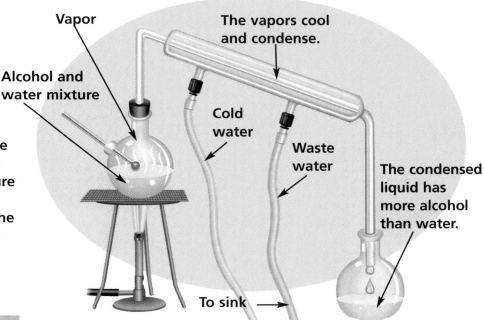

Vapor

The vapors cool and condense.

Alcohol and water mixture

Cold water

Waste water

The condensed liquid has more alcohol than water.

To sink

READING Diagrams

1. What is one way to separate two substances in a mixture?

2. Could you separate sand and wood chips the same way you separate sand and salt? Explain.

3. Make a list of three ways to separate parts of a mixture.

Which Resources Come from Mixtures?

Many of Earth's resources exist as mixtures. Ores are mixtures that provide us with metals and minerals. Seawater is a mixture that can be used as a resource for fresh water, thanks to desalination—another separation process.

Crude oil, our major energy source, is a mixture, too. The diagram below shows a process called *distillation*. We use this process to separate important chemicals out of crude oil.

First, the crude oil is heated until it becomes a gas. Then, the vapors are sent to the tower. There they rise and cool. As they cool, they condense to form liquids.

The substances with large molecules and high boiling points quickly cool into a liquid. The substances with small molecules and low boiling points rise higher in the tower before condensing. The condensed liquids are drawn off as shown.

READING **Cause and Effect** How can we get resources from mixtures?

Distillation

Crude oil is heated until it becomes a gas. The vapors are sent to the tower. There they rise, cool, and condense to form liquids. Substances with smaller molecules and lower boiling points rise higher in the tower before condensing.

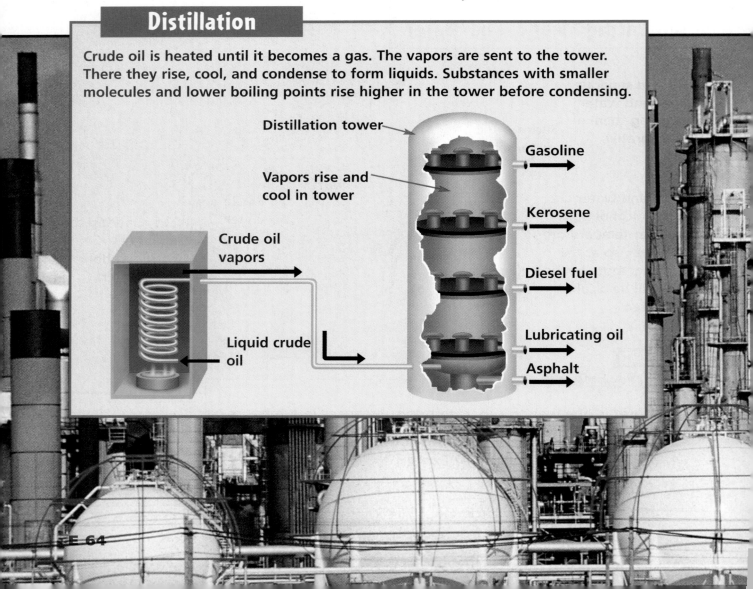

Distillation tower

Vapors rise and cool in tower

Crude oil vapors

Liquid crude oil

Gasoline

Kerosene

Diesel fuel

Lubricating oil

Asphalt

L·I·N·K·S

Why It Matters

Many things you use every day—from the air you breathe to the milk you drink to the steel in your bicycle—are mixtures. Some mixtures need to have just the right amounts of their ingredients each time. For example, you need a certain amount of oxygen in the air you breathe. The amount of iron, carbon, and other metals in steel determines its properties, such as hardness and resistance to rusting.

e-Journal Visit our Web site **www.science.mmhschool.com** to do a research project on mixtures and solutions.

Think and Write

1. How do the properties of sugar and water alone compare with the properties of a sugar-water solution?

2. How are mixtures different from compounds?

3. Air is a mixture of oxygen and nitrogen gas. What type of mixture is air? Why?

4. Oil paints are made of colored particles spread through an oil. Are oil paints solutions, heterogeneous mixtures, or colloids? How do you know?

5. **Critical Thinking** Describe the steps that could separate a mixture of sawdust and salt.

ART LINK

Make a collage. Cut pictures of mixtures from magazines. Paste them on a board. Tell your classmates which are solutions, colloids, and heterogeneous mixtures.

MATH LINK

Make a graph. Air is a solution of gases. Research what the gases are and how much of each gas is in air. Show the results in a graph.

WRITING LINK

Writing a Story Many dishes, such as salad, a casserole, and pizza, are made from a mixture of foods. Often the mixture tastes better than the ingredients by themselves. Write a story about a dish like this. Tell it from the dish's point of view. Do all the ingredients get along?

TECHNOLOGY LINK

Science Newsroom CD-ROM Choose *Here's the Solution* to learn how the three types of mixtures are similar.

LOG ON Visit **www.science.mmhschool.com** for more links.

Got Milk?
Got Butter?

The success of mammals on Earth is helped by what they feed their newborns: milk produced by their mothers. Humans also raise other large mammals to produce milk for them.

A mammal's milk is seven-eighths water, but the other eighth has nearly everything needed for good health! Some food value comes from the lactose, or milk sugar, dissolved in it.

Milk has a lot of fat globs. Because they're lighter than water, the globs rise to the top of a container. Gravity pulls the heavier liquid down. The fat globs merge to become cream. Milk with little or no fat is skim milk.

Many people prefer skim or low-fat milk. The fat in milk contributes to weight problems, heart disease, and possibly other diseases.

← Cream
← Milk

Milk you buy has vitamins D and A added to make it more nutritious. It's been pasteurized—heated to kill disease-causing bacteria. The heating also makes some milk proteins inactive and slows down the spoiling.

Milk is homogenized by putting it through a fine screen to break fat globs into tiny specks. They're so small that the movement of the other molecules in milk keeps them from rising. For that reason cream doesn't form at the top of homogenized milk.

By constantly moving cream in a closed container, you cause the fat globs to merge. Drain off the thin, watery stuff and you've got . . . butter!

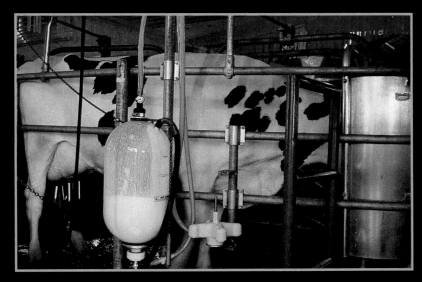
Automatic milking machine

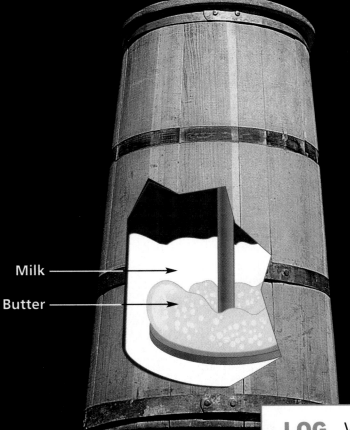
Milk ——→
Butter ——→

An old-fashioned churn stirs up milk to form butter.

Write
ABOUT IT

1. What other foods are vitamins added to? Why do you think that is done?

2. Fat is used to make cells' outer membranes. How does this explain why mammals' milk is high in fat?

LOG ON Visit **www.science.mmhschool.com** to learn more about milk products.

Chemical Changes

Get Ready

How can you tell changes occur? Metal rusts. Milk sours. Bread dough rises when baking powder is mixed into it. A runny egg hardens when it is cooked. What are other changes going on around you?

Inquiry Skill

You infer when you form an idea from facts or observations.

Explore Activity

How Can You Recognize a Chemical Change?

Materials

baking soda

baking powder

cornstarch

salt

iodine solution

vinegar

water

wax paper

permanent marker

4 toothpicks

3 droppers

4 plastic spoons

7 small cups

goggles

Procedure

BE CAREFUL! Wear goggles.

1 Copy this grid on wax paper with a marking pen. Using a spoon, put a pea-sized amount of corn-starch in each of the three boxes in the first row.

2 **Observe** Use a dropper to add five drops of water to the cornstarch in the first column. Stir with a toothpick. Record your observations.

3 **Experiment** Using a different dropper, add five drops of vinegar to the cornstarch in the second column. Stir with a new toothpick. Record your observations.

4 **Observe** Use a third dropper to add five drops of iodine solution to the cornstarch in the third col-umn. Record your observations.
CAUTION: Iodine can stain and is poisonous.

5 **Experiment** Repeat steps 1–4 for baking powder, baking soda, and salt.

Drawing Conclusions

1 **Infer** In which boxes of the grid do you think substances changed into new substances? Explain your answers.

2 FURTHER INQUIRY **Infer** Your teacher will give you samples of two unknown powders. Use what you have learned to identify these pow-ders. Report on your findings.

	Water	Vinegar	Iodine Solution
Cornstarch			
Baking powder			
Baking soda			
Salt			

Main Idea Matter can undergo chemical as well as physical changes.

What Are Physical and Chemical Changes?

Different kinds of changes are going on all the time. In a **physical change**, matter changes in size, shape, or state without also changing identity.

In Lesson 3 you learned about the states of matter. Change of state is an example of a physical change. A substance can change from solid to liquid to gas. The substance does not change its chemical identity in this process. Its state simply changes. The photograph below shows why a change of state is a physical change.

You also learned in Lesson 4 about mixtures. Combining two substances to form a solution is another example of physical change. The two substances do not lose their identities. They can be physically separated from each other to give back the original substances. The photograph above shows this kind of physical change.

Baking soda

Baking soda and water mixture

When baking soda mixes with water, the baking soda seems to disappear. However, when the water evaporates, baking soda is left behind. This is a physical change.

A change of state is a physical change. When the steam—gaseous water—hits the dish, it cools and turns back into liquid water.

Steam condenses to form liquid water.

The photo on page E68 shows a **chemical change**. Chemical changes occur when atoms link together in new ways. The changes cause new compounds to form. The new compounds have properties different from the original substances from which they were formed.

The reaction between vinegar and baking soda is an example of a chemical change. When these two materials are mixed, gas bubbles form. A change in the linking pattern of the atoms in the vinegar and baking soda causes a new substance—carbon dioxide—to form. Other new substances form, too. However, you cannot see them because they remain in the liquid.

Chemical changes are often referred to as **chemical reactions**. The original substances are called the **reactants**. The new substances produced by the chemical reaction are called the **products**. During chemical reactions the atoms in the reactants rearrange to form products with different properties. In the reaction between baking soda and vinegar, the baking soda and the vinegar are the reactants. The carbon dioxide, water, and a chemical called sodium acetate are the products.

READING

Cause and Effect
What happens during a chemical change?

What happens when baking soda and vinegar mix?

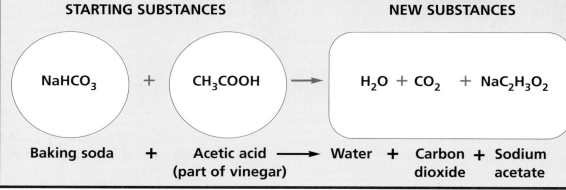

STARTING SUBSTANCES		NEW SUBSTANCES
$NaHCO_3$ + CH_3COOH	→	H_2O + CO_2 + $NaC_2H_3O_2$
Baking soda + Acetic acid (part of vinegar)	→	Water + Carbon dioxide + Sodium acetate

E 71

What Are the Signs of a Chemical Change?

Chemical reactions often show one or more signs that a chemical change has occurred. These signs include a color change, formation of a gas, and formation of light and heat. The reactions on these pages show some of these signs.

Does a chemical reaction occur when reddish brown iodine is placed on a potato? The iodine reacts with starch in the potato. The white starch and iodine change to a bluish black color.

When reddish blueberry juice is mixed with a solution of baking soda, it turns to a greenish color. The green color results from a chemical change in the molecules of the blueberry juice.

The bubbles you see when lemon juice is added to a solution of baking soda are a sign of a chemical change. Carbon dioxide gas forms by the reaction between acid in the lemon juice and the sodium bicarbonate in the baking soda.

Have you ever put hydrogen peroxide on a cut to kill germs? The bubbles tell you that a chemical change is occurring.

What happens when propane gas is released from a tank and ignited? It reacts with oxygen in the air. The light and heat produced are signs of this chemical reaction.

▷ **What are three signs of a chemical change?**

Color Change

When iodine is dropped onto a potato, a color change is observed.

The reaction of blueberry juice and baking soda shows a change of color.

Formation of a Gas

Carbon dioxide gas forms when lemon juice is added to a baking soda solution.

When hydrogen peroxide comes into contact with bodily fluids, it reacts and gives off pure oxygen gas. The oxygen gas, in turn, kills germs in the cut and guards against infection.

Formation of Light and Heat

When you light a match, it gives off light and heat all on its own. This tells you that a chemical change is occurring.

When propane burns in air, it chemically reacts with oxygen.

What Are Some Familiar Chemical Changes?

As a cake bakes, several chemical changes occur. Heat turns the baking soda (sodium bicarbonate) in the cake dough into sodium carbonate, steam, and carbon dioxide gas. The sodium carbonate is a harmless solid that remains in the cake. The steam helps make the cake moist. The bubbles of carbon dioxide help the dough expand and make the cake light and fluffy.

The heat of cooking also chemically changes and hardens the runny white and yolk of an egg. Bacteria in warm milk can change it chemically and turn it sour.

The red powder covering the wheelbarrow above is iron oxide. Iron oxide is commonly known as rust. Rust forms when iron atoms in steel react with oxygen from the air. The reaction is very complex and needs moisture to occur. Steel objects are most likely to rust if they get wet and are not dried right away.

Rocket engines use chemical reactions to produce lots of heat. This space shuttle's main engines are fueled by liquid hydrogen and liquid oxygen. The two react together to make water vapor and the energy the shuttle needs. The shuttle also uses launch boosters containing a solid fuel, aluminum powder. When it burns, it changes to aluminum oxide.

Rust   **Tarnish**

The silver spoon in the photo is partly covered with a tarnish of silver sulfide. The silver sulfide forms when silver reacts with sulfur or hydrogen sulfide in foods or the air. You can even tarnish silver by wrapping it with a rubber band. Sulfur added to strengthen the rubber causes the tarnish to form. Polishes can be used to remove the tarnish and restore the silver's shiny appearance.

> **What are three examples of chemical changes?**

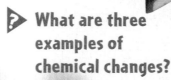

Preventing Rust

You've learned that steel forms rust when exposed to oxygen and moisture. Rusting can ruin metal objects. Can you find a way to stop or slow rusting? In this activity you will experiment to try to find the answer. In order to experiment, you need to do the following things. Form a hypothesis. Design a control. Carry out your experiment. Analyze and communicate your results.

Materials

steel nails

sand paper

paper cups

dilute salt water

goggles

Procedure

BE CAREFUL! Wear goggles.

1. **Hypothesize** The photograph shows a method for making a steel nail rust. Think of a way to protect a steel nail from rusting under such conditions. Write down an explanation of why you think your method will work.

2. **Experiment** To test your method of rust protection, you need a control nail kept under normal conditions. Each experimental nail will have just one condition (variable) change. For example, what if you wanted to make a nail rust? You might leave one nail in a clean, empty jar (the control). You might put another in water. You might put a third in lemon juice. The amount of rusting that occurs is called the *dependent variable*. Write out how you will set up the experimental and control nails for your experiment.

3. **Experiment** Carry out your experiment, and record your observations.

Drawing Conclusions

1. **Infer** Write out a description of how well your hypothesis agreed with your results. Be sure to compare the experimental nail with the control nail.

2. **Communicate** Why did you need a control in this experiment?

Which Are Easier to Reverse – Chemical or Physical Changes?

You would probably agree that turning carbon dioxide gas, water, and sodium acetate back into baking soda and vinegar would be difficult. Simply stirring the three ingredients together would not give you baking soda and vinegar. In general, chemical changes are difficult to reverse. Imagine trying to "unburn" toast or "unspoil" milk!

On the other hand, physical changes can sometimes be easily reversed. Although this is not always true. For example, melting an ice cube can easily be reversed by cooling it until it freezes again. Stirring sugar into water can be reversed by letting the water evaporate.

What changes occur when toast burns? What happens when a candle burns?

However, it would not be so easy to put pieces of paper back together after cutting them from a single page. Still, if a change seems very easy to reverse, it is more likely to be a physical change.

The photograph of a burning candle shows that many changes are happening. Wax melts, runs down the side, and turns solid again. However, some of the wax turns into carbon dioxide gas and steam when it combines with oxygen in the air. This change releases enough heat to make the candle flame you see.

▷ **Why are chemical changes more difficult to reverse than physical changes?**

Why It Matters

Chemical changes harden the yolk and white of your cooked egg. They make cake and bread rise and bake. Chemical changes turn milk sour. They turn fuels into heat to warm your home. Chemical changes even turn the food you eat into energy to keep you going. In what other ways are chemical changes important to you?

e-Journal Visit our Web site www.science.mmhschool.com to do a research project on chemical changes.

Think and Write

1. Is the rusting of a nail a chemical or a physical change?

2. Is the melting of ice a chemical or a physical change? Why?

3. When a match burns, what evidence is there that a chemical change is occurring?

4. **FURTHER INQUIRY** **Experiment** What if you wanted to find out if a cake bakes better with baking soda or baking powder? Design an experiment to test your ideas. Why might you want to use a control?

5. **Critical Thinking** What could you do to protect a bike from rusting?

LITERATURE LINK

Read *Let's Go Spelunking!* to learn about a trip to Howe Caverns. Try the activities at the end of the book.

WRITING LINK

Expository Writing The Statue of Liberty is a famous statue in New York Harbor. What is it made of? How does it look today? How did it look 100 years ago? What could have caused the statue's appearance to change? Research this topic and write a cause-and-effect essay.

MATH LINK

Solve this problem. A car uses fuel at a rate of 25 miles per gallon. How much fuel is consumed after traveling 100 miles?

TECHNOLOGY LINK

 LOG ON Visit www.science.mmhschool.com for more links.

Can Chemical Reactions Make Food Safe or Unsafe?

Why do mold and bacteria grow in foods and spoil them? Are the foods unsafe to eat? What can be done to prevent microorganisms like molds and bacteria from spoiling foods? All the answers involve chemical reactions.

Like all living organisms, molds and bacteria require food. They can "eat" the same foods we eat and multiply in the food. They cause chemical reactions to occur in food, making it spoil.

In some cases, molds and bacteria can be harmful, perhaps even deadly, to people who eat foods in which these microorganisms have grown. Bacteria from contaminated food can multiply in the digestive tract of a person, causing vomiting, diarrhea, and intestinal bleeding. Hamburger, for example, may be contaminated with a bacterium known as *E. coli* O157:H7. Each year, *E. coli* O157:H7 causes about 73,000 illnesses and about 60 deaths in the United States.

To help prevent bacteria and molds from spoiling foods, food manufacturers may add chemicals to kill micro-organisms. Sodium propionate, for example, is a chemical often added to cheeses and baked goods to keep molds from growing. Manufacturers also package foods in airtight containers and bags to prevent spoiling.

While food manufacturers take steps to keep the foods you eat safe, what can you do at home? Chemical reactions slow down as the temperature is lowered. Keeping foods in the refrigerator or freezer is a primary means of preventing the growth of bacteria and molds. The cold temperatures slow down the chemical reactions that make food spoil. Foods such as lunch meats and potato salads should not be kept out of the refrigerator for a long time.

The cheese in the photograph has spots of mold growing on it.

Vacuum-sealed containers prevent bacteria from contaminating food.

LOG ON Visit www.science.mmhschool.com to learn more about bacteria and mold.

Write
ABOUT IT

1. How can molds and bacteria cause food to spoil?

2. What are some harmful effects of eating food contaminated with bacteria such as *E. coli*?

Acids and Bases

Vocabulary

acid, E82

base, E82

neutral, E82

indicator, E84

acidity, E86

alkalinity, E86

pH, E86

Get Ready

Have you ever tried to suck on a lemon? It might have made your cheeks pucker! Lemons taste very sour. Why is this?

Have you ever seen ammonia being used to mop the floor? Why is it a good cleaning agent?

The answer to these questions is that these substances are either acids or bases. What are acids and bases? Are there any other substances in your house that contain an acid or base? How can you find out?

Inquiry Skill

You observe when you use one or more of the senses to identify or learn about an object.

Explore Activity

Which Are Acids and Which Are Bases?

Materials
- red and blue litmus paper
- wide-range pH paper
- plastic cups
- labels
- goggles
- gloves
- apron
- household solutions

Procedure

BE CAREFUL! Wear goggles, gloves, and an apron.

1. **Predict** Which solutions do you think are acids and which are bases? Write your predictions in a chart like the one shown below.

2. **Observe** Vinegar is an acid. Put a small amount in a cup, and mark the cup with a label. Test by dipping a piece of red litmus paper into the vinegar. Record the result in your table. Repeat with a piece of blue litmus paper. Litmus paper is a material that allows you to tell which solutions are acids and which are bases.

3. **Classify** Test all of your other solutions in the same way, and record your results.

Sample	Predict: Acid or Base?	Effect on Red Litmus	Effect on Blue Litmus	Result: Acid or Base?
Vinegar	ACID			ACID
Baking soda				
Lemon juice				

Drawing Conclusions

1. Which samples are acids? How do you know?

2. Which samples are bases? How do you know?

3. **Measure** Now test each sample with a small strip of pH paper. Match the color of the paper to the color scale on the holder, and find the pH.

4. [FURTHER INQUIRY] **Interpret Data** Design and do an activity to test the acidity of the foods you eat. Which foods are acidic? Which are basic? How do you know?

orange juice

diluted ammonia

Main Idea Many important substances in our lives are acids or bases.

What Are Acids and Bases?

How do you know whether something is an **acid** or a **base**? Vinegar, orange juice, and lemon juice are acids. An acid tastes sour and turns blue litmus paper red. Bases, like ammonia and baking soda, taste bitter and turn red litmus paper blue. (You should never test acids and bases by tasting them, however.)

In Lesson 5 you learned about chemical reactions. When you mixed vinegar, an acid, with baking soda, a base, a chemical reaction occurred. Acids and bases can react with each other to form water and a salt.

In a reaction acids "give away" hydrogen particles, or *hydronium ions*. Bases give off *hydroxide ions*.

This is a simplified hydronium ion. Acids release them in solution.

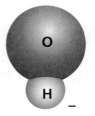

Bases release hydroxide ions, such as this, in solution.

Hydroxide ions are particles that are made up of one oxygen atom and one hydrogen atom linked together. Hydronium and hydroxide ions combine to make water. What is left of the acid and base also combines to make a new substance—a salt.

If you place a blue and a red strip of litmus paper in a glass of water, both strips will stay the same color. This tells you that water is neither acidic nor basic. A solution that is neither acidic nor basic is **neutral**. Water is a neutral substance.

When hydrochloric acid is added to a base, sodium hydroxide, a chemical reaction occurs to produce water and sodium chloride (table salt).

HCl + NaOH → NaCl + H₂O

You can make an acid neutral by mixing it with a base. Likewise, you can make a base neutral by mixing it with an acid. Acids and bases react to form neutral compounds.

The chemical properties, or reactivity, of acids and bases are what make them useful and important. You may know not to add lemon to hot tea with milk. This is because the acid in the lemon can react with the milk, causing it to sour. Acids react strongly with metals, as well. Statues can corrode from the acid found in rain and the atmosphere. The acid in rain is also harmful to plant and animal life.

Acids aren't only harmful, however. Acids are used in batteries to help make electricity. They are used in industry to produce plastics, metals, explosives, textiles, and dyes. They are also used for many functions in your body. All living things use amino acids, for example, to build proteins. All of an organism's muscles and tissues are made up mostly of proteins.

Bases can also be reactive. You may have experienced a bloody nose from smelling ammonia. Ammonia is a strong base that can be corrosive. Bases are often used in cleansers. They can break down grease and oil. Soap is a base you use every day.

Baking soda and baking powder are bases used in cooking. They are often used in baking to make cakes rise. When these bases mix with an acid, carbon dioxide gas is produced. The carbon dioxide gas that is released helps to make cakes become airy and rise.

This statue of George Washington has been corroded by acid in rain.

READING Cause and Effect
What happens when an acid is added to a base?

How Can You Tell if Something Is an Acid or a Base?

Litmus paper has a different color in acids than it does in bases. Litmus is an example of an **indicator**. An indicator is a substance whose color changes when it is mixed with an acid or a base. You can use litmus paper to tell which household materials are acids and which are bases.

Many indicators come from plants. Litmus, for example, is made from certain lichens. Another common vegetable indicator is phenolphthalein (fee·nawl·THAL·ee·in). Phenolphthalein is colorless in acid and pink in base.

Red cabbage juice is another indicator. Add acid to red cabbage juice, and the juice turns maroon. If there is a lot of acid, the juice turns pink. A neutral substance does not change the color. A base turns it green. A very basic substance turns it yellow.

Many household materials can act as indicators. These materials include blueberry juice, beet juice, carrot juice, grape juice, red cabbage, purple hollyhock flowers, and blue iris flowers. Each has one color in an acid and another color in a base.

▷ **What is an indicator?**

Hydrangeas have pink flowers in basic soil and blue flowers in acidic soil. Are these flowers indicators?

Red cabbage juice is an indicator because it changes color in acids and bases. Litmus paper can also be used as an indicator.

Slightly acidic

Slightly basic

Very acidic

Neutral

Very basic

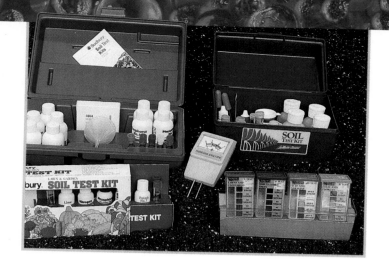

How Can Indicators Be Useful?

The photograph shows a test kit that can be used to find how acidic the soil is. Doing so is important because certain plants grow well only when soil is slightly acidic. The test kit has paper strips that are soaked with an indicator. When a strip is placed in moist soil, it turns a certain color. Matching the color of the strip against the colored scale on the container reveals how acidic the soil is.

Indicators are important in many situations other than gardening. For example, swimming pool water must be routinely checked with a test kit. Aquarium owners or pond owners periodically have to check how acidic the water is to make sure it is healthy for the fish and plants.

▷ **What are some ways indicators are used?**

QUICK LAB

Mystery Writing with a Base

FOLDABLES Make a Half-Book. (See p. R 41.) Label it as shown.

MYSTERY WRITING

1. Dip a cotton swab in baking soda solution. Use it to write a short message to your partner just under the title on the front of your Half-Book.

2. Allow the paper to dry completely. Then give it to your partner.

3. Can you read your partner's message? No? Use another swab to "paint" the paper with grape juice.

4. **Observe** What happened when you painted the paper with the grape juice? Record your observations inside your Half-Book.

5. **Infer** Is the grape juice an indicator? Why or why not? Record your conclusions inside your Half-Book.

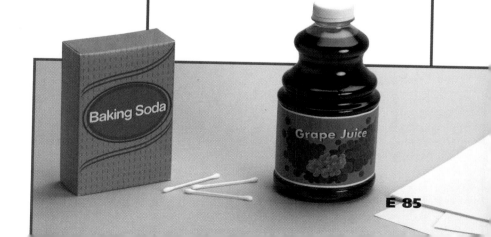

Are All Acids and Bases the Same?

Are all acids equally acidic? Are all bases equally basic? No. Acids and bases have different strengths. The strength of an acid is called its **acidity**. The strength of a base is called its **alkalinity**.

Hydrochloric acid, a laboratory chemical, is much more acidic than citric acid, the acid found in citrus fruits like oranges and lemons. Hydrochloric acid, therefore, has a higher acidity.

Acidity and alkalinity depend on how many hydronium and hydroxide ions are in a solution. The diagram below compares the solution of a strong acid with a weak acid, and a strong base with a weak base.

A scientist named Soren Sorenson developed a scale in 1909 to compare acidic and basic solutions. This scale is called the *pH scale*. The **pH** of a solution tells how acidic or basic the solution is. It measures acidity and alkalinity. Scientists still use this scale today.

The pH of most solutions lies between pH 1 and pH 14. A pH of 1 means that there are a lot of hydronium ions in a solution. The solution is very acidic. A pH of 14 means that there are a lot of hydroxide ions in a

The first solution is a stronger acid than the second because it has more hydronium ions. The third solution is a weaker base than the fourth solution because it has fewer hydroxide ions. Alkalinity increases as the pH increases from 7 to 14. Acidity increases as the pH decreases from 7 to 0.

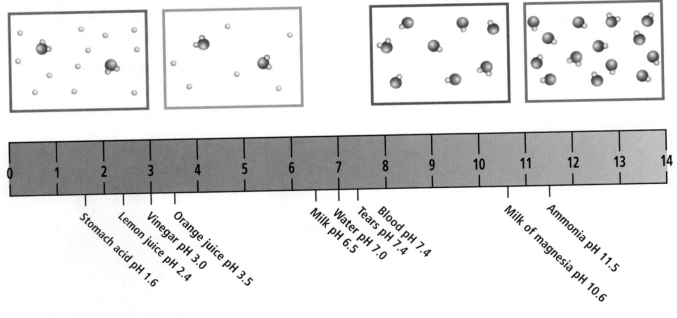

0 1 2 3 4 5 6 7 8 9 10 11 12 13 14

Stomach acid pH 1.6
Lemon juice pH 2.4
Vinegar pH 3.0
Orange juice pH 3.5
Milk pH 6.5
Water pH 7.0
Tears pH 7.4
Blood pH 7.4
Milk of magnesia pH 10.6
Ammonia pH 11.5

pH meter

solution. The solution is very basic. A pH of 7 means that the solution is neutral.

Scientists often use a pH meter to determine the acidity or alkalinity of a solution. Strips of paper called pH paper are also commonly used. This paper changes to a different color depending on the exact pH of a solution.

Your blood has a pH of 7.4. Doctors can use this pH to diagnose certain diseases. The blood of a person with diabetes, for example, has a pH that is lower than normal.

▷ **How can acidity and alkalinity be measured?**

The color match indicates that the solution has a pH of 2, which means that it is acidic.

How Can Acids and Bases Be Used?

Acids and bases are used in many different ways every day. They can be used in your home as cleaning agents. Bleach contains acids, for example. Ammonia, drain cleaners, and window cleaning solutions all contain bases. Bases are good cleaning agents because they dissolve grease, fats, and oils.

Many foods get their flavor from acids. Tomatoes, grapefruit, lemons, and limes all contain acids.

Acids and bases are used in laboratories and in industry to make plastics and textiles. Some minerals can be identified by their reaction with acids. Cotton is often treated with a base to make it look shiny.

The reaction of acids and bases is very useful. You have learned that acids and bases react to make neutral compounds. You may have even experienced this kind of reaction in your own body! Have you ever taken an antacid or milk of magnesia for an upset stomach? Your stomach contains acids to help you digest food. In fact, the pH of your stomach is usually between 1 and 2.

Sometimes there is too much acid in your stomach, causing the pH to go even lower. This may happen when you eat foods that are very acidic or when you are very nervous. The decrease in pH can cause a stomachache.

Products like antacids are basic. When you take them, they react with the extra acid in your stomach. They help increase the pH of your stomach back to its normal level and make you feel better.

 **How can acids and bases be useful?**

Why It Matters

Acids and bases make up many of the compounds around you. They clean your clothes and help you to digest food. Oranges are acidic, but eating one is not dangerous. However, some acids and bases must be treated with care. Use these materials safely. Wear protective eyewear and cover your skin when working with them. The pH scale shows the strength of acids and bases.

e-Journal Visit our Web site www.science.mmhschool.com to do a research project on acids and bases.

Think and Write

1. What kind of particles do acids produce?

2. What are the properties of a base?

3. Your friend wonders if a cleanser is an acid or a base. What test could you do to help him answer the question?

4. What numerical scale describes acidity? How does this scale work?

5. **Critical Thinking** A friend calls you and says he accidentally spilled some acid. Describe what you would tell him to do to clean up the spill safely.

L·I·N·K·S

MATH LINK

Solve this problem. An acid with a pH of 3 is 10 times more acidic than an acid with a pH of 4. How much more acidic is an acid with a pH of 1 than an acid with a pH of 3? With a pH of 4?

ART LINK

Draw a picture. Paint it with lemon juice. Let it dry. Then develop it with grape juice.

WRITING LINK

Persuasive Writing What are the benefits gained from checking and controlling pool water for its pH level? Write a public-service announcement persuading pool owners to check for and control acidity levels.

TECHNOLOGY LINK

LOG ON Visit www.science.mmhschool.com for more links.

Matter and Energy

Vocabulary

kinetic energy, E95
potential energy, E95
conduction, E97
convection, E97
radiation, E97

Get Ready

If you see this electric ray while scuba diving, should you touch it or swim the other way? Don't be shocked. This ray produces enough electricity to power a small motor.

Could you keep an electric ray in your back pack to run your appliances? You use batteries. However, rays don't run out of electricity. Do batteries run out? Do you use past experience to buy the best new batteries?

Inquiry Skill

You interpret data when you use the information that has been gathered to answer questions or solve a problem.

Explore Activity

How Well Do Batteries Provide Energy?

Materials

battery

flashlight bulb

2 wires

Procedure

1 **Experiment** In this activity you will determine which battery may be the best buy. Test variables such as battery type, size, voltage, brand, or cost. Connect the wires to the battery and bulb as shown. Fasten the wires with a battery holder or tape. Record the time the bulb went on and the type, size, voltage, and brand of battery used. Share your data with the class.

2 **Observe** Check the bulb every 15 minutes to see if it is still lit. Record the time it goes off.

3 Repeat using another variable.

Drawing Conclusions

1 **Use Numbers** Divide the time each battery lasted by its cost.

2 Make a graph of the class's results. Which batteries lasted the longest? Which batteries cost the least per hour of use?

3 **Infer** Which batteries are the best buy? The cheapest? The longest lasting?

4 FURTHER INQUIRY Interpret Data Design an experiment to see if a battery will last half as long when it is connected to two bulbs as when it is connected to one. Does it matter how the bulbs are connected?

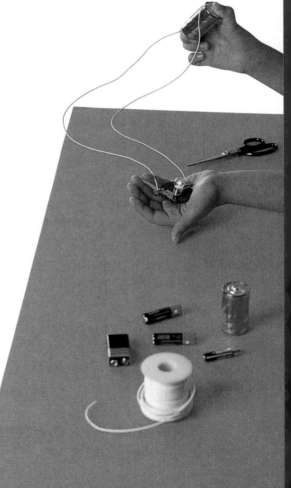

Main Idea Energy has different forms.

What Is Electrical Energy?

You know that a battery can produce enough power to light up a light bulb. How does it do this? What is the "power" in a battery? Where does it come from?

A battery provides electrical energy. Chemicals inside the battery react. These reactions produce electrons. As you learned in Lesson 2, an electron is one of the particles that make up an atom. Each electron carries energy, giving the battery its "power."

When a battery is connected to a light bulb with wires, a closed circuit is formed. A closed circuit means that there is a continuous path for electrons to travel through. The diagram below shows a closed circuit.

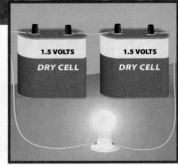

In some cases the amount of electrical energy in a circuit may not be great enough to light certain bulbs. For example, a flashlight battery could not light up a 60-watt light bulb from a lamp. Electrical energy can be measured by the size of the bulb it can light.

Electrons flow from the battery to the light bulb through wires. Some of the energy is given up to the wire in the light bulb, called the *filament*. The filament gets hot enough to glow and give off light. The electrical energy is changed into light and heat.

The rest of the electrons flow back into the battery.

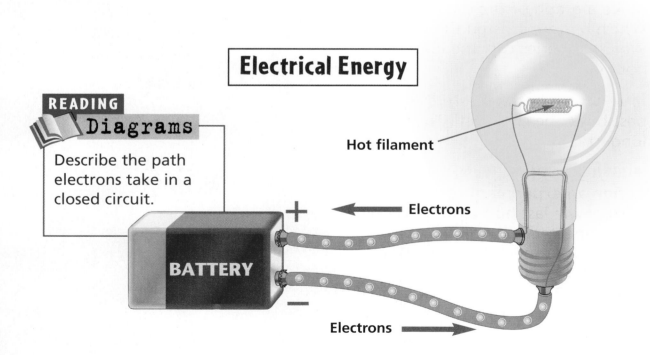

Electrical Energy

READING Diagrams

Describe the path electrons take in a closed circuit.

Hot filament

← Electrons

BATTERY

+

−

Electrons →

After a time the chemicals in a battery have all reacted, and no more electrons can be produced. This causes the battery to go dead.

Measuring Electrical Energy

Electrical energy can be measured in a number of ways. The circuit with two batteries has twice as many electrons flowing as the circuit with one battery. The bulb is brighter when two batteries are present. The brightness of a bulb can measure electrical energy.

We can also use different kinds of meters to measure electrical energy. An *ammeter* measures *amperes*, or *amps*. It tells us how many electrons flow each second. The *voltmeter* measures *volts*. Volts are another measure of electrical energy.

READING Cause and Effect
How does a battery produce electrical charge?

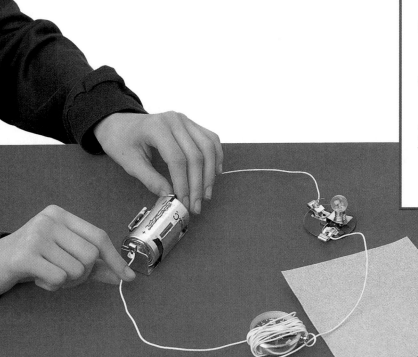

QUICK LAB

Measuring Electricity

FOLDABLES™ Make a Four-Tab Book. (See p. R 44.) Label as shown.

#4	Observe
#5	Observe
#6	Infer
#7	Infer

1. Wrap fine varnished wire around a compass. Remove the coating from the ends of the wire with sandpaper.

2. Turn the compass so its needle stays lined up with the coils of wire.

3. Connect the wire ends as shown to a circuit of a battery and light bulb.

4. **Observe** What do you see that tells you that electricity is flowing in the circuit?

5. **Observe** What does the needle do as you open and close the circuit?

6. **Infer** How might a more powerful battery affect the needle?

7. **Infer** How could the compass needle be used to measure electricity?

What Are Other Forms of Energy?

You've seen how chemical changes in a battery can produce electrical energy. You've also seen how that electrical energy can produce light and heat. All of these things are forms of energy. What exactly is energy? We know energy has many forms, but defining energy can be a little difficult.

A good place to start in talking about energy is to look at what energy can do. Energy is a measure of how much work something can produce.

To scientists work means using a force—a push or a pull—to move an object. Energy is the ability to do work.

Energy is not a type of matter. Matter is something you can often touch or see—solids, liquids, gases. Energy may be thought of as the ability to move matter around.

We can describe energy by its source or by how it is carried. For example, the energy produced by a chemical reaction is called chemical energy. Some typical forms of energy are shown in the table on page E95.

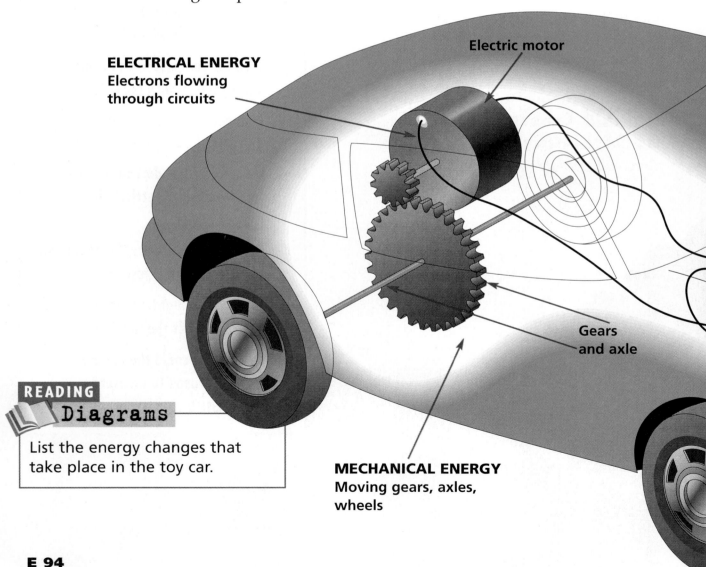

ELECTRICAL ENERGY
Electrons flowing through circuits

Electric motor

Gears and axle

MECHANICAL ENERGY
Moving gears, axles, wheels

READING Diagrams

List the energy changes that take place in the toy car.

Kinetic and Potential Energy

Look at the toy car in the diagram. Electrical energy is being used by the headlights. Electrons are being produced by the battery and are moved through a circuit. When something moves, its energy is called **kinetic energy**. Electrical energy is an example of kinetic energy. Any object that is in motion has kinetic energy.

When the headlights are turned off, the battery stops working. Electrons stop moving, and no new electrons are produced. No energy is being used. However, energy is stored in the chemicals in the battery. This energy is waiting to be used. We refer to stored energy as **potential energy**. Chemical energy is an example of potential energy.

Matter always has at least one of these energy forms.

▷ **What are the two main forms of energy?**

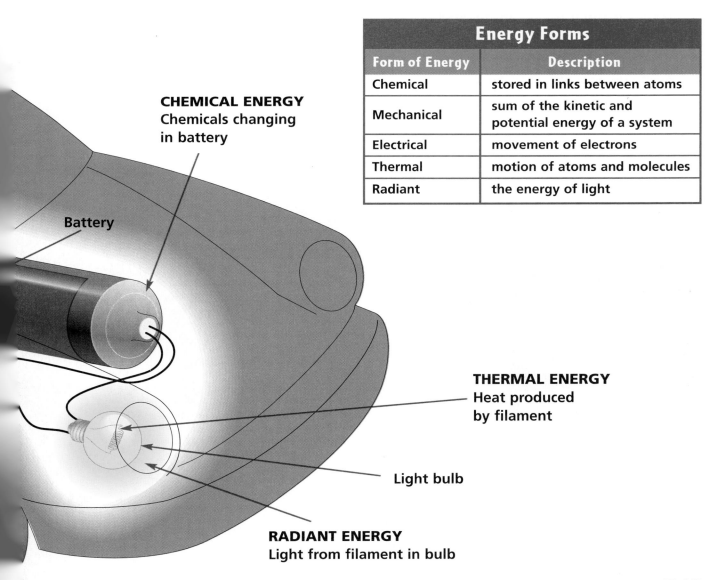

CHEMICAL ENERGY
Chemicals changing in battery

Battery

THERMAL ENERGY
Heat produced by filament

Light bulb

RADIANT ENERGY
Light from filament in bulb

Energy Forms	
Form of Energy	**Description**
Chemical	stored in links between atoms
Mechanical	sum of the kinetic and potential energy of a system
Electrical	movement of electrons
Thermal	motion of atoms and molecules
Radiant	the energy of light

How Can We Describe Thermal Energy?

Have you ever used a thermometer to measure temperature? You have learned that thermal energy is a form of energy that describes the motion of atoms and molecules. Temperature tells us how fast the particles in matter are moving. High temperatures mean the molecules are moving fast and have a lot of energy. Lower temperatures mean the molecules are moving more slowly and have less energy. The movement of molecules is what makes things feel hot or cold.

Heat is the transfer of thermal energy from one object to another.

Heat flows when an object is warmer than its surroundings. Heat always flows from hotter materials to cooler materials, never the other way. Heat flows until objects and their surroundings have the same temperature.

When you hold your hands around a mug of hot chocolate, your body gets warmed. This happens because heat flows from the hot mug into your skin. Thermal energy is transferred from the cup to your hands. Your body gains energy, and your temperature rises as a result. Energy is lost from the mug, however. Its temperature decreases.

▷ **How are temperature and heat related?**

The Sun is the most important source of heat for life on our planet.

These heating coils in an oven are warmed by an electric current. The space inside the oven is warmed by heat flowing from the hot coils.

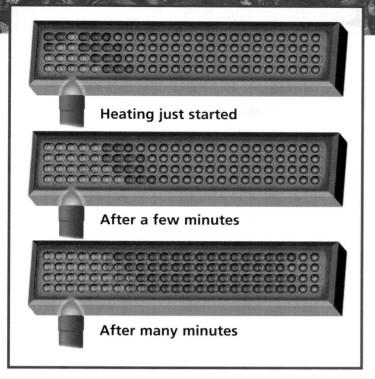

Heating just started

After a few minutes

After many minutes

How Does Heat Move?

When heat flows, it can move in three ways—conduction, convection, and radiation. In **conduction** thermal energy flows through objects as their particles vibrate. Conduction, as shown above, is the way your hand is warmed by a mug of hot chocolate. It usually occurs in solids and between objects that are touching.

In **convection** thermal energy is transferred by the movement of matter. Convection occurs in liquids and gases. In convection hot parts of a material rise, while cooler parts sink. There is a flow of material and heat.

A pot of water is heated by convection, for example. As water is heated on a stove, the water near the burner gets hot and rises to the top of the pan. The cooler water near the top then sinks and gets warmed. Thermal energy is transferred by a cycle of rising and sinking matter.

In **radiation** heat is transferred through electromagnetic rays. Matter is not needed at all in this energy transfer. All objects around us give off radiation. Radiation can travel through space. Radiation from the Sun warms Earth, for example.

▷ **What are three ways that heat can move?**

In convection, cooler materials sink while warmer materials rise in a cycle of motion.

What Materials Conduct Heat Well?

The photograph shows very hot tea in a foam cup. A metal spoon has been sitting in the tea for some time. The outside of the cup is slightly warm. However, the spoon's handle is almost too hot to hold. Why has more heat flowed into the handle of the spoon than into the walls of the cup?

As you learned in Lesson 1, some materials are better at conducting heat than others. The metal spoon is a good conductor of heat. However, the foam cup is a poor conductor of heat. As a result, heat flows quickly from the hot bowl of the spoon to its handle. However, heat flows very slowly from the tea into the foam.

Metals are the best conductors of heat. Why do metals conduct heat so well?

Heat is carried through a material by the motion of molecules. When a metal is heated at one end, the hot molecules vibrate back and forth. They collide with their neighbors, spreading the motion through the material. The spreading of the motion warms up other parts of the material.

The molecules in solids are packed very closely together. This makes transferring energy easier.

In Chapter 10 you learned that the molecules in gases are spread apart. They cannot transfer heat between one

How Materials Conduct Heat	
Material	How Many Times Better Than Air It Conducts Heat
Wood	5
Water	23
Brick	25
Glass	42
Rock	67
Aluminum	8,300
Copper	15,300

another as easily as in liquids and solids. This explains why air is such a poor conductor of heat. Gases are the poorest thermal conductors of all. Look at the table to see how well common materials conduct heat.

▷ **What materials are the best conductors?**

Why It Matters

Energy comes in many forms. The air in your home is warmed by convection of thermal energy. There is energy stored in batteries and energy stored in the food you eat. The Sun gives us light and heat as well. You depend on various forms of energy to live, move, and have a comfortable life.

 e-Journal Visit our Web site **www.science.mmhschool.com** to do a research project on energy.

Think and Write

1. Describe how a battery makes a light bulb glow. Identify the different forms energy takes.

2. Why is energy not a form of matter?

3. How does thermal energy get from place to place?

4. Insulating windows have two layers of glass with air sealed in between. Why is this layer of air important?

5. **Critical Thinking** Two flashlights have the same kind of bulb. One glows more dimly than the other. Why do you think this is so?

L·I·N·K·S

WRITING LINK

Writing That Compares When did Benjamin Franklin discover that lightning is electricity? What was used to light and heat homes before electrical energy? Use the Internet or an encyclopedia to find the answers. Then write an essay comparing what life was like before and after the use of electrical energy became commonplace.

ART LINK

Make a collage. Cut pictures of different types of energy from a magazine. Identify the source of energy being used. Paste your pictures onto a poster. Present your poster to the class.

MATH LINK

Interpret a table. Which material in the table on the preceding page conducts heat five times better than wood?

TECHNOLOGY LINK

LOG ON Visit **www.science.mmhschool.com** for more links.

Chapter 13 Review

Vocabulary

Fill each blank with the best word or words from the list.

acid, E82
alkalinity, E86
chemical change, E71
colloid, E54
conduction, E97
convection, E97
kinetic energy, E95
potential energy, E95
radiation, E97
solution, E54

1. A mixture that looks the same everywhere, even under a microscope, is a(n) _____ .

2. Blue litmus paper turns red when it is dipped in a(n) _____ .

3. Two chemicals react to form a new substance In a(n) _____ .

4. The Sun's energy is transferred to Earth by _____ .

5. An object that is moving has _____ .

6. Energy is usually transferred from one solid to another by _____ .

7. A substance with properties between a solution and a heterogeneous mixture is a(n) _____ .

8. Stored energy is called _____ .

9. Thermal Energy is usually transferred in liquids and gases by _____ .

10. The strength of a base is called its _____ .

Test Prep

11. In a chemical reaction, there may be a _____ .

  A color change

  B formation of a gas

  C heat change

  D all of the above

12. All of the following are poor conductors of heat EXCEPT _____ .

  F wood

  G glass

  H copper

  J air

13. An example of a physical change is _____ .

  A ice melting

  B bread baking

  C a match burning

  D a nail rusting

14. Heat always flows _____.

    F from lighter materials to heavier materials

    G from heavier materials to lighter materials

    H from cooler materials to hotter materials

    J from hotter materials to cooler materials

15. _____ may be used as an indicator.

    A cabbage juice

    B litmus paper

    C a pH meter

    D all of the above

Concepts and Skills

16. Reading in Science What signs are there that baking bread is a chemical change?

17. INQUIRY SKILL Experiment A friend says he removed tarnish from a silver spoon by putting it in the bottom of an aluminum pot containing a hot baking-soda solution. What really removed the tarnish? Describe how you would perform experiments to find out.

18. Critical Thinking A certain material can be separated by physical changes. Can it be a single compound? Why or why not?

19. Scientific Methods What are two things you might see during a chemical change?

20. Safety Whenever you use a cleaning material, you should read the label carefully. Some kinds of cleaning materials should never be used together. What may be one reason for this?

Did You Ever Wonder?

INQUIRY SKILL Predict Gather the following materials: penny, paper clip, nail, aluminum foil, crayon, nickel, barrette, rubber band, scissors, plastic spoon, and metal spoon. Predict which will be attracted to a magnet. Use a magnet and test your predictions.

LOG ON Visit **www.science.mmhschool.com** to boost your test scores.

Dr. Jacqueline K. Barton

Chemist

You probably know that wires can conduct electricity. A wire from a socket carries electricity to a lamp, and light is produced. But what about living material—like the DNA in your body? Can it conduct electricity?

The answer is yes—according to Jacqueline K. Barton. Dr. Barton is a chemist. She studies what substances are made of and how materials react with each other. Dr. Barton took what she knew about the conductivity of metals and started studying DNA.

DNA is in every cell in your body. It determines all sorts of things about you—such as what color eyes you have and how tall you will be.

Some non-living materials with structures like DNA are able to conduct electricity. Many scientists wondered whether DNA could do the same. Thanks to Dr. Barton's experiments, we know that it can. Barton learned that DNA strands are like wires—and your body is full of them!

LOG ON Visit www.science.mmhschool.com to learn more about the work of chemists.

What could be some benefits of using DNA as a wire? Biologists could send electricity through DNA to find possible health problems in people. Some problems might appear as a glow. Others might show up as dips in the flow of current.

Dr. Barton's work may also help doctors treat patients. Her findings could help to develop better ways to treat diseases such as cancer.

TOP 5 A Future in Chemistry

Dr. Barton started her career as a chemist working with metals in a lab. If you become a chemist, here are five places where you might work:

1. Power plant as a nuclear chemist
2. Research company to develop new plastics
3. Drug company to come up with new medicines
4. Hospital as an organic chemist
5. College as a research chemist

Write About It

1. What is DNA?
2. What is Dr. Barton's job?

PROBING the PROPERTIES

Your goal is to describe objects in a collection in terms of their properties.

What to Do

1. List each object in your collection. Leave space next to each name where you can list the object's properties.

2. List as many properties as you can observe for each object.

3. Measure the mass of each object, and record it on your list.

Analyze Your Results

What are all of the objects in your collection made of?

TESTING FOR pH

Your goal is to put eight unknown solutions in order from most acidic to most basic.

What to Do

1. Use eight unknown solutions, pH paper, a pH scale, a pencil, and paper. Dip a piece of pH paper into each solution. Compare the color of the pH paper with the pH scale. Record each pH in a table.

2. Make a new table that shows the order of the solutions from most acidic to most basic. Include the pH of each solution.

Analyze Your Results

1. Which solutions are acids? Which solutions are bases?

2. If you have an upset stomach, it might be because you have too much acid in your stomach. Why are medicines taken for a stomachache usually bases?

UNIT
F

Motion and Energy

Motion and Energy

LOOK!

Runners race past in a blur
of motion. How could you
measure how fast these
runners are moving?

Newton's Laws of Motion

Did You Ever Wonder?

Is it true that what goes up must come down? How can these skydivers appear to float in the air? The skydivers are actually in free fall until their parachutes open. What force pulls them, and all objects, toward Earth? Do all objects fall at the same rate?

INQUIRY SKILL **Predict** Picture each of the skydivers with an open bottle of water. If they tried to drink the water, would the water flow out of the bottles?

Newton's First Law

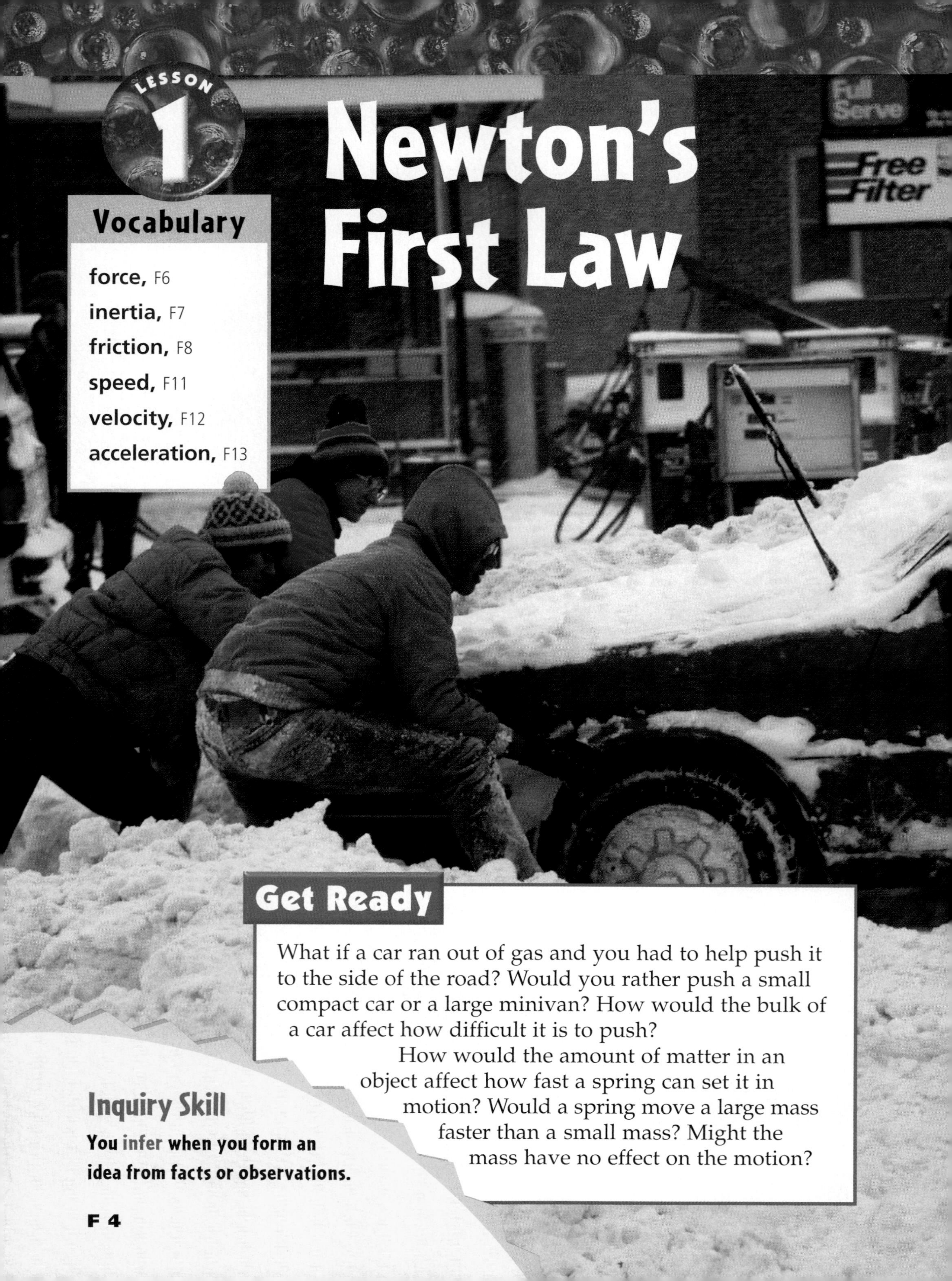

Vocabulary

force, F6
inertia, F7
friction, F8
speed, F11
velocity, F12
acceleration, F13

Inquiry Skill

You infer when you form an idea from facts or observations.

Get Ready

What if a car ran out of gas and you had to help push it to the side of the road? Would you rather push a small compact car or a large minivan? How would the bulk of a car affect how difficult it is to push?

How would the amount of matter in an object affect how fast a spring can set it in motion? Would a spring move a large mass faster than a small mass? Might the mass have no effect on the motion?

Explore Activity

How Fast Does a Spring Move Objects?

Materials

3 masses (washers or AAA batteries)

metal ruler

rubber bands

clock with second hand

graph paper

goggles

Procedure

BE CAREFUL! Wear goggles.

1 Attach a mass to the end of a metal ruler with a rubber band. Hold the ruler tightly against the edge of a table as shown so it can act like a spring.

2 **Use Numbers** Pull the mass back 5 cm (2 in.), and release it crisply. Count and record how many swings the mass completes in ten seconds.

3 **Predict** How will adding more mass to the end of the ruler affect how fast it swings back and forth? Record your predictions.

4 Add a second mass, and repeat the procedure. Repeat again with a third mass.

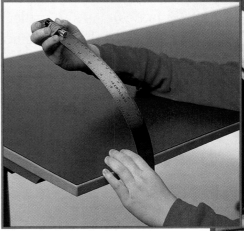

Drawing Conclusions

1 **Infer** Why does the ruler move the attached mass when it is pulled back and released?

2 **Observe** What effect did increasing the mass have on how fast the mass was swung back and forth by the ruler?

3 **Hypothesize** Why do you think the increase in mass had this effect?

4 **Interpret Data** Make a graph of your results. What two variables should you plot?

5 **FURTHER INQUIRY** **Predict** Use your graph to estimate how many swings would be observed in ten seconds when four masses are attached to the ruler.

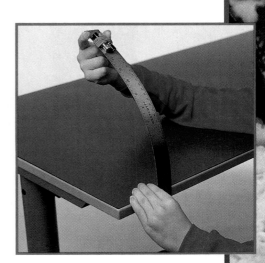

Main Idea Objects that contain more matter are harder to set in motion.

What Does it Take to Make an Object Move?

The students below are investigating how easily objects of different masses are set into motion. First, one student uses a spring scale to pull a toy car from rest through a distance of one meter (39.37 inches). As she pulls, she keeps the reading on the spring scale constant. Her teammate times how long it takes the toy car to travel one meter. Next, the students repeat the experiment using a toy truck that has three times the mass of the toy car.

The results of the experiment show that the toy car traveled the one-meter distance in a shorter time than the toy truck. The amount of pull was kept the same, so why did the car travel faster than the truck? The car traveled faster because objects with more mass are harder to set in motion with a certain push or pull than objects with less mass. The car has less mass, so the pull of the spring scale set it into more rapid motion.

A pull or push that acts on an object is called a **force**. The students' experiment shows you how forces are needed to set objects in motion. As you've seen, objects with more mass move more slowly when acted on by a certain force.

Average Time to Travel 1 Meter with a Steady Pull

An Object's Natural Motion

The mass of an object tends to make the object resist being set into motion. That's why objects with more mass are set into less rapid motion by a certain amount of force. The tendency of an object to resist a change in its state of motion is called the object's **inertia**.

Several centuries ago the famous Italian scientist Galileo began to understand how inertia affects the motion of objects. Galileo imagined rolling a ball down a fixed *incline* (ramp) and then back up ramps of varying steepness, as in the diagram. Galileo had observed that pendulums swing back and forth to the same height. He reasoned that the ball would roll to the same height on any ramp. He realized that if the ramp were less steep, the ball would roll a greater distance and slow down more gradually.

Thinking further, Galileo inferred that if the second ramp were flat, the ball would roll forever at a steady rate (assuming no force is acting on the ball).

Galileo had observed that pendulums swing back and forth to the same height. He reasoned that a ball rolling down one ramp and up another would roll to the same height on any ramp.

To Galileo this meant that the ball's natural state of motion was coasting. Just as it takes a force to set an object in motion, it also takes a force to slow or stop a coasting object. Without any such force, the object will coast forever in a straight line.

▷ **What does it take to change an object's state of motion?**

The ball is released from A. It rolls down the incline, then back up one of the facing inclines. If there is no force acting on the ball, it slows and comes to a stop just as it reaches the starting height.

Incline C is not as steep as incline B, so the ball takes longer to slow down. Galileo reasoned that if there were no incline for the ball to climb, it would not slow down at all—as in D.

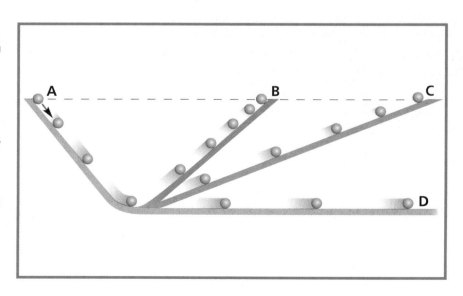

Is Force Needed to Maintain Motion?

The sailboat in the picture is traveling at a steady rate in a straight line. The wind has filled its sails and is pushing the boat forward. Until just a few centuries ago, most people believed that a force was necessary to keep an object traveling at a steady rate, just like the wind pushing the boat.

Galileo realized that this idea was incorrect. He understood that a force called **friction** acts against moving objects. Friction opposes the motion of one object moving past another. If the friction is taken away, no force is needed to maintain motion at a steady rate. An object's inertia is all that is needed to keep it moving.

Forty-five years after Galileo died, Sir Isaac Newton published a complete description of the concept of inertia. This is *Newton's first law of motion*: Objects at rest remain at rest and objects traveling at a steady rate in a straight line continue that way until a force acts on them.

The sailboat needs the force of the wind to keep it moving. That is because the friction between the boat and the water tends to slow the boat down.

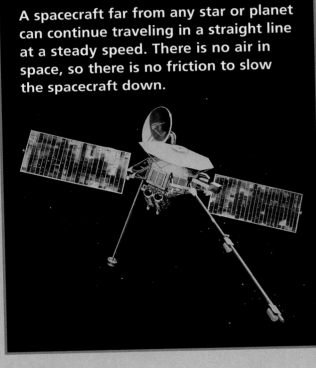

A spacecraft far from any star or planet can continue traveling in a straight line at a steady speed. There is no air in space, so there is no friction to slow the spacecraft down.

How Inertia Works

Newton's first law of motion—the law of inertia—tells us that the state of motion of an object does not change until a force is applied to it. That means, if an object is traveling at a steady rate in a straight line, it will continue to do so until a force is applied to it. Newton's law also means that if the object is sitting at rest, it will continue to be at rest until a force is applied to it. Each of the photographs shows an example of Newton's first law of motion.

The rocket engines must overcome inertia. Their force moves the rocket from rest to high speeds during liftoff. The rocket's momentum is determined by the product of its mass and speed.

▷ Is a force needed to keep a moving spacecraft moving in a straight line?

These race cars could not change their direction of travel without the force of the road surface pushing sideways against the tires.

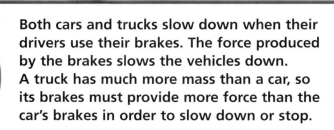

Both cars and trucks slow down when their drivers use their brakes. The force produced by the brakes slows the vehicles down. A truck has much more mass than a car, so its brakes must provide more force than the car's brakes in order to slow down or stop.

QUICK LAB

Using a Position Grid

FOLDABLES Make a Half-Book using graph paper. (See p. R 41.) Label it as shown.

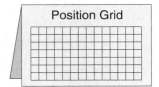

Position Grid

1. A grid has rows and columns. Each is labeled with letters or numbers. You can locate each box in the grid by its letter and number address. Make your own grid. Number the boxes from 1 to 29 across and from A to G down. Inside your Half-Book, explain why the snail didn't want to move. How is a position grid useful?

2. Find each box, and shade it in with a colored pencil.

E27, B8, F24, D15, B29, C20, D5, F14, D29, B3, D11, B16, F3, D7, B27, B2, B11, F27, B20, F12, B23, D8, E17, F20, F23, C6, E2, E24, B10, B1, F10, C29, C2, F17, D24, E8, B15, E14, F1, B12, F5, D16, B21, B24, D27, C5, C10, E29, E7, B5, C14, C24, C16, E20, D2, C27, D10, C8, D17, E28, E10, D6, F25, D20, D14, F8, F29, B19, B14, F11, E5, B25, F2, B28

The snail didn't want to move because he had _____.

Where Is It?

How do you know when you are moving? You are moving when you are changing position. Position is the location of an object. Your position might be in front of, behind, to the right or to the left of some object. Cities or landmarks can be located on a map. The position of each object can be found by using a grid. The position of any object on a map is a comparison of the object's location to other things on the map. We can describe positions of things with a grid like the one covering the map. For example, the location of Atlanta can be described as box J16. You can find the number of Atlanta's position along the top or bottom and the letter along either side.

Find the city in each location.
a. K10   b. H11

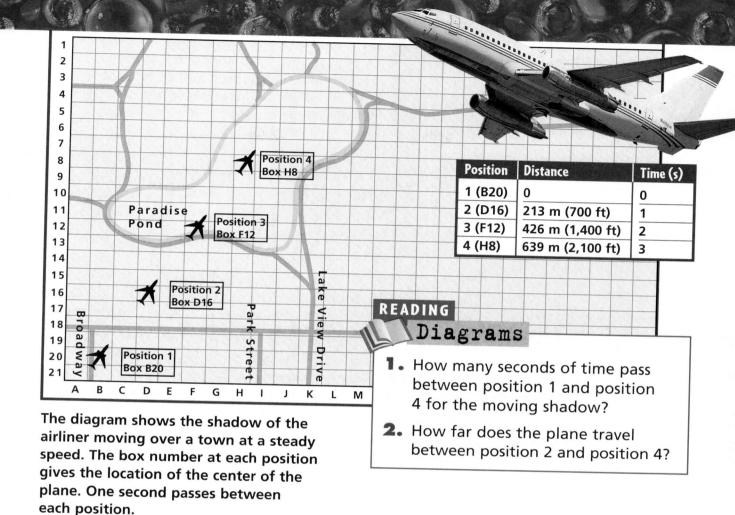

Position	Distance	Time (s)
1 (B20)	0	0
2 (D16)	213 m (700 ft)	1
3 (F12)	426 m (1,400 ft)	2
4 (H8)	639 m (2,100 ft)	3

The diagram shows the shadow of the airliner moving over a town at a steady speed. The box number at each position gives the location of the center of the plane. One second passes between each position.

READING Diagrams

1. How many seconds of time pass between position 1 and position 4 for the moving shadow?

2. How far does the plane travel between position 2 and position 4?

What Speed Is

The airliner in the photo is moving rapidly through the air. How can we tell that it is moving? Think about watching the shadow of the airliner on the ground below, as in the diagram. We can see the shadow sweeping past fixed objects like ponds, homes, or streets. The change in the position of the shadow compared with the surrounding objects reveals its motion, as well as the motion of the airliner.

The table describes the motion of the airliner by giving the position of the airliner's shadow at various times. The position can be measured as the box number of the center of the shadow.

The position can also be measured as the distance traveled past position 1.

As for any moving object, the **speed** of the airliner is how fast its position is changing with time at any moment. When the distance traveled by an object in a given time is known, the speed is found by dividing the distance by the time. The airliner, for example, travels 213 meters (700 feet) in 1 second. Therefore, the airliner's speed is 213 meters per second (700 feet per second) or 213 meters/second (700 feet/second).

▷ **What tells you how fast the plane is moving?**

F 11

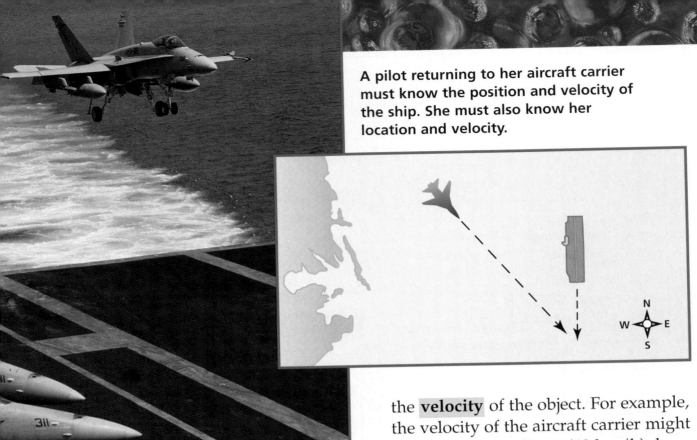

A pilot returning to her aircraft carrier must know the position and velocity of the ship. She must also know her location and velocity.

What Is Velocity?

The pilot of the navy jet is out on a mission. She needs to return to her aircraft carrier before she runs low on fuel. Her position and the position of the aircraft carrier are shown on the map. To get back safely, what information must she obtain from the ship to know in what direction to fly her plane?

First, she must know the position of the ship. She will also need to know the speed and the direction in which the ship is traveling. With this information, plus a knowledge of her own speed, the pilot can decide which direction she must travel in to meet up with the carrier, as shown by the dotted lines.

The speed of a moving object taken together with its direction of travel gives the **velocity** of the object. For example, the velocity of the aircraft carrier might be 40 kilometers/hour (40 km/h) due south, or the velocity of the plane might be 600 km/h to the southeast.

How can you tell the velocity of a car you are riding in? You need to know your speed. The car's speedometer will give you that information. You also need to know the direction you are traveling in. For that, you may need to use a map or road signs.

Two objects can have the same speed but different velocities if they are traveling in different directions. They may also have different velocities if they are traveling in the same direction but with different speeds. The only way two objects can have the same velocity is for the objects to both be traveling in the same direction at the same speed.

▷ **How is velocity different from speed?**

What Is Acceleration?

As long as an object travels in a straight line at a steady speed, its velocity is constant. Newton's first law tells us that an object's velocity will remain constant unless a force is applied to it. What if such a force is applied? How could the force affect the velocity of a moving object?

Both of the photographs on this page show how the velocity of an object can change when a force is applied. The force may change the object's speed, its direction of travel, or both. Any of these changes will change the velocity.

A change in velocity is called **acceleration**. Isaac Newton realized that applying a force to an object would overcome its inertia and change its velocity, causing it to accelerate. A special case of acceleration— *deceleration*—occurs when a force causes the speed of an object to decrease. Look at the photographs. Each photograph

A motor drives these riders in a circle. Even when the riders' speed is constant, their direction of travel is always changing. Therefore, they are accelerating.

shows acceleration due to changing velocity. Which photograph shows a change in direction? Which photograph shows a deceleration?

▷ **How is acceleration related to velocity?**

With the help of its brakes and this parachute, this race car will decelerate—change its velocity and come to a stop.

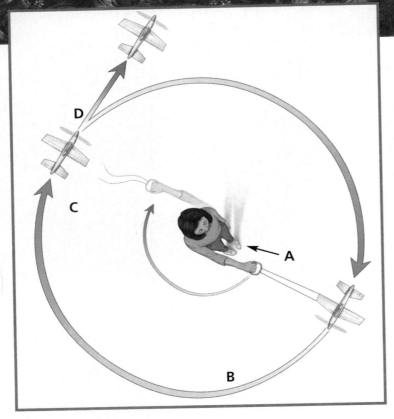

The inward force of the strings (A) keeps the plane on a circular path (B). If the strings were to break (C), the plane would fly off in a straight line (D) at a constant speed due to inertia.

What Keeps Things Moving in a Circle?

A gas-powered model airplane can be tied to a handle with strings. This allows the plane to be flown in a circle. Without strings, the plane tends to fly in a straight line at constant speed—a constant velocity. When it is tied with strings, however, the strings provide a force that pulls on the plane. This force steadily changes the plane's direction of travel, keeping it on a circular path.

Even though the plane's speed remains constant as it flies in a circle, its steadily changing direction of travel means that its velocity is changing and that it is accelerating. Note how the force causing the acceleration—the pull of the strings—is always directed toward the center of the circle.

If the strings tethering the plane were to break suddenly, it would fly off in a straight line at a constant speed. There would no longer be any force to overcome its inertia, and it would travel with constant velocity.

Although Earth and the Sun are much bigger than model airplanes, all of these objects obey the laws of motion in the same way. The pull of *gravity* between Earth and the Sun acts like the strings on the model plane. Gravity is the force that keeps Earth moving in a circular path about the Sun. If the force of gravity were somehow to disappear, Earth would fly off in a straight line into deep space! (You'll learn more about gravity in Lesson 3.)

READING Draw Conclusions
Why is a force needed to keep an object moving in a circle?

Why It Matters

In outer space, spacecraft are not slowed by air resistance. When a pilot tries to dock one spacecraft with another, she sets her craft in motion with a burst of gas. To slow her craft, she applies a burst of gas in the opposite direction. With too little force, her craft may strike the other. With too much force, she may start going backward. It takes great skill to guide a spacecraft.

 Journal Visit our Web site www.science.mmhschool.com to do a research project on force and mass.

Think and Write

1. A boat's motor dies when it is traveling at high speed. The boat slows to a stop. Why?

2. On a wet road, a car drives at high speed. At a sharp turn, the car slides straight out into a field. Why?

3. What do you need to know to find a car's velocity?

4. What is happening when a mass on a spring swings back and forth?

5. **Critical Thinking** If you tie a thread to the middle of a water-filled plastic bottle and pull slowly, the bottle moves. If you pull very rapidly, the thread breaks before the bottle can move. Why?

L·I·N·K·S

MATH LINK

Solve a problem. Absolute motion or rest is misleading. You are speeding faster than most airliners as you read this. Why don't you feel it? Where is the evidence that Earth rotates once every 24 hours? Its circumference is about 40,000 km (25,000 mi). Calculate how fast you and Earth are moving.

WRITING LINK

Expository Writing On a trip to the Moon and back, when would the astronauts be accelerating? When would they be traveling at a constant velocity? What forces would they experience? Research this topic and write a report.

ART LINK

Make a poster. A weather satellite circles Earth at a steady speed. Make a poster that shows its orbit and illustrates why it is accelerating.

TECHNOLOGY LINK

LOG ON Visit www.science.mmhschool.com for more links.

Newton's Second and Third Laws

Vocabulary

balanced forces, F21

unbalanced force, F21

action, F24

reaction, F24

work, F26

simple machine, F26

lever, F26

fulcrum, F26

effort arm, F26

resistance arm, F26

Get Ready

Have you ever been in a hurry on a bicycle? To get moving faster, you pedal harder. The extra force you apply to the pedals makes you reach a greater speed. However, what happens if you are wearing a heavy backpack or carrying a lot of books in your back baskets? Is it just as easy to get up to speed, or do you have to pedal harder to reach the same speed?

How does the amount of force applied to an object affect how fast its velocity changes? What if you kept the force the same but increased the mass of the object? How fast would the velocity change?

Inquiry Skill

You **observe** when you use one or more of the senses to identify or learn about an object or event.

Explore Activity

How do Different Forces Affect an Object's Motion?

Materials

toy car

2 boards with hooks for rubber bands

rubber bands

meterstick

masking tape

goggles

stopwatch

compass

Procedure

BE CAREFUL! Wear goggles

1. Place a 15-cm (6-in.) strip of masking tape on the floor. Hold two boards on either side of the tape with a rubber band stretched between them.

2. **Measure** Pull a toy car back 5-cm (2-in.) against the rubber band to launch it. Use the compass, stopwatch, and meterstick to determine the car's direction, elapsed time, and distance of travel.

3. **Observe** Repeat step 2 twice more. Record your results. Find the average speed.

4. **Predict** What will happen if you use two or three rubber bands to launch the car? Test your prediction.

Drawing Conclusions

1. **Interpret Data** When did the car move farthest on average—when one, two, or three rubber bands were used?

2. **Infer** How is the distance traveled by the car in any trial related to the speed it was given by the rubber band? Why?

3. **FURTHER INQUIRY** **Predict** If you taped a second toy car on top of the first and launched them with two rubber bands, how far would the cars travel? Test your prediction. Explain your observations.

Main Idea As the net force acting on an object increases, the object accelerates more.

What Affects Acceleration?

What if you use a rubber band to launch a toy car along the floor? The rubber band will apply a force to the car, and the force will cause the car to speed up. Once the rear of the car passes the starting line, however, the rubber band no longer is applying force. At this point the car will begin coasting until friction brings it to a stop. The farther the car travels before stopping, the faster it must have been going at the start.

Force and Acceleration

What happens if you add extra rubber bands? Then you are applying more force to the car. As the force increases, the distance the car travels also increases. This, in turn, tells you that the car reaches its greatest starting speed when the force applied to it is greatest.

Sir Isaac Newton realized that forces produce acceleration. In other words, if we apply a force to an object, the object's velocity will change. The object might speed up, slow down, or change direction. It could even change both speed and direction.

Newton reasoned this way: If we multiply the force by a certain amount, we will change the acceleration by the same amount. (This assumes that no other changes are made.) For example, if we triple the force, the acceleration will also be tripled. What if you tried launching your toy car first using one rubber band, then using three rubber bands of the same size? You should see that as the force on the car is increased, the speed it reaches increases by about the same amount. The graph shows an example of how the car's acceleration would be related to the force acting on it, according to Newton's ideas.

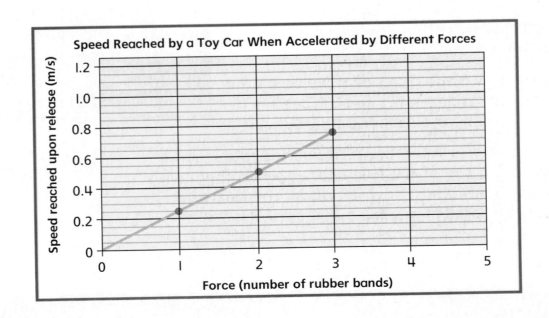

Speed Reached by a Toy Car When Accelerated by Different Forces

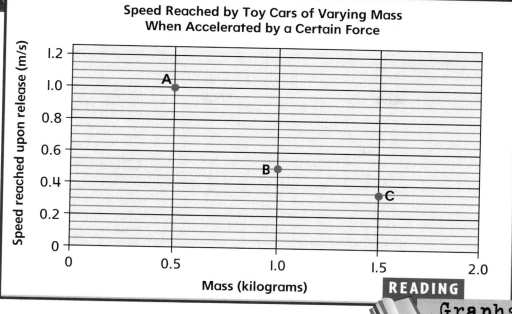

Speed Reached by Toy Cars of Varying Mass When Accelerated by a Certain Force

Using the same amount of force, it is easier to accelerate a less massive object than a more massive object.

READING

Graphs

What would the speed reached be for a mass of 2 kilograms?

Mass and Acceleration

What happens if you tape a second car on top of the first? You double the mass being accelerated by the force from the rubber bands. Now the two cars together will travel only about half as far as one car would alone when launched by the same number of rubber bands. This tells you that doubling the mass resulted in about half the acceleration.

Isaac Newton understood that changing the force isn't the only thing that affects acceleration. He also understood that mass affects acceleration. However, while increasing the force increases the acceleration, increasing the mass decreases the acceleration.

When the mass is multiplied by a certain factor, the new acceleration is obtained by dividing the old acceleration by that factor. (Again, this assumes that nothing else has changed.) For

example, what if the mass of an object being accelerated by a certain force is doubled? The new acceleration would then be the previous acceleration divided by 2. Put another way, if the mass is doubled, the acceleration is reduced to one-half of its previous value.

The relationship between acceleration and force is said to be direct— when one is increased, the other increases. The relationship between acceleration and mass, on the other hand, is inverse—when one goes up, the other goes down. The graph shows an example of how the acceleration of a toy car is inversely related to its mass.

▷ **What two factors determine how great an object's acceleration is?**

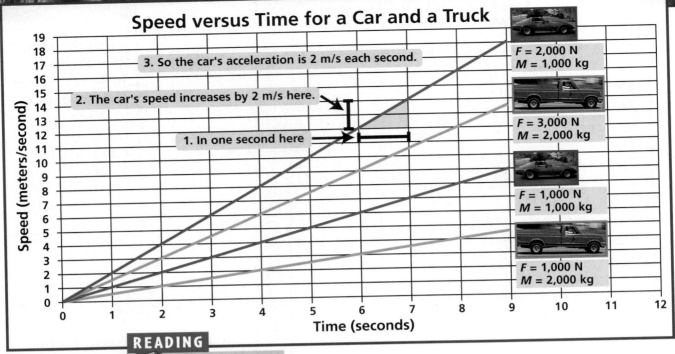

Speed versus Time for a Car and a Truck

3. So the car's acceleration is 2 m/s each second.

2. The car's speed increases by 2 m/s here.

1. In one second here

F = 2,000 N
M = 1,000 kg

F = 3,000 N
M = 2,000 kg

F = 1,000 N
M = 1,000 kg

F = 1,000 N
M = 2,000 kg

Speed (meters/second)

Time (seconds)

READING
Graphs

Describe two ways you could use the information on the graph to calculate the acceleration of the truck when a force of 3,000 N acts on it.

How Is Acceleration Calculated?

You learned in Lesson 1 that acceleration is a change in velocity. Recall that velocity describes both the speed and direction of a moving object. To calculate the acceleration of an object moving in a straight line you first must know three things—the object's starting speed, its new speed, and the amount of time it took for the change to occur.

Look at the lowest blue line on the graph above. In one second, the speed of the car has gone from zero to 1 meter per second. For each second that passes, the car's speed increases by another meter per second. The car is accelerating at 1 meter per second each second. Now look at the top blue line for the same

1,000-kg car. In one second the car's speed now increases by 2 meters per second. That means its acceleration is 2 meters per second each second.

What was changed to make the car's acceleration double? The force acting on the car was changed.

We can write an equation to show how acceleration is related to force and mass: $a = F \div m$. This equation says the acceleration is found by dividing the force by the mass. In the examples shown, forces are in units called newtons (N). A force of 1 newton makes the speed of a 1 kg mass change by 1 meter per second each second.

▶ **What do you need to know to calculate the acceleration an object will have?**

What Are Balanced and Unbalanced Forces?

The plane in the photograph below is flying at a constant speed in a constant direction. Its speed is not changing, nor is its direction of travel, so the plane cannot be accelerating. However, the pilot is using the throttle to make the plane's motor apply a forward force to it. How can the motor apply force to the plane without causing the plane to accelerate?

The explanation is that the force of the plane's motor is exactly offset by other forces acting in the opposite direction, as the diagram shows. In fact, there are a number of forces acting on the plane, but for each one there are others that cancel it out. When all of the forces on an object cancel one another out, the forces are said to be **balanced forces**.

In cases where a certain force is either only partially canceled or not canceled at all by other forces, the force is said to be an **unbalanced force**. For example, what if a plane's motor applies more forward force than the amount of friction and air resistance apply against its forward motion? The friction and air resistance will cancel some, but not all, of the forward force. This will leave an unbalanced forward force acting on the plane.

When we use the equation $a = F/m$ to find acceleration, F always stands for the unbalanced force. This equation

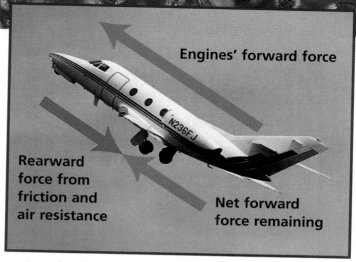

Engines' forward force

Rearward force from friction and air resistance

Net forward force remaining

Are the forces acting on this plane balanced or unbalanced?

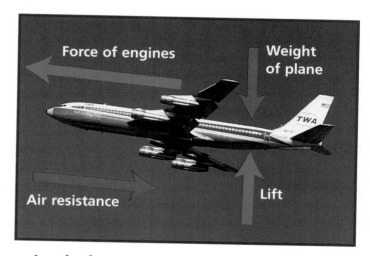

Force of engines

Weight of plane

Air resistance

Lift

Are the forces acting on this plane balanced or unbalanced?

is actually one possible way of stating *Newton's second law of motion*: When an unbalanced force acts on an object, the object's acceleration equals the force divided by the object's mass.

READING Draw Conclusions

What happens to an object's motion when the forces acting on it are unbalanced?

Racing Balloon Rockets

FOLDABLES™ Make a Shutter Fold. (See p. R 42.) Label the shutters as shown.

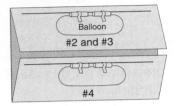

1. Pass thread or string through two short lengths of soda straw as shown. Then stretch the string tightly between two chairs.

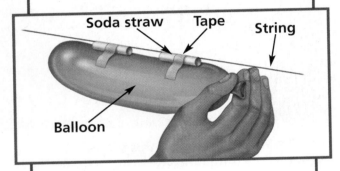

Soda straw   Tape   String

Balloon

2. Inflate the balloon rocket. Hold the neck closed while your partner tapes it to the straws. Let go and record your observations in the Shutter Fold.

3. **Observe** Compare the direction the balloon moves with the direction of the escaping air.

4. **Infer** Is there an unbalanced force on the balloon? In which direction does it push?

Where Does the Force Come From?

The rocket in the picture is accelerating upward due to the force provided by its engine. Fuel has been burned into hot gases in the engine's combustion chamber. The hot gases rush out of the engine nozzle in a downward direction. How is it that gases rushing down can cause the rocket to accelerate up?

If the rocket is accelerating, it must have an unbalanced force acting on it. Clearly, this force comes from the hot gases in its engines. Knowing the unbalanced force and the rocket's mass, we could calculate the acceleration of the rocket with Newton's second law of motion, $a = F/m$. However, as you will see, it takes another law of motion to explain how gases rushing one way can accelerate the rocket in the opposite direction.

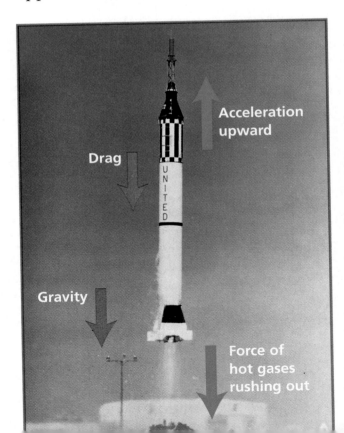

Acceleration upward

Drag

Gravity

Force of hot gases rushing out

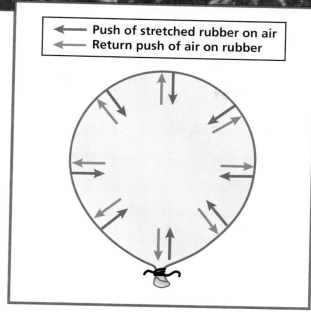

Legend:
← Push of stretched rubber on air
← Return push of air on rubber

All the way around the balloon, the inward push of the stretched rubber is balanced by the return outward push of the air. The balloon neither expands nor contracts, and it is not moved in any direction.

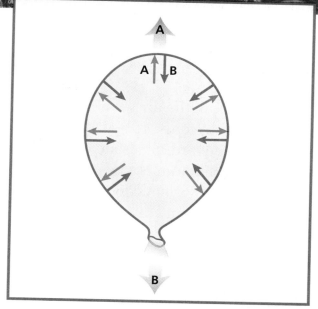

Force A pushes the balloon forward. When the balloon is opened, there are no longer any forces at the opening to offset forces A and B. Force B makes air rush out of the balloon, as shown by arrow B.

Making a Rocket Go

When you blow up a balloon and then release it without tying it closed, it flies through the air. You can take advantage of this behavior to make a balloon rocket. You know that air rushes out one end of the balloon, while the balloon itself moves in the opposite direction. Where do the forces come from that move the balloon and the air?

The air inside the balloon is "squeezed" by the stretched rubber. At the same time, the air resists being squeezed and pushes back on the rubber. When the balloon is inflated and tied off, these pushes are in balance and the balloon neither changes in size nor moves.

What happens if we leave the neck of the blown-up balloon open, instead?

At the point of the opening, there is no stretched rubber squeezing the air. However, there *is* stretched rubber squeezing the air at a point opposite the opening. As a result, there is a net force on the air that pushes it out through the opening.

At the same time, the air pushes forward on the balloon opposite the opening. There is no such push at the opening itself, because there is no rubber surface on which the air can push. Since the push of the air forward on the balloon is not offset by any rearward push, an unbalanced force results that pushes the balloon forward.

▶ **What force makes a balloon rocket go forward?**

How Do Forces Act Between Objects?

In a balloon, the air returns the push of the stretched rubber that squeezes it inward. Sir Isaac Newton understood that one object pushing on another will always receive a push in return. In the same way, the stretched rubber of a balloon receives a return push from the air it is squeezing. The same reasoning also applies to pulling forces.

When one object applies a force to a second, we call this force the **action**. The force the second object returns to the first is called the **reaction**. Think about what happens when a 50-kg student on ice skates pushes forward on another 50-kg student on ice skates. Both of them wind up moving at the same speed, but in opposite directions. Newton realized that while the action and reaction act in opposite directions, they have the same strength. These ideas are summarized in *Newton's third law of motion*: For every action, there is an equal but opposite reaction.

An accelerating race car demonstrates Newton's third law. The car's tires push to the rear on the road surface. At the same time, the road pushes back on the tires in a forward direction. This reaction force is what propels the car ahead.

Gas rushing out of a rocket engine propels the rocket in the opposite direction. The hot gas tends to expand, so it applies an action force to the walls of the combustion chamber. The walls

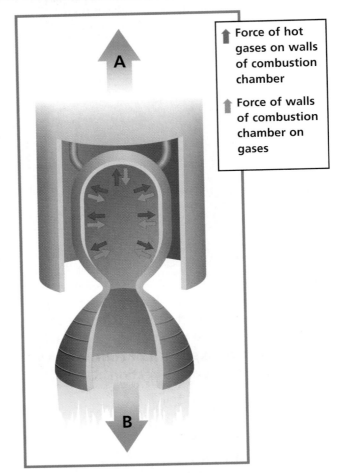

Force of hot gases on walls of combustion chamber

Force of walls of combustion chamber on gases

Action A is an unbalanced force that propels the rocket ahead. Reaction B is an unbalanced force that pushes the hot gases out through the nozzle.

apply a reaction force to the gas similar to the balloon rocket. The gas pushes the rocket ahead, while the walls of the chamber push the gas to the rear, out through the nozzle.

When one object applies a force to another, both objects feel force. The second object feels the action force, while the first object feels the reaction force. If these forces are not balanced by other forces, *both* objects will accelerate.

▷ **What happens when one object exerts a force on another?**

How Do Forces Affect Us?

Everywhere around us, forces act. Newton's laws of motion give us a useful picture of the way forces work. They also tell us how to predict what will happen when forces are applied to objects. Look at the examples of forces on this page. Think about how Newton's laws explain what is occurring in each case.

The bat applied a force to the ball and sent it flying to the outfield. At the same time, the ball applied a force to the bat, in this case enough to break it!

The water coming from this hose is under very high pressure. The water applies a large force back on the hose. The firemen have to use great strength to keep the hose from getting loose and flying around dangerously.

The hot gases in the jet engines push it forward, while the engines force the hot gases rearward.

▷ **How are forces affecting the racing boat?**

The crew on this racing craft push on the water with their oars. The water, in turn, pushes back on the oars and moves the boat forward.

What Is a Simple Machine?

People use forces like pushes and pulls to do work. To a scientist, **work** means using force to move an object through a distance. Holding this book in your hand requires force, but no work is done because there is no movement. Opening this book and turning its pages is easy work. When you have to move a heavy object, work is not easy.

Simple machines are devices with few moving parts that make work easier to do. They lower the force needed to move and lift heavy objects and loads. There are six types of simple machines—levers, wheels and axles, pulleys, inclined planes, wedges, and screws.

Levers

Levers help you lift heavy loads or change the direction of a force. A **lever** consists of a rigid bar that rests on a pivot point or **fulcrum**. The lever turns up or down around the fulcrum.

The part of the lever you apply an input effort force to is the **effort arm**. The **resistance arm** of the lever produces an output force to lift the load. If the effort arm is longer than the resistance arm, the lever changes a small input force into a larger output force. In all machines, applying a small input force over a longer distance produces enough work to move a much heavier load a shorter distance. Both arms do the same amount of work. Energy is not being created.

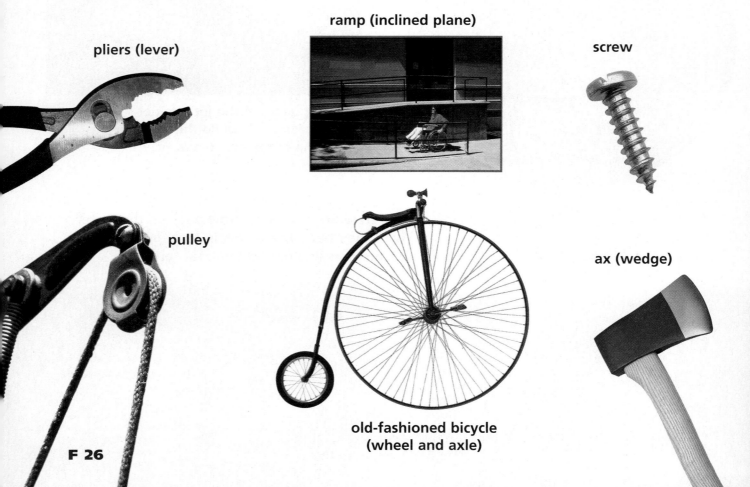

pliers (lever)

ramp (inclined plane)

screw

pulley

ax (wedge)

old-fashioned bicycle
(wheel and axle)

There are three types of levers: first-class, second-class, and third-class. They differ in the positions of the effort arm, resistance arm, and fulcrum.

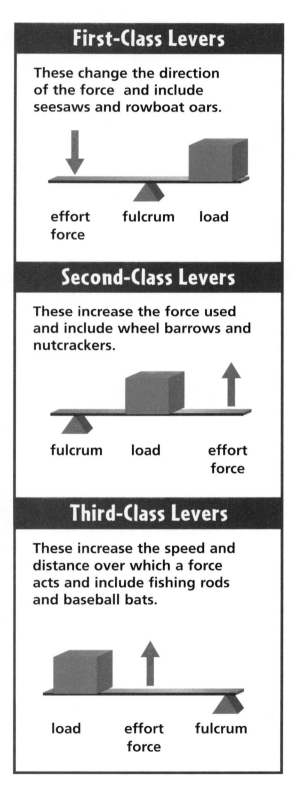

First-Class Levers

These change the direction of the force and include seesaws and rowboat oars.

effort force   fulcrum   load

Second-Class Levers

These increase the force used and include wheel barrows and nutcrackers.

fulcrum   load   effort force

Third-Class Levers

These increase the speed and distance over which a force acts and include fishing rods and baseball bats.

load   effort force   fulcrum

Wheels and Axles

A large-diameter wheel rotates in a circle around a small-diameter axle. A small amount of input force on the wheel becomes a large force on the axle. Doorknobs and screwdrivers use wheels and axles in this way.

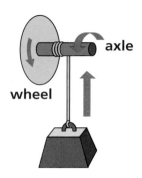

axle

wheel

Pulleys

A pulley is a wheel with a groove in the rim. A rope fits into the groove. A fixed pulley changes the direction of the effort force. However, the input force must equal the load. A movable pulley decreases the effort force needed to move the load. The rope moves a long distance to move the load a short distance. Pulley systems can combine fixed and movable pulleys.

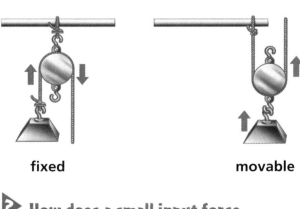

fixed   movable

▷ **How does a small input force become a big output force?**

What Is an Inclined Plane?

An inclined plane is a flat, slanted surface that makes it easier to move heavy objects to higher levels. The slanted surface is the effort arm. The vertical end of the plane is the output arm. The less steep the slope of the effort arm, the longer it is than the output arm and the less effort is needed to move the load up the ramp. Loading ramps for warehouses and gangplanks for ships are examples of inclined planes.

Inclined plane

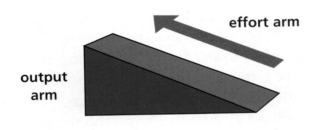

effort arm

output arm

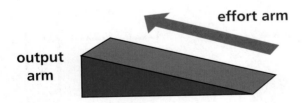

effort arm

output arm

Wedge

Wedges

A wedge is an inclined plane that is used as a tool for cutting or separating things. Some wedges consist of two inclined planes put together back to back so their slanted sides face outward. The thinner the wedge, the greater is the output force. Needles, ax blades, knife blades, and log splitters are examples of wedges.

Screws

A screw is an inclined plane wrapped in a spiral around a cylinder or cone. Screws and bolts are used as fasteners for wood or metal. Drills, corkscrews, and jar lids are also examples of screws.

Screw

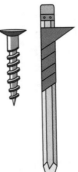

To make a screw, wrap an inclined plane around a cylinder.

▷ **How does an inclined plane make loading a truck easier?**

Why It Matters

In the weightlessness of outer space, it is important to be aware of even small accelerations. While weight seems to disappear in orbit, small accelerations remain, such as gradual slowing due to tiny amounts of air resistance. Measuring these accelerations is important in studying things such as crystal growth and fluid flow in space.

e-Journal Visit our Web site **www.science.mmhschool.com** to do a research project on force and motion.

Think and Write

1. How do you find an object's acceleration from its mass and the force acting on it?

2. How can a boat move at constant velocity if its propeller provides a steady force to it?

3. A 1-kg magnet and a 0.5-kg piece of steel are 25 cm apart. Then they are attracted together. How do they move?

4. How does a lever increase the output force?

5. **Critical Thinking** If you hold a helium-filled balloon in a car with the windows up, the balloon moves forward when the car speeds up and backward when it slows down. Why do you think this happens?

L·I·N·K·S

Read *The Rise and Fall of Galloping Gertie*, to learn about a bridge that was destroyed by wind. When you finish reading, think about how you would design a safer bridge. Try the activities at the end of the book.

WRITING LINK

Personal Narrative What kinds of simple machines do you use every day? Write a letter to a friend telling about the machines you use that make your life easier. Use the correct form for writing a friendly letter.

MATH LINK

Solve this problem. Examine the equation $a = F/m$. Without using numbers, explain what happens to the acceleration if the force increases. Prove it using the equation. What happens to acceleration if mass increases?

TECHNOLOGY LINK

 LOG ON Visit **www.science.mmhschool.com** for more links.

Making It Easy with Machines

You use machines every day of your life. Machines help you make dinner, cut the grass, and visit your friends. The can openers, lawn mowers, and bikes we use today evolved from six basic, simple machines that people have used for thousands of years. Most machines are compound machines, which are just combinations of the simple machines.

These inventions make life much easier. But even with the help of a machine, work is not effortless. To do work, every machine needs an energy source. This can be you, the wind, batteries, or fuel. Car engines burn gasoline to power their motion.

A car is basically a combination of two machines: an engine and a transmission. The transmission uses wheels and axles, levers, and gears to turn work from the engine into rotation of the wheels. At 55 miles per hour, the tires spin 750 times a minute. A car has over 15,000 parts and may seem complicated. But at its heart, it's just a collection of simple machines.

The great thing about machines is that we can use them to make other machines. So our machines get bigger and better every year. In the 1800s, it took a dozen people a full day of hard work to cut down five acres of grain. Today, using a machine called a combine harvester, a single farmer can harvest that much grain in an hour, while listening to music!

Let's hear it for machines!

The levers and wheels of a can opener make it easier to fix dinner.

Put the power to the pedal, and the gears and wheels of a bike will get you where you want to go.

The combine harvester not only cuts down the grain, it also sieves it, threshes it, stores it temporarily, and then pours it into the back of a truck. Quite a combination!

Write About It

1. Name three sources of energy used to make a typical car run. (One may not be so obvious.) Explain how each energy source is used to operate the car.

2. Describe how a machine that you see every day helps you to do work.

LOG ON Visit www.science.mmhschool.com to learn more about machines.

Newton's Law of Gravitation

Vocabulary

gravity, F35
weight, F36

Get Ready

Think about what happens when you drop two objects with very different weights. Does one fall faster than the other? Thanks to scientists such as Galileo and Newton, we now have a good answer to this question.

About 400 years ago, Galileo described a special experiment. Two objects with different weights were dropped at the same time from a tall tower known as the Leaning Tower of Pisa. What do you think happened to the objects in Galileo's experiment?

You drop a golf ball and a table tennis ball side-by-side from the same height. Which do you think will land first?

Inquiry Skill

**You predict when you
state possible results of
an event or experiment.**

Explore Activity

Does Weight Affect How Fast an Object Falls?

Materials

table tennis ball

golf ball

pencil

eraser

goggles

Procedure

BE CAREFUL! Wear goggles.

1. **Predict** Do heavy objects fall faster than lighter objects? Record your prediction and your reasons for making it.

2. **Observe** Stretch out your arms in front of you at shoulder height. Hold the two different balls—one in each hand—at the same height, and drop them at exactly the same time. Listen for them to hit the floor. Which one hit the floor first? Record your results.

3. **Experiment** Repeat step 2 several more times to be sure your observations are accurate. Try dropping a pencil or an eraser at the same time as one of the balls. Record your observations.

Drawing Conclusions

1. **Observe** Which ball hit the ground first?

2. **Observe** When you dropped different objects, which hit first, the heavier or the lighter?

3. **Hypothesize** Suggest an explanation for what you observed.

4. **FURTHER INQUIRY** **Experiment** Take two pieces of paper. Wad one into a tight ball. Leave the other alone. When you drop the two pieces of paper as you did the golf ball and table tennis ball, which will hit the ground first? Test your prediction. Explain your results.

Main Idea We are pulled to the ground by the same force that keeps the Moon orbiting Earth, and the planets orbiting the Sun.

Why Would Air Make a Difference?

The student in the diagram has just dropped a solid rubber ball and a feather from the same height at the same time. The ball has covered a greater distance than the feather in the same amount of time. This means that the ball has fallen at a greater rate. Should we conclude that heavier objects fall faster than lighter objects?

It is important to realize that when the ball and feather are falling, they both must pass through air. Air offers resistance to the motion of objects through it. In the case of the ball and feather, air resistance acts against the feather's motion more than it does against the ball's motion. As a result, the air slows the feather more than it does the ball, and the ball falls farther during the same amount of time.

What would happen, though, if the air were removed so that air resistance disappeared? There is no air on the Moon. If you were to drop a hammer and a feather at the same time on the Moon, would they still fall at different rates? No. Since there is no air resistance, the ball and the feather would fall at the same rate!

Scientists have learned that when the effects of air resistance are removed, objects of different weights do, indeed, fall at the same rate. In addition, air resistance may be too small to matter for objects that are fairly compact. Over short distances such objects fall at the same rate even in air.

> **How does air affect how a feather falls to the ground?**

Do the ball and feather fall at the same rate on Earth as they do on the Moon? Explain.

F 34

Before the parachutes open, these skydivers are in *free fall*—falling toward Earth with the acceleration caused by gravity.

What Makes Objects Fall at the Same Rate?

Aristotle was a philosopher who lived in ancient Greece nearly 2,400 years ago. He believed that heavy things fall faster than lighter things. Aristotle's teachings were accepted for nearly 2,000 years after his death.

In the early 1600s, however, Galileo challenged Aristotle's ideas. Galileo reasoned that objects fall at the same rate (ignoring air resistance). To test his ideas about falling objects, Galileo carried out experiments that involved rolling marbles down ramps. He also talked about dropping two objects with different weights off a tall tower to show that they would hit the ground at the same time. Galileo concluded that objects accelerate steadily as they fall and that an object's weight (or mass) does not affect how fast it accelerates when falling.

We know today that Galileo was right. An object is pulled to Earth by gravity, an attraction between the mass of Earth and the mass of the object. Objects with a large mass are pulled on by gravity with more force,

but they also have more inertia. (Remember that an object's inertia is its resistance to a change in motion.) This extra resistance to motion exactly offsets the greater pull of gravity on them. Therefore, objects with greater mass fall with the same acceleration as less massive objects!

▷ **What force pulls falling objects toward the ground at the same rate?**

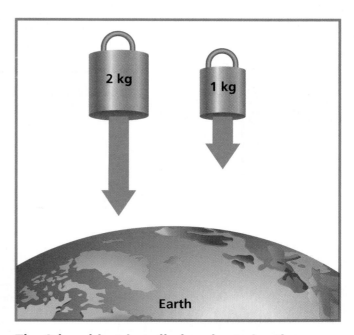

The 2-kg object is pulled on by twice the force, but its mass is also twice as great, so it has the same acceleration as the 1-kg object.

What Is the Acceleration of Falling Objects?

There is a story that says that a falling apple may have set Isaac Newton to thinking about gravity. In the late 1660s, there was a plague (very bad illness that spread very easily) in Cambridge, England, where Newton had gone to college. To avoid the plague, he went home to the countryside. The legend says Newton was sitting under an apple tree one day when an apple hit him on the head. The legend may or may not be true. However, an idea did hit Newton. That idea was that the force that pulls an apple to the ground is the same force that keeps the Moon in its orbit around Earth.

The graph shows how an apple's speed changes as it falls from a tree. Since the apple's speed changes, it must be accelerating. This, in turn, means that it is acted on by an unbalanced force. The force acting on the falling apple is gravity. We give the force of gravity on any object a special name—**weight**. It is the weight of the apple that makes it accelerate to the ground. You can find

Speed Versus Time for a Falling Apple	
Time (s)	Speed (m/s)
0.0	0.00
0.2	1.96
0.4	3.92
0.6	5.88
0.8	7.84
1.0	9.80

READING Graphs

What if the apple fell for a full two seconds? Ignoring air resistance, what speed would it reach?

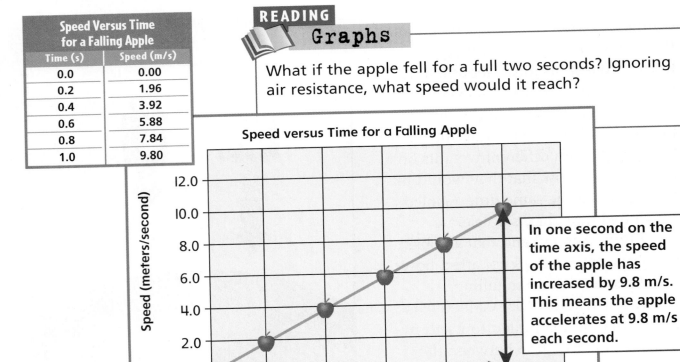

Speed versus Time for a Falling Apple

In one second on the time axis, the speed of the apple has increased by 9.8 m/s. This means the apple accelerates at 9.8 m/s each second.

the weight in newtons of any object by multiplying its mass in kilograms by 9.8. If the apple has a mass of 0.4 kg for example, its weight is 0.4 x 9.8 = 3.92 N.

The weight or mass of an object does not affect how fast it accelerates when falling (if we ignore air resistance). This means that all objects accelerate to the ground at 9.8 meters per second each second. Put another way, the speed of any object falling to the ground increases by 9.8 meters per second each second. However, as you will soon learn, this value is only true for objects falling near the surface of Earth.

Isaac Newton once wrote, "I began to think of gravity extending to the orb [orbit] of the Moon." He wondered if the gravity of Earth could be the force that holds the Moon in its orbit. Just as there is a force between an apple and Earth, there is a force between the Moon and Earth. The force is stronger if the objects are more massive, but it is weaker the farther they are apart. The Moon is much more massive than an apple. However, the Moon is also much farther from Earth's surface than an apple hanging on a tree is. Even so, the same force that pulls the apple to the ground keeps the Moon from flying off into outer space. A combination of the Moon's inertia and the force of gravity between Earth and Moon keeps the Moon orbiting Earth.

▷ **How fast do falling objects on Earth fall toward the ground?**

The Moon's Acceleration

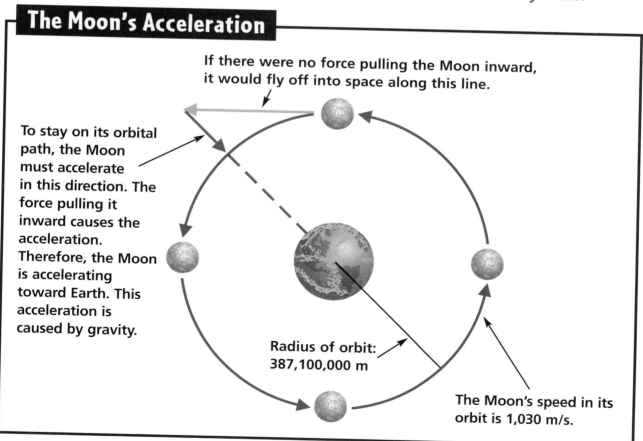

If there were no force pulling the Moon inward, it would fly off into space along this line.

To stay on its orbital path, the Moon must accelerate in this direction. The force pulling it inward causes the acceleration. Therefore, the Moon is accelerating toward Earth. This acceleration is caused by gravity.

Radius of orbit: 387,100,000 m

The Moon's speed in its orbit is 1,030 m/s.

How Can Gravity Be Universal?

When Isaac Newton discovered that Earth's gravity held the Moon in orbit, he next applied his ideas to the planets in the solar system. Could the Sun's gravity hold the planets in their orbits? First, Newton had to work out how the strength of the force depends on the mass of the Sun and each planet.

Newton decided that as mass increases, the force of gravity also increases. From his third law of motion, he knew that two objects pull on each other due to gravity. Then he reasoned that increasing the mass of either object will increase the force of gravity.

In thinking about the Moon, Newton had already inferred how gravity would change with distance. Putting all of his ideas together, he arrived at another law. This is *Newton's law of universal gravitation:* The force of gravity between two objects increases with the mass of the objects and decreases with the distance between them squared.

Newton's law of gravity is "universal" because it applies to any objects, not just moons, planets, and stars. We could find, for example, the force of gravity between two cars in a parking lot. For light objects the force of gravity is quite weak—it will not pull two parked cars together. For massive objects like moons, planets, and stars, though, the masses are so large that the force of gravity becomes very large also.

▶ **What does it mean to say that the law of gravity is universal?**

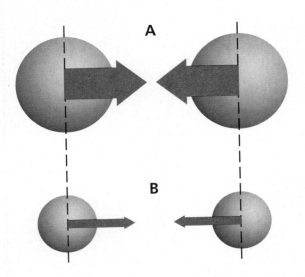

The force of gravity between two objects increases as their masses increase.

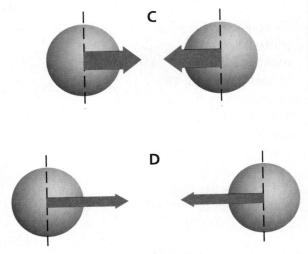

The force of gravity between two objects decreases as the distance between them increases.

What Do I Weigh on Other Worlds?

The Sun, planets, and moons in the solar system have different masses and radii. This causes the force of gravity at their surfaces to vary from world to world (for a gaseous planet, the "surface" is the top of its atmosphere). As the mass of any world increases, surface gravity tends to be stronger. However, as the radius increases, surface gravity tends to weaken. How would your weight change from one world to the next?

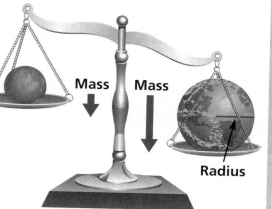

Table 1 lists gravity multipliers for solar system bodies. These values show the combined effect of the objects' different masses and radii on surface gravity compared with Earth. You can use the gravity multipliers to find your weight on other worlds. Just multiply your weight on Earth by the gravity multiplier for the new world. On Neptune, for example, your weight would be your weight on Earth multiplied by 1.1.

Table 1

Object	Gravity (Earth = 1)
Sun	28
Moon	0.16
Mars	0.38
Jupiter	2.6
Saturn	1.07
Neptune	1.1
Venus	0.91
Mercury	0.38
Uranus	0.91

Procedure

1 **Analyze** Study Tables 1 and 2. Look carefully to see how numbers were used in the examples in Table 2.

2 **Use Numbers** Copy and complete Table 2.

Drawing Conclusions

1 **Predict** A student who weighs 95 pounds on Earth has a mass of about 43 kg. What would the student's mass be on each world above?

2 **Infer** Saturn has much more mass than Earth, but your weight on Saturn is about the same as on Earth. How is this possible?

Table 2

World	Weight of a 250-Pound Astronaut	Your Weight in Pounds
Sun	7,000 lb	
Moon		
Mars	95 lb	
Jupiter		
Saturn		
Neptune		
Venus		
Mercury		
Uranus	227.5 lb	

Weight = 50 lb

Older Bicycle

Weight = 30 lb

Newer Bicycle

When Is Added Weight Helpful?

We are accustomed to gravity giving things on Earth weight, including our own bodies. Sometimes, though, weight causes problems. How would it feel to ride up a hill on an old bicycle like the one on the left? Compared with the newer one on the right, the older bike is so much more massive that it would take a lot more force to accelerate it. Which would you rather ride?

Older bicycles were made with steel frames. While steel is strong, it is also very heavy. Some modern bicycle frames are made with steel alloys, titanium, aluminum, or carbon fiber.

These materials are a great deal lighter than plain steel, and bikes made with them are much easier to pedal. Of course, the lightweight materials are also much more expensive than steel!

In cycling, weight does offer certain advantages. The weight of the rider and bicycle presses the tires against the ground. This downward force creates increased friction between the tires and the road, giving the tires traction. If it were not for the friction, the tires could not push on the road surface to drive the rider forward.

Bicycle racers often travel on a circular path at high speed. There must be a force acting inward on them to change their direction of travel. The banked track they are riding on uses their weight to help provide this force. The weight of each bike and rider presses into the track through the tires. The track, in turn, pushes back through the tires on each bike and rider. Due to the tilt of the track surface, some of this return push is directed inward and can act as the force that changes each bike's direction of travel.

The banked surface makes it easier to go around the turn.

READING Draw Conclusions
How is added weight helpful in cycling?

Why It Matters

On a flat road, the only force available for making cars go around a turn is the friction between the tires and the road surface. In wet or icy weather, the friction may not be strong enough, and the cars can slide off and crash on the turn. If the road is banked like the bicycle race track, though, the inward push of the road surface helps cars to make the turn. The same sort of banking is also done when making auto racetracks.

e-Journal Visit our Web site www.science.mmhschool.com to do a research project on gravity.

Think and Write

1. What causes objects to fall?

2. Ignoring air resistance, why do objects with different masses fall at the same rate?

3. A rubber ball is dropped off a tall tower. After one second, how fast will it be traveling?

4. **INQUIRY SKILL** **Use Numbers** Two planets in a distant solar system have the same radius but different masses. On which world would you weigh more? Why?

5. **Critical Thinking** How could you carry out a demonstration on Earth of a feather falling at the same rate as a bowling ball?

L·I·N·K·S

MATH LINK

Solve this problem. Look at the tables on page F39. How much would the astronaut weigh on a planet with 1.5 times as much gravity as Neptune?

WRITING LINK

Writing a Story You are a passenger on a space-shuttle flight. You're in orbit. For the first time, you cannot feel your weight. Write a story describing what it feels like to be weightless. Include dialogue with a friend on the ground. Turn your story into a play to perform.

MUSIC LINK

Write a song. Think about what it might be like to live on a world where you weigh half as much as you do now. Write a song describing your experiences.

TECHNOLOGY LINK

 LOG ON Visit www.science.mmhschool.com for more links.

RIDE THE "VOMIT COMET"

It's called the "Vomit Comet," and students can't wait to go on it! It's not an amusement park ride, but it can feel like one. The Vomit Comet is a special NASA aircraft used to train astronauts in weightlessness. Two weeks out of the year, NASA also allows college students aboard. The students conduct research on how weightlessness can affect things, and they learn firsthand what zero gravity feels like.

After testing and training on the ground, it's time for the students to fly. Onboard they help bolt their equipment to the floor. Padding covers the floor, walls, and ceiling. All the seats have been removed except for a few rows in the rear. A deep roar of the engines means the first climb has begun. Weightlessness will begin in a few seconds.

The Vomit Comet flies up and down fast like a roller coaster ride. It levels off at 7,315 m (24,000 ft), and the pilot tells passengers to get ready. First, the plane climbs another 3,048 m (10,000 ft) at high speed. At the top of the climb, passengers experience weightlessness for about 25 seconds. Then, the plane dives 3,048 m (10,000 ft) at high speed. Each climb and dive is called a parabola. Every flight has about 32 parabolas, so passengers have about 13 minutes of weightlessness!

At first, weightlessness is scary. That's because you feel like you're falling. Then, you feel excited because you realize you're floating in space! The hardest part for the students is concentrating on what's happening with their experiments.

They have only 25 seconds before the dive!

The dive feels very different. Your body feels much heavier than usual. You can hardly lift your arms. Any movement can make you feel very dizzy. That's because the force you feel pulling down on you is twice the force of gravity.

By the ninth or tenth parabola, some students suffer from motion sickness. They head for the seats in the rear and strap themselves in. It's up to the others to finish the experiments. When it's over, even the sick students say it was the ride of a lifetime. For a short time, they felt just like an astronaut!

Astronauts in training experience several minutes of weightlessness on the Vomit Comet.

What Did I Learn?

1. The Vomit Comet is

 A an amusement park ride.
 B a NASA aircraft used to train astronauts in weightlessness.
 C a special section for student experiments on the space shuttle.
 D a strange object from outer space.

2. About how long are the students weightless on a Vomit Comet flight?

 F about 13 minutes
 G about 25 seconds
 H about a day
 J about 30 minutes

 LOG ON Visit **www.science.mmhschool.com** for more amazing stories and facts about gravity.

Chapter 14 Review

Vocabulary

Fill each blank with the best word or words from the list.

acceleration, F13
balanced forces, F21
force, F6
gravity, F35
inertia, F7
reaction, F24
speed, F11
unbalanced force, F21
velocity, F12
weight, F36

1. How fast the position of an object changes is its _____.

2. An object's speed in a certain direction is its _____.

3. A change in a velocity in a certain amount of time is called _____.

4. How much an object weighs depends on its mass and the force of _____.

5. An object's tendency to resist a change in motion is its _____.

6. An astronaut on the moon has the same mass as she did on Earth, but has less _____.

7. For every action, there is an equal but opposite _____.

8. Pushes or pulls which completely cancel one another out are called _____.

9. A push or pull that acts on an object is called a(n) _____.

10. Pushes or pulls which are not cancelled by other pushes or pulls are called _____.

Test Prep

11. Gravity is a _____.
  A velocity
  B speed
  C force
  D weight

12. When object A exerts a force on object B, object B _____.
  F doesn't move
  G exerts a reaction force on object A
  H doesn't affect object A
  J exerts an action force on object A

13. A mass accelerates because _____.
  A it has inertia
  B it is moving
  C it isn't moving
  D a force is acting on it

14. An object is accelerated when it is acted on by _____.
  F an unbalanced force
  G a balanced force
  H inertia
  J velocity

15. A baseball and a sheet of paper are dropped at the same time from the same height. If there is no air resistance _____.

   A the baseball will land first

   B the paper will float slowly through the air

   C the baseball will float slowly through the air

   D the baseball and the paper will land at the same time

Concepts and Skills

16. Reading in Science How did Newton conclude that the same force that pulls an apple to the ground also keeps the Moon orbiting Earth? Write a paragraph explaining your answer.

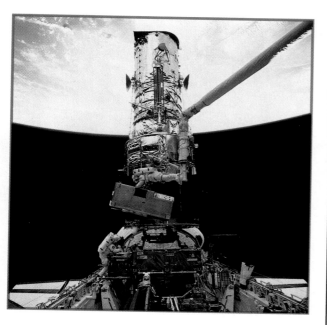

17. Safety Why do seat belts help protect passengers when a car stops quickly? Write a paragraph explaining your answer.

18. Scientific Methods How could you find out how much an object moving in a circle is accelerating? Write up a design for an experiment that would test this.

19. INQUIRY SKILL **Use Numbers** What would a 100-kg astronaut weigh on a planet with five times the gravity of Uranus? Write a paragraph explaining how you would find the answer.

20. Critical Thinking You are sitting on a playground merry-go-round holding a cup of water. What happens to the water in the cup as the merry-go-round spins faster and faster? Write your ideas. Describe how you might test them.

Did You Ever Wonder?

INQUIRY SKILL **Make a Model** Draw a girl on a trampoline. Draw her going up, coming down, and at rest. Digital scales in her sneakers provide data to a wireless readout. She weighs 396 N (about 88 lbs). Predict her weight in each position. Discuss your drawings.

LOG ON Visit **www.science.mmhschool.com** to boost your test scores.

Sound Energy

Did You Ever Wonder?

How do the instruments in an orchestra, such as the Boston
Pops, produce such beautiful sounds? Each instrument—violin,
tuba, drum, clarinet—has its own way of producing sound.
The sounds combine to make beautiful music. Noise is also sound.

INQUIRY SKILL Classify What examples of everyday sound are noise?
What examples are music? How is music different from noise?

Sound Waves

Vocabulary

vibration, F50

matter, F51

sound wave, F51

compression, F51

rarefaction, F51

Get Ready

Do you know that without earphones you could not hear your radio on the Moon? Why do you think this is true? If you place your hand over the speaker of a radio, you can feel the sound. Try it. Why does it happen? Would you be able to feel the sound on the Moon?

What causes sound? Keep in mind that sounds can be different. How could you build an instrument to test your ideas?

Inquiry Skill

You predict when you state possible results of an event or experiment.

Explore Activity

What Makes Sound?

Materials

wood or plastic ruler

long rubber band

plastic or foam cup

clear tape

ballpoint pen

scissors

goggles

Procedure

BE CAREFUL! Wear goggles.

1 As you do this activity, observe how sounds are made and changed. Poke a hole in the bottom of the cup. Cut the rubber band. Insert one end into the hole. Make two or three knots in the end to keep it in place.

2 Tape the cup and the stretched rubber band securely to the ruler as shown.

3 **Observe** Hold the cup next to your ear. Pluck the rubber band. Watch a partner do the same thing. Record what you hear and see.

4 **Experiment** Put one finger on the rubber band, hold it against the ruler, and then pluck it again. What happens to the sound?

Drawing Conclusions

1 **Infer** What did you observe that made your instrument work? How can you explain what makes sound?

2 What happened to the sound when you changed the rubber band with your finger? Explain why, based on your observations.

3 **FURTHER INQUIRY** **Predict** What do you think will happen to the sound if you stretch the rubber band tighter? Untape the end of the rubber band and pull it a bit tighter. Retape the end to the ruler. Repeat steps 3 and 4. How do the results compare with your prediction? Give reasons for what happened.

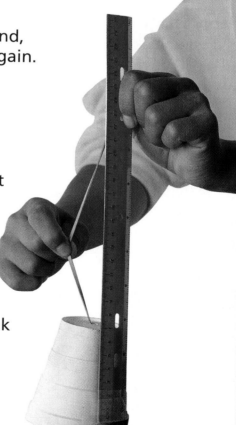

Main Idea Sound is provided by the vibrations of objects.

What Makes Sound?

Sound is provided by making something move back and forth. You can't produce a sound without making something move. If you pluck a rubber band, the rubber band moving back and forth produces twanging sounds. This back-and-forth motion is called a **vibration**. Unless something vibrates, there can be no sound. Many vibrations are too fast for you to see. You may not see the bat vibrating when the ball hits it, but you can still feel it.

Energy Transfer

If you pluck a guitar string, you can see it moving back and forth. You provide the energy necessary for this vibration when you pluck it. This energy is transferred to the rubber band and causes it to vibrate. When you touch the rubber band, you can feel it vibrating.

What can you notice if you place your fingers gently against your throat while you talk or hum? You can feel a vibration. You feel the vibration of your vocal cords. Vocal cords in your throat vibrate when air moves past them, allowing you to speak.

What vibrates when you play a guitar? When the strings of a guitar or violin are bowed or plucked, they begin to vibrate. They produce sounds. However, not all instruments rely on strings. Sounds can also be produced by vibrating surfaces and by vibrating columns of air. The instruments in each section of the orchestra have their own characteristic ways of producing sounds. In each section different materials vibrate.

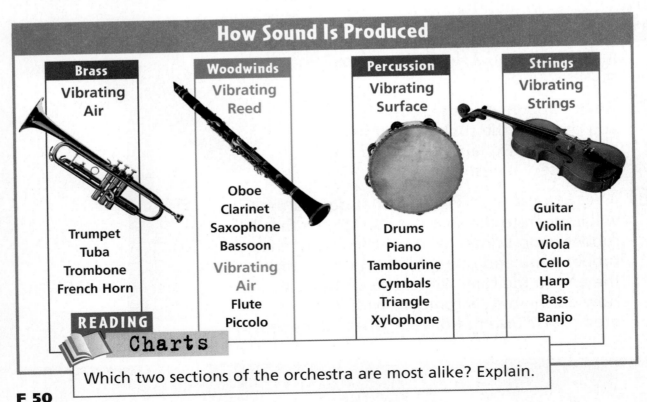

How Sound Is Produced

Brass	Woodwinds	Percussion	Strings
Vibrating Air	Vibrating Reed	Vibrating Surface	Vibrating Strings
Trumpet	Oboe	Drums	Guitar
Tuba	Clarinet	Piano	Violin
Trombone	Saxophone	Tambourine	Viola
French Horn	Bassoon	Cymbals	Cello
	Vibrating Air	Triangle	Harp
	Flute	Xylophone	Bass
	Piccolo		Banjo

READING Charts

Which two sections of the orchestra are most alike? Explain.

Sound Waves

Sound is a vibration that travels through **matter**. Matter is anything that has mass and takes up space. Matter can be a solid, liquid, or gas. Some types of matter are made of pieces too small to be seen, called *molecules*. Molecules are the smallest pieces that matter can be broken into without changing the kind of matter.

How does the sound made by a vibrating string travel? When a string vibrates, it makes molecules of gases in the air next to it vibrate. The molecules squeeze together, then spread apart. The vibrating molecules near the string then make the molecules next to them start to vibrate.

The vibration continues to spread. A vibration that spreads away from a vibrating object is a **sound wave**. It carries the energy from the vibrating object outward in all directions.

READING **Cause and Effect**
What has to happen to make sounds travel?

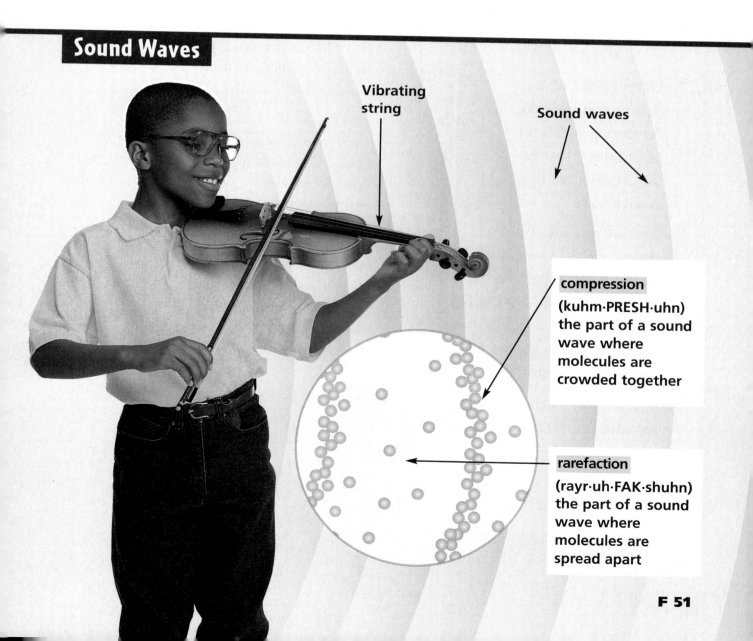

Sound Waves

Vibrating string

Sound waves

compression
(kuhm·PRESH·uhn)
the part of a sound wave where molecules are crowded together

rarefaction
(rayr·uh·FAK·shuhn)
the part of a sound wave where molecules are spread apart

QUICK LAB

Sound Carriers

FOLDABLES Make a Three-Tab Book. (See p. R 43.) Label as shown. Record your observations in the Three-Tab Book.

Wood

Air

Water

1. **Observe** Put a wind-up clock on a wooden table. Put your ear against the table. Listen to the ticking. Lift your head. How loud is it now?

2. **Use Variables** Fill a sealable pint-size plastic bag with water. Seal the bag. Hold it against your ear. Hold the clock against the bag. How well can you hear the ticking? Move your ear away from the bag. How loud is the ticking now?

3. **Interpret Data** Rate wood, air, and water in order from best sound carrier to worst.

4. **Experiment** How would you test other materials, like sand?

What Else Can Sound Go Through?

When you hear sounds, what is usually around you? Air! You can hear sounds in the air. When sound waves reach your ear, they make parts inside the ear vibrate. Since air is a mixture of gases, you may conclude that sound can travel through gases. It travels as sound waves.

Solids

Can sound also travel through solids and liquids? You can tell that sound travels through solids just by putting your ear onto a tabletop. If someone taps the table at the other end, you can hear the tapping louder than if you lift your head away from the table.

Liquids

If you do any underwater swimming, you probably can tell that you can hear sounds in water. You can hear someone calling you from above the surface. You can also hear sounds in the water around you.

▷ **How can you tell that sound travels through liquids and solids?**

Why It Matters

Sound waves can travel through all forms of matter. Without matter, sound waves could not travel. Can you hear sounds in a vacuum? No. A vacuum is a place where there is no matter.

e-Journal Visit our Web site **www.science.mmhschool.com** to do a research project on sound waves.

MATH LINK

Solve this problem. A cricket chirps 20 times per minute. How many is that per hour?

WRITING LINK

Explanatory Writing Study the sign-language chart. Write a paragraph to explain how to use sign language.

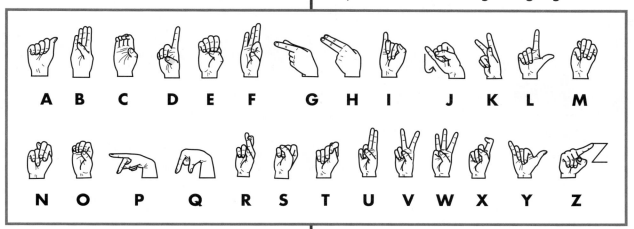

A B C D E F G H I J K L M

N O P Q R S T U V W X Y Z

Think and Write

1. What is needed to make sound?
2. What can sounds travel through?
3. How does a vibrating guitar string make sound?
4. How does a drum make sound?
5. **Critical Thinking** What if you put a ticking clock in a box and pump all the air out? The clock is on a thin string so that it is not touching the walls of the box. Would you hear the clock ticking?

LITERATURE LINK

Read *Making Sounds,* to learn how a sound effects studio makes sounds for the movies. When you finish reading, think about how you would make sound effects for a school play. Try the activities at the end of the book.

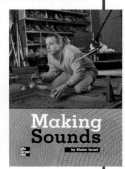

Making Sounds
by Elaine Israel

TECHNOLOGY LINK

LOG ON Visit **www.science.mmhschool.com** for more links.

Pitch and Loudness

Vocabulary

pitch, F56

frequency, F57

hertz, F57

volume, F58

decibel, F58

Get Ready

How have people made music since ancient times? Shepherds have used instruments like this simple one for centuries. They use the instruments to call their flocks or keep them quiet.

Each musical instrument has a sound all its own. As you play an instrument, you make the sound change. What causes the sound to change? Test it by building a homemade instrument from simple items like straws.

Inquiry Skill

You experiment when you perform a test to support or disprove a hypothesis.

Explore Activity

How Can You Change a Sound?

Materials

12 plastic drinking straws

scissors

metric ruler

masking tape

Procedure: Design Your Own

1 **Predict** Work in pairs to make a homemade instrument. Start with straws. Blow over one end of a straw. Will there be a difference if you seal the other end with tape? Record your prediction.

2 **Observe** Tape one end, and blow over the open end. Describe what you hear. Does it work better with or without one end taped?

3 **Classify** Repeat with different lengths cut from a straw. Try at least four lengths. How are the sounds different? Arrange the straws in order to hear the difference.

4 **Experiment** Flatten one end of a straw. Cut the end to a point. Wet it. With your lips stretched across your teeth, blow into that end of the straw. Try to make different sounds with the straw. How might you modify the instrument the girl is using?

Drawing Conclusions

1 **Infer** Why do you think the sounds changed when you cut different lengths of straw? Hint: What is inside a straw—even if it looks empty?

2 **Communicate** Write a description of your instruments for a partner to build them exactly as you did. Include measurements taken with a ruler.

3 FURTHER INQUIRY **Experiment** Try other materials to make other instruments. Try such things as bottles with water, craft sticks, and so forth. Tell what causes the sound to change in each case.

STEP 4

$\frac{1}{2}$ cm { Cut into point.

Close up.

Bend down the straw $\frac{1}{2}$ cm.

Main Idea Pitch and loudness are two characteristics of sound.

What Is Pitch?

Some sounds are "higher" than others; some sounds are "lower." *High* and *low* are words that describe the **pitch** of a sound. In the sixth century B.C., the Greek mathematician Pythagoras (pi·THAG·uhr·uhs) observed that a longer string produces a sound with a lower pitch than a shorter string.

Changes in Pitch

What can you do to a rubber band to make different sounds? If you pluck a rubber band to make sounds, then you can change the pitch by shortening the rubber band. You make it shorter by pressing a thumb over part of it so less of it vibrates. A shorter string vibrates faster and produces a higher pitch.

A second way you can change the pitch is to stretch the rubber band tighter. This causes the rubber band to vibrate faster and, therefore, to produce a higher-pitched sound. The pitch of a vibrating string is also related to its thickness. Compare the strings of this guitar.

Did you know that the length and thickness of your vocal cords, and how you tighten or relax them, affects the pitch of your voice?

Singers can sing a range from high to lower notes by tightening and relaxing their vocal cords. Men usually have longer and thicker vocal cords than women, so men's voices tend to be lower pitched than women's voices.

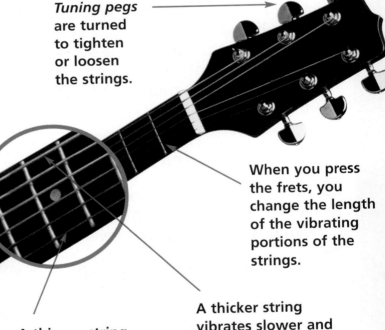

Tuning pegs **are turned to tighten or loosen the strings.**

When you press the frets, you change the length of the vibrating portions of the strings.

A thinner string vibrates faster and produces a higher-pitched sound than a thicker string.

A thicker string vibrates slower and produces a lower-pitched sound than a thinner string.

Sound Waves

You can't see sound waves, but scientists study them with an oscilloscope. This device makes a "picture" of sound waves. An oscilloscope allows you to compare the waves of sounds that have different pitches.

Frequency

The higher the pitch, the more "squeezed together" the waves are. Higher-pitched waves have a greater frequency. Frequency is the number of times an object vibrates per second.

Frequency describes vibrations and sound waves. Pitch describes how your brain interprets a sound. A flute has a high pitch. A bass guitar has a low pitch. Frequency and pitch are related: the higher the frequency, the higher the pitch; the lower the frequency, the lower the pitch.

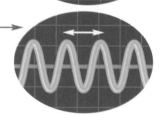

Oscilloscope

Length of a sound wave produced by low-pitched sounds

Length of a sound wave produced by higher-pitched sounds

Frequency is measured in units called **hertz**. A frequency of one vibration per second is one hertz (Hz). *Hertz* comes from the name of Heinrich Hertz (1857–1894), a German physicist who studied sound and radio waves.

Humans hear from about 20 Hz to about 20,000 Hz. Sounds with a frequency higher than 20,000 Hz are *ultrasonic*—too high to be heard by humans, but not by some animals.

> **How are frequency and pitch related?**

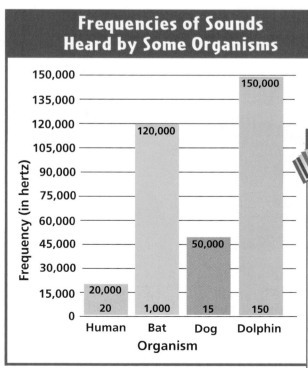

Frequencies of Sounds Heard by Some Organisms

Frequency (in hertz)

Organism	Low	High
Human	20	20,000
Bat	1,000	120,000
Dog	15	50,000
Dolphin	150	150,000

READING Graphs

A range graph shows differences between highest and lowest.

1. Arrange organisms in order of range of hearing, from greatest to least.

2. Put organisms in order of the highest frequencies they hear.

What Is Volume?

A sound wave makes the molecules of gases in air vibrate. The back-and-forth distance they vibrate is based on how much energy the sound wave carries. The more the energy, the greater the distance. The more the energy, the greater the height of the wave as it appears on an oscilloscope. Which of the waves below is carrying more energy?

What is the difference between a yell and a whisper? A sound's **volume**—how loud or soft it is—depends on the amount of energy in a sound wave. To make a louder sound with a rubber band, pluck it harder. A loud sound has more energy than a soft sound and produces a taller wave on an oscilloscope.

You can also make a sound louder by increasing the amount of surface that vibrates. For example, when a cup is attached to a rubber band, the cup and rubber band vibrate together.

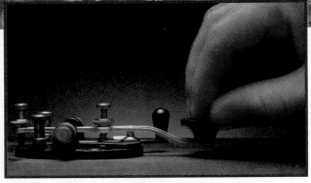

Another way to communicate is by using Morse code—a series of long and short taps sent out by telegraph.

Together they make a louder sound than just a rubber band alone.

Volume is measured in units called **decibels** (dB) with an instrument called a decibel meter. On the decibel scale, a sound that measures 50 dB is 10 times louder than one that measures 40 dB. The same 50-dB sound is 100 times louder than a 30-dB sound—that is, 10 x 10 times louder. The 50-dB sound is 1,000 times louder than a 20-dB sound—10 x 10 x 10 times louder.

READING **Cause and Effect**
Why do sounds differ in volume?

Today's telephones date back to Alexander Graham Bell, who invented the telephone in 1875. Where do you think the word *decibel* came from?

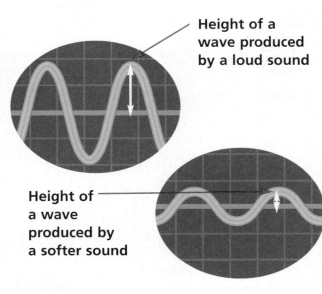

Height of a wave produced by a loud sound

Height of a wave produced by a softer sound

Making Tables and Graphs

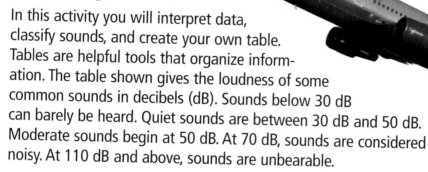

In this activity you will interpret data, classify sounds, and create your own table. Tables are helpful tools that organize inform-ation. The table shown gives the loudness of some common sounds in decibels (dB). Sounds below 30 dB can barely be heard. Quiet sounds are between 30 dB and 50 dB. Moderate sounds begin at 50 dB. At 70 dB, sounds are considered noisy. At 110 dB and above, sounds are unbearable.

Procedure

1 **Classify** Determine which sounds are barely audible (can barely be heard), quiet, moderate, noisy, or unbearable.

2 **Communicate** Make your own table to show how you classified the sounds.

3 **Communicate** Make a data table to record how many quiet, moderate, noisy, or unbearable sounds you hear in one hour. Make a graph to show your results. "Number" is the vertical axis. "Kind of Sound" is the horizontal axis.

Drawing Conclusions

1 **Interpret Data** How much louder is a soft radio than your house at night? A classroom than a house at night?

2 **Interpret Data** How much softer is normal con-versation than thunder?

3 **Communicate** Make a chart listing loud sounds in the environment. What can you do to protect your ears from harm done by each loud noise?

Loudness of Some Sounds	
Sound	Loudness (in decibels)
Hearing limit	0
Rustling leaves	10
Whisper	20
Nighttime noises in house	30
Soft radio	40
Classroom/office	50
Normal conversation	60
Inside car on highway	70
Busy city street	80
Subway	90
Siren (30 meters away)	100
Thunder	110
Pain threshold	120
Loud indoor rock concert	120
Jet plane (30 meters away)	140

How Is Sound Recorded?

What if there were no favorite recordings of music? Fortunately, Thomas Alva Edison first recorded sound back in 1877. Today sound is recorded like this.

A microphone includes a diaphragm, a coil of fine wire, and a magnet. When you sing, speak, or play music into the microphone, sound waves make the diaphragm vibrate. The pitch of the sound determines how fast the diaphragm vibrates. The loudness of the sound determines how far the diaphragm moves with each vibration.

The vibration of the diaphragm makes the coil of wire vibrate near the magnet. Each vibration produces a tiny current of electricity. The coil sends this electric pattern to an amplifier.

The tiny pulses of electricity coming from the coil are very weak. The amplifier makes them up to 50,000 times stronger.

Blank tapes are coated with scrambled magnetic particles. During recording, the electric current from the amplifier arranges the particles on the tape into a pattern—a "code" for the sounds.

When you push "play," the process reverses. The magnetic particles on the tape create a current in the coil. This current vibrates a stiff paper cone in the speaker. This creates the sound waves you hear.

Compact discs do not store sound in magnetic patterns. Instead, a computer in CD-recording equipment translates the sound waves into a code. The code is a combination of 1s and 0s.

Then a laser beam uses the code to cut millions of tiny pits into a blank compact disc. About 85,000 pits cover only one inch of the disc.

When you play a CD, a laser beam shines on it. The flat parts of the CD reflect light back to a small computer. The computer changes the pattern of these reflections back into sound.

Microphone

▷ **What steps are involved in recording and playing a CD?**

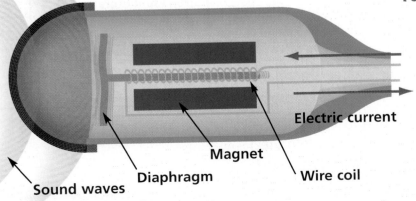

How does a microphone work? Sound waves make the diaphragm in the microphone vibrate. That makes the coil of wire vibrate, sending an electric pattern to an amplifier.

Sound waves

Diaphragm

Magnet

Wire coil

Electric current

Why It Matters

Next time you strum a guitar, pound a drum, or sing a tune, keep in mind what you learned in this lesson. The different musical sounds you make on an instrument or when you sing are different pitches. You can play an instrument at different volumes—to make the sounds louder or softer. You sing louder when you take a deeper breath and breathe out harder. You use loudness and pitch to express different emotions, too.

e-Journal Visit our Web site **www.science.mmhschool.com** to do a research project on the effect of pitch and volume on hearing loss.

Think and Write

1. On a stringed instrument, why are some sounds higher than others?

2. How is pitch related to frequency?

3. How can sounds be changed into an electric current?

4. **INQUIRY SKILL** **Communicate** How is loudness measured? How would you set up a table showing the loudness of different sounds?

5. **Critical Thinking** Why do the notes of a musical instrument have different sounds?

L·I·N·K·S

WRITING LINK

Expository Writing How can a dog hear a dog whistle, but a person can't? Research the answer, and write an essay. Draw a conclusion based on the information you find.

MATH LINK

Solve this problem. How many times louder is a loud indoor rock concert than a busy city street? See pp. F58-59.

ART LINK

Make a poster. Illustrate how CDs are made and played.

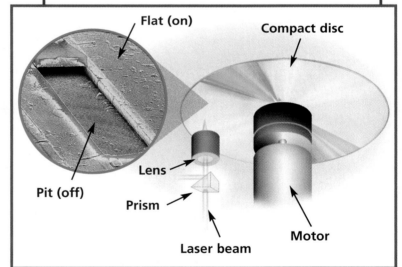

Flat (on)
Compact disc
Lens
Pit (off)
Prism
Laser beam
Motor

TECHNOLOGY LINK

LOG ON Visit **www.science.mmhschool.com** for more links.

Hit That Note!

Ever think of yourself as a musician? Well you are one. When you sing you play an instrument—your voice!

Musical instruments vary in the pitches, or tones, they can produce. It all depends on the frequencies of vibrating parts. Singers produce different tones, too.

You've probably noticed differences in the sounds of some of your favorite singers. The tones they use depend on the vibrations of their vocal cords. Thicker, longer cords vibrate more slowly and have lower tones. Ever wonder why your voice sounds lower when you have a sore throat? It's because your vocal cords are swollen, so they vibrate more slowly!

Here are pitch categories for most human singing voices. Try classifying some of your favorite singers.

	FEMALE	MALE
High pitch	Soprano	Tenor
Medium pitch	Mezzo-soprano	Baritone
Low pitch	Alto (contralto)	Bass

A baritone usually can't hit the high notes a tenor can because of the size and shape of his vocal cords. Likewise a tenor usually can't hit the low notes a baritone can.

When composers write music, they think about the notes that each instrument and voice can produce.

LOG ON Visit **www.science.mmhschool.com** to learn more about music.

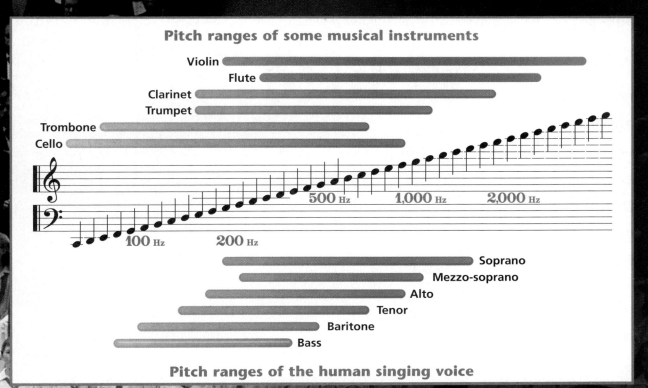

Pitch ranges of some musical instruments

Violin
Flute
Clarinet
Trumpet
Trombone
Cello

100 Hz   200 Hz   500 Hz   1,000 Hz   2,000 Hz

Soprano
Mezzo-soprano
Alto
Tenor
Baritone
Bass

Pitch ranges of the human singing voice

This diagram shows the lowest to the highest notes for each instrument and singing voice. The difference between the highest and lowest is called a range.

Write
ABOUT IT

1. Which instrument shown can reach the highest pitch? About what frequency is that?

2. Which instrument has the greatest range? The smallest range?

Reflection and Absorption

Vocabulary

reflection, F66

absorption, F66

echo, F68

echolocation, F70

Doppler effect, F71

quality, F72

fundamental
frequency, F72

overtone, F72

resonance, F72

Get Ready

What makes a car race at a racetrack so exciting? Is it the speed, the swerves? Is it the roar of the crowd? What would the race be like if it were totally quiet? Would it still be as exciting?

What makes the race so noisy? Describe the racetrack from the photograph. How does the way the racetrack is built contribute to the loud sounds?

What happens when sound "hits" a surface? Does the kind of surface make a difference?

Inquiry Skill

You make a model when you make something to represent an object or event.

Explore Activity

Do Sounds Bounce?

Procedure

1 Collect a variety of hard, smooth materials and soft, textured materials. Place one of the objects on a table. Set up your tubes in a V-shaped pattern on a table, as shown. The V should meet at the object you are testing. Record the name of the object.

2 **Observe** Place a sound maker (clicker or timer) at one end of the V. Listen for ticking at the other end of the V. Rank the loudness of the ticking on a scale of 1 (lowest) to 5 (highest). Record the number.

3 **Experiment** Repeat steps 1 and 2 with the different materials you collected.

Drawing Conclusions

1 **Classify** What kinds of materials are the best reflectors—hard, smooth materials or soft, textured materials? What kinds of materials are the best absorbers?

2 **Make a Model** Draw a diagram of the path of sound from the sound maker to your ear. On your diagram, mark the point in the path where the sound wave bounced.

3 **FURTHER INQUIRY** **Infer** Design an experiment to test the effectiveness of draperies or rugs in absorbing sound in a room.

Materials

2 long cardboard tubes (can be taped, rolled-up newspapers)

sound maker, such as a clicker or timer

hard and soft test materials, such as a book, wood block, cloth, metal sheet, sponge, towel

Main Idea Sounds vary because objects reflect, absorb, or transmit sound differently.

Do Sounds Bounce?

A sound hitting a towel will sound different from the same sound hitting a metal sheet. Why? A sound wave does not act the same way when it hits a hard, smooth surface as it does when it hits a soft, textured surface.

The pictures below show what happens when sound waves come into contact with a surface. When a sound wave hits a surface, some of its energy bounces off the surface. The bouncing of a sound wave off a surface is called **reflection**. However, not all of the sound wave reflects off

the surface. Some of the wave's energy enters the surface, and part of the sound disappears. The disappearance of a sound wave into a surface is called **absorption**.

When a sound wave is absorbed, its energy is changed into heat energy. Sometimes not all of the energy that enters a surface is absorbed. Part of the energy of the sound wave may also travel through a surface and come out the other side—like when you hear a sound through a wall.

How much of the sound wave's energy is reflected or absorbed depends on the kind of material of the surface. When sound waves hit a hard, smooth surface such as the wall around the racetrack, much of the sound wave's energy is reflected. However, when sound waves hit a soft, textured surface such as a towel, less of the sound wave's energy is reflected and more is absorbed.

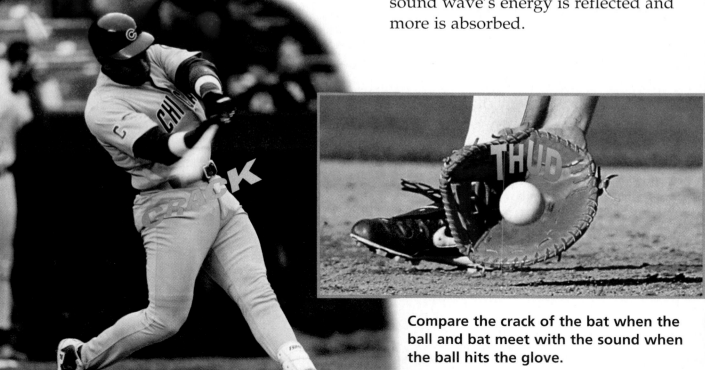

Compare the crack of the bat when the ball and bat meet with the sound when the ball hits the glove.

How Reflection and Absorption Affect Concert Halls

Designing concert halls has always been a tricky business. To get the "right" sound, engineers try to get a good balance of reflection and absorption. Too much reflection results in an empty, hollow sound. Too much absorption deadens the music.

When the London Music Hall was built in 1871, the hall was considered to be one of the great places in the world to hear music. By the 1930s listeners complained that the music did not sound good anymore. Sound engineers were baffled. Nothing in the concert hall had changed since it was built, over 60 years earlier.

Finally, an explanation was found. The concert hall may have stayed the same, but its audience had changed. Most importantly, women were no longer wearing the billowing, layered, sound-absorbing gowns that had been popular earlier. The new styles were shorter and simpler, and didn't absorb sound as well. Overall they changed the balance of reflection and absorption of sound in the room.

▷ Do more sound waves bounce from hard, smooth surfaces or soft, textured surfaces?

The group below is dressed in a style common in the mid- to late 1800s. The billowy gowns and long coats had an effect on sound in a concert hall.

Clap! Clap!

FOLDABLES Make a Four-Column Folded Chart. (See p. R 44.) Label as shown. Record your echo data in the meter columns.

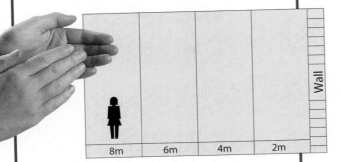

| 8m | 6m | 4m | 2m | Wall |

1. **Observe** Stand about 8 m away from a large wall, such as the side of your school building. Make sure there is plenty of open space between you and the wall. Clap your hands, and listen for an echo. Notice how much time there is between your clap and the echo.

2. **Observe** Move closer to the wall, and clap again. Listen for an echo. Try this several times.

3. **Observe** As you got closer to the wall, how did the time between the clap and the echo change? Did you always hear an echo? Explain.

4. **Experiment** Repeat at different distances. What happens?

What Is an Echo?

Have you ever made an echo? When you yell "hello!" your vocal cords make sound waves that travel away from you in all directions. If the sound wave hits a surface, some of the sound wave's energy will reflect off the surface and travel back to you. A reflected sound wave is called an **echo**. If the echo is strong enough, you will hear yourself yelling "hello!" after you said it! If there is more than one reflecting surface near you, you may hear "hello!" several more times.

If you sing in the shower, you may notice how rich your voice sounds. The hard, smooth walls of the bathroom are often great for making echoes. The echoes reflect back and forth off the walls many times. They make your voice sound rich and mellow, as if background singers were repeating each note you sing.

READING Cause and Effect
How are echoes made?

You hear sound as soon as you make it. After it reaches a reflecting surface, you hear the echo when the waves return.

How Fast Is Sound?

It takes almost no time for an echo to bounce back to you after you yell "hello!" Sound waves travel fast. In air at room temperature (20°C), sound waves travel 343 meters per second, faster than most jet planes. In general, sound waves have a greater speed in a solid than in a liquid, and a greater speed in a liquid than in a gas.

The speed of sound waves depends largely on the molecules of the material—on how tightly packed molecules are and how easily they spread apart and move together. Temperature affects the speed of sound. In general, temperature affects the speed of sound more in gases than in liquids and solids.

> **Will sound travel faster through air or steel?**

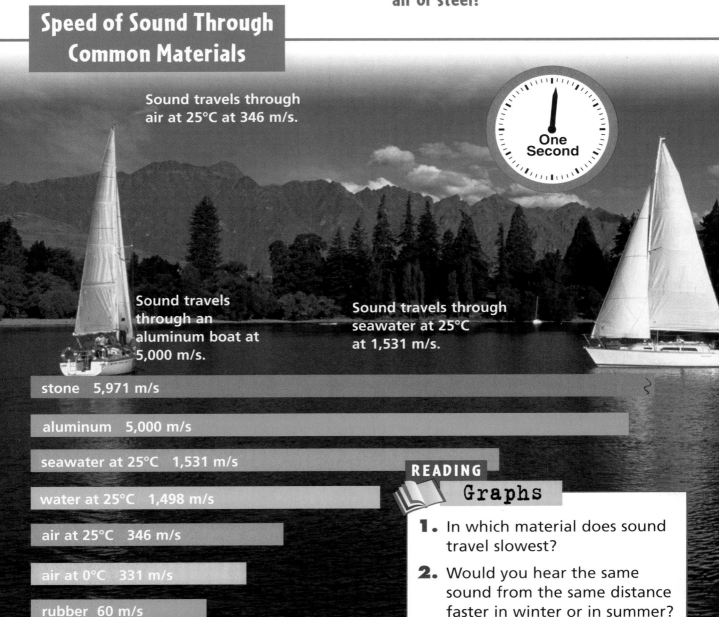

Speed of Sound Through Common Materials

Sound travels through air at 25°C at 346 m/s.

One Second

Sound travels through an aluminum boat at 5,000 m/s.

Sound travels through seawater at 25°C at 1,531 m/s.

stone	5,971 m/s
aluminum	5,000 m/s
seawater at 25°C	1,531 m/s
water at 25°C	1,498 m/s
air at 25°C	346 m/s
air at 0°C	331 m/s
rubber	60 m/s

READING Graphs

1. In which material does sound travel slowest?

2. Would you hear the same sound from the same distance faster in winter or in summer?

What Can Echoes Do?

Sonar, or *s*ound *na*vigation and *r*anging, uses sound waves to detect objects far away. A sonar technician sends out sound waves and then times how long those sound waves take to bounce off distant objects and return.

What if a sonar technician on a ship sends out a sound wave toward the ocean bottom? Sound waves travel about 1,500 meters per second in water.

What if the sound wave takes two seconds to return to the ship? The technician will know that the sound wave took one second to reach the ocean floor and then one second more to bounce back to the surface. He or she will conclude that the ocean is 1,500 meters deep.

Many animals find things around them with a form of sonar called **echolocation**. Whales and dolphins bounce sound waves off objects to find out how far away they are.

Bats are able to live in dark caves because they use a form of echolocation rather than sight to navigate. Bats send out high-pitched squeals and clicks into the air at their prey. Their large, forward-pointing ears pick up the echoes. Using this information, bats can close in on their prey.

▷ **How does sonar use echoes to locate objects?**

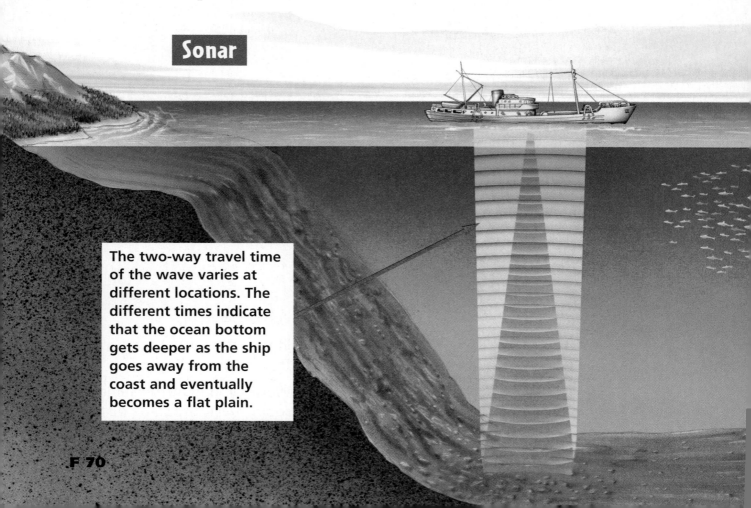

Sonar

The two-way travel time of the wave varies at different locations. The different times indicate that the ocean bottom gets deeper as the ship goes away from the coast and eventually becomes a flat plain.

How Do Moving Sounds Change?

An echo is a copy of the original sound. Both the original sound and the echo have the same pitch. However, have you ever heard a siren blaring as a police car sped past you? If you listened carefully, you may have noticed that the pitch of the siren changed as the police car sped by. As the car came toward you, the siren was higher in pitch. As it sped away from you, the pitch was lower.

Approaching Sound

As the blaring siren approaches, its sound waves crowd together. There are more sound waves reaching your ear each second than there would be if the police car were standing still. The frequency of the sound increases. The pitch is higher.

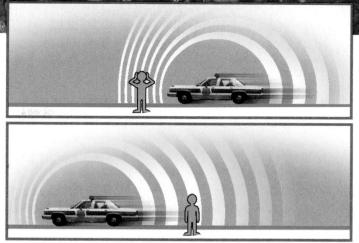

Sound waves from the moving police car bunch together (1) as the car approaches the listener. They spread apart (2) as the police car moves away from the listener.

Departing Sound

As the siren moves away from you, its sound waves spread apart. There are fewer sound waves reaching your ear each second than there would be if the police car were standing still. The frequency of the sound decreases. The pitch of the siren moving away from you is lower.

Change of Frequency

This change in frequency (and pitch) as a source of sound moves toward or away from you is known as the **Doppler effect**. It is named for the 19th century Austrian scientist Christian Johann Doppler, who first described it.

Many radar (*r*adio *d*etection *a*nd *r*anging) devices use the effect to find the speed of objects. Patrol cars detect changes in frequency as a way of detecting speeding vehicles.

Whales and dolphins use a form of sonar to locate things in their environment.

▷ **How does a sound that is moving away from you change in pitch?**

What Is Fundamental Frequency?

How can you tell the difference in voices? What if two people sing the same note—the same pitch—at the same loudness? You can still hear a difference between the two voices. The **quality** of a sound is what makes it different from another sound of the same loudness and pitch. Quality makes a sound unique.

The quality of a sound depends on the vibrations that produce the sound. When a string vibrates, for example, it vibrates at more than one frequency at a time. The whole string vibrates at the **fundamental frequency**, the lowest frequency at which it vibrates.

At the same time, sections of the string are vibrating at higher frequencies, called **overtones**. Each overtone is a different pitch. It is the blend of the fundamental frequencies and the overtones produced that gives each sound its own quality.

Each sound—whether it's a voice or musical instrument, whether produced by a vibrating string or column of air—is different from all other sounds. Each sound has its own blend of fundamental frequency and overtones that allows you to identify it.

What do buildings and bridges have in common with musical instruments? Each has its own natural frequency of vibration. If a vibrating force shakes them at their natural frequency, the vibration builds up. This buildup results in a condition called **resonance**. Resonance can make a violin or trumpet sound louder. However, resonance can also cause great damage to buildings and bridges, making them rattle and sway. Bridges have collapsed as a result of resonance.

Saxophone

If the saxophone and the trumpet play the same note at the same loudness, the sound waves differ because the blend of overtones differs.

Wynton Marsalis

▷ **Why is fundamental frequency important in designing buildings?**

Trumpet

L·I·N·K·S

Why It Matters

Knowing how different materials reflect and absorb sound waves can be helpful at school or home. Your school library probably has stacks of books and other sound-absorbing materials. They help keep the library quiet so you can read and study. Whether you are a student deciding what furniture to put in a room to make it quiet or an architect deciding how to design a building, you must know how different materials affect sound waves.

e-Journal Visit our Web site www.science.mmhschool.com to do a research project on soundproofing.

Think and Write

1. What is an echo? What is necessary in order to hear an echo?

2. How can sound be used to find the depth of the ocean?

3. Why does the same note played on two different instruments at about the same loudness sound different?

4. What kinds of materials reflect sound best? What kinds of materials absorb sound best?

5. **Critical Thinking** Does sound travel with the same speed through all materials? Write a paragraph explaining your answer.

WRITING LINK

Persuasive Writing Research the importance of "tuning" a car's suspension. Why is it especially important for the suspension of a Monster Car? Write an editorial to persuade drivers to "tune" their car's suspension before the next Monster Car rally.

MATH LINK

Solve this problem. Sound waves travel about 1,500 meters per second in water. A ship sends a sound wave to the ocean floor. The echo takes four seconds to return. How deep is the ocean there?

TECHNOLOGY LINK

Science Newsroom CD-ROM Choose *Sounds Good to Me* to learn how sound waves move through matter.

 LOG ON Visit www.science.mmhschool.com for more links.

Sonograms
Seeing with Sound

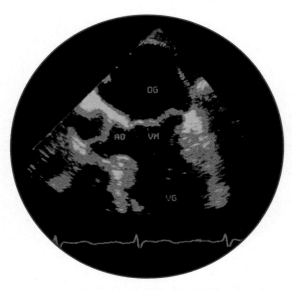

With sonograms doctors can look at organs in hard-to-reach places, such as the heart shown in this sonogram.

What's a sonogram? Does it hurt? Relax! It's a painless medical test that uses sound waves to make a high-tech picture of your internal organs and tissues. Sonograms can be used to look at an unborn baby in its mother's womb (see below) or a beating heart.

Here's how it works. Sound waves are sent through your body using a gadget called a transducer, or probe. The probe is placed on the skin. It sends high-pitched sound waves into your body. The sounds are pitched too high for the human ear to hear.

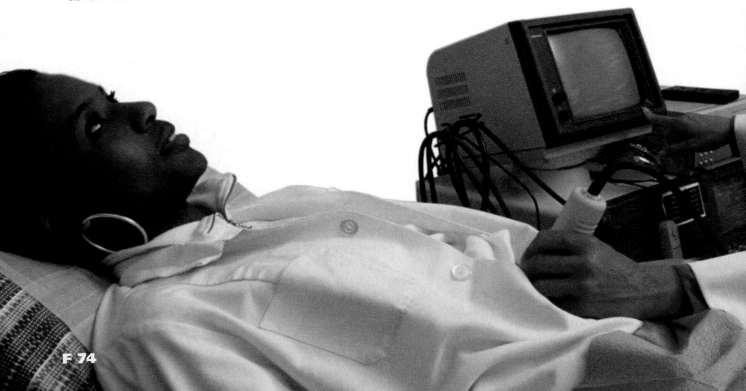

The sound waves travel through your body until they hit a boundary. Here some of the sound waves are absorbed, and some are reflected back to the probe as "echoes." The secret to the sonogram is that sound waves travel through different materials at different speeds. So the time it takes the echoes to get back to the probe depends on whether they traveled through blood vessels, muscles, or organs.

When the echoes return to the probe, they are sent to a computer. The computer keeps track of the time that the different echoes arrive back at the probe. From this the computer can figure out what the sound waves traveled through. It shows what the sound waves "see" during their journey through your body. The computer uses the echoes to calculate the sizes and shapes of your body parts. Then it produces a picture—a sonogram!

Write About It

1. Sonograms can help doctors look at a patient's internal organs without having to perform surgery. Why is this good for patients? and for doctors?

2. Sonograms are often used to take pictures of developing fetuses. Why would this be helpful to doctors?

LOG ON Visit www.science.mmhschool.com to learn more about sonograms.

Chapter 15 Review

Vocabulary

Fill each blank with the best word or words from the list.

> **absorption,** F66
> **compression,** F51
> **decibel,** F58
> **echo,** F68
> **hertz,** F57
> **quality,** F72
> **rarefaction,** F51
> **reflection,** F66
> **sound wave,** F51
> **vibration,** F50

1. The unit for measuring frequency is a(n) _____.

2. An echo is caused by a(n) _____.

3. A sound starts with a(n) _____.

4. Loudness is measured in a unit called a(n) _____.

5. Overtones affect the _____ of a sound.

6. A sound travels as a(n) _____.

7. A reflected sound is called a(n) _____.

8. Sound tends not to bounce off carpets because of _____.

9. When molecules bunch together, that's the _____ stage of a sound wave.

10. When molecules spread apart, that's the _____ stage of a sound wave.

Test Prep

11. If the frequency of a musical note is increased, _____.

  A the note gets louder

  B the note gets softer

  C the note gets higher

  D the note gets lower

12. Echoes are the result of _____.

  F the Doppler effect

  G reflection

  H absorption

  J quality

13. The two parts of a sound wave are _____.

  A compression and rarefaction

  B pitch and quality

  C overtone and resonance

  D absorption and reflection

14. The changing pitch of a moving siren is caused by _____.

  F the Doppler effect

  G reflection

  H absorption

  J quality

15. Two differences we hear in sounds are _____.

   A compression and rarefaction

   B absorption and rarefaction

   C pitch and quality

   D absorption and reflection

Concepts and Skills

16. Reading in Science Write a paragraph explaining how a sound reaches your ear.

17. Decision Making You are organizing a band. Some of the band members want to play their music as loud as possible all the time. Some of them say it is safer for everyone's hearing to play much more softly. How loud would you tell everyone to play? Write a paragraph explaining your answer.

18. Scientific Methods Do people learn better if they listen to Mozart's music than if they listen to rock music? Write up a design for an experiment that would test this.

19. Critical Thinking Do you think louder sounds travel faster than softer ones? Write and explain a hypothesis. Describe how you might test your idea

20. INQUIRY SKILL **Communicate**
Write a paragraph explaining how the instruments below were built to make different sounds.

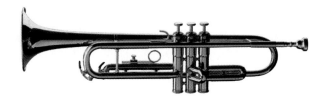

Did You Ever Wonder?

INQUIRY SKILL **Communicate**
In 1947, Chuck Yeager became the first person to fly faster than the speed of sound. Imagine you were flying with him when he broke the sound barrier. What would you have heard at this historic moment?

LOG ON Visit www.science.mmhschool.com to boost your test scores.

CHAPTER 16

Light Energy

Did You Ever Wonder?

How does a lighthouse work? This lighthouse on the coast uses powerful lenses to focus a beam of light so it can be seen far out at sea. How are lenses able to focus light? Are the lenses in a lighthouse the same as the lenses in a pair of eyeglasses?

INQUIRY SKILL Make a Model A lighthouse is 61 m (about 200 feet) high. Its light can be seen at a distance of 30 km (18.6 miles). Why does the distance the light can be seen depend on the height of the lighthouse? Make a drawing to answer the question.

Light and Mirrors

Get Ready

What happens in any city or town when the Sun sets? What if you were in a plane as the Sun was setting and you could look down at a big city? What would you notice as time goes by?

What if you are in a room, sitting near a window and reading? The Sun sets. How does everything in the room seem to change? What do you need to do if you want to keep reading? Is it possible to see objects if there is no light?

Inquiry Skill

You predict when you state possible results of an event or experiment.

Explore Activity

Can You See Without Light?

Materials

small cardboard box with lid

small object to put inside box, such as an eraser, crayon, or coin

scissors

flashlight

Procedure

BE CAREFUL! Handle scissors carefully. Do not put any sharp objects in the box.

1 Can you design a test to find out how well you see without light? Cut a dime-sized hole in the box as shown. Put an object inside the box. Close the lid.

2 **Observe** Look in the box through the hole. What do you see? Write a description of it.

3 Now cut a small hole in the top of the box.

4 **Experiment** Shine the flashlight through the top hole while you look into the box again. Can you see the object this time?

Drawing Conclusions

1 **Communicate** Could you see the object inside the box in step 2? In step 4? Explain any difference in your answers.

2 **Infer** Is it possible to see an object in the dark? Explain.

3 **Predict** Do any characteristics of the object in the box affect the results? Try different kinds of objects. Predict any differences in your results. Test your ideas.

4 **FURTHER INQUIRY** **Predict** How much extra lighting would you need on a dark, cloudy day in order to safely walk around your classroom or your room at home? Would a night-light work? How would you test your ideas safely?

Main Idea Light is a form of energy that is reflected from some objects.

Can You See Without Light?

The Moon looks very bright in the evening sky. However, the Moon does not give off any light of its own.

We are able to see the Moon only because sunlight bounces off the Moon's surface and into our eyes. The dark half of the Moon in the photo is actually a part of the side of the Moon that is not being lit by the Sun. Since sunlight does not reach the Moon there, we cannot see this part of the Moon's surface.

What is light? Scientists know that light, like sound, is not matter. We

You see the Moon because it is lit by the Sun.

could never observe a "piece" of light at rest, taking up space and having mass. Light and sound are both means of transferring energy between points.

The photograph below clearly shows that light carries energy. In fact, light is a form of energy.

A beam of light from a laser carries enough energy to melt the hardest metals.

The Sun

A burner flame

An electric light bulb

How Light Is Produced

All the objects we can see either give off their own light or, more often, reflect the light from a source such as a light bulb or the Sun. The photos show objects that produce light. As you can see, heat is involved in all three cases. Nuclear reactions heat the Sun. Chemical reactions heat the burner flame. Electricity heats the glowing wire of the light bulb.

In a very hot material, the molecules move swiftly. At times when these molecules collide, some energy from the collision may be given off as light.

At other times the molecules themselves vibrate and give off light waves.

Any light source converts energy of one kind into light energy. For example, the Sun makes light from nuclear energy, a burner makes light from chemical energy, and an electric light bulb makes light from electrical energy. The light waves given off by these sources carry the energy away at great speed.

▶ **What can you see in a room that is totally dark?**

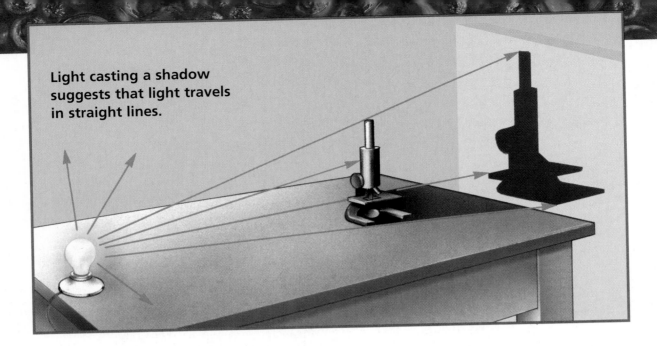

Light casting a shadow suggests that light travels in straight lines.

How Does Light Travel?

Take a look at the drawings below. Which path do you think shows how light travels to your eyes?

In the illustration above, a light bulb casts the shadow of a microscope on a wall. If we draw a straight line from the light bulb to any part of the microscope, we can follow the line directly to that part of the microscope's shadow. This might suggest that light always travels in straight lines. However, this is true only when a substance like air or water remains the same along the whole pathway of light.

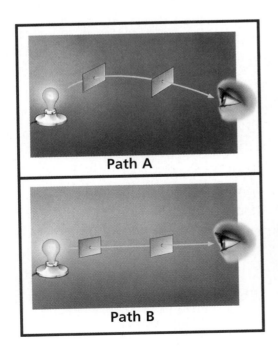

Path A

Path B

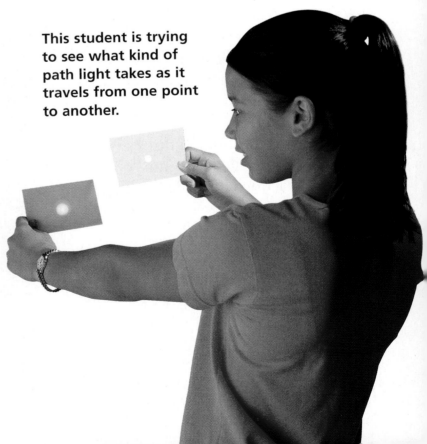

This student is trying to see what kind of path light takes as it travels from one point to another.

In fact, light usually changes direction when it passes from one substance into another. Otherwise, as long as light travels through air or water, it follows a straight line.

Actually, light travels as a series of waves. These waves can be disturbed or bent when they travel past the edge of a thin object or flow through a very narrow opening.

When free of snags, however, light waves move as shown below. If we could follow a point on a light wave as it ripples outward from its source, we would trace a straight line. This beam of light is called a **light ray**.

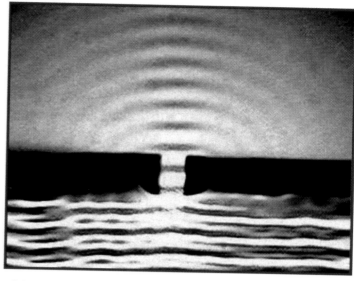

This model uses water waves to show how light waves bend as they travel past very thin objects or pass through very tiny holes.

▷ **How does light travel when it passes from one substance into another?**

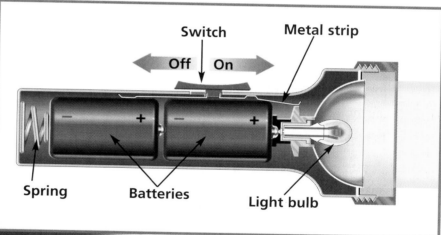

Switch · Off · On · Metal strip

Spring · Batteries · Light bulb

Each small section of a light wave follows a straight path, creating a ray of light.

When the flashlight is on, electric current from the batteries flows through the metal strip and lights the bulb.

QUICK LAB

Follow the Bouncing Light

FOLDABLES Make a Half-Book. (See p. R 41.) Label as shown.

Observation 1 Angles	Observation 2 Angles

1. Hold a small pocket mirror as shown. Adjust it so your partner can see your face in the middle of the mirror.

2. You and your partner should hold a long string taut to the mirror at the point where you see each other's nose. Compare the two angles formed between the string and the mirror. Record your observations in the Half-Book.

3. **Observe** Move a little farther apart. How does the mirror have to be moved for your partner to see your face?

4. **Interpret Data** What did you observe about the angles the string made with the mirror?

How Does Light Bounce Off Objects?

Review how any visible object must either give off its own light or reflect light from another light source. We can picture how light reflects (bounces) off objects using light rays as in the diagram.

How is light reflected by a mirror? When a ray of light reaches your eye from a mirror, where did the light come from before it struck the mirror?

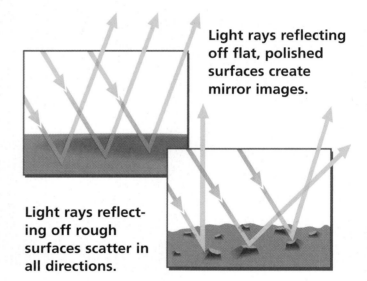

Light rays reflecting off flat, polished surfaces create mirror images.

Light rays reflecting off rough surfaces scatter in all directions.

The Law of Reflection

The angle between an incoming light ray and a surface equals the angle between the reflected light ray and the surface. This is called the **law of reflection**. The illustration below helps to demonstrate this idea.

Light rays that bounce off polished, shiny surfaces can reflect a "picture" of the light source, called an *image*. The things you see when you look in a flat mirror, for example, look very real, almost as if they existed on the other side of a window. However, your experience tells you they are not real— they are just images of the real things in your world. The picture shows how flat mirrors form images.

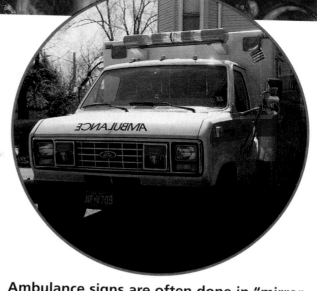

Ambulance signs are often done in "mirror writing" so that they read correctly when seen in a rearview mirror.

The path taken by the basketball shows what a light ray does when it reflects off a surface. The angles between the path of the ball and the floor are equal on either side of the bounce.

Whom does each student see when he or she looks in the mirror?

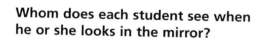

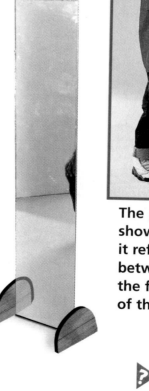

▷ **How does light bounce off a mirror?**

How Do Curved Mirrors Form Images?

Mirrors that curve in on the shiny side are **concave mirrors**, while mirrors that curve out on the shiny side are **convex mirrors**. Curved mirrors form images that are different from those formed by flat mirrors.

How do you think the images formed by concave and convex mirrors will differ from one another? From the image formed by a flat mirror?

Have you ever looked at your reflection in a soupspoon? You may have found that your image looked different depending on whether you were looking at the inside or the outside of the spoon's bowl. You may also have found your image changed,

Inside of spoon

Back of spoon

depending on how far away you held the spoon.

The inside of the soupspoon behaves like a concave mirror. The outside of the spoon behaves like a convex mirror.

Curved mirrors create a variety of images that can be of practical use. Convex mirrors always form reduced, upright images. However, concave mirrors can form many different types of images, depending on the position of the object in relation to the mirror.

The illustrations on the next two pages demonstrate how different kinds of mirrors form images.

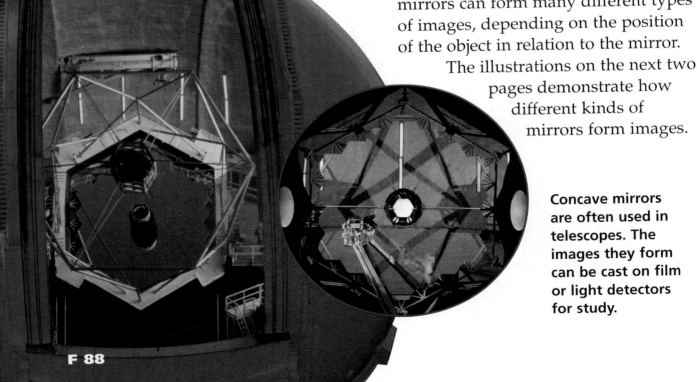

Concave mirrors are often used in telescopes. The images they form can be cast on film or light detectors for study.

Concave Mirrors

Images formed by a concave mirror depend on how far the object is from the mirror. Objects very close to the mirror produce enlarged, right-side-up images. Objects a bit farther back produce enlarged, upside-down images. As the object moves back even farther from the mirror, the image remains upside-down but gets smaller and smaller.

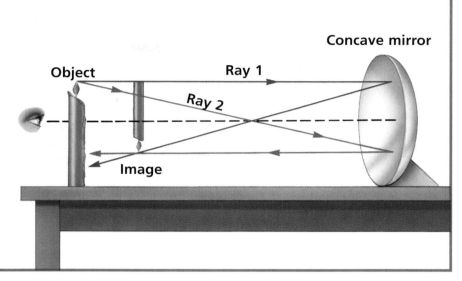

Flat Mirrors

Light rays coming from the candle bounce off the flat mirror and create an image on the other side of the mirror. The image in a flat mirror is always upright, life sized, and left-to-right reversed.

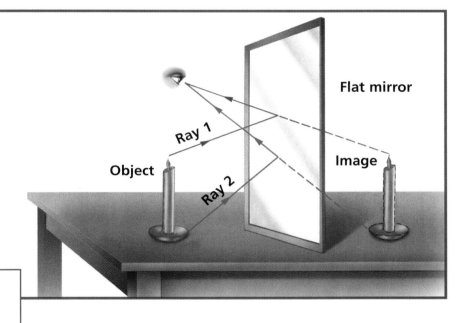

READING Diagrams

1. What happens to the light rays reflected by the concave mirror?

2. Look at the image produced by the concave mirror. How do the image and object compare?

READING Compare and Contrast

How are images formed by curved mirrors different from those of flat mirrors?

How Do Convex Mirrors Work?

A convex mirror is curved like part of the outside of a sphere. It produces an image that is right-side up and much smaller than the object. Convex mirrors are used as side rearview mirrors in cars. They give a wide-angle view. However, the cars seem to be farther away than they really are. Convex mirrors are also used in stores as security mirrors to give a wide view of what's going on in the store.

▷ **Why is a convex mirror useful for store security?**

Convex mirrors provide a wide-angle view.

READING
Diagrams

Examine the ray diagram, and explain how images are formed by convex mirrors.

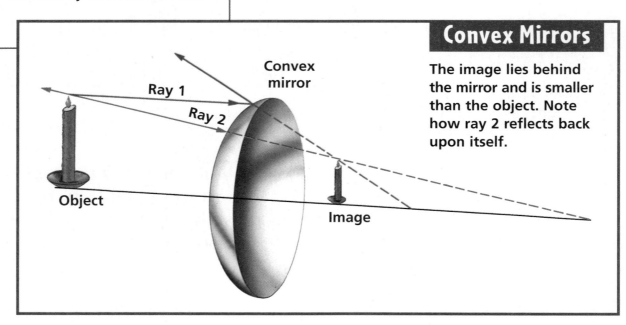

Convex Mirrors

The image lies behind the mirror and is smaller than the object. Note how ray 2 reflects back upon itself.

Ray 1

Ray 2

Convex mirror

Object

Image

Why It Matters

Have you ever gone to a parade and missed almost everything because the people in front of you were taller than you? A simple periscope might have helped. Simple periscopes are tall tubes with mirrors inside that help you see over things that would otherwise block your view. Periscopes are also used in submarines to allow the subs to stay underwater while getting a look at what's going on above the water's surface.

e-Journal Visit our Web site **www.science.mmhschool.com** to do a research project on how mirrors reflect light.

Think and Write

1. Is it possible to see in the dark? Explain.

2. What evidence can you give that light travels in straight lines?

3. How are the images formed by concave mirrors different from those formed by convex mirrors?

4. The rearview mirror on the right side of a car is usually convex. Why is a convex mirror best for this purpose?

5. **Critical Thinking** Describe a demonstration that would show how light carries energy.

L·I·N·K·S

WRITING LINK

Writing a Poem You visit a "fun house" of mirrors and are amazed at what you see. Write a humorous poem describing how you look in these different kinds of mirrors and why.

MATH LINK

Solve this problem. How many 2 x 4 ft mirrors are needed to cover the walls and ceiling of a rectangular room that is 10 x 8 x 8 ft? The room has no doors or windows.

ART LINK

Make a kaleidoscope. Use simple materials. Consult books from the library or the Internet. Draw up a plan to build one. Get permission from your teacher to build it. When it's finished, hold it up to the light. Turn it to see the patterns that form. Describe what you see.

TECHNOLOGY LINK

 LOG ON Visit **www.science.mmhschool.com** for more links.

BULBS: The Bright Idea!

This has been the typical light bulb for more than 60 years. It has a tightly coiled tungsten filament in a bulb that's filled with a special gas.

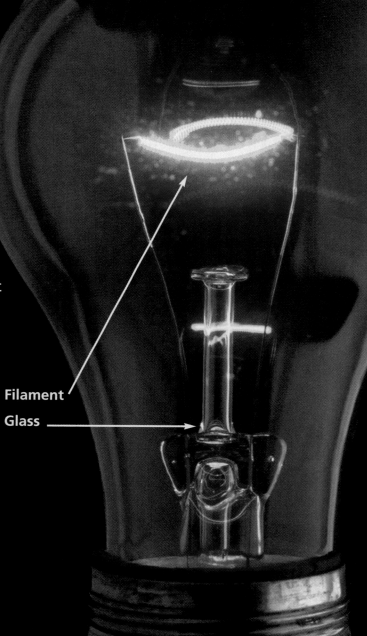

Filament

Glass

Whose bright idea was the light bulb? No one person can take all the credit because you need electricity to light the bulb!

It began in 1800, when Alessandro Volta produced the first steady electric current. In 1820 an inventor put a current through a metal wire, saw a glow, and put it in a closed glass container, creating the first light bulb.

In 1841 someone built the first light with glowing carbon. Other inventors used other kinds of filaments—thin materials that glow when electrified.

Alessandro Volta

Thomas Edison

The first popular light bulb in the United States was a carbon-filament bulb invented by Thomas Edison in 1879. Two years later Lewis Howard Latimer patented an improved bulb with a carbon filament he invented. Latimer was later hired by Edison.

By 1902 metal-filament light bulbs were for sale, but they were very expensive. The General Electric Corporation set up a laboratory to create new bulbs. By 1910 lab workers discovered how to make inexpensive, bright bulbs with tungsten filaments. Sadly, black material coated the inside of the bulbs, dimming the light.

Lab scientist Irving Langmuir found that by filling the bulbs with a special gas, they didn't turn black. By 1934 he'd learned that coiling the filament made the light brighter. Our modern light bulb had arrived!

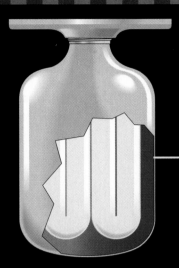

In the 1980s small fluorescent bulbs that screw into ordinary sockets were introduced. These use much less electricity than ordinary light bulbs.

Fluorescent light bulbs were also produced in the 1930s. They use light from a glowing gas to make a coating inside the bulbs glow. Fluorescent lights use less electricity and are cooler than ordinary bulbs.

Write ABOUT IT

1. What's the difference between an ordinary light bulb and a fluorescent light bulb?

2. How has the invention of the light bulb affected the space shuttle? The camera? The automobile?

Lewis Howard Latimer

Irving Langmuir

 LOG ON Visit www.science.mmhschool.com to learn more about electricity.

Light and Lenses

Vocabulary

opaque, F96

transparent, F96

translucent, F96

polarization, F97

refraction, F98

convex lens, F100

concave lens, F100

Get Ready

What are shadows? What kinds of materials cast shadows? Can a window glass cast a shadow? Are shadows always black?

What if you turn off the lights in your room? Then you shine a flashlight on various objects in the room. You look for shadows. Do the shadows differ? Are some sharper than others? If so, why? How do objects cast shadows? Do all objects cast shadows the same way? Are all shadows alike? If light passes through an object, does the object cast a shadow?

Inquiry Skill

You experiment when you perform a test to support or disprove a hypothesis.

Explore Activity

What Can Light Pass Through?

Materials

plastic sandwich bag

paper

waxed paper

aluminum foil

other assorted materials to test

flashlight

clear plastic cup

water (other liquids, optional)

food dye

Procedure

1 Classify Sort the test materials into those that you think light can pass through and those that light cannot pass through.

2 Experiment Use the flashlight to test if light can pass through each of the solid materials. Record your observations. Test if light will pass through water. What about water colored with food dye?

3 Infer How can you test if light passes through gases? Explain. What materials would you need?

Drawing Conclusions

1 Interpret Data Can light pass through all the materials equally well?

2 Interpret Data Can light pass through solids, liquids, and gases?

3 Predict What else might you add to water to see if light gets through—sand, ink, instant coffee? Predict if each lets light through. How would you test your ideas?

4 FURTHER INQUIRY Experiment Design a room from window coverings to lighting, where shadows of objects are always soft and fuzzy, never sharp. What sorts of materials would you use?

Main Idea Light is blocked by some objects and passes through others.

What Can Light Pass Through?

Sometimes when light strikes matter, almost all the light gets through. Sometimes only some light gets through. Sometimes none of it gets through.

- **Opaque** materials completely block light from passing through.

- **Transparent** materials allow light to pass through with almost no disturbance. Transparent materials may or may not color the light, but you can see objects clearly through them.

- **Translucent** materials allow only part of the light to pass through, while also bouncing it in many new directions. Since translucent materials give only a blurry view, they are often used in shower doors. They let some light in, but provide privacy.

Light from celestial objects, such as this galaxy, passes through empty space to reach us.

You might think empty space is opaque to light. After all, light and sound are both waves, and sound waves do need some kind of matter to travel through. However, as the starry night sky shows, light can travel through empty space. We'll learn why in Lesson 10.

Kaleidoscopes use mirrors to turn reflected light into changing patterns. Translucent pieces of colored glass or plastic are often used to create various designs inside.

Which objects in this scene are transparent? Translucent? Opaque?

Controlling Light

In our daily lives, we use many products to control light. You may be familiar with some of the products shown here.

One of the most interesting ways of controlling light depends on **polarization** (poh·luhr·uh·ZAY·shuhn). Light travels in waves. Normally these waves vibrate in all directions. However, light can be *polarized* by some materials. That is, only one direction of light vibrations can pass through them.

Polarized sunglasses use one kind of polarizing material to help us see better on a bright day. On bright days much of the glare we see comes from light reflecting off water and other surfaces.

This reflected light is often naturally polarized to vibrate sideways. Polarizing materials in sunglasses, however, let through only the light that is vibrating up and down. This blocks glare and all other kinds of light that vibrates sideways.

Scientists have also developed sunglasses that change color by themselves! They turn dark in the sunlight but lighten indoors. The lenses

Thin plastic films can be applied to car windows to give them a darker tint. This cuts down on the brightness of the light coming through.

of self-tinting glasses contain very small amounts of a transparent, silver-containing chemical. When struck by bright light, this chemical turns into tiny silver particles. These particles block light and darken the glass.

When taken indoors, the silver particles become transparent again, so the lenses automatically lighten.

READING Compare and Contrast
Compare how light passes through opaque, transparent, and translucent materials.

Self-tinting glasses indoors

Outside in bright light

F 97

How Can Light Rays Be Bent?

The pencil in the photograph certainly appears to be bent. However, the bend is actually just a "trick" that light rays play on our eyes. The illusion is caused when light rays from the lower part of the pencil change direction as they go from water into air. The bending of light rays as they pass from one substance into another is called **refraction** (ri·FRAK·shuhn). The photographs on page F99 illustrate the refraction of a light beam.

How does light affect what you see when it passes through water?

You've seen that light rays may bend as they move from one substance into another. Can light rays move from one substance into another without bending?

Light rays bend as they go from water into air, making the pencil appear to be bent.

How Refraction Works

Imagine skating onto grass from a sidewalk. If you skate straight onto the grass at a 90° angle, you will slow down, but your direction will remain the same. If you skate onto the grass at any other angle, though, one skate will slow before the other. This will cause you to turn in a new direction. The shallower the angle between your original path and the grass, the more your direction will change.

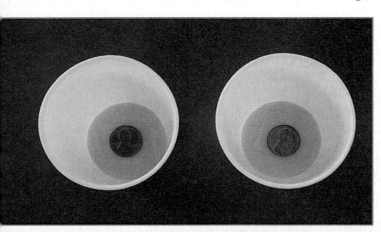

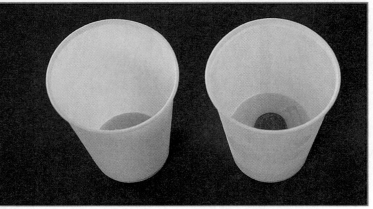

Put a penny in each cup. Add a little water to one cup. Stand away from the table. Can you see both pennies? What would you have to do so that you could see both coins at the same time?

Like a skater, light traveling from one substance into a denser substance slows down. (The denser substance is made of material that is packed together more tightly than the material that makes up the less-dense substance.)

If light strikes the new material head-on, its direction is unchanged. However, if it strikes at any other angle, it gets refracted into a new direction. The amount of refraction increases as the incoming angle gets shallower.

Look at the photos of the skaters. The first skater skates onto the grass at a 90° angle. Both skates hit the grass at the same time. The second skater's skates don't hit the grass at the same time. Why not? How will the path the second skater takes differ from the path the first skater takes? How do the paths the skaters take compare with the paths the light beams take?

▷ **When do light rays bend?**

READING
Charts

1. What happens as the light beams enter the glass? Compare the paths of the two light beams. Why are they different?

2. How do the paths the light beams take compare with the paths the skaters take? Why do you think this is so?

Seeing Through a Lens

FOLDABLES Make a Six-Row Folded Chart. (See p. R 44.) Label as shown.

Step	Observation
1 (Room)	
1 (Book)	
2	
3	
4	

1. **Observe** Hold a convex lens about a foot from your eye. View the image of the room around you. Record what you see. Repeat with the lens quite close to the page of a book.

2. **Experiment** Aim the lens at a light bulb or window. Move an index card back and forth on the other side of the lens until you see an image of the light source cast sharply on the card. Record what you see.

3. **Observe** Is an upright image enlarged or reduced?

4. **Observe** Is an image cast on the card upright or inverted?

5. **Classify** Summarize your observations in a table.

How Do Lenses Work?

Lenses are pieces of transparent materials with curved surfaces that use the refraction of light to make images. **Convex lenses** curve outward, while **concave lenses** curve inward. The diagrams show how these lenses form images.

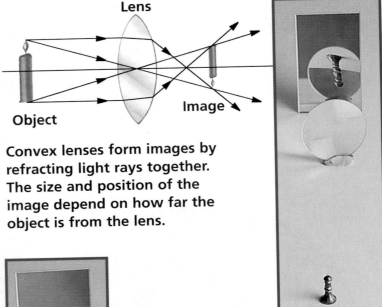

Convex lenses form images by refracting light rays together. The size and position of the image depend on how far the object is from the lens.

Concave lenses form images by refracting light rays apart. These images are always right-side-up and smaller than the object.

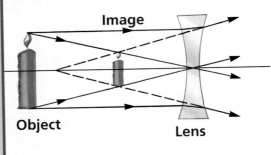

▷ **How do convex and concave lenses work?**

Telescope

Lenses used in telescopes bring you a closer view of distant stars and planets.

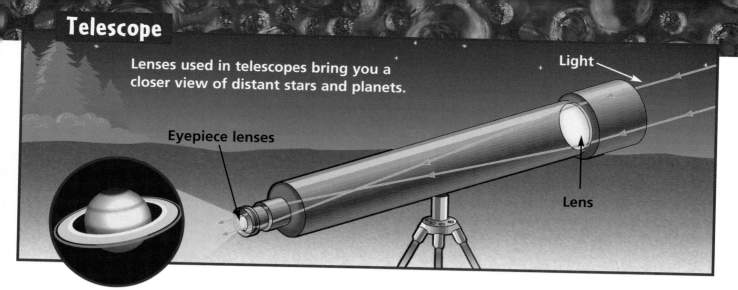

Light

Eyepiece lenses

Lens

Binoculars

Binoculars work like a pair of small telescopes—one for each eye. They are used for viewing distant objects. Unlike most telescopes, binoculars give an enlarged, right-side-up view.

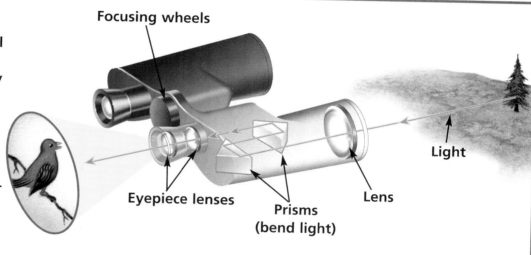

Focusing wheels

Light

Eyepiece lenses

Prisms (bend light)

Lens

Microscope

Lenses used in microscopes help you see a tiny world that is invisible to your unaided eye.

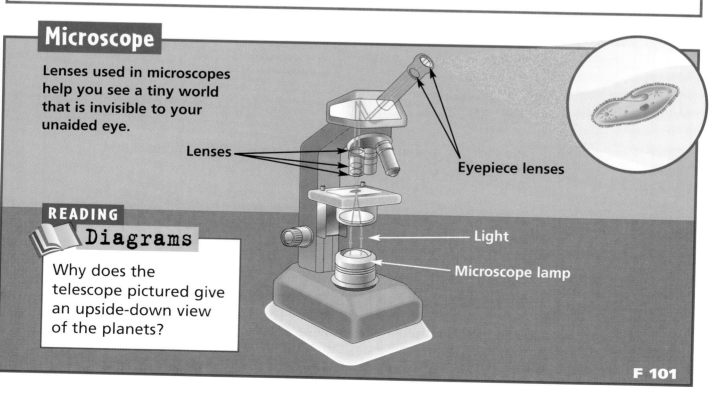

Lenses

Eyepiece lenses

Light

Microscope lamp

READING
Diagrams

Why does the telescope pictured give an upside-down view of the planets?

How Does the Eye Work?

Each of your eyes has a convex lens that casts an image onto the back of the eye. Here a sheet of tissue called the retina converts the light into signals that nerves carry to the brain. Your brain then turns the nerve signals into your view of the world.

The diagram shows how your eyes work. Light from an object reaches the eye and is refracted by the cornea. The refracted light then enters the eye through the pupil and travels to the lens.

The lens of the eye bends the light even more, so that it forms an image on the retina.

Images that form on the retina are sent on by the optic nerve to the brain. The brain then turns these images into your view of the world.

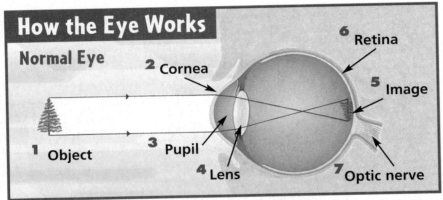

How the Eye Works

Normal Eye

6 Retina
2 Cornea
5 Image
1 Object
3 Pupil
4 Lens
7 Optic nerve

> ? How can lenses help nearsighted eyes work better?

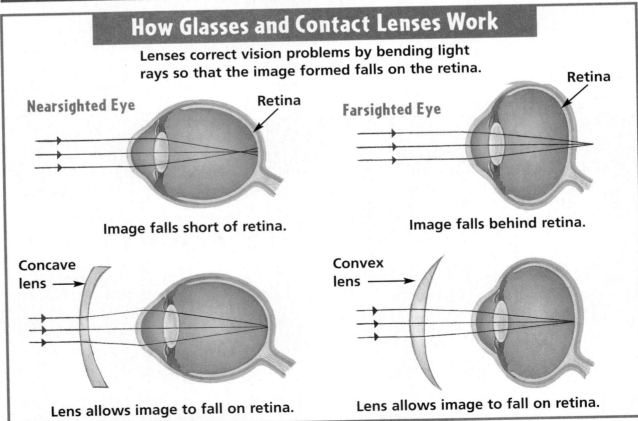

How Glasses and Contact Lenses Work

Lenses correct vision problems by bending light rays so that the image formed falls on the retina.

Nearsighted Eye
Retina
Image falls short of retina.

Farsighted Eye
Retina
Image falls behind retina.

Concave lens →
Lens allows image to fall on retina.

Convex lens →
Lens allows image to fall on retina.

Why It Matters

Light bends as it travels from one kind of substance to another. You can use lenses to focus light and form various kinds of images. The cornea and lens of your eye act as lenses to focus light rays on the retina of your eye. Without this focusing ability, you would not be able to see things clearly.

e-Journal Visit our Web site www.science.mmhschool.com to do a research project on the refraction of light.

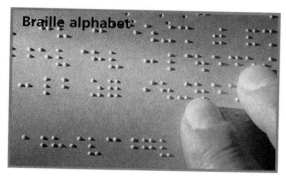

Braille alphabet

Think and Write

1. Give two examples each of opaque, transparent, and translucent materials.

2. What entry angle allows light rays to avoid being refracted?

3. Why are lenses curved?

4. If it weren't for your brain, you might see the world upside down. Why?

5. **Critical Thinking** How can the Sun be visible before it rises above the horizon?

L·I·N·K·S

WRITING LINK

Writing That Compares Lenses affect the way you see things. Write a paragraph that compares and contrasts convex and concave lenses. How are these lenses alike and different?

ART LINK

Make a poster. Research the types of aids available to visually impaired people, and make a poster describing them.

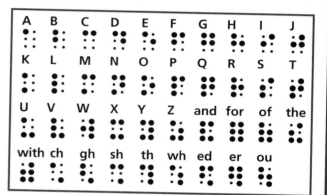

MATH LINK

Solve this problem. A microscope enlarges an object 200 times. How big does the object appear if its actual width is 0.0015 cm?

TECHNOLOGY LINK

 Visit www.science.mmhschool.com for more links.

Cameras — Say "Cheese"!

Even in ancient times, people knew how to make glass. Later they found that curved-glass lenses made an object appear larger or smaller.

One of the earliest devices with a lens was the *camera obscura.* (That's Latin for "dark room.") It was a closed box with a lens on the front, a tilted mirror inside, and glass on the top. The lens allowed light from an object into the box. The light hit the mirror and reflected an image of the object onto the glass.

A "bull's-eye" lantern was also an enclosed box with a lens. When a light was placed inside the box, a narrow, bright beam shone through the lens. The lantern was used in lighthouses.

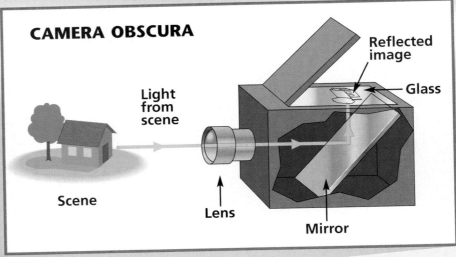

CAMERA OBSCURA

Light from scene

Reflected image

Glass

Scene

Lens

Mirror

Like the bull's-eye lantern, lenses have also been used in light-houses. They create beams of light that can even cut through fog.

Someone placed an image on a transparent sheet and placed it between the light and the lens of a bull's-eye lantern. The image was projected outside the box! The device became known as the "magic lantern," and many people attended magic-lantern shows!

The lens and chamber of the eye are like a small camera obscura. Sometimes an image is formed either too far in front or too far in back of the eye. This can be corrected by adding other lenses in front of the eyes—glasses or contacts!

Some chemicals change color when light shines on them. Inventors put a surface coated with such chemicals at the back of a camera obscura. After many improvements this became the most common way of taking pictures. No one called it a camera obscura anymore. They just called it a "camera"!

MAGIC LANTERN

CAMERA

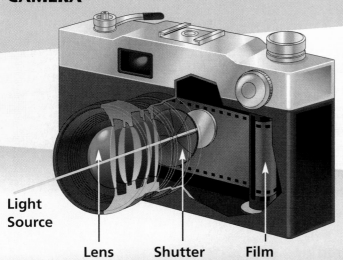

Light Source

Lens   Shutter   Film

What Did I Learn?

1. The word *camera* comes from the Latin phrase for

A dark room.
B image taker.
C picture.
D image maker.

2. Which one of these was used to produce a lighthouse's beam of light?

F bull's-eye lantern
G camera obscura
H magic lantern
J camera shutter

 LOG ON Visit www.science.mmhschool.com to learn more about lenses.

Light and Color

Get Ready

Does a red object always look red? Stage lights can be used to change the color an object appears to be. Why does an object that is one color in normal light look different in certain colors of light, but not in others? Why do you see a color at all? What color will a blue object appear to be if you look at it under a blue light? Under a red light? How could you test your ideas even if you did not have a red or blue light bulb?

Inquiry Skill

You predict when you state possible results of an event or experiment.

Explore Activity

What Is Color?

Materials

red, yellow, blue, and green cellophane sheets

white paper

crayons

red, yellow, blue, green, and black squares of construction paper

flashlight

Procedure

1. **Observe** Instead of using colored light bulbs, shine a flashlight at a sheet of white paper through each of the cellophane sheets. Record what you see.

2. **Predict** Is there a difference if you observe the paper by looking through colored cellophane instead? What color will each of the colored squares appear to be through each of the cellophane sheets? Check your predictions.

3. **Make a Model** Use the crayons to make additional colored squares to view through the cellophane sheets.

4. **Communicate** Make a table that shows what color each square appears to be through each of the cellophane sheets.

Drawing Conclusions

1. **Communicate** What color does the red square appear to be when viewed through the red cellophane sheet? Why? What color does the blue square appear to be when viewed through the red cellophane sheet? Why?

2. **FURTHER INQUIRY** **Predict** What do you think would happen if you looked at the red square through both the red and blue cellophane sheets at the same time? Try it to test your prediction.

Main Idea White light is a combination of all colors.

How Do You Get Color from White Light?

When Sir Isaac Newton passed a beam of white sunlight through a **prism**—a triangular piece of cut and polished glass—in a dark room, he was startled to see a band of rainbow colors. He called the color band a **spectrum** after a word meaning "ghostly vision."

Newton wanted to know more about the colors cast by the prism. Where did they come from? He believed that white sunlight was actually a mixture of all the colors. The prism simply spread the colors out by refracting each one at a different angle. Red is refracted the least, violet the most.

Later, Newton predicted that if the spectral colors cast by one prism were passed through a second prism, the colors would recombine into white light.

The result proved his prediction was right. White light is really made up of many colors, including red, orange, yellow, green, blue, and violet.

Rainbows

The rainbow colors you see after a storm result from water drops that act

READING

Diagrams

How do raindrops break up the Sun's light into different colors?

How Rainbows Form

Rain

Sunlight

Rainbow

Observer

both as prisms and mirrors. The drops bend rays of sunlight at different angles, causing the colors to spread out. Then the various colors reflect off the back of the drops into your eye. As the drawing shows, that is how rainbows form in the sky.

Can you make a rainbow with a garden hose? If you've stood with your back to the Sun and looked at the fine mist from a hose, fountain, or waterfall, you've probably seen a rainbow form.

You can also make a rainbow indoors, as this student (top right) is doing. Fill a clear-plastic cup about halfway with water. Carefully place it on the edge of a table. A third of it should extend over the edge. Hold a piece of white paper directly behind the cup. Shine a flashlight vertically through the bottom of the cup. You should see a rainbow on the paper.

A Recipe for White Light

You've learned that white light is a mixture of an entire spectrum of colors. In the picture at right, the girl is using a color spinner she made from cardboard. She pushed a pencil through the center so that when she twirls it between her palms, others can see the colors mix. She is trying to make the right mix of colors so that others will see white light when she spins the spinner.

What colors would you put on your spinner to try to produce white light?

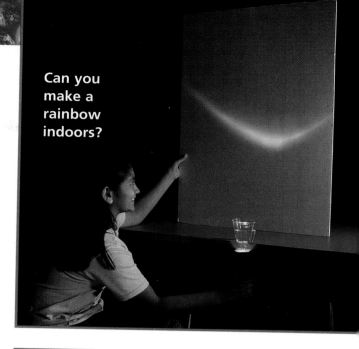

Can you make a rainbow indoors?

READING Compare and Contrast
How do raindrops and prisms produce rainbow colors from white light?

When the spinner is twirled at the right speed, you can see all the colors turn into white.

How Do Colors Look in Colored Light?

A color filter is a material that absorbs certain colors of light and allows others to pass through. The color of an object depends on the color of the light hitting it. What if you looked through colored cellophane sheets as color filters? For example, the red cellophane allows red light to pass through it but blocks other colors.

Try shining a flashlight on a red tomato. Use a sheet of red cellophane as your filter. The tomato still looks red. Now try a green sheet as your filter. Since the tomato can only reflect red light, it now looks black. Try other filters to see how they work.

If you mixed equal amounts of red, green, and blue light, you would get white light, and the tomato would look red. In fact, all of the colors of the spectrum can be created by mixing proper amounts of red, green, and blue light. For this reason we call red, green, and blue the **primary colors** of light.

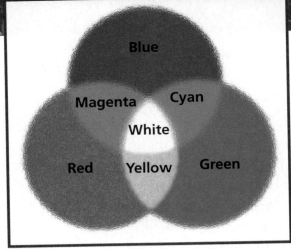

Mixing red, green, and blue light. Note that white is formed in the middle.

Our eyes have cells in the retina that react to colors of light. Some cells react only to red, others only to green, and still others only to blue. If the retina is struck with equal amounts of red, green, and blue light, we see white.

However, if the retina is struck with only red and green light, we see yellow. The drawing above shows some of the different colors that various mixtures of red, green, and blue light can cause us to see.

▷ **How does a red object look in green light?**

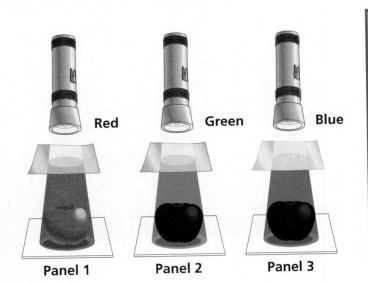

Red   Green   Blue

Panel 1   Panel 2   Panel 3

Stare steadily at the blue square above. This tires the cells in your eye that react to blue light. After a full minute, quickly look at a piece of white paper. What color do you see? Why?

Mixing Colors

You will use pigments—colored substances—in this activity to see the way pigments blend to make other colors.

In this activity you will make a prediction before you do the activity. That is, you will make a reasonable guess about what you expect the results to be. Predict what colors will result when you mix certain colors of food dye together.

Materials

red, yellow, blue, and green food dyes

water

plastic cups

goggles

Procedure

BE CAREFUL! Wear goggles.

1. Place four cups on a piece of paper. Add enough water to each cup to cover the bottom.

2. **Predict** What color will be made by mixing one drop of red food dye and one drop of yellow food dye in the water? Mix well. Record the result.

3. **Experiment** Do step 2 with red and blue dyes. Be sure to make a prediction before you mix the colors.

4. **Experiment** Do step 2 again with yellow and blue, and then with all four colors. Again, be sure to make your predictions before you mix the colors.

Drawing Conclusions

1. **Communicate** What color resulted when you mixed red and yellow?

2. **Communicate** What color resulted when you mixed red and blue? Blue and yellow? When you mixed all four colors?

3. **Infer** What would happen if you used different amounts of each dye? Experiment to find out. Make predictions about the final color before you mix the dyes.

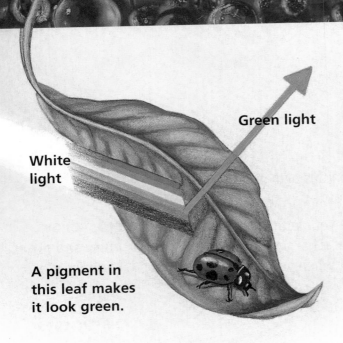

Green light

White light

A pigment in this leaf makes it look green.

What Happens When Color Is Reflected?

When light strikes an object, pigments—colored substances—in the object reflect some colors but absorb other colors. The absorbed colors are missing in the reflected light. The reflected colors mix to produce the color of the object, as shown above.

The leaf in the drawing looks green because it has a pigment that absorbs red and blue light but reflects green light. Some materials reflect all colors and so appear white. Other materials absorb all colors and so appear black.

Colors Made by Blending Paints

Remember that the colors that result when you blend paints are different from the colors that result when you blend colored lights. As you mix colored lights, you keep adding light until you get white.

As you mix pigments, such as food dyes or markers or paints, you keep

subtracting colors until you get black. That is how black is formed at the center of the color wheel below.

Magenta, cyan, and yellow are called the **primary pigments**. Each absorbs one primary color of light and reflects the other two. When properly mixed, these pigments can create any desired color by reflecting a blend of primary colors of light.

Under white light, for example, equal amounts of magenta and cyan would produce the color blue. The cyan would absorb the red out of the white light and the magenta would absorb the green out of the light. Only blue would be reflected.

▷ **What happens when an object absorbs red and green light and reflects blue light?**

READING
Diagrams

What colors would you see if you mixed equal amounts of magenta and yellow? Cyan and yellow?

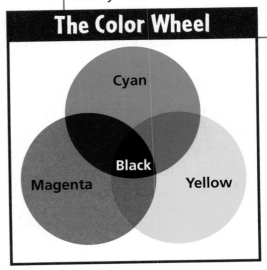

The Color Wheel

Cyan

Magenta

Black

Yellow

Why It Matters

The four-color printing process uses yellow, magenta, cyan, and black plates to make four-color photos. Red is a combination of yellow and magenta. Blue is a mixture of cyan and magenta. Green is a mixture of cyan and yellow. Other colors are formed by mixing various amounts of three or all four color plates.

e-Journal Visit our Web site www.science.mmhschool.com to do a research project on light and color

Think and Write

1. Why do objects appear to be different colors when seen under different-colored lights? When seen through different-colored filters?

2. What happens when white light passes through a prism?

3. What are the primary colors of light? The primary colors of pigments? Why are they different?

4. INQUIRY SKILL Predict What color would be created by mixing red and green light? What color would be created by mixing cyan and yellow pigments?

5. Critical Thinking Where in nature can you see a spectrum? Explain.

L·I·N·K·S

WRITING LINK

Writing a Story What are some of the ways color is important to your life? Write a science fiction story about a world without color. What would life in your story be like?

MATH LINK

Solve this problem. A four-way traffic light requires many lenses. It uses red, yellow, and green colored lenses to control traffic in each direction. How many lenses would you need to build 10 four-way traffic lights?

TECHNOLOGY LINK

 Visit www.science.mmhschool.com for more links.

Invisible Light

Vocabulary

electromagnetism, F118

electromagnetic spectrum, F119

laser, F122

Get Ready

How long does it take to see light when you turn on a lamp in a darkened room? How long does it take for light from a lamp at the end of a long hallway to reach the other end?

It takes about eight minutes for light from the Sun to reach Earth. It can take hundreds, thousands, millions or billions of years for the light from distant stars to reach us.

How does light travel? Sound travels in waves. If light travels in waves, could they be different from sound waves? Explain.

Inquiry Skill

You experiment when you perform a test to support or disprove a hypothesis.

Explore Activity

How Do Waves Move?

Materials

spring toy

meterstick

stopwatch or
digital watch

Procedure

1 One way to experiment with waves is to use a spring toy as a model. Work in groups of three. Two students should stretch the spring toy out 2 meters. One student should jiggle the spring toy slowly up and down to form waves that move along its length.

2 **Observe** The third student should time how long the wave takes to travel from end to end. Repeat several times. Record the results.

3 **Experiment** See what factors affect the size and speed of the wave produced. Compare results when the spring toy is loosely stretched and tightly stretched.

Drawing Conclusions

1 **Observe** In what direction does the wave move? In what direction do the spirals move?

2 **Interpret Data** How does holding it tighter or looser change how the wave moves?

3 **FURTHER INQUIRY**
Experiment Try moving one end of the spring toy with a faster speed of the up and down movement. Again, vary the length of the spring toy. What happens?

Main Idea Waves that produce visible light are part of the electromagnetic spectrum.

How Do Waves Move?

All waves carry energy from place to place. The way a wave carries energy depends on the kind of wave motion.

Remember that sound waves are produced by vibrations. As a string or some other object vibrates, it causes molecules of gas in the air to move back and forth. The energy of the vibration is carried through the air to your ear. In a similar way, sound waves travel through solids, liquids, and gases.

The wave in the spring below moves from left to right. Notice that the particles of matter also vibrate back and forth along the *same* direction—from left to right.

Without particles vibrating back and forth in the direction the sound is traveling, the energy of the sound vibration could not travel. Sound waves cannot travel in a *vacuum*, a space where there is no matter.

By vibrating one end of a spring toy in and out, you can see waves that travel much as sound waves do.

As the wave moves from left to right, how do the water and the ball move?

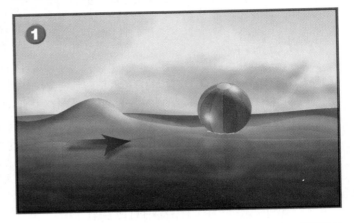

If you toss a pebble into a quiet pond, you can see waves travel across the surface. How does a particle of matter move in the water as the wave moves past it from left to right? Each particle moves in a circle. So does the ball floating on the water.

The waves shown below also move from left to right. How does a particle in the rope or the spring move when a wave passes through it? It does not move back and forth as in a sound wave. It does not move in a circle as in a water wave. It moves up and down.

▷ **Do all waves move the same way?**

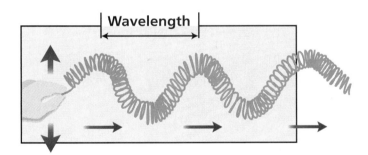

By vibrating one end of a spring toy up and down, you can see waves travel much as waves do on a watery surface.

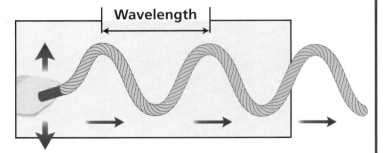

How do the waves made by a jump rope behave?

QUICK LAB

Water Waves

FOLDABLES™ Make a Trifold Book. (See p. R 42.) Label as shown.

60 seconds   30 seconds

1. Fill a shallow pan or tray (20 cm by 28 cm) half full of water. Fold small squares of foil (1 cm by 1 cm) into tiny "boats." Place several boats on the water.

2. At one end of the tray, make waves on the water's surface.

3. **Predict** What do you think will happen to the boats after 30 seconds? After one minute?

4. **Observe** What happened to the boats? How did they move? How far did they move? Were your predictions correct? Use the Trifold Book to record your predictions and results.

5. **Experiment** What happens if you change how fast you make the waves? What happens if you change the number of boats you use?

How Do Light Waves Travel?

Connect both ends of a wire to a battery, then put a compass near the wire. The compass needle moves. The electric charges flowing through the wire create a magnetic field that affects the compass. This is an example of **electromagnetism** (i·lek·troh·MAG·ni·tiz·uhm).

Electromagnetism refers to forces that come from electricity and magnetism. When an electric charge moves in a magnetic field, it produces electromagnetic energy.

In the 1850s, James Clerk Maxwell concluded from his work that light is electromagnetic energy. The electrical and magnetic parts of the energy can carry themselves as a wave moving through space. Electromagnetic waves can travel without matter or through matter.

Electromagnetic waves vibrate back and forth across *(perpendicular to)* the direction in which light travels. Water waves are usually used as models for light waves. The wavelength is the distance from crest to crest. However, light is not just one wavelength. It is many wavelengths. The colors of light are different wavelengths. A prism refracts the different wavelengths in different amounts.

However, all the wavelengths of light travel through empty space at the same speed—over 300 million meters per second. Light slows down when it travels through matter. However, it always travels much, much faster than sound. That's why you see a lightning flash before you hear the thunder.

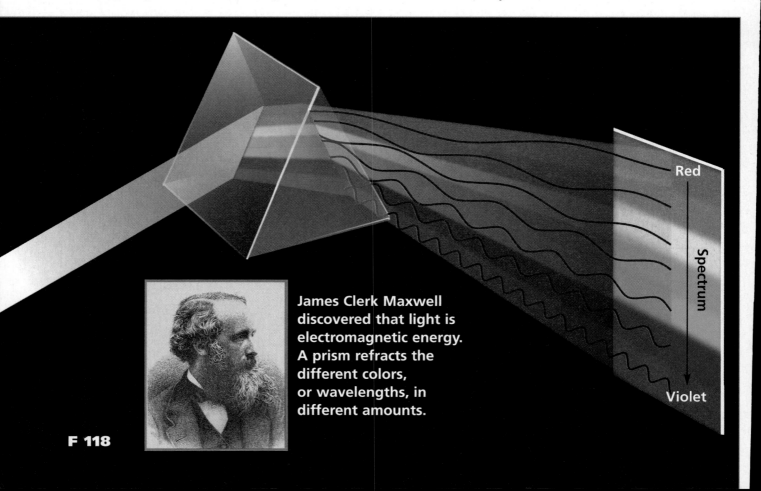

Red

Spectrum

Violet

James Clerk Maxwell discovered that light is electromagnetic energy. A prism refracts the different colors, or wavelengths, in different amounts.

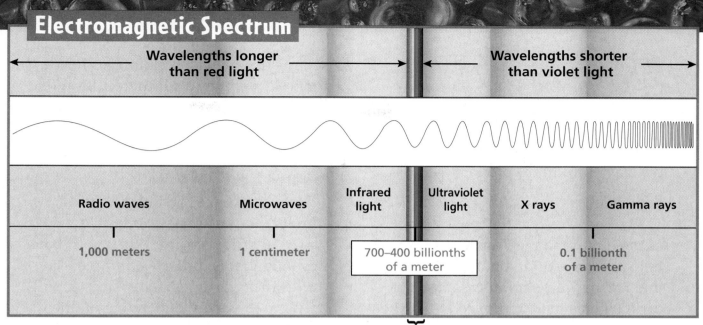

Electromagnetic Spectrum

Wavelengths longer than red light

Wavelengths shorter than violet light

Radio waves	Microwaves	Infrared light	Ultraviolet light	X rays	Gamma rays
1,000 meters	1 centimeter	700–400 billionths of a meter			0.1 billionth of a meter

Visible light

Which kind of wave is the shortest? The longest?

Since Maxwell's work, scientists have formed another idea of how light travels. Rather than as a smooth vibrating wave, perhaps light travels as tiny bundles of energy. Scientists call the bundles *photons*.

Waves or photons? Scientists use both models to explain light. For example, your eye picks up only so many photons of light at any instant. We can see the wavelengths of light that make up the colors of light.

However, there are wavelengths longer than red light and shorter than violet. We cannot see these wavelengths. Together all these wavelengths of light, the ones we see and the ones we cannot see, are called the **electromagnetic spectrum**.

Although we cannot see wavelengths longer than red or shorter than violet, we can detect them, and we can use them in many ways. One way to detect some of this "invisible light" is by using a spectroscope.

READING **Compare and Contrast**
What is one difference between the ways light waves travel and sound waves travel?

Instruments such as this spectroscope (above) allow us to detect forms of light we can't see. This image (right), taken by the spectroscope, analyzes the light coming from an object.

Which Wavelengths Are Longer than Red Light?

The wavelengths of light listed here are longer than red. They are invisible but have important properties and uses.

Radio Waves

Radio waves are the longest waves of the electromagnetic spectrum. You do not see them—and you do not hear them. Broadcast stations use them to carry signals in a kind of code—AM or FM. In AM the height of the waves is changed to carry the signal. In FM the frequency changes. The number of your favorite radio station represents the frequency at which the station sends out radio waves. When these signals are picked up by a radio or television, they produce the sounds and sights that you hear and see.

Radar

Some animals, such as bats and whales, send out sound waves with a high frequency. The echo of the waves helps the animals locate things. Radar works in a similar way. *Radar* stands for "**ra**dio **d**etecting **a**nd **r**anging." Radar uses radio waves that reflect off many objects. The waves can help weather forecasters detect rain and thick fog.

Microwaves

A microwave oven uses electromagnetic waves, too. Microwaves are shortwave radio waves. Water in foods absorbs microwaves very readily. The energy from the absorbed microwaves speeds up the water molecules inside the food. As the water molecules move faster, the food gets hotter. Microwave ovens can heat many foods faster, using less energy than a regular oven.

Infrared Light

Infrared means "just beyond red." Infrared waves are next to visible red waves in the spectrum. When you stand in sunlight, it is the Sun's infrared waves that warm you. All objects give off infrared waves, depending on their temperature. Warmer objects give off more infrared waves than cooler objects do. Special photographic film and electronic sensors can detect infrared light.

▷ **What kinds of electromagnetic energy have longer wavelengths than visible light?**

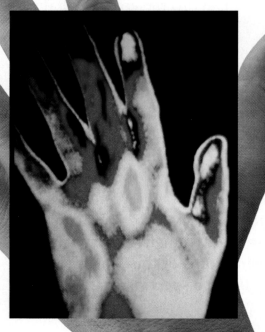

This photograph was taken with film that picks up infrared light.

Which Wavelengths Are Shorter than Violet Light?

The wavelengths of light listed here are shorter than violet light. They are invisible but have important properties and uses.

Ultraviolet Light

Ultraviolet (UV) light is made up of waves just shorter than visible violet light on the spectrum. UV light causes chemical changes. It can produce vitamin D in your body. You need vitamin D for healthy bones and teeth. Ultraviolet light produces vitamin D in milk. Hospitals use ultraviolet light to kill harmful bacteria in equipment used in operating rooms. However, UV light can cause harm. UV light from the Sun can cause a sunburn. Scientists have found that UV light can also cause some forms of cancer on the skin. Cancer is a disease in which cells multiply rapidly with harmful effects.

Earth is protected from much of the Sun's UV light by the ozone layer. The ozone layer is a part of the upper atmosphere that screens out UV light. However, some chemicals produced by factories are eating away at the ozone layer. Thus more of the Sun's UV light will pass through to Earth's surface. Care is being taken to prohibit the chemicals from being manufactured.

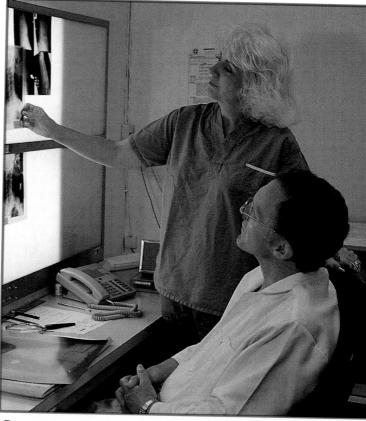

Doctors use light boxes to examine X rays.

X Rays and Gamma Rays

The shortest wavelengths of the spectrum—X rays and gamma rays—have great penetrating power. X rays can pass right through most objects. Thicker or denser objects tend to absorb X rays. This means that X rays can produce a picture when they pass through an arm or leg, or your jaw. The denser objects, such as bones and teeth, can show up very clearly on the finished picture.

▷ **What kinds of electromagnetic energy have shorter wavelengths than visible light?**

What Are Lasers?

You've seen **lasers** in many places—such as at music events and even the checkout counter at the supermarket. Lasers are devices that produce thin streams of light. What makes light from a laser special?

Regular light from a bulb or a candle has many wavelengths all mixed together. As the light travels away from the bulb or candle, it spreads out and gets less noticeable. It gets weaker and weaker the farther it travels.

Lasers produce light that does not spread out or become weaker. Lasers, such as this device using a red ruby, produce light by absorbing flashes of light from a coiled tube. Inside the ruby the absorbed light bounces back and forth between mirrors at the ends of the ruby. As a result, the ruby gives off a light of just a few close wavelengths. The wavelengths are all one color and line up "in step." The beam that comes out of the ruby is narrow and direct.

▷ **What is special about laser light?**

Lasers are used in astronomy.

Flash tube   Ruby crystal

Mirror   **Ruby Laser**   Partial mirror

Laser light does not spread out.

Regular light spreads out as it travels away from a source.

Flashlight

READING
Diagrams

How does laser light compare to light from a flashlight?

Why It Matters

Light has many wavelengths. Only some are visible.

Radar waves help forecasters predict the weather. X rays help dentists and doctors check for cavities and broken bones. Every time you turn on a radio or TV, you are picking up invisible waves of "light."

Some laser beams can be used to melt metals and "crack open" granite. Doctors can use other kinds of lasers to perform delicate surgery. There are even weak laser beams in CD players.

e-Journal Visit our Web site **www.science.mmhschool.com** to do a research project on light.

Think and Write

1. How does light travel? Does it travel the same way as sound?

2. What is radar? How is it used in weather forecasting?

3. How is ultraviolet light harmful? How is it helpful?

4. If a spacecraft were 900 million meters from Earth, how long would it take to send a radio signal from Earth to the spacecraft?

5. **Critical Thinking** What's the difference between a beam of light from a flashlight and a beam of light from a laser?

L·I·N·K·S

LITERATURE LINK

Read *Light Up the Sky with Lasers*, to learn how scientists and artists create laser light shows for planetariums and special events. When you finish reading, think about what you would like to see in a laser light show. Try the activities at the end of the book.

MATH LINK

Make a graph. Use encyclopedias or other reference books to find the wavelengths of the different colors of light. Also research the wavelengths for invisible light in the electromagnetic spectrum. Prepare a color-coded bar graph comparing the wavelengths.

WRITING LINK

Expository Writing Research the history of lasers. Write a report for the class.

TECHNOLOGY LINK

Science Newsroom CD-ROM Choose *Out of Sight* to learn how infrared and ultraviolet light differ from visible light.

LOG ON Visit **www.science.mmhschool.com** for more links.

Chapter 16 Review

Vocabulary

Fill each blank with the best word or words from the list.

concave mirror, F88
convex lens, F100
convex mirror, F88
electromagnetic spectrum, F119
light ray, F85
opaque, F96
primary color, F110
prism, F108
translucent, F96
transparent, F96

1. A straight-line narrow beam of light traveling out from its source is a(n) _____.

2. A mirror that curves in on its shiny side is a(n) _____.

3. A lens that curves outward is a(n) _____.

4. White light is broken up into a rainbow of colors by a(n) _____.

5. A kind of material that allows some light to pass through but may give a blurry view is called _____.

6. Red, blue, or green—each is a _____ of light.

7. A material that light cannot pass through is called _____.

8. A material that light can easily pass through is called _____.

9. Microwaves and X rays are part of the _____.

10. A security mirror used in a store is a(n) _____.

Test Prep

11. Light is a form of _____.
   A heat
   B electricity
   C energy
   D sound

12. Which of the following is translucent?
   F a car windshield
   G a convex mirror
   H a frosted light bulb
   J a concrete block

13. Which is NOT found in the electromagnetic spectrum?
   A X rays
   B infrared light
   C FM radio waves
   D sound waves

14. Sunglasses that reduce glare are _____.
   F transparent
   G translucent
   H cloudy
   J polarized

15. Objects that light can easily pass through are called _____.

   A translucent

   B transparent

   C opaque

   D cloudy

Concepts and Skills

16. Scientific Methods Copy and complete the diagram to show what happens to a light ray as it passes through the lens. Write a paragraph explaining your diagram.

17. Product Ads How does TV advertising use light and color to capture your attention? Write a paragraph giving three examples.

18. Reading in Science What is the difference between the primary colors of light and the primary colors of pigments? Why won't combining colors of paints give you the same results as combining colors of light? Write a paragraph explaining your answer.

19. INQUIRY SKILL **Predict** How many different colors do you think you could make using two flashlights, a piece of white paper, one piece of red and one piece of green cellophane? What if you placed the two pieces of cellophane on top of each other and looked through them. Do you think you would get the same result? Write a paragraph explaining your answer.

20. Critical Thinking Cameras let you take pictures by using lenses to focus light onto film. What if you wanted to make a simple camera but didn't have any lenses. Would you be able to use a mirror instead? What kind of mirror might you try? State and explain a hypothesis. Write a paragraph describing how you would test your idea.

Did You Ever Wonder?

INQUIRY SKILL **Communicate** Imagine tonight we experienced a blackout and you had to live one week without electricity and therefore without lights. How would life be different?

LOG ON Visit www.science.mmhschool.com to boost your test scores.

Dr. S. J. Gates

PHYSICIST

Is everything in the universe made up of tiny little strings? Dr. S.J. Gates, a theoretical physicist, thinks so! Physicists study energy and matter, and how the two interact. Gates is trying to discover the basic building blocks of the universe.

Scientists used to think that the tiniest building blocks were "points." To imagine a point, think of a very, very small ball. But Dr. Gates and other string theorists think that the smallest particles may actually look like short strings.

String theory could help scientists unlock some of the greatest mysteries of the universe. "My type of science is about uncovering the 'code' that runs our universe," Dr. Gates says. "So just as DNA is the code of life, superstrings could be the code of existence."

Tiny superstrings may explain how *everything* works.

TOP 5

Jobs for a Physicist

Dr. Gates is a physicist on the go. Ideas hit him anywhere. Where would you work if you were a physicist? We've put together a list of 5 possible places:

1. NASA as a researcher
2. College as a professor
3. Manufacturer as a developer of new products
4. Home as a writer/thinker
5. Museum as a creator of exhibitions

Science and scientists don't have all the answers to a question. New discoveries change old ideas. So we don't know everything about the code that runs the universe. "We try to figure out the new part of the code simply by 'making it up.' Then we check whether what we made up is really the way the universe works," Dr. Gates says. "The imagination is the only thing we have that allows us to make up new ideas."

Write About It

1. What is S.J. Gates trying to discover?
2. Why is imagination so important to science and scientists?

LOG ON Visit www.science.mmhschool.com to learn more about the work of physicists.

It's the **LAW!**

Your goal is to show how Newton's laws of motion work.

What to Do

1. Place a ball in a shoe box open at one end. Facing the open end, slowly push the box forward. Suddenly stop it. What happens?

2. Push against a wall. What do you feel? Record your observations.

Analyze **Your Results**

Relate your observations to Newton's laws.

Good **VIBRATIONS**

Your goal is to make and use an instrument to detect sound vibrations.

What to Do

1. Stretch plastic wrap over one end of a tube. Secure it with a rubber band. Tape a straw to the plastic wrap.

2. Hold the detector still. Talk into the open end while you gently touch the straw. Use a low voice then a high voice. Record your observations.

Analyze **Your Results**

Draw a diagram of your detector showing how energy is transmitted from you to the straw.

COLOR VISION

Your goal is to explain what happens when you look at colored objects through different color filters.

What to Do

1. Predict which color cellophane you need to look through to make an object look the same color or appear black.

2. Test your predictions. Record your observations.

Analyze **Your Results**

Which color cellophane made both a red and a green object appear black? Explain.

Exploring Ohio

Blanding's turtle has a bright
yellow throat and chin.

Timber rattlesnake

Red-spotted newt

Snapping turtle

Toledo

OHIO

Sandusky River

Columbus

INDIANA

Dayton

Miami River

Cincinnati

Scioto River

NTUCKY

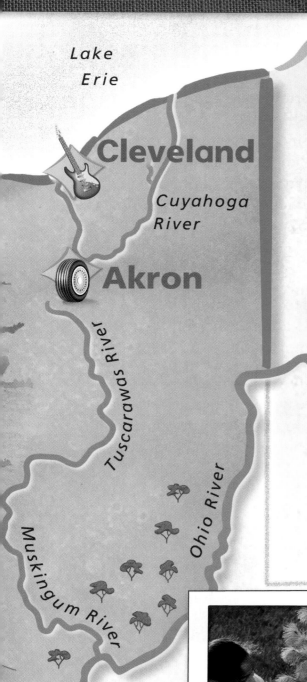

Exploring Ohio

Five-lined skink

Amphibians and Reptiles

Amphibians and reptiles are **vertebrates**, animals with backbones. These animals are **cold-blooded**. A cold-blooded animal cannot automatically keep its body temperature steady. The temperature of a cold-blooded animal can be cool or warm, depending on its surroundings. For example, on a hot day the body temperature of a snake is high. On a cold day its body temperature is low.

Most **amphibians** spend part of their lives in the water and part of their lives on land. *Amphibious* means able to live on land and in water. The skin of an amphibian is always thin, moist, and smooth. As a result the amphibians can take in oxygen through their moist skin.

Reptiles are vertebrates that have scales and breathe with lungs. The skin of reptiles is covered with thick scales or plates. These structures protect reptiles from drying out. Reptiles breathe with lungs from the moment they are born.

Wood frog

Snapping turtle

	AMPHIBIANS	REPTILES
Skin and Claws	▪ Have moist, smooth skin; some have warty skin (toads and newts) ▪ No scales or claws	▪ Have dry skin covered with scales ▪ Claws on their toes
Legs	▪ Most with legs, though some with front legs only	▪ Some without legs: snakes and glass lizards
Breathing	▪ Breathe through skin ▪ Some also use lungs ▪ Larvae and some adults use gills	▪ Breathe with lungs ▪ No gills
Eggs	▪ Have eggs with no outer protective shell	▪ Have eggs with tough leathery or hard outer shell
Larval stage	▪ Most have a larval stage that lives in water	▪ No larval stage
Types	▪ Include frogs, salamanders, and legless amphibians	▪ Include crocodiles, alligators, turtles, snakes, and lizards

Copperhead snake

Red newt

Frogs and Toads

Frogs have rear legs that are built for jumping or hopping. They have thin, smooth, moist skin. True frogs, cricket frogs, chorus frogs, and tree frogs are different kinds of frogs. Frogs can have different colors, shapes, and sizes. Look for warts, spots, stripes, or other patches of color. Some frogs have webbed feet for swimming.

Bullfrogs live in marshes, ponds, and rivers.

Frog larvae are called *tadpoles*. Many tadpole species are herbivores and eat algae. Some are omnivores—they eat plant and animal matter. Adult frogs are carnivores and eat a variety of animals.

Members of the toad family have shorter legs. Most have rough, dry, warty skin. Because their skin is more resistant to drying out, they can live out of water. They return to water to lay their eggs.

American toads live in yards, fields, and woods.

ACTIVITY

INQUIRY SKILL **Classify** You can also identify frogs by their voices. Each species has its own specific song. Frogs usually sing in a chorus.

- Go with an adult to a pond at night where frogs are calling.
- Count the different kinds of frogs you hear.
- Try to estimate the number of frogs you hear of each species.

Salamanders

Salamanders, like frogs and toads, are amphibians. They begin their lives in the water as larvae. Then they undergo metamorphosis and change to animals that are able to live on land. When salamanders are ready to have young, they return to the water. All salamanders are carnivores and eat a wide variety of small animals. Salamanders vary greatly in size, shape, and color.

The **blue-spotted salamander** is one of the smallest salamanders found here. These salamanders grow up to 14 centimeters (5.5 inches). They are found in moist, wooded areas.

The **red-spotted newt** begins its life in a pond. By late summer it develops into a bright red or orange land dweller called an *eft*. Newts remain this way for up to five years. When the newt is ready to reproduce, it returns to the water.

The **tiger salamander** is a mole salamander. It has this name because it spends most of its adult life underground. The tiger salamander is an endangered species.

Where Do Amphibians Live?

There might be an amphibian living within walking distance of where you are right now. Amphibians can survive in many different types of habitats. A **habitat** is the place where an animal lives. Amphibians can be found in forests, woods, meadows, springs, streams, rivers, lakes, ponds, marshes, and swamps.

Wood frog

Forest and woodland

Temporary wetland

Salamanders and frogs live near water. Water is important to all amphibians. Water keeps their skin moist and prevents it from drying out. Mole salamanders spend most of their time underground. Many salamanders lay their eggs in ponds. Frogs also lay their eggs in ponds.

Two-lined salamanders live on land but return to the water to lay their eggs. Still other salamanders live on land only. They lay their eggs under logs or rocks.

Some frogs and salamanders live in temporary wetlands. Unlike permanent wetlands, these wetlands dry up at least once a year. They can be as small as a puddle or larger. These ponds typically have few predators.

Marbled salamander

Permanent wetland

ACTIVITY

INQUIRY SKILL **Classify** With an adult, visit a pond in the spring. Look for and observe tadpoles and salamanders. Record what you see.

- With an adult, use a small net to catch, examine, and release tadpoles and young salamanders.

- Look for amphibian eggs in the pond.

- Remember to return the animals to the pond.

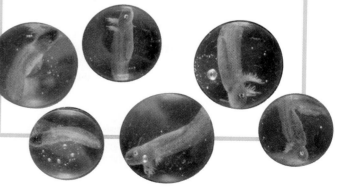

Turtles and Lizards

To identify a turtle, look at the size and shape of its shell. From the side, box turtles have high rounded shells. Spotted and painted turtles have flatter shells. Color patterns on the face, legs, and shell can help to identify different kinds of turtles.

Look for most turtle species in or near ponds, lakes, and rivers. These are **aquatic** turtles. Some turtles spend most of their time in forests or more open areas. These are **terrestrial** turtles.

Spotted turtle

Eastern box turtle

Lizards are different sizes, shapes, and colors. Most have slim bodies and large heads, four legs, and a long tail. Some lizards have rough-looking skin. Others, such as skinks, are smooth, and shiny. Some have stripes, while others are plain.

Lizards can be found in both wet and dry habitats. They live in forested and open country. They may live around your home. Lizards eat invertebrates and other small animals.

Western slender glass lizard

Five-lined skink

Snakes

Snakes are vertebrates with no limbs. They also have no ear openings or eyelids. A snake's body is long. Its skin is covered with scales. As a snake grows it sheds its skin. This process may occur once a year or several times a year.

Most snakes are meat eaters and swallow their prey whole. Their teeth cannot break up food into small pieces. Snakes eat insects, eggs, fish, frogs, and other small animals. Some snakes even eat other snakes!

Some snakes have sharp, hollow teeth called *fangs*. Fangs are used to inject poison into their prey. Despite some people's fear of snakes, most snakes are not venomous and are not a threat to people.

Eastern diamondback rattlesnake

Black racer snake shedding skin

BE CAREFUL!

Leave all snakes alone.

Corn snake

G 9

Where Do Reptiles Live?

There are over 6,000 kinds of reptiles in the world. Reptiles live in a wide variety of places. They can be found in forests, rocky areas, ponds, lakes, and meadows.

In cool climates, reptiles may move from sunny to shady areas during the day. This is so they do not get too hot or too cold. In regions with very cold winters, reptiles hibernate. Although most reptiles do not need water like amphibians, many live in water.

Painted turtles can be found in forests, fields, and vegetated areas, although they are most often observed basking in the sun near shallow bodies of water.

Snakes like this **timber rattlesnake** couldn't survive the freezing temperatures of Ohio's winters. Snakes migrate long distances to reach warm underground dens. There they hibernate and live off the fat they have accumulated over the summer.

Conserving Our Renewable Resources

A **renewable resource** is a resource that can be replaced. It can be replaced in a short time, less than a human lifetime. Plants, trees, wildlife, air, and fresh water are renewable resources.

All living things are adapted to a particular environment. If that environment is threatened, so are the living things. The activities of people can threaten wildlife indirectly by threatening their habitat.

Snowshoe hare

Ohio has lost more than 90% of its original wetlands. Most of Ohio's endangered animals live in or near the water. The **blue spotted salamander** is one of those species. It lives in woodlands next to alder swamps and slow-moving streams.

Ohio has lost much of its vast forest areas. Cutting down too many trees can threaten the plants and animals that live in a forest. Foresters are trying to manage our trees so they are healthier, more plentiful, and continue providing us with the products we need. Planting trees is an important way to maintain our resources.

The government has passed laws to protect wildlife. In some cases these laws protect the species' habitat as well as the animals themselves. New laws are helping to reduce habitat loss from chemicals and other forms of pollution. Some progress has been made, but more work needs to be done to protect wildlife habitats. What ways can you think of to help to protect and maintain Ohio's wildlife?

Ottawa Wildlife Refuge Scientists use different types of investigations to answer questions they are studying. What are two different questions scientists could ask about the Ottawa Wildlife Refuge?

Peregrine falcon

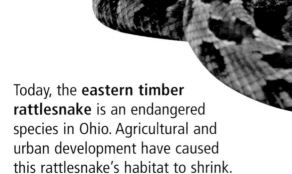

Today, the **eastern timber rattlesnake** is an endangered species in Ohio. Agricultural and urban development have caused this rattlesnake's habitat to shrink.

WE CAN HELP!

- Put litter in its place. Never throw trash on the ground. Do not put anything into rivers or lakes that does not belong there.

- Look, but do not touch. Leave flowers and plants alone.

- Always respect wild animals. Give them their space. Binoculars will help you get a closer look.

- With trusted adults organize a program that cleans up litter in a nearby area.

G 13

Conserving Our Nonrenewable Resources

A **nonrenewable resource** is a resource that cannot be replaced easily. Once a nonrenewable resource is used up, we cannot get more of it.

Nonrenewable resources include metals such as tin, copper, and aluminum. Fossil fuels are also nonrenewable resources. Coal, oil, and natural gas are examples. Fossil fuels take billions of years to form. Once we burn them for energy, they are gone.

Buy a bigger size for things you use often.

REDUCE

REUSE

This milk carton is being reused. Think of some other ways it can be reused.

RECYCLE

Trash put in the garbage gets buried in a landfill.

Items put in the recycle bin are turned into new products. However, this is not always easy. An entire batch of items for recycling can be rejected if it includes the wrong types of plastic. This includes bottle tops. Throw them in the garbage.

Recycling is the process of changing waste into reusable materials. Recycling is important because it reduces the amount of waste sent to landfills and saves natural resources. Recycling, however, has its limitations.

Fifty-five percent of all aluminum cans are recycled. This is because recycling aluminum is cheaper than making new aluminum. Recycling aluminum cans requires less than 10 percent of the energy required to produce a new aluminum can.

Unfortunately, plastic is much more difficult to recycle than materials like aluminum, glass, or paper. Most plastic ends up in a landfill. Only a few kinds of plastic can be recycled economically.

ACTIVITY

INQUIRY SKILL **Communicate**
Interview three trusted adults.

Ask them how they disposed of their household trash when they where young. Then ask them how they dispose of their trash today. How have their actions concerning trash changed? What information helped change their actions?

Write down what they said. Summarize how their ideas changed when they learned more about recycling and the environment.

Making New Cans

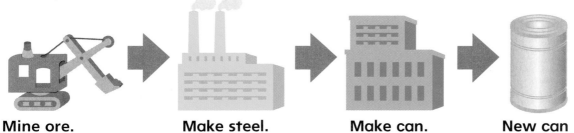

Mine ore.   Make steel.   Make can.   New can

Recycling Cans

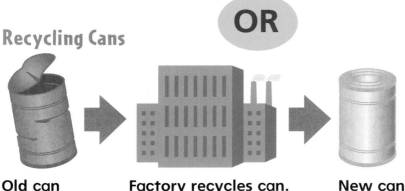

Old can   Factory recycles can.   New can

OR

Most of our plastic ends up in landfills. There it will be covered with layers of soil and remain forever. What are some ways we can save a plastic carton from being sent to the landfill?

Glossary

amphibians (am fib'ē əns) Animals that are able to live on land but must return to water to lay their eggs. (p. G 2)

aquatic (ə kwat'ik) Of or in water, a plant or animal that lives in a water environment. (p. G 8)

cold-blooded (kōld' blud'id) An animal that cannot maintain a steady body temperature. Its temperature depends upon the temperature of its surroundings. (p. G 2)

habitat (hab'i tat') The place where an animal lives. It often has characteristic plants and animals that live there. (p. G 6)

nonrenewable resource (noni'ri nü'ə bəl rē'sôrs) A resource that cannot be replaced easily. (p. G 14)

renewable resource (ri nü'ə bəl rē'sôrs) A resource that can be replaced. (p. G 12)

reptiles (rep'tīls) Animals that have scales, breathe with lungs, and lay eggs on land. (p. G 2)

terrestrial (tə res'trē əl) Of or on land, a plant or animal that lives in a land environment. (p. G 8)

vertebrates (vûr'tə brāts') Animals with backbones. (p. G 2)

Illustrations: Rita Lascaro: p. GI4; Karen Minot: p. GI.

Photography Credits:
All photographs are by Macmillan/McGraw-Hill (MMH) except as noted below:

Unit Opener: David Liebman/David Liebman Photo.

Contents: GI: (bcr) Jon Feingersh/Corbis; (bl) Joe McDonald/DRK Photo; (br) Scott W. Smith/Animals Animals; (cl) John M. Coffman/Photo Researchers, Inc.; (tcr) John Serrao/Photo Researchers, Inc.; (tl) Mary Ann McDonald/Corbis.

Unit G: G2: (bl) John Serrao/Photo Researchers, Inc. G2-G3: E.R. Degginger/Photo Researchers, Inc. G3: (br) Robert Lubeck/ Animals Animals; (t) Joe McDonald/DRK Photo. G4: (bl) E.R. Degginger/Photo Researchers, Inc.; (tcr) Breck Kent/Animals Animals; (tl) Robert J. Erwin/Photo Researchers, Inc. G5: (b) David A. Northcott/Corbis; (c) John M. Coffman/Photo Researchers, Inc.; (tr) Zig Leszczynski/Animals Animals. G6: (l) Darrell Gulin/DRK Photo; (r) Elizabeth A. Domingue. G7: (bl) Kenneth Murray/Photo Researchers, Inc.; (br) E.R. Degginger/Photo Researchers, Inc.; (tr) Zig Leszczynski/Animals Animals. G8: Scott W. Smith/Animals Animals; (bl) Suzanne L. Collins & Joseph T. Collins/Photo Researchers, Inc.; (tl) S.R. Maglione/Photo Researchers, Inc.; (tr) Breck P. Kent/Animals Animals. G9: (b) Kent P. Breck/ Animals Animals; (cr) Joe McDonald/ Corbis; (tcr) Jim Merli/Visuals Unlimited. GI0: (l) Clayton Sharrard/Photo Edit; (r) Jim Zipp/Photo Researchers, Inc. GI0-GII: (bkgd) Michael P. Gadomski/Photo Researchers, Inc. GII: (br) Michael Gadomski/Earth Scenes; (tl) Michael P. Gadomski/Photo Researchers, Inc. GI2: (b) Jon Feingersh/Corbis; (cl) A.B. Sheldon; (t) Steve Kaufman/Corbis. GI2-GI3: (t) Richard Baumer. GI3: (b) Mary Ann McDonald/Corbis. GI4-GI5: (b) Barbar Stitzer/Photo Edit.

For Your Reference

Science Handbook

Health Handbook

Units of Measurement

Units of Measurement

This bottle of juice has a volume of 1 liter.

That is a little more than 1 quart.

She can walk 20 meters in 5 seconds.

That means her speed is 4 meters per second.

Table of Measurements

International System of Units (SI)	English System of Units
Temperature Water freezes at 0°C and boils at 100°C.	**Temperature** Water freezes at 32°F and boils at 212°F.
Length and Distance 1,000 meters (m) = 1 kilometer (km) 100 centimeters (cm) = 1 meter 10 millimeters (mm) = 1 centimeter	**Length and Distance** 5,280 feet = 1 mile 3 feet = 1 yard 12 inches = 1 foot
Volume 1,000 milliliters (mL) = 1 liter (L) 1 cubic centimeter (cm³) = 1 milliliter	**Volume of Fluids** 4 quarts = 1 gallon 2 pints = 1 quart 2 cups = 1 pint 8 fluid ounces = 1 cup
Mass 1,000 grams (g) = 1 kilogram (kg)	**Weight** 2,000 pounds = 1 ton 16 ounces = 1 pound

Use a Hand Lens

You use a hand lens to magnify an object, or make the object look larger. With a hand lens, you can see details that would be hard to see without the hand lens.

Magnify a Piece of Cereal

1. Place a piece of your favorite cereal on a flat surface. Look at the cereal carefully. Draw a picture of it.
2. Look at the cereal through the large lens of a hand lens. Move the lens toward or away from the cereal until it looks larger and in focus. Draw a picture of the cereal as you see it through the hand lens. Fill in details that you did not see before.
3. Look at the cereal through the smaller lens, which will magnify the cereal even more. If you notice more details, add them to your drawing.
4. Repeat this activity using objects you are studying in science. It might be a rock, some soil, or a seed.

Observe Seeds in a Petri Dish

Can you observe a seed as it sprouts? You can if it's in a petri dish. A petri dish is a shallow, clear, round dish with a cover.

1. Line the sides and bottom of a petri dish with a double layer of filter paper or paper towel. You may have to cut the paper to make it fit.
2. Sprinkle water on the paper to wet it.
3. Place three or four radish seeds on the wet paper in different areas of the dish. Put the lid on the dish, and keep it in a warm place.
4. Observe the seeds every day for a week. Use a hand lens to look for a tiny root pushing through the seed. Record how long it takes each seed to sprout.

Use a Microscope

Hand lenses make objects look several times larger. A microscope, however, can magnify an object to look hundreds of times larger.

Examine Salt Grains

1. Look at the photograph to learn the different parts of your microscope.

2. Place the microscope on a flat surface. Always carry a microscope with both hands. Hold the arm with one hand, and put your other hand beneath the base.

3. Move the mirror so that it reflects light up toward the stage. Never point the mirror directly at the Sun or a bright light. Bright light can cause permanent eye damage.

4. Place a few grains of salt on the slide. Put the slide under the stage clips. Be sure that the salt grains you are going to examine are over the hole in the stage.

5. Look through the eyepiece. Turn the focusing knob slowly until the salt grains come into focus.

6. Draw what the grains look like through the microscope.

7. Look at other objects through the microscope. Try a piece of leaf, a human hair, or a pencil mark.

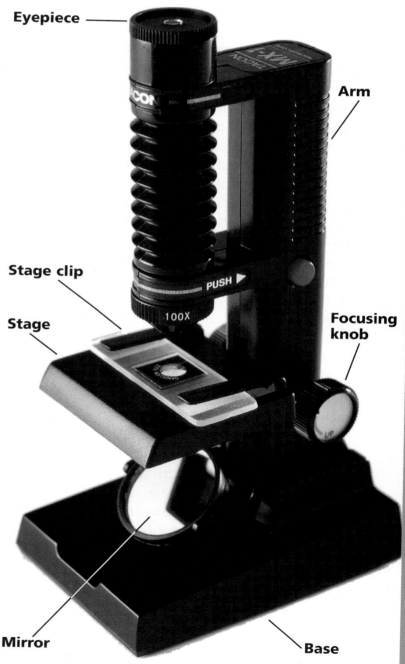

Eyepiece

Arm

Stage clip

Stage

Focusing knob

Mirror

Base

Measure Time

You use timing devices to measure how long something takes to happen. Some timing devices you use in science are a clock with a second hand and a stopwatch. Which one is more accurate?

Comparing a Clock and Stopwatch

1. Look at a clock with a second hand. The second hand is the hand that you can see moving. It measures seconds.
2. Get an egg timer with falling sand or some device like a wind-up toy that runs down after a certain length of time. When the second hand of the clock points to 12, tell your partner to start the egg timer. Watch the clock while the sand in the egg timer is falling.
3. When the sand stops falling, count how many seconds it took. Record this measurement. Repeat the activity, and compare the two measurements.
4. Switch roles with your partner.
5. Look at a stopwatch. Click the button on the top right. This starts the time. Click the button again. This stops the time. Click the button on the top left. This sets the stopwatch back to zero. Notice that the stopwatch tells time in minutes, seconds, and hundredths of a second.
6. Repeat the activity in steps 1–3, using the stopwatch instead of a clock. Make sure the stopwatch is set to zero. Click the top right button to start timing the reading. Click it again when the sand stops falling. Make sure you and your partner time each other twice.

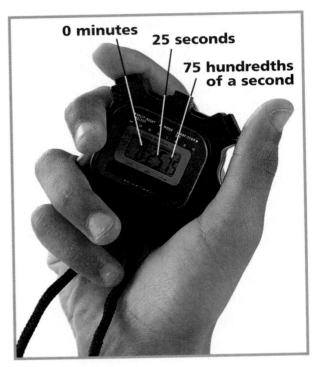

0 minutes **25 seconds** **75 hundredths of a second**

More About Time

1. Use the stopwatch to time how long it takes an ice cube to melt under cold running water. How long does an ice cube take to melt under warm running water?
2. Match each of these times with the action you think took that amount of time.

   a. 00:14:55
   b. 44:39:45
   c. 10:23:00

   1. Taking a shower
   2. Saying the Pledge of Allegiance
   3. Recess

Measure Length

Find Length with a Ruler

1. Look at this section of a ruler. Each centimeter is divided into 10 millimeters. How long is the paper clip?
2. The length of the paper clip is 3 centimeters plus 2 millimeters. You can write this length as 3.2 centimeters.
3. Place the ruler on your desk. Lay a pencil against the ruler so that one end of the pencil lines up with the left edge of the ruler. Record the length of the pencil.
4. Trade your pencil with a classmate. Measure and record the length of each other's pencil. Compare your answers.

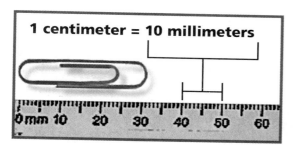

1 centimeter = 10 millimeters

Measuring Area

Area is the amount of surface something covers. To find the area of a rectangle, multiply the rectangle's length by its width. For example, the rectangle here is 3 centimeters long and 2 centimeters wide. Its area is 3 cm x 2 cm = 6 square centimeters. You write the area as 6 cm^2.

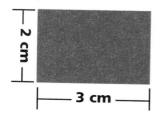

2 cm

3 cm

Opposite sides of a rectangle are parallel. The adjacent sides are perpendicular to each other (at right angles). Rectangles have symmetry. When folded in half, both halves are identical in size and shape. This is known as congruence. The two halves fit over each other exactly.

Find Length with a Meterstick

1. Line up the meterstick with the left edge of the chalkboard. Make a chalk mark on the board at the right end of the meterstick.
2. Move the meterstick so that the left edge lines up with the chalk mark. Keep the stick level. Make another mark on the board at the right end of the meterstick.
3. Continue to move the meterstick and make chalk marks until the meterstick meets or overlaps the right edge of the board.
4. Record the length of the chalkboard in centimeters by adding all the measurements you've made. Remember, a meterstick has 100 centimeters.

Estimating Length

Try estimating the length of objects in the room. Then measure the length, and compare the estimation with the measurement.

Measure Mass

Mass is the amount of matter an object has. You use a balance to measure mass. To find the mass of an object, you balance it with objects whose masses you know. Let's find the mass of a box of crayons.

Measure the Mass of a Box of Crayons

1. Place the balance on a flat, level surface. Check that the two pans are empty and clean.
2. Make sure the empty pans are balanced with each other. The pointer should point to the middle mark. If it does not, move the slider a little to the right or left to balance the pans.
3. Gently place a box of crayons on the left pan. This pan will drop lower.
4. Add masses to the right pan until the pans are balanced.
5. Add the numbers on the masses that are in the right pan. The total is the mass of the box of crayons, in grams. Record this number. After the number write a *g* for "grams."

Estimating Mass

Once you become familiar with the mass of objects, you can try estimating the masses of objects. Then you can compare the estimation with the actual mass.

More About Mass

The mass of your crayons was probably less than 100 grams. You may not have enough masses to balance a pineapple. It has a mass of about 1,000 grams. That's the same as 1 kilogram, because *kilo* means "1,000."

50   500   100   100   20   20   5   2 2 1

1. How many kilograms do all these masses add up to?
2. Which of these objects have a mass greater than 1 kilogram?

Measure Volume

Volume is the amount of space something takes up. In science you usually measure the volume of liquids by using beakers and graduated cylinders. These containers are marked in milliliters (mL).

Measure the Volume of a Liquid

1. Look at the beaker and at the graduated cylinder. The beaker has marks for each 25 mL up to 200 mL. The graduated cylinder has marks for each 1 mL up to 100 mL.
2. The surface of the water in the graduated cylinder curves up at the sides. You measure the volume by reading the height of the water at the flat part. What is the volume of water in the graduated cylinder? How much water is in the beaker? They both contain 75 mL of water.
3. Pour 50 mL of water from a pitcher into a beaker.
4. Now pour the 50 mL of water into a graduated cylinder.

Find the Volume of a Solid

Here's a way to find the volume of a solid, such as a rock.

1. Start with 50 mL of water in a graduated cylinder.
2. Place a small rock in the water. The water level rises.
3. Measure the new water level. Subtract 50 mL from the new reading. The difference is the volume of the rock. Record the volume in cm^3.

Estimating Volume

Once you become familiar with the volumes of liquids and solids, you can estimate volumes. Estimate the amount of liquid in a glass or can. Estimate the volume of an eraser.

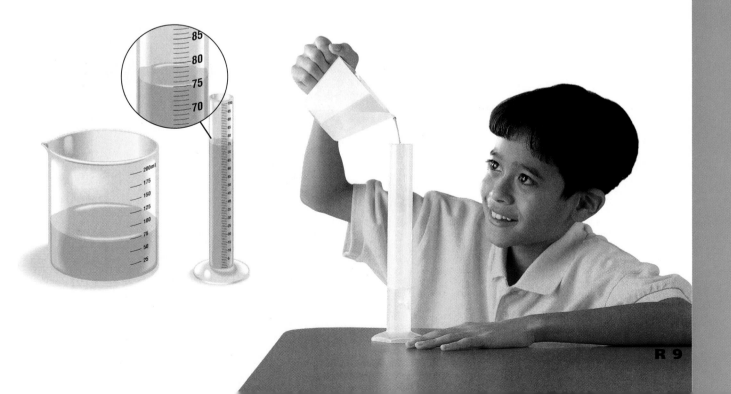

Measure Weight/Force

You use a spring scale to measure weight. An object has weight because the force of gravity pulls down on the object. Therefore, weight is a force. Weight is measured in newtons (N) like all forces.

Measure the Weight of an Object

1. Look at your spring scale to see how many newtons it measures. See how the measurements are divided. The spring scale shown here measures up to 5 N. It has a mark for every 0.1 N.

2. Hold the spring scale by the top loop. Put the object to be measured on the bottom hook. If the object will not stay on the hook, place it in a net bag. Then hang the bag from the hook.

3. Let go of the object slowly. It will pull down on a spring inside the scale. The spring is connected to a pointer. The pointer on the spring scale shown here is a small bar.

4. Wait for the pointer to stop moving. Read the number of newtons next to the pointer. This is the object's weight. The mug in the picture weighs 4 N.

More About Spring Scales

You probably weigh yourself by standing on a bathroom scale. This is a spring scale. The force of your body stretches a spring inside the scale. The dial on the scale is probably marked in pounds—the English unit of weight. One pound is equal to about 4.5 newtons.

A bathroom scale, a grocery scale, and a kitchen scale are some other spring scales you may have seen.

Measure Temperature

You use a thermometer to measure temperature—how hot or cold something is. A thermometer is made of a thin tube with colored liquid inside. When the liquid gets warmer, it expands and moves up the tube. When the liquid gets cooler, it contracts and moves down the tube. You may have seen most temperatures measured in degrees Fahrenheit (°F). Scientists measure temperature in degrees Celsius (°C).

Water boils

Water freezes

Room temperature

Read a Thermometer

1. Look at the thermometer shown here. It has two scales—a Fahrenheit scale and a Celsius scale.
2. What is the temperature shown on the thermometer? At what temperature does water freeze?

What Is Convection?

1. Fill a large beaker about two-thirds full of cool water. Find the temperature of the water by holding a thermometer in the water. Do not let the bulb at the bottom of the thermometer touch the sides or bottom of the beaker.
2. Keep the thermometer in the water until the liquid in the tube stops moving—about 1 minute. Read and record the temperature in °C.
3. Sprinkle a little fish food on the surface of the water in the beaker. Do not knock the beaker, and most of the food will stay on top.
4. Carefully place the beaker on a hot plate. A hot plate is a small electric stove. Plug in the hot plate, and turn the control knob to a middle setting.
5. After 1 minute measure the temperature of water near the bottom of the beaker. At the same time, a classmate should measure the temperature of water near the top of the beaker. Record these temperatures. Is water near the bottom of the beaker heating up faster than near the top?
6. As the water heats up, notice what happens to the fish food. How do you know that warmer water at the bottom of the beaker rises and cooler water at the top sinks?

Use Calculators

Sometimes after you make measurements, you have to analyze your data to see what it means. This might involve doing calculations with your data. A calculator helps you do time-consuming calculations.

Find an Average

After you collect a set of measurements, you may want to get an idea of a typical measurement in that set. What if, for example, you are doing a weather project? As part of the project, you are studying rainfall data of a nearby town. The table shows how much rain fell in that town each week during the summer.

Week	Rain (cm)
1	2.0
2	1.4
3	0.0
4	0.5
5	1.2
6	2.5
7	1.8
8	1.4
9	2.4
10	8.6
11	7.5

What if you want to get an idea of how much rain fell during a typical week in the summer? In other words, you want to find the average for the set of data. There are three kinds of averages—mean, median, and mode. Does it matter which one you use?

Find the Mean

The mean is what most people think of when they hear the word *average*. You can use a calculator to find the mean.

1. Make sure the calculator is on.
2. Add the numbers. To add a series of numbers, enter the first number and press ⊞. Repeat until you enter the last number. See the hints below. After your last number, press ⊟. Your total should be 29.3.
3. While entering so many numbers, it's easy to make a mistake and hit the wrong key. If you make a mistake, correct it by pressing the clear entry key, CE. Then continue entering the rest of the numbers.
4. Find the mean by dividing your total by the number of weeks. If 29.3 is displayed, press ÷ ① ① ⊟. Rounded up to one decimal point, your mean should be 2.7.

Hints:

- If the only number to the right of the decimal point is 0, you don't have to enter it into the calculator. To enter 2.0, just press ②.
- If the only number to the left of the decimal point is 0, you don't have to enter it into the calculator. To enter 0.5, just press ．⑤.

Use Technology

Find the Median

The median is the middle number when the numbers are arranged in order of size. When the rainfall measurements are arranged in order of size, they look like this.

0.0
0.5
1.2
1.4
1.4
1.8 ——— The median is 1.8. This number is in the middle; there are five numbers above it and five numbers below it.
2.0
2.4
2.5
7.5
8.6

Find the Mode

The mode is the number that occurs most frequently. From the ranked set of data above, you can see that the most frequent number is 1.4. It occurs twice. Here are your three different averages from the same set of data.

Average Weekly Rainfall (cm)

Mean	2.7
Median	1.8
Mode	1.4

Why is the mean so much higher than the median or mode? The mean is affected greatly by the last two weeks when it rained a lot. A typical week for that summer was much drier than either of those last two weeks. The median or mode gives a better idea of rainfall for a typical week.

Find the Percent

Sometimes numbers are given as percents (%). *Percent* literally means "per hundred." For example, 28% means 28 out of 100. What if there are about 14,000 trees in the forest and 28% are over 50 years old? How many of them are over 50 years old? Use your calculator. You want to find 28% of 14,000. Press $\boxed{1}\boxed{4}\boxed{0}\boxed{0}\boxed{0}$ $\boxed{\times}$ $\boxed{2}\boxed{8}\boxed{\%}$. The answer should be 3,920.

Mathematical Operations

Addition and subtraction are reverse operations, or inverses of each other. For example:

$2 + 3 = 5$;
$5 - 3 = 2$;
$5 - 2 = 3$.

Similarly, multiplication and division are also inverses of each other. For example:

$6 \times 3 = 18$;
$18 \div 6 = 3$;
$18 \div 3 = 6$.

Mathematical Statements

Mathematical statements using symbols may be true only when the symbols are replaced by certain numbers. For example:

$A < B$

If $A = 2$ and $B = 3$, the statement is true.
If $A = 3$ and $B = 2$, the statement is false.

Use Computers

A computer has many uses. The Internet connects your computer to many other computers around the world, so you can collect all kinds of information. You can use a computer to show this information and write reports. Best of all you can use a computer to explore, discover, and learn.

You can also get information from CD-ROMs. They are computer disks that can hold large amounts of information. You can fit a whole encyclopedia on one CD-ROM.

Use Computers for a Project

Here is how one group of students uses computers as they work on a weather project.

1. The students use instruments to measure temperature, wind speed, wind direction, and other parts of the weather. They input this information, or data, into the computer. The students keep the data in a table. This helps them compare the data from one day to the next.

Use Technology

2. The teacher finds out that another group of students in a town 200 kilometers to the west is also doing a weather project. The two groups use the Internet to talk to each other and share data. When a storm happens in the town to the west, that group tells the other group that it's coming their way.

3. The students want to find out more. They decide to stay on the Internet and send questions to a local TV weather forecaster. She has a Web site and answers questions from students every day.

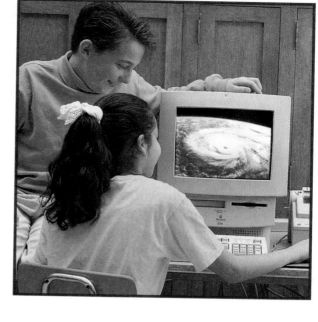

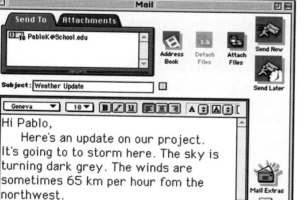

4. Meanwhile some students go to the library to gather more information from a CD-ROM. The CD-ROM has an encyclopedia that includes movie clips. The clips give examples of different kinds of storms.

5. The students have kept all their information in a folder called Weather Project. Now they use that information to write a report about the weather. On the computer they can move around paragraphs, add words, take out words, put in diagrams, and draw weather maps. Then they print the report in color.

Make Graphs to Organize Data

When you do an experiment in science, you collect information. To find out what your information means, you can organize it into graphs. There are many kinds of graphs.

Bar Graphs

A bar graph uses bars to show information. For example, what if you do an experiment by wrapping wire around a nail and connecting the ends of the wire to a battery? The nail then becomes a magnet that can pick up paper clips. The graph shows that the more you wrap the wire around the nail, the more paper clips it picks up. How many paper clips did the nail with 20 coils pick up? With 50 coils?

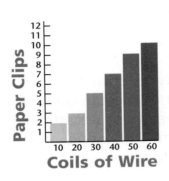

Pictographs

A pictograph uses symbols, or pictures, to show information. What if you collect information about how much water your family uses each day? The table shows what you find.

You can organize this information into the pictograph shown here. The pictograph has to explain what the symbol on the graph means. In this case each bottle means 20 liters of water. A half bottle means half of 20, or 10 liters of water.

1. Which activity uses the most water?
2. Which activity uses the least water?

Activity	Water Used Each Day (L)
Drinking	10
Showering	180
Bathing	240
Brushing teeth	80
Washing dishes	140
Washing hands	30
Washing clothes	280
Flushing toilet	90

A Family's Daily Use of Water

= 20 liters of water

Drinking
Showering
Bathing
Brushing teeth
Washing dishes
Washing hands
Washing clothes
Flushing toilet

Represent Data

Circle Graphs

A circle graph is helpful to show how a complete set of data is divided into parts. The circle graph here shows how water is used in the United States. What is the single largest use of water?

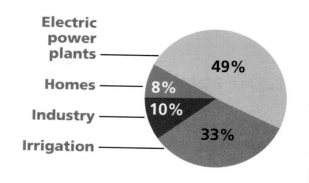

Electric power plants — 49%
Homes — 8%
Industry — 10%
Irrigation — 33%

Line Graphs

A line graph shows information by connecting dots plotted on the graph. It shows change over time. For example, what if you measure the temperature out of doors every hour starting at 6 A.M.? The table shows what you find.

Time	Temperature (°C)
6 A.M.	10
7 A.M.	12
8 A.M.	14
9 A.M.	16
10 A.M.	18
11 A.M.	20

You can organize this information into a line graph. Follow these steps.

1. Make a scale along the bottom and side of the graph. The scales should include all the numbers in the chart. Label the scales.
2. Plot points on the graph. For example, place your finger at the "6 A.M." on the bottom line. Place a finger from your other hand on the "10" on the left line. Move your "6 A.M." finger up and your "10" finger to the right until they meet, and make a pencil point. Plot the other points in this way.
3. Connect the points with a line.

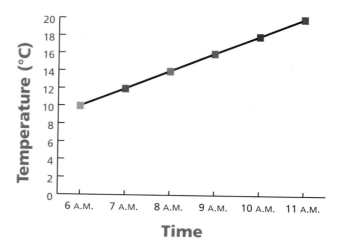

The line graph to the right organizes measurements you collected so that you can easily compare them.

1. Between which two weeks did the plant grow most?
2. When did plant growth begin to level off?

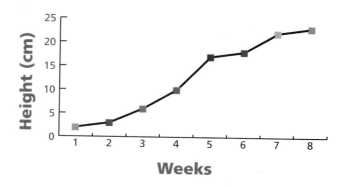

Represent Data

Make Maps to Show Information

Locate Places

A map is a drawing that shows an area from above. Most maps have coordinates—numbers and letters along the top and side. Coordinates help you find places easily. For example, what if you wanted to find the library on the map? It is located at B4. Place a finger on the letter B along the side of the map, and another finger on the number 4 at the top. Then move your fingers straight across and down the map until they meet. The library is located where the coordinates B and 4 meet, or very nearby.

1. What color building is located at F6?
2. The hospital is located three blocks north and two blocks east of the library. What are its coordinates?
3. Make a map of an area in your community. It might be a park or the area between your home and school. Include coordinates. Use a compass to find north, and mark north on your map. Exchange maps with classmates, and answer each other's questions.

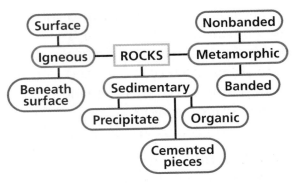

Idea Maps

The map below shows how places are connected to each other. Idea maps, on the other hand, show how ideas are connected to each other. Idea maps help you organize information about a topic.

The idea map above connects ideas about rocks. This map shows that there are three major types of rock—igneous, sedimentary, and metamorphic. Connections to each rock type provide further information. For example, this map reminds you that igneous rocks are classified into those that form at Earth's surface and far beneath it.

Make an idea map about a topic you are learning in science. Your map can include words, phrases, or even sentences. Arrange your map in a way that makes sense to you and helps you understand the ideas.

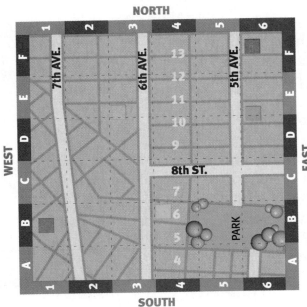

Make Tables and Charts to Organize Information

Tables help you organize data during experiments. Most tables have columns that run up and down, and rows that run across. The columns and rows have headings that tell you what kind of data goes in each part of the table.

A Sample Table

What if you are going to do an experiment to find out how long different kinds of seeds take to sprout? Before you begin the experiment, you should set up your table. Follow these steps.

1. In this experiment you will plant 20 radish seeds, 20 bean seeds, and 20 corn seeds. Your table must show how many radish seeds, bean seeds, and corn seeds sprouted on days 1, 2, 3, 4, and 5.

2. Make your table with columns, rows, and headings. You might use a computer to make a table. Some computer programs let you build a table with just the click of a mouse. You can delete or add columns and rows if you need to.

3. Give your table a title. Your table could look like the one here.

Make a Table

Now what if you are going to do an experiment to find out how temperature affects the sprouting of seeds? You will plant 20 bean seeds in each of two trays. You will keep each tray at a different temperature, as shown below, and observe the trays for seven days. Make a table you can use for this experiment.

Make a Chart

A chart is simply a table with pictures as well as words to label the rows or columns.

The Human Body

Like all organisms, humans are made up of cells. In fact, the human body is made of trillions of cells. These cells are organized into tissues, a group of similar cells that perform a specific function. Tissues, in turn, form organs. Your heart and lungs are examples of organs. Finally, organs work together as part of organ systems. Your heart, for example, is part of the circulatory system.

Levels of Organization

- Cells
- Tissues
- Organs
- Organ Systems
- Organism

Including the skin, or integumentary system, the human body has 11 major organ systems. These body systems each have specific functions, and they also work together as parts of the human body as a whole.

Human Body Systems	
System	**Function**
Nervous System	control
Skeletal System	support
Integumentary System	protection
Muscular System	movement
Circulatory System	transport
Respiratory System	oxygen/ carbon dioxide exchange
Digestive System	food absorption
Excretory System	waste removal
Endocrine System	regulation and control
Reproductive System	reproduction
Immune System	protection

The Nervous System

The nervous system has two parts. The brain and the spinal cord are the central nervous system. All other nerves are the outer, or peripheral, nervous system.

The largest part of the brain is the cerebrum. A deep groove separates the right half, or hemisphere, of the cerebrum from the left half. Both the right and left hemispheres of the cerebrum contain control centers for the senses.

The cerebellum lies below the cerebrum. It coordinates the skeletal muscles so they work smoothly together. It also helps in keeping balance.

The brain stem connects to the spinal cord. The lowest part of the brain stem is the medulla. It controls heartbeat, breathing, blood pressure, and the muscles in the digestive system.

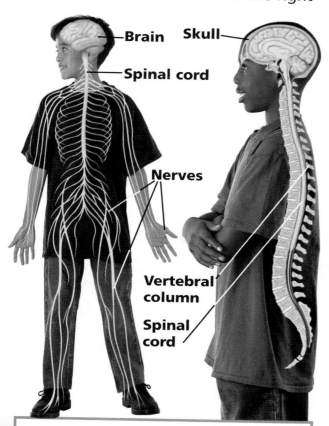

Brain
Skull
Spinal cord
Nerves
Vertebral column
Spinal cord

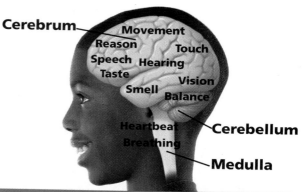

Cerebrum
Movement
Reason
Touch
Speech Hearing
Taste
Vision
Smell
Balance
Heartbeat
Breathing
Cerebellum
Medulla

CARE!

- Wear protective headgear when you play sports or exercise.

- Stay away from drugs, such as stimulants, which can speed up the nervous system.

- Stay away from alcohol, which is a depressant and slows down the nervous system.

Parts of a Neuron

The nerves in the nervous system are made up of nerve cells called *neurons.* Each neuron has three main parts—a cell body, dendrites, and an axon. Dendrites are branching nerve fibers that carry impulses, or electrical signals, toward the cell body. An axon is a nerve fiber that carries impulses away from the cell body.

When an impulse reaches the tip of an axon, it must cross a tiny gap to reach the next neuron. This gap between neurons is called a *synapse.*

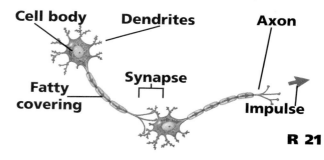

Cell body
Dendrites
Axon
Synapse
Fatty covering
Impulse

R 21

The Senses

Seeing

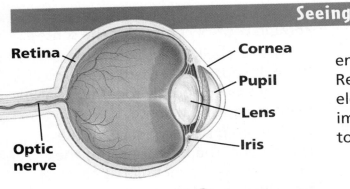

Retina
Cornea
Pupil
Lens
Iris
Optic nerve

Light reflected from an object enters the eye and falls on the retina. Receptor cells change the light into electrical signals, or impulses. These impulses travel along the optic nerve to the vision center of the brain.

1 Light reflects off the tree and into your eyes.

4 Receptor cells on your retina change the light into electrical signals.

2 The light passes through your cornea and the pupil in your iris.

3 Your eye bends the light so it hits your retina.

5 The impulses travel along neurons in your optic nerve to the seeing center of your brain.

Hearing

Sound waves enter the ear and cause the eardrum to vibrate. Receptor cells in the ear change the sound waves into impulses that travel along the auditory nerve to the hearing center of the brain.

1 Your outer ear collects sound waves.

6 Receptor cells inside your cochlea change.

Hammer
Anvil
Stirrup
Cochlea
Auditory nerve
Semicircular canals

2 They are funneled down your ear canal.

3 The eardrum vibrates.

4 Three tiny ear bones vibrate.

5 The cochlea vibrates.

Hearing center

7 The impulses travel along your auditory nerve to the brain's hearing center.

CARE!

- To avoid straining your eye muscles, don't sit too close to the TV screen or computer monitor.

- Avoid loud music. Turn down the volume when wearing headphones.

The Senses

Smelling

The sense of smell is really the ability to detect chemicals in the air. When a person breathes, chemicals dissolve in mucus in the upper part of the nose. When the chemicals come in contact with receptor cells, the cells send impulses along the olfactory nerve to the smelling center of the brain.

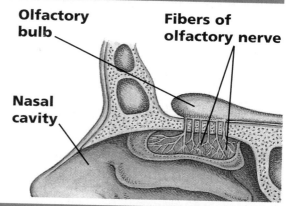

Olfactory bulb

Fibers of olfactory nerve

Nasal cavity

Tasting

When a person eats, chemicals in food dissolve in saliva. Saliva carries the chemicals to taste buds on the tongue. Inside each taste bud are receptors that can sense the four main tastes—sweet, sour, salty, and bitter. The receptors send impulses along a nerve to the taste center of the brain. The brain identifies the taste of the food, which is usually a combination of the four main tastes.

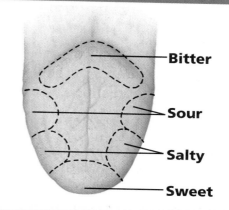

Bitter

Sour

Salty

Sweet

Touching

Receptor cells in the skin help a person tell hot from cold, wet from dry, and the light touch of a feather from the pressure of stepping on a stone. Each receptor cell sends impulses along sensory nerves to the spinal cord. The spinal cord then sends the impulses to the touch center of the brain.

CARE!

- To prevent the spread of germs, always cover your mouth and nose when you cough or sneeze.

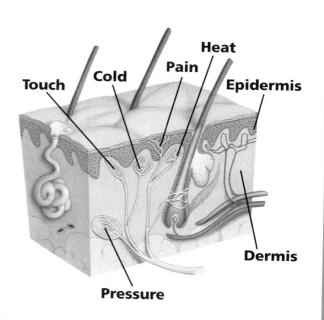

Touch Cold Pain Heat

Epidermis

Dermis

Pressure

The Skeletal System

The body has a supporting frame, called a skeleton, which is made up of bones. The skeleton has several jobs.

- It gives the body its shape.
- It protects organs in the body.
- It works with muscles to move the body.

Each of the 206 bones of the skeleton is the size and shape best fitted to do its job. For example, long and strong leg bones support the body's weight.

CARE!

- Exercise to keep your skeletal system in good shape.
- Don't overextend your joints.
- Eat foods rich in vitamins and minerals. Your bones need the minerals, calcium, and phosphorus to grow strong.

The Integumentary System

The skeleton and the organ systems are covered by an outer layer of skin. The skin is the largest organ of the human body. It is part of the integumentary system. Other parts of the integumentary system are your hair, nails, and glands in the skin. The skin has several functions.

- It protects your internal organs.
- It protects your body from injury and infection.
- It helps regulate body temperature.
- It helps remove wastes.

The Skeleton

Skull
Clavicle
Sternum
Humerus
Rib
Pelvis
Radius
Ulna
Vertebral column
Patella
Femur
Tibia
Fibula

Joints

The skeleton has different types of joints. A joint is a place where two or more bones meet. Joints can be classified into three major groups—immovable joints, partly movable joints, and movable joints.

Types of Joints

Immovable Joints

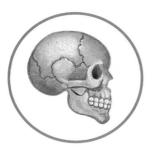

Head

Immovable joints are places where bones fit together too tightly to move. Nearly all the 29 bones in the skull meet at immovable joints. Only the lower jaw can move.

Partly Movable Joints

Partly movable joints are places where bones can move only a little. Ribs are connected to the sternum, or breastbone, with these joints.

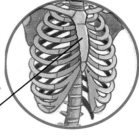

Sternum   **Ribs**

Movable Joints

Movable joints are places where bones can move easily.

Gliding joint

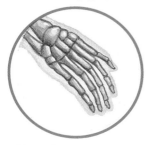

Hand and wrist

Small bones in the wrists and ankles meet at gliding joints. The bones can slide against one another. These joints allow some movement in all directions.

The hips are examples of ball-and-socket joints. The ball of one bone fits into the socket, or cup, of another bone. These joints allow bones to move back and forth, in a circle, and side to side.

Ball-and-socket joint

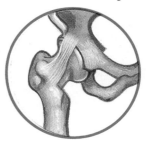

Hip

Hinge joint

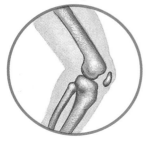

Knee

The knees are hinge joints. A hinge joint is similar to a door hinge. It allows bones to move back and forth in one direction.

The joint between the skull and neck is a pivot joint. It allows the head to move up and down, and side to side.

Pivot joint

Neck

R 25

The Muscular System

Three types of muscles make up the body—skeletal muscle, cardiac muscle, and smooth muscle.

The muscles that are attached to and move bones are called *skeletal muscles*. These muscles are attached to bones by a tough cord called a *tendon*. Skeletal muscles pull bones to move them. Muscles do not push bones.

Cardiac muscles are found in only one place in the body—the heart. The walls of the heart are made of strong cardiac muscles. When cardiac muscles contract, they squeeze blood out of the heart. When cardiac muscles relax, the heart fills with more blood.

Smooth muscles make up internal organs and blood vessels. Smooth muscles in the lungs help a person breathe. Those in the blood vessels help control blood flow around the body.

CARE!

- **Exercise to strengthen your muscles.**
- **Eat the right foods.**
- **Get plenty of rest.**
- **Never take steroids unless your doctor tells you to.**

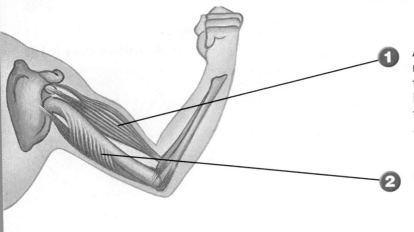

1 A message from your brain causes this muscle, called the biceps (BIGH·seps), to contract. When a muscle contracts, it becomes shorter and thicker. As the biceps contracts, it pulls on the arm bone it is attached to.

2 Most muscles work in pairs to move bones. This muscle, called the triceps (TRIGH·seps), relaxes when the biceps contracts. When a muscle relaxes, it becomes longer and thinner.

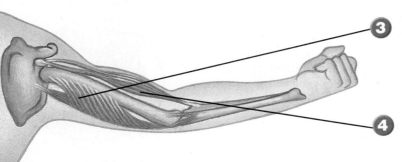

3 To straighten your arm, a message from your brain causes the triceps to contract. When the triceps contracts, it pulls on the bone it is attached to.

4 As the triceps contracts, the biceps relaxes. Your arm straightens.

Stimulus and Response

The nervous system, the skeletal system, and the muscular system work together to help you adjust to your surroundings. Anything in the environment that requires your body to adjust is called a *stimulus* (plural: stimuli). A reaction to a stimulus is called a *response*.

As you learned, nerve cells are called *neurons.* There are three kinds of neurons: sensory, associative, and motor. Each kind does a different job to help your body respond to stimuli.

- The job of your sensory neurons is to collect information from stimuli and send it to your brain and spinal cord. When you touch a sharp tack, sensory neurons alert your brain. The sensory neurons carry the message that your finger has touched a tack (stimulus) to the associative neurons in the brain and spinal cord.
- Associative neurons pass impulses from sensory to motor neurons. The message is interpreted and sent to the motor neurons.
- Motor neurons carry impulses from your brain and spinal cord to your muscles. The motor neurons cause your finger to move away from the tack (response).

In addition to responding to external stimuli, your body also responds to internal changes. Your body regulates its internal environment to maintain a stable condition for survival. This is called a *steady-state* condition.

Nerve Response

Nerves respond to a sharp object.

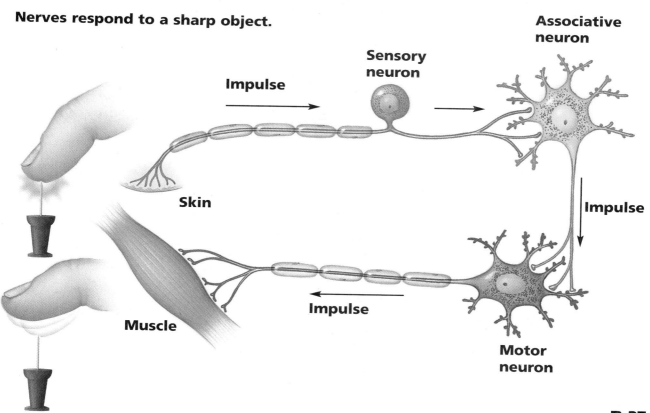

Impulse

Skin

Sensory neuron

Associative neuron

Impulse

Muscle

Impulse

Motor neuron

The Circulatory System

The circulatory system consists of the heart, blood vessels, and blood. Circulation is the flow of blood through the body. Blood is a liquid that contains red blood cells, white blood cells, and platelets. Red blood cells carry oxygen and nutrients to cells. White blood cells work to fight germs that enter the body. Platelets are cell fragments that make the blood clot.

The heart is a muscular organ about the size of a fist. It beats about 70 to 90 times a minute, pumping blood through the blood vessels. Arteries carry blood away from the heart. Some arteries carry blood to the lungs, where the cells pick up oxygen. Other arteries carry oxygen-rich blood from the lungs to all other parts of the body. Veins carry blood from other parts of the body back to the heart. Blood in most veins carries the wastes released by cells and has little oxygen. Blood flows from arteries to veins through narrow vessels called capillaries.

Pulse Rate and Pulse Points

You can tell how fast your heart is beating by checking your *pulse rate*. Take your pulse by putting the first and second fingers of one hand on the inside of the wrist of the other hand, just below the thumb. What you feel is the blood being pumped by your heart through arteries that lie close to the surface of the skin. Count the number of times you feel your heart pump in one minute. This is your pulse rate.

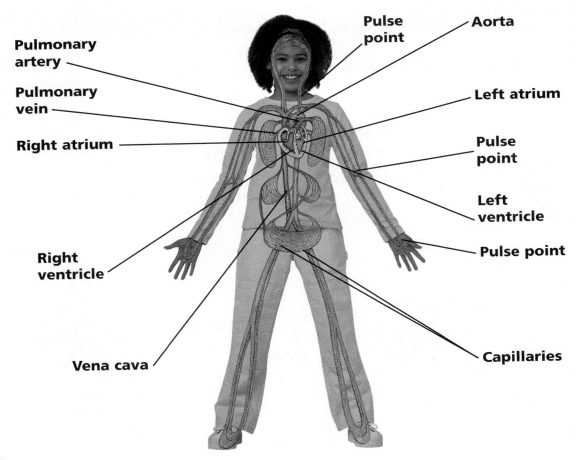

Pulmonary artery

Pulmonary vein

Right atrium

Right ventricle

Vena cava

Pulse point

Aorta

Left atrium

Pulse point

Left ventricle

Pulse point

Capillaries

The Heart

The heart has two sides, right and left, separated by a thick muscular wall. Each side has two chambers for blood. The upper chamber is the atrium. The lower chamber is the ventricle. Blood enters the heart through the vena cava. It leaves the heart through the aorta.

The pulmonary artery carries blood from the body into the lungs. Here carbon dioxide leaves the blood to be exhaled by the lungs. Fresh oxygen enters the blood to be carried to every cell in the body. Blood returns from the lungs to the heart through the pulmonary veins.

CARE!

- Don't smoke. The nicotine in tobacco makes the heart beat faster and work harder to pump blood.

- Never take illegal drugs, such as cocaine or heroin. They can damage the heart and cause heart failure.

How the Heart Works

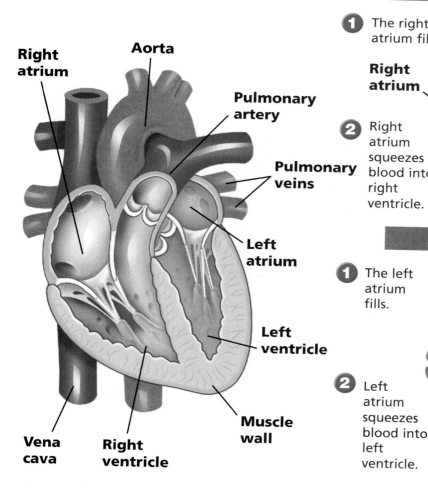

Right atrium

Aorta

Pulmonary artery

Pulmonary veins

Left atrium

Left ventricle

Muscle wall

Vena cava

Right ventricle

To the Lungs

1 The right atrium fills.

Right atrium

2 Right atrium squeezes blood into right ventricle.

3 Right ventricle squeezes blood into pulmonary artery.

One-way valve

Right ventricle

From the Lungs

1 The left atrium fills.

2 Left atrium squeezes blood into left ventricle.

3 Left ventricle squeezes blood into aorta.

Left atrium

One-way valve

Left ventricle

The Respiratory System

The process of getting and using oxygen in the body is called respiration. When a person inhales, air is pulled into the nose or mouth. The air travels down into the trachea. In the chest the trachea divides into two bronchial tubes. One bronchial tube enters each lung. Each bronchial tube branches into smaller tubes called bronchioles.

At the end of each bronchiole are tiny air sacs called alveoli. The alveoli exchange carbon dioxide for oxygen.

Oxygen comes from the air a person breathes. Two main muscles control breathing. One is located between the ribs. The other is a dome-shaped sheet of muscle called the diaphragm.

To inhale, the diaphragm contracts and pulls down. Other muscles pull the ribs up and out. This makes more room in the chest. Air rushes into the lungs and fills the space.

To exhale, the diaphragm relaxes and returns to its dome shape. The lungs get smaller and force the air out.

CARE!

- **Don't smoke. Smoking damages your respiratory system.**
- **Exercise to strengthen your breathing muscles.**
- **If you ever have trouble breathing, tell an adult at once.**

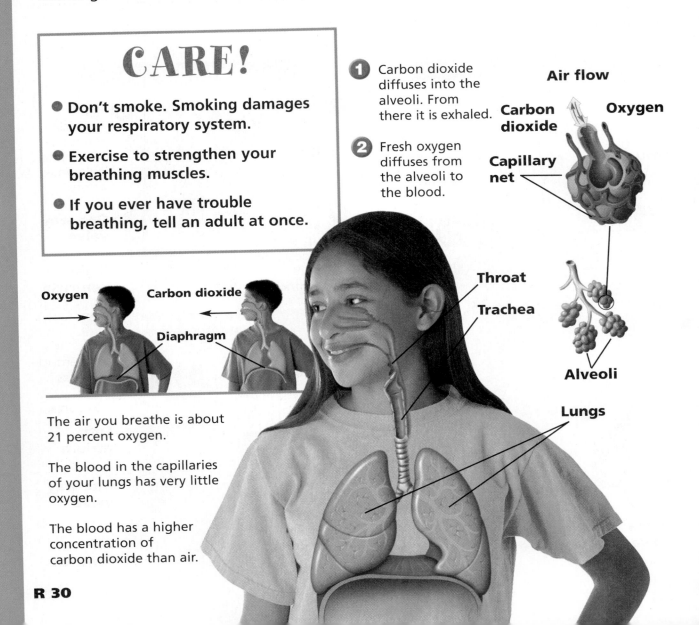

① Carbon dioxide diffuses into the alveoli. From there it is exhaled.

② Fresh oxygen diffuses from the alveoli to the blood.

Air flow

Carbon dioxide   **Oxygen**

Capillary net

Throat

Trachea

Alveoli

Lungs

Oxygen   Carbon dioxide

Diaphragm

The air you breathe is about 21 percent oxygen.

The blood in the capillaries of your lungs has very little oxygen.

The blood has a higher concentration of carbon dioxide than air.

Effects of Exercise

Any type of exercise uses your muscles. When you exercise, your muscles need three things:

- They need oxygen.
- They need to remove wastes.
- They need to get rid of heat.

When you exercise, several things happen to your body. Your heart beats faster, you breathe heavier and faster, and you sweat.

If you are going to be exercising for more than a couple of minutes, your body needs to get oxygen to the muscles or the muscles will stop working. Your body increases the flow of oxygen-rich blood to working muscle as follows:

- Your rate and depth of breathing increase to take in more oxygen.
- Your heart beats faster so that it can pump more oxygen-rich blood to the muscles.

Sweating helps remove both wastes and heat that result from exercise.

The Digestive System

Digestion is the process of breaking down food into simple substances the body can use. Digestion begins when a person chews food. Chewing breaks the food down into smaller pieces and moistens it with saliva. Saliva is produced by the salivary glands.

Digested food is absorbed in the small intestine. The walls of the small intestine are lined with villi. Villi are tiny fingerlike projections that absorb digested food. From the villi the blood transports nutrients to every part of the body.

The shape of the small intestine's villi increases the amount of nutrients that can be absorbed from the food.

CARE!

● Chew your food well.

● Drink plenty of water to help move food through your digestive system.

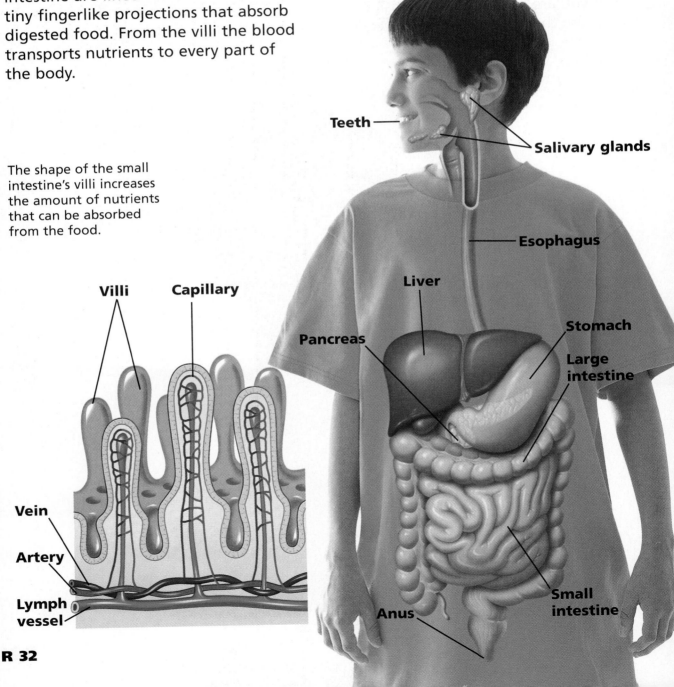

Teeth

Salivary glands

Esophagus

Liver

Stomach

Pancreas

Large intestine

Villi

Capillary

Vein

Artery

Lymph vessel

Anus

Small intestine

The Digestive System

Mechanical and Chemical Digestion

Digestion is both mechanical and chemical. Chewing is the first step in digestion. Chewing is *mechanical digestion*, the physical process of breaking food down into smaller pieces. As you chew, saliva begins to break the food into simpler molecules. This is *chemical digestion*.

After you swallow your food, both mechanical and chemical digestion continue in the stomach. Stomach muscles churn food particles into smaller pieces. Glands lining the stomach produce strong digestive juices.

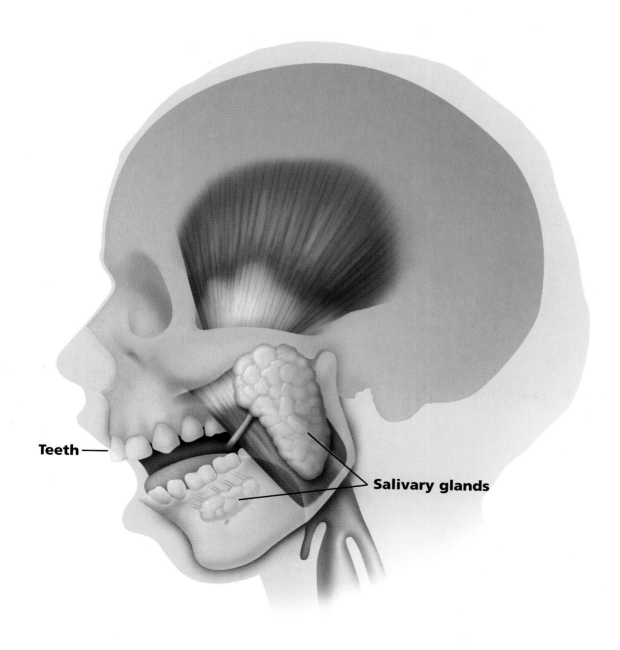

Teeth

Salivary glands

The Excretory System

Excretion is the process of removing waste products from the body. The liver filters wastes from the blood and converts them into urea. Urea is then carried to the kidneys for excretion. Each kidney contains more than a million nephrons. Nephrons are structures in the kidneys that filter blood.

The skin takes part in excretion when a person sweats. Glands in the inner layer of the skin produce sweat. Sweat is mostly water. Sweat tastes salty because it contains mineral salts the body doesn't need. There is also a tiny amount of urea in sweat.

Sweat is excreted by the sweat glands onto the outer layer of the skin. There it evaporates into the air. Evaporation takes place in part because of body heat. When sweat evaporates, a person feels cooler. On hot days or when exercising, a person sweats more to keep the body from overheating.

How You Sweat

Glands under your skin push sweat up to the surface, where it collects.

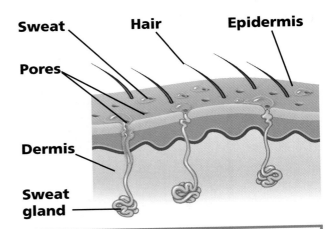

Sweat Hair Epidermis
Pores
Dermis
Sweat gland

How Your Kidneys Work

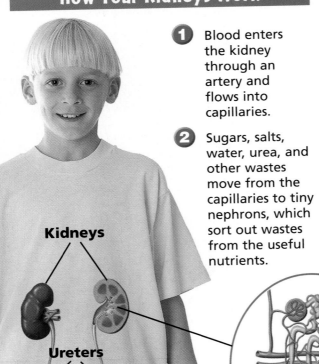

Kidneys
Ureters
Bladder
Urethra

1. Blood enters the kidney through an artery and flows into capillaries.

2. Sugars, salts, water, urea, and other wastes move from the capillaries to tiny nephrons, which sort out wastes from the useful nutrients.

CARE!

- Drink plenty of water to help the kidneys do their job and to replace water loss from sweating.

- Wash regularly to avoid body odor, clogged pores, and skin irritation.

3. The nutrients return to the blood and flow back out through veins.

4. Urea and other wastes become urine, which flows down the ureters.

5. Urine is stored in the bladder and excreted through the urethra.

Artery
Vein
Capillaries

The Excretory System

Removing Excess Heat

In addition to waste removal, one of the skin's most important jobs is to maintain internal body temperature. The skin does this by removing excess heat. Two things happen when you exercise: your face gets red and you sweat. Both are ways of getting rid of excess heat.

The nervous system, the circulatory system, and the skin all work together to regulate body temperature. The diagram below shows what happens when your body heats up as a result of exercise.

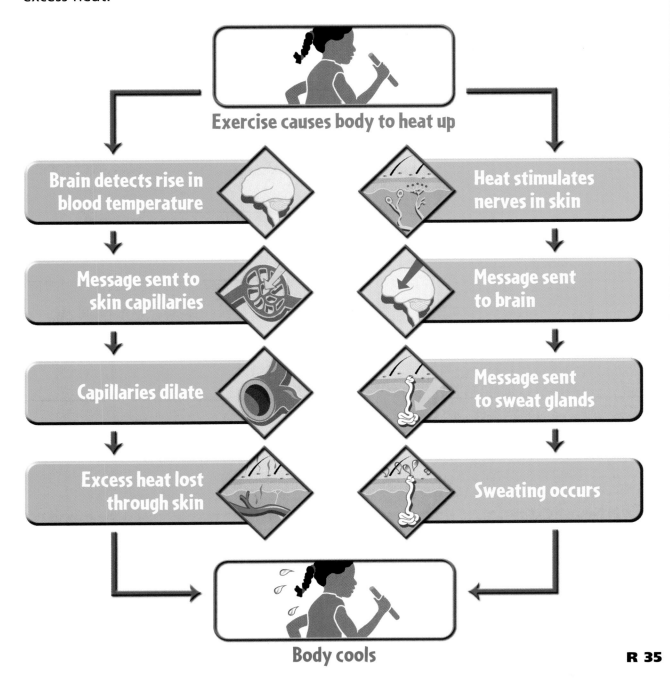

Exercise causes body to heat up

Brain detects rise in blood temperature

Heat stimulates nerves in skin

Message sent to skin capillaries

Message sent to brain

Capillaries dilate

Message sent to sweat glands

Excess heat lost through skin

Sweating occurs

Body cools

The Endocrine System

Hormones are chemicals that control body functions. A gland that produces hormones is called an endocrine gland. Sweat from sweat glands flows out of tubes called ducts. Endocrine glands have no ducts.

The endocrine glands are scattered around the body. Each gland makes one or more hormones. Every hormone seeks out a target organ, the place in the body where the hormone acts.

The endocrine glands help to maintain a *steady-state* condition in your body. They can turn the production of hormones on or off when they sense that too little or too much is being produced.

CARE!

- Doctors can treat many diseases, such as diabetes, caused by endocrine glands that produce too little or too much of a hormone.

Some Glands in the Endocrine System

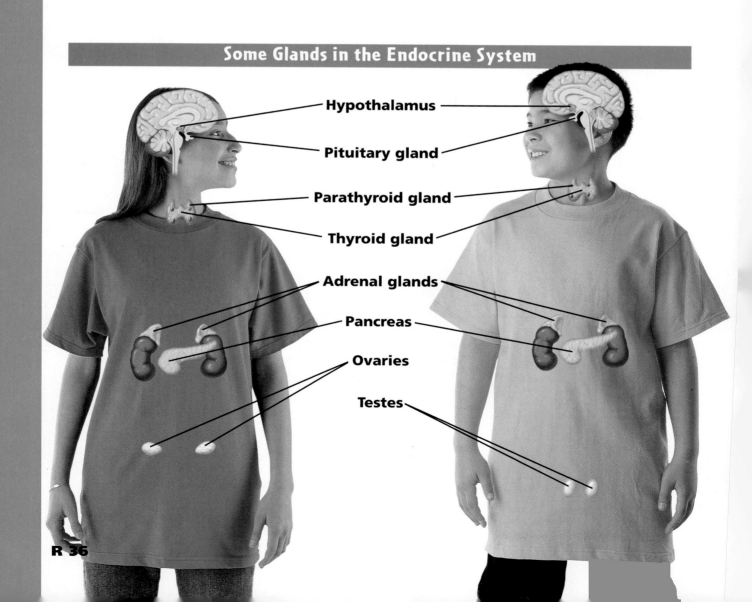

Hypothalamus

Pituitary gland

Parathyroid gland

Thyroid gland

Adrenal glands

Pancreas

Ovaries

Testes

The Reproductive System

The testes are the male reproductive organs. At puberty the testes begin to produce sperm. Sperm move through sperm ducts, where they mix with fluid from endocrine glands.

The ovaries are the female reproductive organs, which contain eggs. After puberty one mature egg is released about once every 28 days. The egg moves to the oviduct, a narrow tube leading from the ovary.

The Male Reproductive System

Sperm move from the testes through sperm ducts, where they mix with fluid from the glands. The sperm and fluid move through the urethra.

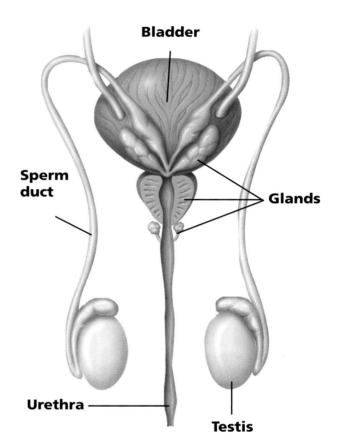

Bladder

Sperm duct

Glands

Urethra

Testis

CARE!

- **Abstinence is the only sure way to avoid sexually transmitted diseases.**

The Female Reproductive System

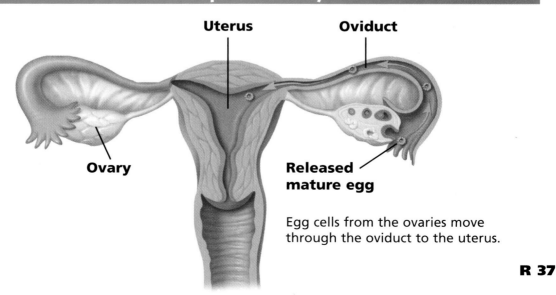

Uterus

Oviduct

Ovary

Released mature egg

Egg cells from the ovaries move through the oviduct to the uterus.

The Immune System

The immune system helps the body fight disease. Inside some bones is a soft tissue known as red marrow that fills the spaces in spongy bone. Red marrow makes new red blood cells, platelets that stop a cut from bleeding, and germ-fighting white blood cells.

There are white blood cells in the blood vessels and in the lymph vessels. Lymph vessels are similar to blood vessels. Instead of blood, they carry lymph. Lymph is a straw-colored fluid surrounding body cells.

Lymph nodes filter out harmful materials in lymph. Like red marrow, they also produce white blood cells to fight infections. Swollen lymph nodes in the neck are a clue that the body is fighting germs.

CARE!

- **Be sure to get immunized against common diseases.**
- **Keep cuts clean to prevent infection.**

1 A bone is covered with a tough but thin membrane that has many small blood vessels. The blood vessels bring nutrients and oxygen to the living parts of the bone and remove wastes.

2 Inside some bones is a soft tissue known as marrow. Yellow marrow is made mostly of fat cells and is one of the body's energy reserves. It is usually found in the long, hollow spaces of long bones.

3 Part of the bone is compact, or solid. It is made up of living bone cells and nonliving materials. The nonliving part is made up of layers of hardened minerals such as calcium and phosphorus. In between the mineral layers are living bone cells.

4 Red marrow fills the spaces in spongy bone. Red marrow makes new red blood cells, germ-fighting white blood cells, and platelets that stop a cut from bleeding.

5 Part of the bone is made of bone tissue that looks like a dry sponge. It is made of strong, hard tubes. It is also found in the middle of short, flat bones.

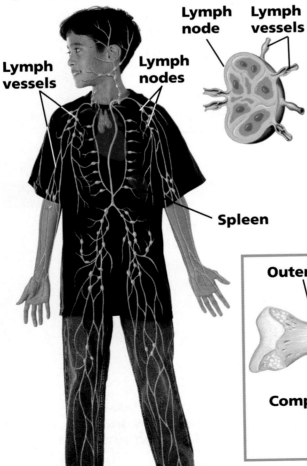

Lymph node

Lymph vessels

Lymph vessels

Lymph nodes

Spleen

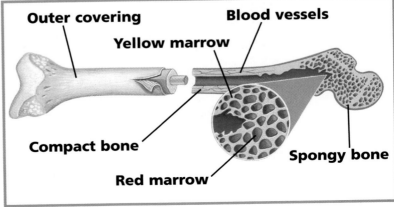

Outer covering

Blood vessels

Yellow marrow

Compact bone

Spongy bone

Red marrow

Infectious Diseases

A disease is anything that breaks down the normal functions of the body. Some diseases are inherited. Others are caused by harmful materials in the environment. Many diseases, however, are caused by organisms.

Disease-causing organisms include bacteria and viruses. Diseases caused by these organisms are called *infectious diseases* because the organisms enter, or infect, the body.

Human Infectious Diseases		
Disease	**Caused by**	**Organ System Affected**
Chicken pox	Virus	Skin
Smallpox	Virus	Skin
Polio	Virus	Nervous system
Rabies	Virus	Nervous system
Influenza	Virus	Respiratory system
Measles	Virus	Skin
Mumps	Virus	Salivary glands
Tuberculosis	Bacteria	Respiratory system
Tetanus	Bacteria	Nervous system
Food poisoning	Bacteria	Digestive system

White blood cells are your body's main protection against infectious disease. The white blood cells leave the blood vessels or lymph vessels to fight disease organisms in your tissues.

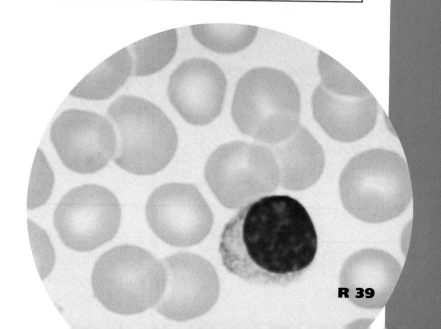

Staying Healthy

Physical fitness is the condition in which the body is healthy and works the best it can. It involves working the skeletal muscles, bones, joints, heart, and respiratory system.

Occasionally
Inactive pastimes such as watching TV

2–3 times a week
Leisure activities such as gardening, golf, softball

3–5 times a week Aerobic activities such as swimming; sports activities such as basketball, handball

Daily Substitute activity for inactivity—take the stairs, walk instead of riding

Activity Pyramid

CARE!

- Stay active every day.
- Eat a balanced diet.
- Drink plenty of water—6 to 8 large glasses a day.

There is more to fitness than exercise. To make sure your body gets all the nutrients you need, you should eat a balanced diet. *A balanced diet* includes all the major food groups.

A balanced diet provides the calories, or energy from food, that you need to stay healthy. The number of calories needed varies from person to person, depending on their metabolism. *Metabolism* is the rate at which you burn energy. It is determined by weight, age, sex, and level of activity.

Fats, oils, and sweets
Use sparingly

Milk, yogurt, and cheese group
2–3 servings

Meat, poultry, fish, dry beans, eggs, and nuts group
2–3 servings

Vegetable group
3–5 servings

Fruit group
2–4 servings

Bread, cereal, rice, and pasta group
6–11 servings

Food Guide Pyramid

FOLDABLES™

by Dinah Zike

Folding Instructions

So how do you make a Foldables data organizer? The following pages offer step-by-step instructions—where and when to fold, where to cut—for making 11 basic Foldables data organizers. The instructions begin with the basic shapes, such as the hot dog fold, that were introduced on page xv.

Half-Book

Fold a sheet of paper ($8\frac{1}{2}$" x 11") in half.

1. This book can be folded vertically like a hot dog or …

2. … it can be folded horizontally like a hamburger.

Folded Book

1. Make a Half-Book.

2. Fold in half again like a hamburger.

This makes a ready-made cover and two small pages inside for recording information.

Two-Tab Book

Take a Folded Book and cut up the valley of the inside fold toward the mountain top.

This cut forms two large tabs that can be used front and back for writing and illustrations.

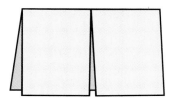

Pocket Book

1. Fold a sheet of paper ($8\frac{1}{2}$" x 11") in half like a hamburger.

2. Open the folded paper and fold one of the long sides up two inches to form a pocket. Refold along the hamburger fold so that the newly formed pockets are on the inside.

3. Glue the outer edges of the two-inch fold with a small amount of glue.

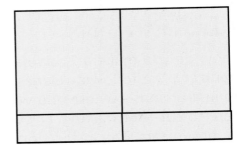

Shutter Fold

1. Begin as if you were going to make a hamburger, but instead of creasing the paper, pinch it to show the midpoint.

2. Fold the outer edges of the paper to meet at the pinch, or midpoint, forming a Shutter Fold.

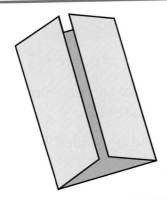

Trifold Book

1. Fold a sheet of paper ($8\frac{1}{2}$" x 11") into thirds.

2. Use this book as is, or cut into shapes.

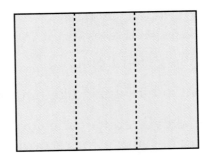

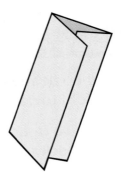

Three-Tab Book

1. Fold a sheet of paper like a hot dog.

2. With the paper horizontal and the fold of the hot dog up, fold the right side toward the center, trying to cover one half of the paper.

3. Fold the left side over the right side to make a book with three folds.

4. Open the folded book. Place one hand between the two thicknesses of paper and cut up the two valleys on one side only. This will create three tabs.

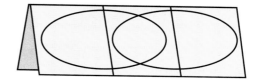

Layered-Look Book

1. Stack two sheets of paper ($8\frac{1}{2}$" x 11") so that the back sheet is one inch higher than the front sheet.

2. Bring the bottoms of both sheets upward and align the edges so that all of the layers or tabs are the same distance apart.

3. When all the tabs are an equal distance apart, fold the papers and crease well.

4. Open the papers and glue them together along the valley, or inner center fold, or staple them along the mountain.

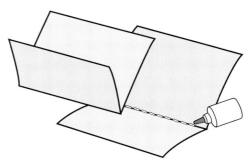

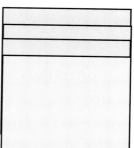

Four-Tab Book

1. Fold a sheet of paper ($8\frac{1}{2}$" x 11") in half like a hot dog.

2. Fold this long rectangle in half like a hamburger.

3. Fold both ends back to touch the mountain top or fold it like an accordion.

4. On the side with two valleys and one mountain top, make vertical cuts through one thickness of paper, forming four tabs.

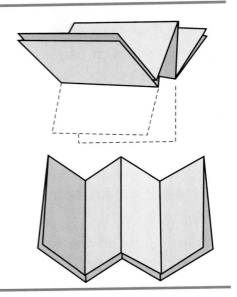

Four-Door Book

1. Make a Shutter Fold using 11" x 17" or 12" x 18" paper.

2. Fold the Shutter Fold in half like a hamburger. Crease well.

3. Open the project and cut along the two inside valley folds.

These cuts will form four doors on the inside of the project.

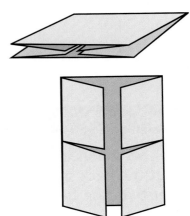

Folded Table or Chart

1. Fold the number of vertical columns needed to make the table or chart.

2. Fold the horizontal rows needed to make the table or chart.

3. Label the rows and columns.

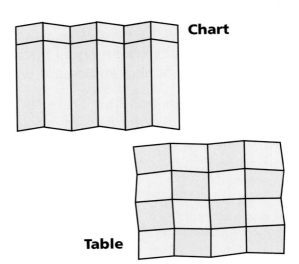

Chart

Table

Glossary

This Glossary will help you to pronounce and understand the meanings of the Science Words introduced in this book. The page number at the end of the definition tells where the word appears.

A

abiotic factor (ā′bī ot′ik fak′tər) A nonliving part of an ecosystem. (p. B6)

absorption (əb sôrp′shən) The disappearance of a sound wave into a surface. (p. F66)

abyssal plain (ə bis′əl plān) The vast flat lands beyond the continental shelf that cover almost half of the deep ocean floor. (p. C90)

acceleration (ak sel′ə rā′shən) Change in velocity with respect to time. (pp. F13, F22)

acid (as′id) A substance that tastes sour and turns blue litmus paper red. (p. E82)

acid rain (as′id rān) Moisture that falls to Earth after being mixed with wastes from burned fossil fuels. (p. C65)

acidity (ə sid′ə tē) The strength of an acid. (p. E86)

action (ak′shən) The force one object applies to a second, as in Newton's third law of motion, which states, "For every action, there is an equal but opposite reaction." *See* **reaction**. (p. F24)

adaptation (ad′əp tā′shən) A characteristic that enables a living thing to survive in its environment. (pp. A46, A106)

aerial root (âr′ē əl rüt) A root that never touches the ground but can take in moisture from the air. (p. A31)

aerosol (âr′ə sōl′) A type of colloid in which liquid drops or solid particles are spread throughout a gas. (p. E60)

air mass (âr mas) A large region of the atmosphere where the air has similar properties throughout. (p. D70)

air pressure (âr presh′ər) The force put on a given area by the weight of the air above it. (p. D33)

alkalinity (al′kə lin′i tē) The strength of a base. (p. E86)

alternative energy source (ōl tûr′nə tiv en′ər jē sôrs) A source of energy other than the burning of a fossil fuel. (p. C104)

amphibian (am fib′ē ən) A vertebrate that lives part of its life in water and part of its life on land. (p. A95)

anemometer (an′ə mom′i tər) A device that measures wind speed. (p. D64)

PRONUNCIATION KEY

The following symbols are used throughout the McGraw-Hill Science Glossaries.

a	at	e	end	o	hot	u	up	hw	white	ə	about
ā	ape	ē	me	ō	old	ū	use	ng	song		taken
ä	far	i	it	ôr	fork	ü	rule	th	thin		pencil
âr	care	ī	ice	oi	oil	ů	pull	th	this		lemon
ô	law	îr	pierce	ou	out	ûr	turn	zh	measure		circus

′ = primary accent; shows which syllable takes the main stress, such as **kil** in **kilogram** (kil′ə gram′).

′ = secondary accent; shows which syllables take lighter stresses, such as **gram** in **kilogram**.

aneroid barometer (an'ə roid bə rom'i tər) A spring enclosed in a pleated metal can that expands or contracts to indicate changes in air pressure. (p. D34)

angiosperm (an'jē ə spûrm') A seed plant that produces flowers. *See* **gymnosperm.** (p. A68)

aquifer (ak'wə fər) An underground layer of rock or soil filled with water. (p. C75)

asexual reproduction (a sek'shü əl rē'prō duk'shən) The production of a new organism from only one cell. (p. A62)

asteroid (as'tə roid') "Minor planet." One of many small, rocky objects that orbit the Sun between the orbits of Mars and Jupiter. (p. D19)

asteroid belt (as'tə roid' belt) Region between Mars and Jupiter where most asteroids are found. (p. D19)

atmosphere (at'məs fîr') The blanket of gases that surrounds Earth. (pp. C26, D32)

atom (at'əm) The smallest unit of an element that retains the properties of that element. *See* **molecule.** (p. E26)

aurora (ə rôr'ə) The northern or southern lights that appear in the night sky, especially in polar regions. (p. D32)

B

bacterium (bak tîr'ē əm) *sing., n. pl.* **bacteria** (-ē ə) A member of either of two kingdoms of one-celled living things that have no nucleus, or center, in their cell body. (p. A19)

balanced forces (bal'ənst fôrs'əz) Forces that cancel each other out when acting together on a single object. (p. F21)

barometer (bə rom'i tər) A device for measuring air pressure. (p. D34)

base (bās) A substance that tastes bitter and turns red litmus paper blue. (p. E82)

basin (bās'in) The floor of an ocean, containing mountains, valleys, and plains. (p. C84)

bench mark (bench' märk') A plaque left by surveyors to tell the exact location and elevation of a place. (p. C6)

benthos (ben'thos) Organisms that live on the bottom in aquatic ecosystems. (p. B72)

bird (bûrd) A vertebrate that has both feathers and wings. (p. C95)

biomass (bī'ō mas') Energy from plant matter or animal waste. (p. C106)

biome (bī'ōm) One of Earth's large ecosystems, with its own kind of climate, soil, plants, and animals. (p. B64)

biotic factor (bī ot'ik fak'tər) A living part of an ecosystem. (p. B7)

boiling point (boil'ing point) The particular temperature for each substance at which it changes state from a liquid to a gas. (p. E37)

buoyancy (boi'ən sē) The upward push of a liquid on an object placed in it. (p. E12)

C

cambium (kam'bē əm) The layer in plants that separates the xylem from the phloem. (p. A31, A32)

camouflage (kam'ə fläzh') An adaptation in which an animal protects itself against predators by blending in with the environment. (p. A108)

carbon cycle (kär'bən sī'kəl) The continuous exchange of carbon dioxide and oxygen among living things. (p. B53)

carnivore (kär'nə vôr') An animal that eats another animal. (p. B20)

carrying capacity (kar'ē ing kə pas'i tē) The maximum population size that an area can support. (p. B35)

cell (sel) The smallest unit of living matter. (p. A6)

chemical change (kem'i kəl chānj) A change of matter that occurs when atoms link together in a new way, creating a new substance different from the original substances. (p. E71)

chemical formula (kəm'i kəl fôr'myə lə) A way to write a compound's name using symbols. The letters tell what elements are in the compound, and the subscripts tell the number of particles in the compound. (p. E25)

chemical reaction (kem'i kəl rē ak'shən) Another name for chemical change. (p. E71)

chemosynthesis (kē'mō sin'thə sis) In tube worms the process by which bacteria create nutrients from hydrogen sulfide and oxygen, using chemical reactions rather than light. (p. C93)

chlorophyll (klôr'ə fil') A green chemical in plant cells that allows plants to use the Sun's energy for making food. (p. A6)

cirrus cloud (sir'əs kloud) A high-altitude cloud with a featherlike shape, made of ice crystals. (p. D44)

classification (klas'ə fi kā'shən) The science of finding patterns among living things. (p. A10)

cleavage (klē'vij) The tendency of a mineral to break along flat surfaces. (p. C34)

climate (klī'mit) The average weather pattern of a region. (p. D84)

climate zone (klī mat' zōn) A region that has similar weather patterns based on temperature, precipitation, wind, distance from a coast, mountain ranges, ocean currents, and vegetation. (p. D84)

climax community (klī'maks kə mū'ni tē) The final stage of succession in an area, unless a major change happens. (p. B84)

cold front (kōld frunt) A front where cold air moves in under a warm air mass. (p. D72)

colloid (kol'oid) A special type of mixture in which the particles of one material are scattered through another and block the passage of light without settling out. (pp. E54, E60)

comet (kom' it) A "dirty snowball" orbiting the Sun — a mixture of ices, frozen gases, rock, and dust left over from the formation of the solar system. (p. D19)

commensalism (kə men'sə liz'əm) A relationship between two kinds of organisms that benefits one without harming the other. (p. B27)

community (kə mū'ni tē) All the living things in an ecosystem. (p. B11)

complete flower (kəm plēt' flou'ər) A flower that has sepals, petals, stamens, and pistils. (p. A78)

compound (kom'pound) Any substance that is formed by the chemical combination of two or more elements and acts like a single substance. (p. E24)

compression (kəm presh'ən) **1.** The part of a sound wave where molecules are crowded together. (p. F51) **2.** A movement of plates that presses together or squeezes Earth's crust. (p. C8)

concave lens (kon kāv' lenz) A lens that is thicker at the edges than at the middle. As it curves inward, it spreads light rays apart, making images appear smaller. (p. F100)

concave mirror (kon kāv' mir'ər) A mirror that curves in on the shiny side. (p. F88)

condensation (kon'den sā'shən) *n.* The changing of a gas into a liquid. (pp. B50, D39) —**condense** (kən dens') *v.* (p. E37)

PRONUNCIATION KEY

a at; ā ape; ä far; âr care; ô law; e end; ē me; i it; ī ice; îr pierce; o hot; ō old; ôr fork; oi oil; ou out; u up; ū use; ü rule; u̇ pull; ûr turn; hw white; ng song; th thin; <u>th</u> this; zh measure; ə about, taken, pencil, lemon, circus

conduction (kən duk'shən) *n.* The passing of heat through a material while the material itself stays in place. (p. E97) —**conduct** (kən dukt') *v.* (p. E14)

conifer (kon'ə fər) Any of a group of gymnosperms that produce seeds in cones and have needlelike leaves. (p. A69)

conserve (kən'sûrv') To save, protect, or use resources wisely. (p. C39)

constellation (kon'stə lā'shən) Patterns formed by groups of stars in the night sky. (p. D12)

consumer (kən sü'mər) Any animal that eats plants or eats other plant-eating animals. (pp. B7, B20)

continental rise (kon'tə nen'təl rīz) A buildup of sediment on the sea floor at the bottom of the continental slope. It is a zone of sand and mud that stretches from the slope down to the deep-sea floor. (p. C90)

continental shelf (kon'tə nen'təl shelf) The underwater edge of a continent. (p. C90)

continental slope (kon'tə nen'təl slōp) The steep slope leading down from the continental shelf toward the sea floor. (p. C90)

contour plowing (kon'tür plou'ing) Preventing erosion by plowing across rather than up and down a slope. (p. C51)

contract (kən trakt') To shrink, as when a material gets colder. (p. E41)

convection (kən vek'shən) The flow of heat through a liquid or a gas, causing hot parts to rise and cooler parts to sink. (p. E97)

convection cell (kən vek'shən sel) A circular pattern of air rising, air sinking, and wind. (p. D55)

convex lens (kon veks' lenz) A lens that is thicker at the middle than at the edges. As it curves outward, it brings light together, making images appear larger. (p. F100)

convex mirror (kon veks' mir'ər) A mirror that curves out on the shiny side. (p. F88)

coquina (kō kē'nə) A sedimentary rock formed from seashell fragments. (p. C44)

Coriolis effect (kôr'ē ō'lis i fekt') The curving of the path of a moving object caused by Earth's rotation. (p. D57)

cortex (kôr'teks) The layer of tissue just inside the epidermis of a plant's roots and stems. (p. A30)

cotyledon (ko'tə lē'dən) A tiny leaflike structure, also called a seedleaf, inside the seed of an angiosperm. (p. A72)

crop rotation (krop rō tā'shən) Growing different crops each year so that the soil does not use up the same kinds of minerals year after year. (p. C51)

crossbreeding (krôs'brēd'ing) Producing offspring by mating individuals from two distinct breeds or varieties of the same species. (p. A112)

cross-pollination (krôs'pol'ə nā'shən) The transfer of pollen from one flower to another. (p. A80)

crust (krust) The rocky surface that makes up the top of the lithosphere and includes the continents and the ocean floor. (p. C7)

crystal (kris'təl) The geometric shape a mineral forms when its atoms and molecules get into fixed patterns. (p. C32)

cumulus cloud (kū'myə ləs kloud) A puffy cloud that appears to rise up from a flat bottom. (p. D44)

current (kûr'ənt) An ocean movement; a large stream of water that flows in the ocean. (p. C86)

cycad (sī'kad) One of the evergreen gymnosperms that resemble palms and have seed-bearing cones. (p. A69)

D

decibel (dB) (des'ə bel') A unit that measures loudness. (p. F58)

deciduous (di sij′ü əs) Said of a plant that loses its leaves each fall. *See* **evergreen.** (pp. A69, B70)

deciduous forest (di si′jə wəs fôr′ist) A forest biome with many kinds of trees that lose their leaves each autumn. (p. B70)

decomposer (dē′kəm pōz′ər) Any of the fungi or bacteria that break down dead plants and animals into useful things like minerals and rich soil. (pp. B7, B21, B56)

delta (del′tə) Fan-shaped region formed by deposits of sediments found at the mouth of a river. (p. C21)

density (den′si tē) A measure of how tightly packed the matter in an object is. (pp. C35, E8)

deposition (dep′ə zish′ən) The dropping off of bits of eroded rock. (p. C13)

desalination (dē sal′ə nā′shən) Getting fresh water from seawater. (p. C73)

desert (dez′ərt) A sandy or rocky biome, with little precipitation and little plant life. (p. B69)

dicot (dī′kot′) An angiosperm with two cotyledons in each seed. *See* **monocot.** (p. A72)

dinoflagellate (din′ə flaj′ə lāt′) A protist containing chlorophyll that has two flagella for motion. When they overreproduce, they can cause "red tides." (p. A14)

distillation (dis′tə lā′shən) The process of separating the parts of a mixture by evaporation and condensation. (p. E64)

diversity (di vûr′si tē) A wide variety of traits in individuals from the same population. (p. A114)

Doppler effect (dop′lər i fekt′) The change in frequency (and pitch) as a source of sound moves toward or away from you. (p. F71)

downdraft (doun′draft′) A downward rush of air caused by the falling of rain during a thunderstorm. (pp. D55, D76)

E

echo (e′kō) A reflected sound wave. (p. F68)

echolocation (ek′ō lō kā′shən) Finding an object by using reflected sound. (p. F70)

ecological succession (ek′ə loj′i kəl sək sesh′ən) The gradual replacement of one community by another. (p. B82)

ecology (ē kol′ə jē) The study of how living and nonliving things interact. (p. B11)

ecosystem (ek′ō sis′təm) All the living and nonliving things in an environment, including their interactions with each other. (p. B6)

effort arm (ef′ərt arm) The part of a lever that applies force to the resistance arm. (p. F26)

electromagnetic spectrum (i lek′trō mag net′ik spek′trəm) All the wavelengths of visible and invisible light in order, from short (gamma rays) to long (radio). (p. F119)

electromagnetism (i lek′trō mag′ni tiz′əm) The production of magnetism by electricity (and the production of electricity by magnets). (p. F118)

electron (i lek′tron) A particle in the space outside the nucleus of an atom that carries one unit of negative electric charge. (p. E27)

element (el′ə mənt) A pure substance that cannot be broken down into any simpler substances. (p. E22)

PRONUNCIATION KEY

a at; ā ape; ä far; âr care; ô law; e end; ē me; i it; ī ice; îr pierce; o hot; ō old; ôr fork; oi oil; ou out; u up; ū use; ü rule; ů pull; ûr turn; hw white; ng song; th thin; th this; zh measure; ə about, taken, pencil, lemon, circus

elevation (el'ə vā'shən) The height of a place above sea level. (p. C6)

embryo (em'brē ō') The immature plant inside a seed. (p. A82)

emulsion (i mul'shən) A type of colloid in which one liquid is spread throughout another. (p. E60)

endangered species (en dān'jərd spē'shēz) A species that is in danger of becoming extinct. (p. B36)

epidermis (ep'i dûr'mis) An outermost layer of such plant parts as roots and leaves. (pp. A30, A34)

erosion (i rō'zhən) The picking up and carrying away of pieces of rocks. (p. C10)

evaporation (i vap'ə rā'shən) The slow changing of a liquid into a gas. (pp. B50, D38, E38)

evergreen (ev'ər grēn') Said of a gymnosperm that keeps its leaves for at least a few years. *See* **deciduous**. (p. A69)

expand (ek spand') To spread out, as when a material gets hotter. (p. E41)

extinct (ek stingkt') A species that has died out completely. (p. B36)

F

fault (fôlt) A crack in Earth's crust whose sides show evidence of motion. (p. C6)

fault-block mountain (fôlt blok moun'tən) A mountain formed by blocks of Earth's crust moving along a fault. (p. C9)

fertilization (fûr'tə lə zā'shən) The joining of a sperm cell with an egg cell to make one new cell, a fertilized egg. (pp. A62, A81)

fertilizer (fûr'tə lī'zər) A substance used to add minerals to the soil. (p. B56)

fibrous root (fī'brəs rüt) One of the many hairy branching roots that some plants have. (p. A31)

filament (fil'ə mənt) The wire in a light bulb that gives off light and heat. (p. E92)

fish (fish) A vertebrate that lives its whole life in water. (p. A95)

flood plain (flud' plān') Land that is likely to be underwater during a flood. (p. C21)

foam (fōm) A type of colloid in which a gas is spread throughout a liquid. (p. E60)

fog (fôg) A cloud at ground level. (p. D44)

fold mountain (fōld moun'tən) A mountain made up mostly of rock layers folded by being squeezed together. (p. C8)

food chain (füd chān) The path of the energy in food from one organism to another. (p. B18)

food web (füd web) The overlapping food chains in an ecosystem. (p. B20)

force (fôrs) A push or pull exerted by one object on another, causing a change in motion. (p. F6)

fossil (fos'əl) Any remains or imprint of living things of the past. (p. C45)

fossil fuel (fos'əl fū'əl) A fuel formed from the decay of ancient forms of life. (p. C64)

fracture (frak'chər) The characteristic way some minerals break in uneven patterns. (p. C35)

freezing point (frēz'ing point) The temperature at which a substance changes state from a liquid to a solid. (p. E37)

frequency (frē'kwən sē) The number of times an object vibrates per second. (p. F57)

friction (frik' shen') A force that opposes the motion of one object moving past another. (p. F8)

frond (frond) The leaf of a fern. (p. A61)

front (frunt) A boundary between air masses with different temperatures. (p. D71)

fruit (früt) The ripened ovary of a flowering seed plant. (p. A70)

fulcrum (fůl'krəm) The pivot point of a lever. (p. F26)

fundamental frequency (fun'də men'təl frē'kwən sē) The lowest frequency at which an object vibrates. (p. F72)

fungus (fung'gəs) *n.,* **fungi** (fun'jī) *pl.* Members of a kingdom that contains one-celled and many-celled living things that absorb food from their environment. (p. A17)

G

galaxy (gal'ək sē) A collection of billions of stars. Our Sun belongs to the Milky Way galaxy. (p. D20)

gas (gas) A form of matter that does not take up a definite amount of space and has no definite shape. (p. E36)

gel (jel) A type of colloid in which a solid is spread throughout a liquid. (p. E60)

gem (jem) A mineral valued for being rare and beautiful. (p. C38)

geologist (jē ol'ə jist) A scientist who studies rocks to tell how they formed and to predict when an earthquake may occur. (p. C16)

geothermal energy (jē'ō thûr'məl en'ər jē) Earth's internal energy. (p. C104)

germination (jûr'mə nā'shən) The sprouting of a seed into a new plant. (p. A83)

ginkgo (ging'kō) *n., pl.* **ginkgoes** A large gymnosperm with fan-shaped leaves. (p. A69)

gnetophyte (ne'tō fīt') One of the gymnosperms that are closely related to flowering plants and live in both deserts and the tropics. (p. A69)

grassland (gras'land') A biome where grasses, not trees, are the main plant life. Prairies are one kind of grassland region. (p. B66)

gravitropism (grav'ī trō'pi'zəm) The response of a plant to gravity. (p. A44)

gravity (grav'i tē) The force of attraction between any two objects due to their mass. (pp. D8, F35)

groundwater (ground wô'tər) Precipitation that seeps into the ground and is stored in tiny holes, or pores, in soil and rocks. (pp. B51, C74)

gymnosperm (jim'nə spûrm') A seed plant that does not produce flowers. *See* **angiosperm**. (p. A68)

H

habitat (hab'i tat) The place where a plant or animal naturally lives and grows. (p. B12)

hail (hāl) Pellets made of ice and snow. (p. D47)

hardness (härd'nis) How well a mineral resists scratching. (p. C34)

herbivore (hûr'bə vôr') An animal that eats plants, algae, and other producers. (p. B20)

heredity (hə red'i tē) The passing down of inherited traits from parents to offspring. (p. A110)

hertz (Hz) (hûrts) A unit for measuring frequency. One hertz equals a frequency of one vibration per second. (p. F57)

heterogeneous (het'ər ə jē'nē əs) Differing in kind or nature; dissimilar; not homogeneous. (p. E54)

high-pressure system (hī'presh'ər sis'təm) A pattern surrounding a high pressure center, from which winds blow outward. In the Northern Hemisphere these winds curve to the right in a clockwise pattern. (p. D59)

PRONUNCIATION KEY

a at; ā ape; ä far; âr care; ô law; e end; ē me; i it; ī ice; îr pierce; o hot; ō old; ôr fork; oi oil; ou out; u up; ū use; ü rule; u̇ pull; ûr turn; hw white; ng song; th thin; <u>th</u> this; zh measure; ə about, taken, pencil, lemon, circus

host (hōst) The organism a parasite lives in or on and is harmed by. (p. B26)

humidity (hū mid′i tē) The amount of water vapor in the air. (p. D38)

humus (hü′məs) Decayed plant or animal material in soil. (pp. B9, C49)

hurricane (hûr′i kān′) A very large, swirling storm with very low pressure at the center. (p. D78)

hybrid (hī′brid) An organism produced by the crossing of parents that have different forms of the same trait. (p. A112)

hydrocarbon (hī′drə kär′bən) Compound made only of hydrogen and carbon atoms. (p. E32)

hydroelectric plant (hī′drō i lek′trik plant) A factory where running or falling water spins a generator to make electricity. (p. C104)

hydrosphere (hī′drə sfîr′) Earth's water, found in continents and oceans, including the fresh water in ice, lakes, rivers, and underground water. (p. C26)

hydrotropism (hī drot′rə piz′əm) The response of a plant to a nearby source of water. (p. A45)

hyperthermia (hī′pər thûr′mē ə) The overheating of the body that can be caused by overexposure in a hot, dry climate. (p. D90)

I

igneous rock (ig′nē əs rok) A rock formed when melted rock material cools and hardens (p. C43)

image (im′ij) A "picture" of the light source that light rays make in bouncing off a polished, shiny surface. (p. F89)

imperfect flower (im pûr′fikt flou′ər) A flower with either a stamen or a pistil, but not both. (p. A78)

incomplete flower (in′kəm plēt′ flou′ər) A flower that lacks sepals, petals, stamens or pistils. (p. A78)

indicator (in′di kā′tər) A substance such as litmus paper whose color changes when it is mixed with an acid or a base. (p. E84)

inertia (i nûr′shə) The tendency of a moving object to keep moving in a straight line or of any object to resist a change in motion. (pp. D8, F7)

inexhaustible resource (in′eg zôs′tə bəl rē′sôrs′) A resource that cannot be depleted or used up easily. (p. B58)

inherited trait (in her′i təd trāt) A characteristic that is passed from parents to offspring. (p. A110)

inner planet (in′ər plan′it) A planet between the Sun and the asteroid belt (Mercury, Venus, Earth, Mars). (p. D16)

insolation (in′sə lā′shən) The amount of the Sun's energy that reaches Earth at a given time and place. *Insolation* is short for *in*coming *sol*ar radi*ation*. (p. D30)

instinct (in′stingkt′) An inherited behavior, one that is not learned but is done automatically. (p. A110)

insulate (in′sə lāt′) To prevent heat from passing through. (p. E14)

intertidal zone (in′tər tī′dəl zōn) The shallowest section of the marine, or ocean, ecosystem, where the ocean floor is covered and uncovered as the tide goes in and out. (p. B73)

invertebrate (in vûr′tə brit) An animal that does not have a backbone. (p. A16)

ionized (ī′ə nīzd′) Electrically charged by radiation, as gas particles of auroras in the night sky. (p. D32)

isobar (ī′sə bär′) A line on a weather map connecting places with equal air pressure. (p. D59)

K

kinetic energy (ki net′ik en′ər jē) The energy of any moving object. (p. E95)

land breeze (land brēz) Wind that blows from land to sea. (p. D56)

laser (lā´zər) A device that produces a thin stream of light of just a few close wavelengths. (p. F122)

lava (lä´və) Magma that reaches Earth's surface. (pp. C9, C43)

law of reflection (lô uv ri flek´shən) The angle between an incoming light ray and a surface equals the angle between the reflected light ray and the surface. (p. F87)

lever (lev´ər) A simple machine made of a rigid bar and a fixed pivot point, called the fulcrum. (p. F26)

light ray (līt rā) A straight-line beam of light as it travels outward from its source. (p. F85)

lightning (līt´ning) One of the huge electric sparks that leap from clouds to the ground in thunderstorms. (p. D76)

limiting factor (lim´ə ting fak´tər) Anything that controls the growth or survival of a population. (p. B34)

liquid (lik´wid) A form of matter that takes up a definite amount of space and has no definite shape. (p. E36)

lithosphere (lith´ə sfîr´) The hard outer layer of Earth, about 100 km thick. (p. C26)

long-day plant (lông´dā plant) A plant that blooms when there is much more daylight than darkness. (p. A46)

low-pressure system (lō´presh´ər sis´təm) A pattern surrounding a low-pressure center, in which winds blow in toward the center. In the Northern Hemisphere, these winds blow to the right in a counterclockwise pattern. (p. D59)

luster (lus´tər) The way light bounces off a mineral's surface. (p. C33)

magma (mag´mə) Hot, molten rock deep below Earth's surface. (p. C9)

magnetic (mag net´ik) The property of a material like iron in which the particles line up pole to pole, causing it to be attracted or repelled by a magnet. (p. E15)

mammal (mam´əl) A vertebrate that feeds its young milk. (p. A95)

mare (mär´ā) *n., pl.* **maria** (mär´ē ə) Dark-colored land on the Moon that is dry and flat and is surrounded by mountains and ridges. (p. D10)

mass (mas) A measure of the amount of matter in an object. (p. E6)

matter (ma´tər) Anything that has mass and takes up space. (pp. E6, F51)

meander (mē an´dər) Bends or s-shaped curves in a river. (p. C21)

melting point (melt´ing point) The particular temperature for each substance at which it changes state from a solid to a liquid. (p. E37)

membrane (mem´brān) A thin envelope surrounding the nucleus of a cell. (p. A18)

metal (met´əl) Any of a group of elements found in the ground that conducts heat and electricity. (p. C38)

PRONUNCIATION KEY

a at; ā ape; ä far; âr care; ô law; e end; ē me; i it; ī ice; îr pierce; o hot; ō old; ôr fork; oi oil; ou out; u up; ū use; ü rule; u̇ pull; ûr turn; hw white; ng song; th thin; <u>th</u> this; zh measure; ə about, taken, pencil, lemon, circus

metamorphic rock (met′ə môr′fik rok) A rock formed under heat and pressure from another kind of rock. (p. C46)

meteor (mē′ tē or) A chunk of rock from space that burns up as it travels through Earth's atmosphere. A "shooting star." (p. D19)

meteorite (mē′tē ə rīt′) A chunk of rock from space that strikes the surface of Earth or the Moon. (pp. C14, D19)

mid-ocean ridge (mid ō′shun rij) Chain of mountains that wind along all the world's major oceans. (p. C91)

mimicry (mim′i krē) An adaptation in which an animal is protected against predators by its resemblance to another, unpleasant animal. (p. A106)

mineral (min′ə rəl) A solid material of Earth's crust with a definite composition. (p. C32)

mixture (miks′chər) A physical combination of two or more substances that are blended together without forming new substances. (p. E52)

molecule (mol′ə kūl′) A particle that contains more than one atom joined together. (p. E30) *See* **atom**. (p. E26)

monocot (mon′ə kot′) An angiosperm with one cotyledon in each seed. *See* **dicot**. (p. A72)

mountain breeze (moun′tən brēz) A cool night wind that blows down a mountain slope to replace the warmer air in the valley. (p. D56)

mutualism (mū′chü ə liz′əm) A relationship between two kinds of organisms that benefits both. (p. B24)

N

neap tide (nēp tīd) The slightest changes from high to low tide that occur when the Sun, the Moon, and Earth form a right angle or are perpendicular to each other. (p. C89)

nekton (nek′tən) Organisms that swim through the water in aquatic ecosystems. (p. B72)

neutral (nü′trəl) Neither acid nor base. (p. E82)

neutron (nü′tron) A particle in the nucleus of an atom that has no net electric charge. (p. E27)

newton (nü′tən) A basic unit measuring the amount of pull or push a force produces. (pp. E7, F20)

NEXRAD (neks′rad′) A new form of Doppler radar that is used to track storms. The word stands for *NEXt generation of weather RADar*. (p. D81)

niche (nich) The role of an organism in a community. (p. B12)

nitrogen cycle (nī′trə jən sī′kəl) The continuous trapping of nitrogen gas into compounds in the soil and its return to the air. (p. B54)

nonrenewable resource (non′ri nü′ə bəl rē′sôrs′) A resource that cannot be replaced within a short period of time or at all. (pp. B58, C64)

nonvascular (non vas′kyə lər) Containing no plant tissue through which water and food move. (p. A15)

nucleus (nü′klē əs) **1.** A dense structure inside the cell. (p. A18) **2.** One of the airborne dust particles around which water condenses as droplets or ice crystals before falling as precipitation. (p. D46) **3.** An atom's dense center, where most of its mass is. (p. E27)

O

omnivore (om′nə vôr′) An animal that eats both plants and animals. (p. B21)

opaque (ō pāk′) Completely blocking light from passing through it. (p. F96)

orbit (ôr′bit) The path of a planet traveling around a star. (p. D6)

ore (ôr) A mineral containing a useful substance. (p. C38)

organ (ôr′gən) A group of tissues that work together to do a certain job. (p. A9)

organism (ôr′gə niz′əm) Any living thing that can carry out its life on its own. (p. A6)

organ system (ôr′gən sis′təm) A group of organs that work together to do a certain job. (p. A9)

outer planet (out′er plan′it) One of the five planets beyond the asteroid belt (Jupiter, Saturn, Uranus, Neptune, Pluto). (p. D16)

ovary (ō′və rē) A structure containing egg cells; the base of a pistil in a flower. (p. A78)

overtone (ō′vər tōn′) One of a series of pitches that blend to give a sound its quality. (p. F72)

ozone layer (ō′zōn lā′ər) A layer of ozone gas in the atmosphere that screens out much of the Sun's UV (ultraviolet) rays. (p. C63)

P

parasitism (par′ə sī tiz′əm) A relationship in which one organism lives in or on another organism and benefits from that relation-ship while the other organism may be harmed by it. (p. B26) —**parasite** (par′ə sīt′) (pp. A71, B26)

perfect flower (pûr′fikt flou′ər) A flower with both male and female parts, that is, both a stamen and a pistil. (p. A78)

permafrost (pûr′mə frôst′) A layer of perma-nently frozen soil found in arctic and antarctic regions. (p. B68)

pH (pē′aitch′) The scale that tells how acidic or basic a solution is. (p. E86)

phloem (flō′em) The tissue through which food from the leaves moves down through the rest of a plant. (pp. A31, A32)

photon (fō′ton) The tiny bundles of energy by means of which light travels. (p. F119)

photoperiodism (fō′tō pîr′ē ə diz′əm) The flowering response of a plant to changing periods of daylight and darkness. (p. A46)

photosynthesis (fō′tə sin′thə sis) The food-making process in green plants that uses sunlight. (p. A36)

phototropism (fō tot′rə piz′əm) The response of a plant to changes in light. (p. A44)

phylum (fī′ləm) *n., pl.* **phyla** (-lə) One of the large groups in the animal kingdom. (p. A16)

physical change (fiz′i kəl chānj) A change of matter in size, shape, or state without any change in identity. (p. E70)

pioneer community (pī′ə nîr′ kə mū′ni tē) The first community thriving in a once lifeless area. (p. B83)

pioneer species (pī′ə nîr′ spē′shēz) The first species living in an otherwise lifeless area. (p. B83)

pitch (pich) How high or low a sound is. (p. F56)

planet (plan′it) Any of the nine major objects that travel around the Sun and shine by reflecting its light. (p. D6)

plankton (plangk′tən) Organisms that float on the water in aquatic ecosystems. (p. B72)

plate (plāt) One of the moving pieces of Earth's crust that has been broken by upward pressure from the mantle. (p. C7)

plate tectonics (plāt tek ton′iks) A scientific theory that Earth's crust is made of moving plates. (pp. B90, C7)

polarization (pō′lər ə zā′shən) Allowing light vibrations to pass through in only one direction. (p. F97)

pollen (pol′ən) Dustlike grains in the flower of a plant that contain its male sex cells. (pp. A70, A74, A84)

PRONUNCIATION KEY

a **a**t; ā **a**pe; ä f**a**r; âr c**a**re; ô l**a**w; e **e**nd; ē m**e**; i **i**t; ī **i**ce; îr p**ie**rce; o h**o**t; ō **o**ld; ôr f**o**rk; oi **oi**l; ou **ou**t; u **u**p; ū **u**se; ü r**u**le; ù p**u**ll; ûr t**u**rn; hw **wh**ite; ng so**ng**; th **th**in; <u>th</u> **th**is; zh mea**s**ure; ə **a**bout, tak**e**n, penc**i**l, lem**o**n, circ**u**s

pollination (pol′ə nā′shən) The transfer of a pollen grain to the egg-producing part of a plant. (p. A74)

pollute (pə lüt′) *v.* To add harmful substances to Earth's land, water, or air. (p. C50) —**pollutant** (pə lü′tənt) *n.* Something that pollutes. (p. C50) —**pollution** (pə lü′shən) *n.* A polluted condition. (p. C50)

population (pop′yə lā′shən) All the members of one species in an area. (p. B11)

potential energy (pə ten′shəl en′ər jē) Stored energy. (p. E95)

precipitation (pri sip′i tā′shən) Any form of water particles that falls from the atmosphere and reaches the ground. (pp. B51, D46)

predator (pred′ə tər) An animal that hunts other animals for food. (pp. A106, B21)

prey (prā) A living thing that is hunted for food. (p. B21)

primary color (prī′mer′ē kul′ər) Red, green, or blue. Mixing these colors can produce all the colors of the spectrum. (p. F110)

primary pigment (prī′mer′ē pig′mənt) Magenta, cyan, or yellow. Materials with any of these colors absorb one primary color of light and reflect the other two. (p. F112)

primary succession (prī′mer′ē sək sesh′ən) The beginning of a community where few, if any, living things exist, or where earlier communities were wiped out. (p. B82)

prism (priz′əm) A cut piece of clear glass (or plastic) with two opposite sides in the shape of a triangle or other geometric shape. (p. F108)

producer (prə dü′sər) Any of the plants and algae that produce oxygen and food that animals need. (pp. B7, B20)

product (prod′ukt) A new substance produced by a chemical change. (p. E71)

prop root (prop rüt) One of the roots that grow out of a plant's stemlike main roots and help prop up the plant. (p. A31)

property (prop′ər tē) A characteristic of matter that can be observed, such as mass, volume, weight, or density. (pp. E6, E24)

protective coloration (prə tek′tiv kul′ə rā′shən) A type of camouflage in which the color of an animal blends in with its background, protecting it against predators. (p. A109)

protein (prō′tēn) A substance rich in nitrogen that the body uses for growth and the repair of cells. (p. B54)

protist (prō′tist) A member of a kingdom that contains one-celled and many-celled living things, some that make food and some that hunt for food. (p. A18)

proton (prō′ton) A particle in the nucleus of an atom that carries one unit of positive electric charge. (p. E27)

Q

quality (kwol′i tē) The difference you hear between two sounds of the same loudness and pitch. (p. F72)

R

radar (rā′där) A device for tracking the position and path of a distant moving object. (p. D80)

radiation (rā′dē a′shən) The transfer of heat through electromagnetic rays. (p. E97)

rarefaction (rârə fak′shən) The part of a sound wave where molecules are spread apart. (p. F51)

raw material (râ mə tîr′ē əl) Material not yet refined, manufactured, or processed. (p. B58)

reactant (rē ak′tənt) An original substance at the beginning of a chemical reaction. (p. E71)

reaction (rē ak′shən) The force with which an object responds to an action, as in Newton's third law of motion. (p. F24)

reflection (ri flek′shən) The bouncing of a sound wave off a surface. (p. F66)

refraction (ri frak′shən) The bending of light rays as they pass from one substance into another. (p. F98)

relative humidity (rel′ə tiv hū mid′i tē) A comparison between how much water vapor is in the air and how much the air could hold at a given temperature if it were full, or saturated. (p. D39)

renewable resource (ri nü′ə bəl rē′sôrs′) A resource that can be replaced in a short period of time. (pp. B58, C62)

reservoir (rez′ər vwär′) A storage area for fresh water supplies. (p. C75)

resistance arm (ri zis′təns arm) The part of a lever that applies force to the load the machine acts against. (p. F26)

resonance (rez′ə nəns) In an instrument or object, a unique blend of the fundamental frequency and its overtones. (p. F72)

resource (rē′sôrs′) Any material that helps support life on Earth. (p. C26)

respiration (res′pə rā′shən) The release of energy in plants and animals from food (sugar). (p. A37)

response (ri spons′) What a living thing does as a result of a stimulus. (p. A44)

reptile (rep′təl) An egg-laying vertebrate with thick, dry skin. (p. A95)

revolve (ri volv′) To move around, or orbit, another object. (p. D10)

rhizoid (rī′zoid) One of the hairlike fibers that anchor a moss to the soil and take in water from the soil. (p. A58)

rhizome (rī′zōm) The underground stem of a fern. (p. A61)

rock (rok) A naturally formed solid in the crust made up of one or more minerals. (p. C42)

rock cycle (rok sī′kəl) Rocks changing from one into another in a never-ending series of processes. (p. C52)

root cap (rüt kap) A thin covering made up of cells that protect the root tip of a plant as it grows into the soil. (p. A30)

root hair (rüt hâr) Any of the threadlike projections from a plant root that absorb water and dissolved minerals from the soil. (p. A30)

rotate (rō′tāt) To make a complete spin on an axis, causing one day on a planet. A day differs in length from planet to planet. (p. D9)

runoff (run′ôf) Precipitation that flows across the land's surface or falls into rivers and streams. (pp. B51, C20)

S

savanna (sə van′ə) A tropical grassland with some trees and shrubs. (p. B66)

scanning tunneling microscope (scan′ing tun′əl ing mī′krə skōp′) A device that uses electric current flowing through a needle to trace the contours of atoms and magnify them as much as 30 million times. (p. E26)

scavenger (skav′ən jər) A meat-eating animal that feeds on the remains of dead animals. (p. B21)

sea breeze (sē brēz) Wind that blows from sea to land. (p. D56)

sea-floor vent (sē′flôr′ vent) An opening in a mid-ocean ridge where mineral-saturated water boils up from the seafloor crust. (p. C93)

seamount (sē′mount′) A huge underwater volcanic mountain that may emerge from the ocean surface as an island. (p. C90)

PRONUNCIATION KEY

a **at**; ā **ape**; ä **far**; âr **care**; ô **law**; e **end**; ē **me**; i **it**; ī **ice**; îr **pierce**; o **hot**; ō **old**; ôr **fork**; oi **oil**; ou **out**; u **up**; ū **use**; ū **rule**; ù **pull**; ûr **turn**; hw **white**; ng **song**; th **thin**; <u>th</u> **this**; zh **measure**; ə **about, taken, pencil, lemon, circus**

secondary succession (sek'ən der'ē sək sesh'ən) The beginning of a new community where an earlier community already exists. (p. B82)

sediment (sed'ə ment) Pieces of material carried and deposited by water or wind (p. C20)

sedimentary rock (sed'ə men'tə rē rok) A rock made of bits of matter joined together. (p. C44)

seed (sēd) An undeveloped plant with stored food sealed in a protective covering. (p. A68)

seed coat (sēd kōt) The outer covering of a seed. (p. A82)

seed dispersal (sēd di spûr'səl) The movement of a seed from the flower to a place where it can sprout. (p. A83)

self-pollination (self'pol'ə nā'shən) The transfer of pollen from an anther to a stigma in the same plant. (p. A80)

sexual reproduction (sek'shü əl rē'prō duk'shən) The production of a new organism from a female sex cell and a male sex cell. (pp. A62, A81)

shear (shîr) A movement of plates that twists, tears, or pushes one part of Earth's crust past another. (p. C8)

short-day plant (shôrt'dā plant) A plant that blooms when there is more darkness and less daylight. (p. A46)

simple machine (sim'pəl mə shēn') A machine with few moving parts, making it easier to do work. (p. F26)

smog (smog) A mixture of smoke and fog. (p. C64)

solar system (sō'lər sis'təm) The Sun and the objects that are traveling around it. (p. D6)

solid (sol'id) A form of matter that has a definite shape and takes up a definite amount of space. (p. E36)

solubility (sol'yə bil'i tē) The ability of a substance to be dissolved by another substance. (p. E58)

solute (sol'ūt) A substance that is dissolved by another substance to form a solution. (p. E57)

solution (sə lü'shən) A mixture of substances that are blended so completely that the mixture looks the same everywhere. (p. E54)

solvent (sol'vənt) A substance that dissolves one or more other substances to form a solution. (p. E57)

sound wave (sound wāv) A vibration that spreads away from a vibrating object. (p. F51)

spectrum (spek'trəm) A band of colors produced when light goes through a prism. (p. F108)

speed (spēd) How fast an object's position changes with time at any given moment. (p. F11)

spore (spôr) Cells in seedless plants that grow into new organisms. (p. A58)

spring (spring) A place where groundwater seeps out of the ground. (p. C75)

spring tide (spring tīd) The greatest changes from high to low tide that occur when the Sun, the Moon, and Earth are lined up. (p. C89)

state of matter (stāt uv mat'ər) One of the three forms that matter can take—solid, liquid, or gas. (p. E36)

stimulus (stim'yə ləs), *n., pl.* **stimuli (-lī)** Something in the environment that causes a living thing to react. (p. A44)

stomata (stō'mə tə) *pl. n., sing.* **stoma** Pores in the bottom of leaves that open and close to let in air or give off water vapor. (p. A34)

storm surge (stôrm sûrj) A great rise of the sea along a shore caused by low air pressure. (p. D79)

stratus cloud (strā'təs kloud) A cloud that forms in a blanketlike layer. (p. D44)

streak (strēk) The color of the powder left when a mineral is rubbed against a hard, rough surface. (p. C34)

strip farming (strip fär′ming) Trapping runoff by alternating tightly growing grasses with more widely spaced plants. (p. C51)

subscript (sub′skript′) A number in a chemical formula that tells the number of atoms in the compound. (p. E25)

surveyor (sər vā′ər) A specialist who makes accurate measurements of Earth's crust. (p. C6)

suspension (sə spen′shən) A mixture in which suspended particles can easily be seen. (p. E59)

symbiosis (sim′bē ō′sis) A relationship between two kinds of organisms that lasts over time. (p. B24)

T

taiga (tī′gə) A cool forest biome of conifers in the upper Northern Hemisphere. (p. B67)

taproot (tap′rüt′) A root that has few hairy branches and grows deep into the ground. (p. A31)

temperate (tem′pər it) Free from extremes of temperature. (p. B66)

tension (ten′shən) A movement of plates that stretches or pulls apart Earth's crust. (p. C8)

terracing (ter′is ing) Shaping hillsides into steps so that runoff and eroded soil get trapped on the steps. (p. C51)

texture (teks′chər) An identifying quality of a rock based on how coarse, fine, or glassy it is and on how angular or rounded it is. (p. C42)

threatened species (thret′ənd spē′shēz) A species that is in danger of becoming endangered. (p. D36)

thunder (thun′dər) The noise caused by lightning-heated air during a thunderstorm. (p. D76)

thunderhead (thun′dər hed′) A cumulonimbus cloud in which a thunderstorm forms. (p. D76)

thunderstorm (thun′dər stôrm′) The most common severe storm, formed in cumulonimbus clouds. (p. D76)

tissue (tish′ü) A group of similar cells that work together at the same job. (p. A8)

topsoil (top′soil′) The dark, top layer of soil, rich in humus and minerals, in which many tiny organisms live and most plants grow. (p. B9)

tornado (tôr nā′dō) A violent, whirling wind that moves across the ground in a narrow path. (p. D77)

trade wind (trād wind) A belt of winds around Earth moving from high pressure zones toward the low pressure at the equator. (p. D58)

translucent (trans lü′sənt) Letting only some light through, so that objects on the other side appear blurry. (p. F96)

transparent (trans pâr′ənt) Letting all light through, so that objects on the other side can be seen clearly. (p. F96)

transpiration (tran′spə rā′shən) The loss of water through a plant's leaves. (pp. A35, A38, D39)

trench (trench) A deep valley in the sea floor. (p. C91)

tropical rain forest (trop′i kəl rān fôr′ist) A hot biome near the equator, with much rainfall and a wide variety of life. (p. B71)

tropism (trō′piz′əm) A response of a plant toward or away from a stimulus. (p. A44)

PRONUNCIATION KEY

a **at**; ā **ape**; ä **far**; âr **care**; ô **law**; e **end**; ē **me**; i **it**; ī **ice**; îr **pierce**; o **hot**; ō **old**; ôr **fork**; oi **oil**; ou **out**; u **up**; ū **use**; ü **rule**; u̇ **pull**; ûr **turn**; hw **white**; ng **song**; th **thin**; <u>th</u> **this**; zh **measure**; ə **about, taken, pencil, lemon, circus**

troposphere (trop'ə sfîr') The layer of the atmosphere closest to Earth's surface. (p. D32)

tube worm (tūb wûrm) Large wormlike animals that live near sea-floor vents and obtain their food through bacterial chemosynthesis. (p. C93)

tundra (tun'dra) Large, treeless plain in the arctic regions, where the ground is frozen all year. (p. B68)

ultrasonic (ul'trə son'ik) Said of a sound with a frequency too high to be heard by humans. (p. F57)

unbalanced forces (un bal'ənst fôrs'əz) Forces that do not cancel each other out when acting together on a single object. (p. F21)

updraft (up'draft') An upward rush of heated air during a thunderstorm. (pp. D55, D76)

vacuum (vak'ū əm) A space through which sound waves cannot travel because it contains no matter. (p. F116)

valley breeze (val'ē brēz) A cool wind that blows up a mountain slope and replaces the slope's rising Sun-warmed air. (p. D56)

variable (vâr'ē ə bəl) One of the changes in a situation that may affect the outcome of an experiment. (p. A48)

vascular (vas'kyə lər) Containing plant tissue through which water moves up and food moves down. (p. A15)

velocity (və los'i tē) The speed and direction of a moving object. (p. F12)

vertebrate (vûr'tə brit) An animal that has a backbone. (p. A16)

vibration (vī brā'shən) A back-and-forth motion. (p. F50)

volume (vol'ūm) **1.** A measure of how much space an object takes up. (p. E6) **2.** The loudness or softness of a sound. (p. F58)

warm front (wôrm frunt) A front where warm air moves in over a cold air mass. (p. D72)

water cycle (wô'tər sī'kəl) The continuous movement of water between Earth's surface and the air, changing from liquid to gas to liquid. (pp. B51, C74)

water table (wô'tər tā'bəl) The top of the water-filled spaces in the ground. (p. C75)

water vapor (wô'tər vā'pər) Water in the form of a gas. (pp. B50, D38)

watershed (wô'tər shed') Area from which water is drained; region that contributes water to a river or river system. (pp. C20, C68–C69)

weather (weth'ər) What the lower atmosphere is like at any given place and time. (p. D34)

weathering (weth'ər ing) Breaking down rocks into smaller pieces. (p. C10)

weight (wāt) The force of gravity between Earth and an object. (pp. E7, F36)

well (wel) A hole dug below the water table that water seeps into. (p. C75)

wind (wind) Air that moves horizontally. (p. D55)

work (wûrk) The use of force to move an object a certain distance. (p. F26)

xylem (zī'ləm) The tissue through which water and minerals move up through a plant. (pp. A30, A32)

Y

year (yîr) The time it takes a planet to orbit the Sun. A *year* is different from planet to planet. (p. D7)

Index

A

Abiotic factors, B6–7
Absorption, of sound, F66–67
Abyssal plain, C90
Acceleration, F13, F18–20
  calculation of, F20
  of falling objects, F36–37
  force and, F18
  importance of understanding,
    F29
  mass and, F19, F20
  of the Moon, F37
Acid rain, C11, C65, C81
Acidity, E86–87
Acids, C65*
  identifying, E81*–82, E84–85
  importance of understanding,
    E89
  reaction with bases, E82–83
  reactivity of, E83
  strength of, E86–87
  uses of, E88
Action, F24
Adaptation, A42–51, A46,
    A104–120
  camouflage as, A108–109
  competition as, A47, B23
  mimicry as, A106–107
  root growth as, A43*
  in sowbugs, A105*
  in taste, A107
  thorns as, A107
  tropisms, A44–45
Aerial roots, A31
Aerogels, E16
Aerosol, E60
African violets, A86
Agnatha, A98
Agriculture, B76–77
Air
  cleaning up, C66
  composition of, D33
  cooling of, D40
  dirty, C61*
  dust in, D33

nitrogen in, B54
pollution of, C64, C67
as solution, E56
water in, D39
Air masses, D70–71, D78
Air pollution, B38
Air pressure
  altitude and, D33
  changes in, D53*–54
  convection cells and, D55
  hurricane formation and,
    D78–79
  isobars, D59
  measuring, D34
  storm surges and, D79
Air resistance, F34
Air sac (swim bladder), A98
Air temperature
  altitude and, D32
  importance of understanding,
    D35
  measuring, D34
  relative humidity and, D39
  Sun's angle and, D29*–31*
Algae, B28, B73
  blooms, B30
  green, A18, A64
  as producers, B7
Alkalinity, E86–87
Alloys, E56
Alternation of generations, A63
Alternative energy sources,
    C104–105, C106
Altitude
  air pressure and, D33, D54
  air temperature and, D32
  climate and, D87
Altocumulus clouds, D45
Altostratus clouds, D45
Aluminum, C38, E23
Alvin (submersible), C92–93
AM, F120
Amazing Stories
  coral reefs, B42–43
  icy survival, E18–19
  milk vs. butter, E66–67
  planetary weather, D22–23

weightlessness, F42–43
Ammeter, E93
Ammonia, B54, B56, E83
Amperes, E93
Amphibia, A95, A98
Amphibians, A16
Amplifier, F60
Anaconda, B71
"Ancient" bacteria kingdom, A19
Anemometer, D62
Anemones, A16, A96
Aneroid barometer, D34
Angiosperms, A15, A64, A68,
    A69, A71–75
  aromatic flowers, A84
  cotyledons, A72–73, A82
  importance of understanding,
    A75, A85
  life cycle of, A74
Animals, A16, A90–120. *See also*
    Populations
  adaptation of, A104–120
    camouflage, A108–109
    mimicry, A106–107
    sowbugs, A105*
    taste, A107
    thornbugs, A107
  carbon cycle and, B53
  classification of, A16
    importance of understand-
      ing, A21
  as consumers, B7
  crossbreeds, A112–113
  in deciduous forests, B70
  diversity among, A114
  habitat change and, B13*, B36
  hoofed, B66
  hybrids, A112*
  importance of understanding,
    A101, A115
  inherited vs. learned traits in,
    A110–111
  invertebrates, A95, A96–97
  life cycles of, A102–103
  in nitrogen cycle, B55
  plants vs., A16
  in prairie ecosystem, B10

* Indicates an activity related to this topic.

*Indicates an activity related to this topic.

*Indicates an activity related to this topic.

*Indicates an activity related to this topic.

*Indicates an activity related to this topic.

*Indicates an activity related to this topic.

*Indicates an activity related to this topic.

Credits